AF251779

THE

KNOWLEDGE OF GOD,

OBJECTIVELY CONSIDERED.

BEING

THE FIRST PART OF THEOLOGY

CONSIDERED

AS A SCIENCE OF POSITIVE TRUTH,

BOTH INDUCTIVE AND DEDUCTIVE.

BY

ROBERT J. BRECKINRIDGE, D.D., LL.D.,

PROFESSOR OF THEOLOGY IN THE SEMINARY OF DANVILLE, KENTUCKY.

NON SINE LUCE.

NEW YORK:

ROBERT CARTER & BROTHERS,

LOUISVILLE: A. DAVIDSON.

1859.

STEREOTYPED BY
T. B. SMITH & SON,
82 & 84 Beekman-st.

PRINTED BY
E. O. JENKINS,
28 Frankfort-st.

TO

THE PENITENT AND BELIEVING FOLLOWERS

OF

THE SAVIOUR OF SINNERS

THIS ATTEMPT TO VINDICATE THEIR FAITH

IS REVERENTLY DEDICATED,

IN THE DEEP CONVICTION, THAT NEXT TO THE APPROVAL OF GOD, THEIRS

IS THE VERY HIGHEST TESTIMONY IT COULD RECEIVE.

CONTENTS.

	PAGE
PRELIMINARY STATEMENT	ix

BOOK I.

MAN·

ARGUMENT OF THE FIRST BOOK	1
CHAP. I.—The actual condition of Man individually considered	3
II.—The moral condition of Man as it is socially exhibited	11
III.—The ruin of the Human Race universal and irremediable—the cause and the mode of its occurrence	22
IV.—The Divine interposition to save Man	36
V.—Inquiry into the Being of God; and the manner thereof	47
VI.—The immortality of Man	58

BOOK II.

THE MEDIATOR.

ARGUMENT OF THE SECOND BOOK	71
CHAP. VII.—Jesus of Nazareth—the Son of God, and the Saviour of the World	73
VIII.—Immanuel.—The Mystery of the Incarnation	90
IX.—The Mediator between God and Man	105
X.—The Humiliation, and the Exaltation of the Mediator: his two estates	119
XI.—Offices executed by the Mediator:—Christ the great Teacher	139
XII.—Offices executed by the Mediator:—Christ the great High Priest	161
XIII.—Offices executed by the Mediator:—Christ the only King in Zion	177

BOOK III.

GOD.

	PAGE
ARGUMENT OF THE THIRD BOOK	197
CHAP. XIV.—The Names of God; Revealed by Himself as the basis of our Knowledge of the Godhead	199
XV.—The Mode of the Divine Existence: Unity of Essence: Trinity of Persons	222
XVI.—The Doctrine of the Holy Ghost	239
XVII.—The Perfections of God: General Classification of the Divine Attributes	260
XVIII.—Primary Attributes of God: such as appertain to him, considered merely as an infinite being	267
XIX.—Essential Attributes of God: such as appertain to him considered as an infinite, Personal Spirit	273
XX.—Natural Attributes of God: such as appertain to him considered with reference to the eternal distinction between the True and the False	284
XXI.—Moral Attributes of God: such as appertain to him considered with reference to the eternal distinction between Good and Evil	291
XXII.—Consummate Attributes of God: such as appertain to him considered as the sum of all infinite perfections	310

BOOK IV.

SOURCES OF KNOWLEDGE.

	PAGE
ARGUMENT OF THE FOURTH BOOK	317
CHAP. XXIII.—Our Knowledge of God; General Statement concerning the manifestations of God	321
XXIV.—God manifest in his Works: God the Creator of all Things	332
XXV.—God manifest in his infinite dominion—the God of Providence	345
XXVI.—God manifest in Human Nature; the Word made Flesh	366
XXVII.—God manifest in the New Creation: God the Holy Ghost	382
XXVIII.—God manifest in Revelation—the God of the Sacred Scriptures	405
XXIX.—God manifest in the Conscious existence of Man: God the Maker and Renewer of the Human Soul	420

CONTENTS.   **vii**

BOOK V.

SUM AND RESULT.

PAGE

ARGUMENT OF THE FIFTH BOOK 443

CHAP. XXX.—The Primeval State of Man 447

XXXI.—The Covenant of Works 461

XXXII.—Origin of Evil: Breach of the Covenant of Works: Fall of Man: Ruin of the Human Race 483

XXXIII.—The Sum and Result of Human Existence: with the Sum and Result of the Knowledge of God objectively considered 503

XXXIV.—The Finite and the Infinite coalesce in Religion: Gospel Paradoxes: Their influence and Solution 521

A FEW PRELIMINARY WORDS.

I HAVE thought that it would have been of great advantage to mankind, in many ways, if it had happened that each century of the past had left to us in a distinct form, its systematic view of divine truth, according to the general attainments of that age, and the general faith of the earnest Christians thereof. And such a vast and constantly accumulating store of the means of estimating the perpetual life of the church of God, and of aids to a complete understanding of the Word of Life, would be only the more important if each particular contribution to it, had come from the bosom of one or other of the grand movements of the church in each particular age, and from some hand which God had used therein. It has, in general, happened far otherwise. From the bosom of most of the Christian centuries, nothing of the sort I have intimated has reached us, and probably nothing of that sort existed in those centuries. From many other centuries, what has come down to us, so far from being either systematic or complete, was in its very nature fragmentary and partial. And what we have really received from all the past, out of the bosom of orthodox Christianity, in the way of complete and systematic treatment of the whole knowledge of God unto salvation—great as is its value in some respects, and numerous as have been such attempts; appears to me to leave theology as a pure science of positive truth, in the disordered condition of many inferior sciences, and more really than they, needing to be restated in a form, as far as possible general, but at the same time simple, natural, and complete. Perhaps the spirit of our existing Christianity amongst the orthodox, is not unsuitable to such an attempt. Perhaps the type of Christian life in the church of which I am a minister, affords some advantages toward its execution. Perhaps such an endeavor springing from the midst of that immense reaction toward the divine life in man, which signalized that church in this age—retrieving its destiny and modifying the Christianity of our times, might not be without its use —if it could survive. Perhaps there are special reasons why, holding the views I do, occupying the position I hold, and led by Providence as I have been, my brethren who have exacted this service at my hands might be excused, and why those who might, perhaps justly, condemn my attempt as rash, might, in their charity, excuse me.

I have not aimed to produce a compend of Theology. I aim to teach Theology itself. In this, God alone, and by means of the manifestations which he makes of himself, is the absolute source, as he is the sole object of knowledge unto salvation. It is this Knowledge of God unto salvation, which I accept and develop, as a science of absolute truth : and these manifestations of God to man, which are the sole means of this knowledge, which I attempt to demonstrate, to classify, and to expound. Creation, Providence, the Incarnation, the Work of the Spirit, the Sacred Scriptures and the Self-conscious Existence of the human soul : these are the only manifestations of God to man—the only sources of the true Knowledge of God, by man. The grand departments of this Knowledge of God, are God himself—the God-man who is Mediator between God and men—and man himself in his self-conscious existence, as created and re-created by God. As to books, in such a science as this, and in such an attempt as this, the Bible is the only one having any authority. And yet I am far from undervaluing the immense advantages I have derived from the labors of others; without which, indeed, I could have done nothing. The fruits of such attainments as I have painfully made, will manifest themselves to the learned who may honor me by considering what I advance. I know too well that the Spirit of God has been in his church always, to treat with unconcern the deliverances of her great teachers, much less her own well considered utterances of her constant faith : and I perceive clearly enough, that on such a subject as this, and after so many centuries of exalted effort, any claim of proper originality touching the subject matter, would be merely a confession of folly, of ignorance, and of error, The general doctrine of this Treatise is in the sense of the unalterable faith of the church of the living God—in the sense of all the ancient confessions of that church—in the sense of the orthodox confessions of the Reformation—in the sense of the standards of the Westminster Assembly—which constitute the confession of so large a part of the Christian world, and, amongst the rest, of my own church. The details which have been wrought out by learned, godly, and able men in all ages, of many creeds, and in many tongues, have been freely wrought into the staple of this work, when they suited the place and the purpose, and turned precisely to my thought. That for which I alone must be responsible, is that which makes the work individual : the conception—the method—the digestion—the presentation—the order—the spirit—the impression of the whole.—If, however, I had not supposed that the portion of this work which made it peculiar, was capable of being used to the great advantage of the noblest of all sciences, commonly denied either the name or the treatment of a science, I should not have considered it my duty to make such a publication.

While I have evaded nothing, the very conception on which I proceed, makes all fundamental truths absolutely vital; while such as are obscure, dubious, or secondary, are just as necessarily reduced to their true position. Upon some points which have always agitated the Christian mind, I have spoken with a certain reserve, dictated alike by the appreciation I had of the true nature of those questions, and of my official position as a Teacher of Theology appointed by a church, whose Standards were framed by men holding almost opposite views on those points, and wisely avoiding defining them as of faith. It is also proper to say, that in the treatment of questions demanding the most rigid analysis or the most compact demonstration, these high processes, great as is my trust in them, have never been so confidently relied on, as to lose sight for a moment, of the necessity of that true spiritual insight into divine things, upon which such an attempt as this must rest, above all. The thoughtful reader will recognize the justice of these observations, and perceive the effect which the principles involved in them must exert upon an attempt to recast in a form at once natural and complete, the great science of Christian Theology.

In such works as this, *method* is second in *importance* only to the conception of the nature of the subject matter to be treated. That which I have adopted, like my conception of Theology itself, seems to be perfectly simple and clear. Systematic Theology is usually divided into Exegetic, Didactic, and Polemic: that is Theology as deduced directly from the original Text of the Word of God—Theology as systematically deduced from the whole of divine Revelation according to the whole proportion of faith—and Theology as defended from all untruth. Now, according to my idea, the whole Knowledge which we have, or can have, of God unto salvation, divides itself into three simple, obvious, and exhaustive classes— or aspects, if that expression is preferred. In the first place, the whole of that Knowledge may be considered and treated as *mere Knowledge*— like any other complete and positive knowledge : that is, it is not only capable of a purely *Objective* treatment, but to be understood clearly it must be treated in that manner. In the second place, that Knowledge of God, in its intimate and transforming effects upon man, in his inner life, his nature, his condition, his destiny—is not only capable of a complete *Subjective* treatment, but is fully comprehensible in its effects, only so far as it is considered in that manner. This distinction, moreover, accords with the fundamental distinction of Philosophy, as applied to man ; and, what is better, with the primeval effort of our intelligence, in taking account of itself, to distinguish the internal from the external. But the Knowledge of God Objectively considered, and the Knowledge of God Subjectively considered—each takes in the whole sum and result of Exgetic and Didactic Theology—and presents that whole sum and result, once as pure, systematic truth unto salvation—and once as pure, systematic truth actually saving man. As to Polemic Theology—it is very obvious that it is simply the systematic confutation of all untruth, militating against the salvation of man; and that the only absolute way of doing this, is to confront it with divine truth, whether Objective or Subjective, unto salvation. There are, therefore, three great aspects of divine Knowledge unto salvation, whenever that Knoweldge is considered either as positively certain, as constituting a true science, or as capable of being taught in a manner either natural or exhaustive. These are the knowledge of God considered Objectively, considered Subjectively, and considered Relatively. This volume embraces the first of those three portions of Christian Theology—the first of those three aspects of Divine Truth: and its main object is to present in a perfectly distinct and connected manner, and to demonstrate as positively certain, the sum and system of divine Knowledge, simply as Knowledge, unto salvation.

I am not aware that either the conception I have of this immense subject, or the method I adopt in developing it, or the order I pursue in treating it—has been distinctly recognized hitherto, as a basis either of inquiry or instruction in Theology. There is this explanation of the ordinary method of treating divine Knowledge, as appears to me in a manner at once arbitrary and artificial; that the idea has possessed the minds of learned teachers, that God himself, in his blessed Word, had observed no particular method of stating, or even of revealing divine truth. But if this were strictly true, it would not justify us in substituting an arbitrary and artificial method for a natural and scientific one, when we expressly set out to give systematic instruction. Because divine truth, being of itself perfect at every stage of its development—having no error in it—never requiring any modification of what is once known, by reason of any further revelation added; is necessarily capable of systematic reduction at every stage of its progress, and from any point of view. Moreover, the nature of God and his relations to all truth are such, that it very illy becomes us to say, that with reference to himself, his statements are not equally systematic in every order, and to whatever extent he might make them. Absolutely considered, what we should say is that divine truth is necessarily revealed after a divine method. When we apply the idea that there is no method in divine revelation, not to God, but to ourselves; it seems to me, that we are, if possible, more mistaken than before. For, in effect, we are naturally incompetent to acquire Knowledge, in any proper sense, independently of perceiving between the parts of Knowledge, relations to each other which are both permanent and systematic: so that, on the condition supposed, we could know divine truths only as so many isolated propositions, wholly unfruitful: and we could know them even in that manner, only with this perpetual badge of apparent untruth, that they refused not only to accord with any known truths, but even to accord among themselves. Besides, it is demonstrably certain on the face of the sacred record, that all Revelation has been given in a perfectly systematic manner, with reference to human intelligence—that it all professes expressly to be one glorious whole, and demands of us in terms, that to which our very nature obliges us, namely, the interpretation of it all according to its own proportion, and as an outbirth of the eternal counsel of God. The only possible question for us, therefore, is a choice of methods: and so they practically admit, who adopt some method, and follow some system, even while they imagine God does neither with regard to us. If it shall be found that the method I adopt is in harmony with the fundamental principle of all Reformed churches, touching the sufficiency of the Scriptures—and with the fundamental impulse of the Christianity of this age, touching the pursuit of divine Knowledge upon the sacred text—and with the fundamental spirit of Philosophy in its present posture: then it will stand, and it will bear fruit.

Within certain limits, the possible order of developing this most difficult part of Knowledge attainable by man, is somewhat more indeterminate than either the method of treating the subject, or the conception of the subject itself. Naturally the Subjective Knowledge of God might perhaps go first in order; since it is the true inward Knowledge of him which prompts us to the diligent search of all outward Knowledge of him, and to the clear statement and defence of both these Knowledges against all errors. Still this Subjective Knowledge in its power and efficacy, is not the mere force of truth by itself—but of truth accompanied by the power of God, and acting upon a soul divinely restored to the likeness of God. On the other hand, the Relative Knowledge of God, that divine Knowledge confronting all opposing systems, beginning with the settlement of the claims of the divine Word itself, and clearing the whole area where truth may expatiate freely; might apparently demand the lead in the studies of those, who are prepared to enter upon such inquiries in all their great proportions. And then the Objective Knowledge of God, might justly urge as a ground of precedence in the order of treatment, the extreme directness of the way which opens into it, and through it to both the other aspects of divine Knowledge. Unquestionably, there is no proper order, but one of these three: unquestionably, neither of these is absolutely and universally preclusive of the other two, as the starting-point of our inquiries. Whether we observe it or not, divine truth so far as we master it and use it, falls into this division, no matter what artificial methods may obscure it and encumber us, in our efforts to obtain it. And under each of these aspects of it, a complete view of divine truth—at least in its outline—is indispensable to the perfect comprehension of the particular view specially considered: while each of the three special views of it, is supplemental to the other two special views of it: and while all three of them unitedly, make but one complete whole. It is truth complete in itself—complete in its effects—complete in its antagonism to error: self-completeness—effective completeness—victorious completeness.

It is in the sense qualified by these considerations, that the Treatise now published is called the First Part of Theology—and that the Objective view of the Knowledge of God, is given the first place in a work designed if the Lord permit, to embrace in the end the whole subject, in a form at once thorough and simple. If the execution bears any proportion to the design, this volume contains a distinct outline of the whole Knowledge of God attainable by man unto salvation, Objectively considered· Its whole conception is that the Knowledge of God unto salvation is a science of positive truth, both inductive and deductive. Commencing with elements simple and undeniable, the progress is always direct and always cumulative—like the progress of any other science of positive truth. All Polemics are turned over to their proper place and treatment, under the Relative consideration of divine truth; at the head of which will stand the establishment of it, and the body of which will embrace the defence of it. Divine Knowledge is a Gospel: it is the folly and wickedness of man which make it appear to be an arena—and rob the systematic treatment of it of so much of its unction. The order in which I have sought to develop my method of treating this divine Knowledge, commencing with man as he is—conducts us by the shortest way immediately to the Mediator between God and men—and through him to the transcendent glory and mystery of God : after which the very nature and sources of this whole Knowledge are subjected to scrutiny—and then the sum and result of all, is brought face to face with the sum and result of all the dealings of God with man· What appears to me to be attainable is, that all confusion should be escaped, that all dislocation of truth should be avoided, that clear statements should become really convincing proofs, that the grand proportion of faith should reign without distortion, that the sublime science of God should emerge distinctly from the chaos of endless disputations, and that the unction of a glorious gospel should pervade the whole.

The narrowness of the space I had allotted to myself, when compared with the boundless nature of the theme, every where embarrassed me. I fear the corresponding evils may embarrass the reader. He may justly complain that much is omitted—and that the whole performance is too elliptical and condensed. I have sought such remedies as were in my power. If I may so speak, the whole system is presented three times: once, in the whole volume; once in the tables of contents at the heads of the chapters; and once in the Arguments prefixed to the several Books. Moreover, while the whole volume contains a system so compact, that the loss of any chapter would mutilate the general argument; on the other hand nearly every chapter, and certainly each of the five Books, might be published as a separate treatise. I am not aware that a single topic—I believe I may say a single sentence—foreign to the absolute purpose of the Treatise, has been allowed a place in this Volume. The whole system of division and notation—books, chapters, paragraphs, subdivisions—has followed the sense and the course of the general and particular argument and proof, with perfect strictness. The style attempted is wholly devoid of ornament, and aims only at being clear, simple and direct. The tone of the work—that crowning mark—the reader, will, of course, determine for himself. If the effect of the whole shall be, to make the common reader desire to become a better man—to make the careful student resolve to become a better theologian, to make both of them aware that infallible Knowledge of the living God, unto salvation, is attainable by man: then I shall not only be consoled with one more proof that I have not lived in vain, but shall have one more reason to glorify God for condescending to use my poor endeavours in his cause.

BRÆDALBANE, near Lexington, Kentucky,
    August, 1857.

THE KNOWLEDGE OF GOD,

OBJECTIVELY CONSIDERED.

ARGUMENT OF THE FIRST BOOK.

The supreme importance of the knowledge of God to us, arises from the decisive influence of that knowledge upon our personal destiny both in this world, and the next: a matter which concerns us more nearly than all things else united. But to know our own nature and condition is the first step toward making the knowledge of God available :—while the study of ourselves, as the only work of God made in his own image, is the simplest and surest commencement of the systematic study of him. This First Book, therefore, of a Treatise devoted to the thorough consideration of God as an object of knowledge, proposes to discuss and settle the fundamental truths which determine the position of man before God. In the First Chapter, man contemplated as an Individual Being—a separate force in the universe—is carefully considered. In the Second Chapter, this consideration is extended to him contemplated in all the permanent relations in which he successively, and unavoidably coöperates with other beings like himself—to wit, as one of a race organized into Households, into Nations, and into Religions. It is shown in both Chapters that man's estate, in all its possible aspects, is one of sin and misery: and in the mean time, all the chief questions touching both his nature and his estate, both individual and social, are discussed in their order, and the foundations of his being laid open. In the Third Chapter, it is shown at large that this ruined condition of man is universal and irremediable—except by means of some Intervention of God inscrutable to human reason: and as part of the proof of the universality of the ruin of the human race, its own unity is proved. It is then shown how Revealed Religion accepts and solves this problem of man's ruin and deliverance. and its first explanation of the cause and mode of the ruin itself is exhibited. The Fourth Chapter is devoted to a general exposition of the fact, the manner, the objects, and the principles of the divine Interposition which has actually occurred : and herein the Plan of Salvation is summarily exhibited. As the whole of this necessarily depends on the Being and Perfections of God, we are led immediately to the question of the divine Existence and Nature : and the Fifth Chapter is devoted to a demonstration of the eternal existence of an Infinite Spirit, who is the First Cause of all things, the Creator and Ruler of the Universe, the Jehovah of the Sacred Scriptures, and the Saviour of sinners.   And then in the Sixth Chapter, which is the last one of this First Book, the Immortality of this fallen creature, thus rescued by his Infinite Creator and Redeemer, at so great a cost, is demonstrated according to its proper nature, and by a method competent to prove the truth of the Christian idea of that Immortality, and the falsity of every other idea of it.   A complete survey of man is thus accomplished ; while it is the knowledge of God himself in the light of which the survey is made; and that divine knowledge is augmented at every step of the survey.   Besides all truths herein set forth which may be considered inferior or incidental to the chief results of this Book, those which follow and which are fundamental, are firmly established, namely, The fall and ruin of the human race : The irreparable nature, of itself, of our estate of sin and misery : The divine Interposition to save man : The Infinite Existence and Perfections of the God who has thus interposed to save man : The Immortal Existence of man, in whose nature God has become Incarnate.

CHAPTER I.

THE ACTUAL CONDITION OF MAN—INDIVIDUALLY CONSIDERED.

1. Concerning the Nature of Man.—2. His Individualism.—3. Personality.—4. Personal Destiny.—5. Sense of Accountability.—6. Perversion of these Elements.—7. Sense of Blameworthiness.—8. Sense of True and False.—9. Sense of Good and Evil.—10. Our Faculties Incompetent to the complete Application of these Distinctions.—11. Our Nature Depraved. Fallen, but Susceptible of Recovery.—12. Our Evil Passions, and their Indulgence. Universal Pollution.—13. Our State of Sinfulness a State of Misery also. The Hope from Thence.—14. Nature and Universality of that Misery.—15. The Condition of Man in Contrast with that of Irrational Creatures, of Lost Spirits, and of Devils.—16. The Bearing of the Original Elements of his Nature upon its Present Pollution and Misery.—17. Conclusion.

1. IN examining the condition of man, as he exists before us, we are to form an estimate of him, according to the received chronology, after nearly six thousand years of progress. If after all the vicissitudes of that vast period, we find in him distinguishing and universal traits, which have existed through all time and in all conditions, and have survived every influence which has borne upon him, we need not hesitate to pronounce them necessary and indestructible parts of his nature.

2. The simplest view which can be taken of him, is as an individual being—acting by himself and for himself, upon his own responsibility and to his own ends, in the midst of innumerable beings like himself. Wants, which, however they may press on others, are peculiarly his: passions, which, however they may be common to all, burn in him with a special fervor: purposes, which, though they may actuate all, urge him with an intimate force: hopes, which every one may cherish, but to accomplish which, is, with him, the very end of his being. And so in every thing, the separate action, the intense individualism, the personal development, the immediate responsibility of each particular being, in one word his separate life and personality is

his most obvious, as it is his most inherent and fruitful characteristic.

3. The Scriptures teach us that God created man in his own image. If this be true, the result already noticed is the one most certain to occur. In all the universe there is no absolute and purely independent existence, but God only. And it is only so far as created and dependent existences are made in his image, and conform to the mode of his being, that each one would be a separate power in the universe, precisely proportionate to its resemblance to him. On the other hand, this fundamental peculiarity of man affords a kind of evidence at once striking and particular, of the mode of that unsearchable existence in the image of which his own was fashioned—an existence, namely, absolutely personal, and wholly distinct from the universe which he has created. These are truths of the highest importance, and will demand careful attention hereafter.

4. One of the most distinct and unalterable conditions of this separate and yet dependent existence of man, is that his eminent responsibility should be a personal responsibility—each one answering for himself directly to his Creator. However much and however variously we may be involved with others, and whether in their blessings or their miseries—still our destiny is pre-eminently a personal destiny. It is our personal freedom, our personal intelligence, our personal dependence, our personal accountability—terminating, at last, in a personal destiny, shaped under the personal dealing of God with each one of us.

5. The corresponding indwelling sense of our personal accountability is one of the most marked and universal characteristics of our nature. Even in our intercourse with our fellow-creatures, we habitually and continually proceed upon the truth, as though it was indisputable and universally accepted, that they are responsible to us, and we to them, not only for such things as human laws take cognizance of—but for all things. And that inherent conviction, which lies in the very depths of our being, that we are personally accountable to a power separate from us and infinitely superior to us, which men in all ages and places have called God ; opens before us the whole field of the religious history of the human race. Our dependence on him is felt to be absolute : his dominion over us to be illimitable. Endowed, as we feel ourselves to be, with freedom and intelligence ; to be

destitute of a sense of accountability under these conditions, cannot occur, and cannot be conceived of, except as we conceive of
whatever else we call a monster. Here, then, on the one hand,
is the basis in us of all that we call religion : on the other hand,
the clear manifestation that religion, in its widest sense, is as
natural to man, as it is natural for him to be what he is, and to
occupy the place he does in the created universe.

6. The outworking, in blindness and error, of this powerful
individualism on the side of our religious nature ; this sense of
personal accountability, striving to please God or to propitiate him
—or to satisfy the demands of our religious instincts—has been
the foundation of all the false human religions which have existed,
and of all their folly and wickedness. On the other hand, the
attempts to allay the pungency of this sense of personal accountability to God, by false and insufficient methods, have been
constant marks of the perversions of all true and divine religion
at any time in the world. The papal superstition by coming
between God and man and relieving the soul by assuming its
burdens and obligations : the Pelagian heresy by mitigating the
nature and the power of sin : the madness of universalism by
robbing the justice of God of all terror to the wicked : these,
and innumerable forms of obscuring the way of life, do no more
really assail the majesty of God, than they pervert the intimate
life of the human soul.

7. In the midst of these striking peculiarities of our nature
—if not indeed at the root of them all—lies that profound sense
of our own insufficiency and blame-worthiness, which is so signal
an exponent of our present condition on earth, and so conspicuous
an element in every change of which that condition is susceptible.
Every human being in estimating every other human being, perceives and admits that, of themselves, they are not perfect, and
cannot render an account of themselves with absolute security
and satisfaction, in the face of any perfect rule of conduct : and
every one, in carefully judging himself, sees and feels only the
more keenly as he has the more variously and the more thoroughly
tried himself, that he is not perfectly sufficient for any part he
was ever called to act, and that he is not perfectly exempt from
blame-worthiness in any serious crisis of his being. So thorough
and so universal are the causes upon which all this depends, that
no matter what rule of conduct or of judgment is laid down for

us, or what we lay down for ourselves, we never come up to the prescribed rule, with absolute fulness, if the rule itself satisfies the reason and conscience of him who attempts to follow it. No law which we violate can acquit us ; and even if it were possible that it could, our case would be only the more pitiable. For our heart and our understanding would take part against the law itself, and our very rule of right become either a means of pollution, or an object of contempt to us ; while our very sense of blame-worthiness sets out with the admission, that we have come short of some standard which we ourselves approve. How strange a condition is that in which our actions come short of our intentions—in which our conduct does not satisfy our reason—in which our passions stand as perpetual culprits at the tribunal of our conscience !

8. There is, doubtless, an eternal and ineffaceable distinction in things, which we express by saying some of them are true and some of them are false. At any rate, such a distinction, let it be founded as it may, exists for us ; and nature has provided us with the faculty of perceiving it, and using it, and being guided by it. It is upon the steadfastness of this distinction that the certainty of all our knowledge depends ; as it is upon our capacity to perceive the distinction itself wherever it exists, that our ability to increase in knowledge rests. It is here precisely that our rational nature expatiates, and here is the foundation of all the relations subsisting between that rational nature and every thing in the universe exterior to ourselves. If it were not so in both respects, it is impossible for us to understand how our condition could be superior to that of the brutes.

9. Nor is this all. Not inferior in any respect to the distinction already pointed out, there exists another as eternal and ineffaceable as it—or at any rate it exists as absolutely for us ; and nature has provided us as distinctly with the capacity to perceive it, to use it, and to be guided by it. We express this distinction by saying, that in the nature of things some of them are good, and some of them are bad ; and we express the feeling in us corresponding to them respectively, by saying we approve the good, and condemn the bad. Upon the steadfastness of this distinction rests the entire fabric of the moral universe—amongst the rest our own moral nature : and upon our ability to perceive the distinction and to be affected by it, depends our capacity to

increase in all moral excellence. The fitness of all our relations to God ceases the moment we obliterate this distinction :—the very ideas of duty, of virtue, and of happiness, become incomprehensible ; nor is it possible to conceive how we could exist afterwards, except as idiots or as demons.

10. It is in the midst of these great characteristics of our nature that we encounter one of those profound contradictions, of which the number is so great and the effects so remarkable, that the very structure of our being and the total manner of its operation, exhibit the clearest proofs of its having received some fearful shock. The rational faculties of man do not enable him to determine either absolutely or invariably, what particular things are true and what are false ; nor do his moral faculties enable him to determine in like manner, what particular things are good and what are evil. The reality of these distinctions is perceived to exist as a fundamental part of the order of the universe, and corresponding operations of our rational and moral nature are felt and known to be immediately connected with them. But our faculties, in their present state, are so far from being adequate to avail themselves perfectly and universally thereof, that they are liable to the greatest mistakes and the grossest impositions touching both the true and the good. While these deplorable results occur in a very low degree in certain departments of human intelligence and effort, they occur in a very high degree in others ; and it is especially in man's spiritual life, and in all his moral relations to God and to his fellow-creatures, that they manifest themselves with the greatest intensity.

11. Our present condition, then, may well be called a depraved condition ; and it is of our spiritual life in its most fundamental characteristics that we may thus speak with peculiar emphasis. Man, as he now exists, cannot rely with certainty and security upon the conclusions of his understanding and the dictates of his conscience in the highest and most important concerns of his soul. And yet so urgent and so universal are his religious wants, and so deeply seated in his nature is the sense of his dependence, his accountability, and his blame-worthiness, that he will accept any thing as true rather than believe nothing, and cling to any thing as good, rather than be deprived of all trust. There is thus exhibited to us continually and on every side, the

proof of that terrible phenomenon which the Scriptures call the Fall of Man ; and at the same time, the power with which the spiritual element in his nature still struggles—the proof of his susceptibility of that divine restoration which is provided through the Son of God.

12. With the reason and conscience of man in such a state as has been described, it would be idle to look for purity of heart and life, even if his passions were slow and dull. But when we consider their violence, the innumerable occasions of indulging them, the urgency of the temptations which assail them, and the nature of the present gratification afforded by their indulgence, there is surely no reason to marvel that the life of each individual person and the common life of the whole race, should exhibit so little which reason can approve, or true religion allow, or a righteous God fail to condemn. If reason, or conscience, or nature, or God, imposes any rule of duty upon individual men, the violation of which is in any respect sinful, we see in the very nature of man as he actually exists, how the whole world must necessarily abound with iniquity just in proportion to the extent and the purity of the rule of duty thus prescribed to us. And this terrible conclusion to which the very nature of the case drives us, does not rise to the still more terrible reality exhibited as the actual and constant result of the moral conduct of mankind in their natural state, as attested by the universal experience of all ages. The whole world lieth in sin, and the whole race of man is guilty before God.

13. One great end gained by striving to train a sinful race to virtue, is that a standard of judgment is erected for them, which, if they come not up to it, may at least suffice to keep them from being at ease while they fall below it, and may thus prevent them from pursuing sin as a means of happiness. When we consider how difficult it is to wean men from vice, even after they are fully persuaded that vice is not good for them ; it is easy to see how hopeless would be all attempts to bring them to repentance, if it were in the order of providence that they could be happy in sin. It is, therefore, not only a most pregnant necessity, but it is besides an unspeakable mercy, that the state of sin into which man is fallen is also a state of misery : since, naturally considered, therein lies the chief hope of his recovery.

14. The detailed exposition of the nature of that misery which

is entailed on man in his present sinful condition, will occupy us hereafter. It may suffice at present to direct our attention to the greatness and the universality of it. Whether we consider the shortness of his life, its utter uncertainty, the unsatisfying nature of all earthly things while it lasts, or its certain, painful, and most generally sinful termination ; whether we contemplate the physical evils which embitter it ; the poverty, the toil, the sicknesses, the sufferings, the oppression, the famine, pestilence and sword, and all the countless ills to which flesh is heir ; whether we turn our thoughts to the moral evils which defile and degrade us, poisoning all the enjoyments of our present state, and rendering us unfit for any better state to come ; whether we turn our eyes for comfort into our own hearts and find them all polluted, or turn them to our perishing fellow-creatures and find them as miserable as ourselves, or to God and feel that he has forsaken us, or to the grave and find that it is no refuge for us, or to eternity and behold only darkness and despair : there is nothing left for us but to confess the greatness and the righteousness of the condemnation we have incurred, and to seek deliverance from it, through deliverance from the sin that produced it.

15. Still, however, we must be careful to estimate truly the other side of the case presented for our consideration. Compared even with our own conception of what is perfect in spirituality, in intelligence, and in physical existence, we must indeed pronounce our present condition to be at once depraved and miserable. Yet, on the other hand, compared with the condition of the brutes that perish, with that of idiots or maniacs, above all with that of lost spirits or devils, our condition is one of great eminence —crowned with a dominion at once just and illimitable over the creatures of God, and endowed with ability to use that dominion, in innumerable ways, for the great glory of God, and the boundless good of his creatures.

16. Man is not always suffering, nor is suffering itself an unmixed evil : nay, it is the parent of many blessings. Man is not always deceived in determining what is true : nay, the conquests of his intelligence may be inconceivably vast. Man is not always misled in seeking for what is good : nay, he may know and do enough to make his pathway through life seem like one of beauty and light. The accountability which he feels, however it may be perverted, is the most enduring restraint to the evil within him ;

the dependence he admits is the constant testimony of his nature
to the being and goodness of his Creator ; the sense of blame-
worthiness which his conscience courageously stirs up in his soul,
is the foundation of all his struggles to release himself from the
dominion of sin and advance in the path of virtue. His very
individualism, however it may be perverted into utter selfish-
ness and cruelty, yet powerfully separates him to God, and to his
own self-dominion, in the midst of the multitudes around him
who encourage each other to forget God, and hurry each other on
to perdition : and the powerful bias of his nature—not indeed to
true religion—but to religious ideas and emotions in general,
greatly as it may be abused and corrupted, opens in the very
depths of his being, an access for the truth that may save him.

17. Such is man as he actually exists before us. Such are
we all. Differing, no doubt, widely from each other, as one or
other true or good, false or evil thing, may disturb the ordinary
balance of human nature ; but all alike in the grand characteristics of our being, and considered in the simplest light as individual persons. This is the being concerning whom it is altogether indispensable that we should have clear and just ideas,
if we would truly comprehend or rightly interpret that great salvation offered to him through the Mediator.

CHAPTER II.

THE MORAL CONDITION OF MAN—AS IT IS SOCIALLY EXHIBITED.

I. 1. The Social Principle Fundamental in Man.—2. The Household. Domestic Life.—
3. Scope thereof. Duty.—4. Here, if anywhere, Man is True and Pure.—5. Result here.—6. Desperate Manifestation of our Fallen Estate. II. 1. Civil Society
a Necessity of Nature and an Ordination of God.—2. The End of this Organization of the Social Principle. Its Capabilities.—3. Its Intimate Nature. Its Habitual Perversion by Man.—4. The Vast and Habitual Wickedness of States, as
such.—5. The Civil Career of Man as Complete a Proof of his Depravity, as his
Personal and his Domestic Career. III. 1. Man's Temporal Capacities are exhausted, when considered as an Individual, as a Member of the Household, and
a Member of the State.—2. Moral Capabilities beyond those Three Conditions.—
3. Religious Ideas.—4. Their Relations to the Social Principle in Man.—5. The
Permanence, Force, Blindness, and Depravity, of the Religious Instincts of
Man.—6. Frightful Demonstration of his Depravity.—7. Ruin of Man's Estate,
Socially and Religiously as, before personally, ascertained.

I.—1. THE social principle in man is as powerful as his individualism, and operates as steadily. To the former of these two
principles we must look as the foundation of all that distinguishes
man, considered personally : to the latter as the basis of our attempts to explain all that distinguishes him, when he acts in con-
cert with others. It is the play of these two principles upon each
other—the preponderance of the one or the other—or the just
balance of both of them, that gives its fundamental character to
every form of association that exists amongst men. Whatever
tends to the highest personal development of man, and at the
same time to the highest purity and efficiency of his associated
action, may be said to combine in perfection, these two grand
principles of his nature. Supposing man to possess even a profound instinct, much more a clear perception of the great necessities of his being, and of the general method of attaining them,
no more convincing proof need be sought of the perversion of his
nature, than the deplorable fact that after nearly sixty centuries
of what he calls progress, he is still unable to obtain general

security and freedom, much less exalted development and civ-ilization.

2. The simplest form in which human association occurs, the one which is most intimate of all, and elemental to all others, is that of the household. The relations of husband and wife, of parent and child, of children of the same parents to each other, of masters and those who are held to service in any way, of guardian and ward, and very largely of personal friends to each other, together with those frequent though they may be considered casual relations, which charity and hospitality, and the thousand impulses of our nature, establish amongst private persons, constitute that vast portion of the business of our earthly existence which we call our domestic life.

3. Our sense of duty, which is the noblest of all the natural impulses of man, and capable of bearing the richest fruits, is the conscientious recognition of the obligation we lie under to be faithful to every being, and every relation we sustain. Many duties have a perfect obligation, that is, they are of that nature that they can be precisely measured, and precisely enforced : such as the duty of universal truth, honesty, and the like. But many others are duties of imperfect obligation, that is, they are of that nature, that no rules that man can lay down, or enforce by any outward means, can either exactly determine them, or adequately enforce them : such as the duty of obedience to parents, gratitude to friends, humanity to inferiors, and the like. It is precisely in the wide range of our domestic life, that the amplest scope is offered for the faithful discharge of these duties of imperfect obligation : and it is precisely the considerations which spring from the bosom of that life, that ought to impel us to the exact discharge of these duties.

4. If the mind of man can be trusted at all, with the determination of what truth requires of him, it would seem as if he might be thus confided in, in what relates to his own family. If the heart of man may ever be relied on to pursue what is good, we can hardly doubt that his own wife and his own offspring are the proper objects of such a confidence. If the dictates of humanity are ever listened to by him, or the calls of piety ever reach him, or the ties of gratitude ever bind him, or the yearnings of affection ever prompt him to labor or to suffer, or any generous or disinterested emotion ever conquers him into self-

denial; surely his own hearthstone is the spot, and they who constantly surround it are the objects, toward which he will turn in these habitual manifestations that the life of God is not wholly dead within him. For this is the very field in which God has set before him the surest and the highest earthly recompense for well-doing; and these are the very beings, of all that the world holds, whom he can the most surely bless, and whom he must the most truly love.

5. Do we find that ordinarily things work after this fashion? In a few Christian households perhaps, yes, to a certain extent. With a few pure and generous spirits, speaking after the manner of man, perhaps, yes, again. With multitudes, to a partial extent, and in a certain sense, perhaps, yes, again. But over the wide earth, and through the long ages, surely, no. Every one of these relations has the seal of nature's most enduring laws; but nature is incapable of enforcing her own laws, and can only seek a compensation in the fearful punishment of their breach. Every one of them has the express recognition of God, both in the order of his providence, and the word of his grace; but God does not miraculously interpose to oblige man to respect his ordinations, and therefore fallen man does not respect them, even when his own immediate happiness is at stake.

6. If what might be called the private history of mankind were written, perhaps the very darkest page of it would be that which recorded the domestic crimes and miseries of the race. Connubial unfaithfulness and unkindness, paternal and maternal cruelty and neglect, natural affection of near kindred turned into indifference or hate, friendships violated and trusts broken, humanity transformed into cruel injustice, and gratitude and reverence, and pity and love, with all fear of the true God utterly banished from the habitations of countless millions of his sinning and suffering creatures. Alas! it is not in the domestic, any more than in the individual life of man, that we can find any evidence that he is not depraved. All ties are not, indeed, broken by all, even in a state of nature. But all ties are not only broken, but despised, by innumerable multitudes. And such as observe them all with simplicity and completeness, if such can be found, will be the first to profess that they have not accomplished this in their own strength.

II.—1. It is only in the reveries of philosophers that we find theories to account for the origin of human society, upon the notion of its being merely a spontaneous compact amongst men. The social state is an ordination of God : the civil power is instituted by him : the commonwealth is as really divine in its origin and sanction as the church itself : and they who bear rule in the former, are no less called thereto of God, and no less responsible to him for the manner in which they discharge their trust, than they who bear rule in the latter. The end of the commonwealth is no doubt peculiar to itself, and the means also are peculiar ; but the one and the other are appointed of God. The gathering together in a dominion of that sort, is a universal impulse of our nature, implanted by him from whom that nature was derived, and responsive to the divine ordination that such dominion should exist. So that if man can plead any thing with certainty, it is that in his efforts to perfect his condition by means of human society, he is sustained by the will of God, by the law of nature, and by his highest impulses and necessities. In such an attempt, so warranted, we might reasonably expect complete success. But we find nothing of the sort.

2. The restraint and punishment of the wicked, and the protection of the innocent and the upright from that rapacity and cruelty which wickedness begets, are amongst the chief reasons assigned by the Almighty for the institution of all civil authorities amongst men.[1] There is a certain sense, therefore, in which the very existence of human society carries with it a divine and perpetual proof of the depravity of mankind, and in which the perpetual continuance of the power, under the sovereign providence of God, is a perpetual demonstration of the continued wickedness of man. The very advantages which society confers are capable of being made the means of extending the dominion of evil ; and the augmented and concentrated forces thus accumulated and directed to the dishonor of God and the ruin of every true interest of man, have found no remedy adequate to their restraint, but in those seditions, revolutions, convulsions and conquests, with which the annals of every people are crowded. Still while every form of civil administration is, from its very nature, liable to be made the instrument of cruelty and pollution, and all have been so used ; yet every form into which the civil power can be cast, is also from its nature, compatible with per-

---

[1] Romans, xiii. 1–7.

sonal purity in man. In every one there is a perpetual struggle between the principle of individualism and the principle of socialism. In every one the grand problem which has continually and vainly solicited a solution, is the perfect preservation of individual rights ; and at the same time that civilization and the public force should be advanced to the highest pitch. No doubt the freest institutions have done the most toward the accomplishment of these great ends ; yet even they are compatible with the general reign of Atheism, idolatry, and superstition. Even that wild hope of universal freedom and equality, to be realized, at last, in a political millennium for all lands and races, which has sunk so deeply into the heart of man, and which burns so fiercely in these latter ages, is not incompatible with the highest offences against God, and the blackest crimes against his creatures.

3. When the public will, the public intelligence, and the public force are put in operation, no matter how, and no matter under what forms, that which necessarily results, and besides which nothing can result is, that certain rules acquire force, to which we give the name of law—these rules are expounded and administered, and then they are executed and enforced. These are the inevitable results of the independent action of every body politic ; and there is no action of any body politic, no matter whether its form be despotic, or limited, or free, which can result in any thing not capable of being classed as a legislative, judicial, or executive act. Now what is to be noted is, that all these things, in all their infinite variety, may be done, and have been done through all ages, in absolute forgetfulness or in utter contempt of God, the great lawgiver, ruler, and judge of men. Society in every form exhausts itself to set up that which it thinks not of God as it sets it up, and which for aught it knows or cares, may be the most opposite from him, and most offensive to him : nay, does it many a time, most sinfully and foolishly, under pretence of serving him by means which he abhors. How often is nature herself set at naught, the clearest lessons she teaches utterly despised, the most precious rights she bestows trampled under foot ? How often are all the individual and all the domestic rights of man ruthlessly disregarded ? How constantly does organized power do, what none but the most abandoned individual would do ? Nor is it to those despotic rulers

who have been monsters of iniquity, that allusion is had, nor yet to the fierce and unusual proceedings of well-ordered commonwealths in times of peril. It is the general current of human affairs as administered by the ordinary authorities amongst men, in all ages and all lands, which obliges us to see that habitually, man as clearly shows in the conduct of the state, as in the bosom of his family, that he is by nature an alien from the commonwealth of Israel, and without God in the world.

4. If we pass from this narrow view of society considered in its own organism and its internal action, and contemplate in a broader light the action of states upon each other, the principles which regulate that action, and the results to which it is designed to lead, how immense is the evidence which all history has accumulated, that the public conduct of nation with nation, since the world began, has been immeasurably more such conduct as became robbers and savages, than such conduct as became wise and just men! The public records of the past, are for the most part records of suffering and crime : suffering inflicted in a career of victorious wickedness—crime perpetrated against the weak and the conquered. Nor have the arts of peace which states have habitually practised against each other, been less foreign from the spirit of doing unto others as we would that they should do unto us, than the cruelties of war have been foreign from the spirit in which men love their neighbors as themselves. Nor does it weaken the force of such enormous proofs of the true nature of man, to extenuate the general conduct of the race nationally considered, by showing that love of country, love of glory, love of power, love of liberty, or any other lofty or heroic impulse which men are accustomed to applaud, actuated and misled them. The terrible fact that they were misled still remains. Their violation of all obligations, human and divine, that conflicted with their interests or their passions : the wide tendency of the wickedness of states to obstruct the march of civilization and to retard the progress of the human race : the general influence of their conduct in diminishing the aggregate happiness and virtue of mankind : none of these things can be excused at that bar where suffering humanity impeaches its rulers as cruel and incompetent—and where reason and religion impeach humanity itself, and its rulers altogether, as sinners, in all these things, exceedingly before God.

5. We cannot pass over this portion of the subject in the most cursory manner, without being shocked with the evidence it affords of the deplorable wickedness of our race. Even the virtues which are begotten by the movement of society across the track of ages, and which could have no existence but from the existence of government, and country, and society in its organized form, derive a part of their lustre from the terrible shadows which give them prominence. And while they prove—what so many other proofs confirm, that the entire image of God is not so totally effaced in man, that he is lost past redemption, they do not shake in the least, the still more abounding proofs that no more of that image is left in man, than may suffice to prove that he once had it in perfection, and that it is yet possible he may be restored to it. Morally considered, his civil career is not less a failure and a wreck, than his domestic and his individual career has been already shown to be : a failure and a wreck, occurring with more uniformity, and liable to fewer and feebler exceptions in this, than in either of the preceding relations in which he has been contempated. The kingdoms of this world must be converted into a kingdom for the Lord and his Christ, before the earth can be made a fit habitation for God.

III.—1. Man's position as an individual, as a member of the family, and as a citizen—that is his personal, his social, and his civil state, present to us a continuous and connected view of his entire being, capacity, and operation, so far as all things which relate merely to this world and terminate in it are concerned. Whatever we are capable of doing at all, of earthly things, we can do either as individual persons, or as members of the family, or of the state. Every capacity of man, temporally considered, is exhausted in these three methods of development and effort ; and we may be perfectly certain that whatever he has not done or exhibited, in one or other of them, he has not done or exhibited at all. So that when we have a just view of his nature as thus presented, we have a complete view of his nature as it actually is. God, who does all things with absolute perfection, has thus ordered and disposed the life of man on earth in such a manner, that it must necessarily develop itself by means the most simple, and yet the most powerful and comprehensive, affording the completest scope for the exercise of all that is good and true, and presenting the utmost restraints to all that is false and evil, which are compatible with a condition of moral freedom, and if I may now add it, of moral probation.

2. But there are interests of man which do not end with time, and which no blindness and pollution seem capable of making him wholly lose sight of: interests, which though he may be unable clearly to explain, much less adequately to secure, no one else is able to explain away, and he himself is incapable of becoming wholly indifferent to. He is religious—using that word in its wide sense—by nature, as really as he is rational by nature; and of the two, the former is the more urgent part of his being.

3. It is easy to conceive, and it is practically exhibited by disciples of every religious creed, that man may hold religious opinions which do not affect his temporal conduct, at all: and, on the other hand, that he may adopt and hold very tenaciously to religious impressions, and even connect them very strictly with religious rites, without having any clear or even settled intelligence on the subject. The whole subject is capable of being kept apart, as it were, from the life of man, both inward and outward—even in the most strictly individual manifestations of that life, and yet of being preserved, at the same time, by him, very carefully as a fundamental portion of his being. And all this is capable of being done, and is done continually, without any serious regard to the truth or falsity, the goodness or badness of the religion thus cherished.

4. If we add to this, the power of that social principle which binds men together in families, and in its wider operation unites them in communities, and bring it to bear in the religious organization of the human race, we have presented to us in its simplest form the religious element in man, assuming an outward, permanent, public form. There is no absolute necessity, in the nature of things, why this public and social form of religion—whatever the religion may be—should or should not be engrafted on the household estate of man. It might be, or might not be—so far as the inherent nature of the case would determine: it has been, and it has not been, so far as human practice is concerned. In like manner, the religious organization and the civil power have no necessary connection or disconnection with each other: they may be wholly disconnected, and even mutually inimical: or they may

be closely connected, and yet mutually independent: or they may mutually influence each other—or one of them may be absolutely subjected to the other. All these results are possible—all of them have occurred : and they all conspire to prove that the religious element in man is fundamentally distinct from that which develops itself in the household and the state, and that although it is capable of a very close union with it, and is liable to many of the conditions which control it, nevertheless it is a distinct element of itself, and must vindicate for itself, a distinct existence whenever it assumes a public or permanent form. It is, in all its manifestations, essentially an organization not of visible, and therefore temporal interests, but of invisible, and therefore eternal interests : and the question is purely incidental, though of transcendant importance, how far it will accept the control, the union, or the subjection of other recognized interests of man.

5. It is worthy to be noted, as a remarkable evidence of the tenacity with which men cleave to religious prepossessions, and the immense importance they attach to religious organizations, that churches—using the word in its wide sense—have been far more enduring than states : religions more powerful and constant, in their domination, than races of men. It is worthy on the other hand, to be observed, as a remarkable proof of the natural power of the human conscience, when roused to the contemplation of spiritual truth, that all great thinkers have always been infidels, as touching the popular religion of their country, when that religion was false : that no false religion, when once actually subverted and destroyed, has ever been able to regain, in another age, or land, or race, its lost sway. It is impossible, in this place, to attempt even the most cursory survey of the various systems of religion which have prevailed amongst men. In general, besides the Jewish and the Christian, there is a form of Theism, more or less pure, of which Mohammedanism has been the most remarkable example ; a form of Theism, exhibited in idolatrous worship of certain representatives of the true God, of which the ancient Persians had the most striking example ; Polytheism, more or less pure ; Polytheism, blended with direct idolatry ; Idolatry simply expressed ; the worship of living creatures ; Devil worship ; the worship of dead men ; the worship of the uni-

verse itself; the worship of the evil passions of men idealized into gods—not to mention the nameless forms of folly and sin which have been superinduced upon the true religion of God, in the manifold corruptions of it. When we contemplate this frightful array, merely as a manifestation of the blindness, on the one hand, and the amazing power, on the other, of man's religious instincts, it must be considered altogether the most astonishing view that can be taken of the nature of our depraved race. Perhaps it is not too much to say, that men have perpetrated no crime—committed no excess—exhibited no pollution—shown no cruelty—indulged in no brutal folly—of which the religions which they have set up, as the means of enabling them to live in acceptable intercourse with their gods in this world, and thus of bringing them to the eternal enjoyment of those gods, have not afforded at once the example and the vindication.

6. Considered as indications of the moral condition of mankind, the religious systems which have challenged the belief, and sustained the hopes of the overwhelming mass of our race, from the remotest ages to the present moment, and those still professed by the vast majority of living men, can be viewed only with dismay and horror. The wonder is, that nature herself, even in her most degraded form, did not utterly revolt at the audacious insults they offered to God under the pretence of adoring him, and the infinite atrocities they committed on each other, and the inexpressible self-degradation they inflicted on themselves, under the pretence of perfecting their own being. It is idle merely to say that the whole case reveals the most incontestable evidences of the blindness, the depravity, and the degradation of man. It does far more. It demonstrates, in the very matter in which it was most necessary and most certain that he would appear to the highest advantage, namely, in his express and direct relations with God, that the extent of his spiritual ignorance and pollution is incapable of belief, if he had not confessed it all himself, and that nothing short of the monuments he has himself set up could have adequately illustrated the depth of such consummate and abounding iniquity.

7. And such, we mournfully repeat, is man; man as he presents himself to our view, in all the affecting and ennobling relations of his domestic, his civil, and his religious life. This is

what mother, and wife, and child, and friend, have found and left him; and this is their recompense and his. This is what the state finds, and makes, and leaves him. This is what he declares concerning himself to God—in the most formal and permanent of all testimony. This is what he has been from the moment he forsook God; and this—it is capable of the clearest demonstration—is what he must continue to be while he exists on earth, unless God himself shall extricate him from an estate at once so depraved and so miserable.

CHAPTER III.

THE RUIN OF THE HUMAN RACE UNIVERSAL AND IRREMEDIA-
BLE—THE CAUSE AND THE MODE OF ITS OCCURRENCE.

I. 1. The Ruin of our Race, and the Proof of that Ruin, Universal.—2. Unity of the
Human Race. Summary of the Proof.—(a.) We must Accept the Cosmogony of
Moses, or Deny the Inspiration of the entire Scriptures.—(b.) God's entire Dealings with the Race, and the Absolute Nature and Career of the Race, prove its
Oneness.—(c.) Such also, is the Universal Testimony of the Race itself, and of its
entire History.—(d.) Scientifically, as well as Historically and Divinely Certain.—
(e.) Connected Utterance of Thought in Speech. Gift of Tongues.—(f.) The Testimony of Philosophy.—(g.) If the Case had been otherwise, the Certainty of it
would necessarily have been Absolute.—3. Difference between Fallen Angels
and Fallen Men, in the particular herein disclosed. Different Dealings of God
with the two.—II. 1. This Universal Ruin of Man is Irremediable, of itself, or by
him.—(a.) Not only no Tendency to Spontaneous Restoration, but a Tendency
to greater Guilt and Misery, Personal, General, and Perpetual.—(b.) The Ruin has
its Root in Man's Nature, which must be Changed to Repair the Ruin, and this
God only can do.—(c.) The Misery of Man being the Product of Sin, is absolutely
Irremediable while Sin Continues.—(d.) The Nature of the Case exacts, not the
Restoration, but the Perdition of Man.—(e.) There was no Remedy possible, or
even conceivable, except the Sacrifice of Christ.—(f.) Not only the Fact, and the
Knowledge, but the Enforcement of a Divine Remedy, necessary.—(g.) Man's
Condition of Sin and Misery Utterly Helpless.—2. This Irremediable and Uni-
versal Ruin as Just as it is deploraable.—III. 1. Inscrutable Nature of our Con-
dition and Destiny.—2. Revealed Religion Accepts, and Solves, this Fearful
Problem.—3. Its first Explanation of the Cause and Mode of this Ruin.—4.
Completeness of it. 5. Conclusion.

I.—1. THE sinful and miserable condition of man in his natural
state, as it has been explained in the two preceding chapters, is
not only that of the race in general, but is also that of every individual of the race. Among the innumerable proofs of this which
the word of God points out, and which are forced upon us in
the most convincing manner, as often as we allow the daily occurrences of life to direct our attention to the true import of such
things ; there is one continually insisted on, which is so sad and
so impressive that any single occurrence of it ought to be con-

clusive ; and which is, besides, so universal and so constant, as to be always before the face of all mankind. What is death ? And why does it desolate the whole earth, and every household on its broad surface with irresistible and pitiless ravages ? It is God only who has solved this terrible enigma.[1] Death, he tells us, had not, at first, any place in the universe : it entered it afterward : it entered by sin. By the offence of the first man, and that offence an act of disobedience to God, sin entered, and entering reigned unto death. In its own nature, it alone of all maladies tends always to destruction—never toward restoration ; for every time our fallen nature conceives, it brings forth sin ; and in its progress and completion, sin always produces death.[2] And the sole reason why death has passed upon all, is that all have sinned. So that even before the promulgation of the law, even from Adam to Moses, the world was full of dead men's bones : and so that, even during that long period, and even admitting that sin against positive law cannot be imputed nor the effects thereof follow, before the law itself exists—yet even then death reigned even over those who, having committed no actual transgression, proved by their fate, that our very nature is sinful. It is in Adam that all die.[3] For God hath made of one blood all nations of men for to dwell on all the face of the earth.[4] By nature every child of Adam is a child of wrath.[5] Every triumph of death is a testimony unto us, at once of our origin and our pollution.

2. It may be worth while to point out briefly some of the more obvious proofs of this fundamental truth that the whole family of man is one race, descended from one man and one woman ; seeing that all the dealings of God with us, and the whole current of divine revelation proceed upon the constant assumption that it is so, and his word abounds with the most explicit declarations of its certainty, while the truth itself has encountered the most steadfast opposition, and still finds some of the highest names amongst living philosophers arrayed against it.

(a) The Mosaic Cosmogony might be true, and yet the authenticity and the inspiration of the record which contains it, might not be capable of proof ; that is, the facts stated may be true, while it may be also true that Moses did not record them, and also

[1] Romans, v. 12–21. [2] James, i. 15. [3] 1 Corinthians, xv. 22.
[4] Acts, xvii. 26. [5] Ephesians, xi. 3.

true that the person who did record them, whoever he was, was not inspired. But the reverse is wholly impossible. If the personal story of Moses is true, and if he, being inspired by God, actually wrote the books which pass under his name, then it is impossible for his account of the creation of the visible universe to be false. But Moses, thus inspired and thus writing, has told us repeatedly and in the most precise manner, that God created Adam, and then formed Eve out of a part of his person, and that from these two, male and female, all the families of man are descended. The first nine chapters of Genesis contain a clear account of the creation and fall of man, and of the progress and ruin of the race till its destruction by the flood and its re-establishment afterward in the family of Noah. The tenth and eleventh chapters contain a precise account of the peopling of the earth by the descendants of Noah, and a detailed statement of the nations and races, embracing the confusion of human language in the plain of Shinar, and the dispersion and settlement of mankind, down to the time of Abraham ; the whole embracing a period of nearly two thousand years. Subsequent portions of the divine writings bring down this general history of man about twenty-two centuries further, and terminate it in the bosom of the Roman Empire, when that empire was at the height of its glory. Now if the Old and New Testaments are inspired books, the Cosmogony of Moses, and as a part of it the unity of the human race, is as certain as that Jesus Christ is the Saviour of the world.

(*b*) The whole course of God's dealing with the family of man, and the whole influence of those dealings upon every portion of the race in every age of the world, and every condition of civilization—incontestably prove that they are, and that God has always considered and treated them as being one and the same race. Where the moral, intellectual, and physical qualities of any number of human beings are essentially identical : where the same providential, and the same gracious, and the same disciplinary dealings of the same gracious God essentially surround them all, and affect them in a precisely similar way : where the same pollution involves them all, the same susceptibility of recovery exists in all, the same nature pervades all, the same law applies to all, the same Saviour is suitable to all, the same truth is applicable to all : it seems to be the merest absurdity, the merest affectation and pedantry of science, to question the absolute identity of the race, and to assert its original and fundamental diversity upon inferior and secondary differences, such as are liable to occur to every race, even in a degree immeasurably greater than has been manifested in the human race.

(c) Passing from the divine to the purely human aspect of the subject, there are considerations which seem to be overwhelmingly conclusive. At the head of these we may place the historical argument. Profane history reaches with certainty only to the era of the Persians : we glean fragmentary information only, of earlier ages, from Egyptian, Assyrian, and Chaldean remains : before all, and parallel with all after the dawn of profane history, we have the sacred history from the beginning of the world down many centuries into the bosom of certain history : and since the canon of Scripture was closed, we have innumerable records, embracing at length every family of man. Now it may be asserted with the greatest confidence that in all this track of ages, and in all this mass of knowledge, there does not exist a solitary fact, or a single historic monument, which is not perfectly compatible with the unity of the whole race embraced by the whole narrative : but that innumerable facts and countless monuments are scattered thickly throughout this vast period of nearly six thousand years, which are utterly irreconcilable with any other belief than that the human race is one race. That it is so, is the testimony of the race itself, throughout its whole career : and all the means of forming an opinion which it has preserved for us, renders it absolutely certain that its testimony is true.

(d) We may not wholly pass by three separate arguments, founded upon three separate sciences, one of them essentially physical, one of them chiefly logical, and one of them pertaining to the higher philosophy : I allude to the arguments drawn from Physiology, Philology, and Ethnology. Touching the first, it may be confidently asserted that the more familiar we become with the great truths and facts of our physical being, the more assured is the conviction that the differences which exist amongst men are but secondary, while the resemblances are thorough and original. The mode of production, growth, decay, and death, is precisely the same in all men. One fundamental and most complicated structure pervades the whole race : the same vital organization, the same vital laws : the same healthful, and the same morbid manifestations : the same senses arranged and used in the same way, and capable of the same culture and abuse : the same mental faculties, in the same order, and depending in the same manner upon the physical organization and the personal culture : the same moral nature connected in the same mysterious way both with the body and with the mind : the same passions, the same will, the same religious instincts, the same freedom, the same intelligence, the same depravity, and all similarly affected by temperament and the nervous system. Doubtless the culture of ages under favorable circumstances places one portion of the race, in many respects far above another portion, in many physical, as well as in many moral and intellectual respects. But while the immense power of culture upon all races is undeniable even to the extent of producing changes as great as are compatible with the preservation of essential unity : it may well be doubted whether any culture is capable of producing any diversities of whatever kind, greater than are to be found accidentally produced amongst individuals of the same variety, indeed in the very same household. If this be so, and we feel sure it is so, the declaration that two children having the same parents, but differing widely from each other in certain respects, are not of the same race ; is not so great an absurdity as the declaration that two children of Adam, whose differences are considerable, but not so great as in the former case, are members of different races.

(e) The power of connected expression of thought in speech, is one of the most astonishing gifts which God has bestowed on man, and is one of the most exalted marks which distinguishes every member of the human family, from every other creature. As soon as God had created man in his own image, he blessed him and spoke to him in articulate language.[1] And afterward he brought unto him every beast of the field, and every fowl of the air, to see what he would call them :[2] so that to hear the voice of God, and to speak in accordance with the will of God, are the first recorded acts of the first created man. The whole earth was of one language and one speech, and all people were one people from the Deluge till God confounded their language that they could not understand one another's speech, at Babel in

[1] Gen., i. 27–30.   [2] Gen., ii. 19, 20.

Shinar, and scattered them abroad from thence upon the face of all the earth.[1] At the end of eighteen centuries there were assembled in Jerusalem on the great day of Pentecost, devout men out of every nation under heaven; amongst whom fifteen languages, wherein they were born, are expressly enumerated by the Apostle; and their amazement and confusion at hearing Galileans speak them all, is recorded as one of the striking incidents of that glorious day;[2] and surely amongst all miracles, that gift of tongues was one of the most unsearchable. Considered in the light thus gathered from the word of God, there is no marvel that we find everywhere, this peculiar and unbroken connection between man and the connected utterance of thought by speech: no marvel that we find the most profound relations between the forms of thought and the forms of speech: no marvel that there should be families of tongues answering to families of nations: no marvel that we should find in all tongues the traces of one primeval language: no marvel that we should discover in the structure of all human speech, those everlasting principles of logic, of metaphysics and of philosophy, which belong to thought itself, and which are a part of the life of the soul which clothes its thought in speech. But there is great marvel that such wonderful things should distinguish every man that ever existed, and should separate every one of them from every creature besides, and yet should be thought insufficient to establish a common nature, and common origin for the race.

(*f*) Rising a step higher we hear the testimony of the youngest, and one of the fairest daughters of philosophy. Let us separate the universal race of man into the peoples, and families, and nations, apparently so diverse from each other, and many times so hostile to each other; so widely separated as they seem in their religions, their manners, their institutions, and their laws. Let us trace them across the long track of ages, following all their great wanderings, watching over their various developments, studying their alternate conquests and subjugations, beholding their mixtures and their separations, their achievements and their decay. It is not simply individual man, nor yet the form which society puts on, now here, now there, whose history we would know: it is society itself, the peoples, the families, the nations, thus so long and so variously manifested, that we ques-

Gen., xi. 1–9.   [2] Acts, ii. 1–13.

tion about those mysteries of which history so long thought it beneath her high province to take cognizance. And now what is the response which is uttered only more and more distinctly and confidently, as more and more carefully the life of all the peoples, and families, and nations, is explored? Is it that they are distinct races, having each, or even many, a distinct origin, a diverse nature, another destiny? Far otherwise. Nations the most remotely situated with reference to each other have been proved to be members of the very same family. Peoples now thoroughly homogeneous have been shown to be the product of many varieties mingled together. Families once supposed to have little in common, have turned out to be branches of the self-same stock. Beneath all the diversified differences which time, and chance, and culture have begotten, there is everywhere manifest the common nature, the common endowment, the common characteristics of man, as man: those grand marks which distinguish him as utterly distinct from every creature, except that single man whom God created in his own image, and the innumerable race which has sprung from his loins.

(*g*) It is not without its use to remark how totally every hypothesis which denies the unity of the human race is destitute of any positive or even rational foundation, and how completely the origin of mankind is hid in darkness the very moment we depart from that account of it which the Scriptures set before us with perfect distinctness, and which all the knowledge we possess thoroughly confirms. This consideration alone ought to be decisive. The existence of man upon earth is comparatively recent: and at the very commencement of that existence his condition appears to have been one of exalted civilization. The oldest monuments that have existed are the most stupendous and imperishable: the earliest records that exist are still the most venerated and influential which the human race possesses. How could such people be utterly ignorant of their own origin, when they could almost clasp hands with the primeval man? How could Noah be ignorant of Adam, or Abraham of Noah, or Moses of Abraham, or the whole Jewish people, with all their prophets and apostles, be ignorant of Moses? The thing is impossible; and the knowledge thus delivered to us, is exact, simple, coherent, and complete. The moment we reject it we are first to suppose that men did not know what, situated as they were, they could hardly avoid knowing ; and then we are to follow the guidance of a crowd of shallow pretenders, and bitter scoffers, who cannot possibly know that which they pretend to know, interspersed here and there with a few fanciful men of learning, who substitute the solemn declarations of God with conceits unworthy of a reasonable man.

3. This course of reflection, so far from being barren, leads us to take notice of the remarkable difference in the dealings of God with two classes of his fallen creatures, namely, fallen men and fallen angels : a difference founded in some degree as we may venture to believe, on the total difference of the nature of angels from the nature of men in the very particular which has just been discussed. Adam stands to the whole family of man as their natural head and common progenitor : the oneness of their blood, their common brotherhood, and the unity of the race all depend upon their common relationship to him. Herein also is laid the necessary ground for that relation of Adam to all his posterity, which we express by calling it a federal relation, a covenanted headship : a relation constituted by God in the Covenant of Works, between himself on one side, and Adam for himself, and for all his posterity on the other. Moreover this natural and this covenanted headship of Adam, this mode of existence of the human race, and this relation of the race to God under the Covenant of Works, explicate clearly many aspects of the fall of man, and the effects of that great catastrophe upon all mankind descending from Adam by ordinary generation. Thus too, if we may for a moment so far anticipate our subject, the sublime fact and the infinitely glorious method of redemption for fallen man ; the very constitution of the person, and the whole nature of the work of the divine mediator between God and man : all involve the great fact of the unity of the human race, and all contemplate and respect the great principles which are illustrated in the Covenant of Works, the fall of man, and the ruin of the human race. So pregnant are the fundamental truths, even those apparently the most remote, which enter into these vast themes. With the other race of fallen creatures, every thing is different. The celestial intelligences are pure spirits, each one created, none descended from the rest :[1] whether they be thrones, or dominions, or powers, or principalities, or hierarchies, or cher-

<hr>

[1] Math., xxii. 30.

ubim, or seraphim, none are related to each other as man is related to his brother man, as all men are related to their common progenitor. Now there is no method known to us, no method intimated in the word of God, whereby a fallen creature can be restored to the lost image and favor of God, except only by the taking of the nature of the fallen creature into indissoluble union with the divine nature, in the person of the Son of God ; and then the outworking by this divine Mediator of all that may be required to save the lost. This is the single method which infinite wisdom and infinite power, directed by infinite beneficence has found effectual to the solution of that greatest problem which involves the glory of God.[1] In the case of man, the unity of the whole race, the absolute oneness of the nature of all, made one incarnation, one sacrifice of the Mediator, effectual and complete.[2] In the case of the fallen angels a separate appearing, a separate sacrifice of the Son of God would seem to have been necessary as often as a single fallen angel wholly distinct from other fallen angels was saved by him. Wherefore the Scripture saith : " Verily, he took not on him the nature of angels, but he took on him the seed of Abraham."[3]

II.—1. There are, no doubt, precious and fruitful elements in human nature defaced and weakened as it is ; and the glorious image of God in which it was originally created, is still discernible upon it. It is not what it was at first, it is depraved ; but it is still human nature, though enveloped in ruin which covers the whole race and involves the entire being. The thing we are now to consider, is not how much our ruined race can accomplish, not of what it is susceptible by means of any further superhuman influence manifested upon it : but directly, whether or not it is capable, of itself, of extricating itself from the estate into which it has fallen, and restoring itself to the estate in which it was created. If not, its ruin is as irremediable as it is universal. The latter has been proved : let us now consider the former.

(a) Whatever may be the cause of man's condition, it is abundantly evident that all the efforts yet put forth by him, have produced no spiritual amelioration, although so long put forth, and put forth in every form and condition of which his being is naturally capable. Whatever individual cases of ame-

---

[1] 1 Cor., i. 24–30   [2] Heb., ix. 26–28.   [3] Heb., ii. 16.

lioration might be supposed to have occurred, their force is spent on the individual, leaving his posterity in the state of depravity common to man. There is a tendency, extremely constant if not invariable in every individual, to grow worse and not better as he advances from childhood to manhood, and then to old age ; a tendency to be found in the life of society itself, considered altogether : so that the very notion of spontaneous restoration, whether in individuals or in societies, is inconsistent with the actual nature of things.

(*b*) The change required is one of nature not of condition : all our meditations have chiefly concerned man's nature, and have looked to his condition only as developing that nature. But it is impossible that any creature can change its own nature. For every creature, man amongst the rest, has a derived existence, which follows the laws of its being, and which the creature can no more change than he can create himself.[1] The particular change moreover, which is needed in man, as a moral and accountable creature, involves not only a willingness, but a strong desire for a total revolution in his own nature ; which desire and willingness are inconceivable and impossible, while he is left to act freely in his own nature : for that of itself cannot so abhor itself, as to seek its own radical change. But if this desire is implanted in him from without, as for example by God, that is God's gracious remedy, not the effect of man's own spontaneous effort after re-creation.

(*c*) If there be such distinctions as virtue and vice, happiness and misery, as it has been shown there are, they must exist by virtue of the law of nature, or the law of God, or both : and they must so exist that happiness goes along with virtue, and misery with vice : for to suppose the contrary would be to put an end to the moral nature of man, by abolishing all moral distinctions in God, in nature, and in man. But it has been abundantly shown that man is naturally both vicious and miserable, and moreover that it is wholly beyond his power to change his own nature. It necessarily follows that the viciousness of his nature, and the misery of his condition are wholly irremediable by him.

(*d*) The suffering which follows transgression, and the happiness which attends virtue, are incontestable proofs that the affairs of the universe are under the control of an infinite Ruler ;

---

[1] Jeremiah, xiii. 23.

that the nature of his eminent dominion is strictly moral: and that he administers his government with perfect righteousness, and infinite exactness, so far as we can observe and understand it.   Under such a government as this, even if the Scriptures had not explicitly told us that every transgression and disobedience must receive its just recompense of reward,[1] it would be wholly inconceivable how such a rebellious and daring transgressor as man, could, if left to himself, escape out of the hands of God, or answer at his dreadful bar.

(e) Moreover, if we leave out of the question, the remedy provided, and the deliverance offered by God in Christ, it is beyond the power of our utmost faculties to conceive how there could be any remedy for such a case as ours, under the administration of an omnipotent moral ruler ; much less to contrive one ourselves, and least of all to conceive, to contrive, and then to execute it.   And God himself being judge, there was no remedy which even his own infinite wisdom could devise, or his own boundless power could execute, except that inconceivable remedy in the blood of his only-begotten Son.[2]

(f) And again: even after this remedy is plainly and fully made known to man, if he be left to himself, it is of no avail. For his old man is not the subject of such a law, as the change in his condition involves, to wit, the perfect law of God; nor is it possible to make that old man subject to that law: for the law itself is foolishness unto him.[3] So that not only a divine remedy, and the divine communication of that remedy to him, but the divine enforcement of it on him, are all indispensable to the extrication of man from his depraved and miserable estate.

(g) And again : supposing, for a moment, that man was once in a better condition, which indeed his heart still whispers to him he was ; and supposing also that the Scripture account of his fall is true : how can it be conceived as possible, that a being who when he was pure and wise deliberately rejected God, should be really able, or should sincerely desire, when in a state of pollution, both to recover the estate which he had forfeited, and then retain it, after thus marvelously recovering it, better than he retained it before he forfeited it ?   That is to say, we are to admit that a desperately wicked man desires and is able

<hr>

[1] Heb., ii. 2.   [2] Rom., i. 16, 32.   [3] Rom., viii. 6, 7

to do a thousand-fold more to recover the lost favor of God, than the same man when righteous would do to retain the favor of God before he lost it, when it is of the very nature of sin to do nothing, and of righteousness to do every thing that pleases God.

2. It is therefore perfectly certain that the fearful misery of man's estate admits of no remedy whatever, except by first remedying the sin from which it flows: that the sin itself is wholly irremediable and therefore the misery too, by any thing that man can do : that any remedy whatever, when we come to look at the whole case fairly, seems to ourselves utterly inconceivable : and that if any remedy really exists, it must result from the direct interposition of God, prompted by considerations drawn from within himself; an interposition which man has no title to demand, and the considerations which could prompt it hid in the bosom of God. We may well bewail a condition so deplorable : but there is no rational ground on which we can gainsay it, no righteous one on which we can complain of it.

III.—1. The exact cause of this universal and irremediable estate of man, and the time and manner of the falling of a calamity so terrible upon him, the entrance in short of moral and physical evil into the world, and its dreadful reign, lie beyond the pale of philosophy, of natural religion, and even of scientific morals, in their widest application. To these all, it is an inscrutable mystery that man should be as he is, full of paradoxes and inexplicable contradictions : and the cause of his being what he is, is to them wholly unsearchable. That God is himself the direct cause of the sin and suffering of man : that there are two first causes, one good and one evil : that it is of the nature of matter to produce sin and suffering, and that matter is eternal and creative : that all sin and suffering have a tendency to purify the immaterial part of man, and that his soul is passing through an infinite series of habitations, rising higher in each : that man has no soul at all, nor any immortality, and that all he calls evil, whether moral or physical, is the mere result of organization and accident, and will soon terminate with him, in the dust : that there is no God at all, and that the total moral and physical derangement of the universe, proves that there is none, and that all things are fortuitous : that every thing is God, man himself being one of the possible forms of the divine outbirths, one of the modes of one of the Attributes of God, and that our notions of creation and providence, of accountability and punishment, are themselves the real cause of most of the evils of our estate, which are really self-inflicted : that these sins and evils are confined to this life, and are the results of mere imitation and false training, and will have no effect beyond death, after which all men will be eternally blessed : that there are innumerable gods and other intelligences above man, some good, some bad, of whom man is the victim and the sport : that there is in all things, and over all things, an inexorable fate, one of whose decrees placed us in the condition in which we find ourselves.   Such are mere examples of the views and faith of some of the most wide-spread schools of philosophy, religion, and morals, that have prevailed in this ruined world of ours.   Proofs the most incontestable both of the power and the blindness of our religious instincts, and of the inscrutable nature of our condition and destiny.

2. Let it be remembered, that upon any theory of morals, of religion, or of philosophy, the facts themselves are to be accounted for, or are to be left, an equal blot upon them all.   So that even if the religion we profess, and which we call divine, should have failed to account for what none else can account for, and to explain what none else can explain, so far as that difficulty went, the question between it and all other systems would remain where it was.   But if it accepts this grand problem of our nature and our universe, as one which it behooves it to solve, as a religion professing to be divine, and to be given expressly on account of this very condition of man : and does actually, completely, and satisfactorily solve it : I do not see how its claims to a superhuman intelligence founded on that great and before impossible achievement, are to be resisted. And, moreover, when the complete solution it offers, not only accords perfectly with all we know of ourselves, and our past existence, and present condition, but throws a flood of light backward and forward, over the whole subject of our primeval and our eternal relation to God, as well as our present nature and estate ; it seems to me impossible to doubt that a power far above any we possess has, at last, interposed.

3. This, then, briefly, is the solution offered.   It is admitted, that originally moral evil, and physical evil, which is its result, had no place in the universe of God.   It is asserted that amongst

the primeval creatures of God, called angels, some rebelled, fell, and were condemned by God. That God when he created man formed him in his own image, and made with him a covenant of eternal life, upon condition of perfect obedience. That man, under the temptation of Satan, one of the fallen angels, broke his covenant with God, disobeyed, fell, and incurred the penalty of that covenant, not only for himself, but as the natural and as the federal and covenanted head of all who should descend from him by ordinary generation. And that the actual state of man as a creature of God, is fully explained by the fact that he now lies under the penalty and curse of that violated covenant, the sweep of which and its condemnation are universal and eternal.[1]

4. Each one of these points, and many others connected with them, require full elucidation as fundamental parts of revealed theology. At present they are stated exclusively as containing the only explanation ever offered to man which is worthy of the vast subject to which it relates, and which is in itself absolutely complete, of the true manner and circumstances of the entrance of sin into the universe, of the mode in which man fell under its pollution and penalty, and of the influence of the fall upon his nature and destiny.

5. The absolute universality, the irremediable nature, and the fearful cause of the ruin which has fallen upon man, are thus exhibited, in some slight degree, before us, as we advance our researches into a subject which so deeply concerns us all.

[1] Genesis, i., ii., iii.

CHAPTER IV.

THE DIVINE INTERPOSITION TO SAVE MAN.

I. 1. The Interposition of God Sovereign, Gracious and Effectual, through the Word made Flesh.—2. Natural Grounds of Hope.—3. Insufficiency of Human Speculation.—4. Divine Revelation. The Son of God. The Holy Spirit.—II. 1. The Method and Principle of God's Interposition.—2. It is, and must be, essentially Gracious.—3. The Possible Results considered. The Actual Result proved.—III. 1. The Motive and Manner of the Divine Interposition, alike Supernatural.—2. The Fact and Mode of that Interposition dependent on the Nature of the Being and Perfections of God. The Infinite Beneficence of an Infinite Spirit, possessing in Himself the Source of all Truth, all Goodness, and all Power, the Root of our Salvation.—3. The Infinite Manifestation of God's Saving Grace could be made only through the Incarnation and Sacrifice of his Only Begotten Son.—4. The Purpose of God to repair the Ruin of Man was made known from the Fall of Man, and was itself Eternal.

I.—1. WITH the blessed word of God in our hands, many things become perfectly clear to us, which but for its teachings would have been, as to some of them, extremely uncertain to us, while others would have remained in profound obscurity, if indeed it had ever occurred to us to meditate upon them at all. Whether God would or would not interfere to ameliorate the ruined condition of man, or to extricate him out of it, are questions far beyond any ability of ours to answer: nay it is not certain that we should, of ourselves, ever have had a just conception of what our true condition was. God vindicates to himself his infinite sovereignty in interposing at all ; and then again in making his interposition effectual : while at the same time he continually asserts both the ruin and the helplessness of man. They who receive power to become the sons of God, receive the Son of God, by reason of being themselves born of God. Born, says the Apostle John, not of blood, nor of the will of the flesh, nor of the will of man, but of God.[1] So that the divine power and the new birth, are not only explicitly declared to be the cause and

[1] John, i. 12–14.

tht means, but every other possible cause and mean is expressly
stated and denied. That which is not hereditary in man, that
which man cannot accomplish for himself, and that which no
man can do for another, is exactly that which is impossible;
since these three categories embrace every human way of influencing the nature and condition of man. The sole remaining
way is divine. God interposes through the Word made flesh.
In doing so, he does it, not only sovereignly, but freely, graciously, justly, effectually, wonderfully: the grand end being his
own glory: the subordinate end being the salvation of man.

2. It is equally true, on the other side, that we could not know
beforehand that God would not interpose to save us: still less
would it have been possible for us to know that he could not do
so. There were indeed, if they had been known and considered
by us, grounds on which to rest a vague hope, perhaps even a
vague expectation, that in some unsearchable manner, he both
could and would do for us far above all we could ask or even
think. We might have founded something on the very nature
of our own inner life: ruined and yet hoping; sinning and yet
discontented with our sins and with ourselves on account of them;
the ruins of a better nature struggling within us; glimpses of
an immortal life caught by the dark soul; the idea of annihilation and the idea of eternal misery alike appalling to us; strong
aspirations for peace with God, without knowing wherein it consisted or how it might be obtained. We might have founded
something also on what we naturally know of God: so many proofs
of his mercy and goodness, exhibited in so many ways to so many
of the unthankful and disobedient; such proofs of his absolute
dominion and irresistible power, combined always with such condescension and forbearance; so many intimations in nature and
in providence, that we ought to trust that he who had gone so
far would go still farther—yea even to the utmost, to bless and
save us. And we might have founded something too on the mixed
and contradictory state of all things here below, looking for their
correction in a future and better state of existence, and longing
for some purifying influence from above to fit us for the service
and enjoyment of God in that higher world.

3. The end of all our hopes, our reasoning, and our meditations is, however, to turn the whole subject back upon God and
over to him absolutely, as far above any solution by us. It is

needless to add anything to the immense diversity which we find in the speculations of mankind upon such a subject. As one or other view of the case has pressed on the mind of man and occupied it supremely; it has conducted him to a peculiar view of God, of nature, of religion, of morals, and ultimately of the nature and operations of his own mind and soul, utterly different from the views taken by him who occupied himself with a different aspect of the case. We pass all by, as being, however curious in themselves, altogether subordinate in an inquiry into Revealed Theology.

4. It is here then that we come immediately to the question of a Divine revelation. I observe at once, that the method I adopt adjourns the detailed treatment of that great question to what is commonly called the department of Polemic Theology: at the head of which it will be discussed. In the meantime I will assume as true, authentic, and inspired oracles of God, the Scriptures of the Old and New Testaments : and will suggest, continually, such incidental proofs as naturally arise. Under every aspect of the subject, it is obvious, that any interposition which it might please God to make for the deliverance of man, must, to be effectual, be made in such a way as will establish its own reality, and make known with certainty what God says and does. We are to remember that we can have no adequate conception of God, nor indeed any certain knowledge of him at all, except through the manifestations he makes of himself to us. The supreme manifestation which he makes of himself to fallen men, is in Jesus Christ his Son our Lord ; and next to this, is the Divine Scriptures, wherein the whole will of God is made known to us for our salvation : and akin to both is the work of the Holy Spirit within us, awakening, quickening and sanctifying the soul. It is of no consequence to determine at this point, in how many ways God has actually manifested himself to man ; much less to inquire in how many ways he might make his will known to us. For us, here is the complete volume of his word : here is his only begotten Son, the Mediator between him and us : here is the Divine Spirit, sent by the Father and the Son. Omitting for the present, every other manifestation of God, these are divinely certain and effectual ways in which Jehovah manifests himself for our salvation ; and therein is the proof at once, and

the method of his interposition to deliver man from his estate of
sin and misery.

II.—1. We are not competent to suggest any reason which
would have precluded an Almighty Ruler from restoring man
after his fall, to the position he occupied before that fall ; at the
same time, by his omnipotent power, restoring every portion of
his universe to the condition it occupied before the entrance of
sin. Another, and another, and a thousand trials, might have
been given to Adam. To what end, we are equally incompetent
to say. The actual conduct of God reveals to us what so many
other parts of his conduct establishes, and what no part of it con-
tradicts—namely: that it is a universal rule of the Divine procedure, from which God never departs, and from which he would
not then depart, even to extricate the universe from sin and death,
not to repeat a second time, precisely what had failed before:
not to allow a second opportunity, so to speak, precisely on the
same conditions, which were despised and rejected before. Even
when the fundamental principle is the same, the circumstances,
or the method of its application is changed. They who would not
stand in holiness under a covenant of works, shall never be restored to holiness by a covenant of works, nor stand thereby any
more forever. And this principle, sublime as it is, and infinitely
fruitful as it must become in the dominion of a God of unwasting
fulness, and whose dominion is over all, and through eternity,
lies in a manner, at the foundation of God's interposition to save
men, and rightly considered, throws a remarkable light upon the
manner in which the benefits of that interposition can be, and
actually are, applied to us. The mode in which man is saved is
not the converse even of the way in which he was lost ; much
less is the principle of the two results the same. On one side it
is the wages of sin which make death inevitable : on the other,
it is the gift of God, that eternal life becomes ours through
Jesus Christ our Lord.[1] How much heresy and folly as well as
bad philosophy this simple but grand truth obliterates !

2. We are not competent to assert, that even if man had
been restored to innocence and another trial, or ten thousand
successive trials had been allowed to him on precisely the same
conditions as those under which he fell, he would have maintained his primitive state and reaped the promised reward. The

---

[1] Romans, vi. 23.

interposition of God, therefore, to save him, or his ultimate perdition, was inevitable, even on that hypothesis : and if an interposition of God, then, first or last, a gracious interposition : and therefore, viewing the subject on the human side of it, as before on the divine side of it, we arrive at the same result, namely, a mode of saving him wholly different from the mode in which he fell, or no mode of saving him at all. All this involves, besides, as we shall see more fully hereafter, that the estate into which man will be brought by the interposition of God to save him is not, and cannot be, similiar to the one from which he fell ; but must be essentially different from it. The restored man cannot possibly be what the unfallen man was : but must be essentially different, both in himself, and his relations to God and to the universe. It follows, moreover, that a state of perfection, to a being who has moral freedom, who is morally accountable, and who has a dependent being, affords no absolute security against a lapse which shall entail utter ruin. Two examples only have occurred in the universe, as far as we know, of races thus situated ; those namely of angels and of men. The first resulted in the fall, and the ruin without recovery, of part of the heavenly intelligences : and all the rest of them are indebted to the interposition of God, for their continuing steadfast. The second resulted in the fall of the whole race of man ; with the rational possibility of the recovery of them all, and the divine certainty of the recovery of the elect, through the interposition of God.

3. The interposition of God in the case of fallen man, is obviously susceptible in the nature of the case, of either one of three results, each of which is rationally possible, no two of which could occur, while some one of them must come to pass. Either the whole race of man must be restored and saved : or the divine interposition must prove so far ineffectual that none will be restored and saved : or a part of the race will be restored and saved, and the remainder fail of restoration and salvation. One or other of the results is obliged to occur; because taken together they completely exhaust the possibilities of the case. If we were to consider the probable effect of the divine interposition, it is most likely we should decide that of the three possible events, the one most likely to occur, would be the restoration of the whole race of man : and if our judgment were influenced exclusively by considering the divine element which enters into

the problem, and with our natural bias to exalt such attributes of God as seem to favor our miserable case, and to overlook such as seem to bear against that case, it cannot be doubted that we should rest firmly in this conclusion. If on the other hand, we should restrict our meditations chiefly to the human element which enters into the problem, and should consider man's terrible alienation from God, and from all that is true and good ; we could hardly avoid the conclusion that the second possible result would occur, and that the whole race would find means, if left to themselves, of defeating the most unsearchable mercy of God, rather than accept deliverance on any terms which it would be possible for God to offer, and would perish rather than be holy. In like manner, if we would estimate fairly both the elements— the divine and the human, the mercy of God and obduracy of man in ceaseless and universal conflict with each other, the third possible result would appear to be unavoidable ; and while multitudes would embrace God's rich provision for their salvation, other multitudes, perhaps more numerous, would obstinately reject the counsel of God against their own souls, and even aggravate their perdition by adding the rejection of their Saviour to the previous rejection of their Creator. This last is precisely what has happened since the beginning of time. The whole sum of human experience exhibits to us, as actually and constantly occurring, exactly that which, in the given state of the case, seemed to human reason to be inevitable. And to the same purport are all the declarations of the Word of God, as to the invariable effects of the Gospel amongst men. For while it is never wholly barren, it is never universally fruitful. Everywhere it finds willing listeners who joyfully accept its divine teaching, and everywhere it encounters unbelief and contempt : everywhere men are saved by it, and everywhere men reject it and perish. And herein lies one of those remarkable proofs of which the number is so vast and the weight so crushing, that the Scriptures must needs be true and divine, or the testimony of human reason, consciousness, and experience, must needs be false. The whole Gentile world for eighteen centuries, wherever the Gospel has been preached, is one boundless illustration of that great conclusion of all the Apostles, that God did visit the Gentiles to take out of them a people for his name.[1]   And this is what God is doing still.

____
[1] Acts, xv. 14.

III.—1. It is impossible for us to elevate our conceptions high enough, and extend our survey wide enough, to comprehend the real nature of the overwhelming problem of a just God interposing to save a rebellious universe from the fate it had brought upon itself, even when the knowledge of his purpose to do so comes to us simultaneously with the knowledge that the universe is ruined. We can readily understand that God is under no obligations whatever, to entertain such a problem : and just as readily that every hope of man is involved in its being effectually and mercifully solved. We can perceive clearly that every interposition of God, must be in perfect accordance with all his own infinite perfections, with the nature and condition of man, with the relations of God and man to each other, and with the relations of both to the whole universe. Whatever comes short of the illustration of the infinite perfections of God, and of his own supreme glory, and the highest good of his universe therein, is inconceivable as a motive worthy of him : while whatever is prompted by all these considerations it is inconceivable that he should not do. But could it ever have been conceived to be possible that the most complete of all illustrations of the glory of God, was to be made to the universe in the salvation of lost man ; and that in the achievement of this boundless glory of his love, God would not spare his own Son, but would freely deliver him up for us all !' It is in such aspects as these of the divine nature and acts, that we may well be overwhelmed with astonishment alike at the depravity which can resist such manifestations, and at the madness which can ascribe such conceptions to beings like ourselves !

2. We see at once, from the nature of the case, as well as from the whole manner of treating it, that the mode of God's being—the highest question to which the faculties of man can be directed—enters into the whole matter we are now considering, with a controlling force. Remitting to its proper place the particular discussion of that subject, it will be sufficient at present to accept the short definition commonly adopted by the church of God for more than two centuries, by which to illustrate more fully the foundation laid in the very being of God, for that divine interposition to save fallen man, which is in one sense the fundamental point of Revealed Religion. " God is a Spirit, infinite,

---

¹ Romans, viii. 32.

eternal, and unchangeable in his being, wisdom, power, holiness, justice, goodness, and truth." He who is higher than the heavens, who is deeper than hell, whom no man can know, and no man can reach,[1] is of himself, an all-sufficient, self-existent, infinite Being.[2] In his essence, he is an infinite Spirit, undivided, and without parts, or passions.[3] It is of his nature to possess every perfection, in a manner corresponding to his substance, and therefore infinitely, eternally, and unchangeably. Of these infinite perfections, whose number also is infinite, six are stated in the definition, as amongst the chief attributes of the Godhead known to man. Of these, two, namely his Wisdom and his Power, are manifestly different from each other, and from the other-four, which are alike, namely, his Holiness, Justice, Goodness, and Truth. These differences are sufficiently expressed by saying that Infinite Power appertains to God considered as an Infinite Spirit, possessing Infinite Intellect and Will; that Infinite Wisdom appertains to him considered with reference to the eternal distinction of True and False; and that Infinite Holiness, Justice, Goodness, and Truth, appertain to him considered with reference to the eternal distinction of Good and Evil. That is, we may call his Power an Essential Attribute, his Wisdom a Natural Attribute, and the other four, Moral Attributes. In the first two of these six Attributes of God, namely, his Wisdom and his Power, we perceive nothing on which we could found any hope of his interposing to deliver us; while in three of the four Moral Attributes, namely, his Holiness, his Justice, and his Truth, we perceive much on which to found the most serious, if not insuperable difficulties, in the way of our salvation. And if our knowledge ended here, our hopes would end here also. But he who spake to Moses on the Mount, as he stood ready to receive, on the tables of stone, the divine sum of all wisdom for all ages, proclaimed the name of Jehovah as he passed by his adoring servant, and then proclaimed that Jehovah, even Jehovah God, is merciful and gracious, is long-suffering and abundant in goodness, as well as in truth.[4] And so it is truly added that God is infinite, eternal, and unchangeable, in his Goodness no less than in his Holiness, Justice and Truth. And so there lies in the very being of God, that unsearchable Beneficence, which is the primal foundation of all his unspeakable

<hr>

[1] Job, xi. 7-9.   [2] Exodus, iii. 14.   [3] John, iv. 24.   [4] Exodus, xxxiv. 6.

grace and mercy to us ; to which we can follow back with trembling and adoring hearts, the whole chain of our salvation ; and the power of which is manifest throughout the universe, and most of all in the cross of Christ !

3. We preach, says the Apostle Paul,[1] Christ and him crucified. Whoever needs a sign of the love of God, let him turn to Calvary : whoever needs a proof of the wisdom in which God's love flows to us, let him look on the cross. I preach a deliverer who is God-man : I preach deliverance through that God-man crucified. The wisdom of God prompted by his infinite beneficence, found only that way to save sinners : the salvation of such sinners transcended the power of God, except they be washed in that blood : and then they become divinely wise in the wisdom of God, and divinely strong in the power of God.[2] Through faith in the blood of him whom God hath set forth to be a propitiation for our sins, not only may God be just and the justifier of him which believeth in Jesus, but he loudly proclaims his righteousness in the remission of sins, for which nothing but his forbearance had prevented him from cutting off all flesh.[3] Nor has immaculate truth any longer one word of condemnation even for a nature once utterly false, as soon as that nature is transformed into the likeness of him whose glory was in the fulness of grace and truth, the glory of the only-begotten of the Father,[4] and can claim fellowship with him, by whom is not only the sole access to the Father, but who is himself, the way, the truth, and the life.[5] So that every Attribute of God, of what kind soever, his Wisdom and his Power, his Holiness, his Justice, and his Truth—all prompted and marshalled by the eternal and unchangeable Love in which his infinite Goodness finds expression, concur in the fact, the method, and the result of his wondrous interposition to save lost men, and his still more wondrous purpose to make that interposition and salvation the highest and the broadest illustration of all his infinite perfections, to his supremest glory, throughout eternity !

4. In such inquiries and meditations as these, there is danger of a particular error which is extremely natural, and which we should carefully avoid. In trying to contemplate subjects so immense, and independently of a divine revelation, so obscure :

---

[1] 1 Cor., i. 23, 24.   [2] Rom., i. 16, 17.   [3] Rom., iii. 20- 26.
[4] John, i. 14.   [5] John, xiv. 6.

the weakness of our faculties often obliges us to study them under conditions which may not correspond throughout with the events, and to separate, in thought, things which, in reality, have been continually united. In like manner we are obliged, in order to estimate the influence of many events upon persons differently situated from ourselves, and the significance of those events in a state of knowledge very different from our own, to omit in our reasonings elements, which though well known to us, and of the highest importance, could not have entered into the case, in the particular state of it which it is our province to investigate. In point of fact the fall of man was immediately followed by the promise of our Saviour; there never was a time when God did not interpose to save man : and the whole human family might have possessed, throughout all generations, a knowledge of these truths. Nevertheless, we are bound to consider, and with the light we have are competent to determine, the natural state of man, considered merely as under the fall and independently of any such divine interposition ; since it is certain that millions of the human race in all ages, have continued in total ignorance that there was any Covenant of Grace, or any Redeemer of men : and since all men, while they continue in sin, continue absolutely under the covenant of works, by which salvation is wholly impossible of attainment, and are therefore in their ignorance and pollution, no whit better off than they would have been if a Saviour had never been revealed. We may indeed, go much further and say, that the Covenant of Grace is an eternal covenant, and that it contemplated and repaired the fall of man innumerable ages before man was created. Still, there is an order in contemplating these subjects, real in itself, and indispensable to their adequate comprehension ; but in the using of which we must bear in mind that no method our weakness obliges us to adopt can affect the absolute nature of the principles we discuss, or the facts by which they are illustrated. With God there is no variableness, neither any shadow of turning : what he purposes now, he purposed from eternity : his interposition to save man was no afterthought. And the ruin of the world is only that much more complete, that God has been willing to save it at every step of its downward progress, and that man has continually resisted, evaded, and prevented all the divine methods of making known and enforcing the divine purposes of mercy.

CHAPTER V.

I.—1. The necessity of discussing these questions here.—2. If anything exists at any time, something must have existed always. Something does exist, if nothing else, then he who denies all. Therefore something has existed from all eternity. —3. It is certain that there is a universe exterior to me, which is not me, occupied by existences which are separate from me, the extent of which I do not know. It is incapable of proof, that God may not be one of these: so that Atheism, even if true, could not be proved; and the eternal existence already proved, may be God.—4. The fundamental division and distribution of all dependent existences, into ultimate classes: Existence, Vitality, Intelligence.—5. The certainty of the present existence of both Matter and Mind: and their total dissimilitude. The consequent certainty of the Eternal Existence, of one or other—or both. Forms of Atheism.—6. Detailed proof, that matter, even if eternal, is inert, and uncreative: that spirit is eternal, and is the sole creative power—if there is any such power.—7. Detailed proof that matter is created: that mind is creative as well as eternal. There is an ever-living Spirit—who is God.—8. This Spirit, Ever-living, Creative, Infinite, First Cause, and God, is Jehovah of the Sacred Scriptures.—II.—1. The mode in which the Sacred Scriptures treat this Question. The influence of the progress of thought and knowledge upon our treatment of it. —2. The method here adopted.—3. The God of Natural Religion, and of man considered as a creature.—4. Sufficient if man had not fallen. Fundamental but insufficient for fallen man.

I.—1. THE complete renovation of man's fallen nature as the only method of extricating him from an estate at once depraved and helpless, full of perpetual sin and hopeless misery: and the necessity and reality of the gracious and effectual interposition of God in order to deliver him in that manner: are the great enquiries which have occupied us hitherto. At some point or other, in investigations of this sort, we are obliged to consider certain questions touching God himself; and certain other questions touching man; which lie in a manner at the foundation of all moral disquisitions, but which, in a certain degree, stand apart from the course of their direct movement, and therefore require, in the general method I have adopted, to be treated at such points in our progress as bring us most naturally in contact with them. At present we come upon two of these : one relating to the Existence of God, and the other to the Immortality of man ; both of which I have heretofore assumed as unquestionable. Others have made each of them the logical starting-point of their whole method. Both of them have been eagerly discussed from the very earliest dawn of Philosophy. I will treat them briefly in their order, and in my own manner ; the former in this chapter, the latter in the succeeding one.

2. It is perfectly certain that if there had ever been a period, in which nothing at all existed, it must necessarily have occurred that nothing at all could ever have existed after that, forever: since it is absolutely undeniable that nothing can create itself, and that nothing can produce nothing. That supposed state of universal non-existence, once established, is established forever. If therefore anything at all exists now, it is infallibly certain that, from eternity, there never was a moment, in which something did not exist. Since if there had been such a moment, any future existence of anything, was utterly impossible. It may be very difficult for us to conceive that anything at all can be created, under any circumstances whatever ; but this difficulty is increased a million fold when we deny the existence of an intelligent Creator : and it becomes a self-contradiction, an impossible absurdity, to speak of a creation, when there is not only no creator, but nothing created, and nothing to create : nay, when the very supposition subverts itself, by showing that something capable of supposing does exist, and that therefore there never could have been an instant of universal non-existence. That something does exist, is known to us with complete certainty ; for even if nothing else existed, that which doubts or denies all existence, must exist itself before it can doubt or deny ; or at the very least the doubt and denial must exist. But in reality we are as conscious of the exercise of every faculty of our souls, our minds, and our bodies, as we are that we doubt or deny anything : that is, we have proof which we are naturally incapable of disbelieving, and which in the nature of the case cannot be false, of our own existence. And besides our own personal existence we have proof just as incapable of deceiving us, and as incapable of being discredited, that all the existences around us, and exterior to us, are not parts of ourselves ; but are existences distinct from us.

Whatever may be their nature or origin, they are as real existences as we are ourselves. It is perfectly certain, that something exists now. It follows therefore with absolute certainty, that something, no matter at present, what, has existed from all eternity : and we are utterly incapable, not only of believing, but even of conceiving that the contrary could be true ; any more than we can believe or conceive the possibility of ourselves both existing and not existing, at the same time. The first point therefore is undeniably established. Something has existed from all eternity.

3. Upon examining carefully into the nature of what actually does exist, we find an immense variety and complexity of appearances, an inconceivable multiplication and combination of forces. We observe also an endless concatenation of things and of beings, apparently independent of each other, yet more or less influencing each other. A ceaseless activity of one sort or another, manifested by everything which is subject to our scrutiny. But as we more and more comprehend the nature and the connections of all things that we can examine into, we find them more and more capable of being reduced into order and class, and more and more the subjects of precise knowledge ; and the more we interrogate nature, the more simple and exact, as well as comprehensive, are the answers she returns us. Amongst the simplest and the most certain conclusions at which we arrive, the first in logical importance as connected with the matter before us, is the distinction which is established between our own existence, and all other existences around us. As has been already intimated, we have as deep a conviction and as conclusive evidence, that other things exist, as that we exist ourselves. It is as certain to each one of us, that there are other existences besides ourselves, and exterior to ourselves, as it is that we ourselves exist. Now this first and simplest truth—obvious and hardly worth noting, as one might hastily suppose—draws immediately after it the utter impossibility of establishing the truth of Atheism. Because as there are existences besides myself, and exterior to myself, I must explore the whole universe, and I must be sure that I have explored it all, before it is possible for me to know that one of the existences exterior to myself, some of which have been proved to be eternal, may not be God. Even, therefore, if it were true, that there is no God, it would be a truth,

which in its own nature did not admit of being established, or even ascertained by such creatures as we are. So that Atheism is a pretence of a positive belief of that which does not admit of being proved to be true ; and is therefore the greatest perversion of the rational nature of man, as well as the greatest outrage on all his religious instincts. And the existence of God is a truth of that nature, that, with ten thousand appearances indicating that existence, and ten thousand hopes and aspirations in all rational beings longing for that existence, and ten thousand probabilities pointing to that existence, and the total absence of any sort of indication against that existence, its falsity and God's non-existence are utterly incapable of being proved, even if both were truths. We thus reach a second point in our enquiry : namely, that in this apparently boundless mass of existence exterior to us and distinct from us, filling an apparently illimitable universe, the existence of every part of which proves that existence itself in some form has been eternal ; the existence of what we call God, may be that eternal existence ; and at any rate, that the denial of this is incapable of the slightest positive support, and is contrary to all the indications of the case, all the probabilities of reason, and all the instincts of our nature.

4. To advance another step. Considering all things around us, and especially considering the phenomena of our own existence, we perceive that there is another distinction entirely different from the one just considered, which runs through all existences, and as far as we can discover, pervades the universe, separating all things into two, and but two classes, into one or other of which all things fall of themselves. There is an existence which loves and hates, and fears and hopes, and reasons and judges, and approves and condemns. There is also an existence which possesses, apparently, various qualities or forces, very different from these, such as figure, motion, weight, color, and the like ; but does not possess these. Whatever we know of, possesses one or other class of capacities, and exerts one or other set of functions, as above, and so falls on one side of this universal line of demarcation, or is destitute of one or other class of them, and by that means falls on the other side of it. No matter how close may be the apparent connection between that which does, and that which does not possess the opposite classes of these attributes ; the distinction between them is not only absolute and impassable, but is the only

ineffaceable distinction of that kind that exists in the universe, so far as we know. Whatever appertains to the visible universe, all existences of both the foregoing kinds are liable to a three-fold distribution, which we express by calling them inanimate, animate, or rational. The Apostle John in that remarkable account of the Saviour with which he commences his Gospel, begins by informing us that the existence of the Word was eternal; that the form of its existence was an in-being with God; and that it was God. He then tells us explicitly that this divine and eternal Word, which was afterwards made flesh for our salvation, was the Creator of all things; and explains to us, on the basis of the distinction just stated, that he is the fountain of all Existence, of all Life, and of all Intelligence. As to all that is inanimate, he is simply its Creator: as to all that possesses vitality in addition to mere existence, he is the maker of its organism and the fountain of its life, as well as the author of its existence; and as to all that rises still higher and possesses intelligence as well as being, organism and life, it is his life which is the fountain of light to them. And then he proceeds to explain in what manner a new and better, even a spiritual and eternal life is bestowed upon us as part of the intelligent creatures of God, by this infinite Creator and Redeemer of men.[1] It is the third only of these three classes just distinguished that possesses the attributes I now speak of. And so proceeding on this divine knowledge, we take the second and third classes, to wit, existences that have life, and existences that have both life and intelligence, and separating the last class into two, according to their spiritual condition; we then say, as instinct is to mere animate creation, and reason to the intelligent creation, so is faith to the new creation; that is to all who have been redeemed by Christ and born of his Spirit. But these last distinctions are of use here mainly to illustrate the wide and fundamental one, now immediately engaging us.

5. The names by which men have agreed to signify the two existences, into which all things are separated, whether they be inanimate, animate, or rational beings, have been very various. They call one soul and the other body : one material and the other immaterial . one matter and the other mind : one physical and the other spiritual. It is the reality of the distinction, not the name that is of any importance here; the absoluteness of

---

[1] John, i. 1–14.

the existence of both kinds, and the total difference between their respective natures. It is of no consequence, at present, whether both of them are substances, or neither of them, or one only ; nor what sort of substances either or both of them may be : but only, that they are not substantially the same, but are substantially different. Two things exist which are thoroughly different from each other in all their manifestations, one of which we call mind and the other matter ; and we are just as sure of the existence of both and of the difference between them, as we are that anything at all exists. Both of them exist in each one of us ; and this we know as certainly as we know that either of them exists in us, or that we exist ourselves. Our knowledge is as positive on this point, as it is or can be, in relation to anything whatever : as positive as that there is such a thing as knowledge, or such a thing as doubt. But this being clearly established, it follows, either that both mind and matter must have existed from all eternity ; or else that matter existed from all eternity and produced mind ; or else that mind existed from all eternity and produced matter. One or other of these three alternatives must be true ; for they exhaust the subject ; and no other supposition is possible. We have therefore reached the third step in our enquiry, namely, the certainty of the eternal existence of mind, or matter, or both. In point of fact, many have held to the eternal existence of both ; and the present form of Pantheism is, that thought and matter are the only known attributes of the eternal Being, while all existence is a mode of one of these. The present form of Materialism holds the eternal existence of matter, and the production of mind from it as a mere result or organization. In effect, these on one side and the other, are but forms of Atheism. They are necessarily destructive of the foundations of all religion, whether considered morally or mentally : and taking man as he is, are necessarily productive of inward defilement and outward pollution. It is the eternal existence of an infinite Spirit, before and separate from that of the material universe ; the existence of a personal God, who is an infinite Spirit and the creator of all things ; that is the only form of belief which places man in his true position, as a dependent, rational, and accountable being. It remains therefore to clear this point from uncertainty.

6. Our own personal share in the matter stands thus. We

find in ourselves both these forms of existence, Spiritual and Material, most intimately united, and yet perfectly distinct in their respective natures. We are perfectly sure that we did not create ourselves : perfectly sure that we did not create anything in the universe exterior to ourselves. We are equally certain that no being who is not infinitely superior to us, did or could create us, or anything else : it is, if possible, more certain that a baboon did not create man, than that man did not create him. It is also undeniably certain that man is a form of existence very much higher than any of the forms of mere inanimate existence or any of the mere forces which exist in the universe. It is therefore obvious, that what we are incapable of doing, could not be done by any inanimate existence, or mere force. And as all inanimate existences and all mere forces are in their very nature thus inferior, it is certain that none of them could have created themselves, or us, or anything else. Moreover, the very same state of facts, and the very same method of reasoning, apply to all animate existences which are inferior to man in dignity and power. But it is as certain that man is superior to all animate existences known to us, as that he is superior to all inanimate existences. Therefore the brute creation, singly or unitedly, could no more create themselves or us, than the forces of the universe, gravitation, heat, light, electricity, chemical affinity, and the like, could create themselves, or us. And again, as man is the only form of existence, of which we have knowledge, uniting rational with animate existence ; the only being in whom matter and spirit are found united in their perfection if at all ; and yet he is wholly incapable of any act of creation at all ; it necessarily follows that the union of spirit with matter, whether the matter be animate or inanimate, does not produce an existence which is capable of exercising any creative powers at all, even though the existence formed by this union were of the highest conceivable form. What is more, it also follows in like manner, that if uncreated matter and uncreated spirit had existed only in this united form, and that of the very highest order, from all eternity, we cannot know or believe that they would have possessed in this united form any creative power : the probability, as far as our experience goes, being that they would not. We are driven therefore to the inevitable conclusion, that amongst the logical possibilities stated above (to wit, the eternal existence both of matter and mind—or the eternal existence of matter-producing mind—or the eternal existence of mind-producing matter), several new conditions are to be imposed :—*first*, that inanimate matter, by itself cannot create either matter or Spirit : *second*, that inanimate matter, united with spirit, cannot create either matter by itself, or spirit by itself, or matter and spirit united. We therefore reach the fourth step in our enquiry, namely : that if matter has existed from eternity, it has existed in a form wholly destitute of all creative efficiency, either singly, or when united to mind ; and that if mind exists at all, it must have existed from eternity ; and must be the sole creative force in the universe, if there is a creative force in the universe at all.

7. But to suppose the eternal existence of mind, which, if it exists at all is inevitably certain, both of which have been shown : and to suppose it to possess creative force, if any creative force exists in the universe, which it has been shown it must possess, if it exists eternally, and any creative force at all exists, and that eternal existence has been shown : and then to suppose that inert matter, whose eternal existence cannot be shown, and whose utter inability to create has been shown, should exist side by side with the eternal existence of mind, whose eternal existence has been proved, and whose creative power has been proved, provided any creative power exists in the universe—is self-contradictious, and absurd. For in the *first place*, there can be in the nature of the case but one *first* cause. The most enormous proposition that can be made to human reason is, that there is no cause for anything, and therefore, of course, no first cause : since that there is not only a cause, but an adequate cause, for everything, is the first postulate of reason, and the one upon which every rational process of our understanding proceeds. However overwhelming the proposition may be, that the cause of all other causes, should itself have no cause : it certainly doubles the difficulty to say there are two such uncreated causes. We accept one of them only because the structure of our mind obliges us to take it ; and because the alternative of its rejection is infinitely worse, and utterly absurd, to wit, that in a universe where everything is a cause, there is no cause at all. We reach this proposition of a first cause, by perfectly clear processes : but every one of these processes results in a single first cause—as indeed the very words

in which both the problem and the result are expressed, absolutely imply, to wit, *a first cause*—one cause. It is therefore, a gratuitous absurdity, from which the human mind revolts, and is self-contradictory in terms, to say that eternal mind, creative if anything is creative being proved, may be accepted as a first cause ; but that inert matter proved to be uncreative, and not proved to be eternal, must be accepted as another first cause, side by side with it from eternity. In the *second place*, if mind be shown to be eternal, and creative if anything is creative, as has been done, there is no need for the eternal existence of matter, even if it were creative : since its own creation would be already accounted for as capable of occurring at any time, as well without as with it. But the creation of the first cause is absurd and inconceivable. And moreover even if it were possible to suppose the existence of two first causes, it is ridiculous to do so, when the second first cause is proved to be of itself an inefficient cause ; and when it is further proved that its union with mind, so far from augmenting the creative force of mind, is, to the whole extent of our knowledge, destructive of it. But it has been shown that matter of itself has no creative power, and when united with mind, can add nothing to the creative force of mind : and may destroy that creative force. Therefore it could not, from eternity, be even an efficient cause, much less a first cause, even supposing it had existed from eternity. That which is neither a first cause, a creative cause, nor an efficient cause, cannot possibly be an eternal cause. It can be only an effect. The eternal existence of matter is impossible. It is created by mind. We reach, therefore, by the most rigorous logic, the fifth step in our enquiry, namely, that the only existence which is known to us, which by possibility could have existed from eternity, is a spiritual, immaterial, mental, rational existence. If therefore, we will admit, or if it can be shown, that anything at all exists, and that we are capable of perceiving the proofs of that existence, both of which have been proved ; then it may be demonstrated by an invincible chain of argument, and established with unshaken certainty by a series of irresistible deductions, that there has existed in our universe, from all eternity, a pure Spirit, who is the first cause of all things ; and that from eternity, nothing else has had any existence, except as it has been created by this pure Spirit. There is therefore an ever-living and true God, the Creator of all things : and the manner of his existence is such as we express by saying that as to his essence, he is a Spirit.

8. This pure Spirit, the first cause of all things, must necessarily be equal to all that he does. And it is impossible for us to know or to imagine, that he exhausts his perfections upon anything, or upon all things that he does, much less upon so much of what he does, as we are made acquainted with : but contrarywise, it is easy to show that all he does can be only indications of what he is. But when we contemplate the immensity of his universe, and the glory and beauty of it : and the vastness of his domain, and the majesty and grandeur of it ; we can say no less than that he is an Infinite Spirit : which indeed is unavoidable, alike on the ground of his eternal existence, and his creative power, and his being the first cause. And so the Scriptures teach us that his Power and Glory and Godhead, arc stamped upon the whole universe, and can be read in every line, and heard in every voice thereof.[1] This pure, eternal, infinite spirit, whose being fills immensity, whose power in all its boundless efficacy pervades the universe, the glory of whose being and perfections is manifested in all the works of his hand, and in all the relations he sustains to every living thing, and the absolute, undivided, and uninterrupted sway of whose sceptre and dominion, shows forth, from eternity to eternity, his supreme Godhead : this great Being is Jehovah, the only Living and True God. . And here, as it seems to me, is a demonstration of his Being, and of the nature thereof.

II.—1. The progress of ethical philosophy in general, and of researches into the great domains of mental philosophy, natural religion, and revealed theology in particular, have placed this whole question of the being and nature of God—as a question to be argued and determined at the bar of human reason—in a different posture, no doubt, from that in which it once stood. The Scriptures continually take for granted the being of God who is the author of them ; and very often, and very distinctly, and very variously assert, as grand and unquestionable truths, the fact, and the mode of his existence. But they do not, anywhere, in an express statement, draw out the demonstration either of that fact or that mode : contenting themselves with relying on the nature which God has given to man for a response to their

<hr>

[1] Psalm xix 1–6; Romans, i. 19, 20.

declarations ; and upon the natural and universal convictions of
our race, that these declarations are true.   And human experience
abundantly teaches us the sufficiency of the Word of God in this
as in all other respects : since men do not reject the Scriptures,
and become blinded and abominable because they doubt God's
existence ; but they doubt God's existence, because, having rejected the Scriptures they become abominable and blinded. Still,
all men, and above all they who are set for the defence of the
truth, ought to spare no effort to understand all the mysteries
of God, and no pains in defending them all; and all men are
exhorted by God himself, to be ever prepared to give a reason
for every hope they cherish in divine things. And, as I have
already said, the question we have been considering, stands in a
different posture from what it once did—as indeed do most
questions of a similar kind. The truth of God does not change
—nor indeed does any truth, properly speaking. The compass
of human thought changes, and the circle of human investigation
enlarges : and the light of the divine Word itself becomes clearer
and broader, in proportion to our fitness to behold it ; and the
light thrown upon it from all outward sources, becomes more
distinct and copious, with every advance made by the human
race.

2. It may be stated, therefore, with becoming modesty, that
it will not do for one generation to rely too exclusively on the
labors of the generations which have gone before, in treating any
of those great and difficult questions which lie underneath and
around the moral sciences, any more than other sciences : and
they who do so will have to put up with a great deal that is not
very satisfactory to their own minds, and that will not, very probably, satisfy others, to whom it may become their duty to impart
it. I have thought proper, therefore, not to gather up the general
outlines of the various and very diverse methods by which so
many others before me have proposed to establish the great
truth of the personal and eternal existence of an infinite, spiritual
God ; all of which have in them more or less that is valuable ;
but rather, with what simplicity I could, to state a single process
of reasoning, which after much thought seemed to me to exhibit
a method in addition to many others before adopted, by which
the whole question might be reduced to a brief compass, and be
placed in a clear light, and upon a firm foundation.

3. God thus made known in nature, seen by reason, and accepted by conscience, the creator, the benefactor, and the ruler of the universe, is the God of man, his creature, considered merely as man. This is the God to which natural religion looks: the only one of which natural religion has any knowledge or any need: the only one of which any religion, except that which regards man as a sinner, and reveals a Saviour, can treat: the only one with which any, except such as are taught by the Word made Flesh, can have any relations. This is the God whom man would have served and enjoyed forevermore, if man had not fallen.

4. Since man has fallen, it is not as man merely, but it is as man the sinner, that all his relations with God must be contemplated. In this God, as thus made known to him, there is no hope for the sinner man. Yet this God is the only God. To this God therefore he must be reclaimed—or he must perish: and if he should be reclaimed, it is this God, who must in some marvellous way, reveal himself in a light which nature does not teach—for an end of infinite mercy, which nature does not propose—or even comprehend. God the creator and benefactor of man the creature, must pass over and become God the Saviour of man the sinner. But it is still the same "God over all, and blessed forevermore." While the knowledge of this God is therefore fundamental in Christianity, and is made all the more glorious and precious as the Christian more and more comprehends his being and perfections, and draws nigher and nigher to him through Jesus Christ our Lord ; it is a knowledge, by itself and to the extent which nature alone is capable of attaining it, wholly insufficient to save sinful man. Because it cannot be too distinctly repeated, this is the knowledge of God as known to us in nature and under the Covenant of Works, not the knowledge of God as known to us in grace and under the Covenant of Grace : it is the knowledge of God the Creator, not of God the Saviour : it is the knowledge of God contemplating man as his creature always bound and once able to serve and enjoy him to perfection, not the knowledge of God contemplating man as his fallen and helpless creature, whom he has become Incarnate to save. The same glorious God ; but presented in what different aspects to man !

CHAPTER VI.

THE IMMORTALITY OF MAN.

I.—1. Usual mode of treating the question confines it to the Soul.   2. The Resurrection and Eternal union of the Body with the Soul, totally changes the question.   3. Should totally change the method of Treatment.—II.—1. Scripture account of the original facts of the case.   2. Additional facts, under the Covenant of Redemption.   3. The form of Immortality stated in the Scriptures the only one possible for man.   4. Analysis and extrication of the exact question.   5. Its precise nature and relevancy to the Incarnation of the Son of God.—III.—1. Distinction between the Soul and the Body.   2. Their union in Man.   3. The endless existence of both—and their endless union being proved—the immortality of man is unavoidably certain from his own Nature.   4. Unavoidably certain from the nature of the case—even on supposition of the truth of Atheism.   5. Unavoidably certain from the course of Providence; that is from the nature of things.   6. Unavoidably certain from the nature of God, and the ends of creation itself.—IV.—1. Singleness and brevity of the argument.   2. Sum of it, and certainty of its result. 3. Actual commencement of our personal Immortality.

I.—1. THE usual mode of treating the question of our immortality, when it is considered philosophically, is to confine it entirely to the soul, or, as it is generally expressed, the immaterial part of man.   And so far as the subject could be treated, independently of Divine revelation, it is not possible that it could be considered in any other light ; for the resurrection of the body is purely a doctrine of revealed religion ; and independently of its resurrection or something equivalent thereto, its immortality is manifestly impossible.   Still, however, although we behold incessant, and apparently inevitable changes and decay in all material things, we do not behold and never did behold, the destruction of a single particle of matter ; and it is demonstrably certain, that not a single particle of it is capable of being annihilated, by any force in the universe, except that of the same Almighty power that created it.   In fact the indestructibility of matter, after it has once been created, is capable of a physical demonstration as precise as it is possible to conceive that any moral reasoning could give to the certainty of the continued being of the human soul, after it has commenced its existence.

2. Inasmuch, however, as divine revelation has taught us the doctrine of the resurrection of the human body, and our own researches have taught us the natural indestructibility of matter ; the idea of the immortality of the human body, would very naturally occur to any careful thinker, as a possible thing resulting from these two facts, even in the absence of a positive revelation that it was immortal. That is, accepting the doctrine of the resurrection of the body as true ; the natural immortality of man is placed on a footing widely different from that on which it stood, in the contemplations and discussions of heathen philosophers. It follows that Christian philosophers, in discussing the immortality of the human soul, precisely after the method of the heathen philosophers, as if it were positively the only part of man which could possibly be immortal, follow a vicious method. Because two great ideas are left out, namely, the natural indestructibility of matter, and the resurrection of the body, both of which, no matter how they were obtained, and no matter whether they are true or false, open the subject in an entirely different way from what it must necessarily have been presented without them. For after we have got these ideas, it is impossible to *assume* that they are false. They must be *shown* to be false, before we can proceed with the argument upon the immortality of the soul alone, under the assumption that it *alone* can be immortal. But they cannot be proved to be false ; for one of them is an unquestionable physical truth ; and to disprove the other requires the confutation of the Bible, on the whole ground of its evidences. Therefore, as before said, the method is utterly vicious ; and being hardly satisfactory to the heathen, because, as we now see, it was necessarily incomplete, through their ignorance of some of its determiate elements unwittingly omitted ; it must necessarily be still less satisfactory to us, from its purposely omitting determinate elements, which we know do exist.

3. It is to be noted that the doctrine of a resurrection, which I have already said is an ultimate truth of Revealed Religion, applies exclusively to the body, and exclusively to the human body. And this limitation is of the utmost consequence, on the one hand, in settling the question of a future state for the brutes that perish, that is that do not rise from the dead ; and on the

other hand, the question with the Universalist, as to the effects of the resurrection upon the moral state of man in a future life—which future life if it be moral cannot be determined by a change which is purely physical, as the resurrection of the body is. It is also to be noted, that the change upon the dead soul of fallen man, so to speak, pointed out in the Scriptures as analogous to the change in his physical nature, by the resurrection of his dead body, is what these Scriptures call the new birth. Further, that new birth is no more a natural effect upon the soul, than that resurrection is a natural effect upon the body; and it is as exclusively a doctrine of Revealed Religion as it, and as completely an ultimate truth of revelation. Here again is the highest condition of the soul utterly unknown to all the heathen philosophers. That the human body would rise from the dead, and that the risen body would be united to the soul, they had no suspicion, much less any knowledge. In total ignorance of these fundamental truths, they pursued that method, the best they knew, of discussing the soul's proper immortality, upon the basis almost universal with them, of their belief in the metempsychosis. That Christian philosophers still think proper to follow such a method, and treat the whole subject as if there was any reason to believe that the final condition of the soul is an immortality distinct from the body, is equally remarkable and absurd.

II.—1. The account which the Scriptures give us of this matter is very exact. And the opinions of Moses and Paul are as deserving of our consideration, to say the least, as those of Plato and Confucius; even if it were merely a human theory. They inform us that man was created by God and placed in a condition which insured to him if he had retained that condition, both a blessed and an immortal existence: that by his own fault he lost that condition, and with it the blessedness of his immortality: that as one result of this fall, he became subject to the separation of his soul and body, that is to what we call temporal death; as another result, to the corruption of his whole nature, both during this life and after death, which we call spiritual death; and as a third result, to the banishment both of his soul and his body, separated by death and reunited in the resurrection, from God's presence forever, which we call eternal death.[1]

2. Now even this eternal death involves of itself the idea of

---

[1] Genesis, i. ii. iii. passim; Romans, vi. 23; Matthew, xxv. 41; 2 Thess., ii. 8.

an eternal being. But, in the mean time a new set of facts is stated by the Scriptures, namely : that it pleased God not to leave man in this wretched condition, but to deliver him from it, so as to relieve him from temporal death, by the resurrection of his body ;[1] from spiritual death by the new birth ;[2] and from eternal death, by bestowing upon him an immortal existence of blessedness, after his body had risen from the grave and been reunited to his soul.[3] How it was that God proposed to do all this, is not now to be considered ; nor yet the conditions, as to man, upon which all of it should occur ; nor even the result to man if he should refuse or fail to obtain the full measure of the benefits proposed. But only the specific notion in it all of man's immortality and the precise nature and conditions of that immortality absolutely considered.

3. What we arrive at then, is the distinct conception of the positive immortality of man : the immortality of each one of us, soul and body, personally and absolutely : so that we shall continue to be in eternity, the very being each one of us was here on earth. I say this is the exact sort of immortality the Scriptures teach, and any other sort of immortality is of no kind of consequence to us, and is not worth discussing, except as a mere amusement. For if any other sort existed, it could have no particular relation to our existence here, except as a mere chance that might or might not fall out ; or a mere caprice of God, or of fate, without regard to our past conduct, or our continued conscious existence. It is comparatively of small account to me, as an inducement to do good, or not to do ill, that some other being, in some other sphere, or in eternity, of whose nature and mode of existence I am uncertain, pretending to be me, or called me, may be benefited or injured by my struggles or self-denials : and it is just the same, if that other me who may live eternally in bliss or woe, is not the very me who suffered here that I might hereafter rejoice, or denied myself here that I might not mourn forever. The preservation of our personal identity throughout our future conscious existence, is an indispensable condition, to every conception of an immortality, that shall be for us, either a reward or a punishment, either a good or an evil. But that preservation immortally of our personal identity and conscious existence is impossible, except we be immortal, both in soul and

[1] 1 Corinthians, xv. 42–44.   [2] Romans, viii. 30.   [3] 1 Cor., xv. 51–58.

body. And an immortality that has no moral quality, or in which no moral distinctions exist, or in which moral qualities are confounded and moral distinctions disregarded, is contradictory to the nature of God as a moral ruler, incompatible with the nature of man as a moral and accountable creature, and therefore impossible and absurd. The only immortality possible for man, is that immortality, the conception of which is most plainly stated in the Scriptures, and which is an immortality of his soul and body, in a conscious and identical existence lasting eternally.

4. It is immaterial, logically, to the present argument, how many mutations the soul and the body may pass through ; or how long or how often they may be united or separated in passing through those mutations. The real question is only as to the final and eternal state. It is also immaterial, logically, what that final and eternal state may be, as a state of woe or bliss ; only that it be the just result, and to the very same person, whose conscious and identical existence is thus eternally continued. And, moreover, it is immaterial, logically, to this argument, whether or not the actual immortality of man be considered, so to speak, as natural and the result, either inevitably or intentionally, of the work of God in the creation of man : or whether it be considered as the result in its form and substance, of the interposition of God to rescue man, the result, that is, of the incarnation, sacrifice, and resurrection of Christ : or whether both of these facts be considered as true, the former to the wicked in a natural immortality of woe, the latter to the righteous in a glorious immortality of bliss. The grand point here is that man, in the mode of existence in which he was created, in which he fell, was redeemed, died, and rose from the dead, and was lost or saved ; in that very mode of continued conscious identical existence, this created, fallen, redeemed, dead, risen and saved or lost creature, with a soul and a body, is immortal, and will be eternally wretched or eternally blessed. Logically, I repeat, the case is the same on either of the three suppositions, as to the particular cause of the actual immortality of man. In the light of mere philosophy, the reasonings which many have supposed competent, to establish not only the natural and necessary, but even the indestructible immortality of an immaterial soul, may be said to be of value chiefly in this, that they give occasion to the soul to reveal an argument much stronger than they are, namely, a desire

for immortality so intense, that such reasonings can satisfy it. In the light of Divine Revelation, it far exceeds our province to say that an immaterial soul could not be as easily extinguished as a material body by him who is equally the creator of both. And while it is unquestionably certain that the blessed immortality of the righteous is the fruit of their union with Christ, it is just as certain that the accursed immortality of the wicked is the result of their separation from him. They who separate the blessedness or the misery from the immortality, and while they make the two former or either of them relate to Christ, base the latter in either case on something else ; should very carefully consider what they teach. The actual immortality of man, as taught in the Scriptures, has an immediate relation to the incarnation and resurrection of the Son of God : and everything that can be called death is not more thoroughly the product of Adam's connexion with the human race and with the Covenant of Works, than is everything which can be called life, the product of the connexion of the Son of God with the human race and with the Covenant of Grace. So that while the natural existence of all men still depends on the connexion of all men with Adam, the immortal blessedness of the righteous, is due wholly to Christ. And while the final condemnation of the wicked, as well as all their pollution in every state of existence, find their root in the depraved nature derived from Adam ; yet it is impossible to say that if human nature had never been united to the divine nature, human nature would nevertheless have manifested the same proper immortality of the wicked who would have risen from the dead even if Christ had never risen from the dead. The Apostle Paul argues these points expressly and at large. By man, even the first man Adam, who was a living soul, death came. By man also even the last Adam, who was a quickening spirit, came the resurrection of the dead. And so, as in Adam, all die, even so in Christ shall all be made alive. Every man, however, in his own order : and then he gives an order beginning with the resurrection of Christ, and extending even to " the end," when Christ shall have finished his reign, subdued his last enemy Death, and delivered up the kingdom to God, even the Father.[1] And to the same purport is the general testimony of all Scripture, which represents the Lord Jesus, the Creator, the Redeemer, the Ruler

---

[1] 1 Corinthians, xv. 12–26.

and the Judge of men, as the Lord alike of the living and the dead, of all worlds, all estates, all conditions : hell being as really his prison-house, as the earth is his footstool, or the heavens his throne.[1]

III.—1. So far from denying the thorough difference between the body of man, as material, and the soul of man as immaterial, I have, in a previous chapter, made that fundamental distinction one ground of the demonstration of the being of a pure and infinite Spirit, the Creator of all things. Nor can it be contested that the soul and body of man are capable of being dealt with separately and differently ; for the Scriptures expressly teach, that from their separation, at death, till their reunion at the resurrection, they are dealt with separately and differently : the one, returned to dust, the other gone to retribution, with God. Nor is it intimated that the proper immateriality of the soul is an uncertain, or unimportant truth in psychology, morals, or Religion, whether Natural or Revealed : on the contrary, its distinct proofs, which are clear and conclusive, and which show it to be wholly different in its essence from the essence of what we call matter, are of immense value in proving that all the phenomena which reveal the existence of intelligence, are specifically incapable of being produced by any organization of matter whatever ; and therefore, that all the dogmas of Atheism, Materialism, Naturalism, Pantheism and the like, many forms of which are rife in our own day, are as false in philosophy, as they are baleful in their effects upon the life of man. Nor on the other hand, is it to be held or allowed, that the physical nature of man—as now existing—is either pure or capable of self-purification ; but on the contrary, that it is utterly sinful, and hastening to death on that very account ; and that it is only in and by reason of the resurrection of the Just, that it can be purified and fitted perfectly for spiritual uses, which indeed is the only idea we can have of a spiritual body.

2. Now we are to remember that as to the absolute essence, either of mind or matter, we know nothing at all, and are apparently incapable of finding out any thing at all. As to the existence of both of them, we arrive at the knowledge thereof, in the same general way ; namely by means of the properties, qualities and forces they exhibit ; that is, by their respective

---

[1] Acts, iii. 21 ; Phil., ii. 6–11.

phenomena. By these means we do arrive at the absolute certainty of the existence of both of them ; and have obtained a large acquaintance, and I may add, a constantly-increasing acquaintance with both of them. We can as certainly prove the total and essential difference of the two, as we can prove the existence of either of them. Man is the only being known to us, and probably the only being in the universe, in which both are united into one living personality, with a separate conscious existence, which is made up of them both. And thus we are brought by another process, round to the conclusion already reached, namely that the proper and final immortality of this being, is the continuance of his personal, conscious, separate, identical existence ; that is of a mind and a body, to wit his own mind and his own body forever.

3. Let us observe further, that after clearly establishing the existence of a soul in man, his immaterial part, which has been done ; there is no means by which we could arrive at the certainty of the annihilation of that soul, except a divine revelation, and there is no such revelation. But, except by annihilation, there is no means known to us by which an immaterial soul any more than a particle of matter could cease to exist. Therefore no soul will cease to exist, but all of them will live forever. In the same manner after getting a clear idea of the indestructibility of matter, and of the resurrection of the human body, there is no way in which we can conceive of the annihilation of the human body, any more than of an immaterial soul, except by a direct act of God's omnipotent power, which is incapable of belief, except upon his own declaration ; and he has made no such declaration. Therefore every human body will exist forever. Again, after we are made acquainted with the nature of our own existence, which we are both by reason and revelation, to wit the union of a reasonable soul with a material body ; and after we ascertain the proper immortality of both the one and the other, as has been done : there remains no method of preventing the personal, and continued self-conscious existence of each individual man, except by separating eternally, his soul from his body, and thus destroying his continued, identical existence. But it is impossible for us to know, in this life, that the separation which occurs at death, and which is, so to speak, an anti-natural phenomenon, will continue eternally : but God.

has explained to us its cause and its object, and has expressly assured us that the separation is temporary. And after we have once gotten the idea of the reunion for eternity, of the soul and body, separated temporarily, and for a special reason and purpose at death, no matter how we got that idea ; the eternal existence of man, soul and body, cannot be denied without disproving the truth of that idea. But that idea, which is superhuman and would never have occurred to the human mind, except by revelation from God ; so far from being capable of being disproved, is proved to be true alike by the circumstances in which it arises, by the fact of its existence, and by the mode of its only possible origin. Therefore the eternal union of man's soul and body, both of which have been shown to be immortal, is certain : and the personal, identical, self-conscious existence of man, that is, his proper immortality, is the certain result of all our knowledge, human and divine, concerning his nature.

4. It is also to be observed, that even upon the supposition of Atheism itself, it is not possible to prove that man is not immortal ; nor even to render it probable that he is not. The direct contrary. For, even supposing there is no God, it is still certain that we exist. And if we exist here, and as we are, without any God, there is no reason why we may not exist hereafter also, without any God. But, on the other hand, by whatever means we exist now without any God, we not only might, but must exist hereafter without any God ; unless those means, whatever they are, can be pointed out, and be shown to be insufficient for our future existence, or incompatible with it ; neither of which is possible. On the contrary if man be supposed to have an independent existence, without means exterior to himself, then the end, and the means of his existence, are in and from himself, and his annihilation is impossible, in the very nature of the case. And it is no answer to this to say that death puts an end to his existence : for there are thousands of creatures around us, all inferior to ourselves, to whose existence death appears to put an end ; and yet after awhile we behold them revive in new forms, and pass through various mutations, and at length recur again as they were before their death. Nor is it any answer to say, that as yet we have not seen this occur with man. For, in the *first place*, we do not know except by Revelation, what may have occurred to the souls of the dead, and therefore

to say they are extinct, is the very silliest thing we could say :
and in the *second place*, for any thing we know, the period of
man's mutations may be as much longer than the periods of the
mutations of the inferior creatures, as he is more exalted than
they, and his mutations more glorious than theirs.   Now, if upon
the very strongest hypothesis that favors the annihilation of man,
his immortality can be shown to be, not only probable, but apparently inevitable ; it follows, that as soon as that hypothesis is
robbed of its whole force, as for example by proving the existence
of God, which has been done ; the force of the truth the
hypothesis was designed to subvert, becomes proportionably
greater and more certain.   Wherefore the immortality of man is
certain, from the nature of the case—as well as from his own
nature, as was before shown.

5. If we will consider the nature and course of things around
us, and consider God's relations to them, and their relations to
us ; the impression they make upon the rational faculties of man,
is most distinct, and has been nearly universal amongst the common people in all civilized nations.   This profound and universal
conviction may therefore be said to be the instinctive testimony
of human nature itself, arising under and derived from what we
call the course of providence ; that our race has a proper immortality.   Thus : Here is the infinite Creator of the universe, and
its almighty Ruler and Benefactor, on the one side : here on the
other side, is man the highest of his creatures known to us independently of Revelation, the manifest head over all the rest
of them, and the peculiar object of his care and love—as he shows
in innumerable ways, and through all ages : Here between the
two, so to speak, is the whole created universe beside, over which
and by means of which, a steadfast and all-pervading dominion
and providence, are exhibited on the part of God, directing and
controlling all things, with reference to man himself.   And yet
while the physical universe abides in strength and beauty and
glory from age to age, man, the noblest and most perfect of the
works of God, passes, as in a feverish dream, hurriedly and wildly
through it, and his generations sweep after each other, like
shadows across the face of the vast creation of God.   As to every
thing, except man, all appears to be perfect in its place, and to
its end : while as to him, for whom all else appears to be made
and directed by God, nothing is perfect, either in its place, or to

its end.   Fallen, and depraved, and perishing, yet full of sublime intelligence and of imperishable hopes, his days are like a hand-breadth, and all that he can accomplish while they last is as nothing compared with what he feels he could do, if he were delivered from sin and death.   As to him, even the dealings of God with him, as well as his own dealings with others, are all broken off in the very midst by the stroke of death, and mercies and sorrows alike, and sin and righteousness alike, are cut short before they are half run out, often before the first scene of them is enacted.   And his own inner life is rudely extinguished in the very vigor of its development, when no eye but that of God could see whereunto it would grow.   If all this wild mass of apparently capricious and incoherent results, be considered as the determinate and final purpose of God with regard to man, it exhibits God to us in a light absolutely appalling ; and presents man before us as an object infinitely to be pitied.   But if they are to be considered merely as the first openings of an exalted and eternal existence ; the rudiments of a scheme of providence, which is infinite and everlasting ; the elements of God's dealings with fallen man, in a way of discipline, probation, punishment, and restoration, to be perfectly illustrated and applied throughout eternity : then indeed the case is presented in a light which makes it perfectly comprehensible to us, and most glorious to God.   It seems to me, therefore, that we are forced by the very existence, and nature and ends of divine providence to assert the immortality of man ; that is, that it is rendered certain from the nature of things, as I have already shown that it is certain from the nature of man himself, and from the nature of the case.

6. God, as he is revealed to us in his word, as I have repeatedly said, is God the Saviour of man the sinner : and herein there is no question of man's immortality, since Revealed Religion is full of it.   But God as he is revealed to us in his works, is God the Creator and Benefactor of man the creature.   Contemplated in this light alone, I cannot see how it is possible to think of God merely as the creator and benefactor of man—in which light Natural Religion presents him to us—without perceiving the most conclusive proofs of the immortality of man. For it is impossible to conceive that God created all things, for any reason that was not drawn from within himself, and which

would not terminate upon himself: since every other reason is wholly unworthy of an infinite being, who alone is self-sufficient. Seeing then that God has created all things for his own glory, it is manifest that the more his universe is peopled with exalted intelligences, to whom he may make himself known, to the praise of all his perfections, by means of the works of his hands, the greater is the glory which he will get to himself, as the creator and benefactor of his creatures : and the higher his intelligent creatures rise in knowledge of him, and in conformity to him, and the longer they exist to praise him and rejoice in him, the more completely will he accomplish the very end he had in view in the creation of them, and of all things : while a universe stripped of all intelligent creatures who may behold the glorious works of God, and know and praise him, no matter how full that universe may be of the displays of God's perfections, by means of inanimate and unintelligent creatures, would come utterly short of the whole reason of any creation at all. But it cannot be imagined for an instant, that any human being in this life ever did, or ever can arrive at the full knowledge of God, or of his wonderful works ; while it is certain that the overwhelming mass of our race, die in the most fearful ignorance of both : so that if our existence here is all our existence, the very end of our creation is frustrated, and the very reason why God created us is defeated. On the other hand, if we are to exist throughout eternity, as the head of the rational creation of God, the very surest means to effect God's design in the creation of us, and of all things, are effectually secured ; and the knowledge of the glory of God throughout an intelligent universe, will rise higher and higher, and spread wider and wider for evermore. So that our annihilation is absolutely incompatible with any idea we can form of the purpose of God in the work of creation ; and the proper immortality of man, is certain from the nature of God, as I have already shown it to be from the nature of man, from the nature of the case, and from the nature of things.

IV.—1. These are by no means all the lines of argument by which this inexpressibly momentous truth can be established ; nor do our limits permit any thing more than the great outlines of thought, under each successive head of a demonstration, which however various, requires to be compact.

2. But that which can be proved by the nature of things, by

the nature of the case itself, by the nature of man, by the nature of God, and by a general and comprehensive demonstration embracing the conception of all these elements ; and which has besides the whole compass of divine revelation to sustain and enforce it, may be said, not only to be placed beyond the possibility of question at the bar of reason, but to be laid as one of the deepest foundations of all human belief and conduct.

3. Let us settle it, therefore, in our hearts, that we have and will eternally have, a personal, separate, self-conscious, identical existence of soul and body ; the very soul which this day lives and struggles within the very body which is to be united with it to all eternity. That there is for us a proper immortality, inconceivably glorious or shameful, the first steps of which we are already treading, and the whole complexion of which will be irrevocably determined as we shall run and finish this first and briefest portion of our course, with sorrow or with joy.

THE KNOWLEDGE OF GOD,

OBJECTIVELY CONSIDERED.

ARGUMENT OF THE SECOND BOOK.

As the First Book had for its special subject Man and his nature and estate; so this Second Book, advancing to the next stage of the grand theme of the knowledge of God, has for its special subject the Saviour of Men and his Person and Work. The Seventh Chapter, which is the First of this Book, is a condensed statement designed to give in one clear view, as complete an idea as possible of the historic Christ, as an object of distinct knowledge unto salvation.—In the Eighth Chapter, which is the Second of this Book, the entire doctrine of the Person of Christ—Immanuel—God-man, is demonstrated in all its aspects: this being the ultimate basis upon which, not only the reality but the possibility of salvation for sinners must rest.—The Ninth Chapter, which is the Third of this Book, develops the office which the Second Person of the Godhead became Incarnate that he might execute; namely the office of Mediator between God and Men, under the Eternal Covenant of Grace; the immediate object thereof being the reconciliation of God and Men: and to the full comprehension thereof, the infinite and eternal Dispensation of the Son of God, considered absolutely as God, considered as the Creator of all things, considered as Immanuel—the Mediator and as such head over all things, is carefully settled.— In the Tenth Chapter, which is the Fourth of this Book, the particular portion of the Dispensation of the Son of God which is immediately connected with the salvation of fallen men, is separately and fully considered; and to this end that portion is divided into two parts by the Resurrection of the Saviour; and his whole work as Mediator from his Incarnation till his Resurrection, is considered in the light of those Scriptures which represent him as working out, by his obedience and sacrifice, in a state of unspeakable Humiliation, an everlasting righteousness for us: and the other portion, from his Resurrection onward eternally, is considered in the light of those Scriptures which represent the glorified Redeemer, in a state of Infinite Exaltation, as carrying forward his Mediatorial work in boundless grace, with infinite power and glory, to the present and endless blessedness of his elect: and for a deeper insight into the whole as an object of divine knowledge, a detailed exposition is given of a suggestion of Christ himself as to the best method of considering the immense subject.—In the Eleventh Chapter, which is the Fifth of this Book, it is shown, in the first place, that the boundless work which Christ, as Mediator, performs for us, in us, and with regard to us, is of that nature that we not only understand the whole more clearly, by considering it part by part, but that in its own nature it exacts this mode of treatment; the Word of God itself establishing and constantly maintaining the distinction observable in the Mediator, both as Humiliated and as Exalted, when considered as our Infallible Teacher, when considered as our Great High Priest, and when considered as our only King and Lord: then in the same Chapter, an attempt is made to estimate this Divine Mediator in his Prophetic Office, as our Teacher of all truth unto salvation; in the course of which the whole exercise of that office by Christ, and the confirmation thereof by God are treated of.—The Twelfth Chapter, which is the Sixth of this Book, is devoted to the consideration of the Priestly Office of the Mediator, as executed both in time and in eternity: and therein are discussed those immense questions upon which our salvation depends,—such as the nature of the Priesthood, the Obedience, the Sacrifice, the Satisfaction of Christ in this world, and of his Intercession in heaven; the nature, application to us, and effects of the righteousness wrought out by Christ, the relation of this part of the Mediatorial work to our title to eternal life, and our fitness for that life; and the like.—The Thirteenth Chapter, which is the Seventh and last of this Book, treats of the Kingly Office of the Mediator: wherein the nature of that office is pointed out, and the nature, perpetuity, and endless triumph of his kingdom is demonstrated, and the salvation of every penitent and believing member of it, and the utter destruction of every other Kingdom and of every enemy of the King eternal, are shown to be unavoidably certain; to which are added the statement and solution of the most important questions involved in the main one discussed.—This Book embraces that part of the Knowledge of God commonly called Christology; and its object is to ascertain and settle as an object of positive knowledge, the precise posture of the Lord Jesus Christ in the divine method of saving sinners. The fundamental truths established may be summarily stated thus: The method of salvation is by the Incarnation of God in human nature—and is practically exhibited in the Person and Work of Christ Jesus:—The Son of God, the Second Person of the Trinity, took human nature, to wit a human body and a rational soul, miraculously into personal and indissoluble union with his divine nature, and thus there was constituted of the two natures in the one person of the Son of God—Immanuel—the Mediator—called Jesus Christ of Nazareth: He is the Mediator between God and Men, so constituted under the eternal Covenant of Grace between the Father, the Son, and the Holy Ghost, for the salvation of God's elect, and to him as a Saviour is exclusively committed the whole work of man's salvation, and with it the whole dominion of the Universe: His whole work he perfectly accomplishes—partly in time in an Estate of inexpressible Humiliation ending with his sacrificial death and temporary submission to the power of death—and partly in eternity in an Estate of Infinite Exaltation commencing with his Resurrection from the dead and his open and triumphant Ascent to heaven: The simplest import of the work thus accomplished is, that this God-man, our Lord and Saviour Jesus Christ, as a Prophet reveals to us the Will of God—as a Priest offers himself up as a sacrifice for us—and as a King subdues us unto himself: The end of all is, salvation for lost men—through divine Grace—by Jesus Christ.

CHAPTER VII.

JESUS OF NAZARETH—THE SON OF GOD, AND THE SAVIOUR OF
THE WORLD.

I. 1. The issues of our being.—2. Their immense import. II. 1. Mission of John the
Baptist.—2. Baptism of Christ by John. Christ's Ministry begun.—3. Lineage
of Christ. His life till his Ministry began.—4. The scene and idea of his Ministry.—5. Scope and outline of his Mission.—6. Crucifixion and Resurrection of
Christ.—7. The relation of Christ's sacrifice to the perpetual Ministry in the
Church of God. His Ascension. Outpouring of the Holy Ghost.—8. The Apostles of Christ. Their Power, Duty, and Sufficiency.—9. The second coming of
the Lord. III. 1. These facts all fundamental.—2. The authority on which they
rest.—3. General aspect of the Story of Christ.—4. Infinite efficacy of the means
to the end.—5. The whole plan of Redemption—superhuman in its conception.—
6. The idea of the Person, Work, and Glory of Christ thoroughly superhuman,

I.—1. WE are to bear in mind, that it is not a matter left to
our choice, whether we shall exist hereafter, any more than it
was whether we should exist here. Our being is a dependent
being—produced through the sovereign will of God ; prompted
so far as relates to us, by infinite goodness, but designed for his
own glory in the manifestation of himself. We can easily abuse
that existence to our own unspeakable misery : but we are
wholly unable to rob God of the glory which he will get to himself by means of it, whether we perish, or whether we are saved.[1]
We may get through that portion of our existence which is but
a pilgrimage leading to the grave, with safety and success, and
secure on the other side of the Jordan of death, glory, and
honor, and immortality : but we cannot, by any possibility,
evade the issues that are before us, or escape the destiny which
—on the one hand or on the other—awaits us all.

2. It is this fearful responsibility, this impending catastrophe,
and judgment, and doom, this imperishable bliss or wo, which
there is no escaping : it is all this, which gives to our being such

[1] 2 Cor., ii. 15.

transcendent importance, and which invests every thing that can control the issues of that being with such vast import. If this earth,—such as our being is, in it—were our only home, and the grave to which we hasten our final resting-place,—all the things which surround us here below, would be of little more significance to us, or we to them, than the clouds which decorate the sunset, to him who is closing his eyes on them forever. But when an immortality which cannot be escaped is shown to be our destiny, and God, and heaven, and hell are placed before us as infinite realities, and there is nothing left for us, whether we will or not, but to incur a doom unspeakably dreadful, or to reap a reward beyond all that the heart of man can adequately conceive ; then every thing that approaches us becomes momentous to us, and we to it, in the degree that it may be inwrought with these fearful issues. How overwhelming then, does the case become, when it is God himself who interposes to save us from endless perdition ; and when it is by means of the sacrifice of his only begotten Son, that he proposes to accomplish this ? And how terrible must be the aggravation of our guilt and misery, if we make our way to destruction, in contempt of the majesty of God, and of the blood of Christ shed for us ?

II.—1. In the fifteenth year of the reign of Tiberius Cæsar —Pontius Pilate being governor of Judea, and Herod being tetrarch of Galilee, and his brother Philip tetrarch of Iturea, and of the region of Trachonitis, and Lysanias the tetrarch of Abilene,—Annas and Caiaphas being the high priests of the Jews : the Word of God came unto John, the son of Zacharias, a descendant of Aaron, and a priest of the course of Abia, in the wilderness of Judea. Declaring himself to be a messenger of God, and acting, as he said, under the express commands of heaven, he came into all the region about the Jordan, preaching the Baptism of repentance for the remission of sins. He represented himself to be the forerunner, predicted by the Jewish prophets, who should prepare the way for that Messiah, who was the grand object of all their visions. The burden of his testimony was, that the kingdom of Heaven was at hand, and that there should appear immediately One who was to be so infinitely superior to himself, that he was not worthy to unloose the latchet of his shoes, and who would baptize the people with the Holy Ghost, and with fire : One who when he was divinely pointed out to

him, afterwards, as he earnestly declared, he called the Lamb of
God, who taketh away the sin of the world.[1] The whole Jewish
people were already filled with a mysterious expectation of
the immediate advent of their Messiah ;[2] a feeling kindred
to that strange expectation of the appearance of a great deliverer, which filled the heathen world, at the same moment.
And so all the land of Judea, and they of Jerusalem, went out
to John and were all baptized of him, in Jordan, confessing
their sins.[3] ·

2. Under these circumstances Jesus commenced his public
ministry. The ministry of John as his forerunner, seems to have
terminated when he baptized Jesus in Jordan : for it is written
that it was only when all the people had been baptized, that
Jesus demanded, and that John was persuaded to administer
that rite to him,[4] amidst the most astonishing and miraculous
attestations, to his Divine nature and mission. For the Holy
Ghost descended in a bodily shape, like a dove upon him, and a
voice came from heaven, which said, Thou art my beloved Son,
in whom I am well pleased.[5] And thus every person of the Godhead is exhibited in this wonderful induction of the Saviour into
his work ; and the highest human attestation is superadded : for
John expressly declared that he did not personally know who
was the Saviour of the world : but he knew that he was to be
immediately manifested to Israel ; and he who had sent him to
baptize with water, had made known to him, that he who was to
baptize with the Holy Ghost, should be pointed out to him by
the Spirit himself, descending and resting upon him. He saw
the miraculous proof, and loudly proclaimed its Divine significance, Behold the Lamb of God, which taketh away the sin of
the world.[6] I saw, says John, and bear record that this is the
Son of God.[7]—Nor can it be supposed that a transaction so wonderful, closing that special mission which was the most glorious
ever given to man, and opening the public career of the Lord
himself, was in itself a mere form. Long afterwards, when the
Chief Priests and the Elders of the people demanded of the
Saviour as he was teaching in the Temple, by what authority he
acted as he did, and who gave him this authority—questions

---

[1] Luke, iii. 1–14.   [2] Luke, iii. 15.   [3] Mark, i. 5.
[4] Luke, iii. 21; Mat., iii. 13–15.   [5] Mat., iii. 16, 17 ; Luke, iii. 22.
[6] John, i. 29–36.   [7] John, i. 33.

which they were the very persons authorized to ask ; he pointed them at once, in a manner not explained by him, but wonderfully significant, to the Baptism of John. Jesus answered and said unto them, I also will ask you one thing, which if ye tell me, I in like manner will tell you by what authority I do these things. The Baptism of John, whence was it ? from heaven or of men ? After reasoning and consulting with themselves they answered, We cannot tell. And he said unto them, Neither tell I you, by what authority I do these things.[1] Whatever may have been the significance of this conversation—and it probably was that Christ's Baptism by John had a real though not the highest relevancy, to the authority which Christ habitually exercised about the Jewish Temple and the Jewish Worship ; that significance is immensely increased by the two parables which he immediately proceeded to utter to them—the parable namely of the obedient and disobedient son, and the parable of the owner of the vineyard and his husbandmen who killed his son : parables, which they saw were spoken of them, and of the very matters to which the previous conversation had been directed ; and which Jesus applied directly to their rejection of him,—and the consequent taking of the kingdom of God from them, and giving it to a nation which should bring forth the fruits thereof.[2]

3. Jesus began to be about thirty years of age, when he commenced his ministry ;[3] the age at which the Jewish priests were allowed to enter upon their solemn functions.[4] He was not however of the tribe of Levi, but of that of Judah. And the sacred writers have given us two genealogies—one of his descent through his mother, by the evangelist Luke,[5] back through David and Judah and Abraham to Adam, and to God : the other through Joseph his reputed father by Matthew[6]—commencing with Abraham and tracing down a different descent, but still through Judah and David, to Christ. Of the royal tribe, and of the royal family thereof, to both of which so many and so glorious promises had been made by God ; he was born, so to speak, by accident, in Bethlehem, the city of his father David,[7] in circumstances of great destitution : while yet the angels heralded his birth, with songs of glory to God and of peace to man.[8] The temple of

---

[1] Mat., xxi. 23–27.   [2] Mat., xxi. 28–46.   [3] Luke, iii. 27.
[4] Num., iv. *passim.*   [5] Luke, iii.   [6] Mat., i.
[7] Luke, ii. 1–7 and 22–24.   [8] Luke, ii. 9–14.

Janus was shut in Rome, for the first time during long and bloody ages, in token of universal peace : and wise men from the farthest East, guided by his star, came rejoicing with exceeding great joy to worship him, whom they knew to be born King of the Jews.[1] He was raised in great obscurity at Nazareth in Galilee, out of which, to a proverb, no good thing could come : and he escaped in his tenderest years the sword of Herod the usurper of the throne of his ancestors, only by being an outcast in Egypt, the land of their long oppression—whither he was miraculously led.[2] Of his training we know only that he waxed strong in spirit, filled with wisdom and the grace of God, and grew in favor with God and men.[3] And of all his life, from his miraculous restoration from Egypt in early childhood, till the commencement of his public ministry in the wonderful circumstances attending his baptism by John, and his still more wonderful temptation of Satan in the wilderness,[4]—but a single incident is preserved, and that occurring when he was but twelve years old.[5] That however as well as the drift of all we gather of his private life, shows how deeply and how incessantly the spirit of his sublime mission was upon him, from his youth up : and how in all things, and at all periods of his life, it was his meat and drink, to do the will of him who sent him, and to accomplish that for which he came into the world.

4. At length his public ministry began. In the annals of the human race, there is nothing that approaches it—much less that resembles it. It lasted scarcely three years. It was confined entirely to Judea, a remote province of the Roman Empire, and to the Jewish race—a comparatively small—a conquered—and most peculiar people ; and it terminated in his public execution. And yet during the subsequent eighteen centuries, that brief and strange ministry, and its fruits, have taken deeper and deeper root in the human soul, and have spread wider and wider over the face of the earth : until it can no longer be doubted, that while the earth itself shall last, the destiny of man upon it will be controlled by what Jesus of Nazareth said and did. Those three years, and that ministry, settled, irreversibly, the fate of man. And well and truly might Jesus say, that the judgment of this world had now come, the time to settle its great

[1] Matt., ii. 1–10.   [2] Matt., iii. 13, 14.   [3] Luke, ii. 39–52.
[4] Matt., iv. 1–11.   [5] Luke, ii. 42, etc.

assize, and to cast out the Prince of it ; and that by the sacrifice of himself, he would draw all unto him. And the audible response from heaven,—that God was thereby glorified—and would be glorified—has accomplished its promise, throughout the universe, and been attested by all succeeding ages.[1]

5. The object of his mission, Christ proclaimed to be, to save the world. The immediate motive of it, God's eternal love to his perishing creatures. His own ability to accomplish such a mission, he steadily asserted, as resulting from his Divine fulness, as the Son of God—which he constantly claimed to be.[2] The truth of all his claims he attested in innumerable ways, and amongst the rest by stupendous miracles : and then he sealed his testimony with his blood. He professed to have divine wisdom ; and they who have most attentively considered what he taught, and how he taught it,—and who have the most carefully observed the effects of his teachings, are the last to doubt that he was indeed the way, and the truth, and the life. He demanded and received a divine worship, which by his own doctrine was due only to God, which he declared himself to be :[3] yet he performed scrupulously all the duties of life, as if he were a man—which he acknowledged he was—and his common designation of himself was by that most significant phrase first applied to him by the prophet Daniel—The Son of man.[4] He proclaimed himself a King, and laid the foundation of a kingdom commensurate with the whole world : yet he declared that his kingdom was not of this world, and avowed to those who desired to follow him, that his destitution was so complete, that he had not where to lay his head.[5] He stood forth as a mediator between an offended God, and His sinful creatures, and terminated the case by laying down his life for the party that was wholly in the wrong. The most pure and enlightened of all mortals, the most glorious of all teachers, engaged in the most benign of all missions, and executing it with a divine authority, perpetually exhibited ; he was despised and rejected of men. Set at naught by the fierce multitude, condemned by their rulers, adjudged guilty of blasphemy by the regular authority of the visible church of God, and convicted of treason amid the clamors of his own countrymen, by the tribunals of a usurper, exercising that royal authority which

---

[1] John, xii. 27–33.   [2] John, iii. 1–21.   [3] John, x. 26–29.
[4] Dan., vii. 13 ; Matt., xii. 33–50.   [5] Luke, ix. 58.

had been wielded for so many ages, by his own progenitors ; denied, forsaken, reviled, mocked, scourged, he was executed as a malefactor, with every circumstance of injustice, hatred, and contempt. Yet all this fearful mockery at which the heavens were darkened, and the sun refused to give his light ; and all this ferocious blood guiltiness against the Son of God, at which the earth itself shook with affright ; became, by a miracle of Divine Mercy, the very means of accomplishing the very object which had brought the Saviour into the world. He redeemed us with his own most precious blood.[1]

6. The wonderful story does not end here. Conceived by the Holy Ghost, born of the Virgin Mary, crucified under Pontius Pilate, dead and buried : but that is not all. On the third day he arose from the dead, the first fruits of them that slept. The graves were opened, and many bodies of the saints which slept arose and went into the holy city and appeared unto many.[2] Man had thus exhibited to him for the first time, the absolute reality of the resurrection of the body. A few times, in the course of ages, the dead had been restored to life, to complete a mortal existence which had been cut short ; and there dwelt then at Bethany near Jerusalem, Lazarus a friend of Jesus, whom he had thus snatched temporarily from the grasp of death.[3] Twice in the ancient times examples had been exhibited by God, one in the case of Enoch, one in that of Elijah,[4] and then by Christ himself a third and still more glorious manifestation had been made in his own transfiguration on the mount,[5] of the reality of that incomprehensible change, which at the coming of the Lord at the last trump, shall pass instead of death and resurrection, in the twinkling of an eye, upon all the children of God who are alive and remain unto the coming of the Lord.[6] Widely different from mere restoration to mortal life ; widely different from that transfiguration and translation which awaits the living saints in the great day, a few examples of both of which, men had known : there is now shown to the universe for the first time, in the resurrection of Jesus, followed by the resurrection of the bodies of many of the saints which slept, and which arose and went into the Holy City, the reality of that stupen-

[1] Matt., xxvii. ; Mark, xv. ; Luke, xxiii.; John, xix.   [2] Matt., xxvii. 53, 54.
[3] John, xi. 1–46.   [4] Gen., ii. 24 ; Heb., xi. 5 ; 2 Kings, ii. 1–11.
[5] Matt., xvii. 2 ; Mark, ix. 2.   [6] 1 Cor., xv. 51, 52 ; 1 Thess., iv. 13–17.

dous restoration, and the true form of the immortality of man. And Christ himself, during about forty days, from the feast of the Passover at which he had been crucified, to the eve of the feast of Pentecost, the feast of weeks, as it was originally called, repeatedly appeared, after his resurrection, to his Apostles and other of his disciples, and held familiar converse with them: having been seen by many, on many occasions, and by about five hundred of his brethren at one time, the greater part of whom were still alive, as Paul informs us, when about twenty-six years after that event he wrote his first epistle to the Corinthians.[1] Upon this great fact, of the resurrection of Jesus Christ from the dead, the Scriptures insist as repeatedly, and as earnestly as upon any other fact in his personal history, or in his divine mission: and it is easy to understand why they should do this. For if it be once fixed, it is impossible to discredit any of the preceding and dependent facts connected with his person and his work, or to doubt any of the results which he assures us will follow in connection with that marvellous event: because in it is found a direct and explicit attestation of God himself to the mission of Christ, of a nature altogether indisputable. Whereas, on the other hand, if the fact of the resurrection of Christ could be disproved, his whole mission falls of itself to the ground. Yet even in that case every thoughtful mind would consent that such a combination of stainless purity, goodness, wisdom and force, with cruel and impious imposture, presented a phenomenon at once contrary to human nature and utterly appalling to human reason.

7. He had been crucified at the feast of the Passover, that great national sacrament of the Jews, in which they commemorated their divine deliverance in Egypt, when the angel of the Lord passed over that devoted land, and slew the first born in every habitation of the Egyptians. As they ate their paschal lamb, and commemorated the deliverance of their first born, they sacrificed the lamb of God, and slew the only begotten of the Father. Nor, though they knew it not, was this fearful sacrificial murder less related to all their future than to their great past. Without developing this now, there is one deep and generally unnoticed aspect of the matter which puts in a clear light many things disputed among the people of God. The first born of

---

[1] 1 Cor., xv. 6.

God's people—the male that opens the womb—appears always to have stood in a peculiar relation to God. But in that great and final plague upon Egypt, when the Lord smote all their first born, and· delivered all the first born of Israel, the matter assumed an aspect perfectly distinct: for the blood which was the token between God and his people, was the blood of sacrifice, the blood which pointed to the Lamb of God, who taketh away the sin of the world, to the only begotten of the Father, who is the first born of every creature. And they who perished in Egypt were the males who opened the womb; and they who were spared amongst Israel were the males who opened the womb; and the sacrifice was a sacrament immediately relevant to the sacrifice of the Son of God; and the redemption of the first born in Israel was directly connected with the sacrifice in its form and origin, and directly related to the Son of God, whose sacrifice was thus set forth and commemorated.[1] Sanctify, said God, unto me all the first born, whatsoever openeth the womb; it is mine.[2] After this, when God in the wilderness, had constituted his church in a formal manner amongst his ancient people, founding it upon the covenant of Sacrifice revealed in Egypt, and the still more ancient covenant of circumcision revealed to Abraham, but superinducing upon the sacrament, many rites and ordinances : he established a priesthood in Aaron and his descendants—male after male, and gave the whole tribe of Levi, of which Aaron was, for perpetual service in divine things.[3] Now the thing to be noted is, that this designation of the tribe of Levi, embracing in it the priesthood itself, is expressly a substitution of the males of that tribe, for the first born males of all Israel : thus intimately connecting every thing sacred in the Levitical institutions, on the one hand with the sacrifice of the Passover and with the consecration therein of the first born unto God, and on the other hand, with the divine sacrifice to come, and with the only begotten of the Father, and with whatever new form these ancient and glorious provisions of mercy might put on. I have taken the Levites, saith God, from amongst the children of Israel instead of all the first born that openeth the matrix among the children of Israel ; therefore the Levites shall be mine.[4] And the principles of all these proceedings are universal, and they abide more clearly under the gospel,

<hr>

[1] Exod., xiii. 1–36.   [2] Exod., xiii. 2–16.   [3] Num., iii., *passim*.   [4] Num., iii. 12.

than in the Levitical institutions, or in those which preceded them. And so we are told in express allusion to the calling and functions of the High Priest, that Christ himself was made a High Priest, by Him who said, thou art a priest forever after the order of Melchizedek : and that in like manner as Aaron was called of God, so no man without the call of God may take on himself the honor of ministering in divine things.[1] The first call was of the first born, with sacrifice and miracle : then followed the divine call of Aaron, and the substitution of the Levites for the first born : then came the only Begotten, in whom the first born had been called, and whose blood held forth in that of the paschal Lamb had redeemed them : and last of all came the Apostles, Prophets, Evangelists, Teachers and Pastors, given amongst the chief ascension gifts of the First Born from the dead.[2] The real difference being chiefly here, that the glorified Redeemer calls his ministers of all kinds, by a supernatural call and generation, instead of calling them through a natural generation, as was done before Aaron and in his priesthood. And so the feast of Pentecost, in which they commemorated, year by year, their deliverance from Egyptian bondage, and God's mercies to them, in their own land was chosen by the Lord, as the fit occasion for his own ascension up into glory, and the outpouring of the Holy Ghost : by the one and the other of which, the deliverance of his own elect is made palpable in the leading of Captivity itself captive—and the divine agent of the whole work of grace within them whereby the whole benefits of the Covenant of Redemption are applied to them,—is manifested openly and the great promise of the Father fulfilled.[3] The fact of the ascension of Christ, and the dependent fact of the outpouring of the Holy Ghost, are asserted, attested, and insisted on, in the Scriptures, with a distinctness and earnestness proportioned to their fundamental importance in the economy of Salvation, by Jesus Christ. Exalted, a Prince and a Saviour, at the right hand of God, to give repentance to Israel, and the forgiveness of sins ; it is by means of the Holy Ghost, promised to his people, purchased by his blood, and shed forth in their hearts, that an abiding and living witness is provided of his own glorification, and the sole efficient agent of the life of God in their souls —is entirely exhibited.

[1] Heb., v. 1–6.   [2] Eph., iv. 4–16.   [3] Acts, i., ii

8. The Lord Christ did not personally organize the Christian church during his ministry in the flesh. He lived in the strictest observance of the Jewish religious institutions; and the Scriptures declare that he was a minister of the circumcision for the truth of God, to confirm the promises made unto the fathers; and that the Gentiles might glorify God for his mercy.[1] He purchased the Church with his blood, and he bestowed upon it, as on his elect Bride, infinitely precious gifts, his word, his ministers, and his ordinances; and pointing out to her her boundless inheritance, he bade her possess it and occupy it, remembering always that it was as her head, that he was head over all things.[2] Concerning his apostles especially, three things are to be noted with the greatest care: one relating to their power in the matter of giving a new form to the kingdom of God in the world; one relating to their duty in discipling all nations; and one relating to their divine sufficiency in both respects. As to their *power*, it was the power of the Lord Jesus Christ committed to them and to be exercised in His name.[3] Often before his resurrection, and still oftener, perhaps, after it, the things pertaining to the kingdom of God, were the subject of his distinct instructions to them.[4] Whatsoever ye shall bind on earth shall be bound in heaven; and whatsoever ye shall loose on earth, shall be loosed in heaven: such was the boundless form in which he invested them with power and authority, to take to pieces the fabric of the Jewish church, and to erect in its stead a church for all the families of man. And repeating on a different occasion the same investiture without limit or condition, he prefixed the emphatic declaration that he would give to them the keys of the kingdom of Heaven. His very last assurance to them was, that all power was given unto him in heaven and in earth; and that he was with them always, even unto the end of the world. The entire ministry of all the apostles, as far as it is known to us after the ascension of the Saviour, exhibits the habitual exercise by them of this divine authority; and the New Testament church as held forth in the writings of inspired men, is the product of their labors, and is, both in its substance and its form, of divine obligation. As to the *duty* of the Apostles to subdue all nations to Christ, the testimony of Scripture is, if

[1] Rom., xv. 8, 9.   [2] Eph., i. 20–23.   [3] 1 Cor., v. 4; 2 Cor., xiii. 10.
[4] Matt., xvi. 15–20, xviii. 15–20; John, xx. 19–23; Acts, i. 3.

possible, still more distinct. The scope of divine mercy which had originally flowed over all peoples, was again to be released from the bonds imposed on it by the institutions given to the Jewish people : and mankind having seen a universal form of grace pass over and survive in another form both narrow and peculiar, were now to behold that grace burst through every barrier, and in a form perfectly simple, universal, and effectual become the common heritage of man. The whole world was to be the field of their efforts, and they were to be witnesses unto Christ, first in Jerusalem, then in all Judea, then in Samaria, and then unto the uttermost parts of the earth.[1] Whatever might be intended by the Lord as to the restoration of the kingdom to Israel, or whatever the Apostles might have understood concerning the nature of that great event : it was not to that end, they were sent as Apostles, nor did the times and the seasons thereof, which the Father had put in his own power, appertain to their apostolic office or obligations.[2] They were to be the founders of the new form of the Church of God, and witnesses for Jesus Christ the Head and Lord thereof. And so their commission ran—teach all nations, and having taught, baptize them. Disciple them ; not lord it over them. Teach them to observe all things whatsoever Christ had commanded : and then gather them into the fold of Christ, baptizing them in the name of the Father, and of the Son, and of the Holy Ghost. To this commission also appertain both the assurance of the Lord that he possessed universal and unlimited power, and the promise of his presence with them always, everywhere.[3] We have in our hands the divine record of the manner in which the Apostles discharged these transcendent duties ; a record which, unto us this day, is a repository of Eternal Life. Touching the *sufficiency* of the Apostles for both parts of their work, the Scriptures are as explicit as they are touching the nature of the work itself, and the authority by which they performed it. The risen Saviour opened their understandings, that they might understand the Scriptures : and most especially that they might understand how it behooved him to suffer, to rise from the dead, and to enter into his glory ; and how it behooved them, as witnesses for him to preach repentance and remission of sins in his name among all nations. The ascended Saviour sent the promise of His Father upon them, and

[1] Acts, i. 8.   [2] Acts, i. 6, 7.   [3] Matt., xxviii. 16–20.

ndued them with power from on high, by the Holy Ghost with which they were filled.[1]   There is nothing in the Scriptures more distinctly told, more transcendantly important, or more incontestably established than the descent of the Holy Ghost on the day of Pentecost.   It was the direct and crowning testimony that the Lord Jesus was ascended into heaven, and was set down on the right hand of the majesty on high ; and therefore that his mission was divine, his work accepted, and man redeemed.   It was also the divine Unction of the Apostles, sealing their call, and replenishing them with divine sufficiency to accomplish all that was involved therein.   And it was the beginning of that glorious dispensation of the Holy Spirit, peculiar to that whole period of the church, which extends from that day to the second coming of the Lord, when he shall descend from heaven with a shout, with the voice of the archangel, and with the trump of God, when every eye shall see him, and they also which pierced him, and all kindreds of the earth shall wail because of him.[2] And thus we readily understand how simple and how conclusive was the answer of every Apostle, every time their teachings, their authority, or their sufficiency, was called in question. There was their divine doctrine, and there were the mighty signs and wonders wrought by them.   And thus we understand as well how futile, if not impious, are the claims of those who pretend to Apostolic dignity, authority, and sufficiency, without one single mark of the divine call or the miraculous unction of an apostle, or it may be, even the lowest evidence of being a disciple of Christ.

9. There remains but one more point to complete this general survey.   What relates to that second coming of Christ, to consummate his glorious work, which has been incidentally alluded to, besides which no doctrine of holy Scripture is more largely insisted on by the inspired writers, and hardly any one is so little considered, or so obscurely understood by Christian people. For the present, I content myself with a single remark, which I commend to the careful consideration of the followers of Christ, as they read the word of God, and meditate thereon : Namely that, while the first coming of Christ into the world, is undeniably, the great promise of the Old Testament Scriptures, the

---

[1] Luke, xxiv. 26 and 44–48 ; Acts, i. 4, 5, 8, ii. 1–4.
[2] 1 Thess., iv. 16 ; Rev., i. 7.

second coming of Christ in a manner the most glorious and overwhelming is just as undeniably the great promise of the New Testament Scriptures ; and that in point of fact, this idea is so thoroughly inwrought into the very texture of the Gospel, that it is easier for a Jew to expound the Old Testament Scriptures in an intelligible sense, which shall exclude the idea of the Incarnation of Christ, than for a Christian to expound the New Testament Scriptures in an intelligible sense, which shall exclude the idea of the return of the Son of man, in infinite power and glory to reign upon this earth. It is not the fact of a millennium, about which the faith of the church of God is divided and obscure. For no pious heart can question the fact that Christ is to be believed on in the world, any more than it can question his supreme Godhead, the testimony of the Holy Spirit to him, his dominion over the unseen world, the call of the Gentiles into his kingdom, or that he has been received up into glory ; since it is placed in the midst of all these glorious truths, and expressly declared to be, along with them, amongst the incontrovertible elements of the mystery of Godliness.[1] What is obscure to the church is the mode of this blessed millennium ; the personal relations of the glorified God-man to it, and to this earth, as the scene of it, and to his saints as the subjects of his reign. The relations, also, of it, to so many other stupendous questions, which the Scriptures have connected with it, and which are to receive a solution in some way intimately related to it : the question of God's ancient people,—the question of the heathen world,—the question of Antichrist,—the question of the resurrection of the just and the unjust,—the question of the general Judgment,—the question of the final delivery of the kingdom of Messiah, perfected and completed, to the Father. This outline is sufficient to show how sublime are the events which wait upon the future coming of the Lord ; in whom though now we see him not, yet believing we may rejoice with joy unspeakable and full of glory, knowing that even the very trial of our faith will be found unto praise, and honor, and glory at the appearing of Jesus Christ.[2]

III.—1. Such in the way of a most general statement is, if I may so call it, the personal outline furnished by the Scriptures of the Lord Jesus. To the exposition and establishment of the various points involved it, I shall proceed regularly and so onward,

---

[1] 1 Tim., iii. 16.   [2] 1 Pet., i. 7, 8.

to the successive parts of the great subject of Revealed Theology, as they open around the person the work and the glory of Christ, its central object. For the burden of my whole method lies in this, that the salvation of sinners, is the great end of all ; that God alone could effect this ; and that he effects it only through his Son, our divine Redeemer.

2. All that I have recapitulated in this general way, all that is involved implicitly or explicitly in what has been now delivered, and in all that concerns man's salvation, rests for its support, so far as it has any serious importance for us, on the divine authority of the Word of God. It would therefore be appropriate to discuss in this place and at this point of the development of the method adopted, the whole question of Scripture Evidences. I prefer, however, not to break the continuity of the subject, into the midst of which we have now fully come ; and will therefore take for granted, as I have intimated before, that the canonical Scriptures contained in the Old and New Testament, as commonly received, are the Word of God, reserving the proof for another place.

3. And now in reflecting upon the plan of salvation offered to us by God through Jesus Christ, which has been briefly run over so far as his personal history is concerned, I think it cannot be denied, that his story as delivered to us, is perfectly coherent in its parts, clearly intelligible to the humblest capacity, and entirely consistent with all that we know of God, and of ourselves. Wonderful as the whole is when we seriously consider it, it is hard to imagine any reason except the very depravity which it proposes to heal, why it should not commend itself, upon adequate proof of its verity, to the conscience of every man in the sight of God.

4. It is perfectly obvious also, that the means whereby God proposes to save us, in Christ Jesus, are completely adequate to the end for which they are employed, and are most appropriate to him, to us, and to the exigencies of the case. Marvellous as is the grace displayed, it is not beyond the bounds of divine Love : and the wisdom, and power, and righteousness, and goodness, and truth, though all are unsearchable, yet are they all exhibited in a manner, and to an end, and by a Saviour, infinitely becoming. If fallen and depraved men can be saved at all, they can be saved this way most surely and most gloriously.

5. It is further to be observed that every essential feature of this wonderful interposition of God to save man, is superhuman alike in its conception and in its execution. It depends ultimately upon the mode in which God himself exists, and upon the nature not only of all the attributes of his divine being, but even upon the mode in which those attributes mutually influence each other, so as to make up the infinite glory and perfection of his character. It hangs absolutely upon the eternal and unsearchable counsel of his own will—as the free, sovereign, and inscrutable cause of all things. So that supposing ourselves to have been created before all the rest of God's creatures, and the question of a further and boundless creation, to have been submitted by him to us ;—we could more readily have penetrated the creative counsel of God, and foreseen and contrived his glorious work of creation ; than supposing us to be fallen and depraved, and the question of deliverance and restoration, submitted to us by God, we could have penetrated his redeeming counsel, and foreseen and contrived his more glorious work of salvation. The one and the other is alike and wholly, beyond the compass of human intelligence as a thing to be independently contrived, much less independently executed by man. We can neither tell of ourselves, how a soul can be created at first, or recreated after it has fallen : much less can we, of ourselves, actually create it or actually recreate it : these are the works of God. And of the two the work of redemption is a more illustrious proof of the being of God, and a more complete illustration of his infinite perfections, than the work of creation.

6. And finally, the Lord Jesus Christ considered of himself —is by far the greatest phenomenon, which the universe has ever exhibited. The conception of just such a being, as well as the mode of his production, is altogether superhuman. The relations of such a being,—after the idea of him was obtained—to God, to man, and to the whole universe—are to us when left to ourselves wholly inscrutable. After these relations have been clearly established, the character which the Scriptures ascribe to this man-God is itself utterly above all that human intelligence could suggest, much less could perfectly develop, and least of all develop through protracted centuries, partly by prophecy, partly by personal description,—multitudes of hands in successive ages, and of all possible degrees of skill—working upon the im-

mortal delineation.   And even after the being, its relations, and
its character were perfectly established, the part he should enact
amongst men, the work he should accomplish in the universe—
the power he should exert upon things in heaven, and things on
earth, and things under the earth, and the effects thereof, in time
and in eternity : all these are things inconceivably beyond the
utmost reach of what we feel ourselves, and perceive all others to
be capable of unfolding.   Alas ! how feebly do we realize the
living force of these great mysteries of Godliness, even after they
have been divinely made known to us, not in word only, but in
power ; and how do our weak and sinful natures come short of
the sublime truths they convey, even after we have received
them by the demonstration of the Holy Ghost.—The idea of
Jesus Christ—the Son of God—and the Saviour of the world, as
that idea is developed throughout the Scriptures,—while it replenishes them with a divine fulness, incontestably stamps them
as the product of a Divine Intelligence.

CHAPTER VIII.

IMMANUEL.—THE MYSTERY OF THE INCARNATION.

I. 1. God's work of infinite Mercy.—2. The Composition of the person of Christ to be considered.—3. The controlling influence of the question.—4. Special consideration of it.—(a.) The Word made Flesh is very God, and the only Saviour of Sinners.—(b.) The Word is the Son of God, and has become incarnate.—(c.) Thus God and Man in one Person for ever.—(d.) The two natures eternally united in the Person of Christ, are still distinct from each other.—(e.) Christ has but one Person, to wit the Person of the Son of God.—(f.) This Immanuel is given to be the Mediator between God and Man: and is the Messiah, the Christ.—(g.) He is the only, and all-sufficient Saviour.—(h.) It is this person thus constituted—contemplated as a whole, and not by parts, who works out our salvation.—5. This whole doctrine is a transcendent Revelation.—6. All its parts unite in a perfectly clear, effectual and exclusive system.—II. Relevancy of these grand truths.—1. The effect of this Union of the two natures upon both of them.—2. The mode and nature of this Union.—3. The nature of the necessity that the Mediator must be true God.—4. In like manner that he must be true man.—5. In like manner, that he must be God-man.—6. In all this, the infinite certainty of man's salvation, and the complete manifestation of God's nature and glory.—7. The unspeakable Wonderfulness of the person of Immanuel.—8. And of the mode in which each nature enables the other.—9. The Incarnation is the most absolute manifestation of God, and the Supreme exaltation of human nature.

I.—1. This is a faithful saying, and worthy of all acceptation, that Christ Jesus came into the world to save sinners, of whom I am chief.[1] These words of Paul—like multitudes of similar statements, in every part of the oracles of God—develop the nature of God's work of infinite mercy towards fallen man, with a fulness and distinctness, and yet with a compactness and richness, of which human language seems incapable, except when it is made the vehicle of divine inspiration. First, we have the grand foundation for the whole scheme of redemption,— our sinfulness: then, God's purpose to save us: then the necessity of accomplishing that purpose, by some means which this world does not furnish: then, the means—Christ Jesus—the

---

[1] 1 Tim., i. 15.

very names given to him expressing at once the nature of his person and his work : then, the perfect faithfulness of God in all his gracious dealings with us, and all his statements to us thereof : then, the worthiness of God's offers and God's teachings, of the universal and unqualified acceptation of every human being : and finally, the estimate we should form of ourselves, and the mode in which that should affect us, as we survey the wonderful provisions of God's mercy, and their effects upon us ! It is impossible to contemplate such powers of thought and expression, directed to the development of inscrutable mysteries with the precision of perfect knowledge, without feeling our conviction of the divine reality of these mysteries continually strengthened.

2. Christ Jesus, says the Apostle Paul, came into the world to save sinners.[1] Of the six propositions contained in the general statement of the Apostle, just explained, the two which are embraced in this short portion of it, express in the briefest and clearest manner, first, the nature of Christ's person, and secondly, the nature of his work. It is to the former of these, the person of Jesus Christ, the Son of God, and the Saviour of the world, that our attention is now immediately directed.

3. No article of the Christian faith is more fundamental than this, and not one has been more carefully cherished by the church of God throughout all generations. Upon the supposition of any interposition by God for the deliverance of man, the result of the work must depend, absolutely, both for its certainty and its character, upon the nature of the instrumentality used to accomplish it : and since the mode of God's interposition is by the sending of Christ Jesus into the world, the person of Jesus Christ, immediately becomes the pivot on which the whole scheme must turn. And upon the further supposition, that this interposition of God, by means of Christ Jesus sent into the world, is in the way of a Mediator between himself and fallen man, then, again, the person of this Mediator becomes still more obviously the key to all our knowledge of God's dealings with us as sinners, and the means of all our access to God. In divine truth, as in all other truth, there is such an intimate concatenation of the parts with each other, and such a dependence of every part upon the fundamental thesis, that the slightest error touching that must needs be pernicious, and may be fatal. Since then, the

[1] 1 Tim., i. 15.

person of Christ is that rock whereon the church is built,[1] and the foundation of all the mysteries of God's will concerning man's deliverance,[2] and, in a manner, the repository of every revealed truth,[3] we must needs know him, if we would obtain that eternal life which God bestows upon man, no otherwise than through him, and which consists indeed, in the true knowledge of him, and of God by him. For the Saviour himself has said—addressing himself directly to the Father, and speaking of himself—Thou hast given him power over all flesh, that he should give eternal life to as many as thou hast given him. And this is eternal life, that they might know thee, the only true God, and Jesus Christ whom thou has sent.[4]

4. Of the coming of Christ into this world, and of his life, death, resurrection and ascension into heaven, and second coming, I have spoken generally in the preceding chapter. Something has also been said in a general manner of the doctrine of the Gospel involved in each of those aspects of the person and work of Christ, as Immanuel, that is, God with us. Entering now more carefully into what relates to the person of Christ, we gather from the word of God the doctrine which follows in a series of dependent statements.

(a) The Word which was made flesh, a phrase by which the Apostle John designates the Lord Jesus Christ, as he explains to us himself, existed from eternity, existed eternally in a form of in-being with God, and was himself eternally God. So existing, he was the real and only Creator of all things, according to the testimony of the same Apostle, and did not hesitate to claim, even when in the flesh, not only equality, but oneness with the Father.[5] That this divine word made flesh, was the only Saviour of men, is the very burden of the whole Gospel of this Apostle, who tells us himself that he wrote it in order that men might believe that Jesus is the Christ, the Son of God ; and that believing they might have life through his name.[6] To the same purport on both sides, is the testimony of the Apostle Paul, who tells us that Christ Jesus was in the form of God, and thought it no robbery to be equal with God : but made himself of no reputation, and took upon him the form of a servant, and was made in the likeness of man ; and being found in fashion as a man

---

[1] Matth., xvi. 16.   [2] Eph., i. 9, 10.   [3] 2 Cor. iv. 6.
[4] John, xvii. 2, 3.   [5] John, i. 1–14 and x. 30.   [6] John, xx. 31.

humbled himself, and became obedient unto death, even the death of the cross.[1]

(*b*) When the fulness of time was come, God sent forth his Son, made of a woman, made under the law, to redeem them that were under the law, that we might receive the adoption of sons. And because we are sons, God hath sent forth the Spirit of his Son in our hearts, crying, Abba, Father.[2] This was that divine and eternal Word, now made flesh ; and he dwelt among men, and men beheld his glory, the glory as of the only-begotten of the Father, full of grace and truth.[3]

(*c*) In this manner, the Lord Jesus was both God and man; he was truly God-man. As concerning the flesh, an Israelite, but still, over all God blessed forever, Amen.[4] And this union of the divine and human natures in the person of Christ Jesus, survived death and the resurrection, and will continue through eternity. For being raised from the dead by the mighty power of God, he is set at his own right hand in heaven, far above all principalities, and power, and might, and dominion, and every name that is named, not only in this world, but also in that which is to come ; and God hath put all things under his feet, and hath given him to be the head over all things to the Church, which is his body, the fulness of him that filleth all, in all.[5]

(*d*) While the two natures of the Lord Christ, the divine and human, are thus indissolubly united in his person, and will continue so united forever ; at the same time these two natures are, and will forever be, distinct in him. The Evangelist Luke has recorded with great particularity, the interview between the angel Gabriel and the Virgin Mary, in which he announced to her that the Holy Ghost should come upon her, and the power of the Highest overshadow her, and that she should conceive in a superhuman manner, and bring forth a son whom she should call Jesus, and who should be the Son of the Highest, to whom the Lord God would give the throne of his Father David, whose reign over the house of Jacob should be eternal, and of whose kingdom there should be no end.[6] And immediately following this narrative, the same Evangelist gives us an account of the remarkable interview betweeen the Mother of Jesus and her kins-woman, the mother of John the Baptist, before the birth either

[1] Phil., ii. 6–8.　　　[2] Gal., iv. 4–6.　　　[3] John, i. 14.
[4] Rom., ix. 5.　　　[5] Eph., i. 20–23.　　　[6] Luke, i. 26–38

of Jesus or John ; in which, being filled with the Holy Ghost as they spoke with each other, the general facts already given are set forth in another form.[1]   Now it is in him that all the fulness of the Godhead dwelleth bodily.[2]   It is in this manner, and it is with relation to the person of Christ, that God was manifest in the flesh, justified in the Spirit, seen of angels, preached unto the Gentiles, believed on in the world, and received up into glory.[3]   And it is still of Jesus Christ, God-man, and so the Saviour of the world, the ruler of the universe, the final judge of men, the true God and everlasting life, that the Scriptures bear such continual and such explicit testimony.

(e) These two natures, the divine and the human, thus indissolubly united in Christ, subsist in such a manner that there are not two persons, but only one person of the two natures, namely, the person of the Son of God, the second person of the adorable Trinity.   For, saith Isaiah to the house of David, Behold the Lord himself will give you a sign : a virgin shall conceive, and bear a Son, and shall call his name Immanuel.[4]   His very name, as well as the whole declaratian of Isaiah, according to the comment of Matthew, importing the oneness of his person as well as the union of both natures in it ; for Immanuel, being interpreted, is, God with us ; it is one person, who is God-man : all of which, moreover, the Apostle in the same passage makes perfectly clear in his own inspired statement, of the nativity of Jesus Christ.[5]   And the various and explicit statements of all the New Testament writers, do not contain any new doctrine ; but only identify the individual, in whom the promises of God and the predictions of his Prophets in all ages, had found their accomplishment ; when, at last, the child is born, the Son is given, upon whose shoulders the government should be, and whose name should be called Wonderful, Councillor, the Mighty God, the everlasting Father, the Prince of Peace.[6]

(f) The Word of God made flesh,—Immanuel—the God-man, with a person thus constituted, was given to be the Mediator between God and man.   As to the origin of this gift of Christ to man as a Mediator with God, it is in the Decree of God, from all eternity.   For the blessed God, the Father of our Lord Jesus Christ, hath chosen us in him before the foundation of the world,

---

[1] Luke, i. 39–56.   [2] Col., ii. 9.   [3] 1 Tim., iii. 16.
[4] Isaiah, vii. 13, 14.   [5] Matth., i. 18–25.   [6] Isaiah, ix. 6, 7.

having predestinated us to the adoption of children by Jesus Christ to himself, according to the good pleasure of his will, to the praise of the glory of his grace, wherein he hath made us accepted in the beloved.[1] As to the efficiency thereof, it is from the beginning of the world. From the first word of promise, which indeed was uttered in the form of a threat to the great seducer of man, that the seed of the woman should bruise the head of the serpent,[2] to the very last earnest call of the Spirit and the Bride, that men should come and take freely of the water of life ;[3] the whole word of God, and the whole of the forty-one centuries which it covers, intimate no name whereby any sinner can be saved, but the name of Jesus Christ of Nazareth ;[4] while the whole word has taught always, and under every dispensation ; and the whole of human experience confirms its teaching, that he is, and always was, able to save to the uttermost, all that do, or ever did, or ever will, come to God by him.[5] As to the manifestation of this Mediator in the flesh,—that was, when the fulness of the time was come, according to the eternal counsel of God, that he should set forth his Son, made of woman, made under the law, to redeem them that were under the law;[6] when the due time had arrived, according to the judgment of the eternal Son of God, for him to give himself a ransom for all.[7] He who was thus given in the Decree of God, from all eternity, in his divine efficiency to save sinners from the beginning of time,— and in his perfect manifestation to all men, from his Incarnation ; was no other than the Messiah, whom the Prophets had so long foretold,[8] manifested in the flesh as Jesus of Nazareth.[9] The Scriptures set forth his life, his death, his resurrection and his ascension to heaven ; his glorious gospel, according to his command, has been preached to men, through eighteen centuries ; the church purchased with his blood, still abides in strength, under that form which his Apostles gave to it, by his own authority and through his own Spirit ; and his followers confidently and unanimously expect his own return in transcendent power and glory.

(*g*) This divine person, Immanuel, the Son of God and the Son of man, the Mediator between God and man, is the only, as

---

[1] Eph., i. 3–6.   [2] Gen., iii. 14, 15.   [3] Rev., xxii. 17.
[4] Acts, iv. 12.   [5] Heb., vii. 25.   [6] Gal., iv. 4, 5.
[7] 1 Tim., ii. 6.   [8] John, i. 45 and viii. 56.   [9] Luke, ii. 1–14.

he is the all-sufficient Saviour of the world. For there is one God and one Mediator between God and men, the man Christ Jesus, who gave himself a ransom for all.[1] It is precisely because he is both God and Man, that he is qualified to be the Mediator between God and man ; and his very names, all of them, imply both the nature of his person, and the nature of his work.

(h) All the office work of this Mediator, looking to the salvation of man, or having any bearing thereon, is not to be considered as the special work of one nature or the other nature indissolubly united in his person ; but is to be considered as the work of the person thus formed of these two natures, that is, the work of him who is God-man, the work of Immanuel, the work of the Mediator. We are not to divide our Saviour, for his fitness to be our Saviour lies precisely in this, that the two natures are hypostatically united in him. There are innumerable statements of the word of God, which place this whole subject in the clearest light ; and there is not a single utterance of the Saviour himself either during his ministry, or after his resurrection, that can be made to signify a purpose on his part to divide his two natures, even in contemplation, in anything that related to his Mediatorial work. As if to guard us against this very error, the writers of all four of the Gospels, seem intentionally to designate the Lord merely by his name Jesus, when they speak of him after his resurrection, and therefore when we would be most liable to lose sight of his human nature. Even when they record his last commission to them, investing them with powers and imposing upon them duties, commensurate with the whole world, and making to them declarations and promises, which involve in their very nature, his absolute Godhead ; it is still Jesus who thus commissions and instructs them. It is Jesus who claims omnipotence and says to them, all power is given unto me, in heaven and in earth ; who commands them to teach all nations to observe all things whatsoever he had commanded them, and to baptize them in his name, as the Son, along with the names of the Father, and the Holy Ghost ; who appropriating the most unsearchable attributes of God, promised to be with all of them, always, and everywhere.[2]

5. It is impossible to conceive of anything that can lie more entirely out of the reach of our knowledge, when left to our-

---

[1] 1 Tim., ii. 5, 6.   [2] Matt., xxviii. 18–20.

selves, than every part of this subject does. The whole of it claims to be, and must necessarily be, divinely revealed to us. God abundantly declares, throughout his word, not only that it is a most clear and certain revelation, but that it is the revelation of the most glorious of all his works, and of the very highest counsels of his eternal will : a revelation by means of which the whole perfections of his infinite being, so far as it is possible for us to comprehend them, will be made known. That the whole subject is full of mystery, not only need not be disguised, but must therein exhibit one of the surest marks of its heavenly origin and devolopment, its eternal verity and efficacy.

6. If, however, we will accept this revelation as indeed God's message of infinite love to us, and sit down at the feet of Jesus Christ to learn its mighty import, and to become imbued with its divine efficacy ; we shall soon perceive that the mysterious facts revealed in it form a simple, comprehensive and most wonderful system of connected and dependent truths, all looking to the one grand result. We shall see that as far as we can comprehend, they perfectly explain, in themselves, their own nature and necessity, as well as their absolute relevancy and sufficiency to the end they are set forth to produce. We shall understand clearly at the same time, the utter impossibility of attaining that glorious end, upon any other supposition but that of their absolute truth, or in any other manner, except that exhibited through them. Man can be saved in this manner. He cannot be saved in any other, known to us, or conceivable by us.

II. Having, therefore, established the grand truths themselves, which relate to the mystery of Christ's Incarnation, and stated them one by one in their natural order, let us now endeavor to explain their relevancy to each other, to the great object had in view, and to God and to our own destiny.

1. According to the Scriptures, the divine existence is as to its essence, absolutely one ; but as to the mode in which that essence exists, it is a three-fold personality ; all of which will be more fully explained, when I come to treat expressly of the Trinity. The Second Person of this adorable Trinity, is he who became incarnate, as heretofore explained. Now this incarnation, consisting in the assumption of the nature of man into union with the divine nature, had this result, immediately, that the separate existence, the person, so to speak, of the Man Jesus,.

was swallowed up in the person of the Son of God ; and the effect was, not a new being with two natures and two persons, but another nature only, to wit, that of man united with the divine nature, in the person of the Son of God.   It is a hypostatical,—that is, a personal union.   The effect produced on the part of God is, not that a new person is added to the adorable Trinity, but that a new nature, to wit, human nature is assumed into union—to wit, personal union, with the divine nature, in the person of the Second Person of the Trinity.   And the effect produced on the part of man is, not that human nature has become divine, nor that human personality has ceased, as to the race ; but that human nature has been assumed into personal union with the Godhead—in the person of the man Jesus.   What the results are which flow hence, on both sides, belong to another part of the general subject, and will be considered hereafter.

2. Christ, therefore, the Son of God, became man, not by infusing the divine nature into the human nature, nor by mixing the two natures together, nor by ceasing to be divine himself, nor by making man divine ; but by assuming to himself a true human body, and a true human soul, and thus taking human nature into personal union with the divine nature : the two natures being kept perfectly distinct, but being eternally united, hypostatically, that is personally, in the person of the divine Word. This union was effected and the Christ of God was constituted, by a divine and superhuman conception, by the power of the Holy Ghost, in the womb of the Virgin Mary, and, as to the human nature of Christ, out of the substance of her body.   By this superhuman generation, Christ became a true man, yet free from the pollution of original sin, and the curse and penalty of the Covenant of Works ; and by being made and born of the Virgin Mary, of the lineage of David, and Judah and Abraham, —all the promises and prophecies, touching that part of the matter which related especially to the Jewish people, had their accomplishment.   And as being true God and sinless man, we have the key which unlocks all that is otherwise inexplicable in his personal history, his doctrine and his work : and get down to the very foundation of his ability to save sinners, so as that God might be just while he justified them.

3. We can see, as soon as God has opened the subject to us, that it was altogether indispensable for the Saviour of sinners, to

be true and very God ; and, when it is further made known to us, that their salvation necessarily involves just what Christ, as the Redeemer, performed, the " needs be" of that condition becomes overwhelming. An infinitely meritorious obedience, and an infinitely meritorious sacrifice are both absurd, unless predicated of an infinite being : so that the divine dignity and worth of the person of Christ, lie at the root of the necessity which required the Saviour to be made under the law ; and that necessity is absolutely paramount, in every view we can take of the nature and dominion of God. To overcome death, hell and eternal wo ; to rescue us from enemies so numerous, so insatiable and so much more powerful than ourselves ; our Redeemer must be divine. To give divine efficacy to his own work of obedience, of sacrifice, of instruction and of dominion over us ; to purchase and to pour out upon us, the Spirit of all life, all truth and all holiness, and thereby—in the renewing of our souls and the sealing of all blessings unto them—fit us for the eternal service and enjoyment of God ; our Redeemer must be very God, of very God. And so of all his work. It is to be observed carefully, that it is the Second Person of the Trinity, the Son, the Word, and neither the Father nor the Holy Ghost, that assumed our nature ; so that obviously, we sustain, and must eternally sustain relations to him most intimate and most distinct from those we sustain to the other persons of the Godhead. It is he who stood in the middle personality of the Godhead, that is to stand in the midst between us and God : he who, by eternal generation, was the Son of God, who is set forth to bring many sons and daughters to glory : he, from whom, with the Father, the Spirit eternally proceeds, who is to open a way for the outpouring of that Spirit on all flesh : he who created all things by the word of his power, who will re-create all things by the word of his grace.[1]

4. In the same manner, it becomes obvious to us why the Mediator should be man. Not sinful man, for then every part of his work of redemption becomes at once impossible ; and herein we apprehend the reason of those careful and repeated explanations of the miraculous conception of Christ's human body, and the still deeper necessity of the method adopted by infinite wisdom, that the man Jesus though descended from Adam, should not, by a descent through ordinary generation,

[1] Eph., i. 10.

incur the curse and penalty of the broken Covenant of Works, and so inherit a polluted nature. He must be true man with a living body and a rational soul, but with human nature unpolluted by the Fall; and so he was. And then, the divine Mediator can advance human nature, far beyond its original condition; and then he can obey the law of God, and satisfy all the claims of that perfect rule of human duty, and suffer in our stead, its fearful curse and penalty; he can, in our nature, be touched with a sense of all our infirmities, and intercede for us therein, continually at the throne of God; through him, as our elder brother, we can now receive the adoption of Sons of God, have access with boldness to the throne of the infinite Majesty, and become joint-heirs with him, the heirs of God to an inheritance incorruptible and undefiled, that fadeth not away, but is reserved in heaven for such as are kept by the mighty power of God through faith unto salvation.[1]

5. Nor is it less apparent why the Mediator should be both God and man, than why he should be either one or the other; that is, why these two natures should not only be possessed by him, but should be personally united in him; and as the Mediatorial work is for eternity, and the relations created by its performance, are eternal, why this hypostatical union in Christ, should also be eternal. His very fitness to be the Mediator between God and man, depends upon this. The glory of God and the good of his whole universe throughout eternity, were involved in all the acts, and most especially in the final award of a Mediator appointed by himself and acting in his behalf; while every hope of man founded upon the conduct or decisions of a Mediator between him and God, must necessarily depend upon the nature, character and fitness of him in whose hands his case was lodged. The actual Mediator, not only possessed the very nature of both the parties between whom he was to arbitrate; but both of those natures were indissolubly united in his person. He Mediated between his Father on one side, and his brethren on the other. Not the highest angel before God's throne, was worthy or was fit to have the glory of God and the fate of the universe thus committed to him; and it had been a mere mockery of man, to commit such a case as his, for arbitration, to the mightiest and purest creature who found his whole blessedness

[1] 1 Peter, i. 1–9.

in obedience to God, and who could not endure so much as the bare recital of man's sins, without throwing up his case with horror. As the case actually stood, the divine Mediator could not but decide everything for God, and everything against man. But at this very point, when nothing but despair awaited us— the very nature of the Mediator saved us. He decided openly for his righteous Father ; but instead of casting off his polluted brethren—he bowed his own head to the stroke their guilt had merited, and received into his own bosom the just punishment of their sins. He washed them in his blood, and presented them faultless, before God. All that is involved in all that Christ does for our souls in this life ; all that is involved in whatever secures to us a better life to come ; all that is involved in our fitness and our title to take part in the eternal reign of Christ and the saints in glory; connects itself, directly or indirectly, in some part or other of the plan of salvation, with the person of Christ, and therefore depends upon the manner in which his person is constituted.

6. The Mediator is called Jesus, because he saves his people from their sins.[1] He is the Christ of God, replenished without measure by the Holy Ghost, and possessing by his nature, by covenant and by unction, all ability, all authority and all fitness, as the Son of God and the Saviour of the world. And thus as Mediator of the Covenant of Grace, he executes the offices of a Prophet, of a Priest and of a King, both in his estate of humiliation and his estate of exaltation. From one end to the other, it is all an unsearchable mystery of godliness, revealed to us from heaven ; and if any particular part of it can be said to be more wondrous than the rest, and to enter most pervadingly of all into the whole matter of salvation, it is perhaps this very union of the divine and human natures in the person of Immanuel : for except upon the supposition of the supreme Godhead and the vicarious atonement of Jesus Christ, I cannot see that the ruin of man is less irremediable than that of devils. If we may enter a little further into the particulars of a matter so far above our natural knowledge, and yet so fruitful and so precious ; we may observe, that as touching this hypostatical union of the two natures, in Immanuel, as relates to its original efficiency, it was the act of the Divine Nature ; that its authoritative designation

---

[1] Matt, i, 21.

was the act of the Father; that the formation of the human nature, was the act of the Holy Ghost; and that the assumption of flesh was the act of the Son; and the Covenant of Grace of which the whole is an outbirth, was the act of the Father, and the Son and the Holy Ghost. And thus, the divine nature, and all the persons of the Godhead, severally and unitedly, concur therein, and are glorified thereby.

7. In the whole universe there is no union like unto this personal union of the divine and human natures, in Immanuel. There are, indeed, examples wherein the general principle of the most intimate union of natures, or persons, or existences, is shown in the most remarkable manner to be one of the deepest and most fruitful of all the principles that pervade the universe: the most remarkable of which are the union of the three persons of the Trinity in the substance of the Godhead; the mystical union of believers with Christ; the natural union of the soul and the body in man; and I may add the typical union of man and wife, whereby God illustrates the union of Christ with his Church. But all of these differing widely from each other, differ not less widely from the personal union of two natures in the God-man. In the Trinity it is the unity of three persons, in one nature: in Christ, it is the unity of two natures in one person. The union between Christ and the believer is mystical, and therein neither is the human person or nature of the believer swallowed up; but in Christ, the human personality is swallowed up, and the human nature is indissolubly united with the divine. The union of the soul and body in man, makes of both a single personality and a single nature, and is itself natural; but the union in Christ is wholly supernatural, wherein the personality of man is lost, while his nature is preserved, and united both with another nature and another personality. And though the union of husband and wife is such that Christ himself declared that they were no more twain but one flesh, and so what was literally true of the first pair is mystically true of all others,[1]—a great mystery, says the Apostle Paul, but yet real and analagous to the union between Christ and the Church,[2] still it is a union which, so far from uniting two natures in one, relates only to two persons of the same nature, and so far from swallowing up either personality, places both of them in a new relation, out of which

i Matt., xix. 5, 6.   ² Eph., v. 27–33.

arise innumerable duties, both new and mutual. There is no marvel therefore, that in contemplating such an existence as that of Immanuel, the prophet should begin the unparalleled list of names by which he distinguishes him, with the name Wonderful.[1]

8. And finally, we must bear in mind the intimate and mutual communication with each other which these two distinct natures united in the person of Christ, must necessarily have by virtue of their union in that indissoluble manner. This ineffable communication takes place immediately in the person of the Son, in which they are united. Moreover, through the immeasurable fulness of the Holy Ghost with which the Son is replenished, he fills the human nature united with his nature, with all fulness of habitual grace. On the other hand, every act of every office of the Mediator, whether as a Prophet, or a Priest, or a King, finds expression in his estate of humiliation, through some service, or some suffering, peculiar to his human nature ; and even in his state of exaltation, the same use and service, though not necessarily involved in every expression of the Godhead of the Son, are of perpetual recurrence in all that relates immediately to the salvation of the elect. At the same time, it is the divine nature which communicates all their worth and dignity to all the acts of the Mediator, which find expression through the human nature ; which acts, however, could never have been performed, but for the human nature. God has but one nature, and man has but one nature ; but the God-man has two natures, both of which are equally his ; and both constituting a single personality, their intercommunion is inconceivably complete. And though both natures must remain distinct, and each preserve its own essential properties, and each operate according to its own substance ; yet there is but one being—even Immanuel —constituted by both, and that in the personality, not of the man Jesus, but of the Son of God. So that we arrive at the conclusion reached before, by another process, that it is Christ, taken wholly, who performs every work on which our salvation depends.

9. Such, most imperfectly set forth, are the relevancy and mutual dependence of some of the most important truths, which are involved in the mystery of the incarnation and result from

---

[1] Isa., vii 14　viii. 8; ix. 6.

the manner in which the person of the Messiah is constituted. Since the creation of man, the most stupendous event in the history of humanity, is its assumption into union with the divine nature. The manifestation of God in human nature, is not only the most absolute manifestation of God which human nature can be conceived capable of understanding, but is the highest exaltation of human nature to which it is conceivable that human nature can attain. As we advance we shall see more and more plainly and completely, that in the person of Christ, his whole work hinges, and that our whole destiny depends upon that work. Infinitely glorious in all that he is, and all that he does, the Scriptures propose him to us, as our only deliverer. The knowledge of him is not only the root, but is the sum of all other knowledge ; and our state can in no way be so truly decided, as by determining what we think of him.[1]

[1] Mat., xxii. 41–46.

CHAPTER IX.

THE MEDIATOR BETWEEN GOD AND MAN.

I. 1. The ruin of man irremediable of itself.—2. The unsearchable nature of the divine Interposition.—3. No other mode of salvation conceivable by man, or possible in itself.—4. The Mediator—considered on the side of his human nature.—5. And on the side of his divine nature.—II. 1. All God's dealings with men committed to this Mediator.—2. Nature, conditions, objects, difficulties of the Mediation by Christ.—3. Summary of the fundamental and controlling elements of this Way of Life.—4. The infinite glory of the Everlasting Dispensation of the Mediator.— (a.) From Eternity.—(b.) Creation of Angels.—(c.) Fall of the Angels, War in Heaven.—(d.) Creation of the Visible Universe.—(e.) Fall of Man, Origin of New Creation.—(f.) The Incarnation.—(g.) His Resurrection.—(h.) His Ascension into Heaven.—(i.) His second coming.—(j.) His delivery of the Kingdom to the Father.—5. The simplicity of Redemption as a Way of Life: its boundless sublimity as an Object of Knowledge.

1.—1. THE sin of man, his consequent loss of the favor and image of God, and the pollution and misery into which he was thereby plunged ; all united make up for him an estate, as we have already shown, from which it was impossible for him to deliver himself, and from which, in consequence of the depraved condition of his nature, he was not willing to be delivered upon any terms that would be at once effectual and compatible with the infinite perfections of God. It is a condition which we can not too emphatically assert to be irremediable on the side of man ; and this very fact adds the last condition to its fearful ruin. There was no eye that pitied him ; there was no arm that could save him.

2. That in these circumstances God should have been prompted to interpose for the deliverance of man, can, as has been fully shown, be accounted for only upon grounds existing absolutely in his own nature. They could have no respect whatever as to their efficient or meritorious cause, to man or to his fate ; but in regard of him, they must have been on the part of God purely sovereign and perfectly gratuitous. But that God should

so love the world, as to give his only begotten Son, that whoso-ever would believe on him—not only might not perish, but might have everlasting life,[1] is such a manifestation, that none but a demon could consider it any thing else than unsearchable riches of grace : while that he should propose, by the salvation of such creatures, from such an estate, by such means, to make the very highest manifestation of his own perfections, to his own eternal glory, is such an illustration of the nature and character of God, as could never have been conceived by the highest created intelligence.

3. It is not the part of such creatures as we are to determine with positiveness, what the infinite and adorable God might do : nor to pronounce upon the mysteries that may be contained in his unfathomable being, whether they be of his power, his wisdom, his knowledge, his righteousness, or his love. But meekly and earnestly searching into all that we can know of him, by every means, and bowing our spirits reverently before every intimation that he is pleased to give us of himself; it is our part to believe every word of his upon which he allows us to hope, and to accept every intimation of his will he causes to be communicated to us, whether through his works, his providence, his Word, his Spirit, or his Son. When, therefore, one of the greatest, as well as one of the last of those whom he has inspired that he might teach us, makes it the express ground of his glorying with the saints at Rome, in the gospel of Christ, that it is the power of God unto salvation to every one that believeth ; we need not hesitate to declare, that the reason he adds is the true reason why this gospel has that power ; namely, because therein the righteousness of God is revealed from faith to faith. Nor need we shrink from adding, as he has added, that except by means of that divine righteousness, and that living faith, and that Christ the author of the one and the object of the other, there was no power of God unto salvation, and there could be no Gospel, but only the wrath of God revealed from heaven against all ungodliness and unrighteousness of men.[2] And when we hear the same inspired teacher assuring the church at Corinth that although the Jews required a sign, and the Greeks sought after wisdom, yet he had nothing to preach but Christ crucified ; who though he might be a stumbling-block to the Jews and foolishness to the

---

[1] John, iii. 16.   [2] Rom., i. 16–18.

Greeks was, nevertheless, unto them which are called, both Jews and Greeks, Christ the power of God and the wisdom of God : we may confidenly assert with him, that by that divine power and wisdom through a preached gospel, revealing the Son of God crucified for us, we are of God in Christ Jesus, who of God is made unto us wisdom, and righteousness, and sanctification and redemption. Nor need we fear to add, that independently of Christ crucified and to the exclusion of him there is no power of God, and no wisdom of God, whereby sinful men may be called ; whereby they can obtain either divine wisdom or righteousness or sanctification or redemption, or whereby they can be saved.[1] Not only then, may it be confidently asserted, that no way of salvation is actually revealed to man, except that which is held forth by the cross of Christ ; but we come short of uttering the full mind of God as revealed to man if we fail to add, that the salvation of sinners by any other means is absolutely incompatible alike with the nature of his almighty power and with the nature of his infinite wisdom, and is therefore in itself utterly impossible.

4. There is one God and one Mediator between God and men, the man Christ Jesus.[2] Now observe ; there is a God : and there is but one. These are the fundamental truths of all religion. Observe again ; there is a Mediator between God and men : there is but one : he is the man Christ Jesus. These are the fundamental truths of the Christian religion. The man Jesus, of the seed of David, born of the Virgin Mary, at Bethlehem of Judea, was miraculously conceived by the power of the Holy Ghost in her womb and made of her flesh, truly, perfectly and entirely possessing a human nature. He was not begotten or born according to ordinary generation, any more than Adam was ; and so he was not polluted with original sin, was not made under the curse or penalty of the Covenant of Works, had no part in the imputed guilt of Adam's first transgression, and was not subject to death in any form : but was holy, harmless, undefiled and separate from sinners.[3] He was called Jesus by the express command of the angel of the Lord, because he should save his people from their sins,[4] which was done in exact accordance with the prediction of Isaiah seven centuries and a half

1 Cor., i. 17–31.   2 1 Tim., ii. 5.   3 Heb., vii. 26.   4 Mat., i. 20–23.

before, that he should be Immanuel.[1] This on the side of human nature, is the Mediator between God and men.

5. On the side of his divine nature the Scriptures are equally explicit. Fear not, said the angel of the Lord, as he came upon the shepherds of Judea and the glory of the Lord shone round about them, and they were sore afraid ; fear not, for I bring you good tidings of great joy which shall be to all people. For unto you is born this day, a Saviour, who is Christ the Lord. And this shall be a sign unto you ; ye shall find the babe wrapped in swaddling clothes lying in a manger. And suddenly there was with the angel a multitude of the heavenly host praising God, and saying, glory to God in the highest, and on earth, peace, good will toward men.[2] Now observe : it is Christ the Lord : true God, of true God : as before true man of the seed of David. Very God and very man—and therefore Christ. One God, the Almighty : one Man even Jesus ; of the two, one Mediator between God and men even Christ the anointed one. This is the testimony of men and angels, of earth and heaven, at the moment of his birth. And like unto it is the testimony of God and man, of heaven and earth, when his race was finished and he had led captivity captive. When the day of Pentecost was fully come and the Holy Ghost was poured out upon the Apostles, devout men from every nation under heaven, heard that day, in Jerusalem, each in his own tongue the wonderful works of God. And Peter closed his first great discourse, with these memorable words : Therefore, let all the house of Israel know assuredly, that God hath made that same Jesus, whom ye have crucified, both Lord and Christ.[3] And the Holy Spirit sealed this testimony on the spot ; for on the same day about three thousand souls gladly received the word, and were baptized and added unto them.[4] And still the same testimony is lifted up, by all the redeemed. There is a Saviour, even Christ the Lord. That same Jesus, the crucified, hath God made both Lord and Christ. The good tidings and the great joy have spread continually for more than eighteen centuries, and they are still spreading to all people. The highest glory to God is being reaped and will be more and more richly gathered forever. Peace on earth, peace that passeth all understanding is shed abroad in the hearts of men ; peace with God, peace with one another, peace to their

<hr>

[1] Isaiah, vii. 14.   [2] Luke, ii. 8-14.   [3] Acts ii. 36.   [4] Acts ii. 41.

own souls precisely in proportion as they accept this Saviour. Good will towards men, of which the gift and the advent of this Mediator between God and men are the highest proof the universe affords, reigns upon earth exactly in the degree that the spirit of that universal brotherhood amongst men, which has been restored by that same Jesus who was crucified, supplants the spirit which shed the blood of him whom God hath made both Lord and Christ. This on the side of the divine nature is the Mediator between God and men.

II.—1. Into the hands of this Mediator, God has committed all his dealings with the children of men. To him, since all the prophets witness, that through his name whosoever believeth in him, shall receive remission of sins.[1] Such was the conclusive testimony of the Apostle Peter as to the matter of salvation, on the memorable occasion of the baptism of the first Gentile converts in the persons of Cornelius of Cæsarea and his household. Not less clear is the revelation by the Apostle Paul concerning Jesus Christ our Lord, which was made of the seed of David according to the flesh, and declared to be the Son of God with power according to the Spirit of holiness by the resurrection from the dead.[2] So that according to the judgment of these two apostles the remission of sins is committed absolutely to him, and is made to depend exclusively on faith in him: and so he, the seed of David and the Son of God, and thus our Lord Jesus Christ, is declared to be the Son of God with power. And the proof of all this adduced by them is the unanimous testimony of all the prophets, Christ's own resurrection from the dead, the testimony of the Holy Ghost, and the direct proclamation of God himself. And the Apostle John, treating expressly of the person of Christ, of the work he came to accomplish, and of his ineffable fitness and fulness for it ; tells us that the Word was made flesh and dwelt among us and we beheld his glory, the glory as of the only begotten of the Father full of grace and truth.[3] The proof of all this alleged by him lay before him, and before all men not then only but throughout all the generations that have followed. For although the world which he had made knew him not when he came into it ; and although his own received him not when he came unto them ; yet to all who did receive him and believe upon him he gave this sublime and un-

---

[1] Acts, x. 43.　　　[2] Rom., i. 3, 4.　　　[3] John, i. 14.

erring evidence concerning himself, and he continues to give it still, and will give it while the world shall last, namely, to them gave he power to become the sons of God. And that, as to the matter, and in the manner thereof, not in any wise hereditary, nor in any wise self-produced by them, nor in any wise the product of any human power besides : but simply his own bestowment of a divine fitness and a divine right to become sons of God.[1] Thus then stands the case. On the one hand, he has been made like unto his brethren in all things, that he might be a merciful and faithful high priest, in things pertaining to God, to make reconciliation for the sins of the people ;[2] and on the other hand he is able to save them to the uttermost, that come unto God by him, seeing he ever liveth to make intercession for them.[3]

2. All this idea of the Mediation of Jesus Christ between God and men involves and carries with it certain other profoundly important ideas. Its very existence depends upon the fact of there being a breach, an alienation, a controversy between God and man : yea a controversy so fearful and deadly, that God so to speak, will not pass it by, and yet of himself and simply as God cannot adjust it : and man, on his part is either so mad that he will persist in braving God, or else so helpless and undone that his case has gone beyond all remedy from him, or else— which is true—both of these damning maladies afflict him at once. Now, moreover, it must needs be, that before all mediation, there must be on one part, or on both a willingness at least, if not a desire for reconciliation and a readiness to do whatever may be needful thereunto. But here on the part of man, his case is so deplorable, that having first apostatised from God, and robbed him as far as he was able, of all the glory which he proposed to himself in his creation ; he had gone on in a course of constant rebellion against God, and continual self-degradation, until in the depths of his pollution, religion itself was made a chief means of insulting the majesty of heaven, and until the only living and true God had become the special object of horror and aversion to man. Again, there could be no Mediation properly so called, unless upon terms either mutually agreed upon, or else dictated by one party and submitted to by the other, which whatever they might be, involve the idea of a binding obligation

----

[1] John, i. 10–13.   [2] Heb., ii. 17.   [3] Heb., vii. 25.

upon both the parties, or at least upon the one having the power and the right to dictate. The distance between God the Creator and man the creature is so immense, and that between God the Saviour and man the sinner is so immeasurable, that it is only in a sense appropriate to these relations that we can speak of terms of mediation between God and man, or attach to them the nature of a covenant. And yet, the Scriptures constantly represent all the dealings of God with man, from the beginning of man's existence under the idea of covenant relations subsisting between God and men; their original ruin having been produced by the breach of the Covenant of Works in Adam, and their salvation being possible only through the Covenant of Grace in Christ. This whole subject of the covenants between God and men, is fundamental in its relations to Christian doctrine, and will be treated separately hereafter. Still further, the object of the Mediator being specific; namely, the reconciliation of the parties between whom it is undertaken, whatever is done by the Mediator must be done unto that end, and in that spirit, and in the very terms so far as they may have been specifically settled, of the covenant under which the mediation is undertaken. Christ, therefore, as the Mediator between God and men, is the Mediator of a covenant which looks to reconciliation between them; his very mission is a gospel: the terms of the covenant springing only from the beneficence of God, it becomes in its very nature a covenant of grace; while the end and mode of its execution as regards man makes it a Covenant of Redemption; and while as compared with all that had been attempted before, the Scriptures call it the new and better covenant. It is obvious, herein, how on the one side a clear conception of the Covenant of Grace, and on the other, of the Person and Office of Christ, as the Mediator of that covenant, is indispensable in order that we may comprehend in any tolerable degree, on the one hand the work and the glory of the Messiah, and on the other the blessings and the benefits which are bestowed on us through him. And to add but one more consideration, the Mediation of Christ, even supposing all the terms of it fully settled, and the parties to it fully aware that there is no other way to reconciliation, and the Mediator himself perfectly qualified and wholly inclined to do all that can be done; is still environed with difficulties arising out of the nature of the parties, and the nature of the breach between them, which to human reason would appear utterly insuperable. For one of the parties has given infinite offence, while the other has acted with infinite rectitude ; the offending party is in his nature finite, the party offended is in his nature infinite : the one wholly unable to do the least good or satisfy for the smallest offence,[1] the other demanding perfect obedience and insisting on complete satisfaction.[2] Nay the very order of things is wholly reversed. For amongst men, it is the weak and the offending who are supposed to desire and sue for peace ;[3] but here it is the infinite God, to whose felicity we can add nothing, and whose essential glory we cannot tarnish, who beseeches fallen men to be reconciled unto him, and sends his only begotten Son on that amazing errand.[4] And not the least wonder of all is, that the fallen, polluted, offending party to this mediation of unsearchable love, should have added to the guilt which already no eye pitied, and from which no arm could save, the inconceivable atrocity of rejecting and then murdering the Mediator himself, with every circumstance of ignominy and cruelty : and that this very act should turn to such account, that he whom they had taken and with wicked hands had crucified and slain, should prove to have been delivered up by the determinate counsel and foreknowledge of God,[5] and should in this very way become Lord, both of the living and the dead.[6]

3. The office of the Mediator : the composition of his person out of the two natures of God and man : the Covenant of Grace of which he was the Mediator : the work which he performed as Mediator between God and men : the Mediatorial kingdom which he redeemed : the sending of the Comforter as his vicar in that kingdom, during his personal absence at the right hand of God : the blessings conferred upon believers as members of his mystical body; and the ruin which awaits all their enemies and his ; the second coming of the Lord, and the final solution with infinite power and glory of every problem begotten by all these immense truths and forces : and at the bottom of the whole, the eternal counsel of God, whence all these wonders spring, and according to which they are all directed with an unsearchable wisdom, and by an Almighty power, through an unutterable fulness of grace and truth ; these are the grand and awful themes of God. They

---

[1] 2 Cor., iii. 5 ; Job, ix. 3.   [2] Deut., xxvi. 26 ; Mat., xviii. 34.
[3] Luke, xiv. 31, 32.   [4] 2 Cor., v. 18–21.   [5] Acts, ii. 23.   [6] Rom., xiv. 9.

constitute in its glorious outline the Plan of Salvation of which, as we contemplate it as a stupendous scheme of divine mercy, they are the elemental parts. Everything else which enters into the scope of God's dealings with the children of men, falls, by a vital necessity into such an order and place, as will make it coherent with these living and controlling realities. In them is found the method by which the divine proportion of faith is determined. Out of them, as a whole, or out of each one of them separately, or out of any two or three of them combined, flow all the streams that make glad the city of our God. In them explicitly or implicitly the whole power of God unto salvation is contained and is held forth. And in them and by means of them is that living force of the word, the ordinances, and the spirit, by which Christianity is no longer a belief or an emotion only, no longer a doctrine or an institution merely, but is an imperishable, an irresistible, and an eternal power.

4. Contemplated in this light, the Mediator considered in what he did while he tabernacled in the flesh ; in what he was before he assumed human nature and became incarnate ; in what he now is, and what he will be and do through everlasting ages ; is for us, assuredly, the grand object that fills immensity and eternity. His Dispensation, using that word in its most comprehensive sense, and using it because we have none that is more comprehensive, is from everlasting to everlasting. And as eternity came rolling forward from the past ; and as time and created things were projected so to speak into its awful cycle ; and as time and created things will pass out of that cycle once more ; and as eternity and eternal things will roll on unshaken in that future abyss, before which our reason shrinks : still, at all periods, and amidst all events, the person of the Son of God is in all and above all. And the successive parts and aspects of his Dispensation, are the things which mark and divide, illustrate and control all the parts and interests and events, of time and creation ; and all the parts and movements of grace and of eternity, whether going before time and creation or whether following after them, are relevant to us in the way of mercy, only as they are relevant to him, and to God's love made manifest through him. Let us make this more specific.

(*a*) Before any effort of creative power was put forth, even from eternity he was with God, and was God ; the central person in that infinite being, the unity of whose essence is the first principle of all true religion and acceptable worship. This is the first period of his everlasting Dispensation. We should mean nothing by asking how long it was after eternity began, before the heavenly intelligences were created.

(*b*) Then came the creation of angels. When, as regards our measures of time, God has not told us. This was the second period of his absolute Dispensation; and the first period of his Dispensation as a creator; for he made them all: and he will rule over them all forever. How long it continued before any of the angels fell, is wholly unknown to us.

(*c*) Then followed the war in heaven; the fall of those mighty angels who kept not their first estate, and their visitation by the Son of God with the vengeance of eternal fire. This is the third period of his dispensation: and in it we have the first exhibition to us, of the nature of his moral government, and of the unutterable certainty and completeness of his exercise of penal justice. How long this period lasted with a portion of the angels still in glory, and a portion in the pit before the creation of man, we know not.

(*d*) Then we reach the period at which time began; the creation of the heavens and the earth and all that in them is, in the space of six days and all very good: all created by the Son of God, and all, by the word of his power. The period of man in the image of God, and of God's covenant with him. This is the fourth period of the absolute Dispensation of the Son of God, and the second period of his Dispensation as a creator. We know not, with reference to the efflux of eternity, how or where to place this work of creation: nor do we know what relation it bore in regard of the length of time, to either of the periods relating to the angels, to their creation or to their fall. Nor do we know how long this period of man under the Covenant of Works continued: nor even with certainty, when it occurred, computing backward from our own day.

(*e*) We come next to the fall of man, the first intimation of the Covenant of Redemption, and the promise of the Son of God, as the Mediator thereof. This is the fifth period of his absolute Dispensation, and perhaps it is proper to say, the third period of his Dispensation as a creator; for the new birth is as really a creation by God, and is as really so declared to be, as the work of mere spiritual creation of the angels, or that of combined physical and spiritual creation of man. And I add, this is the first period of his Dispensation as a Saviour. During this period, which reaches to the incarnation of Christ, the covenant of grace was administered variously; but all the while without any change of Christ's personal relation to the dispensation.

(*f*) Then came his Incarnation. The Word was made flesh. It is not positively certain at what precise period after the creation of man, or after his fall this stupendous event occurred. There is some room for doubt, and the learned are not agreed, even as to the exact length of time back to it from our day. We know, however, from the word of God, that it occurred precisely at the point of time, when according to his own counsel, all things had been made ready for it. This is the sixth period of his absolute Dispensation, and the second period of his Dispensation as a Saviour. The life of Christ in the flesh on earth continued during about thirty-three years: his public ministry about three years: but the duration of neither period is settled with absolute certainty. And it may be observed here, in general, that nothing whatever as touching the person, the office, or the work of Christ, or man's salvation thereby, depends upon the exact determination of those questions of chronology of which the number is considerable, and about which the learned have so ardently disputed; but which God, apparently with design, has left more or less obscure.

(*g*) The next period is that marked by the resurrection of Christ from amongst the dead, the first fruits of them that slept. This is the seventh period of his absolute Dispensation; it is the fourth period of his Dispensation as a creator, for herein, and by means of it is the resurrection of the body; and it is the third period of his Dispensation as a Saviour. His human body slept in the grave, under the power of death; his human soul was in the bosom of God; and his divine nature, then as always filled immensity. In this as in all things it behooved him to be made like unto his brethren; whose souls and bodies, like his soul and body, are separated during the period that elapses between their death and resurrection; their bodies sleeping in the grave, their souls dwelling with God. Moreover Christ's human soul and body were united again by the breaking of the power of death, which could not hold him; and so will the souls and bodies of all believers who shall ever die, be reunited by the breaking of the same power of death as to every one of them. Precisely here is a great point remaining to be more considered by the church. Will believers like Christ also dwell on earth in their resurrection bodies ? Is he, after breaking the power of death and after rising from the grave, made like unto his brethren in the estate which preceeded his ascension, as he was in taking flesh, in dying, in sleeping, and rising from the dead ? Is that, or not, the type of the Millennial kingdom ? Is it a type of any estate yet in reserve for the people of God ?

(*h*) We arrive next, at the ascension of Christ into glory, his sitting at the right hand of the Majesty on high and his sending forth of the Holy Spirit. This is the eighth period of his absolute Dispensation; the fifth period of his Dispensation as a creator, for therein his new creation is produced and exhibited, in a manner and with a power never before seen, extending from Pentecost to his second coming : the Dispensation of the Holy Ghost with power as the vicar of the Son of God amongst men. It is also the fourth period of his Dispensation as a Saviour. This is the point in the development of the unsearchable mystery of Christ, unto which we are now come. To-day we stand thus : In the eighth Dispensation of the Son of God : in his fifth Dispensation as creator of all things : in his fourth Dispensation as the Saviour of sinners. What the Apostle Paul said eighteen centuries ago, we can say still. We do not as yet see all that was promised in the Covenant of Grace, bestowed on him as the Mediator of that covenant ; but we have seen a great deal ; all, up to the point of his being crowned with glory and honor. And we are sure of all the rest.[1]

(*i*) The next Dispensation of the Lord Jesus Christ, will be his return in glory to raise the dead, to judge the world and to reign in righteousness with his saints. This will be the ninth Dispensation of the Son of God ; his sixth Dispensation as creator, for in it, he will make all things new ; his fifth Dispensation as a Saviour. That will be his Millennial Dispensation ; in regard to which, as I have several times intimated, his people are so much divided and perplexed ; and in regard to which therefore, when speaking incidentally in a general survey of this sort, it is the more proper to avoid all extreme statements. This is

[1] Heb., ii. 9.

what the Apostle Paul declares concerning the matter, when
writing expressly of it to the church of Corinth. As all die in
Adam, all shall rise in Christ. The order of that resurrection
is this : first Christ ; secondly they who are Christ's—which will
occur at his coming : thirdly, the changing of the living saints
in a moment, at Christ's coming, and after the resurrection of
the righteous dead ; then the reign of Christ till all things are
put under him, and every enemy under his feet : the last enemy
being death. Then cometh the end : and Christ's work having
been fully accomplished, he will deliver up the kingdom to the
Father.[1] And this if fully accepted and believed, involves all
that we can need for our satisfaction and abounding comfort.

(j) And this brings us to the end of all that God has revealed
to us concerning his Son Jesus Christ, the only Mediator between
God and men. For it is mauifest, says the Apostle Paul, that
although God hath put all things under his Son, as Mediator of
the Covenant of Grace, yet he who did put all things under him,
is himself necessarily excepted.[2] Exalted now, far above all
principalities and powers, and made head over all things to the
church, which is his body ;[3] reigning in the heavens until the
time of the restitution of all things which God hath spoken by
the mouth of all his holy prophets since the world began ;[4] urging forward the dispensation of the fulness of times, through
which God is gathering together in one, all things which are in
heaven and which are on earth, even in Christ ;[5] when the infinitely glorious end shall be fully reached, he will deliver up the
kingdom which he redeemed, perfected, judged and reigned over
to God, even the Father ; and the Son himself shall be subject
unto him that put all things under him, that God may be all in
all.[6] The counsels of eternity so far as they related to the power,
the work and the glory of Christ, the Mediator of the Covenant of
Grace will have been perfectly accomplished. The salvation of
sinners will have been absolutely and eternally perfected ; and
the Lamb's book of life in which is the record of the names of
the children of the kingdom,[7] and which is the proof of their
ingrafting into Christ and their complete salvation by him,[8] will
be openly displayed.[9] And then the kingdom itself upon this

---

[1] 1 Cor., xv. 22–28, and 51–57.   [2] 1 Cor., xv. 27.   [3] Eph., i. 20–23.
[4] Acts, ii. 21.   [5] Eph., i. 10.   [6] 1 Cor., xv. 24–28.
[7] Phil., iv. 3.   [8] Rev., iii. 5, and xiii. 8.   [9] Rev., xx. 12.

eternal record of it, will be delivered up : and the record itself
with every soul inscribed in it, shall pass under the direct dominion, and into the eternal fruition of God as God, the glorified
Mediator of it having thus entered upon his tenth Dispensation,
as the Son of God, his seventh Dispensation as creator of that
unspeakably glorious condition of the universe, and his sixth
dispensation as the Saviour of sinners, thus made perfectly blessed
in the full fruition of God to all eternity.[1]

5. The end of our faith is the salvation of our souls. It is
only by the mighty power of God, that we can be kept even
through faith unto salvation. The trial of our faith, though
that trial of it be a token of its preciousness in the sight of God,
yet is often by fire, that it may the more assuredly apprehend
and the more perfectly receive Christ who is the object of it, and
salvation which is the end of it. Nor need we wonder at the
depth or the fulness of the mystery of this salvation, when the
very prophets who predicted it, enquired and searched diligently
without fully comprehending what and what manner of time or
things the Spirit of Christ which was in them, did signify when
it testified beforehand, the sufferings of Christ and the glory
which should follow. Nor is there any occasion for us to be cast
down or to be deterred from the fullest inspection of these glorious and life-giving mysteries, when we learn that this superadded
vastness and complexity by reason of the gospel preached unto
men, and the Holy Ghost sent down from heaven, filled even the
angels of God with a holy curiosity and a longing desire to look
into them.[2] In one respect the way of life is infinitely simple.
In another respect it is unfathomable. But the most simple
parts of it hang directly upon the most unfathomable : and the
most unfathomable lead us directly to the most simple. Just so
it is here. For nothing is more obvious and more level to the
humblest comprehension than the reconciliation of enemies by
the intervention of a mutual friend. And yet this simple idea
when applied to God and man, carries us step by step and by
absolute necessity, through all the mysteries of the Godhead, and
all the mysteries of human nature ; and then brings us back to
the first and simple truth, laden with priceless treasures of wisdom and knowledge.

<hr>

[1] Rev., xxi. 27.   [2] 1 Peter, i. 7–12.

CHAPTER X.

THE HUMILIATION AND THE EXALTATION OF THE MEDIATOR: HIS
TWO ESTATES.

I. 1. The estates in which Immanuel executes his office of Mediator.—2. Doctrine
of the two preceding chapters applied.—3. Statement and division of the subject.—4. The peculiar aspect which this twofold condition of Christ gives to the
sacred Scriptures, and to Christian experience.—5. A more perfect division of his
estates intimated by Christ. Doxology of the Lord's Prayer.—6. Detailed exposition of it, with reference to the present subject.—II. 1. What constitutes the
humiliation of Christ.—2. The fact and method of his incarnation and life on
earth.—3. His crucifixion. Cause and import of it.—4. His very office, no less
than his incarnation and sacrifice, a humiliation.—III. What constitutes the exaltation of Christ.—1. His resurrection.—2. His ascension to Heaven.—3. His dominion at the right hand of the Father.—4. The infinite glory of his second coming.—IV. 1. The necessity both of the humiliation and the exaltation of Christ.
—2. The matter as revealed, and why so revealed.—3. Its relevancy to the
eternal decree of God.—4. Its posture in the infinite nature of the case.—5. Its
solution of the relations of God and man, and of the relations of the Mediator to
both.

I.—1. In the two preceding chapters it was the Person and
the Office of the Lord Jesus Christ, which occupied our attention : the mystery of the Incarnation and the mystery of the
Mediation of the Son of God. We have seen the divine fitness
of his person—Immanuel—so marvellously constituted to perform
the work of redeeming love : and we have seen the office which
he executed, that of Mediator between God and men—in the
whole of that divine work. The whole of what God does for
man through this Mediator, so far from being confined to man's
brief existence on this earth, covers the whole of his immortal
existence : and the crucifixion of Christ divides his Mediatorial
work into two portions, as distinct in their nature, as the two
portions of the existence of man on the opposite sides of the
grave. For the aid of our weak faculties in discerning and then
in profiting by the truth, these obvious distinctions are made the
ground of a separate treatment of the two portions of the work

of the Mediator as divided by his death ; and a separate treatment also of the applicability of both portions of Christ's work
to the necessities of man as his existence also is divided by the
tomb.   And so we speak of the two Estates in which the Mediator executes his office : calling one of them his estate of Humiliation, and the other his estate of Exaltation.   It is to the
illustration of these two estates, that this chapter is devoted.

2. What has been shown to be true of the Person and of the
Office of Christ, is equally true concerning both the Estates in
which he executes that office : namely, that his two distinct natures
inseparably united in one person, are no more to be confounded
and no more to be divided when we contemplate the estates in
which his office of Mediator is discharged, than when we contemplate him directly as Immanuel in the mystery of his Incarnation, or contemplate him in his office as the Mediator between
God and men.   It is the person constituted out of both natures ;
it is the office filled by a days-man who has both natures ; and
in like manner it is the humiliation and exaltation of him in
whom both natures are thus united.   It is in vain to say, the
Godhead can neither be humiliated nor exalted ; in vain to say
the human nature cannot possess or exercise any attribute of the
Godhead.   All such cavils are swallowed up as soon as we accept
that mystery which is greater than all that such cavils can suggest and which itself solves them all ; the mystery of Immanuel,
God manifest in the flesh : and if we accept not that mystery,
all reasonings on the subject are vain, and all salvation for men
is as hopeless as any salvation for devils.   It is Christ who is humiliated ; it is Christ who is exalted.   Whoever Christ is, it is he
who as Mediator wholly discharges his whole office in these two
estates so widely different from each other.   The infinite God has
many names and many appellations by which he makes himself
known and by which he is adored : but his personal, incommunicable, specific name, expressive of his very essence, is Jehovah.
And so the Son of God has many names and many appellations,
most glorious and most precious : but his name Christ, Messiah
—the anointed of God—one the Greek and the other the Hebrew
expression of the ideas fundamentally involved in his whole nature
and work, designates precisely who it is, that is both humiliated
and exalted : the very same, namely, who is Immanuel, and who
being God-man, is Mediator.

3. It is obvious that Christ's estate of humiliation, might be divided into many portions. As, for example, into the period from his Incarnation to the commencement of his public ministry—the period embracing that ministry—the period of his trial and crucifixion—and the period during which he remained under the power of death. Still however all these periods constitute a perpetual humiliation. In the same way Christ's estate of exaltation might be divided into his resurrection from the dead—his continuance upon earth during about forty days after his resurrection—his ascension up into glory—his reign over all things, at the right hand of the Majesty on high—his second coming to judge the quick and the dead—his infinite reign with the saints—his delivery up of the perfected kingdom to the Father—and his abyss of glory to all eternity. Nevertheless all these are but parts of one perpetual exaltation which becomes more and more ineffable, until our faculties are lost in every attempt to grasp it. It is simpler, therefore, and puts these sublime questions more within our reach to limit the estates in which Christ executes the office of Mediator to two only, as exhaustive of the subject: his estate, namely, of Humiliation, and his estate of Exaltation. The former extending from his conception to his resurrection—and embracing all that relates to his life, his sufferings, his temptations, his crucifixion, and his remaining under the power of death. The latter commencing with his resurrection, and extending through eternity.

4. It is this twofold position of Messiah, as at one time a Redeemer humiliated even to the cross, and at another time a Ruler exalted even to the throne of the universe, which throws over the Scriptures an aspect so peculiar. The representations by prophets and apostles, at one time of his sufferings, his trials and his temptations, contrasted with the representations by prophets and apostles at another time of his transcendent glory and blessedness: are well calculated to perplex the hearts of weak believers and to seduce us into a state of mind in which we are habitually and unduly engrossed with one or the other aspect of the subject. It seemed almost impossible for the ancient people of God to bring themselves into sympathy with those revelations, which made known to them the infinite humiliation which awaited Messiah: while they joyfully laid hold on every promise of his coming glory. For us the difficulty is reversed. The demonstration of the sufferings of Christ has been made by the

fact itself, palpable to the weakest faith, and enters fundamentally into the present form of all religious teaching and life: while the glory of Messiah, beyond what has yet been manifested to the universe, takes the place in our minds which his humiliation occupied in the minds of his ancient people. They had daily proof of his infinite power: but they had never seen him nailed to the cross. We have daily proof of everything, up to the point when Jesus was crowned with glory and honor: but now we see not yet all things put under him.[1] And so the habitual form of insufficiency in our spiritual life, is the reverse of theirs, but no less real; unless it were true, that the highest exaltation of Christ is of less moment to us, than his lowest humiliation. The Apostle Paul, in a very short passage, has set the whole matter in a position of wonderful force and light.[2] The original condition of Christ was that he was in the form of God, and thought it no robbery to be equal with God. After that, he made himself of no reputation, and took upon him the form of a servant, and was made in the likeness of men: and being found in fashion as a man, he humbled himself, and became obedient unto death, even the death of the cross. What followed was that God hath highly exalted him, and given him a name which is above every name: that at the name of Jesus every knee should bow, of things in heaven, and things in earth, and things under the earth: and that every tongue should confess that Jesus Christ is Lord, to the glory of God the Father. This sublime statement is introduced, let us remember, with the most earnest appeal, founded upon all our consolation in Christ, and all the comfort of our Christian love, and all the fellowship of the Spirit, that this mind should be in us, which was also in Christ Jesus.[3] This mind which made him consider it no robbery to be equal with God, when he was in the form of God: this mind which induced him to humble himself to death, even the death of the cross, when he was found in fashion as a man: this mind which fitted him for the ineffable dominion and glory and blessedness, to which God hath exalted him. So that all parts of the work of Christ ought to find expression in our inner life; and every form of the mind that was in Christ ought to find its image in us: and then we may confidently hope that we shall not only be made conformable unto his death, and have

---

[1] Heb., ii. 6–9.   [2] Phil., ii. 5–11.   [3] Phil., ii. 1–5.

fellowship with his suffering, but shall also know the power of his resurrection, and be fashioned in a glory like unto his glory and according to the working whereby he is able even to subdue all things unto himself.[1]

5. Unspeakably important, therefore, in every point of view, is this whole question of the different estates in which Christ executes his office of a Mediator : important to the right understanding both of the way and nature of salvation, and not less so to the perfect cultivation and development of the life of God in our own souls. After what I have said of the classification long adopted by the people of God, and herein followed by me as simple and exhaustive of the subject : I may add that it is not the nomenclature, nor exactly the classification I would adopt if I were treating a subject which could be considered in any respect new, or concerning which any one can now feel authorized to disregard wholly as a public teacher the settled nomenclature and ideas of the Church of Christ during so many ages. Still it is my duty to say, that it appears to me Christ himself has suggested both a different nomenclature and a more complete method, in a passage whose force has been wonderfully and, as far as my knowledge extends, universally overlooked, by those who have discussed these great subjects in a systematic manner. Of all the written compositions which the human race possesses, the most remarkable, beyond all doubt, are the Ten Commandments which Moses declares were delivered to him by God, and the Lord's prayer, which Matthew informs us was uttered by the Saviour as part of his wonderful sermon on the mount, and which, as appears by the testimony of Luke, he habitually taught his followers.[2] Both of these are very brief. But the former contains, in four statements the sum of all our duty to God, and in six statements the sum of all our duty to man : while the latter contains in ten statements, occupying hardly ten lines, not only the rule, but the very substance, of the most complicated, the most boundless, the most various, and the most urgent of all the manifestations of man—namely his devotional feelings. If Jesus and Moses had produced nothing else—these two gifts would have placed them above all the benefactors of mankind. In the case of Jesus, the prayer of which I have spoken, was not uttered as on his own behalf, but was taught to

----

[1] Phil., iii. 8–21.   [2] Exodus, xx; Mat., vi. 5–15; Luke, xi. 1–13.

the multitudes as for the benefit of all men. And it formed a portion, as already intimated, of that most remarkable discourse of the Saviour, in which he explained the manner in which all the law, all the prophets, all righteousness, were perfected and completed in him: nothing of the past destroyed—but every-thing, and each after its kind, fulfilled, accomplished, completed, terminated, perfected, in him. And so in this boundless array, the matter of acceptable worship, and prayer as a fundamental part thereof, fell into its place and was treated with the rest; and the form given closes with this sublime Doxology.—" Thine is the kingdom, and the power, and the glory, forever. Amen." It is in this Doxology, that the Saviour intimates, as I suppose, the natural division of his whole work as Mediator between God and man ; and affixes to each part, its specific designation—of his kingdom, his power, and his glory. His kingdom meaning the portion answering exactly to his estate of Humiliation : his power and his glory, together, answering to his estate of Exalta-tion : but Christ dividing this estate into two, of which the former extends from his resurrection to his second coming, and the latter from that second coming onward through eternity. It is well that the established division and nomenclature, so nearly represent the substance of Christ's Mediatorial work ; and that they do not depart even from the form of it, more seriously than they do. But it had been better, and that to an extent we can-not fully appreciate, by a more careful search into the Divine Word, to have hit precisely not only upon the substance, but also upon the very form and the very nomenclature intimated by Christ. But let us examine this somewhat more closely.

6. It is not meant to be asserted that the word " *kingdom*" used with reference to Christ and his Mediatorial work, is con-fined exclusively to the period of his personal Ministry. On the contrary this very Doxology teaches us that the Messianic king-dom will extend beyond the personal ministry of Christ, and will cover a period after his resurrection during which power, even the power of the Holy Ghost will be the great characteristic of the kingdom ; and that afterwards another period extending to eternity will commence on the second coming of the Son of God, when glory, or as it is sometimes expressed, both power and glory will especially distinguish the kingdom. The Messianic kingdom is first manifested to men under the visible headship of Messiah

himself, during the personal ministry of Christ : and so, while it is called, under that form, by many other names, it is called emphatically βασιλεια, the *kingdom*, or the kingdom of God, or of heaven ; and I believe the Scriptures will be searched in vain for the application of the word *power*, δυναμις, or the word *glory*, δοξα, to the kingdom, as descriptive of it, while it abode in that form.   The very burden of the testimony of John the Baptist as the forerunner of Christ was. that the kingdom of heaven was at hand : nay, that Christ, though unknown, was standing in their midst.[1]   What Jesus himself began to preach was, " the Gospel of the Kingdom :"[2]   What he sent forth his twelve apostles to proclaim to the lost sheep of the house of Israel, forbidding them to go into the way of the Gentiles, or to enter into any city of the Samaritans, was that the kingdom of heaven is at hand.[3]   And what he sent the seventy disciples to teach in every place to which he purposed to come himself, was that the kingdom of God is come nigh unto you.[4]   And this is the same kingdom, and the same portion of it, namely, his own tabernacling in the flesh, full of grace and truth, and manifesting in himself the glory of the only begotten of the Father, to which he alludes in that Doxology, as a matter for which every soul that prays should magnify the name of God.   As to the next aspect of the Messianic kingdom, the portion of it held forth with *power*, even the power of the Holy Ghost, and which should reach from the ascension of Christ till his second coming : the Scriptures seem to be equally explicit.   The Saviour, speaking to his apostles of his early departure to the Father to prepare a place for them—and of his purpose to come again, and receive them unto himself : says to them, I will pray the Father and he shall give you another Comforter, that he may abide with you forever : even the Spirit of Truth, whom the world cannot receive, because it seeth him not, neither knoweth him : but ye know him for he dwelleth with you, and shall be in you.   That Comforter, adds Christ, is the Holy Ghost, whom the Father will send in my name ; he shall teach you all things, and bring all things to your remembrance, whatsoever I have said unto you.[5]   And again : when the Comforter is come whom I will send unto you from the Father, even the Spirit of Truth which proceedeth from the

[1] John, i. 26.   [2] Mat., iii. ; Luke, iii. ; Mat., iv. 23.   [3] Mat., x. 5–7.
[4] Luke, x. 1–10.   [5] John, xiv. *passim.*

Father, he shall testify of me.[1] And again : It is expedient for you, that I go away : for if I go not away the Comforter will not come unto you ; but if I depart I will send him unto you. And when he is come he will reprove the world of sin, of righteousness, and of judgment : of sin, because they believe not on me : of righteousness, because I go to my Father and ye see me no more : of judgment, because the prince of this world is judged.[2] And to the same purport, are innumerable statements of the word of God. But what believer doubts, that the dispensation which is passing over us, is the dispensation of the Holy Ghost, and that it is he alone who is the author of the new birth, and of all divine life in the soul of every child of God ? It is the period of the Messianic kingdom, manifested with that divine power which was exhibited so marvellously on the day of Pentecost—and which will continue till the glory of Messiah shall be personally manifested, at his second coming. And now of that second coming, and of the infinite glory thereof, how repeated and how explicit are the testimonies of God ? One of the last of inspired men, quoting by name, the words of one of the first, proclaims this constant doctrine of divine revelation, in its most compact form : Behold the Lord cometh with ten thousand of his saints, to execute judgment upon all.[3] This is that Lord Jesus who shall be revealed from heaven with his mighty angels, in flaming fire, taking vengeance on them that know not God, and that obey not the gospel of our Lord Jesus Christ : who shall be punished with everlasting destruction from the presence of the Lord, and from the glory of his power : when he shall come to be glorified in his saints, and to be admired in all them that believe.[4] This is the kingdom, and this the power of it, and this the glory of it—for which the Lord Jesus teaches every pious heart to rejoice in God, while time endures : and which the saints are to commemorate throughout endless ages. These are the estates intimated by Christ himself, in which he founds, redeems, perfects, and reigns over his kingdom : the first distinguished by the personal ministry of Christ, the second distinguished by the power of the Holy Ghost as the vicar of Christ, the third distinguished by the inconceivable glory of Christ when he comes again to take it, judge it, perfect it, and deliver it up to the Father. And the divine nomenclature itself is un-

<hr>

[1] John, xiv. 26.   [2] John, xvi. 7–15.   [3] Jude, 14, 15.   [4] 1 Thess., i. 7–10.

speakably fruitful. For the careful use of it unlocks many of
the prophecies of the New Testament Scriptures and especially
those uttered by Christ—by determining their chronological order :
and the faithful adherence to it, sheds abundant light upon the
proportion of faith, touching many doctrines which enter profoundly into every period, and especially the third one of Christ's
kingdom. Many prophecies which are obscure, and many doctrines which perplex us in the absence of this knowledge, fall
naturally and clearly into their place, whether in the great current of events, or in the great scheme of faith, as soon as we
observe whether it is βασιλεια, or δυναμις, or δοξα—the *kingdom*—
the *power*—or the *glory*, to which they specially appertain. And
this, of itself, is abundant confirmation of the truth of the exposition here given. Nor is it without its use to have pointed
out, how the long accepted method of treating these great questions of the humiliation and exaltation of Christ, may be
brought into a near harmony with the method suggested by
Christ himself; without suddenly changing a large part of the
nomenclature of systematic Theology, and recasting a considerable portion of the form of it.

II.—1. The nature and the efficacy of the work which Christ
performs in his estate of humiliation and his estate of exaltation ;
as well as all that relates to the offices of prophet, priest and
king, which, as Mediator, he executes in both estates : belong to
a different part of the subject, and will be treated in their proper
place. Having endeavored to gain a clear insight into the nature
of these estates, and their relation to the plan of salvation, and
to the person and work of Christ ; it is necessary to point out in
a more particular manner, those circumstances which the most
distinctly characterize them both, and invest them with such
great importance.

2. All our conceptions of the humiliation of our Saviour, to
approach any thing like truth, must start with the recognition
of his estate before he took flesh. The glory of which he emp-
tied himself, in order to become man, was indeed a glory which
we cannot fully apprehend ; but which we know to have been
the highest of all glory—for it was the glory of an existence, a
dominion and a blessedness commensurate with that of God, and
essentially identical with it. How much is involved in saying
that all this glory was obscured, laid aside, put off in the very

fact of any incarnation—we cannot tell : but the reason why we cannot tell is, that the humiliation exceeds at its first step, all we can imagine, much less utter. Then comes the particular form of the incarnation ; and another step to a lower humiliation is taken—in that the nature he is to assume is a nature fallen and depraved—a nature degraded in the face of the whole universe—a nature lying under the curse and penalty of the broken covenant between God and man. Another step is taken, and a new humiliation occurs, in all that was peculiar and personal in the condition as a man, which he assumed, and in which he lived and died : a condition condemned to ignominy as a Jew, and to toil, privation and obscurity as a man, all aggravated by his illustrious descent from a long line of kings, and by the insolent dominion of foreign rulers, oppressing him and his people from the throne of his ancestors. Still another step and another humiliation in all that is involved in his being made under the law—his own law : not only that law given to sinful men as a rule of duty and of judgment, in itself eternal, but all those peculiar institutions of the Jewish people, which made them at once the most peculiar form both of a nation and a church. And thus unutterably humiliated in the very fact and method of his incarnation, his whole life was exposed to sorrows, indignities, and sufferings, the acuteness of which was far beyond our conception : one perpetual scene of contradiction and misconstruction by sinful men, whose very companionship was a ceaseless trial to his infinitely pure spirit : one conflict after another with the great enemy of God and man, amidst fierce temptations, and fiery trials, and the hidings of his Father's face, and agonies which even inspired men who witnessed them strive in vain adequately to depict. Yet through a life of perfect sufferings he was shown to be perfect himself. The perfection of all goodness and love, the perfection of all wisdom and power, the perfection of all purity and righteousness, the perfection of all majesty and glory—all exhibited through the perfection of suffering, during a life ordained and chosen as a life of perfect humiliation—unto an end to which nothing but such a life could lead. It seems to me that the conception and development of such a life as this, wholly without a parallel amongst the works of man ; and the relevancy of such a life to the salvation of men, as the first fundamental point in realizing the establishment of a kingdom at once infinitely pure, universal and irresistible ; leads us at once out of the domain of merely human things, and ushers us broadly into a domain which merely human thoughts could never have opened to us.

3. A death corresponding to such a life, crowned it. We are to remember that he was not subject to death, being sinless : and that he could not die by violence, even if he had been subject to death, without his own consent, since he was divine. But, as the righteousness of his life in the way of active obedience was indispensable to the justification of his followers, so also was the righteousness of his death as a sacrifice for their sins : the righteousness, in both cases, of the God-man. A death of unspeakable humiliation crowning a life of unspeakable humiliation : and in both cases a climax which we can trace, but far more terrible than we can comprehend. That he should incur the stroke of death at all was an infinite humiliation ; and that he should lie under the power of it for one instant was a fearful aggravation of that humiliation. For death is the fruit of sin ; and he who hath the power of death is the devil ; and it is through the law that sin becomes the sting of death. Herein lay the stupendous mystery—that death is conquerred by incurring its stroke, that sin is atoned for by enduring its penalty, that the law is satisfied by fulfilling it even to blood—that Satan is vanquished in the very act of his apparent triumph. But it is not less a stupendous mystery of humiliation, than of wisd. n or love. And so the death itself is aggravated by every circumstance of cruelty, ignominy and shame. Rejected by the people whose king he was—sold at the price of a servant by one of his own apostles—delivered up as an impostor and a blasphemer by the proper authorities of the visible church of God—condemned as a traitor by the Roman governor in obedience to the furious clamor of the Jewish people—denied or deserted by nearly all his immediate followers—he was buffeted, scourged, spit upon, and led to the most horrible death, under the scoffs and derision of men, and the hiding of God's face from him. The bitterest cry that human ears have ever heard, was that cry from the cross —Eloi, Eloi, lama sabachthani ! And we may confidently assert, that except upon the simple basis of the facts as set forth in the Scriptures, the crucifixion of Jesus Christ, taken in all its circumstances, is the very darkest spot in the whole compass of God's dealings with the human race. Accepted as the means—

the only means—of salvation to man ; accepted as the means—the very highest means—of glorifying God throughout eternity ; then we understand it all—and it becomes illustrious as a display of God's redeeming love, precisely as it becomes overwhelming as a proof of Christ's utter humiliation. Wrested from their true intent, these dealings of God become appalling: accepted in their simple and awful majesty, they are full of unsearchable riches of grace.

4. We cannot separate either the life or the death of the Lord Jesus from the office which he executed both in his life and in his death : for the very object of his incarnation was to execute that office. He became Immanuel, precisely that he might become Mediator : and his whole humiliation is the humiliation of the Word made flesh. But herein is a new source of humiliation. Everything involved in his assuming and executing the office of Mediator, is of itself a humiliation just so far as it identifies him with man, or makes him responsible, in the face of the universe, for the fate of man. The brotherhood of such a race is ignominy enough. But it is infinitely more to incur the guilt of their imputed sins—to bring down on his head the wrath of God because he stood in their place—to expose himself for them to the malice of the Devil, to the claims of the law, to the power of the grave—to place himself in a position where his very office would demand that our offences should cause his death, and that our justification by God should be the condition of his resurrection.[1] Here was a spectacle for men and angels and devils, the most amazing that ever was or could be, whether it is considered in itself, or whether it is considered relatively to what he was as a perfect man, or relatively to his person as God-man, or to his work as Mediator between God and man, or to his own eternal God-head as the divine Word. A life of humiliation—a death of humiliation—an office of humiliation ! On every side infinite humiliation : and yet on every side infinite grounds on which to judge, that all humiliation was in itself impossible. No statement can express, nor can any heart adequately conceive, the extent of the humiliation of Christ. And yet, except as the humiliation of Christ enters into the very essence of God's plan of saving sinners, and except as the reality and the efficacy of that humiliation are beyond all doubt, the very life of the whole

<hr>

[1] Rom., iv. 25.

method of divine grace ; no heart can conceive why Christ should have been humiliated at all, while every heart can suggest ten thousand reasons against it, if it were possible to consider it either needless or unfruitful.

III. The Estate of Christ's exaltation, attaches to him as God-man, and so Mediator between God and men, in the same manner as it has just been shown that his estate of humiliation does. What we consider and treat herein as one single estate, is divided by the Saviour in the Doxology heretofore expounded, into two estates ; namely, the first of power, the second of glory. It is enough to say at present, that the first, second, and third subdivisions of this general head, embrace the kingdom with power ; while the fourth subdivision embraces the kingdom with glory ; all constituting the Exaltation of Christ.

1. In his resurrection from the dead, the Lord Jesus conquered death, and broke the power thereof, and delivered them who had been in bondage through the fear of death. Free from sin—he never saw corruption : but made an open demonstration that he was the Son of God with power in the resurrection from the dead. He proved that divine justice was satisfied : that the elect of God were justified : that he who had the power of death, that is the Devil, was subdued : and that in and by his own resurrection, all men would rise from the dead—and of that number, his own brethren to eternal glory. God, in the resurrection of his Son, gave a divine and immediate attestation to him as the Saviour of the World—ratifying thereby every part of his previous ministry—proving him to be the Lord of the living and the dead —the judge of the world—the head of the church, and as such invested with all power in heaven and upon earth ! How boundless and how overwhelming are all the questions solved forever by this first step in the exaltation of Christ ! How clear and perfect is the light thrown over the greatest and the darkest problems which the shadow of death had covered throughout all ages ! And is it not fit it should be so ? Is it not most becoming ? The Incarnation of the Son of God—his resurrection from the dead—and his second coming to judge the world—the kingdom, the power and the glory of the Mediator : these are the three grand and closing eras of the Messianic kingdom. The second of the three we have now seen accomplished : the first was very

nearly connected with it : the third still impends over us, after the lapse of so many centuries.

2. The ascension of the Lord up into glory was the next step in his exaltation. David foretelling the triumphant ascent of the Lord on high, and applying to him the language quoted by Paul when explaining to the saints at Ephesus the nature of Christ's ascension gifts ;[1] intimates that thousands of chariots and of angels, even as they surrounded the Lord on Sinai should bear him to the skies. And so, doubtless, the cloud which received him out of the sight of his apostles, as he was rapt from their presence upon Olivet, was this glorious retinue of the heavenly hosts marshalling back the Son of God victorious over the grave.[2] What a day was that in heaven ! The glory of the Son no longer veiled from the spirits around the throne. Captivity itself led captive—Christ openly triumphing over his enemies far above all heavens—and openly lavishing upon his elect Bride, the most costly and precious gifts. To prepare a place for his brethren, and to prepare a place for himself, at God's right hand, till the restitution of all things ; these are the immediate objects of that sublime return to glory.[3] In our nature, and as our head —glorified and making manifest in the heavens the glory to be hereafter made manifest upon earth ; the special form of his triumphant ascent to the realms of light, is the open recovery of his visible dominion over the angelic hosts, his open leading captive him who had before led all captive, and his open bestowment of all his ascension gifts on men. About to sit down on the right hand of the Majesty on high, his return thither is signalized with glory, with triumph, and with gifts, worthy of the King eternal, immortal, and invisible !

3. And then he sits down beside the Father on his throne—a Prince and a Saviour, exalted to give repentance to Israel and the remission of sins. That same Jesus, whom with wicked hands they crucified and slew, hath God made both Lord and Christ. And from the highest heaven he proclaims,—To him that overcometh will I give to sit with me in my throne, even as I also overcame, and am set down with my Father in his throne.[4] The God-man is exalted to the highest dominion and power and glory and joy, over the whole universe. He sheds forth, with the

[1] Psalm lxviii. 17, 18; Eph., iv. 8, 11–13. [2] Acts, i. 9–12.
[3] John, xiv. 2–4; Acts, iii. 21. [4] Rev., iii. 21.

Father, the Holy Ghost—his vicar in his kingdom with power—
his everlasting justifier—the witness of him in his person, his
office, his work, and his estate, and the channel to men of a new
life, of all truth, of all holiness, and of every good and perfect
gift purchased by the blood of the Son of God. For himself,
he is the satisfying portion of all who have rested from their
labors : the perpetual intercessor for all who are still in the vale
of tears : the only King in Zion : the Ruler of the universe :
the Lord of lords, and the God of gods ! Thus far has the Dispensation of Christ advanced in its infinite and eternal progress.
At this point it stands and will stand till the second coming of
the Lord, if it may be conceded to human weakness to contemplate as in repose, an infinite activity operating throughout the
universe with a force at once ceaseless and divine ; but operating
after a method peculiar to itself and different from the method
that preceded it, and that will follow it. The aspect of the
kingdom in this world has always an analogy in the aspect of it
in the unseen world : and the analogy to that unseen aspect of
it, represented by the reign of Christ at the right hand of the
Father, is the Dispensation of the Holy Ghost with power in the
kingdom here below. It is that which now exists.

4. If we could allow ourselves, for a moment, to suppose that
the plan of salvation revealed in the Scriptures was purely of
human conception ; it seems to me that nothing is more certain
than that the mind of man would have considered the catastrophe fully reached, and the matter absolutely complete, when the
main figure was exalted to the throne of the universe, and the
main action accomplished in a complete provision for the perpetual salvation of successive generations of men, through all
time. To man, the subject is exhausted, and everything is
dramatically complete, when Christ has been infinitely exalted,
and every dependent event has been perfectly solved. But God's
thoughts are not as our thoughts. And so the conception which
Christ gives us of the consummation of his kingdom, reveals to
us a further aspect of it, when his exaltation shall have a new
manifestation, and the great glory of that kingdom find its expression in his own second coming, without sin, unto salvation.
Time is to have an end : the dead are to arise : every soul of
man is to be judged. The earth is to be burned up, and the firmament is to melt with fervent heat, and the heavens are to be

rolled together as a scroll and a new earth and a new heavens are to emerge : Satan is to be bound for a thousand years and then to be loosed for a little season, and then to be cast into the lake of fire—where death itself shall die. There is to be a kingdom of infinite glory and blessedness : and then it is to be delivered by Christ to the Father. We may dispute, as we like, over these sublime realities, and we may group them, and expound them, one way and another, to suit our own foregone conclusions. But still they are realities which no man can call himself a Christian, and deny. And in the midst of them all, always, the Scriptures exhibit to us the Son of Man, in unutterable glory, surrounded by all his holy angels, perfecting and reigning over his kingdom, distributing immortal crowns to his followers, and taking immortal vengeance on his enemies. Preliminary, it may be, to these stupendous events, there are others less imposing, but still only less imposing than they, which are also to receive a solution which the Scriptures uniformly connect with the person and glory of Christ, in his second coming. The question of God's ancient people—the question of the heathen world—the question of the great Eastern apostacy—the question of the still greater Western apostacy—the question of the World powers—the question of the Bride of the Lamb, till that great day shall come ! Who can imagine the glory of Messiah—who can conceive of his exaltation—when he shall take to himself his great power, and in his own glory and the glory of the Father, reappear in the midst of such a scene of things ? Or how shall we lift up our hearts to that height he will have reached, when his whole Mediatorial work is thoroughly completed, and the kingdom is delivered up to the Father—and Messiah, as very God, all and in all, thenceforward throughout eternity, shall draw still nigher to the glorified saints, and reign still more palpably over the universe, which he created, which Satan and sin had ruined—which he had in a manner so glorious and so wonderful, redeemed, recovered, restituted, recapitulated in himself ! What is man that he should sit in judgment upon revelations like these—penetrating the most august counsels of Jehovah, and delivered to us, for the most part, in fragments and outlines, too remote and too vast almost for distinct comprehension ?

IV.—1. On the day on which the blessed Lord rose from the dead, he joined himself to two of his disciples as they walked from Jerusalem to Emmaus, and their eyes being holden that they should not know him, he communed with them of the matters immediately relating to himself. When they had uttered what was in their hearts, he said to them, Oh ! fools and slow of heart to believe all that the prophets have spoken : ought not Christ to have suffered these things, and to enter into his glory ? And beginning at Moses and all the prophets, he expounded unto them in all the Scriptures, the things concerning himself.[1] It is not, therefore, without an infinite necessity of some kind, that Christ was both humiliated and exalted. There was a "needs be" recognized and enforced by Christ himself, both that he should suffer as he did, and that he should enter into his glory.

2. The most obvious form of that "needs be," is immediately suggested by the words of Christ. All the prophets had so declared ; and their words must be fulfilled. The plan they revealed, was the plan adopted by God, and the plan adopted by God must be accomplished. His wisdom in adopting it, and his veracity in proclaiming it, alike rendered its accomplishment an inevitable necessity. Nor is it possible to imagine a more distinct assurance than is here given by the Saviour, of the divine reality and the divine certainty of all that is written in the Jewish Scriptures. Still, this obvious view goes much deeper. For it is no more certain that what is revealed is true, than it is certain that it is revealed because it was both true and certain. This humiliation and this exaltation of Messiah, must needs be ; and therefore all the prophets have said so. Strictly speaking, salvation is of grace, and thus in a certain sense, there is no necessity that any salvation should be provided : while yet, in another sense, grace itself is of the very nature of God, and for that reason there is salvation. If any way of salvation at all—then of necessity, the way that is most suitable to all the divine perfections, and that is most for the glory of God : that is to say, the way that is best. And so revelation itself can make known to us, only the right, the proper, the best, and in that sense the necessary. We may go further and say, we are not able to conceive how it was possible for man to be saved in any other way, or upon any other conditions : and we may add that no other way has been intimated by God as possible, but on the other

----

[1] Luke, xxiv. 13–27.

hand the Scriptures abundantly assure us, that there is no other way : which has been proved in another place. Taking the case, therefore, just as it is presented throughout the Scriptures : considering the nature of God as it is therein revealed to us, and the whole question of salvation as therein developed : there is that infinite fitness both in the humiliation and the exaltation of Christ, which constitutes in a divine sense, the very highest "needs be." It became him for whom are all things, and by whom are all things, in bringing many sons unto glory, to make the Captain of their salvation perfect through sufferings.[1] And such a High Priest became us, who is holy, harmless, undefiled, separate from sinners, and made higher than the heavens.[2]

3. Perhaps, also, after it has been made known to us by God both that he will save sinners, and how he will save them : and after we have come to apprehend in some good degree, the nature and perfections of God—and the results, on either hand, of his interposing to save man, or of his refusal to interpose : we are in a position to comprehend that the free, sovereign, and gracious interposition of God, precisely in the manner he has interposed, was an inevitable part of that eternal Decree of God, whereby he works all things according to the counsel of his own will. In such a crisis, of such a universe, under the dominion of such a God, the overwhelming "needs be" is for such an interposition, after such a method. I have pointed out in another place, how it is the infinite goodness of God, which amongst all his perfections lies at the foundation of every hope of salvation, which the sinner, personally considered, could cherish. But we now encounter a wider aspect of this vast subject : and I may add a few words in further illustration of the remarkable language of the Saviour, bearing directly on it.

4. We are to consider the manner in which man fell—the manner in which he was tempted—the motives which overcame him. We are to consider the relations which both Eve who tempted Adam, and Satan who tempted Eve, bore both to Adam and to God. We are to consider that, on supposition of God's refusal to interpose, Satan was completely triumphant, sin and misery became the everlasting condition of the universe, the human race became forever unfit for the destiny designed for them in their creation, and the glory of God in the illustration of his

<hr>

[1] Heb., ii. 10.   [2] Heb., vii. 26.

perfections became limited and obscured. On the other hand, we are to consider, that on supposition of God's effectual interposition, Satan would be vanquished, sin and misery would be restrained and turned to the glory of God—death would be abolished—the universe would be purged and restored to the dominion of God—the human race would be recovered and advanced in purity and blessedness—and all the perfections of God would be displayed in the most illustrious manner, to his own infinite and eternal glory. All these are considerations clearly arising from the statements of the Word of God ; and the problem involved in them had this solution which is presented in the plan of salvation : that is, summarily stated with reference to the matter under our immediate consideration, in the Humiliation and Exaltation of Christ. With reference to his Exaltation, touching which the "needs be" involved in the language of the Saviour was especially emphatic ; there is no difficulty in perceiving, that after his Humiliation had actually occurred, his Exaltation was an absolute and unavoidable necessity. For any other supposition than that the risen Lord ought to enter into his glory, involves the whole case in self-contradiction ; for the fact of any Humiliation is dependent upon the fact of his being a divine person ; and if that is true his Exaltation is not only infinitely fit but absolutely inevitable—while if it is false, there was no Humiliation, and the whole case falls into hopeless absurdity.

5. Now, upon the supposition of the whole case between God and men as it stands up to this point, the relevancy and completeness of this method of developing the whole Office-work of Christ as Mediator, by means of his two estates of Humiliation and Exaltation, are not only perfectly obvious ; but the whole case after getting to this point, breaks down of itself, unless it is allowed to progress by some method of exposition essentially involving the same principles and the same results touching the Mediatorial office and work of Christ, considered as a suffering, and considered also as a triumphant Saviour. The whole controversy between us and God, is infinitely to our dishonor, and must end in our destruction. And so every Mediator must find, and must decide. Unless, therefore, he is both able and willing —after deciding against us, to do something that will save us ; we are ruined, and the Mediation breaks down, as to any attain-

ment of its fundamental design, namely, peace between us and God. But the Mediator does undertake for us : and what he does in both estates, is the result of that undertaking : and the whole is perfectly relevant to his Office and Person and Work, so far as we are concerned—if it only prove effectual. That it does so, is what makes the plan of salvation of inestimable value to us. As relates to the Mediator himself, everything depends upon his willingness and his ability to reconcile us to God upon the terms everywhere set forth in the Scriptures ; and which as to the Mediator, have been summarily recounted in this chapter. If he is willing and able to obey and suffer for us ; if he is willing and able to present us faultless before God : then the whole design of the Mediation can be perfectly accomplished—and his whole Humiliation and his whole Exaltation, are perfectly relevant to that design, and perfectly complete in themselves. On his part, it is a work of boundless love. As relates to God—we are to remember that the Mediator is his only begotten Son ; and that he spared not this Son, but delivered him up for us all.[1] It is well for us to speak of the need there was that God's justice should be satisfied, that his law should be magnified, that his righteous dominion should be restored. But the things that shine most conspicuously in the sufferings and the triumph of the Saviour of the world, are the eternal Beneficence of God, and his eternal love for us in which it finds expression, through every part of the Mediatorial work and reign of his Son, our Lord ! The deeper the humiliation of the Son of God, the more intense is the proof of that amazing love which the Father has bestowed on us ; and the higher the exaltation of the Saviour of sinners, the more illustrious is the assurance, that he who gave us Christ, will with him freely give us all things !

[1] Rom. viii. 32.

CHAPTER XI.

I. 1 The threefold office of Christ, as Mediator of the Covenant of Grace.—2. He is
our Prophet, our Priest, and our King.—3. These offices perfectly distinct, but indissolubly united to each other in the person of Christ.—4. The glory and the
burden of these united offices, which the Son of God humbled himself to execute.
—5. The order of their execution.—II. 1. The Prophetic office of Christ especially considered.—2. Idea of it, stated by God through Moses and the ancient
prophets.—3. Illimitable power appertains to this office in Christ.—4. Divine wisdom appertains to it.—5. The great Teacher is true God.—III. The actual teaching of Christ.—1. Always and under all Dispensations of the Covenant of Grace,
Christ the fountain of all truth unto salvation.—2. Christ is not only entitled to
the glory, and responsible for the truth and efficacy of all Scripture: He is himself the concrete of it all.—3. The manner in which his personal teaching, developed, fulfilled, and supplemented all that was known before.—4. The sublime conception that truth must supplant force, and teaching supplant violence, as the
means of universal conquest, is the key of Christ's ministry.—5. The habit and
power of Christ as a teacher.—6. Christ's method as a teacher—parables—analysis and illustration of them.—7. Christ's prophetic office in his estate of exaltation.
The power of the Word and ordinances. The perpetual presence of the Holy
Ghost.—IV. Divine confirmation of the prophetic office of Christ.—1. The general testimony of the life of Christ—the direct testimony of the Scriptures—the
proof from prophecy and the internal evidences suggested.—2. Taking the Scriptures as a whole, the relation of Christ to their total contents renders the divinity
of his prophetic office an unavoidable necessity.—3. Everything concerning
Christ and the Scriptures is explicable and glorious or inexplicable and monstrous
—according as he was or was not a teacher sent from God.—4. The miracles of
Christ.—(a.) Their suprising number.—(b.) This power absolute and unlimited in
Christ: and derived from him by all others whoever possessed it.—(c.) So performed as to exhibit his dominion over the whole universe—and his possession of
every divine attribute.—(d.) The substance of the way of life as taught by Christ,
may be deduced from Christ's miracles and the Scripture account of them.—5.
The divine nature of the question herein discussed.

I.—1. As the Mediator of the Covenant of Grace, alike in
his estate of Humiliation and in his estate of Exaltation, Christ
in all the glory, and all the burden of his office, was as one ex-

pressly called thereto of God.[1] Possessed of infinite power and acting under the commandment of the Father[2] he was at last unspeakably exalted by him, to be head over all things to the church which is his body, the fulness of him that filleth all in all.[3] While his office carried with it in one respect an infinite honor—it carried also an infinite burden. To teach his church all that it was needful for it to know—but to do this, in great part, under infinite humiliation : to reconcile us to God, and acquire thereby the highest glory and joy, but to accomplish this by the sacrifice of himself : to conquer and to establish for himself an endless kingdom, but to endure everything in the accomplishment of this sublime work. The whole work of Christ is performed as Mediator of the Covenant of Grace : he performed the whole of it as a suffering or as a triumphant Saviour : and in both these estates it is liable to a threefold division according as we contemplate him as our Teacher, as our Atoning Sacrifice, or as our Lord and Master.

2. Considered in this light the whole work which Christ performs for his people, as their Mediator with God, he performs as their *Prophet*, as their *Priest*, or as their *King*. In discharging his office as Mediator, whether reference be had to God or to man, as the parties to the Mediation, which, through infinite grace has been undertaken by him : or to the two estates of Humiliation and Exaltation, in which he executes that office ; every function which he performs must be referred to him as the Prophet, as the Priest, or as the King constituted by the Covenant of Grace—and accomplishing its unsearchable mercy. His general office of Mediator, therefore, becomes subdivided into his Prophetic,[4] his Priestly,[5] and his Kingly[6] offices.[7]

3. These offices of Christ though united in his person, are perfectly distinct in their own nature ; and the contemplation of his Mediatorial work as performed for us, through them, is indispensable to the clear understanding of the Scriptures—which constantly present it to us in this manner. Nor is there any method of evading or altogether setting aside the teachings of God's word touching the person and work of Christ, and the benefits secured to us by the Covenant of Redemption, more

---

[1] Heb., v. 4, 5.   [2] John, x. 18.   [3] Eph., i. 23.
[4] Deut., xviii. 15–18 ; Luke, xxiv. 19.   [5] Psalm cx. 4, and Heb., v. 5.
[6] Psalm ii. 6, and Mat., ii. 2.   [7] Psalm cx. 2–4, and Heb., i. 1–3.

common, or more insidious, than that of confounding these offices
of the Mediator with each other, and so obscuring and rejecting
the great doctrines of grace which they illustrate and confirm.
On the other hand, these offices of Christ, though perfectly distinct are no more to be disconnected than they are to be confounded : just as the two natures in the person of Christ, are
neither to be confounded nor disconnected.   It is the same Christ,
the only Mediator, who performs them all.   It is for the same
general assembly of the first born whose names are written in
heaven, that they are performed.   It is unto the same end—the
salvation of believers that he executes them all.   And it is
through the same ministry in the flesh, and the exaltation and
reign afterwards, that, by means of these functions of the office
of Mediator discharged by Christ, God and men are reconciled,
and that eternal salvation is secured to us.   It is Christ Jesus,
who of God is made unto us, wisdom and righteousness, and
sanctification and redemption.[1]

4. The inexpressible dignity conferred upon the Mediatorial
office, as well as the glory and burden of the work, from the
union of these three functions in it—is such, that of all who
have been types of Christ, whether as to his person, his work or
his office, not one is set forth in the Scriptures as being invested
with the full discharge of them all—much less with the regular
possession of them.   There were those who were at once prophets
and kings : of whom David and Solomon were the most eminent.
There were those who were both kings and priests : of whom the
most remarkable was Melchizedec.   And there were many who
were both priests and prophets ; of whom, perhaps, were all the
High Priests who answered for God to the people, by Urim and
Thummim.   But to be prophet and priest and king all together,
even in such a sense as would present only a perfect type of the
whole office which Christ was to humble himself so as to discharge, was never permitted to the children of men.   Moses and
after him Samuel, the two most illustrious men that preceded
Jesus of Nazareth—and the former by far the more illustrious
of the two—made the nearest approach that has existed towards
exhibiting to us, in dim outline, a type of those offices, all of
which are united only in the person of the Son of God, as the
Saviour of the world.

[1] 1 Cor., i. 30.

5. In respect of the relevancy of these offices of Christ, to the parties who, so to speak, were involved in the result of his Mediation, it is obvious that his priestly office had a more direct relevancy to God, who by means of it especially was propitiated towards man : and that his prophetic and kingly offices had a more direct relevancy towards men, who are especially taught the way of salvation, and guided therein through them. And indeed, in a very important sense, the two last named offices have their foundation in the first one ; since without the work of Christ as our priest to satisfy divine justice and redeem us from destruction, there is no teaching that can avail, nor any guidance that can be sufficient to lead us to God. Still, however, as in his public ministry on earth, Christ has entered, in his estate of humiliation, upon the great work of instruction first—and that of satisfaction next, and that of dominion last of all, although all are in some degree discharged together ; the usual method of treating his offices is in the order of prophet, priest, and king, which accords entirely with the natural order of the subject. We commence therefore, with his prophetic office.

II.—1. Christ, the Mediator, executes the office of prophet by making known unto men the whole will of God necessary to their salvation. The design of his Mediation is to reconcile us to God. In order to that, one indispensable part of his work is to make known to us, all that it imports us to know of God and of ourselves ; of the relations in which we stand to him as creatures and as sinners ; of the mode of reconciliation to him ; of the salvation which we shall thus obtain ; and of the ruin which will overtake us, if that is neglected. Dealing with us according to his own nature, and according to ours also—God condescends to restore to us the knowledge which we have lost—and to superadd what relates to the new method of his dealing with our fallen race. Life and immortality in a new form, are offered to men through Jesus Christ ; and it is one great part thereof that he becomes our divine Teacher in all things pertaining to that eternal inheritance.

2. "I will raise them up a prophet," saith God to Moses— "from among their brethren, like unto thee, and I will put my word in his mouth, and he shall speak unto them all that I shall command him. And it shall come to pass that whosoever will not hearken unto my words which he shall speak in my name, I

will require it of him."[1] A prophet, that is, who receives directly from God, and delivers to men, divine instruction, which if they reject they shall perish. A prophet raised up immediately by God, from the midst of his brethren—in a manner altogether different from that in which ordinary prophets are raised up by God. A prophet, like unto Moses, not only in both these particulars—namely, that the manner of his raising up, and the manner of God's communication with him are thus marvellous ; —but also, that as Moses was a glorious ruler, and executed at intervals the priestly office—as well as habitually the sublime functions of a teacher, taught himself immediately of God : so this predicted Mediator, should be at once and fully a Prophet, a Priest, and a King. A Prophet moreover, who like Moses, should redeem a people from bondage, and found a glorious kingdom—give it laws and ordinances, lead it through a howling wilderness, and plant it in triumph in the promised land. Only that his work should be infinitely broader and deeper and more glorious—the redemption by him more illustrious—the triumph through him more complete—and all the results imperishable and eternal. For at the best, Moses in all his greatness was faithful only as a servant in the house of God ; but Christ Jesus as the Son of God, in his own house ; which house, says Paul, are we, if we hold fast the confidence and the rejoicing of the hope firm unto the end.[2] Beyond all doubt Jesus of Nazareth is he, of whom Moses and all the prophets did write :[3] that great Teacher sent from God, of whom they all did testify. It is he by whom the people that walked in darkness, have seen a great light—and whom on that account, Isaiah called the Counsellor.[4] He whom from the very earliest period, God's inspired messenger revealed to man as the Interpreting angel—as well as their Ransom.[5] He whom the prophets made known as the Pastor, sent from God, to feed his chosen flock.[6] And when he came into the world—while the testimony of all men unto him was, that never man spake as he spake ; and the testimony of his immediate followers was, that he and he alone, had the words of eternal life : his own unqualified declaration was, "I am the light of the world."[7]

[1] Deut., xviii. 18, 19.   [2] Heb., iii. 1–6.   [3] John, i. 45 ; Acts, iii. 22, and vii. 27.
[4] Isaiah, ix. 2–7.   [5] Job, xxxiii. 23, 24.
[6] Ezek., xxxiii. 23 ; Isaiah, xl. 2, and Jer., xxiii. 4, 5.   [7] John, viii. 12.

3. It appertains to the prophetic office of Christ, that he should possess supreme power. Power by which he may not only secure the absolute certainty, that his divine teachings shall be made known outwardly, and in his own good time and way to the whole family of man : but that still more unsearchable power, by which, with an irresistible efficiency, he may open the mind of man, and turn his heart to the knowledge and the belief of his word. To this office also a boundless and uncontrollable power over the universe appertains : in the exercise of which he confirms the reality of his heavenly mission as the Teacher sent from God, and establishes the truth of his doctrine, by miracles performed by his own proper Godhead.[1]

4. To the prophetic office of Christ it also appertains, that he should possess divine and infallible wisdom. Such power as has been already shown to appertain necessarily to this office, could be exercised beneficently only by one possessed of a wisdom, commensurate with itself. The supposition of infinite power lodged with wisdom less than infinite, if it be not in itself self-contradictory and absurd, since power is necessarily either self-destructive, or limited by our ability to use it—would establish a kind of spiritual system for the universe, utterly incompatible with all the knowledge we possess of it, and of God. Christ has expressly declared that no man knoweth the Father, save the Son, and he to whom the Son will reveal him ;[2] and in like manner he has asserted, that he is himself the way, the truth, and the life.[3] It is through him, that the Comforter himself leads us into all truth : for the things which he shows us are the things of Christ ; and the things of Christ are all that the Father hath. So that with a divine and an infallible wisdom—the world may be convinced of sin, of righteousness, and of judgment—and thus know, through Christ, all that is needful for salvation.[4]

5. It is to be observed, that in every classification we attempt to make of so many of the Attributes of God as are known to us, they fall, of themselves, into certain great divisions. Amongst these classes, some are known to us more distinctly and by more various methods than others ; some result from the very idea of his infinite existence, and some from particular aspects of that incomprehensible being. This vast subject will fall under special

[1] Luke, xxiv. 31, 32, 45, and John, viii. 32, 36, and Luke, vi. 19, and Mark, v. 30
[2] Mat., xi. 27.   [3] John, viii. 14.   [4] John, xvi. 7–15.

consideration hereafter: but at present it is to be observed, that while every attribute of God—of which we have any knowledge, is ascribed to the Mediator and involved in the offices he executes; some of them are so manifestly at the very foundation of his ability to execute one or other of those offices—that we cannot conceive of his being the Mediator without them. Thus, Infinite Power is inseparable from Infinite Will guided by Infinite Intelligence: the whole of which appertain to an Infinite Spirit, and to nothing else: and infinite Wisdom is not conceivable except in connection with an Infinite Moral and Rational Existence. To open the soul of man, to sanctify the conscience of man, to control the reason and the will of man, to teach truth that may be made available to all this, and to enforce it all with illimitable power of every kind: all this is the work of God. Now, since all these and similar attributes of God, are found ascribed to Christ in every part of his office and work as Mediator, and are here shown, both from the word of God and the necessity of the case, to lie at the very foundation of his Prophetic office: it is apparent here as everywhere, that the entire plan of salvation which turns absolutely upon the person of Christ, is subverted the very moment we deny his supreme Godhead. By the personal union of the human and divine natures in Christ, as has been shown in a former chapter, such infinite and divine unction is communicated to the human nature, and such ineffable intercommunication exists between the two natures in his person —and such fulness of the Godhead dwelleth in him bodily; that upon the supposition of such a being, for such an end—both of which points have been heretofore fully established, we can not only see clearly how infinite power and wisdom should reside in Christ, as the great Teacher of Men—but we cannot see how it could possibly be otherwise.

III. In the execution of the Prophetic office of Christ, there may be said to be two general stages or parts of the glorious work; namely the actual Teaching, and the divine Confirmation both of the Teacher and of that which he taught: the actual exercise of the office—of divinely and infallibly teaching men the whole will of God unto salvation, and then the infinite confirmation by God of the whole truth delivered—and of Christ himself, the great Teacher thereof.

1. With respect to the first of these, namely the making

known unto men of the entire way of salvation and the whole means thereof, and declaring the whole will of God relating thereto ; Christ has always been, and will for ever remain the great Teacher—the Prophet of his people.[1] All the prophets and Apostles were but his servants and Disciples—and spoke only as they were moved by his Spirit.[2] He alone taught with an absolute, personal authority, freedom, confidence, wisdom and fulness.[3] While he was on earth he did this in his own person,[4] and as a minister of the circumcision,[5] but with the authority of a lawgiver ;[6] and also by his servants and Disciples chosen and fitted by himself.[7] Before he was incarnate he did it by Prophets, Priests and Scribes of the earlier Dispensations.[8] Since his resurrection and to the end of time, he has done it and will do it, first by his Apostles and then by Ministers, called and qualified by himself for their great work.[9] Always and under all circumstances—with a divine power operating internally, by the Word, upon the minds of men.[10] And since the day of Pentecost in a peculiar manner, by the Holy Ghost, sent down from Heaven and abiding in the hearts of his people—their comforter, and his witness, till he shall return again without sin unto salvation.[11]

2. There are various points touching the exercise of the prophetic office by Christ, as an actual Teacher, which even in the briefest statement of it—need to be distinctly insisted on— as being pre-eminently characteristic in themselves, and of supreme importance to us. Amongst these, at the very threshold, we are to understand that Christ has made himself absolutely responsible for the whole contents of the Jewish Sacred Books, and for the whole contents of the Books written by Apostles and Evangelists selected by himself to record the story of his life, to perpetuate his personal teachings, and to expound the whole doctrine of Salvation. His attestation to the Scriptures of the Old Testament, as being of divine origin and authority, is perfectly

---

[1] Isaiah, lxi. 1–4; Psalm ii. 6, 7; Luke, iv. 18; Mat., xvii. 5, and xxiii. 8–10; Acts, vii. 37, 38; Heb., iii. 1, 2.

[2] Mat., xi. 27; 1 Peter, i. 10, 11, and iii. 19; Eph., ii. 17; Neh., ix. 30.

[3] Mat., v. 22, 28, 32, 34, 44, and vii. 28, 29; Mark, i. 22.

[4] Heb., ii. 3.   [5] Rom., xv. 8.   [6] Mat., vii. 29.   [7] Mat., x. 40; Luke, x. 16.

[8] Heb., i. 1; 1 Peter, i. 11, 12, and iii. 18, 19; 2 Peter, i. 19–21; Hosea, iv. 6, 7 Mat., ii. 5, 6, 17, and xxiii. 37.   [9] 2 Cor., iv. 6, and v. 19, 20; Eph., iv. 8–13.

[10] Acts, xvi. 14; Eph., i. 19; Luke, xxiv. 32, 45.

[11] John, vi. 45; Acts, xvi. 14, and i. 4–8; John, xiv. 16, 26; Acts, ii. 23.

emphatic, and the whole body of the Scriptures of the New Testament presents one continual picture and record of himself, all directed to the one object, that men might believe that he is the Christ, and that believing they might have everlasting life. Nay more : it is his Spirit which inspired them all, and their very name—the *word of God*—identifies them with him as God the Word, and identifies them with him again, as the Word made flesh. Whatever these Scriptures may be, they are the eternal monument of the Great Teacher : a monument more stupendous than all others united, which have been erected in the Universe ; and above all else stupendous in this, that Christ himself, in his person and his work, presents to all rational creatures, the sum of the whole teachings which the whole written word presents to the same creatures in another form. The great Teacher not only points the way, but he is the way ; he not only teaches all truth, but he is the very truth ; he not only brings life and immortality to light, but he is the true God and eternal life. Amongst all wonders none is greater than this. Christ is subjectively, the very sum of revealed Religion, taken objectively. The great Teacher is the concrete form of all divine knowledge ever communicated to man.

3. When we consider the substance of the personal teaching of Christ—two things strike us as infinitely remarkable ; namely the wonderful manner in which he develops the ancient Scriptures, and the fulness and authority with which he supplies whatever they had left obscure. Amongst the most remarkable extended examples we might take the Sermon on the Mount as recorded by the Apostle Matthew.[1] But in truth the whole ministry of Christ is full of examples. I am not come, said he, to destroy the law or the prophets, but to fulfil ; and his teachings abound with applications of this great principle to every aspect of revealed truth, and every form in which we can imagine that truth to be perfected, or accomplished, or exhausted. The law is fulfilled by being perfectly obeyed, by having its widest applications so explained as to make it almost a Gospel—by developing from it the great law of love—and then by submitting to its direst penalty and becoming the end of it for righteousness. Truths before revealed in part, or fully revealed only under types, are laid open and developed by him, so as to be perfectly

[1] Mat., chaps. v. vi. and vii.

clear and simple, and to possess a force which did not before appear in them. The prophecies in part accomplished, and in part more clearly set forth, and in part supplemented with new predictions, carrying forward the prophetic history with increased distinctness, to the consummation of all things, are thus fulfilled in every sense. The types, and shadows, and ceremonies, and ordinances, are sometimes dismissed as being completely exhausted, sometimes replaced by others more complete, sometimes illustrated and continued, sometimes finished by their own nature and limitation; but all of them are in some sense fulfilled by Christ. All the duties of life are put more clearly on their true bases, illustrated more fully in the light of a more perfect revelation, and their amazing breadth, and their infinite significance, and the immutable relations between duty and truth, and between goodness and greatness, are set forth in expositions which are most inadequately described when we say nothing human approaches them. In one word, and as the sum of all—in the hands of the Lord Jesus, all the Institutions of the ancient patriarchs, which were Institutions contemplating the human race as so many distinct families, but which were applicable to every family in the world; and all the Institutions of Moses, which designedly separated the people of God from all other people, and established them under a Theocracy absolutely distinct and peculiar : all passed over into a new and glorious form, and without any distortion of anything that had gone before, but on the contrary fulfilling, perfecting, completing everything—the Messianic Kingdom stood forth capacious as the Universe itself, and pregnant with all truth, all blessedness, and all force.

4. The very conception of teaching as a power fit and adequate, which was personal to Christ, distinguishes the exercise of his prophetic office, almost as remarkably as either of the circumstances already pointed out. The conception of a universal kingdom by universal conquest, was one of the earliest, and considering the unity of the human race, one of the most natural, as it was one of the most steadfast, that took possession of the great powers of the earth. Four times at least, the idea was realized, by the four universal monarchies of which the Scriptures teach so largely, and whose career is the very staple of all profane history, down to the complete overthrow of the Roman Empire, and the total reconstruction of society in modern times,

Nor is it a little remarkable that this conception was abandoned by the World-Powers, only after the complete initiation of the true universal kingdom, the Messianic kingdom, under the power of the Holy Ghost ; nor less so, that simultaneously with this abandonment by the World-Powers, the conception was taken up, as against the true Kingdom of Christ, both by the great Apostacy of the East under Mahomet and his successors, and the great Apostacy of the West under the Roman Pontiffs— all striving for universal dominion by conquest. But here lies the ineffaceable distinction between the Messianic conception of universal dominion and every other conception of it : that the Messianic kingdom is to be established and maintained by in- struction, by light, by consent—while every other universal do- minion is one of conquest, of force, of violence. Put up again thy sword into his place,[1] was the command of Christ to his fol- lowers, at the very crisis of his own fate ; and such, as concern- ing the spread of his kingdom, is its very conception and whole spirit. No conception can be more simple or more august ; while none could be more distinctly anti-natural, as the whole history of man has shown. Nothing more sublime has ever appeared, than the confidence of Christ both in the truth which he taught, and in the power of that truth to supplant violence as the prin- ciple of universal dominion. Teach all nations ; teach them precisely what I have taught you ; neither more nor less. This is the basis of his universal dominion. And all succeeding ages have so proved that the preaching of the Cross is the power of God,[2] that even misbelievers accept, after their own fashion, the great conception of the great Teacher—and lavish against the preaching of the truth, a part of that violence on which they rely for the conquest of men.

5. Nor was his method of teaching truth less distinctly char- acteristic of Christ. He gathered no special audience, he had no fixed place, he made no preconceived discourses : but in the temple, or on the way-side—in the desert, on the sea-shore, from the mountain-top ; from house to house, from village to village, from city to city, from tribe to tribe ; now disputing with learned sceptics, now rebuking fierce bigots, now warning hypocritical formalists ; now teaching with infinite tenderness the humble seeker after truth, now confounding great scholars and doctors,

[1] Mat., xxvi. 52.   [2] 1 Cor., i. 18.

now solving the doubts which perplexed wise and anxious hearts ; now seated in earnest converse with some beloved household, or even some single disciple, or some single outcast; now pouring forth to countless multitudes, who forgot the wants of nature as they waited from day to day at his feet, those words of eternal wisdom and love which have nourished the pure in heart through all succeeding time. A few of his immediate followers have preserved for all mankind, in a few brief narratives, a small portion of those unparalleled teachings,[1] which during three years were continually on his lips and which were personally heard, it may be, by many millions of our race. The power of his teaching both in the substance and in the form of it—the power of his overwhelming presence as a teacher, was so transcendent, that in all his history there is not the slightest intimation that a single human being was ever wholly unconcerned under it. Sometimes they shouted hosanna—and sometimes they shouted crucify him : but no one was ever indifferent when they saw that wondrous man, and heard those wondrous words. He taught them with absolute fulness, he taught them with absolute authority, he taught them concerning all truth and all duty, he taught in a way that no one ever taught before or since. Yet he taught them so simply that the very weakest could understand all that the very greatest could understand—so clearly that every one could know all that could be known.

6. The habitual form in which Christ cast his teachings, is too remarkable to be passed over without special notice : the more so as there is no room to doubt that even to our own time, the nature and significance of it, are not fully appreciated. All these things, says Matthew, spake Jesus unto the multitude in parables and without a parable spake he not unto them.[2] The reason of this remarkable habit is given by Christ himself, in explaining to his disciples the parable of the sower ; for he tells them, unto you it is given to know the mysteries of the kingdom of God ; but to others in parables that seeing they might not see, and hearing they might not understand.[3] And at the very close of his ministry he said to his apostles, these things have I spoken unto you in parables ; but the time cometh when I shall no more speak unto you in parables, but I shall show you plainly of the Father.[4] And the first passage above cited from Mat-

[1] John, xxi. 25.   [2] Mat., xiii. 34.   [3] Luke, viii. 10.   [4] John, xvi. 25.

thew's gospel is immediately followed by this quotation from the seventy-eighth Psalm, which the Apostle applies to Jesus, That it might be fulfilled which was spoken by the prophets saying, I will open my mouth in parables : I will utter things which have been kept secret from the foundation of the world.[1] We are thus distinctly told that teaching by parables, was not only the constant habit of Jesus, but that it was predicted of him as such, and that it was a peculiar mark of his personal ministry—and was not to continue after that ministry had ceased. Moreover, that the special reason for adopting this method of instruction was to veil the mysteries of the kingdom of God ; which mysteries should involve things, thus veiled in parables, which had been kept secret till then, but which Christ should utter in this form ; and finally that the followers of Christ were entitled to know these mysteries, thus veiled in parables. Therefore Christ expounded to them many of his parables, which confessedly they did not understand before the explanation. Mark adds[2] that Christ in explaining the parable of the sower remarked on the ignorance of his apostles, intimating apparently, that they might understand from the explanation he was about to give, the method of expounding all parables. Considering all these statements we can understand how it is, that besides the charm of the parables of the Lord, derived from their very form, and which makes them so effective as a vehicle of instruction ; and besides the obvious lessons of wisdom and prudence and piety which lie on the surface of all of them, and which are all that men commonly seek for in them : there is in every one of them, some precious secret of the kingdom of God, veiled indeed, but still comprehensible to all to whom it is given to know the mysteries of that kingdom. It is this hidden treasure which renders the parables of the Lord, perfectly unique in the literary history of mankind : and consecrates that form of instruction to him, in a way altogether unapproachable by man. It is this abounding richness which makes them separately of such inestimable value to the children of God ; and which makes them when taken together, a complete summary of divine truth. As one example taken nearly at random, the Saviour, in the parable of Lazarus and Dives has taught mankind in a few sentences, occupying half a page, and uttered without premeditation to certain Pharisees

---

[1] Mat., xiii. 35.   [2] Mark, iv. 12.

who had derided him ; more fully and more precisely, all that relates to the vast, obscure and multiplied questions of the state of man after death, than is to be found in all the utterances of all beings except himself, before and since.[1] The certainty of man's immortality ; the certainty of future, eternal, and separate retribution, to the just and the unjust ; the certainty that the issues of our being in the world to come depend on the nature of our life here ; the certainty that goodness and not greatness, virtue and not success, is the decisive matter for eternity ; the certainty that the truths revealed in the Jewish Scriptures are adequate to the direction of men's lives and the salvation of their souls, and that repentance and faith are the conditions of salvation ; the certainty that no portents, whether physical or spiritual—not even a messenger from the dead, are adequate to any such end. Can there be any doubt that except Jesus, the earth till then had never contained one single person to whom all these great and dark questions stood exactly in the light, in which he has placed them for us ?

7. It has already been pointed out, that it appertains to the prophetic office of Christ, to make known to man the whole will of God unto salvation ; and that Christ has most emphatically set forth the whole truth of God, contained in the Old and New Testaments, as being complete unto that end ; the latter by uttering and enacting it, the former by ratifying and attesting it— both by inspiring the whole by his Divine Spirit. This divine truth thus identified with Christ becomes by the very terms of the statement, a rule at once complete and infallible, both of human conduct and human belief ; that is both of duty and of faith to the whole extent that both of them appertain to salvation. The great Teacher is responsible for it all—and he is entitled to the use of it all in the execution of his sublime office. And we must remember that all these terms are used in their widest sense. Thus taken, the Word of God is a light and a power unto salvation. It is a two-edged sword within us separating between the very joints and marrow. A discerner of the very thoughts and intents of the heart, it is the only effectual instrument, in the whole work of man's salvation. He who has substituted instruction for violence, has taken the sword of the Spirit, instead of the sword whose use he prohibited ; and in

[1] Luke, xvi. 19–31.

these sacred writings is contained that very truth, in which he manifested that sublime confidence, that it would win for him a universal and an endless dominion. Whatever is lacking to men who never enjoyed the divine power of his personal presence and instruction, is supplied by the divine presence of the Holy Ghost in their hearts. It is he who is the only effectual agent— as divine truth is the only effectual instrument in the whole work of regenerating and sanctifying the soul of man. The relations both of this instrument and this agent of man's salvation, to man himself, are controlled and determined by man's relation to Christ. The whole work of the Spirit has absolute relevancy to the person, and work, and word of Christ ; and whatever difference may be apparent in the relations of the Holy Ghost to the Messianic kingdom, and to the work of salvation carried on in its bosom, in different ways under different dispensations ; the whole difference is always attributable to the different position of Christ himself, with reference to the kingdom. Since the descent of the Holy Spirit on the day of Pentecost ; since the completion of the personal work of the great Teacher on earth, and the resumption of his prophetic office at the right hand of the Majesty on high, which preceded that descent: beyond a doubt—as has been abundantly proved before—the aspect of the kingdom of Christ is correspondingly changed, and therewith the aspect of divine truth and the work of the Holy Ghost. It may be confidently asserted that the Word and the Spirit of God—and the ministry and ordinances of the kingdom of Christ, as they all relate to the prophetic office of Christ, do more and more manifestly prove themselves to be the power of God unto salvation, as the long ages pass away. And thus do all things more and more illustrate that prophetic office, both as Christ executed it during his estate of Humiliation, and as he has continually executed it in his estate of Exaltation, proving how transcendent he was as the great Teacher of mankind, and how illustrious a part that office was of his divine work as Mediator between God and man.

IV. With respect to the divine confirmation of Christ's prophetic office—it is impossible to develop even in the feeblest manner, the actual work of Christ as the great Teacher of mankind, without exhibiting at every step proofs of his divine fitness for his office, and of his divine authority therein. The very story of what he does, is a perpetual demonstration of what he is.

There are however overwhelming proofs distinct in themselves—some of them nearly connected with the work itself—some of them quite separate from it, which confirm to us in the most remarkable manner, the divine power of the Mediator in his prophetic office. Some of the most obvious of these proofs will be briefly suggested.

1. If we are asked to produce evidence to sustain the claims of some great captain, we point at once to the victories he has won. Upon the same principle we point to the administration of great statesmen—to the works of great poets—to the researches of great scholars—to the discoveries of great philosophers—to the lives of great philanthropists. Supposing this kind of evidence to be of any value—and it is manifestly of the very highest value,—it establishes the mission of Christ as a divine Teacher, in a manner more various and more conclusive than any other disputed point, was ever established by that kind of evidence. I will not in this place lay particular stress on the direct and innumerable testimonies of the Scriptures themselves to the supreme Godhead of the great Teacher ; because, as these very Scriptures have been identified in the most intimate manner with Christ himself, the caviller might say, this is merely Christ's testimony to himself ; and I will not stop now to expose that cavil. Moreover I will only suggest the conclusive nature of the proof furnished by the whole compass of prophecy as it bears, from the beginning of time, upon the person and work of Christ ; and as it has been manifesting itself by its perpetual fulfilment, since the ascension of Christ, precisely as it was restated, supplemented, and completed by himself, and by those selected and qualified by him. And further still I will merely direct attention to the irresistible force of the confirmation derived from a complete survey of what is specially called the internal evidences, that the intelligence, wisdom, and knowledge of the Saviour were divine. Still however every one of these three immense departments of proof, may be asserted to be overwhelming in its own nature, and overwhelming in its application to the question of the divinity of Christ's prophetic mission. For the testimony of the Godhead to itself, is the very highest testimony which can be borne ; and the perfect knowledge of all things, and amongst the rest, of all future things, is divine omniscience ; and the direction of that boundless omniscience into the soul of man bear-

ing with it a perfect remedy for all the deadly maladies of that soul, is to the soul itself, the most conclusive form in which infinite wisdom can be exhibited.

2. But there are broad and unequivocal aspects of the Word of God as connected with the prophetic office of Christ, which seem to me wholly irresistible in the confirmation they afford. Take the Scriptures as a whole —and consider the claims of Christ as a divine Teacher to depend absolutely on the estimate which human reason ought to form of these writings—taken altogether and viewed as the product of one mind. Unquestionably the supposition of their being the product of one single human intellect is utterly ridiculous : for the whole of human intelligence has not been able to produce any single complete portion of them. But that one and the same intelligence does pervade every part of them, is just as manifest as that there are such writings. The moment we admit the relation which Christ's prophetic office bears to the Scriptures—that moment all doubt ceases as to what Christ is. But the moment we deny the relation which Christ's prophetic office bears to the Scriptures, that moment we change the whole character of the Scriptures themselves. The Word of God—God the Word—and the Word made flesh—all stand or fall together. And if there be in this universe anything that stands more firmly, than the word of eternal life—the divine Saviour of sinners—and the self-existent God, all united ; it has not hitherto fallen to the lot of man to find it out. Moreover, the grand conception of these Scriptures—and the central object of the whole of them, is Christ himself—and salvation by him for lost sinners. What may be boldly asserted, is that every part of this conception of Christ which pervades the Scriptures, is wholly superhuman : and that every use to which the conception of such a being is put, throughout the Scriptures, is wholly superhuman : and that the tenacity with which they hold to and develop the conception, and the grand use to be made of it, is if it were possible still more superhuman. This is not the way in which man conceives of things. Nor is it the way in which he develops them : nor are these the ends he proposes : nor is this the method by which he accomplishes what he proposes. There is not one capital truth which enters into the plan of salvation, which every thousandth human being even adequately understands : not one of them which any human being ever understood

at all except as it was taught him through the prophetic office of Christ. We might as well say that the universe itself is an out-birth of some human conception—as to say that the Christ of the Scriptures is. And moreover, we are now in a position to estimate the power of God's word—the power of Christ's prophetic office, at the end of about thirty-three or four centuries since the days of Moses, and of about eighteen centuries since the days of the Son of Man. Here is the Great Teacher himself; here is the totality of his instructions, which have survived through all ages; here are the fruits of his teachings covering the whole known history of man, and now lying palpably before our eyes. An immense portion of the human race has, in all ages, neglected this Great Teacher; and other immense portions have perverted his teachings; and others still have followed other teachers. So that every aspect of the case, necessary for the most decisive judgment is exhibited to us. Is it within the compass of human ignorance and folly to doubt what judgment every enlightened mind must render? Viewed, therefore, in its totality—viewed in its great and pervading conception—and viewed in the sum of its practical effects upon the human race—the word of God, and by consequence the prophetic office of the Son of God to which we owe that word—are divine. And this is the emphatic and perpetual testimony of the Holy Ghost. A testimony rendered both to Christ and to the word of life. Rendered to Christ in every conceivable way during his ministry on earth: rendered of Christ in every conceivable way since his ascent up into glory. Rendered to the teaching of Christ, incessantly, while he taught in the flesh: rendered to the word taught with divine power, from the day of Pentecost to this day. It is the testimony of the Spirit of Truth, to the truth itself: the testimony of the Holy Spirit, to that true holiness, which divine truth begets and nourishes: the testimony of the Quickening Spirit, to that new life, begotten by himself, and which is nourished in holiness by divine truth. If divine testimony is worthy of credit, Jesus Christ is a divine teacher.

3. It is impossible to admit for a moment, that the Lord Jesus—such as all testimony proves him to have been—could have designedly imposed upon his followers, by pretending to be, what he was not. Nor would it help the case of the unbeliever at all, to allege that he was deluded himself, and in that way

deceived others. He was no fanatic—no impostor. His life was a life of immaculate purity. A life absolutely incomprehensible upon the supposition that he was a mere man—much less a weak and sinful man ; yet perfectly comprehensible, consistent and glorious, when considered as the life of a divine Teacher, actuated by the spirit of a divine mission, as Mediator between God and men. This is what he uniformly testified of himself ; and the testimony of God and men, sustained his own.[1] All his disciples,[2] even Judas who betrayed him,[3] the wife of Pilate who judged him,[4] the centurion who watched his death-struggle,[5] the Roman governor who condemned him,[6] nay the Jews themselves[7]—all testified that his life was one of unspotted purity and unapproachable perfection. His death—though it appertains more especially to his priestly office—attested and confirmed his prophetic work. The *Faithful Witness* ($\delta\ \mu\alpha\rho\tau\epsilon\nu\varsigma\ \delta\ \pi\iota\sigma\tau\sigma\varsigma$)[8] is the title given to him, in the last record of him, by the last and best loved of his Apostles. And throughout all succeeding ages, all who have sealed with their blood, their testimony for the truth as it is in Jesus, have been honored with this title of their Master—martyrs—that is faithful witnesses. Led to crucifixion for blasphemy and treason—crimes which in their own nature, the Son of God and the Ruler of the universe could not commit— he refused to modify a single word he had uttered ; avouched with perfect simplicity, to the Sanhedrim of the Jews, and at the bar of Pontius Pilate, all that he had publicly taught, and willingly laid down his life, not only as a sacrifice for sin, but also as the most solemn attestation of the office he bore, and the truth he had taught. If the perfect fitness of a whole life, be any attestation to the ruling idea of that life ; if death willingly encountered, is any proof of the depth of personal convictions : then the life and the death of Jesus of Nazareth, do clearly prove, that he was in the highest of all senses a Teacher sent from God.[9]

4. Above all other attestations, in the judgment of God himself, as the direct and unquestionable proof of the divine mission of his Son as a Teacher—and of the infallible truth of

---

[1] Mat., iii. 17 ; Isa., liii. 11.   [2] Acts, iv. 27 ; 1 Pet., ii. 22.   [3] Mat., xxvii. 4.
[4] Mat., xxvii. 19.   [5] Luke, xxiii. 47.
[6] Luke, xxiii. 4–22 ; John, xix. 4–6 ; Mat., xxvii. 24.   [7] John, viii. 46.
[8] Rev., i. 5.   [9] 1 Tim., vi. 13.

his doctrine : Jesus Christ added this, that he performed an immense multitude of the most astonishing miracles. I omit for the present all discussion of the nature of miracles and of the proof which may be thought necessary to establish their existence : and observe here, that taking the Scriptures as our guide—and considering miracles as the most obvious proof of the divine mission of Christ—and the divine truth of his doctrine : the case would stand thus :

(*a*) The number of the miracles of Christ exceeds the whole number ever performed, by all other persons united. The learned Jews compute, that from the beginning of the world till the destruction of the first temple, but seventy-four miracles are known to have been performed—exclusive of those wrought by Moses, and on his account, which amounted to seventy-six more—making in all one hundred and fifty, for a period of more than thirty-three centuries. It is perhaps impossible to compute the number performed by Christ, during about three years. But when we consider, that besides the particular and single miracles, which he was daily performing—it is a common mode of stating his wonders, that he healed many of various diseases—that he cast out *many* devils—that he cleansed *many* lepers—that he healed *many* blind, and lame, and halt, and deaf—that he restored *many* dead to life—that he fed *many* thousands again and again ; when we reflect that, as was expressly told the disciples of John the Baptist, when they came to enquire concerning Christ, this was his constant habit—and the perpetual proof of his being the Son of God ; and when we hear the Apostle John declare, that what has been recorded of the acts of Christ, are but a selection and sample of what he actually performed ; we cannot avoid the conclusion that the number of his miracles must have been immense.[1]

(*b*) According to the Scriptures this power of working miracles, was immediate and absolute in Christ. He exercised it at his pleasure—and in his own name—and by virtue of a divine plenitude residing in himself.[2] Not so only, but this power of working miracles was capable of being conferred by him upon others, and was actually and largely so conferred by him. Nay, that all the miracles ever wrought by others, in any age of the

---

[1] John, xx. 30; Luke, vii. 21, 22; Mat., iv. 24; Mark, iii. 10, and vi. 35, 36; John, xxi. 25.   [2] Mat., viii. 2, and ix. 28; John, v. 18–21.

church, were wrought—in fact—and as to most of them in form, in his name and by virtue of his authority and power.[1]

(c) The miracles of Christ were performed in such a manner as to exhibit his supreme power and Godhead, with regard to every department of nature, and creation. The elements—all of them: the inferior animals: man, both in his soul and his body —both in life and death: angels, both good and bad: the grave, and death, and Satan. Insomuch, that upon the most careful examination of the works of creation, nothing can be found that has not in some way been made tributary to· the exhibition of Christ's miraculous power: and in the closest scrutiny of the Bible nothing can be discovered which is especially ascribed to Jehovah, as a proof of his being, or an illustration of his attributes—which it cannot be shown, that the same Scriptures declare to have been done by Christ, or else distinctly ascribed to him. It is not conceivable that any demonstration could be more thorough and complete.

(d) The miracles of Christ have also this stupendous proof, in themselves, that they were wrought, and that they do completely verify all that they were performed to establish: namely —if they be reduced to systematic order—in a way of classifying the particular truths touching Christ, his person, his work, and his offices, which they, respectively, bear the nearest relation to: they will be found to contain, and to present in a complete form, the whole plan of salvation. Insomuch, that if we had no record of Christ, except what is contained in his miracles, and his own explanation of them, we should be able to learn the way of life through them. This is at once a proof of the miracles themselves and a use of them hitherto overlooked: which is the case also with the parables of the Lord, as already intimated. But I cannot avoid the belief, that in both cases the aspect I venture to suggest is one of the grandest aspects in which both the parables and miracles of the Lord stand connected with his prophetical office. For, of the parables, it is a thousand times easier to believe that they are the product of a divine intelligence, than to believe that all the mysteries of the kingdom of God, were accidentally concealed in them, and that in a systematical manner, by a person who did not know what he was doing, nor even

[1] Acts, v. 15, 16, and xix. 11, 12; Mat., x. 1; Luke, x. 1,9,19; Mark, xvi. 17, 18 Acts, iii. 12–16.

the existence of one of the mysteries he was teaching. In like manner, it is a thousand times easier to believe that Christ was divine and did work innumerable miracles : than to believe either that a series of amazing transactions illustrating the most mysterious attributes and counsels of God, and the most sublime truths that exist, should have been illusive, and accidental, and fraudulent, and no miracles at all: or to believe, that, although they were real miracles, they were performed by a person who was totally ignorant of their nature, and even of the very truths concealed under his own stupendous acts.

5. There is much that remains untouched of this glorious work of our Saviour, in his leading us from darkness into his marvellous light, and from the power of Satan unto God. This much, however, may suffice, perhaps, to direct our minds in the proper channel of investigation—while it sets before the sincere enquirer, some of the cardinal truths upon which the people of God, in all ages have rested with confidence and joy, and upon which the gospel itself reposes as a way of life to man. It is for us, not only to accept Christ as our prophet, but to accept his divine teachings in the full comprehension, and the earnest love of them. It is in this manner, only, that they become a lamp unto our feet, and a light upon our path ; or that we can be transformed, from glory to glory, even as by the Spirit of the Lord. It is when we obey the commandment, that we know the doctrine, whether it be of God.

CHAPTER XII.

OFFICES EXECUTED BY THE MEDIATOR: CHRIST THE GREAT
HIGH PRIEST.

I. 1. Summary of the personal facts which historically contain and set forth the Priestly Office of Christ.—2. Expiation by bloody sacrifices, at once propitiatory and vicarious, a fundamental idea in the religion of all nations.—3. Origin and perpetuity thereof.—4. The First Born and the Passover.—5. The Priesthood and the Sacrificial system.—II. 1. The idea of Priesthood and Sacrifice, in connexion with Christ.—2. Developed.—3. Not after the order of Aaron.—4. But after that of Melchisedek.—5. Conception of it as vested in Christ.—6. The Lord our Righteousness.—7. The manner in which this is possible and actual.—III. 1. The obedience and sacrifice of the Lord Jesus—and thereby the everlasting righteousness whereby men may be saved.—2. Christ obeys for us and suffers for us.—3. The propitiatory sufferings of Christ.—4. They were vicarious.—5. The infinite worth and efficacy both of the obedience and the sacrifice of Christ.—IV. 1. The intercession of Christ.—2. Nature thereof.—(a.) He makes it in Heaven, as our High Priest.—(b.) Through the perpetual application to us of the Virtue of his own Mediatorial Work.—(c.) Giving us access with confidence and acceptableness, to God.—(d.) Making our persons and services acceptable to God—and giving us peace and joy therein.—(e.) In some degree making us Priests unto God, in our offerings unto him.—3. General view of this part of Christ's Priestly Office.—4. Except upon the condition of the vicarious satisfaction for sin by Christ—the salvation of man is impossible.

I.—1. AMONGST the things that relate to the person and work of the Lord Jesus, these are clearly stated in the Scriptures : namely, that he was conceived by the Holy Ghost, in the womb of the Virgin Mary : that he lived a life of spotless purity—but at the same time of great privation, trial and suffering : that he scrupulously obeyed the law of God in all things : that he was rejected of the Jews—and accused by them, before the tribunal of the Roman governor of Judea : that he was condemned and crucified—under circumstances of great cruelty, injustice and ignominy : that he endured, before his crucifixion, and especially on one remarkable occasion in the garden of Gethsemane, inex- pressible anguish, and that upon the cross his torture was unutterable : that upon the third day after his crucifixion, he rose from the dead, and about the fortieth day after his resurrection ascended into heaven : that on the day of Pentecost, not many days after, the Holy Ghost was wonderfully and miraculously poured out : that in his infinite exaltation, at the right hand of the Father, he ever liveth to make intercession for his people— and that his intercession is always prevalent : and that he will come again in great glory, to judge the quick and dead. These facts, I repeat, are distinctly stated and continually insisted on in the Scriptures, as constituting an outline of what may be called the personal history of Christ. They are all intimately related to each other : they all mutually illustrate and confirm each other : and taken together they constitute a connected and clear exhibition of one aspect of the Mediatorial work of Christ. For these are, historically, the facts which contain and set forth, the Priestly Office of the Mediator between God and men. As they are obscured by human glosses, or explained away by the perverse ingenuity of wicked men, the Priesthood of the Messiah is rendered more and more indistinct, and the fundamental ground of our salvation crumbles away. As they are accepted in their fulness, and interpreted in the sense ascribed to them by God, the work of Redemption by Jesus Christ, as the great High Priest of our profession, stands palpably before us in its infinite certainty and efficacy.

2. The idea of the existence of God, and our accountability to him, has been discussed in a former chapter. Whether as the result of a primeval revelation never utterly lost, or from whatever source, the whole human family has held the belief, that the anger of God might be propitiated : and that sacrifice, in some form or other was the mode of doing this, most acceptable to him. There is one fact, infinitely humiliating to our nature, which places in the clearest light the strength of these universal convictions, and, at the same time illustrates the abjectness of that fear of God, and the cruelty of that sense of guilt, by which the depraved soul of man is actuated when left to itself. There is no nation of whose religious rites a complete account has been presented, which has not been stained with the blood of human sacrifices ; and every form of Pagan and idolatrous worship which the world ever saw, has offered up the souls and bodies of human beings, to propitiate false gods. Nor is it of small

moment to remark, that throughout the whole world, all bloody sacrifices in all the varied forms of their religions, have been considered by themselves, not only strictly expiatory but absolutely vicarious. This, practically, has been the fundamental and universal basis on which the human race has sought to obtain peace with God: expiation, by way of bloody sacrifices—including those of their fellow men—in a sense, at once, propitiatory and vicarious.

3. However we may be shocked with the cruelty of many heathen rites, and wonder at the folly and brutality which defaced them; we have only to remember that our whole race had a common head, first in Adam and afterwards in Noah; and that sacrifice and oblation, have been essential parts of the true worship of God in every age and under every dispensation: and then we can easily trace, and in the ignorance and degradation of mankind, easily account for any perversion of those universal notions of sacrifice and expiation, which we find so clearly revealed by God, and so deeply seated in the convictions of mankind. From the very beginning, the patriarchal worship before the flood and after it, exhibited no formal method of access to God, in which the pardon of sin was not signified and sealed in the blood of victims: and the Mosaic dispensation, as the outward and instituted means of reconciliation with God, was not only throughout and thoroughly a sacrificial system, but its fundamental doctrine was that the blood made atonement for the soul—and that without shedding of blood there is no remission.[1] To say that all these sacrifices were only typical, is but to point us with more distinctness to the real sacrifice of which they were the types, ordained by God himself. And the more clearly it can be shown that the blood of beasts cannot purify the soul, the more obvious is it that the blood of which God himself has made the blood of beasts the constant emblem, can cleanse us from all iniquity.

4. We have seen heretofore, that the first born of God's people, consecrated of him in Egypt commensurately with the institution of the Passover—a priesthood and a sacrifice—all typical of Christ, were laid together at the very foundation of the ancient dispensation.[2] We have seen them, by express command of God, exchanged in the wilderness for the tribe of Levi.[3] And then this tribe was given for the service of the sanctuary to

<hr>

[1] Lev., xvii. 11; Heb., ix. 22.   [2] Ex., xii. and xiii.   [3] Numbers, iii. 1–13.

Aaron and his sons, who were also of it—and who were to wait exclusively on their priests' office, to which they were consecrated by such emphatic proceedings under such express directions by God.[1] And so amongst the Jews—the priestly office, and the sacrificial system, come down side by side from Moses to Christ—across all those centuries, during which, the Scriptures of the Old Testament were being delivered to the church : and God was preparing in all things, that fulness of time, in which the great High Priest should be revealed, and by one offering of himself perfect forever them that are sanctified.[2]

II.—1. Of all the work of Christ as our Mediator, no part, perhaps, is so formally and largely explained in the sacred Scriptures, as that which is involved in his priestly office. One entire epistle—and one of the most extended of all—is devoted expressly to the explanation of this vital subject. And to leave nothing undone that might place it in the strongest light, the great Apostle of the Gentiles, whose vast labors amongst the most enlightened heathen whom the world ever saw, had given him the largest insight that man ever had of the exact posture of the whole question as it lay in the natural mind : was called of God to treat it fully and for all time, and all men, in a discussion with those who of all that lived, must needs have been most familiar with the same question as it lay in the mind of God, as revealed in his ancient Scriptures. It is Paul, arguing to the Hebrews, but for the human race, the question of priesthood and sacrifice, as it touched on one side the person and work of Christ, and on the other the salvation of man.

2. That Messiah should be a priest, was the burden of the Old Testament Dispensation, whether moral, prophetical or typical. That Christ was a priest—is alike the burden of the New Testament Dispensation. Without this, both Dispensations are empty and incompetent. With it, both are pregnant with the wisdom of God and the power of God. To this nakedly, neither Jew nor Greek, had anything to object : for neither of them had any idea of any religion, that did not embrace a priesthood, as a fundamental element. But what sort of a priest ? In what sense ? After what order ? And with what sacrifice ? These were all vital questions : and with every one of them the matter assumed a new and more difficult aspect.

[1] Lev., viii. [2] Heb., x. 14.

3. Not a priest after the order of Aaron—is most certain. Because undeniably, Christ came of the tribe of Judah—concerning which tribe God not only spake nothing touching the priesthood, but he had most plainly prohibited—and that under the penalty of death, any one who was not of the tribe of Levi and descended from Aaron himself, from intruding into the priestly office.[1] A marvellous statute, whereby God obliged himself, and staked the whole Jewish dispensation upon the hazard, that Aaron should have male issue from generation to generation. For sixteen centuries, it is certain he had :—for eighteen centuries more, the world has had no special interest in this marvellous continuance of the race of Aaron—but there is reason to believe, it abides until now.

4. After what order then ? David has told us plainly, and Paul has largely explained it. " The Lord said unto my Lord, Sit thou at my right hand, until I make thine enemies thy footstool." " The Lord hath sworn and will not repent, thou art a Priest forever, after the order of Melchizedek."[2] That Melchizedek, says Paul, who was king of Salem, and priest of the Most High God, who met Abraham returning from the slaughter of the kings and blessed him : and of whom Moses had given an account so remarkable, so many ages before.[4] This is the order of the priesthood of Christ : the order of Melchizedek, and not the order of Aaron.

5. It is an order, before and above, and not under and after, the dispensation of types and shadows. An order of the Most High God—and not of a ceremonial system. An order with the power of an endless life—and not after the law of a carnal commandment.[5] It is an order of Royal Priesthood : for Melchizedek was king, as well as priest : king of righteousness, and king of peace :[6] not an order of simple priesthood merely like that of Aaron. An order so kingly, that he who had it blessed Abraham, as being greater than he, and therein greater by office not only than the whole Jewish Dispensation, priesthood and all : but greater even than the dispensation of promise which Abraham had as the father of the faithful. An order, above the Law and above the Gospel itself ; for both of them hung on it.

---

[1] Heb., vii. 14; Numb, xviii. 7. [2] Psalm cx. 1–4. [3] Heb., vii. 1.

[4] Gen., xiv. 17–19. [5] Heb., vii. 15. [6] Heb., vii. 2.

[7] Heb., vii. 2, and 4–10.

It is an order not limited like that of Aaron, to begin at a certain age, and end at another : not limited again, to a special tribe and family : not bound for its efficacy, to a certain place, and period, and rites : not changed by death, and chance : not constituted by a mere induction and continued by an endless succession : not marked by every badge of weakness and decay, even to the changing of the law under which it stood, and to the ceaseless manifestation by constant sacrifice for himself, of the individual sinfulness of the very priest. But it is an order so sublime, that it did not behoove it to count any descent at all, since it came immediately from God. Christ being without mother as to his divine nature, without father as to his human nature, as the Son of God held by order and office an eternal priesthood ; constituted by the oath of God under an everlasting covenant ; to be exercised at all times, and in every place even in heaven itself, and with infinite liberty and fulness ; and without any to succeed him in his unchangable priesthood. Wherefore, as was most becoming and most needful, he was holy and harmless and undefiled, and separate from sinners, and made higher than the heavens. Wherefore again, he had no occasion to offer any sacrifice for himself ; and the single offering which he made of himself, for the people—was so infinite—that it perfected forever all them that believe, that he is able to save them to the uttermost that come to God by him, seeing he ever liveth to make intercession for them.[1]

6. This immaculate holiness, and infinite dignity of our great high priest, appertained of necessity to the person of him who should fill such an office.[2] But besides this personal necessity in view of his fitness for the office itself, there is the further need thereof resulting from the mode in which his office is exercised for, and instead of, sinners whom he proposes to reconcile to God. For it is written, Behold the days come, saith the Lord, that I will raise unto David a righteous branch, and a king shall reign and prosper, and shall execute judgment and justice in the earth. In his days Judah shall be saved, and Israel shall dwell safely : and this is the name whereby he shall be called—THE LORD OUR RIGHTEOUSNESS.*[3] And again, By the obedience of one, shall many be made righteous.[4] And

---

[1] Heb., vii. *passim.*   [2] Heb., vii. 26, 27.   * יְהֹוָח צִדְקֵנוּ

[3] Jer., xxiii. 5, 6.   [4] Rom. v. 18, 19.

again, He hath made him—who knew no sin, to be sin for us : that we might be made the righteousness of God in him.[1] And again, What the law could not do, in that it was weak through the flesh, God sending his own Son, in the likeness of sinful flesh, and for sin, condemned sin in the flesh : that the righteousness of the law might be fulfilled in us.[2] So that the conclusion is irresistible—that Christ, by his perfect obedience to the law of God—has obtained whatever righteousness, obedience to that law conferred : that he did this for us, and in our stead ; and thereby procured, that the righteousness of the law was fulfilled in us, and that we are made the righteousness of God in him.

7. The obedience and the sufferings of Christ, were constant and inseparable through his whole life : for every act of suffering was an act of obedience too—and every act of obedience was a humiliation, in respect to his infinite being. But in the contemplation of his work as our High Priest, with reference to the law of God, and the righteousness which it exacts, and the sanctions by which it is sustained ; there is a very obvious distinction between obeying its precepts, and enduring its penalty : and therefore a very obvious difference between Christ's paying our debt of obedience to it, and his paying our debt of suffering under it.—One general division separates every system of laws, human and divine, into two clearly distinct parts ; and into two only. There is, first, the preceptive portion of the law—wherein is set forth what is commanded and what is forbidden. And secondly, the penal portion thereof, wherein is set forth the penalty for transgression. For it is to be considered that where there is no penalty, there is no law, but merely advice or instruction. And, moreover, that in its very nature, law, properly speaking, can confer no reward, and bestow no grace, in the proper sense of those terms. It establishes a rule of rectitude : to this, it exacts obedience : when that obedience is rendered—it is satisfied—and he who renders it is righteous according to that standard : and then he takes, not as of reward, nor as of grace, but of right, whatever the law had proposed as the condition of obedience. If obedience is refused, there is nothing left, but to inflict the penalty. In the nature of the case, therefore, it is not possible, for any law to save any

<hr>

[1] 2 Cor., v. 21.   [2] Rom., viii. 3 4.

transgressor ; nor—on the other hand, to confer any reward on the righteousness of those who obey it. But the righteousness which results from the perfect keeping of the law of God, is a divine righteousness, since the law itself is divine. And this righteousness was due from us : because the obedience which produces it was due from us. As long as we live we owe this obedience : and, therefore, leaving out of view, all our past transgressions, we owe it still, and as sinners are wholly unable to render it. It is this debt of obedience on the part of the sinner, to the preceptive portion of the law of God, which Christ has discharged—and it is this righteousness, original and actual, which the law required in the perfect keeping of itself, which Christ has obtained for us, by his obedience : just as it is the debt we owe to the penal part of God's law, on account of our sins, original and actual, which he has paid, and thereby secured the full remission of the whole penalty, as to us, by the sacrifice of himself, through which he has merited forgiveness for us. His obedience is rendered, in his office of Mediator, and his work as High Priest. It is rendered to God, for us—the law being the absolute rule thereof. When rendered, being perfect, the law is satisfied, and the divine righteousness which obedience to it confers, appertains immediately, and of absolute right, to the person of Christ. But there, the whole case would end, if it were not for two further considerations. The first is, that the divine nature of Christ, gives to his obedience, and therefore to his righteousness—both original and actual, both active and passive —an infinite dignity and value. The second is, that as all this obedience has been rendered by him, as our Mediator, and our High Priest, in our nature, and in our place—all whereby he was enabled to render it, and all that results from his having rendered it, inures to our advantage, both in the sight of the law, and in the sight of God who gave it ; and we are considered and treated, just as we would have been, if we had rendered that obedience ourselves. We can see, therefore, how the facts stated at the commencement of this chapter, concerning the life of Christ, lie at the foundation of his obedience, as the first part of his priestly work, and of our salvation thereby ; and how completely all our hopes depend upon him.

III.--1. Seventy weeks, said Gabriel to the prophet Daniel, are determined upon thy people and upon thy holy city, to finish the transgression and to make an end of sins, and to make reconciliation for iniquity, and to bring in everlasting righteousness, and to seal up the vision and prophecy, and to anoint the Most Holy.[1] But now, in Christ Jesus, says Paul, ye who sometime were far off, are made nigh by the blood of Christ. For he is our peace, who hath made both one, and hath broken down the middle wall of partition between us : having abolished in his flesh the enmity, even the law of commandments contained in ordinances : for to make, in himself of twain, one new man— so making peace : and that he might reconcile both unto God, in one body by the cross, so making peace.[2] Such statements— and the number of them scattered through every part of the word of God is almost beyond computation—do not admit of being interpreted except in such a sense, as will attribute the everlasting righteousness whereby alone men can be saved, to the obedience unto death, of the Lord Jesus Christ. Upon any other hypothesis than that explained by the Scriptures, the person and work—the life and death of Christ—constitute the most inscrutable and appalling exhibition, of the nature and character of God. That the only perfect life ever passed on earth, should have been one continued scene of humiliation and sorrow, and should have terminated in ignominy and blood, is, by itself and when left without any adequate explanation, the highest providential exhibition of God's aversion to human excellence, or his inability to protect it. But when God himself is made a direct party to this fearful proceeding, and when the victim is acknowledged to be related to him by ties of inexpressible tenderness and force : the divine participation in the anguish, and sacrifice of Christ, becomes unutterably dreadful, unless there be that in it, which will explain and justify the awful tragedy. To say, that God spared not his only begotten Son, and stop there : would have been felt by every human heart, to have been an impiety and a blasphemy, on the part of Paul. When he adds, that he delivered him up for us all, we feel that a wholly different aspect is put on the amazing transaction : and that an infinite field of divine glory and mercy lies all around it. And when he completes the proposition, by asserting, that God will with Christ, freely give us all things, nay that the certainty he will do this is far greater than the certainty that he has al-

<hr>

[1] Dan., ix. 24.   [2] Eph., ii. 13–16.

ready done the other : then the whole case stands revealed to us in its infinite proportions, its boundless motives, and its eternal objects : and we can participate in his rapturous demonstration, that nothing shall be able to separate us from the love of God, which is in Christ Jesus our Lord.[1]

2. The obedience and sacrifice of Christ, are then two great acts of his priesthood, whereby he makes satisfaction to God, and reconciles us to him. An obedience and a sacrifice, never disconnected, but capable of being, to a certain extent, contemplated apart : commencing with his conception in the womb of the Virgin Mary, manifested throughout his whole life on earth, and consummated by his death on the cross. It is the very nature and end of the priestly office—as the Scriptures plainly tell us, that they who exercise it, are ordained for men, in things pertaining to God, that they may offer both gifts and sacrifices for sin.[2] So Christ, our great High Priest, hath not only loved us, but hath given himself for us, an offering and a sacrifice to God, for a sweet smelling savor.[3] He who was the brightness of God's glory, and the express image of his person, and who upheld all things by the word of his power ; before he sat down on the right hand of the Majesty on high, had first, by himself, purged our sins.[4] For the very object of his coming into the world, and the very will of God which he came to execute, was that we might be sanctified through the offering of the body of Jesus Christ, once for all.[5] As our surety and in our stead, he has made full payment of all our debt to God as sinners in his sight, and set us free.[6] By his sufferings he has made perfect satisfaction to the justice of God, appeasing his wrath, by the sacrifice of himself ;[7] just as by an absolute and perfect obedience, he has obtained God's favor and kingdom for us.[8] By his sufferings meriting for us the forgiveness of our sins ; as by his fulfilling the law, he procured for us righteousness : both of which, are required for our justification : wherein not only are our sins pardoned, but our persons and services are accepted as righteous in the sight of God only for Christ's sake.[9] We need not perish under the penal sanctions of the law of God, on account

---

[1] Rom., viii. 32–39.   [2] Heb., v. 1.   [3] Eph., v. 2.   [4] Heb., i. 3.

[5] Heb., x. 5–10 ; Psalm xl. 6–8.   [6] Heb., vii. 21–25.

[7] Isa., liii. 5, 6 ; Job, xxxiii. 24 ; Phil., ii. 5–8 ; 1 Peter, ii. 24 ; 1 Tim., ii. 6.

[8] Eph., i. 6 ; Rom., v. 19.

[9] Rom., iii. 22–25, and iv. 5 ; 2 Cor., v. 19–21 ; Eph., i. 6, 7.

of our sins ; and we may be saved, through Christ, without that perfect obedience to the law, which it exacts of us, and which we cannot render. Christ obeys for us, and suffers for us.

3. It is wholly impossible for us to comprehend the extent of these propitiatory sufferings of Christ, in whatever light we attempt to consider them. His bodily sufferings, throughout his life, and in his death : his inward anguish from the ceaseless contradiction of sinners, and their ingratitude, stupidity, degradation, and pollution, as a source of inexpressible distress to a being absolutely perfect, in a life-long intercourse : the hiding of the face of God from him, and the unutterable bitterness of his anguish therein : the fearful temptations of Satan, once and again let loose upon his soul : the sins of the world imputed to him, who alone of all the world, knew no sin : the curse of the law and its tremendous penalty fallen upon him ; carry the awful action to its highest pitch. Upon the cross, the utmost fury of every separate portion and source of his agony, pours over him in one combined and overwhelming torrent ; accursed of the law—forsaken of God—denied by his followers—assaulted by the devil—enduring the penalty of sin—betrayed—condemned —mocked—crucified : he succumbed at last to the king of terrors —and with one loud and bitter cry—bowed his head—and gave up the ghost ! Such a spectacle, the universe had never seen ! In all the universe, God alone comprehended what it meant !'

4. It was for us, and for our sins. It was our glorious Lord, making, as a priest, a vicarious atonement for us. He was himself the sacrifice as well as the priest, and he offered up himself. Most needful was it. For the justice, the holiness, the truth of God alike demanded it : and all his threatenings, and all his promises, and all his types, absolutely required it. And most true and exact and complete was it. For, he was delivered for our offences.[2] While we were yet without strength, in due time, Christ died for the ungodly.[3] He was wounded for our transgressions, he was bruised for our iniquities, the chastisement of our peace was upon him, and with his stripes we are healed : and the Lord hath laid on him the iniquity of us all.[4] He was

---

[1] 2 Cor., v. 22; John, iv. 6, 7, viii. 48–52; Luke, iv. 2; Isa., liii. 5–10; 1 Peter, ii. 24; Mat., xxvi. 27, 28, and 67; Luke, xxii. 44; Rom., v. 7, 8; Rev., xix. 15; Mat., xxvi. and xxvii.   [2] Rom., iv. 25.

[3] Rom., v. 6; 2 Cor., v. 15; Mat., xx. 28.   [4] Isa., liii. 5, 6.

the Lamb of God which taketh away the sin of the world.[1] He redeemed us from the curse of the law by being made a curse for us.[2] He hath purchased us with his own blood.[3] He gave his life a ransom for us.[4] Nay, he is our expiation,[5] our propitiation,[6] our reconciliation,[7] our redemption,[8] our healing and our peace,[9] and our Saviour.[10] What more could God say, to make us understand and believe ?

5. As before, in regard to the perfect obedience of Christ, so now, as relating to his sufferings, I recall the facts concerning Christ, of which a summary was made at the commencement of this chapter. In them, are held forth the outline which has now been filled up, concerning this part of his satisfaction to God, by suffering, as before concerning the other part, by obedience. There is not one of those facts, which does not explain completely, some portion of this priestly work of Christ ; and, there is not one of them that is explicable, except in connection with that work. That the sacrifice of Christ should be accepted in the place of the punishment of all believers in hell forever, is utterly impossible, and so the whole priestly work of the Mediator is a pure fraud, and all our hopes founded upon it are absurd ; unless Christ was supernaturally born, and yet a real man ; unless he was true God and true man, in one divine person ; unless his individual righteousness, both original and actual, was absolutely perfect ; unless his sufferings were strictly and really propitiatory, and vicarious ; and unless some signal demonstration, such as that furnished by his resurrection, is afforded by God, that all this work of Christ is accepted by him. And after the work is accepted by God, its benefits could never accrue to us, unless some efficacious mode of applying them to us, and fitting us to enjoy them, like that furnished in the descent and work of the Holy Ghost, which are the purchase of Christ's satisfaction to God, were divinely and certainly assured unto us. Upon these conditions, all distinctly and repeatedly stated in the Scriptures, but upon no others, the infinite dignity and worth of the high priest, God-man, who atoned for us, by the sacrifice of himself, give to his expiatory sufferings, a value and sufficiency, equivalent to the everlasting torments of all believers : and se-

---

[1] John, i. 29, and 2 Cor., v. 21.   [2] Gal., iii. 13.   [3] Acts, xx. 28.
[4] Mat., xx. 28; 1 Tim., ii. 6. [5] Heb., i. 3. [6] 1 John. ii. 2. [7] 2 Cor., v. 18, 19.
[8] Gal., iii. 13.   [9] 1 Peter, ii. 24; Isaiah, liii. 5.   [10] Eph., v. 23.

cure for them results and issues, infinitely certain, and eternal. He who has suffered is God manifest in the flesh ; and his person, majesty, Godhead, justice, goodness, and righteousness, being every way infinite and eternal, made that which he suffered of no less force and value than eternal torments upon all the world besides ; and made all the results thereof, divinely inevitable and immutable.[1] These effects of the whole satisfaction of Christ, as our high priest, immutable before, are confirmed unto the heirs of promise, by two immutable things, added of God, namely his counsel and his oath.[2] They extend to all time, before and after his death on the cross : they extend to the persons of all his children, in all ages : they extend to all the sins of all believers : they extend to every obstacle between God and man. Herein are the infinite power and wisdom of God, made tributary to his eternal love ; through the unsearchable riches of his grace, his divine justice is not only satisfied in the salvation of sinners, but in a manner it exacts, for Christ's sake, that all who have been given to him in the covenant of redemption, should be brought off conquerors and more than conquerors through him who loved them, and gave himself for them.[3]

IV.—1. To intercede for the people, and to bless them, which indeed is but a species of intercession, appertain to the nature of the priestly office : and so, in all ages, amongst all people, and in all religions, it has been understood. It was an express, and important part of the priestly office under the Old Testament Dispensation. Let the priests, the ministers of the Lord, weep between the porch and the altar, and let them say, Spare thy people O Lord, and give not thine heritage to reproach.[4] The very name of the priest,* in both the sacred languages, meant one consecrated to God that he might, as one sacred, offer sacrifices and offerings unto him and intercede with him. And so, of Christ it is written, that he is ever at the right hand of God, where he maketh intercession for us :[5] that in heaven itself, he appears in the presence of God, for us :[6] and that his ability to save us, to the uttermost, depends upon his endless life and ceaseless intercession.[7] The doctrine clearly is,

---

[1] Heb., vi. 18.　　[2] Heb., vi. 13.　　[3] 1 John, i. 9 ; John, xvii. *passim.*

[4] Joel, ii. 17 ; Ex., xxii. 11, 12 ; Deut., ix. 26–29.

* כֹּהֵן,—ἱερευς—*Sacerdos*—Priest.　　[5] Rom., viii. 34.

[6] Heb., ix. 24.　　[7] Heb., vii. 25 ; 1 John, ii. 1 ; 1 Peter, ii. 5.

that he alone, continually appears in our nature before his Father in heaven for his elect, in his own infinite worthiness : making the persons of all believers, and their approaches before God acceptable, by applying the merits of his perfect satisfaction unto them : and through the infinite value of his own obedience and sacrifice, removing and covering over all the pollution of themselves and their good works, and presenting them and their services, as faultless before God.[1]

2. There are various ways in which this intercession of Christ is represented in the Scriptures, as to the things to which it relates, the fruits that flow from it, the modes in which we are interested in it, and the relation it has to Christ's glorious work and purchased kingdom.—Thus :

(*a*) It is as the great High Priest, passed into the holiest of all, that all his intercession is offered : and the intercession itself, is founded upon the work which he, as priest, has performed on earth : and its prevalence depends on the infinite perfection of that work, and its entire acceptableness to God.

(*b*) He makes continual request, for us, and in our names, to God the Father : frees us from the accusations of our enemies before God, and above all from the accusations of Satan, the great enemy of our souls : and covers over our sins, from the sight of God, by applying unto us the virtue of his Mediation : and so reconciles us to God the Father, in our daily offences and shortcomings.

(*c*) He teaches us by his Spirit, in all things, and especially to send up supplication and prayer, for ourselves and others : presents our prayers to God, and makes them acceptable in his sight : gives to us access, with boldness, to the throne of grace : and reconciling us to God as his children, through our brotherhood with Christ, enables us to come to him with confidence, as to our Father.

(*d*) Through the intercession of Christ, our good works are made acceptable to God, and rewarded with infinite fulness and richness ; so that not even a purpose, or desire, for the promotion of his glory, is left without note and price on his part. Our persons also, are accepted of God, in our daily services, trials, infirmities and dangers, and are precious in his sight : and quiet of conscience, and peace of mind, notwithstanding sins, and

[1] Heb., i. 3, ix. 24; Eph., i. 6; 1 Peter, ii. 5.

cares, and anxieties, are made our constant portion while we live near to Christ.

(e) Nay in a manner, we become ourselves priests unto God through the intercession of Christ : for being accepted and sanctified, we have freedom and boldness, to draw nigh, and offer up our souls, our bodies, and all that we have and are, as a reasonable service and living sacrifice unto God the Father. And as a spiritual priesthood, we are permitted to offer, in spiritual sacrifice, our obedience, prayers, and thanksgiving to God :[1] which, however unworthy in themselves, are made acceptable to God, through the merit and intercession of our adorable High Priest.[2]

3. The absolute necessity of this intercession of Christ for his children as they pass, one by one, through this vale of tears : the infinite efficacy of it, which is the very foundation of all our trust in Christ as our very present help in every time of need : the glorious extent of it, commensurate with the design, and therefore with the efficacious effects of the other parts of his priestly work : the administration of it, variously, before his Incarnation, during the days of his flesh and Suffering, and since his Resurrection, and Ascension into heaven : all these are topics which hang upon the more fundamental points already discussed, and which find their solution, not only in the express words of Scripture, but in the controlling relations of the whole subject, according to that divine proportion of Faith, which we are plainly commanded to make the rule of all spiritual instruction.[3]   Other topics also, of the deepest import, and some of them occasions of no small division amongst the followers of Christ, stand related more or less directly to the priestly office of Christ, as the Mediator of the Covenant of Grace : the chief of which will be discussed, as we advance further into the great subject of Salvation.

4. The infinite certainty of the adequate punishment of sin, throughout every portion of the dominions of God, shines forth with overpowering clearness in all that relates to the priestly office of Christ. The soul that sinneth, shall die :[4] this is the fundamental and invariable law, that lies at the foundation of the whole moral government of God. Let us, then, rest perfectly assured, that sin and punishment go together inseparably, under the almighty and everlasting sway of God. An uncon-

---

[1] 1 Peter, ii. 5.   [2] Mark, x. 41, 42.   [3] Rom., xii. 6.   [4] Ezek., xviii. 20.

trollable necessity results from this, that Christ must have made an expiatory sacrifice, and that he must have been possessed of infinite worth in all his work of satisfaction ; or else, that no soul of man can escape hell, through him. As I have shown before, the supreme Godhead of the Lord Jesus Christ, and the absolute vicariousness of the satisfaction made by him, may therefore be confidently asserted, to be the indispensable conditions of our salvation. Upon these two conditions, the salvation of believers becomes not only possible, but inevitable. For if Christ died in their room and stead, and if his sacrifice was infinitely meritorious, their redemption and salvation are made as certain, as their destruction was before. So that the everlasting glory and blessedness of those who are united to Christ, is as certain as that Christ was the Great High Priest of his people, in the sense herein taught after the word of God.

CHAPTER XIII.

I. 1. In the universal belief of his own age, Jesus claimed to be both divine and royal.
—2. The Kingly office of Christ, as Mediator.—3. He is the Son of Jehovah—
and reigns in Zion by his decree.—4. Prophetic account of him, as such.—5. Distinctive facts:—(a.) His person:—(b.) His manner of holding and ruling his
kingdom:—(c.) On the throne of David—after Judah has lost the sceptre:—(d.)
This is an endless kingdom—under an everlasting King, who shall be called
Jesus:—(e.) There shall be an endless increase of his dominion and peace—amidst
the ruin of all other kingdoms:—(f.) The zeal of Jehovah will accomplish this:—
(g.) Five titles expressive of his character and dominion are bestowed on him.—
6. These titles explained—Wonderful.—7. Counsellor.—8. The Mighty God.—
9. The Everlasting Father.—10. The Prince of Peace.—11. This is King Immanuel—whom they derided as "one Jesus."—II. The kingly aspect of the Mediatorial office.—1. Further and more glorious manifestations thereof.—2. His particular kingdom as Mediator, is spiritual and eternal—3. In both respects it exacts
the perpetuity of his presence, both as divine and regal.—4. The government of his
kingdom:—(a.) It is his by creation—by inheritance—by covenant—by purchase
—by conquest:—(b.) It is utterly incompetent to exist or act, except in and under
Christ:—(c.) Ruler, Lawgiver, and Judge, he must be—and besides must make
us willing and able—or his kingdom must perish:—(d.) It appertains to him to
confer every distinction, every reward, every benefit, and every blessing, both in
time and in eternity.—5. The protection, enlargement, and defence of his kingdom:
—(a.) The gates of hell shall not prevail against it:—(b.) Nor against a single
believing and penitent member of it:—(c.) The efficient cause of all this, is of
that nature, that failure is impossible:—(d.) The unavoidable certainty of infinite
and eternal triumph.—6. Kingly office of Christ—like prophetic and priestly offices—not only supreme, but exclusive.

I.—1. When Paul and Silas had preached at Thessalonica,
during three Sabbath days, that Jesus was the Christ; some of
the Jews, and a great multitude of the Greeks, and a few of the
chief women believed. But the Jews which believed not, stirred
up the city, and a company of lewd fellows of the baser sort,
missing Paul and Silas, haled Jason, who had received them,
and certain brethren with them, before the rulers of the city.
Their fierce cry was, that they who had turned the world upside

down, are come hither also ; whom Jason hath received, and these all do contrary to the decrees of Cæsar, saying that there is another king, one Jesus.[1] So also, the infuriated multitude which led Jesus before Pilate, accused him with perverting the nation, by teaching, as they said, that he himself is Christ, a king.[2] And when Pilate asked him, Art thou the king of the Jews ? he answered and said, Thou sayest it. They platted a crown of thorns and put it on his head, and they put on him a purple robe, and said Hail king of the Jews, and they smote him with their hands. And when Pilate sought to release him, the Jews cried out that he ought to die, by their own law, because he made himself the Son of God ; and by the Roman law also, because whosoever maketh himself a king, speaketh against Cæsar. And Pilate wrote a title in Hebrew, and Greek, and Latin, and put it on the cross : and the writing was, *Jesus of Nazareth, the King of the Jews ;* a title which he refused to change when urged to do so by the chief priests.[3] In the universal popular mind, therefore, of the days of Christ, and of those immediately succeeding, the fixed impression was, that Jesus claimed to be both royal and divine : and the distinct grounds upon which he was arraigned and crucified were blasphemy under the Jewish law, in that he made himself the Son of God, and high treason under the Roman law, in that he made himself a king.

2. That he claimed to be, and that he was, the Son of God ; and the connection of that fundamental truth with our salvation, has been heretofore considered at large. That as the Son of God, and so the Mediator between God and men, one of his grand offices was to be our King, is the subject of our present consideration. And on the threshold of it, we ought to bear in mind that all the treasures both of the prophetical and priestly offices of Christ, are bestowed upon us, by means of his kingly office. His Apostles carry to such a height, the doctrine of his absolute and universal sway, that one of them asserts in the most precise terms, that Christ Jesus, who before Pontius Pilate, witnessed a good confession, is the blessed and only Potentate, the King of kings and Lord of lords.[4] And another Apostle to whom the inmost depths of heaven were opened, saw there one called "The word of God," clothed in a vestment dipped in blood, followed by the armies which are in heaven, treading the

[1] Acts, xvii. 5–7.   [2] Luke, xxiii. 1.   [3] John, xix. 1–21.   [4] 1 Tim., vi. 13–15

winepress of the fierceness of the wrath of Almighty God ; and on his vesture, and on his thigh a name written, King of kings and Lord of lords.[1] So that even to the most careless reader of the Scriptures, the need is, not to prove the Kingly Office of Christ, but to illustrate its nature and fruits.

3. Notwithstanding the rage of the heathen, the vain opposition of the nations, the hatred of the kings of the earth, and the counselling together of its rulers against the Lord and against his Anointed ; still, saith God, who holds them all in derision, I have set my king upon my holy hill of Zion ; I will declare the decree ; the Lord hath said unto me, Thou art my son : this day have I begotten thee. Ask of me and I will give thee the heathen for thine inheritance, and the uttermost parts of the earth for thy possession. Thou shalt break them with a rod of iron : thou shalt dash them in pieces like a potter's vessel.[2] That is to say, there is a divine King, the Son of Jehovah, constituted by an eternal decree, which is at last declared to men : his throne is in Zion, where he reigns over and in the bosom of the church of the living God, and thereunto he is anointed by God himself : the heathen also, even to the uttermost parts of the earth, shall be his inheritance and his possession, and he shall rule them with a rod of iron : when his wrath is kindled but a little, all his enemies perish from the way : but all they that put their trust in him are blessed.[3] If it were possible to doubt that all this applies to Christ, that doubt is removed by its being repeatedly quoted in the New Testament as expressly describing him. A single sentence of it is quoted three times, by a single Apostle. In one instance to show that God had fulfilled in Christ his promise to the Fathers, beginning with that primeval promise that the seed of the woman should bruise the head of the serpent :[4] in another to show the infinite superiority of Christ to all the angels of God :[5] and in the third to illustrate the manner in which he was glorified of God in the kingly as well as in the priestly office.[6]

4. Perhaps the most special and comprehensive statement of the Kingdom of Christ, and in connection with it of the person and glory of Christ himself, which is contained in the word of God, is that most remarkable one uttered by the prophet Isaiah,

---

[1] Rev., xix. 11–16.   [2] Psalm ii. 6–10.   [3] Psalm ii. *passim.*
[4] Acts, xiii. 33 ; Gen., iii. 15. [5] Heb., i. 5.   [6] Heb., v. 5.

in the midst of the thick darkness then overhanging the Messianic Kingdom. Unto us a child is born, unto us a son is given : and the government shall be upon his shoulder : and his name shall be called Wonderful, Counsellor, the Mighty God, the Everlasting Father, the Prince of Peace. Of the increase of his government and peace there shall be no end, upon the throne of David and upon his kingdom, to order it, and to establish it, with judgment and with justice from henceforth even forever. The zeal of the Lord of Hosts will perform this.[1] Nor is there any part of this statement, or any idea contained in it, either explicitly or implicitly, which is not, in other portions of the Old Testament Scriptures again and again applied to Christ ; and which is not repeatedly and habitually, throughout the New Testament Scriptures used as descriptive of his person and his work, as being the only wise God and the King eternal, immortal and invisible, to whom honor and glory are due forever and ever.[2]

5. Herein, then, it is revealed to our faith, that touching the Kingly Office of the Mediator, the great facts stand thus :

(a) That he is born as a child, and given to his people as one of their own sons. Namely God manifest in the flesh, which is the first incontrovertible truth of the mystery of Godliness ; and which has been heretofore fully discussed.[3]

(b) That he shall possess and execute the government personally, immediately, and directly : holding it in his own right, as purchased by his own blood, and conquered by his own word and Spirit : the burden, as well as the glory of it, shall be upon his own shoulder, and he shall execute all things in it, by his own authority, efficiency, and virtue, personally or through his divine Spirit.[4]

(c) That the throne and kingdom of his father David, shall be the immediate and original seat of his dominion, which shall have no end. Shiloh has come and the sceptre has departed from Judah.: but it is only that it may pass into the hands of the true Lawgiver, who shall wield it forever, and unto whom shall the gathering of the people be.[5]

(d) That he shall order and establish this particular dominion with justice and judgment, forever. For, thy throne, O God

<hr>

[1] Isa., ix. 6, 7.   [2] 1 Tim., i. 17.   [3] 1 Tim., iii. 16.
[4] John, xvi. 7, 16.   [5] Gen., xlix. 10.

is forever and ever : the sceptre of thy kingdom is a right sceptre.[1]   The Lord God shall give unto him the throne of his father
David ; and he shall reign over the house of Jacob forever : and
of his kingdom there shall be no end.   And thou shalt call his
name Jesus.[2]

(e) That there shall be an increase of his government and
with it of peace : peace with God that shall know no end: peace
in the church of God : peace of conscience : spiritual peace.[3]
At the same time a dashing and breaking to pieces of all other
powers and dominions :[4] and the extension of his dominion from
sea to sea, and from the river to the ends of the earth.[5]

(f) That the zeal of Jehovah himself, will perfom all this.
For he will remove every obstacle, and crush every hindrance,
and break over every barrier whether presented in the weakness and sinfulness of his people, or in the enmity of men and
devils.[6]

(g) That the titles which God uses to designate this everlasting and universal King, and to set forth, as far as titles can,
his nature, his dominion and his acts, and to illustrate as fully
as by that means may be done, his character and renown, are
these, namely : Wonderful, Counsellor, the Mighty God, the
Everlasting Father, the Prince of Peace.

6. These titles declare unto us the person, and the attributes
of Christ as he is the King in Zion, and as he is the King of
kings.   The first of these is his name *Wonderful.**   His name,
says the prophet, shall be called *Wonderful;* thus heaven and
earth shall express their sense of what he is, and what he does.
As regards his person, he is Immanuel : as regards his work he
is the Mediator : as regards his Estates they are infinite Humiliation succeeded by infinite Exaltation : as regards his Offices
he is Prophet, Priest and King, in both Estates.   In all things
he is Wonderful.   No less so in what he does than in what he
is.   He is the Creator of the Universe ; the Preserver and Benefactor of men and angels and all inferior creatures ; the Redeemer of his elect.   In every point of view, Christ is so utterly
removed from all comparison with all else, and is so unspeakably
above and separate from all other excellence, and glory ; that

---

[1] Psalm xlv. 6.   [2] Luke, i. 31–33.   [3] Rom., v. 1 ; Eph., ii. 14–17.
[4] Psalm ii. 8, 9.   [5] Zech., ix. 10.   [6] 2 Kings, xix. 31.

* אֶלֶפ—*Mirabile.*

the Holy Ghost applies to him the title of Wonderful as the foundation of all the rest of his titles : expressing thereby not only what he is, of himself, but what he is in respect of every thing signified by every other title applied to him.

7. Thus he is next called *Counsellor.** He is the Wonderful Counsellor : the Wonderful in Counsel. So that the eternal and universal government which is upon his shoulder, is executed with infinite wisdom and counsel : and not one act of it was ever or ever will be performed inconsiderately or unskilfully : nor will one ever be reversed. And this boundless wisdom in counsel, directed by an authority infinitely kingly, not only guides the universe and all that is in it : but it is accessible to the humblest of his people, for his ear is ever attentive to their cry. Freely and unchangeably, by the most wise and holy counsel of his own will, hath God from all eternity ordained whatsoever comes to pass : and yet in the Wonderful Counsellor has this been so done, both as to men and as to events, that no violence is offered to the freedom of the one, or to the contingency of the other.[1]

8. The name which follows is *The Mighty God.*† He is invested with all strength and might, as well as with all wisdom and counsel. The Lord is wonderful in working as well as wonderful in counsel.[2] All power, in heaven and in earth, is given unto him ; and he hath promised to exert it all, in support of those who teach all nations all his commandments. So that the infinite might as well as the unsearchable counsel, in all the wondrousness of both, are made tributary to the Kingly office and authority of Christ. The Wonderful, as he is the Counsellor, and as he is The Mighty God, sits upon the throne of David, God's King upon his holy hill of Zion, the King of kings and the Lord of lords. So that while he rules the universe, exalted far above all principality and power, and might and dominion, as head over his church, and therein head over all things :[3] he condescends with exceeding greatness of power, to usward who believe, to work in us both to will and to do ; and that with an infinite goodness and satisfaction on his part, towards us in all our attempts to work out our own salvation.[4]

9. There follow two additional titles, which in some respects, may be said to depend upon, and flow from those already con-

---

* יוֹעֵץ—*Consiliarius.*   [1] Eph., i. 11; Acts, ii. 23.   † אֵל גִּבּוֹר—*Deus Fortis.*
[2] Isa., xxviii. 29.   [3] Eph., i. 22.   [4] Phil., ii. 12, 13 ; Eph., i. 19–23.

sidered, and which yet in other respects have a substantive character of their own. For although it is not possible to conceive that the things signified in the three preceding titles should appertain to Christ, without those which are signified by the two which succeed, following thereupon ; yet it is very conceivable that the latter might exist, without necessarily implying the existence of all the former. Wherefore these two are distinctly added. First, namely, that he is *The Everlasting Father :*[*] The Father of Eternity. Which is expressed in the fourteenth Psalm by saying, Thy throne, O God, is forever and ever.[1] Which words the Apostle Paul says were uttered by God to his Son, and which are applied by him explicitly to Jesus Christ, as a part of his crushing argument that we shall perish if we neglect the great salvation which is offered to us in him.[2] Nor is it conceivable that a kingdom which is administered by the Author of Eternity, and which can never be destroyed, nor changed, but is ruled over by infinite wisdom and almighty power, to the very end of consuming all other kingdoms, should fail to be the Kingdom of the God of Heaven.[3]

10. The last title of the whole, and the second of these last two, is *The Prince of Peace.*[†] He is the procurer of Peace between God and men : which indeed is the end of his mission to this earth. He is the Author of Peace in every human soul in which Christ is formed the hope of glory. Peace on earth, is the final heritage he will bestow on it, when the kingdoms of this world shall have been made into a kingdom for the Lord and his Christ. To the wicked there can be no peace. The only alternative which can be offered to them, or which can be conceived of as possible, is either submission to the Prince of Peace, and restoration through him to God : or everlasting enmity and warfare between them and God. A warfare, every act of which is attended by increased pollution and wretchedness, on their part ; and which by no possibility could end otherwise than in their utter perdition. It is in this fearful conflict, and as its result, that the vengeance of God is poured out upon devils and wicked men ; that the earth is ravaged ; and that hell, the prison house of despair, becomes the abode of all who are finally impenitent. Nor will it be the least of the horrors

---

[*] אֲבִי־עַד—*Pater Æternitatis*   [1] Heb., i. 8.   [2] Heb., ii. 3.
[3] Dan., ii. 44.   [†] שַׂר־שָׁלוֹם—*Princeps Pacis.*

of those who dwell therein, that their enmity to God is as impotent, as it is cruel and causeless, and that he whom they thus hated and rejected was able and willing to have saved them.

11. We must recollect that all these things appertain to the kingly office of Christ. These titles belong to him as he is a King : and all these effects follow from the exercise of his royal functions : and all these descriptions apply to his kingly person. The child promised who was the Son of God, and to whom such glorious appellations are given, to whom such majestic acts are ascribed, by whom such infinite advancement is obtained, is King Immanuel. They crowned him with thorns, and nailed him to the cross, and called him in derision "one Jesus." But that glorious brow will wear to eternity, the crown of the universe ; and those pierced hands grasp the sceptre of a dominion which extends over every created thing ; and at the slightest whisper of that despised name, every knee in heaven and earth and hell shall bow, and every tongue confess. Nor is it less carefully to be borne in mind that it is as the head of the Mediatorial kingdom that all these titles are ascribed to our Saviour, and all this infinite weight of glory achieved by him. This kingly authority extends indeed far beyond the limits of the Covenant of Grace, under which he is appointed Mediator between God and men : but it is as Mediator of that covenant that he becomes a king and that he erects his throne on Zion. Thus being the head of his church, the headship over all things is added to him : and the King of saints becomes King of kings and Lord of lords. His whole dominion and authority, his whole counsel and might, as well as all the riches of his wisdom, and all the merit of his sacrifice, along with all that is wonderful in what he is and what he does, and all that is immeasurable in that vastness wherein he is the very author and father of eternity : all, all are held and exercised for the glory and blessedness of that kingdom of Grace, which he has founded and which he will save : which he is now gathering and perfecting, and which he will at last present faultless before God.

II. This general statement and exposition of the doctrine of God's word concerning the kingly office of Christ, enables us to reduce to a few distinct propositions the substance of what the Scriptures teach us concerning that aspect of the Mediatorial office. Thus :

1. Christ is truly and really a King : as much so as he is a Prophet or a Priest. As he is all three, and as he discharges all the offices of them all both in his estate of Humiliation and Exaltation, his Mediatorial work is complete, and his Mediatorial office fully accomplished. Thereupon he is entitled, first on his own account, and secondly on behalf of his people, to every thing that was promised him in the Covenant of Grace : and he must receive it all. For he is a king not only in that he possesses the ordinary kingdom of Providence which appertains to him as the creator of all things : but he is a King also as he possesses the kingdom of Grace, the Mediatorial kingdom, which has been given to him by the Father, on account of his obedience unto death. As has been repeatedly said, it belongs to Christ's Mediatorial work to execute all his offices personally, and all of them both in Humiliation and Exaltation, both upon earth and in heaven. Hitherto he has executed his prophetical and his priestly, and in a certain sense, his kingly office personally, and in Humiliation on earth : and while he executed the two first of these offices in glory before his incarnation, he has since his Ascension in our nature, executed them both personally in that nature in Exaltation in heaven, making the glory of both perfectly manifest to the universe. There seems to be wanting to complete the sublime analogy some further and more illustrious personal manifestation on earth of the kingly office of Messiah in our nature : a manifestation of his dominion on the throne of his father David, of his dominion over that kingdom purchased by his blood. And the declarations of the word of God, that this is to occur, are clear and full. But in what sense, under what circumstances, at what period, the church of God, as I have several times intimated, has long been and still remains, much divided in opinion. Coming face to face with the great question here, it is enough to say, in this brief recapitulation, that the Scriptures leave us no place for doubt, concerning the fact of a future and transcendantly glorious manifestation on earth, of the Messianic kingdom and of the glorified Saviour as the Ruler thereof.

2. This true kingdom of Christ, which is entirely distinct from his priesthood, and also from his prophetic office, the extent and nature of which have been explained, is a spiritual and eternal kingdom. The church of God, which is strictly the per-

sonal kingdom of Christ, taken in one sense, is visible ; in another it is invisible : and in both senses it is universal or Catholic. The former consists of all those throughout the world, that profess the true religion, together with their children :[1] the latter of all, in all ages, who shall be gathered into one under Christ the head, and is the Bride of the Lamb.[2] Taken in both of these senses, the true kingdom of the Lord Jesus, is not of, nor is it to be confounded with, the kingdoms or governments of this world, which are separate ordinations of God for their own appropriate ends.[3] But all its power, object, and ends are exclusively spiritual, so far as time and earth are concerned. Moreover it is eternal. While the earth lasts, Christ will have a people and a kingdom in it, which is the salt of it, and for the sake of which alone God does not, as yet, destroy it : and when the end of all things here below shall fully come, the kingdom of the Lord Christ, shall thereby only be made more glorious and blessed forever more.

3. With respect to the infinite dignity, and the supreme wisdom and power of Christ, as a king, little perhaps need be added here, to what has been said in the former part of this chapter. It is obvious, on the one hand, that the power of controlling the will of man, so that it shall certainly and yet freely choose God as its portion, and this by means of an effectual spiritual working, whereby the conscience is sanctified, and the heart renewed, and the spirit restored to the lost image of God, utterly transcends all human ability : and yet, on the other hand, if these things be not provided for, and that effectually and constantly, it is equally manifest that the kingdom of Christ must cease from amongst men. Which is all one, as saying, that a divine power and wisdom must be continually present and operative, and yet perpetually regardful of the wonderful nature of man, in order to perpetuate the kingdom of Christ on earth. In their nature these are regal, and not prophetical nor yet sacerdotal powers. Appertaining to Christ as a king, they give such unspeakable majesty to his person and office, that even in their exercise by the Divine Spirit, who was purchased by his blood, they have such relevancy to Christ, that the second one of the incontrovertible points of the whole mystery of Godliness, is

<hr>

[1] 1 Cor., vii. 14.   [2] Eph., i. 10, 22, 23.
[3] Luke, xvii. 20; John, xviii. 36.

declared to be, that he who is God manifest in the flesh, is God justified in the Spirit.[1]

4. The administration of the kingly office of Christ, imposes the necessity of exercising two distinct functions with reference to his kingdom : namely the Government of it, and the Protection of it : embracing whatever is involved in its enlargement, as well as in its defence. I will consider these in their order : and first, of the Government of the kingdom, the matters which follow are to be noted.

(a) Every thing in the nature of the kingdom of Christ, makes it not less peculiar as a kingdom, and his subjects peculiar as a people, than he is peculiar as a king. It belonged to him originally by creation : but long ago it revolted from him. It belongs to him also by inheritance, seeing he is the only begotten of the Father, to whom, originally as God, it belonged, and who gave it to him. It belongs to him also by covenant, and purchase ; he having undertaken to reduce it back into obedience to God, by reconciling it to him in his work of Mediation, and in effecting this, having redeemed the kingdom and every member of it, with his own most precious blood. It belongs to him by conquest, too ; for he has reconquered it from the prince of this world, the spirit that worketh in the children of disobedience, the devil who led it captive at his will : and every particular member of the kingdom is a special monument of this reconquering love of Christ, through which every one of them has been translated from darkness into light, and from the power of Satan unto God.

(b) Such a kingdom as this, must needs be governed in a manner, every way remarkable, by a king, who is himself, both as to his person and his work, the wonder of the universe. For as has just been shown, every subject of the kingdom was once a rebel and a criminal not only ; but a faithful subject of another kingdom, whose ruler is the implacable enemy of Christ. And what is, if possible, still more deplorable, every one of them would immediately revolt from Christ, and return to their allegiance to Satan, if Christ should withdraw his immediate and absolute dominion over them, and leave them to choose and act for themselves. It is a kingdom, therefore which is wholly incompetent to govern and direct itself ; much less to preserve and

[1] 1 Tim., iii. 16.

extend itself. There is not even so much as one single member of it who is worthy to be trusted, nay, I will add, who is willing to be trusted with any other power, or authority or dominion, or even any function or regimen in it, whether over himself, or over any other, except only such and so far as continually implies the presence and the help of Christ himself.

(c) There is no help therefore but that the kingdom must perish ; or Christ must be to it both Lawgiver, and Judge, and Ruler. Nor does this even, express the extent of the need of him, and of what he must do, in the government of his kingdom. For after his laws are made, we should comprehend them most inadequately, and obey them most unwillingly ; and after his judgments and decrees are rendered, we should receive them neither in the power nor the love of them ; and every act of executive authority over us, on his part, would be accepted with indifference or aversion. Left to ourselves, even under a perfect lawgiver, and judge, and ruler, we should see no beauty in him that we should desire him, and would do continually what we have so often done already, namely we should despise and reject him.[1] Besides all the external government of his kingdom, which rests upon Christ, in the way of giving his most holy Law, and his most blessed Gospel ; and in the way of administering both through all the ordinances and office bearers, instituted by him ; and in the way of controlling, directing and determining all things to the outward establishment and guidance of his kingdom ;[2] there remains that further work, whereby a true, willing, and inward obedience to his will, and a righteous conformity to his law, and a joyful submission to his authority are begotten and wrought in the souls of all the subjects of his kingdom.[3] For unless all this is effected, it is impossible for such a kingdom as that of Christ, composed of such subjects as fallen men, to be established or to endure. And there is no power revealed to us, or even conceivable by us, except that which belongs to Christ, as the Mediator, and which is exerted by him, and through his Spirit, and word, and ordinances, whereby such effects can be produced.

(d) To the kingly government of his church by Christ, it also appertains to bestow upon the subjects of his kingdom,

---

[1] Isa., liii. 2, 3.   [2] Isa., xi. 2, 3 ; Psalms xlv. and cx.
[3] Psalm xxiii. 3, cxliii. 10 · Cant., i. 4.

whatever blessings, and honors, and rewards he has been graciously pleased to attach to their new obedience and their faithful endeavors for his glory. This is partly, during this life; but chiefly in the Great Day and throughout eternity. All these benefits and distinctions whether in this life, or in that which is to come, are bestowed upon the children of the kingdom, not on account of any merit in them, or in any of their works; for it has been shown all along, that personally, there is nothing meritorious either in them or their works, when judged by the perfect law of God. Godliness indeed hath the promise of the life that now is and of that which is to come.[1] But it is only through the merits of Christ, and by faith in him. Nay even then it is of his royal bounty. For the wages of sin is death: and eternal life is simply the gift of God through Jesus Christ our Lord.[2] But this embraces all things, and both worlds. For the kingdom of God is righteousness and peace and joy in the Holy Ghost:[3] and to believers all things appertain, whether Paul, or Apollos, or Cephas, or the world, or life, or death, or things present, or things to come; all are theirs; and they are Christ's; and Christ is God's.[4] Therefore when we have by God's grace fought a good fight, and finished our course, and kept the faith; we may confidently and joyfully trust that there is laid up for us a crown of righteousness, which the Lord, the righteous Judge shall give us at that day: and not to us only but to all them also that love his appearing.[5] Blessed be God, this is the distinguishing characteristic of the kingdom of Christ Jesus our Lord; that it is not a kingdom for the administration and execution of punitive or vindictive justice; but for the exhibition of grace and mercy. In it penitent rebels are not only pardoned, but through the infinite goodness and by the benign power of God, they are turned and moved, are inclined and enabled to a sweet submission, and a loving obedience to him who both loved them and washed them from their sins in his own blood, and hath made them kings and priests unto God and his Father; to him be glory and dominion forever and ever.[6]

5. And now secondly of the Protection and therein of the defence and enlargement of Christ's kingdom, we are to note the things which follow.

[1] 1 Tim., iv. 8.
[4] 1 Cor., iii. 21–23.
[2] Rom., vi. 23.
[5] 2 Tim., iv. 7, 8.
[3] Rom., xiv. 17.
[6] Rev., i. 5, 6.

(*a*) The whole kingdom of Christ, and every true member of it, are special objects of the care and love of their king. Although particular portions of the visible church universal, may err and fall away by reason of false brethren unawares crept in ; or may be uprooted by persecution and oppression, and so by both means may fail, as by both means portions thereof have failed : yet that the whole kingdom should fail, and that the dominion of Christ amongst men, through his church should be put down, and that the church itself, as a visible institute of God, should wholly disappear from amongst men, is utterly impossible. The Christ, the Son of the living God, is laid as the chief corner stone and foundation of this building of God ; and we have his plighted word, that the gates of hell shall not prevail against it.[1] And to this purport are innumerable testimonies of the word of God ; and the whole of his providence during the entire existence of man on this earth, is a constant and living illustration of the import of these testimonies : and the whole power, and wisdom, and glory, of Christ, are staked upon their truth. Thanks be to God, we have seen the worst of this : and the malice of hell and of wicked men is vain. It will occur no more, that the kingdom of Christ will be confined to a few wanderers who have no certain dwelling place. Much less will it ever again be limited to a single household. And least of all will its glorious Lord ever again be crucified, dead, and buried !

(*b*) What is true of the whole kingdom, taken in its absoluteness, is true also of each individual member of it. Not that some of them may utterly perish, although the whole of them cannot : for that all of them cannot perish is before proved, in proving that the kingdom itself cannot fail : so that the analogy cannot stop even logically, in this form. But as the kingdom itself cannot fail, by reason of its relations to Christ, and Christ's promises to it, so for the same reasons not a single child of God can perish ; however much, each one of them, by reason of the remains of original sin, may for a time, fall away from the life of God in their souls. There are three modes, by which it is conceivable, that particular believers might utterly fall and perish ; and but three. 1. They might voluntarily relapse into sin, and being forsaken of God, perish. 2. God might withdraw himself from them, without any special blame on their part, and

____
[1] Mat., xvi. 13–20.

so leave them to be destroyed. 3. Their enemies and God's, might be able to snatch them out of the hand of God, and drag them to perdition. In either of these three ways, we can easily understand that the children of God might be utterly and finally separated from him : but we cannot conceive of any other mode of arriving at that fearful result, which, when duly considered, does not resolve itself into one or another of these three modes. But each of these three possible modes, is distinctly considered in the Scriptures, each one of them is explicitly provided against, and God has emphatically declared that his children shall not perish by either of the three. As to the first mode, it is written, My grace is sufficient for you :[1] and again, I will never leave thee nor forsake thee :[2] and again, I have never seen the right eous forsaken.[3] As to the second mode, it is written, All things work together for good to them that love God, to them who are the called according to his purpose :[4] and again, that nothing shall be able to separate us from the love of God, which is in Christ Jesus our Lord.[5] As to the third mode, it is written, My sheep hear my voice, and I know them, and they follow me ; and I give unto them eternal life ; and they shall never perish, neither shall any pluck them out of my hand. My Father which gave them me is greater than all : and none is able to pluck them out of my Father's hand.[6] And of like import are innumerable statements of the word of life. God will, therefore, according to the riches of his grace, and the faithfulness of his promises, bring all those whom he hath begotten again to a lively hope by the resurrection of Jesus Christ from the dead, to an inheritance incorruptible, undefiled, and that fadeth not away reserved in heaven for them. And thereunto they shall be kept by the power of God, through faith unto salvation : and rejoicing with joy unspeakable and full of glory, shall receive the end of their faith even the salvation of their souls.[7]

(c) The efficient cause of this complete and everlasting protection of the kingdom of Messiah, and of every true member of it ; the effectual working whereby the glorious enlargement and final victory of the church will be accomplished, and the growth in grace, and final perfection, and salvation of every true believer infallibly secured : is of that nature, that all defeat,

---

[1] 2 Cor., xii. 9.   [2] Heb., xiii. 5.   [3] Psalm xxxvii. 25.   [4] Rom., viii. 28.
[5] Rom., viii. 31–39.   [6] John, x. 27–29 ; Eph., i. 4–12.   [7] 1 Peter, i. 1–9.

mischance, failure, or mistake is utterly impossible. For the sacerdotal intercession of Christ, is effectual for salvation, even to the uttermost ; and he ever liveth to make that intercession :[1] an intercession in which the Holy Spirit unites in a manner so wondrous, that the Scriptures say it is with groanings which cannot be uttered ![2] Add now, the divine kingly power of Christ, and hear him saying of his followers, I give unto them eternal life : they shall never perish :[3] I will raise him up at the last day : he that believeth on me hath everlasting life :[4] upon this rock will I build my church and the gates of hell shall not prevail against it.[5] And now to this all prevalent sacerdotal intercession, and to this irresistible power of the divine king, add the effectual working of the divine Spirit, sent by Christ, the king in Zion ; even that Holy Spirit of God, whereby we are sealed unto the day of redemption.[6] And then consider if the efficient cause of all that Christ has undertaken to do, is not complete : if the effectual working whereby he proposes to accomplish all that he ever promised to do, is not irresistible ?

(*d*) The prophet Daniel, expounding in a few sublime words, the career and the end of all the universal world-kingdoms ; and the ultimate triumph of the Messianic kingdom over all kingdoms ; told Nebuchadnezzar, the very head of the whole immense series of godless empires, that the fate of all of them was, that they should be utterly destroyed by the kingdom of God. Then, said Daniel, was the iron, the clay, the brass, the silver, and the gold, broken to pieces together, and became like the chaff of the summer threshing-floors ; and the wind carried them away, that no place was found for them : and the stone that smote the image became a great mountain and filled the whole earth.[7] And the great wonder which the Apostle John saw in heaven, even the wonder of a woman clothed with the sun, and with the moon under her feet, and upon her head a crown of twelve stars, travailing in pain to be delivered : and the wonder of a great red dragon having seven heads and ten horns, and seven crowns upon his heads, and whose tail drew the third part of the stars of heaven, and did cast them to the earth, who stood before the woman ready to devour her child as soon as it was born : found its complete solution in the birth of a man-child, who was to rule

---

[1] Heb., vii. 25 ; Rom., viii. 34.   [2] Rom., viii. 26.   [3] John, x. 28.
[4] John, vi. 44–47.   [5] Mat., xvi. 18.   [6] Eph., iv. 30.   [7] Dan., ii. 35.

all nations with a rod of iron, and who was caught up unto God
and to his throne.[1] And this testimony to the final and utter
destruction of all the world-powers, and the complete and universal triumph of the kingdom of the Son of God, borne by the
great Apocalyptic Prophet of the Ancient Dispensation, and by
the great Apocalyptic Apostle of the New Dispensation ; is only
a clear utterance of what is asserted and implied through the
whole word of God. It only makes emphatic what is involved
in the very structure and end of the whole plan of salvation, as
revealed in the Scriptures : what appertains to the very person
and office, and work, and kingdom, and power, and glory, of him
in whom all fulness dwells ; by whom God reconciles all things
unto himself ; in whom all things in heaven and earth are to be
gathered together in one throughout the whole dispensation of
the fulness of times ; and at whose name, which is above every
name, every knee shall bow in heaven, in earth, and in hell !'[2]
The very conception of the covenant of grace, and the very conception of Christ as the Mediator of that covenant, involves the
conception of a kingdom without limit and without end, which
Christ as a Priest will redeem, which Christ as a Prophet will
instruct, and over which Christ as a King will rule. Neither
one of these sublime conceptions is stationary in any part of the
Scriptures, nor is either one of them separately developed therein. By a steadfast march, at once of God's adorable providence,
and God's infallible revelation, they become more and more distinct, and more and more dependent on each other, from the
beginning to the end of the word of God, and throughout all the
actual dispensations recorded therein. And when the word of
life closes, the prophetic history of all ages and all dispensations
which are to follow, is the history of the progress of these conceptions, still further realized, to the glory of God in the perfect
development and completion of them, through all time and then
through eternity. The further we advance side by side with the
Messianic kingdom along the course of ages ; and the greater
the compass over which God's providence illustrates every part
of God's revelation, especially the prophetic portion of it ; and
the wider the range of our vision of all divine things in all ages
which have preceded our age : the more confidently ought we to
be able to rely on our sober and deliberate conclusions, concerning

[1] Rev., xii. 1–5.   [2] Col., i. 19, 20; Eph., i. 10; Phil., ii. 9, 10.

all these great mysteries of God. Nevertheless, their very vastness, together with the certainty that a spiritual illumination is
indispensable to their adequate comprehension, and that even
with this, in the degree commonly vouchsafed to the people of
God, innumerable errors have been committed, by such as have
attempted to develop what is future, with the same confidence
we may feel in expounding what is past : ought to make us feel
habitually that our posture as interpreters is very different with
reference to all the past, from what it is with reference to any
portion of the future of the kingdom of our Lord. God gives
us to know the former, in all completeness : he gives us to know
the latter only in sublime outlines. The one is for our present
salvation : the other is for our future glory and blessedness.

6. It only remains to observe that the kingly office of Christ,
like his prophetic, and his priestly offices, is absolute and exclusive, as well as perpetual. Christ is the only Teacher whose
authority and sufficiency are divine and infallible ; and all other
teachers whether of duty or of truth, are trustworthy only so far
as they accord with him ; and are competent only so far as they
are taught by him. Christ is the only Priest, whose sacrifice, or
oblation, or intercession, or benediction, are of themselves acceptable to God or prevalent with him ; and all other priests who
offer sacrifice, or oblation, who make intercession, or utter benediction, irrespective of him, do so in mere blindness, or insult
the majesty of God in all their acts. In the same manner, Christ
is the only King in Zion ; and as such he is the supreme ruler of
the universe. Passing by this latter aspect of his exalted dominion, there are multitudes of questions of the highest importance,
both doctrinal and practical, which are determined by the perpetual headship of Christ over the church, in every period of it ;
and multitudes relating to the faith, to the life, and to the form
of his church, which are determined by the exclusiveness of that
universal headship. The freedom of the church from all other
dominion, depends absolutely upon the completeness of Christ's
dominion over her. The purity, the vitality, the comfort, the
peace, the advancement, nay the very perpetuity and glory of
the church, all depend upon the exclusiveness with which Christ
reigns over her, and his divine Spirit lives within her. And that
which occurs to nothing else is that which is her most peculiar
characteristic : namely, the perpetual revival in her bosom of her

simple, original life : the perpetual recurrence of the same life under innumerable forms and amidst all the vicissitudes of an endless progress. She has no rule of duty but the divine Law, no ground of hope but in the Gospel of the kingdom, no light but the light of life, no power but through the divine Spirit, no authority except to save sinners, no end but to glorify God. All this, she may possess in every human condition, and possessing it she abides, in apparent helplessness an irresistible power upon earth, and will shine with increasing glory throughout eternity.

THE KNOWLEDGE OF GOD,

OBJECTIVELY CONSIDERED.

ARGUMENT OF THE THIRD BOOK.

THREE great ideas are involved in the conception of salvation: the idea of God; the idea of man; and the idea of the Mediator between God and man. Three terms, with a signal limitation to each, contain the problem as stated by the great Apostle to the Gentiles, namely; God, who is to be worshipped in the Spirit; Christ Jesus in whom we rejoice; and the Flesh in which no confidence is to be placed. It is this idea of God involved in salvation—this chief term in the great problem, to which this Third Book of the Knowledge of God is particularly devoted. The two other ideas—the two other terms—have been separately developed in the two preceding books. Salvation for fallen man by Jesus Christ, through divine grace: thus far we have come. And now, with the God-man advanced to the throne of the universe, our Infinite Teacher—we advance our inquiries into the very Being and Perfections of the God of all grace. The Fourteenth Chapter, which is the First of this Third Book, is devoted to the obtaining of a complete idea of God, by means of the first, the simplest, and the most constant form of revelation of himself: to wit, the Names by which he made himself, his Nature, and his Perfections known from the beginning; and which disclose the permanent and systematic knowledge thereof. The Fifteenth Chapter, which is the Second of this Book, aims to demonstrate the mode of God's existence, as being that of an Infinite Spirit, in the absolute unity of whose essence three divine Persons eternally subsist: the nature and method of such an existence is carefully discussed, and the doctrine of the Trinity is deduced, explained, and established: and therein it is shown that upon any other conception than this of the Being of God, the Scriptures are incomprehensible, and the salvation of man impossible: and that this conception of God is not only as distinct and comprehensible as any other conception of him; but that, as the matter stands, it is infallibly true and certain. In the Sixteenth Chapter which is the Third of this Book, the doctrine of the Holy Ghost, the Third Person of the adorable Trinity, is treated at large: and this is done with special relation to the nature, office, and work of the Spirit, in his connection with the person, office and work of Christ; and in his connection with the salvation of lost men: wherein the supreme Godhead, and the divine Personality of the Spirit are demonstated, and his constant relation to all saving knowledge of God, and the particular nature of the sin against him, are explained. The Seventeenth Chapter, which is the Fourth of this Book, considers the Godhead in its peculiar unity, and discusses and establishes a classification of the divine Perfections whereby all the attributes of God cognizable by man may be contemplated distinctly under a few classes founded on distinctions inherent in the nature of the case, and on laws fundamental in the nature of man; and thus become objects of exact knowledge. The Eighteenth Chapter, which is the Fifth of this Book, discusses the first class of the divine Perfections, called God's Primary Attributes: such namely, as arise from the simplest idea we can form of him as an Infinite, Eternal, Unchangeable, Self-Existent Being. The Nineteenth Chapter, which is the Sixth of this Book, discusses the second class of the divine Perfections, called God's Essential Attributes: such namely, as arise out of his essence, and are inseparable from our conception of him as an Infinite, Personal Spirit; to wit, Infinite Understanding, Will, and Power. The Twentieth Chapter, which is the Seventh of this Book, discusses the third class of the divine Perfections, called God's Natural Attributes: such namely, as have direct relevancy to the ineffaceable distinction between the True and the False, and therefore to the Rational nature both of God and man. The Twenty-First Chapter, which is the Eighth of this Book, discusses the fourth class of the divine Perfections, called God's Moral Attributes: such namely, as have direct relevancy to the further and ineffaceable distinction between Good and Evil, and therefore to the Moral nature both of God and man. The Twenty-Second Chapter, which is the Ninth and last of this Book, discusses the fifth and last class of the divine Perfections, called God's Consummate Attributes: such namely, as transcend the conception upon which each previous class rests, and embrace the Perfection of many Infinite Perfections: as the Life, the Oneness, the All-Sufficiency, the Omnipresence, the Blessedness of God. This is the living and true God to whom sinners have access through the divine Redeemer: the Jehovah whom we are to worship in Spirit, and whom to know aright is life eternal. Besides the immense questions incidentally examined in this Book, the fundamental truths established may be summarily stated, thus: The knowledge of God unto salvation was always revealed to man: the revealed mode of the divine Existence, namely, one Infinite Essence in which three divine Persons eternally subsist is the only conceivable mode consistent with the salvation of sinners: the Holy Ghost, the Third Person of the adorable Trinity is very God, and so the Renewer and Sanctifier of the human soul: the Godhead, contemplated in the attributes of its Infinite Essence, is an object of certain knowledge—and those divine Perfections are susceptible of rational classification: these Perfections, Attributes of the Infinite Essence of God, disclose him to us in his eternal self-existence—a Personal Spirit filling immensity, distinct from the universe, and its Creator and Ruler who possesses those Perfections in immeasurable fulness, both as to the boundless number of them, and the absolute completeness of each one of them; and who, by means of the knowledge of himself, makes lost men partakers of his own Blessedness.

CHAPTER XIV.

THE NAMES OF GOD; REVEALED BY HIMSELF AS THE BASIS OF OUR KNOWLEDGE OF THE GODHEAD.

I. 1. Origin of personal appellations.—2. Peculiar method of their application to God.—3. This difference inherent and fundamental.—II. God revealed in his names.—1. Jehovah. Necessary, and yet voluntary eternal Self-Existence.—2. Proper name of God.—3. Superstitious disuse of it by the Jews.—4. Spread of this fanaticism to the Greek and Latin churches. Result thereof in the Latin church.—5. Result in the Greek church. Sum of the three results.—6. The name Jehovah expressly includes the Son, and the Spirit, as well as the Father, in the Essence of the Godhead.—7. Well known to the Patriarchs.—III. I Am and Jah—names of the divine Essence.—1. *I Am* explained. Applied by Christ to himself.—2. *Jah*, the name of the divine Essence in the simplest conception of God, explained with the two preceding.—3. Its use in the Scriptures.—IV. 1. Nature and sum of the foregoing names. Additional names of God.—2. El, Almightiness of God.—3. The Lord of Hosts. Force of this name.—4. Infinite dominion of God.—V. 1. Most High. Infinite Exaltation of God.—2. Adonai. Its peculiar form and force. Special application to Christ.—3. Shaddai. The All-Sufficiency of God. Habitual appropriation by Christ.—4. Elohim. Great peculiarities of this name. The first and oftenest used of all. Exposition of its force and use.—5. These names of God are a real and systematic, as they are the original revelation of the Godhead.—VI. 1. Distinction between names and descriptive phrases.—2. Special necessity of the present enquiry.—3. Its fundamental relation to the true knowledge of God.

I.—1. WHEN there was but a single human being in the world, there was no need that he should have a personal appellation, such as we call a proper name ; since the name distinctive of the race which was to spring from him, would completely and forever distinguish him. Therefore God called him, simply, man.* When God formed a help-mate to the man, he distinguished her, in the same manner, and called her woman,† the general appellation of all her kind, that should afterwards exist. It was only after the fall and curse, that Adam, to designate his wife as the mother of all living, gave her the personal appel-

---

* אָדָם—*homo.*　　　† אִשָּׁה—*fœmina—uxor*, from אִישׁ—*vir, maritus.*

lation of Eve,* which distinguished her from all other women, as the universal mother of mankind.[1] And as every human being has been added to the race, and has needed to be distinguished from all other human beings, he has received some personal designation, which we call his name. It is a very remarkable thing to observe, in what various ways the different races of men have managed a matter so simple as this, at first sight, might appear. Few treatises would be more curious, and in some aspects instructive, than one carefully and learnedly prepared on this subject.

2. Following the analogy of the case already stated as to man, it would seem altogether probable, if not indeed in some sort necessary, that there should be but one name of God, in any one language, supposing the fundamental truth of the absolute unity of the Godhead, to be known to those who use that tongue. And this notion would seem to apply with its greatest force, to those languages in which it pleased God to reveal the knowledge of himself to mankind : and if there were any difference, then with greater force to the language first and longest used by God for that purpose. The fact however, is very far otherwise : and it ought to teach us great caution in our attempts to establish what we are pleased to call rational canons, by which to determine what God's word ought to teach. For it is altogether undeniable that neither the Greek nor the Hebrew Scriptures, do confine themselves to a single name for God, in the revelations which he has made of himself, in those tongues : it is certain, that there are fewer names of God, considerably, in the Greek than in the Hebrew Scriptures : and it is extremely probable, if not positively certain, that there are more names of God in Hebrew, than in any other tongue in which the true knowledge of him has ever been exhibited.

3. No doubt, it is easy to believe and to comprehend after facts so unexpected are made known to us by the Scriptures, that there are important considerations why God, in the way of aiding our manifold weakness and enticing us to the most careful and assiduous efforts to obtain the knowledge of him, should condescend to reveal himself to us by various names, as well as by multiplied acts, and perpetual disclosures of his being, his nature, and his will. And after he has done so, it is not too

---

* חַוָּה.   [1] Gen., iii. 20.

much for us to say that we may perceive in the facts themselves, abundant intimation that the analogy which seemed at first so obvious, from the case of man to the case of God, is altogether unfounded and illusive ; because the nature of man and the nature of God are altogether dissimilar. The nature of man is such, that each man being one personality, and no man being any more ; each one, to be distinguished by a proper name at all, must have one proper name, no matter of how many parts that proper name may be made up : and no one can have more than one proper name, without incurring the risk of confusion. Man, means every male that has a human body and a rational intellect, and an immortal soul : and Cain means a particular individual man : and Abel means a special and different one ; and so on of all : and we get not only a distinct, but a complete idea, in each case. But God exists in such a manner as we learn from himself, and could learn no otherwise, that we should have a totally false conception of him if we supposed there was but one personality in his being, since, in point of fact, there are three personalities in his being. And, therefore, if we knew him by only one single name, however exact might be our con· ception of the unity of his being, simply as a unity : it would be a false conception even of his unity itself : for the very unity of the essence of God, is a unity in which three divine persons subsist, and not a unity like that of our nature, which is represented by a single personality. With us, the soul and the body unitedly make one person : and we give that person a name : Abraham, Pontius Pilate, Marcus Tullius Cicero, or any other. With God the unity lies not, as with us, in the mode of existence, but in the essence of the being ; for according to the mode, there are three persons ; while according to the essence, in which these three persons subsist, there is absolute unity. It is very obvious, therefore, that to obtain a similar result in the two cases, namely distinct and complete ideas of the being spoken of, there must be a very different system of nomenclature resorted to in the two cases. And it is equally manifest that the further back we go into the revelations of God, the more copious, it is to be presumed, will be those appellations assumed by him, to present a distinct and complete idea of himself to the human mind. So that even in this apparently subordinate part of divine knowledge, a department more curious than fundamental, as we might lightly consider it, we see that if we would not err, we must not follow human subtilty, but must walk according to divine light. So walking, we find even from the beginning, that divine proportion of faith which underlies all the Scriptures, and that glorious insight into heavenly things which distinguishes every utterance of them.

II. I do not propose to discuss, either doctrinally or philologically, with any special thoroughness, this question of the revealed names of God, meaning thereby the names of God considered simply as God. But having cleared the only point that seemed to stand directly before us, I proceed to state successively the Hebrew divine names, which are commonly allowed by scholars : adding as I pass on, such observations as seem needful to a clear understanding of each particular, and of the conception I have of this original method of the knowledge of God.

1. JEHOVAH.* This word is, apparently, derived from the verb of existence.† Its signification therefore is He who exists. The Apostle John, perfectly expresses its sense, when he says, Grace be unto you and peace, from him which is, and which was, and which is to come.‡[1] There is no single word in any human speech, which expresses its full sense ; otherwise than as men may agree to use any particular name of God, in their own languages, to represent the ideas necessarily comprehended in the word Jehovah, to wit, of a necessary and yet voluntary, eternal self-existence. When I say the name was probably derived from the radical form of the Hebrew verb of existence, I merely speak in accordance with grammatical indications ; for it might with equal, perhaps greater reason be said, that the Hebrew form of the verb of existence is derived from this name of God. To consider questions of this sort, however, belongs to a discussion of the origin of language in general, and of the Hebrew language in particular : which is not the object immediately before us.

2. Some divine names express only, or chiefly, some property ; but it has always been admitted, both by Jews and Christians, that this name expresses not only the essence and being of God —but his eternal and unchangeable self-existence, and that it is his proper name, which is never applied to any creature. There

* יְהֹוָה pointed יֱהֹוִה when preceded or followed by אֲדֹנָי.

† הָיָה—est, fuit.   ‡ ὁ ὢν καὶ ὁ ἦν καὶ ὁ ἐρχόμενος. [1] Rev., i. 4.

are various grammatical reasons, peculiar to the structure of the Hebrew tongue, whose consideration makes it positively certain that this name is the proper name of God ; which will be found stated at large, by various scholars who have expressly treated the subject. It is however enough at present, to say, that the fact itself is repeatedly asserted in the Scriptures, in the most precise manner. And God said moreover, unto Moses, Thus shalt thou say unto the children of Israel, The Lord God of your fathers, the God of Abraham, the God of Isaac, and the God of Jacob, hath sent me unto you : this is my name forever, and this is my memorial, unto all generations.[1] The sublime song of triumph sung by Moses and the children of Israel, at the overthrow of the Egyptians, in the midst of the sea, was sung unto him, whose name is Jehovah ![2] The great plea of David with God, why the enemies of the eternal King should be utterly destroyed, is that men might know, that he whose name alone is Jehovah, is the most high over all the earth.[3] And amongst all the multiplied predictions of Christ, hardly one is more ample or more majestic, than that in which Isaiah introduces Jehovah, speaking of himself and of Messiah, and declaring I am Jehovah : that is my name : and my glory will I not give to another ![4]

3. So great has been the superstitious reverence of the Jews for the name Jehovah, that they neither write it nor pronounce it, and as a people have done neither from a period anterior, in all probability, to the advent of Christ. When they have had occasion to write it, they have always substituted certain signs for it : and instead of pronouncing it when they come to it, in their Scriptures, they pronounce some other name of God, generally Adonai. Indeed Jewish scholars nearly without exception, long held, and many still hold that the vowel points used in the Hebrew Scriptures with the word Jehovah, are those belonging to the consonants which make the word Adonai, and not to those which make the word Jehovah : and that the true vowels, and therefore the true pronunciation of the latter word are utterly lost : so that to pronounce it as we do, is, as they say, at once silly and blasphemous. The diligent student will find in the works of learned Christians, devoted to these subjects, all these matters

---

[1] Exodus, iii. 15, and xx. 2.   [2] Exodus, xv. 3.
[3] Psalm lxxxiii. 18.   [4] Isaiah, xlii. 8.

fully discussed, and cleared up. They are studies, not without a certain high value to those who are set for the defence of the truth : and perhaps I ought to add for the encouragement of those teachers of divine truth who feel authorized to neglect them—-that the pursuit of them is as far from being difficult, as the neglect of them is from being either safe or reputable. No child of God can know any thing about the revelation which God has given us of himself, which will not richly repay the toil of learning it. Indeed I may be allowed to add, that no one can know any thing at all that may not be, in some unexpected change of life, of the utmost value to him : while we ought to be assured that idleness and indifference to knowledge are amongst the most expensive of all vices : for they not only squander our present time, but they mortgage, at terrible usury, our future usefulness and influence in life.

4. It may be as well to add that the superstition of the Jews just alluded to, touching the name Jehovah, spread very widely over the Christian church, in the ages succeeding the apostles, and almost universally, during the middle ages, over the Latin and Greek churches. The reasons for this unhappy and most injurious fanaticism were, however, obvious enough. Amongst the Latin Fathers, as they are called, who wrote in the Latin language and were members of the Roman church, whose writings have come down to us, the great mass, during ten centuries preceding Luther, probably knew not even the letters of the Hebrew alphabet : while Jerome and the small number who understood somewhat of that tongue, got their knowledge, and with it many Jewish prejudices and follies from such Rabbis as they chanced to obtain instruction from. Instead of transferring the name Jehovah into Latin, as we have partially done into English, they translated it by the Latin name Dominus ; and did not even signify by any special mark as we do with general, though not with universal accuracy, as we will see presently, by small capitals, where Jehovah is translated LORD, that this special name of God was used in the particular passage. The ignorance, therefore, became the natural vehicle of the superstition, both of which were so congenial to the general spirit of the Romish church : and until the Reformation of the sixteenth century, and the revival of learning, which immediately preceded it, there was hardly left in the western church any suspicion of the folly, much

less any way to correct it.   God had ceased to be known as Jehovah, in all the wide dominions of antichrist ; a fact of terrible
significance, still too much overlooked, in the prevailing shallow
mode of waging the battle of the Lord with that fearful superstition.   After suppressing and then forgetting his adorable name,
the pollution of his worship and the perversion of his doctrine,
were altogether natural.   And then the working with all deceivableness of unrighteousness, fairly brought them, who perish, step
by step in impiety and folly, until the supreme act of their religion came at last to consist, in transubstantiating a piece of
bread into Jehovah-Tzebaoth (the Lord of Hosts), then adoring
it, then eating it, and then murdering every one who would not
do the like !

5. With the Greeks the case was more peculiar and excusable,
and, perhaps on that account, had a very different result.   Among
the Greek Fathers the knowledge of Hebrew appears to have
been almost as rare as amongst the Latins : and as amongst the
latter hardly one besides Jerome, so amongst the former hardly
one besides Origen can be named, who knew that tongue ; while
amongst all the fathers hardly one is a less safe guide than Origen.   The Greeks could, no doubt, pronounce the name Jehovah ; just as we can pronounce many sounds which are not
natural in our language, and which, therefore, we have no combination of letters to express.   But it is manifest, they could not
express the pronunciation by any combination of the letters of
their own alphabet ; as any one will see who makes the attempt,
or who examines the attempts made by Greek scholars themselves.   And therefore they could not transfer the word Jehovah
into Greek by any use of Greek letters.*   The word was of
course ineffable to them ; and they used various terms and
phrases to express the intractable nature of this glorious name
of God in their language.   The fact itself is extremely curious :
and when we consider the providential use of the Greek language, in the early spread of the Gospel, and in being made the

---

* The Greek language has no *j*, which we substitute in the word Jehovah for the
initial *y*, of the Hebrew ; it has no *y*, as a consonant ; it has no *v*, as a consonant ; it
has no *h*, except in composition with and always after *t*, or *p*, or *c*, thus θ, ϕ, χ: or
except as a mere aspirate with initial vowels ; and it has amongst its vowel sounds,
nothing to represent the Hebrew *sheva ;* that is, of four consonant letters, two vowels,
and sheva, which make the Hebrew word Jehovah, the Greeks have only the two
vowel so nds in their language.

permanent receptacle of the Christian revelation, we hardly dare
to pronounce it accidental. The nature of God's being, when it
came to be fully explained by God himself, in the complete exhibition of the plan of salvation ; seems to have required, in order
to be adequately comprehended by man, a new nomenclature, in
a tongue more copious and delicate than that in which he had
hitherto revealed himself. And so retaining in that venerable
tongue, all that he had, till then, revealed concerning his essence
and operation ; he chose this new speech, in some respects so different from the other, as the vehicle of those more explicit statements, concerning the mode of his being and action without
which, the work of Christ was wholly incomprehensible. It was,
if we may venture to express it in that manner, a new starting
point assumed along with and at the moment of, a new and more
explicit manifestation of himself. No longer a question of the
self-existent God, named from his essence and his attributes :
but a question of the Father, the Word and the Spirit, acting,
and revealing themselves in man's salvation, as the divine personalities which subsist and act, in the unity of that infinite essence. The Jew in his superstition, refused to utter the proper
name of that divine essence : the Latin, in his fanatical ignorance, accepted the superstition of the Jew : the Greek had no
means of expressing the word in his own tongue. But God used
his tongue to express perfectly every idea contained in it, and
to add what further it was needful for us to know. Yet the history of the church has sufficiently shown, that to know God as
we should, we must know him wholly as he has revealed himself : since it is not to our curiosity but to our faith that he is
revealed.

6. It is of great importance to remark that the name Jehovah is unquestionably applied, in the old Testament scriptures,
both to the Son and to the Holy Ghost, according to the declaration of Christ and the belief of the writers of the New Testament
scriptures : so that if any of them were inspired, there is an end
of the question of the supreme Godhead of Christ and of the
Spirit. As that question is not now under discussion, I content
myself with one proof as to each aspect of it. As to the Son ;
In the book of Numbers, it is said that the people much dis-
couraged, because of the way, spoke against God and against
Moses. And the Lord, (Jehovah) sent fiery serpents among the

people, and they bit the people ; and much people of Israel died.[1] And then the people confessed, they had sinned against Jehovah. And Moses bade them "pray unto Jehovah," and he also prayed for them.   And the Lord commanded Moses to make a fiery serpent and set it on a pole : And Moses made it of brass ; and whosoever was bitten and looked on the serpent, lived.   Now, Christ himself, when expressly teaching Nicodemus the way of salvation, tells him that this whole transaction illustrated and pointed to his own crucifixion, and its effects.[2]   And Paul, if possible, more directly to the present intent, says, Neither let us tempt Christ, as some of them also tempted, and were destroyed of serpents.[3]   As to the Holy Ghost ; In the same book of Numbers,[4] it is related that God, angry at the insolence of Miriam and Aaron towards Moses, suddenly appeared, and addressing himself directly to them, explained that he communicated with Moses in a manner altogether peculiar and glorious : but as to every other prophet, said he, I, the Lord—(Jehovah) will make myself known unto him in a vision, and will speak unto him in a dream.[5]   But Peter tells us that no prophecy of the scripture is of any private interpretation ; and that no prophecy came in old time, by the will of man ; but holy men of God spake as they were moved by the Holy Ghost.[6]   The personal appellation of God, in his essence, as the self-existent and eternal Jehovah, therefore includes the Son, and the Spirit, as really as the Father.

7. The last observation I will make on this most glorious name of God, is that it was well-known to the patriarchs and their cotemporaries.   Thus God said to Abraham, I am the Lord (Jehovah) that brought thee out of Ur of the Chaldees, to give thee this land to inherit it.[7]   At the destruction of Sodom, Lot said to his sons-in-law, the Lord (Jehovah), will destroy this place.[8] Abimelech king of Gerar, pleading with God, in the matter of Sarah, said, Lord (Jehovah) wilt thou slay also a righteous nation ?[9]   Laban gave Rebeckah to the servant of Isaac, and said, to him, let her be his wife, as the Lord (Jehovah) hath spoken.[10] And so in multitudes of other places.   The passage in Exodus,[11]

---

[1] Num., xxi. 5–9.
[2] John, iii. 14, 15.
[3] 1 Cor., x. 9.
[4] Num., xii.
[5] Num., xii. 6.
[6] 2 Pet., i. 21.
[7] Gen., xv. 7.
[8] Gen., xix. 14.
[9] Gen., xx. 4.
[10] Gen., xxiv. 51.
[11] Ex., vi. 3.

where God tells Moses that he had appeared unto Abraham and Isaac and Jacob, as God Almighty, but was not known to them as Jehovah; plainly means that though the patriarchs knew that name, they did not understand its import; God having revealed to Moses himself, first of all, that it peculiarly designated the divine essence, and was the foundation of all the divine attributes.

III. I AM and JAH. Besides the name Jehovah, there are two other names, I am, Ehje,[1] the one now under consideration, and Jah,[2] the next following one, which seem unquestionably to be expressive of the essence of the divine being, and to be employed to express it, and in some degree to explain it.

1. This name differs much less from the name Jehovah, than its English pronunciation would allow us to suppose. Speaking grammatically, it differs from it, in fact, only as Ehje is the first person singular, and Jehovah is the third person singular, of the future form of the same verb.[3] They really differ no more than *I will be*, and *he will be*, or *I am* and *he is*, differ in English. This name occurs as applied, in this way to God, only three times, it is supposed, in the Old Testament : all three in the third chapter of Exodus. When the Lord appeared unto Moses, in Mount Horeb, in the burning bush—and would send him to deliver his people out of Egypt : Moses desired to know what answer he should make to the people, when, having told them the God of their fathers had sent him, they should demand, What is his name ? And God said unto Moses, I AM THAT I AM ; and he said Thus shalt thou say unto the children of Israel, I AM hath sent me unto you.[4] If the words of the answer itself were not perfectly explicit, the whole context would render it certain, that God here revealed to Moses one of his essential and eternal names, as a token from him to his people, of the stupendous deliverance, which he was about to work out for them. The Lord Jesus, in a direct discussion with the Jews as to his own authority and dignity, applies to himself this very name of God, and the eternal existence involved in it. For, Jesus, said unto them

---

[1] אֶהְיֶה.   [2] יָהּ.

[3] הָיָה fuit: to be. The one has י, and the other ו, in the second syllable, letters constantly exchanged for each other: The י and א, in the first syllable of each being only the sign of the third and first persons, respectively.

[4] Ex., iii. 14.

verily, verily I say unto you, Before Abraham was, I am.[1]* It was impossible for them to understand this except in one way; so they took up stones to cast at him: and Jesus obscuring himself by a miracle, passed through the midst of them out of the temple. Ehje is, *I will be :* or as the Hebrew future is very often used for the present, and the past, and for all three when continued action is denoted, it is simply as rendered by Christ himself, I AM. It is one of the proper names, of the immutable, self-existent God, by which he desires his people to know and honor him; especially in seasons of great trial, demanding great trust.

2. Jah† is the last of the Hebrew names of God supposed to be personal and exclusive to him, and to be derived from the essential nature of his being. The Greek translators following the Jewish superstition before alluded to, with regard to the name Jehovah, substituted Adonai for it, and translated both words Lord.‡ They probably considered Jah to be either the first syllable of Jehovah, or very closely related to it. The prophet Isaiah says, in the Lord Jehovah,§ is everlasting strength;[2] from which it would appear, as both names are used together, that they do not designate precisely the same thing in God. What may be the exact difference, it is not so easy to determine. The Jews themselves say that Jah denotes especially, the clemency of God. Jerome who considered that Jah was not derived from Jehovah, but contrary-wise, Jehovah from Jah, by doubling it, supposed it expressed the invisibility of God: while Maimonides, the great Jewish scholar, applied it to the eternity of God's essence. Perhaps, (and this is my own opinion), the word is an original independent Hebrew root, which, if it ever had a particular meaning in that tongue, independent of its use and sense as the name of God, has lost it, as for us: and designates simply, and perhaps always did, the primeval idea, HE IS, which man can form of that infinite being, who calls himself, in addition Ehje, I WILL BE, and Jehovah, WAS, AM and WILL BE. JAH is God, in our naked conception of him: EHJE, is God in his continuing

---

[1] John, viii. 58.

* אֶהְיֶה אֲשֶׁר אֶהְיֶה : this the LXX. translate ἐγω εἰμι ὁ ὤν : and Jerome, if he is the translator of the Latin Vulgate, *sum qui sum :* our English version as before seen, *I am that I am.* † יָהּ. ‡ Κυρίος.

§ Jah—Jehovah. [2] Isaiah, xxvi. 4.

self-existence : JEHOVAH, is God in his existence from eternity
to eternity.

3. The word Jah is used occasionally in the Old Testament,
especially in the Psalms : but, as compared with other names of
God, very much less frequently than most of them. Its use in
composition, at the end of proper names, is very common, and it
is the last syllable of Hallelujah, which occurs in so many emphatic passages, both of the Old Testament and the New, as if
to intimate to us, that our fundamental conception of God is
peculiarly connected with our chief relation to him, which is one
of praise and adoration. That it is one of the names of God,
assumed by himself and peculiar to himself, it seems impossible
to doubt. David says, Extol him that rideth upon the heavens,
by his name JAH,[1] where his name is merely transferred into
English. And the whole book of Psalms, closes with the solemn
appeal, Let everything that hath breath praise the Lord (Jah).[2]
Our translators manifestly considered this name of God, essentially one with the name Jehovah ; and have therefore translated
it by the word Lord, printed in small capitals. An error to be
regretted on various accounts, amongst the rest because it mis-
leads the ignorant, and gives needless trouble to the learned.

IV.—1. The three Hebrew names of God hitherto considered,
are supposed, as I have already said, to appertain in a special
manner to the divine essence itself. The names which remain
are believed to appertain rather to certain properties, perfections,
attributes, or habitudes so to speak of this divine essence, which
are peculiar to it, as God. These latter, however are not the less
really names of God, than the former ; but they differ from them
obviously, in their mode of application to him ; and they differ
also in that respect, somewhat amongst themselves. These differences are in some respects grammatical, belonging to the very
nature of the language, and showing in that a designed difference,
in the character of the names applied to God. In other respects,
they are of a still higher and more intractable kind, showing a
profound reason in the subject-matter, the doctrine, the being
himself, why the distinction in his names, and the mode of using
them, should be preserved. The simplest mode of expressing the
general result of all these differences between the names already
considered, and those yet to be spoken of, perhaps is to say that

---

[1] Psalm lxviii. 4.   [2] Psalm cl. 6.

the former, are personal and proper names of the divine being, and belong exclusively to him: while the latter, are indeed his names also, but neither exclusively personal nor proper to him. The names of the former kind express his self-existence, his eternity, his unchangeableness, and his infinitude: but the first one (Jehovah) expresses this completely, as of the eternal essence of the being who proposes himself to his creatures, as their God: the second one (Jah) expresses that being in the simplest sense of his actual existence and therewith in his special claims upon the boundless trust of his creatures: and the third one (Ehje) expresses the same being in the continuing existence of his infinite essence, and therewith in his special claims upon the adoration and praise of his creatures. This is my idea of the force of these three names of the divine essence : which I state not without diffidence. Amidst the boundless contentions of scholars, over the rind of the subject, they seem to me, to have overlooked the part of the matter, which was the most important to us, and the most clearly intimated in the Scriptures. Nevertheless, a certain reserve is always becoming on our part, when we think we see plainly, what others have denied or overlooked : while yet it is impossible to avoid too carefully, all shallow and artificial methods of examining and explaining God's word.

2. The name EL,* is used very commonly throughout the Old Testament scriptures to designate God ; and as far as I can discover, without exception, to express his power, greatness and majesty. Not simply God, so much as the great God ; the infinitely exalted, the almighty.[1] Our translators make it, God of Gods, in the exalted passage in which the prophet Daniel foretells, and characterizes the wildest extravagance of folly and impiety in him who shall rise up to resist him, in the latter day.[2] Such a name can apply properly and primarily only to the true God : however it may be sometimes applied to others ; differing in this use from the personal names of God. As for example, to idols : and to angels : and to inferior creatures. It is compounded in the names of persons and places : such as Israel, Bethuel, and multitudes like them. In the names of angels also, such as Michael, Gabriel, and many more. Indeed the names of nearly all the angels known to us end in El : a very curious

---

* אֵל Deus Deorum: Fortissimus omnium fortium : God of gods.

[1] Daniel, xi. 36.   [2] Daniel, xi. 36.

fact, which has not been sufficiently attended to ; nor, as far as I can discover, is any angel at all mentioned by name in the scriptures, before the Babylonish captivity, a fact also not a little singular. David gives it as the peculiar characteristic of angels, that they excel in strength,[1] which answers precisely to the generic addition of this name of the Almighty to the name of every one of them, if indeed that is true of their countless hosts.

3. LORD OF HOSTS.[*]   The word TZEBAOTH, is never used as a name of God, by itself ; but it is found very frequently in conjunction with some other name of God.[2]   Thus in the matter of David's strong desire to build a house for God, at first approved by Nathan and afterwards prohibited by the express command of God, yet with many and great promises to David and his seed ;[3] we have complete examples of the use of this remarkable name of God, in connection with other names.   Many years after that event, David, narrating it to Solomon, and charging him to perform what the Lord God of Israel had denied to him, repeated distinctly the personal reason of the divine prohibition, which Nathan had only intimated in a general manner to him.   The word of the Lord came to me, he tells Solomon, saying, Thou hast shed blood abundantly and hast made great wars : thou shalt not build a house unto my name, because thou hast shed much blood upon the earth in my sight.[4]   When the matter occurred both the great Prophet and the great King, were profoundly affected by it : and the narrative of the event, and the prayer of David, preserved by Samuel, form one of the most instructive passages in the history of the Old Testament church. Hardly any where in so short a compass is the name of God used more frequently, more earnestly, or more variously.   In the prayer of David, occupying only twelve verses,[5] the name of God occurs about twenty times, under five distinct forms : namely, Jehovah ; Adonai-Jehovah ; Jehovah Elohim ; Elohim ; Jehovah-Tzebaoth Elohim and Jehovah Tzebaoth Elohai.   In our English version four forms only are used, namely : Lord ; Lord God ;

---

[1] Psalm ciii. 20.

[*] צְבָאוֹת, Jehovah Tzebaoth Elohim, (1 Samuel, viii. 26,) צָבָא, exercitus : Tzebaoth, the plural : Hosts, the Lord of Hosts, God of Hosts, יְהֹוָה צְבָאוֹת, and אֱלֹהִים צְבָאוֹת.

[2] Isa., i. 9, and iii. 5 ; Psalm lxxx. 8–15, and lxxxiv. 9.   [3] 2 Sam., vii. 1–17.

[4] 1 Chron., xxii. 8 ; 2 Sam., vii. 1–17.   [5] 2 Sam., vii. 18–29.

God ; Lord of Hosts. In two instances the name Tzebaoth, now under consideration occurs in this passage ;[1] in both of them, following Jehovah: and in one preceding Elohim and in the other preceding Elohai, which is a form of the same word. In both instances our translators render Jehovah Tzebaoth, Lord of Hosts, and separate the latter part of the name, Elohim, Elohai, rendering it God, and attaching it to the following word : thus Lord of Hosts, God of Israel ; and Lord of Hosts, God over Israel. Indeed this use runs through the whole prayer, and is common throughout the scriptures : thus giving one name to God, and adding another name to point out his special relation to the special matter there treated of. Thus Jehovah of Hosts, is in a very special manner, the God of Israel. And it is most affecting and instructive to hear David, the greatest and the best of all kings and all conquerors, appealing with intense earnestness, humility and confidence to God, by his very name of Lord of Hosts : at the very moment when the desire of his own heart was denied to him, as being unsuitable in another respect of God, just because God had so continually blessed and prospered him in his service, in this very respect of God, as the God of armies ! Nothing could more obviously confirm what has been all along intimated, namely, that there are in the nature of God, as it must be comprehended and appreciated by us, profound distinctions on which all his revealed names rest ; which distinctions belong to the very foundations of our knowledge of God, and which it, therefore, supremely imports us to look into.

4. The word Tzebaoth, is never rendered as if it were a name of God : but always in our English scriptures, descriptively ; as Lord of Hosts, God of Hosts. When however it is put in apposition with another and unquestionable name of God, as Jehovah or Elohim, the form, as well as the sense, renders it certain that the two words united, make one name of God : thus Elohim-Tzebaoth, or Jehovah Tzebaoth : like Christ-Jesus, or Lord-God ; or any similar form ; of which the use is so common, and the number so great in the scriptures, throughout every part of them. As a name of God it gives a most exalted conception of his power, glory, wisdom and dominion, as the creator, preserver, and ruler of all things, and especially as the protector and defender of his people. All existing things, angels, worlds, men,

<hr>

[1] 2 Samuel, vii. 26, 27.

all inferior creatures, and all endless varieties of existences, in all their innumerable hosts, through all their countless generations, in all their infinitely diversified manifestations ; spring from the hand, and are upheld by the power, and guided by the wisdom of him who names himself not as by individuals, but as by hosts of them, Jehovah Tzebaoth Elohim, The Lord God of Hosts.

V.—1. MOST HIGH, ELJON.* This name of God occurs very frequently in the Hebrew Scriptures: especially in the Psalms and the Book of Daniel. The Proto-Martyr Stephen, in the remarkable discourse which preceded his death, applied it with great emphasis, under its Greek form,† in quoting the sublime words, which the prophet Isaiah says were spoken to him by Jehovah.[1] The use of the name in the Book of Psalms is remarkable ; as a single example may suffice to show. He that dwelleth in the secret place of the Most High, shall abide under the shadow of the Almighty. I will say of the Lord, He is my refuge and my strength ; my God : in him will I trust.[2] We have in these few, and most impressive words, four of the names whereby the Supreme being has made known his nature, to man : The one now under consideration, Eljon, Most High ; one already fully considered, Jehovah, Lord ; and two remaining to be considered, Shaddai, Almighty ; and Elohai, God. And then the remainder of the Psalm, one of the most sublime compositions ever seen by man, is devoted to the exposition of the safety, triumph, and blessedness of the righteous, in Eljon, The Most High ! It has been denied that this is properly a name of God : they who do this, contending that it should rather be considered one of the numerous epithets applied to God, than one of his names ; and urging in support of that judgment, mainly these two considerations, namely, that the word is apparently an adjective, and that it is frequently joined, apparently as such, to unquestionable names of God. The answer to both suggestions, is obvious : namely that it is the common habit of the Scriptures both of the Old Testament and the New, to unite two, three, and occasionally even four names of God in a single expression ; and that to deny that an adjective, as well as a verb, a particle, or a part of a noun, can be capable of the use in question, is mere empiricism. The constant use of this word in the

---

* עֶלְיוֹן, Ὑψίστος, Excelsus, Altissimus: Most High.   † Ὑψίστος.
[1] Acts, vii. 48; Isaiah, lxvi. 1, 2.   [2] Psalm xci. 1, 2.

Scriptures as a name of God and the repeated intimations that it is his name, put the matter out of question : for these are the only sources of our knowledge on the subject.   Nor can any one imagine a more appropriate ground, than the infinite exaltation of God in his nature, his perfections, his works and his acts, for one of his glorious names ; or a more fit thing to reveal to man, by a specific name, and as one of the foundations of our knowledge of God, than that very exaltation of his glorious being ?

2. ADONAI, Lord.* This name of God is rendered by our translators with the same word (Lord) used to render the name Jehovah : distinguishing them by the mode of printing the two ; that is using small capital letters when the word in the original is Jehovah.   Very frequently both names occur together ; thus, Adonai-Jehovah : and in such cases our translators render and print them Lord-GOD, using the small capitals for the latter word.   Adonai is perhaps exactly equivalent to the Greek Κυριος, which in the writings of the Apostles is applied continually to Christ, as Adonai is applied more than a thousand times to God, in the Old Testament Scriptures.   The idea conveyed by this name is that of infinite dominion and activity combined : The Ruler, The Disposer, The Sustainer, The Lord !   Nor is its use less obvious, than it is frequent, as an example will plainly show. The prophet Isaiah has recounted a most glorious vision he had, in the year that king Uzziah died, that is about seven centuries and a half before Christ ; in which he saw the Lord (Adonai), sitting upon a throne high and lifted up, and the train which surrounded him, filling the whole temple.   Above stood the seraphim ; and the prophet heard them crying one to another, Holy ! Holy ! Holy ! is the Lord of Hosts (Jehovah-Tzebaoth) : The whole earth is full of his glory.   He also heard the voice of the Lord (Adonai) saying, Whom shall I send and who will go for us ?   And then he asked the Lord (Adonai) how long the stupidity and obduracy of his people should continue.   And the Lord (Jehovah) replied, pointing out the desolations—and in-

* אֲדֹנָי. This is a peculiar plural form, of the singular אֲדוֹן, *Dominus*. It is some. times used in the plural, construct. as אֲדֹנֵי (Deut., x. 17.), sometimes also in the plural absolutely, אֲדוֹנִים (Malachi, i. 6).   Most frequently, as I have given it above, with preceding the י, as (Gen., xv. 2).   As I have already said, this form of the plural in י, preceded by ָ, is irregular, and is intentionally used to distinguish it as a mere name of God.   The plural in י, preceded by ָ, would signify, not simply God, but *my* God.   This form when used absolutely is applied only to God.

timating some mercy, in store for the children of Israel. Now it will be observed that the name Adonai is used interchangeably with the name Jehovah, and with the name Jehovah of Hosts.[1] But the particular reason why I have selected this passage to illustrate what so many hundreds illustrate as well: is that it is quoted with great emphasis in the New Testament Scriptures, and applied directly to Christ. Christ himself, explaining why he taught in parables, cites the words which Isaiah heard from Adonai-Jehovah-Tzebaoth, concerning the obduracy and desolation of Israel ; and told his disciples that these terrible words were fulfilled in the generation around him.[2] And still more explicitly, the Apostle John, who after quoting one of the most emphatic of the Messianic prophecies of Isaiah,[3] in such a way as to apply it to Christ, proceeds to quote from the vision Isaiah had of Adonai-Jehovah-Tzebaoth, the words which as we have just seen, Christ had cited and applied ; and then adds, these things said Esaias, when he saw his glory and spoke of him.[4] The glory Isaiah saw, was the peculiar glory of Messiah ; who in the ineffable Trinity is thus distinguished as Lord God of Hosts !

3. SHADDAI,* the Almighty, the All-sufficient. Our English translators have uniformily rendered this name of God, by the word Almighty. The name is used very frequently in the Jewish Scriptures : and the Greek form of it is applied again and again with the greatest emphasis, to the glorified Redeemer, in the New Testament. I am Alpha and Omega, the beginning and the ending, saith the Lord, which is, and which was, and which is to come, the Almighty :[5] which is precisely tantamount to Christ's saying to John, in the Hebrew tongue, I am Elohim-Jehovah-Shaddai ! The name is applied, not to the very essence of God, but to that unsearchable peculiarity of the divine nature, which we call its All-sufficiency. Like those names which are derived from his very essence, this which carries us so deeply into the nature of the Godhead, is never, in its simple form applied to any thing but God : and even in composition, less frequently than they. It is used for the first time in the Scriptures, in that interview between God and his servant Abraham,

---

[1] Isa., vi., *passim.*　　[2] Mat., xiii. 10–17.　　[3] Isa., liii.
[4] John, xii. 37–41.　　* שַׁדַּי, Παντοκρατωρ, *Omnipotens.*
[5] Rev., i. 8, iv. 8, xi. 17, xvi. 7.

wherein God changed the patriarch's name, and gave him the covenant of circumcision, and promised him a son, Isaac, with whom, and in whose seed, his covenant should be everlasting: an occasion, it must be allowed, of the most transcendent interest, in all its consequences, to the whole family of man.[1] Confining ourselves to the matter immediately before us, we note that it was under these wonderful circumstances that God revealed himself to the Father of the Faithful, as El-Shaddai, The All-sufficient God. And when Abram was ninety years old and nine, the Lord (Jehovah) appeared to Abram and said unto him, I am the Almighty God (El-Shaddai); walk before me, and be thou perfect. And I will make my covenant between me and thee, and will multiply thee exceedingly. And Abram fell on his face; and God (Elohim) talked with him.[2] In these few lines, we have four names of the supreme being: namely, Jehovah, El, Shaddai, and Elohim. That is, according to the Hebrew, Jehovah-El-Elohim is Shaddai, and desires Abraham to understand that it is as El-Shaddai that he makes this wondrous covenant with him. In English, it stands thus: Jehovah-Lord-God, is the Almighty, and makes this covenant of circumcision, which embraces the Messiah, and all the future of the kingdom of heaven, under his name, God Almighty! Multitudes of examples equally clear, abound in the Scriptures.

4. ELOHIM-ELOAH,[*] God. These two names of God remain to be considered: and they differ from all that have gone before. They are not, like Jehovah, Ehje, and Jah, derived from his essence; nor are they like El, Tzebaoth, Eljon, Adonai, and Shaddai, founded upon some infinite peculiar property of the supreme being. They seem intended rather to embrace every divine property and perfection: to hold forth the great being, Summum Numen, as comprehending in himself every Attribute which the Scriptures reveal, and which man can conceive as appertaining to him whom he calls God. They differ also from all the preceding names of God in this remarkable particular, that they allow grammatical affixes at their end: which none of the others do, and which is wholly inconsistent with the Hebrew use of all proper names. Being however, unquestionably names of God, they are distinguished from all his other names, by being called

---

[1] Gen., xvii., *passim.*   [2] Gen., xvii. 1–3.   [*] אֱלֹהִים אֱלַהּ.

Appellatives.* It has been supposed that the name Jehovah expressed the unity of the essence of God, and the name Elohim the Trinity of persons in that essence : an opinion not sustained by the grammatical reasons usually adduced to support it. And it is certainly untrue to say that Elohim is never used except with reference to the Trinity of Persons in the Godhead, and Jehovah never except with reference to the Unity of God's Essence. Of all the revealed names of God, Elohim is the first and by far the most frequently used in the Jewish Scriptures. In the first chapter of Genesis, and to the fifth verse of the second chapter, no other name of God occurs with reference to the whole work of creation, and the appointment and sanctification of the sabbath ; while the name Elohim occurs about thirty-five times. In the fifth verse of the second chapter, the name Jehovah appears, for the first time ; but in connection with and always preceding Elohim. Thenceforward through the second chapter, which recapitulates the work of creation in general, and that of the Garden of Eden, and of Adam and Eve in particular, and wherein the Covenant of Works is revealed ; it is Jehovah Elohim to whom every thing is ascribed ; that combined name alone being used, and that occurring ten or twelve times. Throughout the third chapter, which recounts the fall of man, the breach of the Covenant of Works, the entrance of sin into the world, and the curse of God upon man, upon the earth and upon the tempter, and gives the first intimation of the Covenant of Grace, it is still Jehovah Elohim who does all : Elohim separately, being used three times, in the conversation between the woman and the serpent. The first time the name Jehovah is used separately, is in the fourth verse of the fourth chapter, in the matter of Cain and Abel ; throughout which, as also through the matter of Lamech and his wives to the end of the chapter, the name Jehovah is used separately ; except that, in the twenty-fifth verse, Elohim is used separately, when the birth of Seth is spoken of. No other name of God but these two, and they only in the manner above set forth, occurs in these four chapters. In this place it is not possible to develop the ideas which these statements suggest. But when we con-

* These names are found in the Scriptures under the following forms: אֱלֹהִים־אֱלֹהַּ אֱלֹהֵי־: and with the final affixes אֱלֹהַי my God אֱלֹהָיו his God, אֱלֹהֶיךָ thy God, etc.: the form with the affixes being very various.

sider the marvellous and perfectly unique character of this portion of the word of God, there seems to be an unspeakable fitness
in the connection which the statements I have made points
out between the transcendent events recorded, and the transcendent aspect in which he who is the author of those events, is
exhibited to the universe. It is God made known to us in those
names by which, on the one hand every perfection of his infinite
being is intimated to us, and on the other hand the self-existent
and eternal nature of that infinitely perfect being is held before
us. It is this God of whom we have this primeval revelation :
itself full of overpowering majesty, and fraught with the first
existence and the whole fate of the universe ! And the events
themselves are such as could appertain only to such a God.
A universe created : a covenant of eternal life established : the
universe and the covenant destroyed together : both recovered
by a still more glorious covenant of divine grace ! It is the
Lord, God, Creator, Saviour !

5. In conducting this inquiry, it has not happened that it
was necessary to speak particularly of the persons of the Godhead, except occasionally and incidentally, especially of the Son
of God. The subject matter has been God, considered simply as
God : considered in the first great outlines in which he reveals
himself to man, by the names which he assumes in order to make
his absolute Nature and his most peculiar perfections known to
us. His eternal self-existence : His infinite Godhead, as the
Most High ; the All-sufficient ; the Lord of Hosts ; the boundless Ruler and Disposer ; the Great Being, full of all perfection.
This, it appears to me, is a true and systematic Revelation : the
fundamental type of all Revelation touching the being and
perfections of God. Being so, it would necessarily occur, that
as to God the Father, all these are primary Revelations of him.
And with the complete volume of divine truth in our hands,
nothing is easier than to show that all these primary truths of
the Godhead, apply to every divine person inseparably united in
the essence of that inscrutable existence ; and therefore that
they apply, and that the Scriptures clearly teach that they do
apply, as really to the Son, and, to the Holy Ghost as to the
Father. But it does not appear to me necessary or pertinent to
develop that in this place.

VI.—1. Without entering too far into the subject, it may be

observed that in the Hebrew, as in all other languages, there are multitudes of phrases, and epithets, whose primary sense may have no particular relevancy to God ; but which are capable of such an application, and which are actually so applied as necessarily to mean him. The Scriptures are full of instances of this sort. Yet we cannot on this account, say that such phrases and epithets become, in any proper sense, names of God. If we say the Nazarene, the crucified, the man of sorrows : we may be understood, at once, as meaning the Saviour. But these are not in any proper sense, names of the Son of God.

2. It may be observed in the same general way, that both the Greek and the Latin languages, as well indeed as our own and all others of which I have any knowledge, are much more limited in the names by which they express the existence and perfections of God, than the Hebrew. $\Theta\epsilon o\varsigma$ and $\kappa\upsilon\rho\iota o\varsigma$: Deus and Dominus : God and Lord : almost exhaust, in these languages respectively, the proper and peculiar appellations of the supreme being. In translating the Hebrew Scriptures, or using their divine teachings in any other tongue, a great danger of confusion and error must result from this singular richness of that language, compared with the singular poverty of others. A danger which renders such general expositions as that herein attempted, a necessary part of all systematic inquiries into the true Knowledge of God.

3. If we will take the trouble to reflect we shall perceive that a very small part of the distinct ideas we obtain on any subject, have any fixed names appropriated to them ; and that this is one reason why the general progress of mankind in knowledge is not more rapid, and why the minds even of educated persons, so frequently exhibit confusion and perplexity on subjects with which they might be presumed to be familiar. In the same manner when we have arrived at a degree of knowledge concerning the supreme being, sufficiently precise to give to the conception which we have of him, a distinct name, or in other words to give that name to him : it is easy to see, not only that we have already reached a certain exact amount of information, but that by this means we are most certain at once to retain it and to extend it. It is not therefore an idle curiosity, but it is a solid and enduring process, by which to systematize and extend our knowledge of God, as he has revealed himself to us, that we

are fostering when we push soberly but thoroughly, such inquiries as these into the very root of God's revelations to us. And they occupy no place so appropriately as one at the very entrance of those immense inquiries which concern the mode of his intimate existence, and constant manifestation. To these, by our method, having proved the Lord Jesus, as the Great Teacher, to be on the throne of the Universe ; and now finding in the very names of the Godhead which he possesses, the type of all Revelation ; we are fully come—seeking in his glorious light, that light which for us exists nowhere else.

CHAPTER XV.

THE MODE OF THE DIVINE EXISTENCE: UNITY OF ESSENCE: TRINITY OF PERSONS.

I. 1. The method of man's salvation determined by the mode of God's existence.—2. General nature of this relation.—3. Particular explanation of it.—II. 1. Salvation is possible only through the Father, the Son, and the Holy Ghost.—2. These three Divine Persons must co-operate, or all men must perish.—3. This great mystery thoroughly practical and fundamental.—III. 1. The scriptural idea of God. The decisive nature of this fact.—2. The unity of the Divine Essence. The Godhead under that aspect.—3. God is an Infinite Spirit—subsisting in three Persons and one Essence.—4. This Unity of Essence, and this Trinity of Persons, alike fundamental.—5. Elemental truths recapitulated. Doctrine of the Trinity.— IV. 1. Aspect of the Godhead considered in its Unity of Essence and Trinity of Persons.—2. Peculiar sense in which the word *Person* is applied to the Godhead. —3. Divine origin of this knowledge of God.—V. 1. General results of Divine truth, bearing on the relation of the mode of God's being to the plan of salvation. —2. The names of God in this respect, both as they are essentially, and as they are personally applied.—3. One essence: oneness of essence: consubstantial: triune—not triplex.—4. Distinctions between the Divine Essence and the Divine Persons: and between the Persons themselves. Salvation for man impossible, unless God exists in this manner.—VI. 1. The Unity of the Divine Essence, rendered more obvious by means of the Divine Persons.—2. The scriptural use of the names of God, with respect to the Divine Essence and the Divine Persons.—3. The revealed method of the Divine existence perfectly distinct and systematic.— 4. The doctrine of the Trinity and the plan of salvation, stand or fall together.— 5. The exact points of the mystery of this particular mode of the Divine existence.

I.—1. THE mode in which salvation can be offered to sinful men, must necessarily depend upon the nature of God himself: and as the nature of God and the mode of his existence, must necessarily depend on each other—if they be not essentially the same thing—it follows that the mode of God's existence must determine the method of man's salvation.

2. It might be true that God might fail, or even refuse to reveal to man, any thing beyond the mere fact and method of salvation ; but even in that case, it would be impossible to avoid seeing, that a connection existed which was not explained to us,

and which therefore we might not understand. Just as now, in various parts of God's dealings with us, we clearly perceive that a connection does exist—which it exceeds our capacity to unravel, and which God has not seen fit to explain completely—or, in some instances, at all. As, for example, the connection which exists between the unchangeableness of God, on the one hand, and his being the answerer of prayer, on the other ; concerning which, we know that both are certain, and that they mutually consist with each other : but *how*, we do not perceive. But when God is pleased, not only to point out to us clearly and precisely, that a connection of this sort does exist—as, for example, that between the mode of his own existence, and the method of man's salvation : but when he goes much further than this, and plainly and explicitly reveals to us, the exact nature of the relation of these two sublime mysteries to each other ; it is an unspeakable folly and impiety in us, to shut our eyes to the light of heaven, and harden and stupefy our hearts against the wisdom that is from above.

3. For if, as has been shown in a former chapter, the salvation of man is impossible except through the interposition of God—and impossible even then except as the salvation of a moral, rational, accountable, and yet fallen creature—from sin and its fruits ; and if, as has also been proved, that salvation for that creature is secured by Immanuel, the Mediator, Prophet, Priest, and King : then it follows that the knowledge and fruition of that salvation, are not only dependent, absolutely, upon the knowledge of the divine Saviour as he exists, interposes and acts ; but, in a manner, that knowledge, in the power and the grace of it, is in fact the very salvation itself ; and ignorance thereof, is, in effect, the perdition of the sinner. Well may Christ say, Teach all nations ! And well may we say, that the most childlike faith does not impeach the profoundest meditations of philosophy, when it conducts us directly to the feet of the Great Teacher, for all our knowledge of God.

II.—1. It is thus, only more clearly, that the case is put by the Apostle Paul. What comes by Christ, he argues, is far greater and more glorious, than all that came before ; but, they who neglected the word spoken by angels perished ; therefore, they shall more certainly perish, who neglect the great salvation now offered to them. What great salvation ? Why, that which begun to be spoken by the Lord ; that which God confirmed, with signs and wonders ; that which the Holy Ghost attested, with miracles and gifts.[1]   Can there be the least doubt that it is the Father, the Son, and the Spirit, who are here spoken of by Paul ?*   A divine salvation, more glorious than that made known by angels, is revealed by the Son : it is confirmed by the wonders wrought by the Father : it is attested by the miracles, performed through the Spirit : and, beyond all controversy, men must perish, if they neglect it.

2. What is of the last consequence to us to note is, that the matter here put at risk, is neither more nor less, than our own salvation. They whom Paul calls, respectively, God, the Lord, and the Holy Ghost, perform, each one a part, without which there is no salvation at all ; a part which establishes and completes the salvation itself—works it out, applies it, and makes it effectual. It is of no particular consequence, just here, what those respective parts may be ; the thing that is of consequence, and that is fundamental and overwhelming in its consequence, is, that it is our only hope of salvation ; and that three divine persons, receiving the very highest divine titles known to the Greek Scriptures, are declared to have, each, a part in it—without which, all must fall to the ground.

3. This great question, then, of the mode of God's being, is put by the Scripture itself, in the very front of practical religion. To say we cannot understand it, is to say we cannot understand how we are to be saved. To say we will not consider it, is to refuse to examine the only way by which we can escape perdition. To say we cannot accept God's teaching concerning it, is to give up our last hope of deliverance. Nor is it too much to assert, that starting from this point, every proposition concerning the salvation of sinners, becomes clear in proportion as our views are distinct concerning the mode in which the being of God stands related to the divine scheme of man's redemption ; and that every proposition is obscured, in proportion as our conception is dull, and our faith weak, touching the nature of the Godhead, and the relations of the Father, the Son, and the Holy Ghost, to each other, and to the work of our restoration to God.

III.—1. The prime idea which the Scriptures give us of God,

---

[1] Heb., ii. 1–4.

* Θεος, κυριος, πνευμα ἁγιον, are the divine names used by the Apostle.

is that of a self-existent Spirit, who is infinite, eternal, and unchangeable ; who fills immensity, and who is the creator, the preserver, and the ruler of the universe, and of every created thing therein. We are so familiar with the form of words in which we express the elements of this stupendous idea, that it is only when our attention is aroused, by our being brought in contact with the productions of those ages and races that were destitute of them ; or by its becoming necessary for us to take them apart, and examine them, and recombine them ; that we are adequately impressed with their superhuman grandeur. The bare existence in the human mind, of such an idea of God, as is distinctly set before us throughout the Scriptures, is of itself perfectly decisive. For, if the Scriptures are divine, then the idea is divinely realized, and is true ; but if the Scriptures are not divine, then the idea is the spontaneous and irrefragable natural response of the soul itself to its infinite creator—and is still true. We need hardly ask ourselves, however, where man obtained that idea. For after it has been clearly stated in writing for so many centuries, and after such immense and enduring labors to fix it in the human mind, but a small portion of the human race has ever yet received it clearly—and every part of that race which has received it, has shown itself prone to obscure and to forget it.

2. The unity of the Godhead, the absolute oneness of his self-existent essence, is the fundamental conception of his being. His existence is, therefore, in the very nature of it, anterior to all other existences, and is necessarily preclusive of all being, that does not exist from, and in him. He is self-existent, and therefore infinitely simple and immense ; necessarily from, and to eternity ; boundless in power and in intelligence. His existence is by consequence, infinitely pure, and right, and free ; immeasurably good and blessed. In what particular manner such a being would manifest its life and activity ; or in how many glorious and boundless ways ; we could know only as the result of our personal experience—or by means of his own revelation to us. But we cannot comprehend, organized as we are, and knowing what has been made known to us, how such a being could fail to manifest a life and exert an activity, proportioned to the infinite perfections of his nature : since no existence, of which we know any thing, is exempt from this invariable law,

of all being. It is not possible, therefore, for us to fail to recognize in God, the infinite Creator of the universe—its infinite providential ruler—the eternal giver of all its laws, written and unwritten—natural and moral—the unfailing and satisfying source of all mercy and all felicity—the sure and righteous avenger of all evil and wrong, forevermore. And now, and always, after we have striven the most earnestly to utter, simply and clearly, what we had before learned from God himself; how incessantly are we driven back to the statements of the Scriptures for all just and comprehensive expression of the idea which they alone, have adequately embodied, of Jehovah ! What a testimony is this to the record, which God has given us of himself ! What a proof, that in these sublime mysteries, the very least in the kingdom of heaven is greater than the very greatest ever born of woman !

3. Our blessed Redeemer, in his memorable conversation with the woman of Samaria, at the well of Sychar, said to her plainly, God is a Spirit : and they that worship him, must worship him in spirit and in truth.[1] But it is also said of Christ, The Lord is that Spirit : and where the Spirit of the Lord is, there is liberty :[2] and not less emphatically, The first man Adam was made a living soul, the last Adam was made a quickening Spirit.[3] And, yet again, the Holy Spirit is the name commonly given throughout the Scriptures, especially of the New Testament, to that divine being by whose agency all the grace of God is made effectual in our salvation.[4] In these declarations, therefore, we are advanced in the scope and certainty of our knowledge touching the awful mystery of the divine existence. It is capable of being demonstrated—and that demonstration has been attempted in a former chapter—that the general mode of God's existence, is that of an infinite Spirit ; and now we have this great truth confirmed by divine revelation ; and the further truth added, as already seen, that that infinite Spirit subsists and acts, in man's salvation, as *Father*, *Son*, and Holy Ghost :[*] and now again, and further, that each of these persons is also a Spirit.

4. It is impossible to let the idea of the absolute oneness of the Godhead slip from us, or be in the least encroached upon, without subverting the foundations of the entire spiritual sys-

---

[1] John, iv. 24.   [2] 2 Cor., iii. 17.   [3] 1 Cor., xv. 45.
[4] Gal, iv. 6; 1 John, v. 7; 2 Cor., xiii. 14.   [*] Θεος, κυριος, πνευμα ἁγιον

tem, revealed in the Scriptures—and shutting ourselves out from every hope of the eternal life, brought to light through them. Hear O! Israel: the Lord our God is one Lord,* is the first principle ; and, thou shalt have no other Gods before me, is the first duty, of revealed religion.[1] Yet on the other hand, that there exists a plurality of some sort—and that distinctly three-fold—in this divine nature, is just as clearly certain, from the Scriptures, as that the essence itself is undivided :—certain from their entire tenor, and certain from their distinct and repeated statements. Thus, There are three that bear record in heaven, the Father, the Word, and the Holy Ghost ; and these three are one.[2] And, when Jesus was baptized, the Spirit of God descended visibly upon him, and the voice from heaven said, this is my beloved Son, in whom I am well pleased.[3] And in the memorable conversations with his Apostles, preceding his cruci-fixion, of which the Apostle John has preserved so full an account ; the Saviour in promising the Comforter to his people, has carefully explained the divine relations of the Father, the Son, and the Holy Spirit, to each other, in the matter of our salvation, and to that salvation itself.[4]

5. These, therefore, are the fundamental conditions of the nature of the divine existence, as to the mode of its being, so far as we are informed : first, that the mode of that infinite self-existence, is wholly a spiritual mode : secondly, that, as to the essence of that infinite Spirit, the mode of its existence, is with absolute simplicity and unity : thirdly, that in the unity of that divine essence, that essence hath eternally a method of subsisting and acting, which we express by saying there are three persons in the unity of the Godhead, to wit, the Father, the Son, and the Holy Ghost. These elemental truths make up the leading conceptions contained in the doctrine of the Trinity—and embraced by that word.

IV.—1. It is to be constantly borne in mind, that the sense in which the unity of the Godhead is affirmed, and the sense in which the threefold personality of the Godhead is affirmed, is not, and cannot be, of the Godhead in the same view and con-

---

* ‏יְהֹוָה אֱלֹהֵינוּ יְהֹוָה אֶחָֽו׃‏

[1] Deut., vi. 4; Exod., xx. 3.　　[2] 1 John, v. 7.　　[3] Mat., iii. 16, 17.
[4] John, xiv. 15–26, xv. 26, xvi. 13–16; 1 Cor., xii. 4–6; 2 Cor., xiii. 13 ; Eph., ii. 18. Rev., i. 4, 5.

ception thereof : for in that case there would be a direct contradiction in the terms, in which our fundamental belief concerning the divine existence is stated.   The unity of the Godhead is predicated of the very being itself, of God—of his nature—of his infinite essence : the Trinity, on the other hand, is predicated of the personality of the divine nature—of the mode, that is, in which the divine existence subsists and acts, as one God, in three persons, to wit, the Father, the Son, and Holy Ghost. Even though we may not fully comprehend what is meant either by the essence of God, or the persons of the Godhead ; yet we can perfectly comprehend that different ideas may be, and are expressed by these different terms : and therefore that to assent to both propositions of God's being is as comprehensible, and may be as true, so far as the propositions themselves or their terms are concerned—as to assent to either of them separately, is, or could be, true, or comprehensible.   Precisely as it is true, that even though we may not fully comprehend what is meant by calling God a Spirit—much less by calling him an infinite Spirit ; yet it is perfectly comprehensible, that a spiritual God is widely different from a physical one ; and it is also perfectly comprehensible, that an infinite Spirit, existing as a personal God, is widely different from an infinite spiritual influence, existing, and manifesting itself in a wholly impersonal form.   In one of these three statements, we have the idea of God revealed in the Scriptures ; in another we have the atheistical denial of all separate spiritual existence ; and in the third, we have the idea of God, in every form of pantheistical infidelity.   They are all three, not only perfectly intelligible, but perfectly distinct.

2. We are liable to serious mistakes in examining this immense subject, from the peculiar sense in which the word *person* is used, when applied to the Godhead.   When applied to human nature and human beings, by person, we mean an individual made up of soul and body—and whatever else constitutes a complete and separate being.   No matter how many elements, physical, mental, spiritual, temporal, and eternal go to make up the individual—when all are united and completed, the word person expresses our idea of the particular individual being, in which all these elements are united.   Not so in the application of this term to the Godhead.   By speaking of three persons in one God, we necessarily reject the idea that either of the three is exclu-

sively God ; just as we necessarily express the idea, that each one of them is really God. While in man many things make but one person, in God three persons subsist in one and the same Jehovah. While in man person is the highest and most exclusive conception we have of human nature—in God person is the conception we have of one respect of the mode of the divine existence, and not of the essence and totality of the existence itself.

3. We are to remember also, that of all parts of revealed religion—not one is more completely above our faculties and beyond the pale of our natural knowledge, than this concerning the nature and mode of the divine existence. There is absolutely nothing, independently of an immediate revelation from God, that would ever have led us so much as even to conjecture, that in the unity of the divine nature there existed just three divine persons. Nor is there any reason to doubt that if the plan of salvation were capable of being explained upon any other hypothesis, as applied to God's nature, or if the multiplied declarations of Scripture could possibly be understood in any other sense ; the human mind would have utterly rejected the doctrine of the true mode of God's existence ; that is the doctrine of the Trinity as received by God's people, more or less distinctly, in every age. Most assuredly if man had made the Bible, his nature and his whole history abundantly prove that we should have had a widely different doctrine on the subject of the divine existence, from that which the Bible actually teaches : a proof at once of its divine origin, and of the duty binding upon us, simply to learn and accept what God teaches us on this sublime theme.

V.—1. Keeping strictly to the idea already insisted on, that this doctrine of the Trinity is immediately involved in the whole scheme of God's interposition to save sinful men ; and that while the latter is incomprehensible without the former—the former is most easily and most clearly explicable, by the latter : I proceed to gather up and state in order the remaining truths of Scripture immediately connected with it, in this general aspect of the subject. And as seven chapters have already been devoted to an elaborate consideration directly of the person and work of the Lord Jesus, the second person of the adorable Trinity—and incidentally of the two remaining persons of the Godhead ; it will be less necessary, in what is now to be advanced, to exhibit minutely than to sum up clearly, the divine instruction on the whole subject.

2. The name of God both in the Hebrew and Greek Scriptures, is applied sometimes, essentially and generally to the divine essence which is common to the Father, Son, and Holy Ghost—and so, to the whole Trinity.[1] This use is common throughout the Scriptures. Sometimes it is specially and personally applied, not to the whole Trinity, but to a single person thereof, as to the Father exclusively :[2] to the Son exclusively :[3] to the Holy Ghost exclusively.[4] Neither the former, or essential, mode of using the name of God, nor the latter, or personal, mode of using it, is by itself and exclusive of the other mode of any avail for the salvation of sinners : since as sinners we are amenable in every form and upon every ground ; and if we are saved, that must be done for us which involves and demands, the concurrence of God in every aspect of his glorious being and perfections. In whatever mode he exists and acts towards us, he must be manifested for us, or we must perish. Here then in the supreme Godhead of each person of the Trinity, supposing God to subsist in that manner, is laid the foundation of the possibility that sinners may be saved ; while the revelation of the fact of that mode of existence on the part of God, in connection with the purpose of God in the salvation of sinners—establishes the certainty of that salvation.

3. The Jehovah of the Hebrew, and the *I am*[*] of the Greek, are one and the same : the self-existent. Through the Greek language, the case is easily and clearly stated. First the essence ; and from that the oneness of essence—applied to the three persons of the Trinity.[†] The same in substance ; equal in power and glory. Each is Jehovah, each is *I am*—the self-existent. All are consubstantial ; that is, the same in essence. Of these three persons, Father, Son, and Holy Ghost, let it be noted however, that God is tri-une not triplex ; for the idea of composition is to be wholly rejected. Each one is a divine person,[5][‡] subsisting in the essence[§] of the self-existent.[||] Each one is of the same

---

[1] Mat., iv. 7–10; John, iv. 24.   [2] Mat., xvi. 16; John, i. 1, 2; Rom., i. 8.
[3] Acts, xx. 28; 1 Tim., iii. 16; Titus, ii. 13.   [4] Acts, v. 4; 2 Cor., vi. 16; 1 Cor., vi. 19.
[*] Ὁ ων, και ὁ ἠν, και ὁ ἐρχομενος, ὁ παντωκρατωρ.—Rev., i. 5.
[†] Ὁ ων, οὐσια ὁμοουσια. The self-existent essence—consubstantial.
[‡] [3] Heb., i. 3   [5] Ὑποστασις.   [§] Οὐσια.   [||] Ὁ ων.

substance* with the others; and that substance is but one, and it self-existent—the Jehovah.—A Trinity, not *numero numeranti* —but *numero numerato:* three persons in one essence, not three persons of three essences, nor three essences in one person, nor yet the same essence three times repeated; but one divine essence which subsists and acts in three persons, Father, Son, and Holy Ghost; and these three are one.[1] That is, one God —not one person. The communion† of the persons of the Trinity consists in the oneness of substance, which is common to them all—and total in each of them.[2] They are all consubstantial to, and with each other; that is, they are the same in their divine substance. Wherefore each one of them is equally, by essence, God of himself. Each person being equally God, is equal as to essence, properties, essential operations, power, dignity, glory and honor:[3] and the Scriptures constantly predicate of each all that is essential of every one. All the three divine persons are eternally and inseparably united to, with, and amongst each other: and yet each person has distinct, and incommunicable properties peculiar to itself.[4] For the Son is not the Father, nor is the Holy Ghost the Son; but they are all three distinguished from each other by properties which distinctly mark each, and which are incommunicable and inseparable. That is, they are as really three persons by subsistence, that is by their mode of being, as they are one God by substance and essence. And so deeply are all these truths connected with the plan of salvation, that the denial of them, on the side of the unity of the divine essence, is the foundation of the fatal heresy of Arius, and the denial of them on the side of the divine personality, is the foundation of that of Sabellius.

4. There is revealed to us, besides the general distinction between the essence, or substance of God's being, and the method in which that essence exists—already so often stated—a series of distinctions perfectly comprehensible, between the divine essence and the divine persons—such as those which follow. 1. The person includes the essence; and besides includes the idea of relation, as paternity, filiation, procession: and moreover, the essence must be considered absolutely; the person, relatively. 2 The person is incommunicable; for the Father

* Ὁμοούσιος. [1] 1 John, v. 7. † Κοινωνια. [2] John, x. 30; 1 John, v. 7
[3] Phil., ii. 6. [4] John, i. 1. x. 38, xiv. 10, 11, 20.

cannot be the Son ; and so of the rest ; but the essence is communicable, so far as the persons are concerned—for all three of them partake of it. 3. The essence exists of itself, and has no origin in any sense whatever ; but, in a certain sense, the Son is of the Father ; and the Spirit is of the Father and the Son. So also there are revealed to us certain distinctions amongst the persons themselves ; such as the following. (1.) They differ in name from each other ; one being called the Father, another the Son or the Word, and the third the Holy Ghost ; a distinction of the greatest importance in understanding the plan of salvation.[1] (2.) They differ in their incommunicable properties, which are so called to distinguish them from those essential properties which are common to them all. Thus it is peculiar to the Father that he is unbegotten ; and that he begets the Son ; and that from him and the Son proceeds the Holy Ghost. It is peculiar to the Son, that he is begotten of the Father, and that from him with the Father, proceeds the Holy Ghost. And it is peculiar to the Holy Ghost that he is not begotten—nor yet, as to his personality, of himself—differing both from the Father and the Son, but that he emanates, or proceeds, equally from the Father and the Son.[2] (3.) They differ as to their order of existing. The Father, not only as to his essence, but also as to his person, is of and from himself. The Son and the Spirit, as to their essence, are also of, and from themselves ; but as to their personality, the Son is of the Father, as begotten ; and the Spirit is of the Father and the Son, as emanating, not begotten. (4.) So amongst the divine actions ; while some are of that nature that they are performed mutually, as between the persons of the Trinity—according to the properties peculiar to each person ; others relate more especially to the universe, and the creatures God has formed. Of the former, necessarily, and of the latter, most generally, an order of action distinguishes the persons of the Sacred Trinity, corresponding with their order of existing : the Father acting of, and from himself :[3] the Son acting from the Father :[4] and the Holy Spirit acting from both.[5] And on account of this order of existing and acting, the Father is called the first, the Son the second, and the Holy Ghost the third person of the Trinity. (5.) And thus we may not pass

---

Mat., xxviii. 19; 1 John, v. 7.   [2] John, xiv. 16, xv. 26.
Mat., xi. 25-27; John, xi. 41, 42.   [4] John, v. 19-23.   [5] John, xiv. 26, xv. 16.

by in silence the general distinction, that to the Father is attributed, the fountain and source of all things : to the Son, the
wisdom, counsel, and arrangement of all operations : and to the
Spirit, the power and efficacy, by which every action is accomplished.   (6.) The person of Christ is peculiarly distinguished,
since he is not only to be considered in all that characterizes him
as the Word, the Son, the second person of the adorable Trinity;
but also, as the human nature has been assumed by him into
personal, that is, hypostatical, union with the divine nature, of
which so much has been said in preceding chapters.   In this
assumption by Christ, the human person is lost and swallowed
up in the divine person of the Word, as I have heretofore shown :
else there would be four persons in the Godhead—and one of
them a man ; which would be impossible and absurd.   But the
human nature, in the person of Jesus of Nazareth, remains personally and eternally united to, not confounded with, the divine
nature, in the person of the Son of God—whose nature and person are both divine.   But for the divine personality, in the mode
of God's existence, plainly therefore, the Son of God never could
have assumed human nature : and, but for the essential divinity
of the Son of God, human nature never could have been united
with the divine nature.   Yet plainly, again, but for the existence
of God, as a Trinity of persons in one divine essence ; what
Christ thus did, would have been alike impossible, whether contemplated on the part of human nature, or on the part of the
Godhead.   So that the mode of the divine existence, which we
express in the word, and signify by the doctrine of the Trinity,
is the only conceivable mode of the divine existence which is
compatible with the revealed method of saving sinners.

   VI.—1. These distinctions in the divine persons of the
Trinity, so far from giving any pretext to the wickedness of those
who pretend that we thus divide the Godhead into three parts ;
or the blasphemies of those who allege that by this means we
teach that there are, in reality, three Gods ; do indeed rather
place the unity of the divine essence on a clearer and firmer
basis, than it could otherwise be shown to occupy.   For in this
manner we are enabled not only to define but also to illustrate
that infinite and indivisible simplicity in which God eternally
and unchangeably exists.   For the Son, as he has one Spirit with
the Father, must be one God with him : and the Spirit, as he

proceeds both from the Father and the Son, must be of the same essence with both of them. So that although each hypostasis has something peculiar to itself, that very peculiarity is, by its own nature, the means of proving that the whole divine nature is in each one : whereby Christ could truly say, I am in the Father and the Father is in me.[1] Christ, considered of himself, is God ; but considered with reference to the Father, he is the Son : just as the Father, considered of himself, is God ; but considered with reference to the Son, is the Father. And so all the distinctions of the persons of the Godhead, and all the appellations which express those distinctions, while they denote their own reciprocal relations, indicate, at the same time, the unity of their divine essence, in which there is no distinction whatever.

2. Inasmuch as the Father sustains no relation to the Son or the Spirit, by which in the order of existence, or action, or thought, he could be said to be of or from either of them—either as begotten or as proceeding ; it naturally follows that when the Son or the Spirit is mentioned together with the Father, the name of God, is in that case, more peculiarly applied to the Father, than to the Son or the Spirit. This occurs with great frequency in the Scriptures ; thus keeping before the mind, on the one hand, the unity of the divine essence, and on the other, the order of the divine persons. But when the name of God is used generally and absolutely in the Scriptures, and not with particular reference to the mode of his existence, in three persons ; then it is not the Father that is intended, but the single and simple essence, comprehending the Father, Son, and Holy Ghost. Although the name of God is used many thousands of times in the Scriptures, it is perhaps impossible to select a single instance, in which an attentive consideration of the passage, and a careful comparison of it with other parts, will not satisfy the sober inquirer whether it is used in that place of God indefinitely—meaning his essence, or of the Father, or the Son, or the Holy Ghost : while, in most instances, the use is so obvious that doubt is hardly possible. When we consider the great weakness of our faculties, the small acquaintance we possess with our own nature, and our total natural ignorance of the nature of God ; together with the imperfection of all language in the communi-

[1] John, xiv. 10, 11.

cation of knowledge, of this sort ; it must be allowed to be infinitely remarkable, that the writers of the Old and New Testaments, should have succeeded in a manner so complete, in making themselves perfectly understood upon the most difficult subject ever presented to the human mind. A theory of the divine existence which is found nowhere else, is developed, illustrated, and applied all through the Scriptures, in such a manner that, while the intelligence of an angel could not perhaps go a hair's breadth beyond what is taught, the intellect of a child can receive all that is made known.

3. It is not pretended that the understanding of man is capable of fathoming all the sublime truths which the Scriptures unfold to us, concerning the being of God : nor all the relations of such parts thereof, as appear most simple, to each other, and to the whole subject. But it is undeniable that we are as capable of understanding one exhibition as another ; one theory as another ; one set of facts as another, upon a subject the larger part of which lies beyond the pale of our researches, and in regard to which therefore, we must be taught, if we are taught at all, in a supernatural manner. What is indispensable is, that the proof should be complete and conclusive, that the instruction offered to us is true and divine ; for as to the knowledge itself, which is imparted to us in that manner, the only difference touching it is that the more clearly and the more variously it is communicated to us, the more readily does it impress itself upon those who give heed to the Divine Teacher. Except in this sense, we cannot say that one part is more comprehensible than another ; nor upon these conditions, is it in the slightest degree true to assert that any part, intended to be explained to us, is incomprehensible. We are not asked to comprehend the self-existence of God ; for we do not comprehend even our own dependent existence. But we are taught that God exists—and this fact is not only comprehensible, but far more comprehensible than the opposite fact ; namely, that there is no God at all. Now when to this it is added point by point, that God who thus exists is a Spirit ; that he is an infinite, self-existent, eternal, and unchangeable Spirit ; that in the unity of his immense and almighty being, there subsist three hypostases, which, from their mutual relations, are called the Father, the Son, and the Holy Ghost ; and that the action of the Godhead, upon and within

itself—as well as its action, in every respect, upon the universe and upon all creatures, has respect always, to this unity of essence and Trinity of persons ; what I assert is, that amongst all these sublime truths, one is just as intelligible as another ; as matter of fact, that all are perfectly comprehensible ; that each one is made more obvious, and not more obscure, by the addition of the others ; and that when it is at length perceived that all united, form a vast system of knowledge, the dependence of whose parts is more obvious, the more complete the system is ; then, the more credible and the more perspicuous, does the whole and every particular part become as we advance to the sublime conclusion.   Confining ourselves strictly to the subject under consideration, it may be asserted, that in the whole round of our knowledge, human and divine, there is nothing that impeaches, in the slightest degree these great truths :—namely, 1. That there is a God, and that there is but one ; 2. That he is, as to his essence, an infinite Spirit ; 3. That the method of his existence is by three hypostases ; the same in substance, equal in power and glory.   Nor is there in these propositions any thing either contradictory or incomprehensible ; but on the other hand, they illustrate and confirm each other.   The self-existence, from eternity, of that transcendent being whom we call God, is a proposition which assuredly is not rendered either more obscure or more overwhelming when it is added, that he is an infinite Spirit.   And the further idea, thus obtained, of the majesty and grandeur of his nature, is neither rendered more irrational nor more incredible, when we are informed, that the mode of his being is such as to give the most complete scope for the enjoyment of an infinite felicity—in the divine co-existence, and eternal in-being, of the Father, Son, and Holy Ghost, and to furnish the most entire manifestation of all the divine perfections, by means of their joint, as well as their mutual and their separate action, within the Godhead, and without it ; to, and upon all creatures.   Whoever will ponder the subject will see, that amongst the properties, attributes and perfections, which reason and revelation alike ascribe to God, there are not a few, which we are fully able to conceive of, as having their perfect scope and exercise only upon the condition of a distinct plurality of persons in the divine nature.   Indeed this observation applies in some degree to most of the moral perfections of God ; and completely and with the greatest emphasis to all the results which are represented as flowing from the mutual relations of the Father, Son, and Spirit, in the way of infinite glory, blessedness, and love. Insomuch that the admission or denial of God's existence, simply ; or the admission or denial of the unity and spirituality of his nature ; is not more pregnant in determining all that relates to the universe, and our position in it, than the admission or denial of the mode of God's existence, as that of three persons in one essence necessarily must be.

4. When we come to apply the doctrine of the Trinity to the plan of salvation revealed in the Scriptures, we see at once in that plan, the complete illustration of the being of God as taught in that doctrine ; and the indispensable necessity which pressed the whole case, that the mode of God's existence should be distinctly explained, touching a matter which depends absolutely upon it. The plan of salvation is consistent with the idea that God is an infinite Spirit : but if God is not an infinite Spirit, the plan of salvation is necessarily and absolutely false in all its parts. If God is an infinite Spirit, whose simple and indivisible unity fills immensity and eternity, but the method of whose being is that of three divine, consubstantial, and co-essential persons, in the one divine essence : then again the plan of salvation by the Father, the Son, and the Holy Ghost, fully illustrates that mode of the divine existence, and perfectly accords with it : and it not only may be true, as matter of theory, but it derives from its intimate relevancy to the whole mode of the divine existence, an overwhelming confirmation of its positive truth. But if there is no adequate proof that God exists, as the Father, Son, and Holy Ghost, in the unity of the divine essence ; then there is no certainty that sinners can be saved upon a hypothesis, which derives all its efficacy from the assumption that God does exist in that manner ; but there is a most violent presumption that sinners cannot be saved, in a manner peculiar—and which is defective in the evidence that its fundamental proposition is true. But as soon as this defect of proof is converted into positive proof of the contrary ; as soon as it is established that God does not exist in a unity of essence and a Trinity of persons ; then immediately, the theory of salvation for sinners, founded upon this fundamental deception, becomes not only futile, but impious. In that case, we have nothing tc

teach the nations, nor any authority to baptize them in the name of the Father, and of the Son, and of the Holy Ghost ; and the love of God, and the grace of the Lord Jesus Christ, and the communion of the Holy Ghost, are vain and empty sounds.

5. That which is incomprehensible to us in the doctrine of the Trinity—which the Scriptures do not explain—and which no similitude taken from any thing known to us, adequately illustrates ; and which therefore makes this doctrine so great a mystery, may be stated thus : 1. While we understand that the persons of the Trinity are distinguished from each other, and while we also understand the relations, terms, and acts, which express and illustrate that distinction ; we do not understand the *nature* of that distinction, nor comprehend precisely what it is.   2. While we understand that as to the essence of God, it is absolutely one, and as to his manner of subsisting and acting it is threefold—so that he is one God in three persons ; and while we understand the terms, acts, and relations, in which the distinction between the essence and the personality of the divine nature is expressed and illustrated ; we do not understand the *nature* of that distinction, nor comprehend precisely what it is. In both cases, there is something beyond what is revealed ; and therefore there is that which we do not comprehend ; there is an immense mystery.   But this is no more than must be said of some part of every doctrine that relates directly to the existence of God.   In searching for divine knowledge we gain nothing by endeavoring to fathom what God has left in mystery ; while we only prove our sinful neglect and voluntary ignorance, by making a mystery of any thing that God has clearly explained to us.

CHAPTER XVI.

THE DOCTRINE OF THE HOLY GHOST.

I. 1. The work of the Holy Ghost, in our gratuitous and divine salvation.—2. Nature, and Person of the Divine Spirit.—3. These to be specially exhibited in his connection with Christ and Salvation.—II. 1. The existence of Immanuel a demonstration that the Spirit is the Most High God.—2. The whole work of the Mediator full of proofs of the Supreme Godhead of the Spirit, in essence and person. —3. The Infinite Fitness, authority and ability of the Mediator, the product of the Infinite Unction of the Spirit.—4. As the Inspirer of all Scripture, he and it stand or fall together.—5. The conclusive force of the structure of the Scripture upon the mode of the Divine Existence.—III. Constant Relation of the Spirit to the knowledge of God.—1. Pentecost.—2. Under the ministry of Christ, the Father is the chief object: under the ministry of the Spirit, Christ is the chief object.—3. The Spirit is the author as Christ is the head of the New Creation.— 4. Direct Scripture statements concerning the Holy Ghost.—5. The Spirit of Holiness, of Truth, and of Life.—IV. The sin against the Holy Ghost.—1. There is a sin which is unto Death.—2. It has direct reference to the Holy Ghost and through him to Christ.—3. Its peculiar form is, Blasphemy against the Holy Ghost.—4. The meaning of the term *Blasphemy*, thus used; (*a*) To rob the Spirit of his glory and due, is to Blaspheme him; (*b*) To pretend to do the office and work of the Spirit, is to Blaspheme him; (*c*) These senses of the term being exclusive—Blasphemy against the Holy Ghost is defined.—5. The solemnity, distinctness, and practical importance of this doctrine.—6. Fundamental character of the general doctrine of the Holy Ghost.

I.—1. THE salvation for sinners revealed in the word of God is a gratuitous and a divine salvation. The wages of sin is death; but the gift of God is eternal life, through Jesus Christ our Lord.[1] And the conception, the preparation, and the application to man, of all that whereby they escape the proper wages of sin—and are made partakers of the infinite gift of eternal life is wholly divine. It is God who bestows it all upon us; it is through Jesus Christ our Lord that we receive it all; and in order to receive it we must be born again—and that of the Spirit of God.[2] It is not only that God has brought life and immor-

[1] Rom., vi. 23.

[2] John, i. 12, 13, iii. 5.

tality to light by the Gospel, and that after we had forfeited and rejected both, and rendered ourselves alike unable and unwilling to seek effectually for either of them : nor is it only that Jesus Christ has accomplished for us at so great a cost, all that the Scriptures record concerning him : but it is, that in addition to all that is implied in both of these statements, the divine Spirit executes an infinite agency in making the work of Christ, and the mercy of God effectual to the ends which the Father and the Son have proposed. It is of unspeakable importance to us, therefore, to understand clearly, and to appreciate fully, the teachings of the word of God touching the person and office and work of the Holy Ghost. To sum them up is the particular object of this chapter.

2. It has been heretofore frequently shown, more or less particularly—though in an incidental way, and it was attempted, in the immediately preceding chapter to explain in a formal manner, what is the sum and result of the Scripture doctrine touching the Holy Ghost.* In the unity of the divine essence, the third of the three persons—the same in substance, equal in power and glory—is the Holy Ghost. Eternally proceeding from the Father and the Son—*breathed*—and hence his name—neither made, begotten, nor created, but very God and of one substance with the Father and the Son. It is he, whereby the Father and the Son, in a special manner, reciprocally dwell in each other— and by whom are effectuated the things, which proceed from the Father through the Son. We are now to examine the doctrine touching the mystery of this glorious being more in detail. And we ought to do it the more carefully and soberly—not only because of the immense importance and extreme difficulty of the subject itself ; but also because, in all ages, the minds of ungodly men have been, in a manner, set in them to disparage, to obscure, and to pervert this most precious and fundamental truth.

3. The Book of Genesis opens with the declaration, that in the beginning, when God created the heavens and the earth, the Spirit of God brooded upon the face of the creation.[1] And the Book of Revelation closes with the invitation solemnly reiterated by the Spirit and the Bride—that is the Church and the Holy Ghost—that whosoever will shall take of the water of life freely.[2]

* רוּחַ, πνευμα, Spiritus, the Spirit.   [1] Gen., i. 2   [2] Rev., xxii. 17.

And David and Isaiah both inform us,[1] that it was the Spirit of Jehovah, who thus brooded with almighty power, over the work of creation.   And all the Scriptures are full to the point, that the whole efficient agency of that new creation, through which we enter the kingdom of heaven, appertains to the same divine Spirit.[2]   It belongs to him, therefore, to concur, as Jehovah, in every form of the work of creation—physical and spiritual—original and redemptional—of which any knowledge has been imparted to us by God.   But, in order to contain what needs to be said within allowable limits, I will confine myself at present, more particularly to the relations of the Holy Ghost to the person and work of Christ, and to the life of God in the souls of men—while I attempt to illustrate his supreme Godhead and his divine personality.

II.—1. It has been abundantly proved that the doctrine of God manifest in the flesh—the Incarnation of the second person of the Holy Trinity—is the fundamental doctrine of the New Testament Scriptures, and that upon its truth depends the practical outworking of the Plan of Salvation.   But the Angel Gabriel said expressly to the Virgin Mary, the Holy Ghost shall come upon thee, and the power of the Highest shall overshadow thee : therefore also that holy thing which shall be born of thee, shall be called the Son of God.[3]   So that the Holy Ghost, is the Most High God, who formed the human nature of the Lord Jesus, in the womb of the Virgin Mary : and it is because these facts are so, that God was manifest in the flesh—that Jesus is truly called the Son of God—and that salvation is possible for lost sinners.

2. The whole life and ministry of Christ are full of proofs of the personal presence of the Holy Ghost with him, and therefore of the divine personality of the Spirit : as well as proofs of his infinite possession of the perfections of God, and therefore of his complete participation of the divine nature.   When Christ was brought, as a child, into the temple, Simeon, upon whom " the Holy Ghost was," and to whom it was revealed by the Holy Ghost that he should not see death, till he had seen the Lord's Christ, led of the Spirit, took up the child and blessed God saying, Mine eyes have seen thy salvation.[4]   The open testimony of

---

[1] Ps. xxxiii. 6, 7 ; Is., xl. 12–14.   [2] Tit., iii. 5, 6 ; John, xvi. 7, 8.
[3] Luke, i. 35.   [4] Luke, ii. 25–30.

John the Baptist was, that Christ's baptism of the people should be with the Holy Ghost and with fire : and when he was himself baptized of John, the Holy Ghost descended in a bodily form, like a dove upon him, and a voice came from heaven which said, Thou art my beloved Son ; in thee I am well pleased.[1] It is added that Jesus, being full of the Holy Ghost, returned from Jordan, and was led by the Spirit into the wilderness ; being forty days tempted of the Devil : and then he returned in the power of the Spirit into Galilee.[2] And at Nazareth, where he had been brought up, one Sabbath day in the commencement of his ministry; when they handed him the Book of the Prophet Esaias, he read out of it these sublime words : The Spirit of the Lord is upon me, because he hath anointed me to preach the Gospel to the poor ; he hath sent me to heal the broken hearted, to preach deliverance to the captives, and recovering of sight to the blind, to set at liberty them that are bruised, to preach the acceptable year of the Lord. And then under the fixed gaze of the multitude—so remarkable as to be noted by the sacred record, he said, This day is this Scripture fulfilled in your ears.[3] Now let it be considered, that all these occurrences are taken from a few consecutive pages, of a single Gospel, in the first four chapters of which, are no less than twelve allusions, by name, to the Holy Ghost, and it will readily be seen how constant and how immense is the testimony furnished in the life and ministry of the Lord Jesus, to the nature and work of the Spirit. And it is testimony of a kind, which is, from its very nature, not only decisive, but overwhelming. It is the testimony of one divine person, to another : the testimony of God the Son, to the nature and work of God the Spirit. There is therefore nothing left for us, but to accept the testimony, or to reject it and Christ together : and along with them, the whole fabric of revealed religion.

3. Besides the striking and multiplied testimonies which the Scriptures so carefully record, as having been given by the Holy Ghost, to the person and ministry of Christ, and by Christ to the nature and work of the Spirit—testimonies, whose import has already been explained : there are other representations still more remarkable, in which the infinite fitness of Christ, as well as his authority and ability, are ascribed to the abounding ful-

---

[1] Luke, iii. 16–22.   [2] Luke, iv. 12, 14.   [3] Luke, iv. 16–21; Isa., lxi. 1–3.

ness with which he was made partaker of the Holy Ghost. John the Baptist in assigning unanswerable reasons, why the words of Christ must be the words of God, contents himself with these two, namely, that God had sent him, and that he had given him his Spirit without measure.[1] Isaiah speaking in the name of Christ, in a passage which Christ applied to himself, as we have just seen, declares, that it was because the Spirit of the Lord God was upon him, and because of the divine unction so received, that he preached good tidings to the meek, that he bound up the broken hearted, that he proclaimed liberty to the captive ; and indeed that he performed all his glorious offices, of prophet, priest, and king.[2] David tells us, that this anointing of God, by God, as he expresses it, was an incomparable anointing :[3] and the New Testament writers are constant in their testimonies, that it was by means of it, that all fulness dwelt in Christ.[4] Insomuch that Jesus told the Pharisees that he even cast out devils by the Spirit of God ; and that therein lay the proof that the kingdom of God had come unto them.[5] Indeed the very name of the Son of God made flesh* is a divine and perpetual testimony, to the divinity of the Spirit, by which the Saviour of sinners was infinitely replenished for every part of his work, in his state of humiliation. Nay the very sacrifice of himself—and his resurrection from the dead, were both accomplished, by Jesus Christ, through the Holy Ghost. For it is expressly written, that through the eternal Spirit he offered himself without spot unto God ; and, that he was quickened by the Spirit.[6] And thus the blood of Christ which alone can purge our consciences from dead works, and the resurrection and exalted life of Christ, by which alone, we can be brought nigh to God—both as to the fact of the occurrence of these great mysteries, and as to our participation in their benefits—are directly connected with the supreme Godhead of the Eternal Spirit.

4. Our faith concerning the nature, person and work of the Holy Ghost, must be materially influenced by the judgment we form with regard to the sacred Scriptures, considered in their power, as well as in their truthfulness. Undeniably, if they are worthy of credit at all, their very nature makes the testimony

---

[1] John, iii. 34.   [2] Isa., lxi. 1–3 ; Luke, iv. 18.   [3] Psalm xlv. 7.   [4] Col., i. 19, ii. 9.
[5] Mat., xii. 28.   * מָשִׁיחַ—Χριστος—unctus, anointed—Christ.
[6] Heb., ix. 14 ; Rom., viii. 11 ; 1 Pet., iii. 18.

they bear upon this, as upon all other subjects, absolutely conclusive. But that is not the view of the subject, to which I now allude. These Scriptures let them contain what they may, are nothing less than a gross imposture ; or else they are absolutely, and throughout inspired by the Holy Ghost. There is no point upon which they are more explicit than that all Scripture is given by inspiration of God : and that whatever is profitable for doctrine, for reproof, for correction or for instruction in righteousness is contained therein ; insomuch that they are able to make us wise unto salvation.[1] And what is meant by the Scriptures being given by inspiration of God is clearly explained to us : it means that Holy Men of God spake as they were moved by the Holy Ghost.[2] Here then, in this vast and mysterious work which we call the Bible—altogether the most wonderful monument which distinguishes and commemorates the existence of our race upon this earth—we have the Holy Ghost set before us, in a manner, which enables us to form the very fairest judgment of him. It is true, he has used many different men, through many centuries to speak as he moved them. But however that may have increased the difficulty of his work, he still declares the work to be his—to be divine, and to be able to make us wise unto salvation. Nothing can be more direct or explicit than this mode of putting the question. Nor is there any thing touching the whole question of God and our souls, that we are more competent to determine. As these Scriptures are, so is the Holy Ghost, who is the author of them, and who, in them, professes to teach us with infinite certainty and with divine authority, what man ought to believe concerning God and what duty God requires of man. Either way, the question is settled. For if the rule of faith and duty is perfect, their testimony is irresistible in every point of view : if otherwise their author is condemned by his own work. It is in this manner that humble and even ignorant Christians, derive from the simple study of the word of God, such profound convictions of its divine truth and authority—by being brought face to face with the Eternal Spirit. And it is through sinful neglect of this unerring source of spiritual light and life, that many who consider themselves instructed, and even learned Christians, stagger through life, under a load of doubts and heresies. They may not in either case have an-

[1] 2 Tim., iii. 15, 16.   [2] 2 Pet., i. 21.

alyzed the cause of their spiritual condition.   It is that which I have now attempted to do.

5. There is no aspect of revealed religion in which the nature of God is more remarkably displayed, both as it relates to his infinite Spirituality, to the unity of his essence, and to the subsistence of that one Spiritual essence, in three persons—co-equal and consubstantial ; than in the entire treatment of the whole question of the divine oracles.   The Scriptures are the word of God.   But they are also, in a most peculiar sense, the word of the Son of God—God the Word ; and therein, as has been shown in a former chapter, they are specially appurtenant to Christ the Mediator of the Covenant of Grace, and with intense emphasis to his office as Prophet—the *Great Teacher.* But again, it is the divine Spirit by whom all Scripture is given : he is the Inspirer—he the Revealer.   Representations to the effect of each of these statements, are beyond computation throughout the sacred Scriptures : nor is it possible to comprehend the scope of these Scriptures, nor to interpret a single capital passage of them, nor to understand one fundamental doctrine touching our salvation stated in them, without making account of statements involving all these relations of the Godhead to the written word.   Nor do the Scriptures themselves manifest the slightest consciousness, that there is any thing involved in such statements, which can perplex the believer, or which requires a separate divine explanation.   Whether the utterance is in the name of God, absolutely considered ; or in the name of the Father, or of the Son, or of the Holy Ghost separately ; or in the names of all three unitedly : still it is a divine utterance, and every renewed heart will so recognize and receive it, and every awakened soul will more or less apprehend it, as he is more or less aroused from the torpor of sin.   The use of this exposition here, is to point out the remarkable evidence thus afforded of the nature of the divine existence, in the very structure of the Scriptures, and in the fundamental relations of the Holy Ghost to the person and work of the Son of God, in his office as the great Teacher of all truth unto salvation ; and therein to set before us, in its elemental form, the mystery of the Spirit as one of the persons of the Godhead, and of the substance thereof, in his perpetual relation to the Saviour of the world.

III.—The Spirit of God was always known, wherever any

true knowledge of God existed ; and he was always that person of the Trinity, by which God dwelt in the souls of men, and effectually communicated with them. But the testimonies of his presence and power were greatly multiplied during the life and ministry of Christ. And the crucifixion, and subsequent resurrection and ascension of the Redeemer, were made occasions for additional revelations concerning him ; and for new and glorious exhibitions of his relations to the Father and to the Son, and to the whole work of man's redemption ; as well as for elucidating more perfectly, many things that had been revealed to the fathers, but not understood, or not heeded by men.

1. After the resurrection of Jesus, and in his last interview with his Apostles before his ascension into heaven, he commanded them that they should not depart from Jerusalem, but wait for the promise of the Father, which, said he, ye have heard of me. For John truly baptized with water ; but ye shall be baptized with the Holy Ghost, not many days hence.[1] These commandments, we are expressly told, were given by Christ to his Apostles, " through the Holy Ghost."[2] And it will be observed that they are capable of being comprehended, or executed, only upon the condition, that the doctrine of the Trinity is true, and that it is well understood. For here is Christ, the second person of the Trinity, who was declared to be the Son of God with power, in the resurrection from the dead, giving commandment concerning a remarkable promise of the Father—the first person —to be speedily executed through the Holy Ghost, the third person. And upon the fulfilment of this promise, which was nothing less than the baptism of the Apostles by the Holy Ghost, it is openly stated by Christ before his ascension, must depend the very commencement, and therefore the very existence, and indeed the very possibility of the mission and work of the Apostles themselves. The Apostles, anxious and, even yet, knowing but imperfectly their own vocation, asked him, Lord, wilt thou at this time restore again the kingdom to Israel ?[3] His answer was most remarkable. Paraphrased it would run thus : That of which you inquire, is reserved exclusively to the Father, and the knowledge of it and of its times and seasons, is not for you : Your mission is to be witnesses for me, and you will be qualified and anointed for it by the Holy Ghost, who will come upon you:

<hr>

[1] Acts, i. 4, 5.   [2] Acts, i. 2.   [3] Acts, i. 6.

and this, and not the restoration of the kingdom to Israel, is the promise of the Father to which I allude. And these were his last words to them.[1] When the day of Pentecost was fully come, the great promise of the Father was fulfilled : the Apostles were all filled with the Holy Ghost, and all of them began to speak with other tongues, as the Spirit gave them utterance.[2] Then they comprehended all. And Peter stood up, and speaking to the multitude, said, This is that which was spoken by the prophet Joel.[3] And then he quoted and applied a prophecy uttered eight centuries before : and showed that the time for the pouring out of God's Spirit on all flesh, and for the doing of all wonders, and for the free offer of salvation to all men, had fully come. The great promise of the Father was fulfilled. The Holy Ghost has come upon them : and so, on the one hand, he attests that Christ's work is accepted of God, and that he is the witness that the Son is glorified, and that he has been himself sent by the Father and the Son ; and on the other hand, he baptizes the Apostles, of himself, for their glorious witness-bearing, to the ends of the earth : and then, initiating the kingdom of Christ with *power*—the dispensation of the Holy Ghost—he converted three thousand souls the same day ![4] Looking at this whole matter of the promise of the Father, the glorification of the Son, and the outpouring of the Spirit, on the day of Pentecost : considering the manner in which the whole transaction stands related to the Jewish dispensation, which it closed—to the New Testament Church which it initiated with power—and to the whole economy of salvation—and the whole nature of God as revealed in the Scriptures : I confess myself unable to imagine any thing short of judicial blindness, that can lead a student of the Scriptures to deny that they teach the divine personality, and the supreme divinity of the Holy Ghost.

2. There is another aspect of this intimate relation of the Spirit to the Father and the Son—another proof of the unity of purpose and operation in the Godhead, working out the salvation of sinners—which seems to me to be not less convincing than the one just explained, and not less conclusive as to the nature and office of the Holy Ghost. In all the work of Christ there is a constant reference, by him, to the Father ; and while he

<hr>

[1] Acts, i. 3–11.   [2] Acts, ii. 1–4.   [3] Acts, ii. 14–21.   [4] Acts, ii. 41.

never hesitated to declare absolutely that he and the Father are one ; and while he constantly manifested that his natural form was that of God, and that he thought it no robbery to be equal with God : yet, on the other hand his allusions were continually to him who sent him—to him from whom he received his doctrine—to him whose will he regarded more than his own—to him whose work he came to do, and which it behooved him, in season and out of season, to be about. This double aspect of the character of Christ, is like the double aspect of the prophecies that relate to him. Both of them are, on the one hand, the surest proof of the truth, to them who seek it in sincerity—since a Messiah to suffer and a Messiah to triumph, are both alike predicted ;—and Christ who was divine, and Christ who was human, did actually come : but, on the other hand, both are a terrible rock of offence and stumbling, to those who will see no Messiah in the prophecies, except one who shall suffer only or reign only, and no Christ in the gospel, except one who is human only, or divine only. The real Christ of the gospel wrought out the salvation for man, which sprang from the eternal love of God the Father : and therefore, at every step, the relation of Christ to the Father, and of the Father to salvation through Christ—is exhibited to us. Now when the work is done and Christ is glorified, there arises a new condition of things, as we have seen, in which the purpose of the Father, and the work of Christ are to be effectually applied : and there occurs an agency of the Spirit more glorious than had ever before been exhibited in accomplishing this great salvation. And the point, to which attention is here immediately directed, is, how Christ becomes, under the dispensation of the Spirit, the capital object—just as the Father had been the capital object, during the personal ministry of Christ : how the Spirit, in giving efficacy to the work of Christ, has incessant reference to Christ, just as Christ, in executing the work of the Father, had incessant reference to him : and how this great analogy and proportion of faith, and this glorious working of all the persons of the Trinity—opens to us, at the same time, the economy of salvation, and the infinite being of God. The first of the incontrovertible truths of the mystery of godliness, says Paul, is, that God was manifest in the flesh : the second is, that he is justified in the Spirit.[1] So that

---

[1] 1 Tim., iii. 16.

there is no office, nor any work, nor any exercise of the Spirit in the matter of our salvation, that is without reference to what Christ is and does ; nor is there, in all that relates to the Son of God as he is the Redeemer of men, any thing whatever, that the Holy Ghost does not accept as perfect, and use to the glory of God, with that power and demonstration which appertain to him. Of him, that came by water and blood, even Jesus Christ —there are three that bear witness on earth, namely the Spirit and the water and the blood, and they agree in one : and there are three that bear record in heaven, namely the Father, the Word, and the Holy Ghost, and they are one.[1] And by all this boundless testimony, Christ himself has told us, the Holy Ghost will glorify him. For he will convince the world of sin, because they have not believed in Jesus ; of righteousness, because he is gone to the Father, and we see him no more ; of judgment, because the Prince of this world is judged. And as all things that the Father hath are Christ's ; and it is the office of the Spirit, to take of the things of Christ and show them unto us : he that is the Spirit of truth will guide us into all truth.[2] And so, by him, in a work of infinite light and power, Christ Jesus is of God, made unto us wisdom, and righteousness, and sanctification, and redemption.[3]

3. But there is somewhat more, and if possible still more intimate in the relation of the Holy Ghost, to the person, the work, and the glory of Christ—and therein on the one side, to the Godhead, and on the other, to the souls of men. I have just explained how every thing is accomplished, under the dispensation of the Spirit, in the name and on account of Christ, and so as to justify and to glorify him : and I have previously shown how all is effected by the Holy Ghost himself, beginning on the day of Pentecost when the great promise of the Father, concerning the last days, began to be fulfilled. What I now allude to is, that over and above all that is involved in all this, the Holy Ghost has been put in actual possession, administration and dominion of the kingdom of Christ in this world—so that he is to all intents and purposes his vicar therein.[4] To this he has been appointed by a joint act of the Father and the Son : and his dominion and authority will continue until the Lord Jesus shall return the sec-

----

[1] 1 John, v. 6–8.   [2] John, xvi. 7–15.   [3] 1 Cor., i. 30.
[4] Isa., xlviii. 16 ; Acts, x. 18–20, xiii. 2–4, xvi. 6.

ond time, without sin unto salvation. The divine Redeemer came into the world to offer himself up a sacrifice for sin : and as the time drew near he more and more revealed to his followers his impending death, with the manner and the fruits of it. At length he said to them plainly, Now I go my way to him that sent me :[1] and then added, It is expedient for you that I go away : for if I go not away the Comforter will not come unto you : but if I depart, I will send him unto you.[2] The Comforter he had before expressly told them, proceeded from the Father :[3] that he was the Holy Ghost, whom the Father would send in Christ's name :[4] and that this act of the Father was not only with the Son's consent, but at his request, and performed for the reason that the Comforter might abide with us forever.[5] He is the Spirit of truth to dwell in us and to be with us ;[6] the teacher of all things, and the remembrancer of all things, uttered by Christ :[7] the reprover and convincer of the world :[8] the sole guide of men into all truth, and the only revealer of things to come :[9] the glorifier of Jesus, and the true discloser of all that relates to him.[10] Now all this mass of testimony is found in a few sentences uttered by Christ, and recorded in one of the Gospels. I rest on it, merely as consulting a proper brevity ; for the Scriptures are full of statements of the same import. When we compare it with Christ's commands to his Apostles just before his ascent into heaven—concerning the Father's promise to pour out the Spirit : and with what actually occurred on the day of Pentecost : and with the miraculous administration of the Spirit during the entire period from the day of Pentecost, to the closing of the canon of Scripture : and with the gracious administration of the same Spirit from that day to this—so far as history has informed us, or we have been personally witnesses of the work of the Holy Spirit amongst men : it is utterly impossible to evade the conclusion that the words of Christ were spoken with a divine foreknowledge—that they have been executed with infinite certainty and exactness—and that they have been attended with an almighty power. I pass by many questions naturally springing up in the track of these vast ideas ; as my object is merely to illustrate one fundamental doctrine—the doc-

[1] John, xvi. 5.   [2] Ver. 7.   [3] John, xiv. 26.   [4] John, xiv. 26.
[5] John, xiv. 16.   [6] John, xiv. 17.   [7] Ver. 26.   [8] John, xvi. 8.
[9] Ver. 13.   [10] Ver. 15.

trine of the Holy Ghost. And it seems to me that the considerations thrown together in this paragraph, leave us no alternative
but to accept the doctrine of the divine nature, and true personality of the Spirit, in the sense of one God, in three persons, of
which he is one ; and to accept along with this, the plan of salvation as absolutely dependent upon that conception of the
divine existence : or else, to reject the Scriptures utterly, and
grope through darkness and sin—with Atheism or Superstition
as our only refuge against despair.

4. It may be proper, in a few words, to gather out of the
thousands of references of the Scriptures to the Spirit, some of
the more obvious, in order that in this manner, as well as by
such exhibitions as I have already made, we may the more clearly
perceive and the more intelligently accept, the truth revealed to
us on a subject so momentous. I therefore observe, that the
Holy Ghost must necessarily be a divine person, like the Father
and the Son ; and as to his essence must be along with them,
one and the only true God : *Because*, 1. he is frequently and
expressly called God in the Scriptures.[1] 2. Because he is eternal, immense, omnipotent and omniscient.[2] 3. Because he is
the Creator and preserver of all creatures and all things.[3] 4. Because he dwells in the hearts of believers, as in a temple, which
is declared to be proper only to the true God.[4] 5. Because we
are baptized in his name, as well as in those of the Father and
the Son.[5] 6. Because we are required to believe in him, equally,
as in the Father and the Son.[6] 7. Because he is the author of
all that is spiritually good, and is to be invoked in the same
manner as the Father and the Son.[7] 8. Because it is declared
that no one is good but God, and yet the Spirit is declared to be
good.[8] 9. Because it is revealed that God alone can justify us,
and yet it is revealed that the Spirit justifies us.[9] 10. Because
God is said to be the author of all consolation, and yet the Spirit

---

[1] 2 Sam., xxiii., 2, 3; Isa., v. 8, 9; Acts, xxviii. 25, 26; Luke, i. 68–70; 2 Pet., i. 21;
Acts, v. 4; 1 Cor., iii. 16, 17, vi. 19; 2 Cor., vi. 16, xii. 4–6.

[2] Gen., i. 2; Psalm cxxxix. 7; John, xvi. 13; 1 Cor., ii. 10.

[3] Gen., i. 2; Job, xvi. 13, xxxiii. 3; Psalm xxxiii. 6.

[4] Rom., viii. 9–11; 1 Cor., iii. 16, vi. 19; 2 Cor., vi. 16; Levit., xxvi. 12.

[5] Mat., xxviii. 19; Mark, xvi. 15.   [6] 2 Cor., xiii. 14; Mat., xxviii. 19

[7] 1 Cor., xxii. 14; Rev., i. 4.

[8] Mat., xix. 17; Mark, x. 18; Luke, xviii. 19 · Psalm cxliii. 10.

[9] Rom., iv. 5; 1 Cor., vi. 11.

is called expressly the Comforter.[1]   11. Because while it is taught that God alone can teach men inwardly—it is also taught that the Spirit is the great inward teacher of men.[2]   12. Because although it is declared that we are made free only by the work of God, it is still declared that the Spirit sets us free.[3]   13. Because while all wisdom and power of utterance and gifts of tongues are said to be conferred by God alone, yet the Spirit is said to confer them all.[4]   14. Because the leading of the ancient people of God out of Egypt is declared to be the work of God, and yet it is ascribed to the Spirit.[5]   15. Because the rebellion of Israel which is pronounced to have been against the true and eternal God, is pronounced to have been against the Holy Ghost.[6]   16. Because the divine command that we shall not tempt the Holy Ghost, is precisely similar to the divine command that we shall not tempt God.[7]   17: Because while we are commanded to walk exclusively in the way of the Lord, and hear only his words, we are commanded in like manner, to hear and obey the words of the Holy Ghost.[8]   18. Because those commands and instructions which are repeatedly ascribed' to the true God, are also repeatedly ascribed to the Holy Spirit.[9]   And so we might go on through forms, and statements, and exhibitions, well nigh innumerable, and embracing, first and last, every salient point of divine revelation.   Upon the supposition of such a mode of the divine existence as the doctrine of the Trinity necessarily implies ;   and upon the further supposition of an attempt on the part of God existing in that manner, to save such sinners as we are : it is perfectly obvious that a complete revelation, such as the Bible purports to be, of the method of that proposed salvation—must present in a great multitude of ways and on an immense variety of occasions—the actual nature of the Godhead, and the various relations of the persons of the Trinity to each other, to us, and to the work of redemption : and that all these presentations, without exception, must accord with the absolute

---

[1] Rom., xv. 5 : 1 Cor., i. 3 ; John, xiv. 16, xvi. 26.

[2] Isa., liv. 13 ; John, vi. 45 ; Luke, xii. 12 ; Rom., viii. 26.   [3] 1 Cor., iii. 17.

[4] Exod., iv. 11 ; James, i. 5, 17 ; Mat., x. 19, 20 ; Luke, xii. 14, 15 ; Acts, ii. 14; 1 Cor., ii. 13, xii. 8.   [5] Isa., lxiii. 12–14.

[6] Psalm lxxviii. 40 ; Isa., lxiii. 10.   [7] Deut., vi. 16 ; Mat., iv. 7 ; Acts, v. 9.

[8] Ezek., xx. 18, 19 ; Luke, xi. 28 ; Rev., ii. 7, 17, 29.

[9] Levit., xxvi. 12, 13 ; Psalm xcv. 7, 8 ; Isa., vi. 7, 9 ; Acts, xxviii. 25, 26 ; 1 Cor., iii. 6, vi. 19 ; 2 Cor., vi. 16 ; Heb., iii. 7–9.

reality of God's being and purpose and work. The absurdity of supposing that God could thus speak to us continually, of himself, and of us, and of all the relations between him and us, and not involve in these utterances any clear knowledge of his own being, is one of those imbecile fancies of heresy, near akin to that most puerile atheistical conceit, that an infinite God can act with infinite force continually throughout a boundless universe, and before the faces of intelligent beings, and they, nevertheless, shall see no rational or credible manifestation of his existence. What blinds us in both cases, is voluntary ignorance and abominable wickedness.

5. Amongst these multiplied exhibitions of the nature, office, and work of the Holy Ghost, as revealed in the Scriptures, there is a distinct view of his immediate relations to us, which places the whole subject in an extremely clear light. He is called the *Holy* Spirit—the *Holy* Ghost—most commonly, throughout the Scriptures. A most holy and pure Spirit, and the fountain, cause, and author of all holiness and purity in us. He is called also the Spirit of Truth—as we have seen abundantly.[1] The inspirer of all divine truth ; the true author of all that all holy men of God have spoken, when moved by him ; and our only effectual and inward teacher in the true knowledge of God. He is also called the Spirit of Life : and the Scriptures expressly state that it is not only he who will quicken our mortal bodies, but that it is he who sets us free from the power of sin and death.[2] For as they clearly teach us, we are renewed by the Holy Ghost which God hath shed on us abundantly through Jesus Christ our Saviour :[3] and nothing concerning the kingdom of God is more certain, than that no man can enter it except he be born of water and the Spirit.[4] As for us, we have lost the image of God in which we were created, and we must recover it or perish forever. We must be born again, is the doctrine so pressed by Christ on Nicodemus :[5] and this is it. We are his workmanship, created in Christ Jesus unto good works.[6] Our new man is created in righteousness and true holiness, after God.[7] It is renewed in knowledge after the image of him that created him.[8] The Spirit of life quickens us : and we are renewed in the image of him

[1] John, xiv. 17, xv. 26, xvi. 13. [2] Rom., viii. 2, 12. [3] Tit., i. 4–6. [4] John, iii. 5.
[5] John, iii. *passim*. [6] Eph., ii. 10. [7] Eph., iv. 24. [8] Col., iii. 10.

that created us. The Spirit of truth shows us the things of Christ, and leads us into all truth : and we are renewed in knowledge. The Holy Spirit works in us a real righteousness and a true holiness : and being his workmanship, created in Christ Jesus, unto good works, we are led on, by him, from one degree of grace and strength unto another, until we appear before God, perfect in Zion.[1] He gives us a true, a new, and an immortal life : a life not such as that inherited from the first Adam, who was a living soul, but such as that derived from the Second Adam, who was a quickening Spirit.[2] But this new creation, though as real as the first, is widely different from it. That was an original and primary creation—the dust of the earth became man : and God did it by the word of his power. This is a regeneration of an actual and existing man—fallen and depraved—but rational and accountable—into an heir of God and a joint heir with Jesus Christ ; a new man, and yet the same ; and this creation is by the word of grace, and through the Spirit of truth as well as the Spirit of life. And this whole new life, and this divine truth, upon which the new life is nourished, by the Spirit of God, is unto righteousness and true holiness ; and so it is the Holy Ghost that doth it all. Without entering further into these topics, than is barely necessary to elucidate the point immediately under discussion—I may be permitted to say that there is something infinitely remarkable in this wonderful fitting, not only of the nature, and office, and work, but even of the very appellations of the Eternal Spirit, to all the phases and necessities of the glorious mission he accomplishes, and, to all the wants of the fallen being he restores to God—and to all the infinite blessings and benefits given to him when he has been reclaimed. It is indeed these simple yet profound and powerful outworkings of Scripture truth, which invest our present inquiries with a true spirituality, and tend to make us better men, as we strive to become better Theologians.

IV. There remains one very remarkable aspect of the doctrine of the Holy Ghost, which is so distinctly insisted on in the Scriptures, that it cannot be passed over in silence ; and yet, concerning which there is so much difference of opinion, and, in general, such great obscurity in the minds of Christian people —that it must be considered becoming in each individual teacher

---

[1] Ps. lxxxiv. 7.   [2] 1 Cor., xv. 45.

to speak with much diffidence about it. I allude to what is commonly called the *unpardonable sin;* about which I proceed to sum up briefly, the teaching of the word of God.

1. Whatever may be the particular nature of this sin, it is perfectly clear that there is, as the Apostle John expresses it, a sin unto death ; which, he adds, I do not say that he shall pray for it.[1] And the Apostle Paul teaching the same fearful truth, with the greatest solemnity ; warns us in one emphatic passage, that there are those whom it is impossible to renew again unto repentance :[2] and in another that there are those to whom nothing remains but a certain fearful looking for of judgment.[3] And Christ himself has taught us with the utmost clearness, that there is a sin which shall not be forgiven, neither in this world, neither in the world to come.[4]

2. It is equally certain that this sin has direct and immediate reference to the person, office, and work of the Holy Ghost, and through him to the person, office, and work of the Lord Christ. Not primarily to Christ, for he said, in express reference to this sin, whoever speaketh a word against the Son of Man, it shall be forgiven him : but whosoever speaketh against the Holy Ghost, it shall not be forgiven him, neither in this world, neither in the world to come.[5] And yet, of those whom it is impossible to renew again unto repentance it is said, seeing they crucify unto themselves the Son of God afresh, and put him to an open shame :[6] and of those to whom nothing is left but a certain fearful looking for of judgment and fiery indignation, which shall devour the adversaries, it is said they have trodden under foot the Son of God, and counted the blood of the covenant, an unholy thing, and done despite unto the Spirit of grace.[7] Against the Holy Ghost, therefore, primarily and directly, is this sin perpetrated : and yet against Christ also, as his person and work are exhibited and applied by the Holy Ghost—and so also, once more, against the Holy Ghost, as he is the justifier, the glorifier, the testifier of Christ—or in one word, his Vicar, as I have before expressed it. Against the Holy Ghost, therefore, absolutely, as to his nature, and person : and then further, against the Holy Ghost, as to his office and his work in the matter of our salvation :

---

[1] 1 John, v. 16.   [2] Heb., vi. 1–6.   [3] Heb., x. 27–31.
[4] Mat., xii. 31 · Mark, iii. 29 ; Luke, xii. 10.   [5] Mat., xii. 32.
[6] Heb., vi. 6.   [7] Heb., x. 27–29.

in other words, against the only efficient agent in man's salvation, and against the only effective ground of his agency—is this transgression.   We need not wonder, therefore, that it should be fatal. And we can readily see to what a height the whole case carries the proof of the unity of the Godhead, and the divine nature and personality of the Holy Ghost.

3. The particular nature of this sin against the Holy Ghost, is further and plainly declared. It is repeatedly called blasphemy against the Holy Ghost: and it is never called by any name, or described in any manner inconsistent therewith.   In Matthew xii. 31, Christ calls it, the blasphemy against the Holy Ghost.   In Mark iii. 28, he speaks of him who commits it, as he that shall blaspheme against the Holy Ghost.   In Luke xii. 10, he denounces him that blasphemeth against the Holy Ghost. And in all these places, the Saviour explicitly declares that he who is guilty of this blasphemy shall never be forgiven : and such is the doctrine taught in every other place in the Scriptures, where any clear allusion is made to the subject.[1]

4. It is fundamental, therefore, in any attempt to get a more precise idea of the nature of this sin, than that it is blasphemy against the Holy Ghost, to ascertain what sense our Saviour attributed to the term *blasphemy :* and it is for lack of attending to this that much of the obscurity which environs the subject in the minds of Christians has probably arisen.   Let us then settle that point.   (*a*) They brought to our Saviour one possessed of a devil, blind and dumb ; and he healed him.   The people were greatly amazed, and inclined to believe in Christ : but the Pharisees said, as they commonly did, This fellow doth not cast out devils, but by Beelzebub the prince of the devils. Jesus, expounding the absurdity and impiety of this accusation of the Pharisees—declaring and proving that he cast out devils by the Spirit of God—denounced them as a generation of vipers, incapable of speaking a good thing : and, in the midst of that exposition and rebuke, uttered the terrible words concerning the general nature of the blasphemy against the Holy Ghost, and the absolute certainty that it should never be forgiven.[2]   Here, then, is the precise significance of what occurred : Christ cast out a devil, and said he did it by the Spirit of God : the Pharisees said he did it by Beelzebub : Christ pronounced this blasphemy

<hr>

[1] Heb., vi., 1–6, x. 26–29; 1 John, v. 16.   [2] Mat., xi. 22–37.

against the Holy Ghost. Explicitly, therefore, obstinately to attribute the work of the Spirit to the devil, or to any unclean spirit, and, more generally, to attribute wickedly and knowingly the work of the Spirit to any other than the Spirit, so as to rob the Spirit of his glory and due, is blasphemy against the Holy Ghost, and is unpardonable.[1] (*b*) There is another view of the subject which supplements this, clearly presented, though, perhaps, not so directly. Thus: when the high priest adjured Jesus to tell them whether he was the Christ, the Son of the living God: and Jesus admitted that he was; the high priest rent his clothes, saying, He hath spoken blasphemy; what further need have we of witness? behold now ye have heard his blasphemy. And to this they all agreed, and adjudged him guilty of death; which, if he had not been the Son of God—which he made himself to be—would have been a righteous judgment, according to the Mosaic law.[2] And to this exposition of the law, and of blasphemy, Jesus made no objection, either then or on various other occasions, when substantially the same thing occurred.[3] Explicitly then, it is blasphemy to pretend to be God, or to pretend to do the works of God, when those pretensions are known to be false. And, more generally, it is blasphemy against the Holy Ghost to assume to do his office and work, and knowingly and wickedly to rob the Spirit of his glory and his due, by substituting ourselves, or any thing else, in his room, or by denying the need or the reality of what he doth.

(*c*) Except in these two senses, I find not the Saviour, or the New Testament Scriptures, using or allowing the term blasphemy, with any reference to the Holy Ghost, or to the sin against him. In these two senses I find the Saviour and the writers of the New Testament Scriptures, repeatedly using and allowing the term. I therefore conclude that blasphemy against the Holy Ghost, and by consequence the unpardonable sin, consists in obstinately and wickedly denying and insulting the Holy Ghost and his work, and in attributing to some other than the Spirit works which are put in the place of his works, and which are pretended to be his, or equivalent thereto.

5. Considered in this manner the subject assumes the distinctness, solemnity and immense practical importance, which,

[1] Mark, iii. 22–30.   [2] Mat., xxvi., 63–67; Deut., xxiv. 16; John, xix. 7.
[3] Mark, xiv. 60–65; Luke, v. 20–26; John, x 33.

in the frequent allusions to it in the Scriptures, always invest it. There is hardly any point in which the declarations of Christ are more earnest or clear.   And accepting as true the general doctrine of the Holy Ghost as herein set forth, nothing seems more inevitable than that they who account his regenerating and sanctifying work to be a delusion, a superstition, or a heresy—must perish : that they who substitute idols, or men making themselves to be God, or pretended sacraments, or beggarly elements, or any thing else, as the power that is to save men, instead of the power of the Holy Ghost, thereby seal themselves up in the gall of bitterness, and unto perdition.   And how it is possible that they, who do always resist the Holy Ghost ;[1] they who open their mouths even in their pretended religious rites but to blaspheme the name of God ;[2] they whose very emblems of existence and dominion are covered with names of blasphemy :[3] they whose most sacred functions are set forth by themselves, as being a repetition of the sacrifice of Calvary—and are denounced by God as being a crucifying unto themselves, of the Son of God afresh, and putting him to an open shame ;[4] they, in fine, who throughout all ages, and of whatever name or pretension, and upon whatever pretence reject and dishonor the Holy Ghost ; how is it possible that they should escape that which God has threatened from the very earliest ages of his church ?   They have blasphemed the Holy Ghost.   God has declared that his Spirit should not always strive with man.[5]   There is no other way to be saved. And so by a fearful and inevitable necessity, their sin becomes a sin unto death.[6]

6. In the matter of our salvation it necessarily follows from all that has been said, that the doctrine of the Holy Ghost is absolutely fundamental.   The doctrine, not of a Spiritual influence, but of a divine Spirit : not of God manifesting himself in a particular manner, but of God the Spirit applying to us the benefits of Christ's redemption : not of divine persuasion and Spiritual inducement to us, but of a real and powerful work within us, whereby the Holy Ghost enables and inclines us to work out our salvation—he himself working in us to will and to do according to the good pleasure of God.   All that God the Father has purposed to do for us in his eternal love, or to exact from us

---

[1] Acts, vii. 51.   [2] Rev., xiii. 6.   [3] Rev., xiii. 1.
[4] Heb., vi. 6.   [5] Gen., vi. 3.   [6] John, v. 16.

in his eternal justice : all that God the Son has wrought out for us, in both respects, as Immanuel, Mediator, Prophet, Priest, and King : all this, God the Holy Ghost makes practically and personally available to, and in the redeemed. Without his work for us and in us, salvation is no more possible, than it is without what the Son has done and suffered, or without what the Father has proposed for our deliverance. And if we will but consider our low, depraved and lost condition, we cannot fail to see the inexpressible power and wisdom manifested in what the Spirit does for us, as well as the unutterable condescension exhibited in his method of doing it—in a light corresponding entirely with the eternal love of the Father, and the boundless grace of the Son. Grace, mercy, and peace, from God the Father, and the Lord Jesus Christ, are made the portion of the saints and multiplied unto them only through the Holy Ghost.[1]

[1] 1 Pet., i. 2.

CHAPTER XVII.

THE PERFECTIONS OF GOD: GENERAL CLASSIFICATION OF THE DIVINE ATTRIBUTES.

I. 1. General Statement of the Subject.—2. Summary of the chief methods of classification; (*a*) Proper and Metaphorical Attributes; (*b*) Negative and Positive Attributes; (*c*) Absolute and Relative Attributes; (*d*) Internal and External Attributes; (*e*) Communicable and Incommunicable Attributes.—3. Their insufficiency. —II. 1. Necessity for some classification.—2. The principle on which it should proceed.—3. The first Class: *Primary* Attributes: God considered simply as an Infinite Self-existence.—4. Second Class: *Essential* Attributes: God considered as an Infinite Spirit; under which illustrative statements connected with: (*a*) The Divine Intellect: (*b*) The Divine Will; (*c*) The Divine Power.—5. Third Class: *Natural* Attributes: Infinite Knowledge and Wisdom.—6. Fourth Class: *Moral* Attributes: Infinite Goodness, Justice; and the like.—7. Fifth Class: *Consummate* Attributes: Omnipresence, All-sufficiency; and the like.—8. Connected statement and illustration of the proposed classification.

I.—1. I AM now to pass in review, through several successive chapters, those perfections of God, whose consideration is most necessary to our knowledge of him; and especially those which exhibit him most completely in his relation to us, as our Creator, Ruler and Judge, and also as our Preserver, Benefactor and Redeemer. The whole subject covers the most difficult part of Theology, considered as a science; indeed, the most difficult part of human knowledge; and this was one of the considerations which led me to adopt such a method of teaching the whole science, as would not bring us to this portion of it, until the mind had become familiarized, in some degree, to this kind of inquiry, and certain truths, of the greatest importance in themselves, had been first clearly settled, both concerning God and ourselves. For a similar reason I prefer to pass over the Attributes themselves in a general manner, now that the point for their consideration has been reached, before attempting any detailed consideration of them; and to lay open the grounds of a rational classification of them, by means of which the immense difficulties of their separate consideration, may be, in some degree alleviated.

2. The chief classifications of the Attributes of God which have been heretofore suggested—as far as I have discovered—are these which follow :

(*a*) They have been sometimes distributed into two classes, called respectively, Proper Attributes of God, and Metaphorical Attributes of God. By the former, meaning such as in a proper sense belong to his nature ; and by the latter, such as properly express human affections, or the qualities of created things, applied metaphorically to God. As Justice, Goodness and Wisdom, are Proper Attributes ; but to say of God that he is consuming like fire, raging like a lion, and so on, is only to speak metaphorically.

(*b*) Again, they have been classified as Negative and Positive —having reference, by that distinction, only to our finite manner of conceiving them. And thus God's Infinity, Immensity, Independency, Invisibility, and the like, would be called Negative ; that is, be stated in a way of negation ; while his Wisdom, Goodness, Justice, and the like, would be called Positive ; that is, perfections which are eminent in God as we conceive of him.

(*c*) Others have distinguished them as Absolute and Relative —signifying thereby the relation of some of them to God himself, as being, so to speak, absolute in him ; and the relation of others, both to the creatures and to the absolute Attributes in which they are founded. Thus, Goodness would be considered an absolute Attribute ; while Mercy would be considered a relative one—as being founded in Goodness, but having a special relevancy to the creature ; and in like manner, Immensity would be considered an absolute, and Omnipresence a relative Attribute ; Holiness an absolute, and Punitive Justice a relative Attribute ; and so of the rest.

(*d*) The Attributes of God were divided into Internal and External, during the predominance of the Cartesian Philosophy, in order to accommodate Theology to the exigencies of that system. According to that method, two Attributes, namely, Intellect and Will, are considered Internal ; and all others are called External, as being only Relations or Negations, which are Attributes of God, considered with reference to external things.

(*e*) Perhaps the most general method of their distribution is, to distinguish them into Communicable and Incommunicable ; by the former, meaning such as we find some analogy to, more or less obscure, in the creature ; and by the latter, such as are exactly opposite to what exists in all creatures. The Attributes called Communicable, are especially God's Wisdom, Goodness and Justice ; those called Incommunicable, are chiefly his Independence, Simplicity, Immateriality, Eternity and Immensity.

3. Without discussing any of these classifications, it is very obvious to remark, that their number and the great diversity of the principles upon which they proceed—show plainly the difficulty of suggesting any clear, simple and satisfactory distribution of the infinite perfections to which they are, respectively, applied. And yet, that there are distinctions amongst them is perfectly obvious ; and that these distinctions ought to afford the means of a classification as complete as the distinctions themselves, is equally manifest. Nor can any one doubt, that almost any classification that is not absurd, is a help to our conception of the whole of them ; while a classification which would logically distribute them all in some manner, answerable at once to our manner of conceiving them, and to the distinctions which we perceive to exist amongst them ; would be of the utmost value in promoting our systematic knowledge of this vast and difficult —and yet unspeakably important subject. I have, therefore, ventured to attempt such a classification.

II.—1. The perfections of God are considered and treated in a separate manner, and are classified, only out of the necessity on our part, that we may, in this manner, contemplate God himself, more intelligibly. They are not, in fact, parts of God, nor faculties of God ; but they are God himself. When we mean to say that he knows all things, we express that idea by calling him Omniscient : when we mean to say that he can do all things, we express that idea by calling him Omnipotent : and as both of these facts are true universally, necessarily and inherently in God, we express that idea by saying, these are Perfections or Attributes of God. And so of all his other Perfections.

2. Now as God is manifest in all things, it is impossible even to conjecture in how many ways and upon how many objects, he might, or does, make his Perfections known. In effect every divine Perfection is infinite : and the number of Perfections in

an infinite being is also infinite—since he is subject to no limit-ation, and the aspects in which he is capable of manifesting him-self are illimitable. As every thing he does, has for its founda-tion something that he is, and as every thing that he is, can be conceived of in various relations to every thing else, that he is : the Perfections which in any particular aspect of his being can be shown to belong to him, are apparently boundless. Through-out his blessed Word, the ascriptions of infinite perfections to him, scarcely admit of being numbered. In any systematic treatment of the subject, therefore, what is wanted is, not a vain attempt to enumerate the divine perfections, and give names to them ; but the discovery and clear statement of a method by which such of them as are known to us may be classified and contemplated by our finite understanding, in a manner consistent with its own nature and modes of obtaining knowledge.

3. There are certain Perfections of God which may be con-templated as qualifying his very being, as well as all his other perfections ; conditions, if I may so express myself, without which God, considered simply as God, cannot be said to have a being, or any other perfection. Such are these—to wit : that he is Simple, Infinite, Independent, Self-existent, Necessary, Eternal, Incorporeal, Immaterial, Immense, Incomprehensible, having life in himself. These, and the like, I would place in the first class, and call them the Primary Attributes ; meaning thereby to express the idea, that these Attributes cannot be separated from our conception of the true God ; but that as soon as we say, that such a being exists at all, we must neces-sarily imply, that these, and all such things are true concerning him ; because, such a being as he is, cannot exist except upon these conditions—as inseparable from his existence.

4. There are other perfections of God, which are necessarily implied, in the exercise, by him, of many of those which I would call Primary Attributes ; and which are also necessarily implied, in the mode of his being, as an Infinite Spirit ; perfections, with-out which we cannot conceive of his being a Spirit, at all ; nor conceive, if he is a Spirit, that he either lives, or imparts life—or that he exerts any of his Primary Attributes. As he is a Spirit, and as he must conceive all that he does, he must have an Intellect : and as he is a Spirit, and as he does conceive and act, he must have a Will : and possessing an Intellect and

Will, and acting at all—he must possess Power commensurate with his nature and acts. These I would place in the second class, and call Essential Attributes of God ; intending thereby to express the idea that God, as he is not only God simply considered—but as he is God the infinite, eternal and unchangeable Spirit, must be endowed with Intellect, Will and Power—in a manner corresponding with his being, and with his Primary Attributes. Now there are certain conditions to be predicated of these Essential Attributes of God, which express more distinctly the nature and extent of these perfections themselves ; or which open to us, if we prefer to consider it so, additional perfections of God ; and these can be viewed more distinctly, by considering them as related in a manner, more or less direct, to these Essential Attributes. They are such as the following, to wit :

(*a*) As connected with the divine Intellect :—That, amongst God's Essential Perfections—are, a perfect Intuition of himself, and of all things else ; that he is omniscient, having an unsearchable, incomprehensible and eternal insight of all that ever did, will or could be ;—that he is the Fountain of all Possibilities, and all Ideas, and therefore of all Truth ;—and that, from all eternity ; and by an act of his illimitable Intelligence ; so that it is not possible that he should err.

(*b*) As connected with the divine will : That, amongst the Essential Perfections of God are, such as these, to wit : That his will is infinitely free, pure and active ; that, spontaneously, by one act, and from eternity, in view of all things existing in his infinite understanding, his most perfect will determines all things ; that seeing all motives, all possibilities, all ends and all means, the determinations of his will are complete, immutable and most sure ; that nothing is possible except as he wills it, and that any thing he wills is certain ; and that he wills every thing, not one by one, but all as a part of the boundless scheme which he proposes and the glorious ends he designs.

(*c*) As connected with the divine power : That God does and can do, whatever does not in itself involve a contradiction ; that his Power is of every kind, and extends to every object, and acts in every form and unto every end, and that throughout the universe, and through eternity ; so that no appreciable resistance can be conceived of, to him ; and that no exertion or effort can be conceived of as being made by him ; he is omnipotent.

5. There arises a third ground of distinction amongst the

Attributes of God, as advancing from the primary conception of him merely as an Infinite and Self-existent being—we pass onward through the consideration of him as an Infinite Spirit, and arrive at the view of him, in which he is to be contemplated as an Infinite Spirit, under a particular aspect ; namely, under the aspect of possessing the perfections of that boundless knowledge and wisdom, which have relation to that special distinction which we call True and False. While it is certain that a spirit must possess Intelligence, and an Infinite Spirit must possess infinite Intelligence ; yet the special relevancy of a particular kind of Knowledge and the special Wisdom connected therewith, to a special aspect of his being, and to our special relations to him ; begets a complete, and to us transcendently important distinction amongst the Perfections of God. Here it is founded, as I have observed, on the distinction of the *true* and *false* : in the next class upon the distinction of *Good* and *Evil*. The Perfections of the former kind, I would place in the Third Class, and call them the Natural Attributes of God ; partly, as expressing the nearest approximation of the nature of God to that of the creature. Since of all spiritual things knowledge and wisdom are those in which the creature—which perceives the eternal and ineffaceable distinction between the true and the false, is naturally and universally most capable of growing. And partly, as expressing a distinction—more slight, between them and the class immediately preceding, and more marked between them and the class immediately following.

6. In like manner when we conceive of this All-knowing and All-wise Spirit, which fills immensity, as taking notice of that distinction we express by the words *good* and *evil;* and as being actuated by such affections as Love and Aversion ; and conceive of such qualities as Goodness and Mercy, or Anger and Wrath, as attending their exercise ; and then conceive of these being all ordered in Justice, Truth and Long-suffering ; it is very manifest that a view of him is obtained, different from any hitherto presented. I would therefore establish a Fourth Class, and refer to it such Perfections as Holiness, Goodness, Graciousness, Love, Mercifulness, Long-suffering, Justice, Truth and the like ; and call them the Moral Attributes of God. Meaning thereby such perfections as we find some trace of in our moral nature, and which all point to that eternal and ineffaceable distinction between good and evil, already suggested.

7. And finally, we cannot avoid perceiving that there are other conceptions of God, which cannot be contemplated without exhibiting him to us, in a manner different from any suggested, in the four preceding classes. For there are views of him which necessarily embrace every thing; which necessarily show him to us in the completeness of all his Perfections. I would, therefore, establish a Fifth Class, and refer to it what I will call the Infinite Actuosity of God, that is, the ceaseless movement of his Infinite Life; also his Infinite supremacy, that is the consummate dominion of that Infinite Life of God; also his Omnipresence, his All-sufficiency, his Infinite Fulness or Infinitude, his consummate Perfection, his absolute Oneness and his unutterable Blessedness. And, as expressive of the particular ground of distinction in these Perfections, I would call them Consummate Attributes of God.

8. According to this method we are enabled to contemplate God successively, 1. As he is an infinite being and endowed with the proper perfections thereof: 2. As he is an infinite Spirit, and endowed with the proper perfections thereof: 3. As being both, and endowed with all perfections that belong to both, considered with reference to the eternal and ineffaceable distinction between true and false, which is the fundamental distinction with which our own rational faculties are conversant: 4. As being endowed with all perfections, considered with reference to the eternal and ineffaceable distinction between good and evil, which is the fundamental distinction with which our moral faculties are conversant: 5. As being endowed with all perfections which underlie, which embrace, or which result from the union of all the preceding perfections. And so the classes of his perfections would necessarily be: 1. Those called Primary Attributes, that is, such as belong to an Infinite and Self-existent being, simply considered: 2. Essential Attributes, that is, those belonging to such a being considered essentially as an infinite Spirit: 3. Natural Attributes, that is, such as appertain to an Infinite Spirit considered naturally rather than morally or essentially: 4. Moral Attributes, that is, such as appertain to such a being, considered morally, rather than naturally or essentially: 5. Consummate Attributes, that is, such as appertain to such a being considered completely and absolutely. To the development of these conceptions, and the demonstration of the Infinite Perfections of God as thus classified, the five following chapters will be devoted.

CHAPTER XVIII.

PRIMARY ATTRIBUTES OF GOD: SUCH AS APPERTAIN TO HIM, CON-
SIDERED MERELY AS AN INFINITE BEING.

I. 1. Simplest conception of God.—2. Nature of the Sufficient Reason.—3. Infinite
series.—4. Demonstration of the Being of God.—5. Demonstration of his Attributes.—II. 1. Essence of God incomprehensible. It is the foundation of all that
exists in him.—2. That Essence absolutely necessary and self-existent.—3. All
Attributes inseparable from this Essence.—III. 1. God's Being Independent: and
Eternal.—2. Simple. Incorporeal. Immaterial.—3. Infinite actuosity.—4. The
Fountain of Life.—5. Intelligence.—6. Free Will. God is a Spirit.—7. The
mutual light of Reason and Revelation.—8. Establishment and statement of the
First Class of the Divine Attributes.

I.—1. THE simplest idea we can form of God is, that he is a
self-existent Being, distinct from us and from the universe, who
contains in himself a sufficient ground and reason for the existence of ourselves and the universe. Stated in other words : that
God is a Being absolutely necessary and independent, in whom
and upon whom all things are contingent and dependent.

2. As it is impossible for any thing to be, and not to be ; it
follows that a sufficient reason exists, and can be given, why any
particular thing is, rather than is not: and why it is in a particular mode, rather than in some other. This sufficient reason
being discovered and stated, nothing more can be required concerning the fact or mode of the existence of that thing.

3. In like manner, there can be no such thing, as an infinite
series either of reasons or causes, in such reasoning. For as long
as the question still remains, why—and whence—any thing is ;
the sufficient reason, either of the fact or the manner of its existence, has not yet been found or stated. But as such sufficient
reason does exist, and may be discovered and stated ; it is not
an infinite series, but it is the ultimate reason, the actual first
principle, or first cause that is sought for.

4. What ought to be demonstrated, therefore, concerning the

existence of God, is that simplest idea which we can form of him : namely, a being of himself and absolutely necessary ; upon whom we and the universe are contingent and dependent. Let us conceive, if we can, that God does not exist. What would we mean ? Would we mean that there was no *essence* at all : or no *self-existent* essence : or no *life* in which it ever might be ? Some, or all of these—we must mean—by such a conception : and, no matter which, it is absurd.—Moreover, that which we conceive of as having life of itself, and of its essence, must exist if existence is possible : but this is the conception and definition of God : his existence therefore is necessary, unless existence is impossible.—Moreover, to say that a certain Attribute is contained in the nature or conception of a thing, is to say that it is inseparable from it : but this is true with reference to necessary existence, in God : therefore this is an Attribute of God : that is he necessarily exists.—Moreover—to be able to exist, is an ability,—while to be unable to exist is a debility : but if all existences are merely finite, and not one that is infinite does or can exist ; it follows that every finite, is more powerful, than any infinite existence—which is utterly absurd : wherefore there is no existence at all—or there is an infinite self-existence, which is the cause of all things. Either of these four ways, the necessary existence of God is certain, *à priori*—An infinite series of causes is an absurdity : to assert the endless reproduction of beings whose existence is not of itself, is the weakest form of an absurd infinite series : to allow them self-existence, is to make countless millions of infinite gods, in order to avoid having one true God. That which exists, but not of itself, must have its existence determined by that which does exist of itself : an existence of itself, that is God—has been shown to be inevitable, unless it be impossible : but so far from being impossible—its reality is established by every dependent existence determined by it. Thus *à posteriori* also, the necessary existence of God is certain.

5. The detailed demonstration of that first principle of all religion, I have attempted in a former chapter. I have also discussed the fact and the manner of the intervention of God, to save sinners : the whole doctrine of the Person and Work of the Divine Redeemer, objectively considered : the method of the Divine Existence : and the doctrine of the Holy Ghost. What

I am now to prove and to illustrate, therefore, is the Perfections of this glorious God, existing as has been demonstrated, in three Hypostases in one Essence: commencing with those Primary Attributes which belong to him under our simplest conception of him, and advancing according to the method developed in the previous chapter, through the sublime array, to the highest conception we can form of his consummate Perfections.

II.—1. Let us not deceive ourselves by words and terms, but confess our total inability to define, to describe, or even to comprehend the intimate nature and essence of God. Still, there must be some method of expressing what we do know concerning this incomprehensible Jehovah. And the highest idea we can have of him, or of our being, is that which we call his nature, his essence. In this essence is the foundation of whatever does, or can exist, in the being.

2. Now whatever has its sufficient reason solely in the essence, and proceeds from it only, we call an Attribute of that being. The fundamental conception of God, therefore, is of his essence, from which every thing that appertains to him flows. But the simplest idea of God, as has been shown, is that he hath a being necessary, and of himself. Whence it immediately follows that the essence or nature of his being consists in this, that it is absolutely necessary and self-existent.

3. And this is the precise idea contained in the personal name of God revealed to us.* And the Scriptures abundantly declare this simple, necessary self-existence of God; and that all things are from him and by him.[1] And the Attributes of God, as before explained, are those things which follow from his essence, and cannot be separated from it; being the Perfections of God, which we distinguish by means of their objects, their effects, our manner of conceiving them, and their special relevancy to one or another aspect of the Being of God as revealed to us. In reality, these Perfections of God do not differ among themselves; nor can they be separated from each other: for whatever is in God—is God.

III.—1. God is a being of himself. But a being of himself would exist if nothing else existed. God's existence is, therefore, absolutely independent. It is also absolutely necessary; for we can conceive neither of its beginning nor its ending. God's Be-

* יְהֹוָה—ὁ ὤν—I AM. [1] Isa., xli. 4; Psalm, cxlvi. 6; Acts, xvii. 25; Rom., iv. 17.

ing, therefore, is eternal: that is, he has the total and perfect possession of endless life.

2. Every existence that begins and ends, does so in some union or dissolution of its parts; that is, every being not eternal is compound. But as God's being neither began, nor can end, as has been proved, it follows that there are no parts of which his essence is composed; because it is only by union of its parts and dissolution of its parts, that any being commences or terminates. The Nature of God, therefore, is not compound; but it is perfectly uncompounded and simple. But every bodily existence is necessarily compounded, and has parts: therefore, God, whose Nature is absolutely simple, must be incorporeal. Moreover, every material substance, in like manner as every bodily existence, is necessarily compounded and has parts; therefore, God, whose essence is perfectly simple, must be immaterial.

3. The sufficient reason of the existence of all things is in God. But all things, from the highest to the lowest, are endowed with activity; and that activity, in all dependent existences, exerts itself as long as it is not repressed from without. But God is the source, as Creator, of this ceaseless activity of the creature; and God, by the independence of his own Being, cannot be repressed. It follows, therefore, that the essence of God must be endowed with eternal actuosity. Thus Christ said, My Father worketh hitherto, and I work;[1] indicating not only this ceaseless divine actuosity, but also some transfer of its manifestation in the kingdom of grace. As if he had said plainly—hitherto, in the name and manifestation of my Father—henceforth in mine; by me, with constant reference to my Father—by the Holy Ghost, with constant reference to me.

4. Life, is activity produced by some inward principle or power. But God is eternally active; and must, therefore, have Life.[2] But God exists of himself, and also independently of all others; he must, therefore, have Life of himself and independently.[3] But God contains in himself the sufficient reason of the existence of all things; therefore the sufficient reason of all activity intrinsic in all things, that is all life—is to be sought in God. He is, therefore, the Fountain of all Life. And this is precisely the testimony of the Apostle John, concerning Christ.[4]

5. Now, since the sufficient reason of our own existence, and

<hr>

[1] John, v. 17.   [2] Jer., x. 10.   [3] John, . 26.   [4] John, i. 1–9.

of the existence of the universe, is contained in God, we must seek in him, and not in ourselves, nor in any thing else exterior to God, for that reason. For nothing can occur without a sufficient reason ; wherefore, there must have been with God a sufficient reason, why he should rather create us and the universe, than not do it ; and why thus, and not otherwise. But, in order to determine the sufficiency of the reason, there must be a distinct perception of the thing ; and as God, in creating, must act with sufficient reason, it follows that he must have conceived distinctly, all he was about to create. But the faculty by which he would thus distinctly conceive them, we call intellect, or intelligence. Therefore God must possess intelligence.

6. Moreover, since the universe is from God, and not of itself, it required in God a determination not only to create it, but to create it as it is, and not otherwise. But these determinations presuppose choice and acts of the will. God, of himself, and depending on nothing exterior to himself, chose and determined to create the universe, and to do it after a particular manner. Free will, therefore, appertains to God. But nothing except a spirit, can be endowed with intelligence and free will. God is, therefore, a spirit, possessing intelligence and free will.

7. In contemplating the essence of God, and the attributes which arise directly out of such a view of his infinite being, we perceive that the knowledge we may obtain in that way is immense, and that the foundations of it are most certain ; even while we admit that his essence is itself incomprehensible. Many things which the sacred Scriptures teach us with great clearness, we are able, after we get possession of their fundamental conceptions of God, to deduce from a few great elemental truths. It is thus we can demonstrate so many of the perfections of God —by a double process of reason and revelation. And then afterward, guided in the same manner—and considering the perfections demonstrated in another light—and treating them separately or in combination as new starting points of our inquiries ; we proceed from step to step, until we have surveyed every aspect in which, according to our measure, we are able to comprehend the wonders of the divine existence. It is the knowledge of him, whom to know aright, is life eternal.

8. Thus far we learn this much concerning those Primary Attributes of God, which appertain to him in our simplest con-

ception of his Being, namely : That he is Self-existent, Independent, Necessary, Eternal, Simple, Incorporeal, Immaterial ; that it appertains to him to be eternally Active, to have Life of Himself and Independently, to be the Fountain of Life, and its actual Giver to all things that possess it ; that in bestowing it, and in all things, he manifests Intelligence and Free Will, and proves thereby that he is a Spirit. This is the point to which the demonstration of his Being in a previous chapter brought us by a widely different process. It is hardly necessary to remark, that all these Perfections are infinite Perfections : that all these attributes belong to God in a manner answerable to the divine Essence from which they are inseparable : that is in an infinite manner and with infinite fulness. These, and such as these, are *Primary* Attributes of God, and constitute the first class in a natural division of the divine Perfections, according to the most obvious distinctions observable amongst them.

CHAPTER XIX.

ESSENTIAL ATTRIBUTES OF GOD: SUCH AS APPERTAIN TO HIM CONSIDERED AS AN INFINITE, PERSONAL, SPIRIT.

I. The Infinite Understanding of God.—1. In it is the source, and the rule of all Possibilities.—2. It embraces all things, in all their modes.—3. And in all their order and relations. His Knowledge Infinite.—4. Omniscience.—5. The source of all Essences.—6. The nature of Ideas.—7. The Relation of all existences to the Understanding and Will of God.—8. Divine Foreknowledge.—9. Universal Truths. All truth in God.—II. 1. The Will and Power of God.—2. The determination of the Will of God; with the ground and manner thereof.—3. Objective and subjective reasons as determining the Will of God. Creation of the Universe. —4. Omnipotence of God. Miracles.—5. Immutability of God's most perfect Will. The plenitude of Perfection, in every act of his Will.—6. It is All-sufficient. Infinitely Free. Determines all, with reference to all.

I.—THERE are certain attributes of God which may be most distinctly considered, when they are viewed as depending fundamentally upon, and as immediately connected with, that Infinite Understanding which I have shown in a former chapter, was an Attribute of his infinite substance, and one of the essential and immediate proofs, as well as results, of his being an Infinite, Personal Spirit. I will now consider these.

1. God by his Infinite Intelligence knows himself, and in knowing himself knows every thing that is, in its own nature possible ;—that is, every thing which does not involve a contradiction. Things, therefore, are possible because God represents to himself that they involve no contradiction ; and consequently the conception of them by the Divine Intelligence, as possible, is what makes them so. Wherefore all the possibilities of all things lie in God, and his divine Intellect is their sole fountain; so entirely that if there was no God, there could be no possibility of any thing whatever.

2. In itself considered, every thing is possible which does not involve a contradiction. But this universe existing only con-

tingently, its opposite involves no contradiction ; therefore many others would be possible. But as already proved, the divine Intelligence is the source of all possibilities, and God knows them all—whether any of them actually exist or not : nay God knows all possible things, that never did, and never may exist—as well as all that do, or ever did exist. Possible things may be considered absolutely and separately—or relatively to each other and as reduced into systems. Considered by themselves, he knows all that according to their essence is possible for them ; and considered relatively and systematically, he knows all their relations, to each other and to all things. But there is no other way, but these two, in which any thing can exist ; so that the divine Intelligence necessarily extends to, and embraces all possible things, in all possible modes of existence.

3. If all things which could possibly be united into one system, are considered in that manner, some particular order—no matter what—of all of them to each other would arise from their existing together, or from their succeeding each other ; in this manner the ideas of what we call time and place occur, perhaps arise : and by what has been proved it necessarily follows, that these, whether as realities or as possibilities, with all the accidents of both, are perfectly embraced by the Intelligence of God. All things and all beings, in all times and all places—in all their separate conditions, and all their mutual relations—as they exist together and as they succeed each other ; in one word, that which we call the world, the universe—all of it, always, is absolutely pervaded and taken in, by a single Intuition of the Infinite Intellect. In the same manner other systems beside ours—if they exist, and all that is in them, God knows as he knows us ; and if they exist not, he knows them as possibilities, as distinctly as he knows ours as a reality. But he who being infinite and eternal knows himself, and also knows every existing and every possible universe, together with every existing and every possible being and thing in them all, and together with all the qualities and differences and relations of them all ; he may be truly said to know all that is the subject of knowledge— and the more so as he knows it all at once, and together. And in God, this Supreme Understanding is not a mere faculty, denoting a possibility of acting ; but it is an infinite perfection of that eternal essence, who knows all things simultaneously, with

an intimate and unerring certainty, and in whom no cognition can be separated from an everlasting activity.

4. Now, an Intelligence which extends to all things that are possible, whether they succeed each other, or whether they exist together, must be considered illimitable ; but such is the Intelligence of God ; therefore God hath an illimitable Intelligence. Again : a higher and more perfect Intelligence cannot be conceived of than that which distinctly, by a single act, and simultaneously, conceives all things ; but such is the divine Intelligence ; it is, therefore, most Perfect. Again ; that is incomprehensible, of which we cannot conceive how it is or can be done, but the mode in which the divine Intelligence conceives all things, distinctly, at the same time, and by one act, is wholly beyond our comprehension ; that Intelligence is therefore Incomprehensible. Again : that is Omniscience which knows all things that are the subjects of knowledge ; but God knows himself, and all things that are possible ; his Intelligence is therefore Omniscient. And this Illimitable, Perfect, Incomprehensible, and Omniscient Intelligence, is directed toward and exercised upon every thing and every creature, from that which is most vast to that which is most minute, throughout illimitable space, and boundless creation, and eternal ages.

5. I have shown in the preceding chapter that the essence of God, as a self-existent and necessary being, consists in that self-existence and necessity ; that is, in its certainty. From this, it follows that the essence of all dependent and contingent existences, such as all created existences are, consists in that dependence and contingency ; that is, in the possibility of their existence. But as the divine understanding conceives of all possibilities ; that is impossible of which it does not conceive ; therefore the reason why any thing is possible, is to be sought in the understanding of God. But since the essence of any dependent existence, as an existence, consists in its possibility—as just explained —it follows that the divine Intelligence, as the source of all possibilities, is the source also, of all essences. There is, however, a wide difference between the possibility of existence and the existence itself ; and while the divine Intelligence is the fountain of the former—that is of the essence or possibility of the existence—the divine Will is the foundation of the latter, that is, of the existence itself ; a distinction without which every possible

thing would be obliged to exist and God would be obliged to cre
ate it.

6. The divine Intelligence is not, we must recollect also, a
mere faculty, but is a perfection of God ; an Attribute, and
therefore a divine activity. The representation of possibilities,
that is of the essences of existences, is constantly in it. But
whatever is always actively present with God is essential to him ;
but the representation of possible things is so ; therefore Ideas
are essential to God, who in knowing himself, knows at the same
time, whatever is possible. So that God cannot be conceived of
without ideas of things, without at the same time, conceiving of
him, as without Intelligence. But, these things without which
we cannot conceive of God, and which are essential to him, are
necessary ; and whatever is both essential to God and necessary
is immutable : yet ideas of things, though essential to God, are
not arbitrary, even though different ideas could not exist. There
is a wide distinction between a thing's being necessarily possible,
and its necessarily existing ; and of that necessary possibility,
there is a wide difference between saying it is of God and saying
it is of the thing itself. For a thing is possible because the idea
of it exists in the divine understanding ; but the possibility of
existences constitutes their essence ; yet the necessity of that
possibility depends on the divine understanding ; therefore the
necessity of essences depends on the divine Intelligence, and not,
like the necessity of existences, upon the Will of God, nor upon
his decree. These distinctions, though they may appear intricate, are not only true, but important as bearing upon questions
connected with the origin of evil, and with the Manichean heresy,
which was so long the pest of the church of God.

7. It has been shown that the ideas of things are always actually present in the divine understanding ; that they are essential
to him, and so are necessary and immutable ; it is clear, therefore, that they are eternal. It has also been shown, that the
ideas of things in the divine understanding, the possibility of
their existence, and essence of them, are all but various terms to
express one and the same thing ; for the things are conceived by
God as possibilities, and the possibility of existence is the essence
of contingent existence. It necessarily follows, that if the ideas
of things are eternal, the essence of things has existed from
eternity in the divine understanding ; and as the divine Intellect

is Eternal, the essences of things, that is, the ideas of them, and the possibility of them, are eternal. But they are eternal merely as in the divine understanding, and of God, who represents to himself all things that are possible; for it has been shown, that if there was no God, nothing would be possible; therefore there can be no existence independently of the will of God, nor any possibility of any existence, that is any essence of any, independently of his Intelligence. And so the Scriptures teach us that all the works of God were conceived of by him, and known unto him from Eternity:[1] that his incomprehensible Intellect embraces all things, from the greatest to the least;[2] that his understanding is infinite;[3] that before the Immensity of his Intelligence all creatures and all things, actual and possible, lie open and naked;[4] and that in comparison of the unsearchable perfection of his counsel, and wisdom, and knowledge, there is not only none like him, but none else.[5]

8. There is a distinction between simple intelligence and determinate knowledge.* By the former, which relates only to the divine understanding, God knows all things that are possible, without regard to the question of the actual existence of any of them; so that this knowledge of Simple Intelligence may be said to take no cognizance of the future actual existence or non-existence of any thing. By the latter, which involves the divine will, God knows from eternity all things that would actually exist in the system of the universe. This is called foreknowledge. God, as has been shown, knows all possible things, whether considered separately or in systems; hence he knows all things that are possible, under all possible systems; and all things that will be actual he knows, as being determined by his will. Amongst other things, he knows all that is possible to the souls of men, embracing the whole of their perceptions and thoughts, desires and purposes. And as he conceives all these, and all other possible things, at once, and by a single act, the past and the future are alike to him; and to perceive, to foresee, and to remember all things, as in our weakness we express it, is one and the same act in the infinite Intelligence; that is, all knowledge is in God.

[1] Acts, xv. 18.   [2] Ps. cxlvii. 4; Mat., x. 30.   [3] Ps. cxlvii. 5.
[4] Heb., iv. 13.   [5] Is., xlvi. 5, 9, 10.

* Scientia simplicis Intelligentiæ, aut Scientia naturalis; Scientia visionis aut Scientia libera.

9. The system of the universe contains in itself the total connection of all things that compose it, and whatever is possible by it ; therefore it contains all universal truths. But since God conceives all these existences as embraced in this system, it follows that he knows all universal truth. Again : since God is the only author of all things that are possible, and by consequence the only author of all their essences ; and inasmuch as all universal truths are comprehended under them, he is the author of all universal truths ; that is, all truth is in God. From whence it follows, that all truth is consistent with all truth. Again : as the ideas and essences of all things are eternal, and universal truths are contained in a system of possible things, it follows that universal truths have been in the divine understanding from eternity, and are therefore eternal. Moreover, there can be no new truths ; but eternal truths have been disclosed from time to time, and may yet be more and more disclosed. Again : as all particular truths are comprehended under universal truth, and all universal truths are known to God, it is impossible for God to err. So also, since God knows all things that are possible, he also knows what things are not contained in his ideas as possible ; that is, he knows what things are impossible. And as ideas are essential to God, and as whatever is essential to God is necessary, seeing that God is a necessary being, therefore the knowledge of all things is necessary to him, and his divine understanding, of necessity, knows all things. So much of the Infinite Intellect of God, and of the Perfections connected with it, and flowing immediately from it.

II.—1. He who alone hath immortality,[1] that is, who alone lives by an independent, eternal, and immutable existence, cannot be conceived of as so existing, much less as so existing in a spiritual manner, without conceiving of him as understanding, willing, and acting, in a manner corresponding with the nature of his existence. A directing Intellect, a controlling Will, and Power competent to both, and all of them exerted with an activity corresponding to themselves, and to the nature of God, are perfections which are inseparable from every true idea we can form of the Being of God. They express the perfect manner in which he must act, when he acts in regard of the things which they signify ; and they express still further, that he must needs

---

[1] 1 Tim., vi. 16.

act in regard to such things. To Will and to Do belong to God no less than it belongs to him to Know; and all equally, after their own manner. They are perfections wholly inseparable from each other, and wholly inseparable from a living spirit. And having endeavored to deduce and illustrate that perfection of God called his Intellect, it occurs next in order to do the like concerning his Will and Power; for as we cannot conceive of him as existing without Intelligence, so neither can we conceive of him as existing with it, without at the same time both Willing and Acting.

2. As nothing can occur without a sufficient cause, so nothing can be done without a sufficient reason. The sufficient reasons of all acts are the motives, which induce the performance of them. It follows that whatever God wills, he does it from some motive : and so we commonly speak of the reason, impelling cause, motive, of the creation of the world, the redemption of men, and all other acts of God. As God knows what things are impossible, he can never will what is impossible : therefore whatever God wills is possible. Moreover, as an infinite multitude of things which do not exist, are possible, it follows that mere possibility is not a sufficient motive with God, to will. God knows all things, distinctly, from eternity, and he knows, in like manner, whether there is a sufficient motive for willing any particular thing : the knowledge of the thing, and the knowledge of the sufficient reason for willing it, existing together. But as he wills for a sufficient reason, he wills when he knows the sufficient reason : therefore whatever he wills, he wills from eternity. But as God knows all things, and the sufficient reason for willing any of them, by one act, as well as from eternity : and as he wills not ignorantly and without motive, but according to his knowledge of things, and of the sufficient reason for willing them : it follows, that he wills all things by a single act, as well as from eternity. God is Eternal, Independent, the Fountain of all things : he is therefore the first of all and the creator of all, besides himself : and so it is impossible that he could be obliged, by any thing external to himself, to will any thing. It follows that the determination of his will is from himself, and that what he wills, he wills spontaneously, that is, of his own accord.

3. The objective reason for any thing, is to be sought in the thing itself; the subjective reason is in him who does the thing :

so that the objective reason why God willed the creation of the universe, is to be found in the universe itself, but the subjective reason why he so willed, is in himself—that is, is himself. The reason why God willed to create any thing, is purely subjective, and in himself: the reason why, having willed to create, he would will to create this rather than some other possible universe, is purely objective, and lies in the universe itself, which he willed. The objective reason why God willed to create this particular universe, does, however, carry us back into himself: for the subjective reason why he would will to create any universe, must needs be a sufficient reason, in view of the knowledge which God hath, of himself and all things: and therefore, the particular universe created, and so the objective reason for its creation, must have reference, to that subjective reason, that is, to God. This universe suited the end which God proposed to himself in creation, better than any other possible universe: and therefore, he willed to create it, in preference to all others: and herein lies the objective reason, for its creation. Now this very objective reason establishes the fact, and rests upon it, that this universe differs from all others that are possible ; and that on that very account, objectively, God has willed it, rather than any other. In it, all the particular reasons of all things, whether existing together or successively, resolve themselves at last, into that general one, by which it becomes perfect in its kind :. namely, perfectly adapted to the end God proposed in creation. All particular reasons of all things, are subordinate to the general reason, which is the chief end of all things : so that to act for a sufficient reason, is to act for an end : and therefore God wills and acts for an end. That end itself is most perfect, being eternally conceived by the divine Intelligence, amongst all the possibilities of things ; and being eternally determined by the divine will, as thus seen. And the universe which he created is also most perfect, as unto the accomplishment of that most perfect end ; the divine Intellect conceiving, the divine Will determining, and the divine Power accomplishing all in infinite rectitude, wisdom, and goodness. Nor does it militate in the least against these things, that there should appear to be imperfections in the universe which God has willed and created. For until we know the entire means, and their total operation, which we neither do nor can know, we cannot say which, if any, are imperfect : and until we know the whole end, which we cannot, we can neither say that it is amiss, nor that the means are unsuitable.   And even if we knew, fully, both the means and end, which we do not, we are incompetent to determine the connection and proper operation amongst them all.   And even if this were otherwise, the grand predicate of the whole matter, is, a universe into which sin was permitted to enter, and therefore, a universe which, thus defiled, is perfect only in the peculiar sense before explained, namely, its perfect adaptedness to the infinite end, which the divine Intellect has conceived, and the divine Will determined.

4. As God has actually created the universe, and as it was willed by God as, of all that were possible, the most perfect unto the infinite end whereunto it was created ; it is clear that the Power of God is competent to the production of every thing that is possible : God is, therefore, Omnipotent.   Miracles are effects which flow, neither from the essence nor from the power of creatures, nor from the power of the universe according to the antecedent state of things.   God has made the fact of their existence an immediate proof of the reality both of his own existence and of his interposition to save men.   And it has always been a favorite resort of infidels to attack them, as being alike incapable of occurrence and of adequate proof, or even explanation.[1]   Nothing is more simple than the demonstration of their possibility ; from which easily flows their precise definition, which I have just given ; and then their positive proof, which does not fall under the present exposition.   Thus : the created universe, and every thing in it, exists contingently ; for there is no contradiction involved, and therefore no impossibility in supposing it, and every part of it changed, or even destroyed.   And this is true of every law, operation, creature, and thing, within it ; all exist contingently.   Hence it is perfectly conceivable, it involves no contradiction, and is therefore *possible*, that an Omnipotent Cause, exterior to the created universe—such as God—should be able to produce, and should produce, such effects as would be opposite to the effects which flow from the essence or from the force of creatures or of the universe, according to their antecedent state. These effects are Miracles.   They are possible, therefore, in a double sense.   Intrinsically, because the whole connection of all

<hr>

[1] Acts, ii. 22, x. 38.

things in the universe being contingent, is capable of being changed, and every natural law capable of being suspended. Extrinsically, because there exists, separately from the created universe, a cause—to wit, God—which can do all things by his infinite Omnipotence. Moreover, if it could be proved that Miracles are impossible, it would immediately follow, that creation is impossible, and that there is no God. Because, if miracles are possible, it is because the created universe exists contingently ; and because there exists exterior to it, an Omnipotent Cause. But if the universe does not exist contingently, then its existence is necessary, eternal, and unchangeable, and it had no creator ; and if there exists no Omnipotent Cause exterior to the universe, then there is no God.

5. Inasmuch as God wills by one act, and from eternity, all that he wills, as has been proved ; it follows that he must either change his purpose, from time to time, which is contrary to what has been proved, and which neither Scripture nor reason allows : or that he must, at the same time, both will and not will, which is impossible ; or his will must be the same for ever. Of necessity, therefore, the Will of God is Immutable. Again : God has determined and has revealed that determination to us, obscurely by the light of natural reason, and by his work of creation and providence, and clearly in his most holy word ; to work all things after the most perfect counsel, by the most perfect means, unto the most perfect end. His will, therefore, is most perfect. But as intellect and will appertain only to spiritual existences, and as it has been proved that God has a most perfect intellect, and a most perfect will ; it follows that he is a most perfect Spirit. And this perfection of God is to be taken in its full sense, not as limited to any single attribute, without respect to all the rest of them, and to God himself, who is one with all his attributes. For the highest perfection of God can be understood only of the union of all his divine attributes ; that is, of the entire plenitude of the Godhead. It is only with relation to this plenitude of the Godhead that we can speak of the absolute goodness of any thing in reference to God ; and just as it is only with relation to the suitableness of the entire universe to its chief end, that we can estimate the perfection or imperfection of any of its parts. But finite creatures cannot know and understand either the whole universe, or all its parts,

or its chief end, or the infinite intellect, will, and other perfections of God ; much less his entire plenitude and perfection, as God himself knows and understands them all. Wherefore, no finite creature can judge concerning any of these sublime topics, in the manner that God judges of them. As I observed before with reference to some previous distinctions, and the great doctrines they served to elucidate ; I may add here that these, besides their immediate use, will be found, if carefully considered, to have an important bearing upon the doctrines of God's punitive justice, his wisdom in the permission of evil, and his providence toward his enemies. Nor need there be any doubt of the things advanced. For besides the conclusions of human reason, based on those truths which we certainly know, both from nature and revelation, the chief points are expressly taught in the word of God. For the perfection of this universe to its end, is distinctly declared by Moses ;[1] the determination of the will of God from eternity, is repeatedly taught by Paul ;[2] the omnipotence of God is the theme of some of the highest revelations, by Moses, by David, and by Jeremiah ;[3] the ability of God to do exceeding abundantly above all our thoughts is expressly declared by Paul ;[4] and the will, the purpose, and the acts of God, in working miracles are among the commonest things recorded in the Scriptures for our instruction.

6. God being self-existent, and having no ground of his being in any other existence ; nor yet of his preservation, which is existence continued ; and being, moreover, a most perfect and omnipotent spirit, whose perfection or power could not be augmented ; he needs nothing exterior to himself, either for his preservation or his perfection ; needs no external aids, and being omniscient, can have no increase of knowledge. Again : God knows himself and all things that are possible, and did so from eternity ; and, moreover, that he could bring them all into existence. Wherefore, if the intuition of things different from himself could add any thing to God, he had that intuition equally, whether the things were actually created or not ; so that he hath neither need nor lack of any thing without himself, to add any thing to him in any way ; for in him is absolute All-sufficiency. Again : God being All-sufficient of himself, it was, as to him-

---

[1] Gen., i. 31.   [2] 2 Tim., i. 9 ; 1 Cor., iv. 7.

[3] Gen., xvii. 1 ; Psalm, cxv. 3 ; Jer., xxxii. 17.   [4] Eph., iii. 20.

self, indifferent, whether the universe existed or not ; therefore, there was no intrinsic necessity with God, why he should create any thing ; but God, as has been proved, is perfectly independent ; and, therefore, there could be no extrinsic necessity why he should create any thing ; in the work of creation, therefore, God willed and acted, without any co-action, either external or internal—and, therefore, spontaneously and freely ; the will of God, therefore, is most free. Again : God wills all things by a single act of his will ; and God estimates the perfection of particular things by their relation to the whole universe ; and he willed the universe to be as it is, because, as it is, it most perfectly answers the chief end which he proposed in it ; that is, it is most perfect of its kind ; which perfection consists in this, that all particular things and ends, resolve themselves into the great general chief end. From all which it is clear, that God wills nothing as particular and separate, but that he wills all things in relation to the whole universe. It is because we fail to bear these profound truths in mind, that our views become perplexed on various questions, both speculative and practical : and many difficulties take their rise in the habit of considering and treating particular things, by themselves, as if they alone were to be considered and treated ; and from dwelling only on a single attribute of God, instead of having regard to the method of all the divine perfections. On the contrary, the great canon laid down by the Apostle Paul is, that we must teach according to the proportion of Faith :[1] and the grand principle on which that canon rests, as laid down by the Apostle Peter is, that no part of the revealed will of God is to receive any private, that is, any separate interpretation, as if it were not a part of one divine whole.[2]

[1] Rom., xii. 6.   [2] 2 Pet., i. 20, 21.

CHAPTER XX.

NATURAL ATTRIBUTES OF GOD: SUCH AS APPERTAIN TO HIM
CONSIDERED WITH REFERENCE TO THE ETERNAL DISTINCTION
BETWEEN THE TRUE AND THE FALSE.

1. The Unsearchable Wisdom and Knowledge of God.—2. Nature of these Attributes.
3. Manner of Operation.—4. The Objects of them.—5. Method of their Co-operation with other Divine Perfections.—6. Their Relation to Creation and Redemption.—7. Their Relevancy to the ineffaceable distinction between the *true* and the
false: and the Relevancy of that distinction to our nature and destiny.

1. THE Apostle Paul after concluding one of those immense
surveys of the whole dealings of God with his people, which so
remarkably distinguish his writings; exclaims, Oh! the depth
of the riches, both of the wisdom and knowledge of God, how
unsearchable are his judgments and his ways past finding out.[1]
It is both the unsearchable depth of Wisdom and of Knowledge,[*]
that is in God. And to this extent is the whole testimony of
his word.

2. It has been already abundantly shown that the divine Intellect perceives, at once, of itself and from Eternity, all possible
things in all their possible relations. But according to our finite
method of understanding and representing such a condition of
the divine nature as that statement expresses; something more
than has yet been explained is involved in it, and must follow
after it. This may be expressed by saying that all the conceptions of the divine Intellect are exact and perfect cognitions;
they are Knowledge; and still further they are Knowledge in
that sense which we call Wisdom. In other words that God is
perfectly and infinitely and eternally Wise and Knowing; that
is that universal and illimitable Wisdom and Knowledge are
divine attributes.[2]

[1] Rom., ii. 33.   [*] Σοφιας—γνωσεὠς.

[2] Mat., ii. 27; Heb., iv. 13; Job, xii. 13; Psalm cxxxix. 11; John, xxi. 17;
1 Tim., i. 17.

3. The method, so to express it of these divine Perfections, must be such as will exactly accord with all the other Perfections of God ; as for example, with his Simplicity, Independency, Immensity, Immutability, and the rest. It is not therefore by successive endeavors, and exercises, but it is by one and the same most simple and infinite act, that all Wisdom and Knowledge are in God. Nor is it from time to time, that His Knowledge and Wisdom are augmented ; for as he exists from eternity, and conceives in His infinite Intellect from eternity, all possible things, and all their possible qualities, issues, and relations ; so his Wisdom and Knowledge are from eternity. Nor is it by observing and comparing any thing exterior to himself ; but it is of Himself as the sole fountain of all things, and in the perfect intuition of himself, and of all things in himself—that God knows all things, and is unerringly and unsearchably wise concerning all things. And so, not only do his Wisdom and Knowledge simultaneously, from himself, and eternally comprehend and pervade all things ; but they do this in a manner most intimate, infallible, absolute, instant and immutable ; that is most perfectly. As to this ineffable method of the divine Wisdom and Knowledge, we perceive that it embraces, at once, all things past, present, and to come ; all things that are possible ; and God himself as the fountain of them all. It pervades them all, most perfectly in every way, in which they can exist or be known. It rests not in the effects of things, but penetrates their essences. It is instantaneous, covering at once all times, places, and things. It is unalterably certain, containing even those things, which considered of themselves, are contingent. It is without beginning or end, or change by way of increase or diminution, and so is invariable and everlasting. It is the product not of accidental things—nor even of a divine faculty, but is the result of the perfections of God —which are God himself ; who is not only infinitely wise and knowing himself, and does and disposes all things with infinite Knowledge and Wisdom ; but is the Source and the Cause of whatever Wisdom or Knowledge exists in angels, in men, or in the universe.[1]

4. The objects to which the divine Knowledge and Wisdom extend are all things. This has been so fully illustrated in the preceding chapter, when treating of the divine Intellect, that

[1] John, i. 1–14.

there is no necessity of enlarging on it again, in the same manner. But it may be proper to point out, somewhat more fully,
the remarkable testimony of God's word on this subject, more
especially in its direct application to ourselves. We are taught
in the broadest and most unqualified terms, not only that all
things are naked and opened, unto the eyes of him, with whom
we have to do ; but, the statement is turned in the opposite
direction—and we are informed that neither is there any creature
that is not manifest in his sight.[1] And in one of the most affecting personal passages in all the Scriptures, Peter appealed
to the risen Saviour as the Searcher of hearts—in a manner
which carries the universal proposition of the knowledge of God,
into the very depths of the human soul. Lord thou knowest all
things ; thou knowest that I love thee. And Jesus, probing to
the bottom the heart of his penitent servant, accepted alike the
truth of the universal proposition, and of the particular one deduced from it.[2] Nay this knowledge of God penetrating the
hearts of men, is declared to be more just and perfect than that
which each particular person has of his own heart. For we are
expressly warned that, if our heart condemn us, God is greater
than our heart : and knoweth all things.[3] And even in the
great, and to us who are by nature Gentiles, the decisive matter
of our vocation at all, into the fold of God ; the united testimony
of the Apostles and Elders, after the mature consideration of a
matter which seemed to them so remarkable, was, that it had its
solution in this same stupendous, but undeniable truth. For
beyond a doubt, God had granted unto the Gentiles repentance
unto life ; and equally beyond a doubt, known unto God are all
his works from the beginning of the world.[4] And it is to be
borne in mind that these and all other things are not only to
be considered as being always in the divine Understanding, as
things that might be—which has been proved : nor only as
being determined by the divine Will as things which shall be,
and as accomplished by the divine Power as things which are,
which also has been proved ; but they are to be further considered as being in God and conceived of God, and Willed of God,
and Done of God according to that further sense which we intend
by saying that it was all conceived, willed, and done, with a divine Knowledge and a divine Wisdom : and that God is of him-

<hr>

[1] Heb., iv. 13.   [2] John, xxi. 17.   [3] 1 John, iii. 20.   [4] Acts, xi. 18, xv. 18.

self, infinitely, eternally, and unchangeably Knowing and Wise therein.

5. It has been sufficiently shown that God in willing to create any universe at all, found in himself alone, the sufficient motive thereof; that is, that he is himself the end of all he does. His own glory in the manifestation of his own perfections, is the grand purpose, and the subjective reason, on account of which, is the whole work of creation and redemption.[1] And such is the constant testimony of his word. This particular universe rather than any other, had as the motive and objective reason of its creation—that it was better fitted than any other could be, for the chief end which God had in view, namely, his own glory in the manifestation of all his perfections. Yet although the infinite knowledge of God was, so to speak, subservient to the purposes of his infinite intelligence, and infinite will, and infinite power, in all that relates to the creation of the universe; it is clear on the one hand, that that knowledge, of itself, was not the efficient cause of the possibility of any thing, nor of the existence of any thing, nor of the certainty of any thing; while on the other hand, it is equally clear, that nothing could be known as possible, as created, or as certain unless it was, what it was known to be. On the contrary, the wisdom of God could not concur in the willing or the doing of any thing, which, as to the fact of it (for example, any creation), would not be for the greatest glory of God; and as to the manner of it (for example, this particular creation), would not in the most perfect manner illustrate that greatest glory of God.

6. We perceive, therefore, a substantial distinction, according to our manner of conceiving things, between these divine perfections; and at the same time their perfect accordance with each other, and with every other perfection of God. Seeing imperfection, evil, and sin are in the universe, it follows that they are in it with the knowledge, notwithstanding the omnipotence, according to the will, and not against the wisdom of God. And no higher proof can be given than this—that by means of their existence in the universe, God's perfections will be more completely manifested—and his glory will be greater than if they had not existed in the universe. Nor can any higher conception be formed of the knowledge and wisdom of God, than that they

---

[1] Rom., xi. 36; 1 Tim., i. 17.

can disclose and conduct a method, whereby imperfection, and evil, and sin shall turn to the manifestation of the very highest glory of God. All of which, and much more, is contained in that pregnant Scripture which pronounces Christ crucified to be, not only Christ the power of God, but also Christ the wisdom of God.[1]

7. Intellect and Will appertain exclusively to that which is spiritual ; and Power is inseparable from our primary conception of Will, directed by Intelligence. When we add to the infinite spirit thus endowed, Wisdom and Knowledge as infinite as they, and all as infinite as the essence of which all of them are Attributes ; we may be said to have as complete a conception as we can entertain of the sublime outline of God's *rational* nature, considered separately as far as we are able to do so. Whatever may be the nature of that ineffaceable distinction, which we express by *The True* and *The False;* it is inconceivable that such a Being should not eternally perceive it and eternally respect it. If his own nature is the foundation of the distinction, then the distinction is commensurate with his Being ; that is, it is an infinite and eternal distinction. It is in the light of that distinction that our rational faculties take cognizance of whatever is submitted to them ; it is on its reality that all increase in knowledge and all growth in wisdom on our part depend. Without it, it is not easy, if it be possible, to affix any idea to what we call Intelligence ; and if it be obliterated, we obliterate at the same time the distinction between *Good* and *Evil*, since the Good is always the True, and the Evil is always the False. It is thus the rational nature of God underlies the moral nature of God ; and while both aspects of his Being afford the most distinct means of surveying and comprehending it, the rational goes before the moral. It is thus that unshaken foundations are laid for a true science, both of the mind and the soul of man ; for philosophy in general, and metaphysics and morals in particular. We were created in the image of God, both in knowledge and in holiness. The sum of the glory of the only begotten of the Father, while he dwelt among men as the Word made Flesh, was the glory of the fulness of Grace and Truth.[2] And in the manifestation of the Spirit given to every man to profit withal, to one is given by the Spirit the word of Wisdom—that is divine

[1] Cor., i. 23, 24. [2] John, i. 14.

Wisdom; to another the word of Knowledge, that is divine Knowledge, by the same Spirit.[1] * Our Creator, our Saviour, and our Sanctifier, all deal with us upon the basis of this ineffaceable distinction between the True and the False, which underlies all Wisdom and all Knowledge ; and our own rational nature whether considered in its original, its fallen, its renewed, or its sanctified state, is consciously responsive to that divine dealing and that eternal distinction.

[1] 1 Cor., xii. 7, 8.

* Λογος σοφιας—λογος γνωσεως. But λογος *The Word,* is one of the most emphatic appellations of the Son of God.   What the το πνευμα, *The Spirit* gives, therefore, is *Divine Wisdom—Divine Knowledge.*

CHAPTER XXI.

MORAL ATTRIBUTES OF GOD: SUCH AS APPERTAIN TO HIM CONSID-
ERED WITH REFERENCE TO THE ETERNAL DISTINCTION BE-
TWEEN GOOD AND EVIL.

I. 1. Recapitulation of the Distinctions on which the first three Classes of Divine Attributes rest. The Fourth Class.—2. Infinite Rectitude of God.—3. The true
ground of Moral distinctions.—II. 1. Relation of God's Holiness to his Justice
and his Goodness.—2. That of his Goodness to his will.—3. And to all his Perfections, and to the chief end of his whole work.—4. Goodness of God in itself
and as manifested in Grace, Love, Mercy, and Long-suffering.—5. Nature and
fruits of Divine Grace.—III. 1. The Love of God.—2. Its power and manifestation.—3. Its force as an element, both systematic and living, in our Salvation.
—IV. 1. The Mercy of God, as flowing from his Goodness, through his Love.—
2. Divine Succor for the Miserable.—3. Universal manifestation of Divine Mercy.
Sole Cause of its inefficacy.—4. The Cavil, that it is unequal.—5. That it ought
to prevent, or remove all misery.—6. That it ought to have obliged God to hinder Sin, and thereby hinder Misery.—V. 1. Long-suffering of God.—2. Its immeasurable exercise.—3. Its universal application.—4. The fate of despisers
thereof.—VI. 1. The Justice of God.—2. Particular account of its several aspects.
3. Infinite in God. His Immaculate exercise thereof.—4. Its Relation to the
Infinite Truth of God.—5. The Distributive Justice of God. Unavoidable certainty of Retribution.—6. Fundamental application to all God's dealings with
man.—7. Exacting even the blood of Christ!

I.—1. WE pass next to the consideration of God, by means of
another class of his Perfections, which exhibit his nature and
character to us in an aspect different from any in which the Attributes hitherto discussed have shown him to us. However we
may attempt to express it, there is, to us, a distinction, and
therefore a ground of more precise knowledge, between contemplating God merely as an Infinite Self-existence, and contemplating him as an Infinite Personal Spirit : and then a further
distinction arises when we contemplate him as an Infinite Personal Spirit, endowed with such Attributes as boundless Knowledge and Wisdom, the infinite reality, of which our own rational
nature is a kind of shadow. So far we have come. And now it

is equally clear that a further distinction is perceived when, having reached that point in the development of the vast subject, we address ourselves to the consideration of those Perfections of God, which according to our manner of conceiving, possess a distinctly moral character. For we conceive of God's being, as real, necessary, eternal, and so on, without determining any thing in particular as to its exact mode ; but when we come to consider him as a spirit, and a person, it is no longer possible to conceive of him as destitute of Intellect, and Will, and Power : and so a fundamental distinction is laid in our minds. And then when we conceive of infinite Wisdom and Knowledge directing all the acts of his Intellect and Will, and underlying every exertion of his Power ; he is represented to us in a new light, and a new distinction arises. And then when we conceive of God as having such affections as Love and Hatred ; and conceive of Goodness, and Mercy, and Anger, and Wrath, as attending them ; and conceive of all as being ordered in Justice, Long-suffering, Equity, and so on ; it is very clear that another and most important distinction is afforded, whereby the nature of God may be more nearly contemplated through such Attributes.

2. The first in this great class of the Moral Attributes of God, is his infinite Rectitude, Righteousness, or Holiness, as it is variously called ; which is, indeed, at the foundation of all the rest, and the very basis of his moral character. A perfect being must possess not only all possible separate perfections, but those perfections must co-exist in him, in a perfect relation to each other. Without limit as to their number, and without limitation as to their completeness, the Attributes of God are of that kind, and so exist in him, that being neither different from each other, nor inconsistent with each other, they exclude all imperfection and embrace all perfection. On the one hand, a perfect being cannot be conceived of as wanting Holiness ; for how is that perfect which wants not only an infinite good, but the greatest of all moral perfections ? On the other hand, an infinitely perfect being cannot be conceived of, otherwise than as possessing a constant and unalterable Will to do whatever is right. And every free right action in such a being, must have the sufficient motive and ground of it only in his own essence and perfections ; and therefore no action of his can possibly contradict any of his attributes, or any of his essential determinations ; and therefore the

Holiness of God is well enough defined, to be that supreme love by which he is carried into himself—excluding every thing which is inconsistent with his perfections, and which is not founded in them. All the perfections of God are essential ; they inhere in God ; they are God ; and so they are immutable, and could neither be changed nor substituted by other perfections, any way different from them ; and therefore the Holiness of God is immutable, and could not be changed even by the Will of God. It follows, that God does not Will any thing which is unworthy of his Perfections, and inconsistent with his infinite Rectitude ; and that in the order of thought Holiness is the rule of his Will, and not his Will the rule of holiness ; that is, God wills only such things as agree with all his infinite Perfections, which Perfections do not depend on his Will, but have an inbeing with his Essence.

3. To us, no doubt, all that God wills is right : but in God himself there is a very wide difference between saying, he wills any thing because it is right—that is because it accords with all his Perfections ; and saying any thing is right, that is accords with all his Perfections—merely because he wills it. A distinction which draws after it—remote and subtle as it may be supposed to be—the whole nature of moral good and evil, and the whole economy of salvation. For the necessary and immutable distinction between good and evil ; and the foundation of all religion, both in God and human nature ; and the rule of God's infinite justice ;—and the need of a Saviour ; are all subverted and every logical foundation taken away from them—as soon as the mere will of God is substituted for the perfection of all his attributes, and the Holiness of his adorable nature—as the ultimate ground of moral distinctions, and the fundamental basis of right actions. Good and evil depend on law, not on nature ;* was an apothegm of the ancient atheists—who only substituted nature for God, in the proposition. The number is not small amongst Christian teachers, who, under the guise of evangelical contempt for human reason, and extraordinary devotion to the honor of God's revealed will, still retain in a somewhat different logical form, and perhaps, in a somewhat mitigated degree, the essential poison of the detestable paradox.

II.—1. The infinite Holiness of God—manifested in all his

* Το δικαιον ειναι και το αισχρον ου φυσει αλλα νομω.

ways and in all his works, may be said to be exhibited in a most peculiar manner, in every exercise of his Justice and his Goodness; which are two moral perfections of his nature, which bring him so nigh to us as creatures and as sinners. The Great the Mighty God, the Lord of Hosts, from whom nothing is hid, and to whom nothing is too hard; in the greatness of his counsel and the might of his working, exhibits his loving-kindness unto thousands—but, also, gives to every one according to his ways, and the fruit of his doing.[1] Next after the Holiness of God, therefore, it is proper to consider his Goodness—and then his Justice;—which like it, have also a special relation to his Will.

2. It is in this relation of the Goodness of God to that infinite Will, according to the counsel of which he works all things, that we find the method of all his work of creation, and providence and grace. His boundless Goodness led him to open that fountain of life, which was hid in him from eternity;—and to create a universe, which perfect in itself, and perfect in the glorious end of its existence, might partake of his knowledge and his love; and while it illustrated his perfections, might dwell, at least in the shadow of his blessedness, by an adequate fruition of himself. And when the universe became polluted by sin, there was left for it, in all the divine perfections, no assured refuge except in the eternal Beneficence of God. And when we consider that the universe was created in a manner, and to an end—most perfect; that the whole series of existences, and every particular creature—was endowed with the utmost perfection of which they were all capable, in their place and for their end—and were all related to each other in the same perfect manner: that evil itself, of whatever kind, is directed to some end that is good—and that its introduction into the universe will be made to turn to the highest glory of God, and the highest good of the universe itself: that all this has occurred—by means indeed of all the perfections of God—but in a most peculiar sense because it is of God's nature to be unutterably Good: it becomes impossible for us to conceive that any greater goodness could exist.

3. But the Goodness of God cannot be separated from the other Attributes of God, nor from God himself; for, as has been

---

[1] Jer., xxxii. 18, 19.

shown before, the perfection of the universe is to be estimated with reference to the whole of it, and to its end ; and the perfection of God is to be estimated with reference to all his attributes, and to himself; hence the goodness of God must be considered with relation to the whole universe, and to all the divine attributes ; and so considered, it is that attribute which leads him to bestow upon every creature as much perfection as is consistent with the method and chief end of the universe, and with all his own perfections.   It is not a divine weakness, but it is a divine, and therefore an infinite, Perfection.   To communicate a being, a light, a felicity, a perfection, which, in the comparison, shall be some slight reflection of himself, to dependent existences, is the primary impulse of this Beneficence of God toward the creatures ; and to pity and succor them in whatever miseries, or whatever endeavors toward him, as long and as far as is consistent with his other perfections, is its second impulse toward them.   But immeasurable as may be the riches of the goodness, and long-suffering, and forbearance of God, there are things to which even an infinite Beneficence does neither bind nor impel him ; and the despisers of his Goodness must not expect to escape the judgment of God, nor be surprised to find that obstinate impenitence and hardness of heart are not claims upon his Goodness, but are, for the present, only tribulation and anguish, and for the future treasuries of indignation and wrath.[1] Nor is it for finite, much less for sinful creatures, to order the method, the extent, or the proportion in which this, any more than any other attribute of God, shall either exert itself or display itself.   But the part of such creatures is, to receive with adoring thankfulness whatever measure of goodness is meted out to them, and use it diligently, as at once a blessing and a trust ; knowing that their portion, whatever it may be, is very far beyond what they are entitled to expect, or are likely to use aright, and is the utmost that infinite Goodness could bestow, with a perfect regard either to their advantage, or to the great end of the whole universe, or to the glory of the giver of all good.

4. There is none good but one, that is God.[2] His goodness is infinite, so that all other goodness flows out of him : and with unwasting fulness, all goodness dwells in him ; and unto him, as

<hr>

[1] Rom., ii. 3–11.   [2] Mat., xix. 17.

the chief end, all goodness is referred ; and of himself, in himself, and without himself—he is the eternal and unchangable pattern and measure, as well as the only source of perfect goodness ; so that not only is all Good essential and immeasurable in him as God, but as God creating, governing, and disposing all things, as God redeeming lost sinners, and as God judging the world, he sets himself forth to our apprehension and to our love as being the chiefest among ten thousand, and altogether lovely ;[1] persuading us, yea enabling us, to taste and see that he is Good, and to accept the blessedness that flows from him.[2] For even when we were sometime foolish, disobedient, deceived, serving divers lusts and pleasures, living in malice and envy, hateful and hating one another, the kindness and love of God our Saviour toward men appeared, not by works of righteousness which we have done ; but according to his mercy he saved us, by the washing of regeneration and the renewing of the Holy Ghost.[3] Grace, therefore, and Love and Mercy, to which we may add Long-suffering, are perfections of God, which flow immediately from his unsearchable Goodness ; or, if we prefer to express it differently, they are branches of that Goodness, divers kinds of it—special modes in which it is manifested.

5. The divine declaration is most precise, that it is the grace of God that bringeth salvation.[4] If any sinner shall ever obtain eternal life—it can only be by the gift of God : for death is the wages of sin. And it must be through Jesus Christ our Lord : for as there is but one God—so there is but one mediator between God and man—the man Christ-Jesus.[5] The efficient cause of this Grace of God is his own Goodness and Free-will : the final cause is the salvation of his children : and the glory of his own great name is the chief end. The beginning, the continuance, and the accomplishment, of every good thing we can possess in this life, or in the life to come—depend wholly upon the grace of God.[6] And so we speak of this grace of God as being universal, because all of us, merely as his creatures, partake of it : and yet also as being special, because it is specially given, according to every special end it accomplishes. And we call it prevent-

---

[1] Cant., v. 10–15.   [2] Ps. xvi. 11, xxx. 8, 9.   [3] Titus, iii. 3–5.
[4] Titus, ii. 11.   [5] Rom., vi. 23 ; 1 Tim., ii. v.
[6] 2 Tim., i. 9 ; Phil., ii. 13 ; Rom., iii. 24, xii. 6 ; 1 Cor., xii. 9 ; Titus, iii. 5 ; 1 John, iv. 2 ; Ezek., xxxvi. 27 ; Jeremiah, xxxii. 40.

ing grace, because it precedes all good in us ; and enlightening the understanding, and swaying the heart, and determining the will of man—it both inclines and enables us. And we call it Free Grace, because God bestows it by a free act of his most holy Will, freely upon us. Aud we call it gratuitous grace—because, though it was purchased by the blood of Christ—that blood was not ours to give, nor were we fit, much less worthy, even to receive, much less merit it, except as we were seen of God in him. And we call it efficacious Grace, because it really produces in us those effects which are designed of God, and which are appropriate to its own nature and end. And to crown all, we call it Sovereign Grace, because God the Sovereign Ruler of the universe, neither owes, admits, nor renders any account of the administration of his own royal favor. It is precisely because the goodness of God is bestowed on objects which are, of themselves, unworthy of his favor, that it is called Grace : and therefore we must seek elsewhere than in them, that is, we must seek in God himself, for the sufficient ground and reason of the favor shown to them. The answer is, that it belongs to his nature to be gracious.

III.—1. God, says the Apostle John—is Love. And he adds : In this was manifested the Love of God towards us, because that God sent his only begotten Son into the world, that we might live through him. Herein is Love, not that we loved God, but that he loved us, and sent his Son to be the propitiation for our sins.[1] For God so loved the world that he gave his only begotten Son, that whosoever believeth in him should not perish but have everlasting life.[2] And that sending of his Son, and that propitiation which through the love of the Father he became for our sins—is explained by the Apostle Paul to be, that God spared not his own Son but delivered him up for us all.[3] Upon which amazing state of case, the latter Apostle draws this adoring inference, How shall he not with him also freely give us all things : and the former Apostle this, Behold what manner of Love the Father hath bestowed upon us, that we should be called the Sons of God.[4] In the infinite perfection of God's nature, one shape which his Goodness takes—one result of his perfect and unchangeable Beneficence, is that he should Love. Indifference is no more possible with God, than inaction, or igno-

---

[1] 1 John, iv. 8–10.   [2] John, iii. 16.   [3] Rom., viii. 32.   [4] 1 John, iii. 1.

rance, or any other state opposite to any one of his Perfections. But in the exercise of his Love, as in that of all his Perfections, there is a divine proportion and measure, which takes in all his being ; and a divine procedure according to the nature of his being.

2. Our Love is a passion of the human soul : God's Love is an Attribute of the divine essence—and like every other attribute is free, eternal and unalterable. Springing up within himself, and from himself, as essentially and spontaneously as the infinite Goodness to which it is so nearly related, or the infinite Wisdom by which it is directed ; he is himself the immediate object of this infinite complacency. And then in like manner— is the infinite Love of the Father, the Word and the Holy Ghost, mutually for each other ; in which consists one element of the eternal blessedness of God. And then follows the out-going of God's Love—to the whole universe which he has created. That he loves us, merely as his creatures, is apparent not only in the innumerable blessings which are bestowed on us, even when we are unthankful and disobedient ; but in the bestowment upon us, when he created us of the most exalted rank, and a dominion over all creatures ; and in fitting us for our transcendent position, by forming us in his own image. But all this, great as it is, is nothing, when compared with the proof of his Love, in bringing life and immortality to light, in a new form, through the incarnation and sacrifice of his only begotten Son : and by that means, dictated and executed in boundless Love, snatching us from the perdition which we had incurred by our hatred of him, and of which our pollution rendered us so deserving. The Love of God for sinners—and his hatred of their sins ; his Love of them, and his hatred of all that constitutes them moral objects, either of love or hatred : this is the grand paradox of the spiritual system revealed in the sacred Scriptures—and which even natural Religion, in its degree, tries to hold up continually before us. Human reason absolutely recoils before the solution of that paradox : for, to human reason, the opposite terms of it seem to be precisely contradictory of each other.—And yet, both of them are irrefragably certain : and yet, if both stand, the result would appear to be the degradation of God in bestowing his love on objects which are unworthy of it, and which hate him while they profit by it ; and further on, the righteous perdition

of men, notwithstanding the love of God.—If you will follow that infuriated multitude, which is rushing out of the gates of Jerusalem—you will see God's solution of that paradox.—They knew not what they did, that day, at Calvary! One sentence of the Holy Ghost explains it all : That God might be just, and the justifier of him that believeth in Jesus.[1]

3. Of all the perfections of God this, perhaps, is the one which most nearly touches human nature. Not only in that unmerited goodness manifested towards us with deep and fixed Love, is the most irresistible appeal which can reach the human soul, as long as it is open to any appeal at all : but that of all the dim traces that are left in our fallen nature of any of those divine perfections, in the image of which we were created, the deepest and most enduring point towards this attribute of God. With a power of analysis and combination altogether superhuman, the whole duty of man towards God is summed up by Moses in four propositions ; and his whole duty to his fellow men, in six propositions ; which are called, respectively, the first and second tables of the Law.[2] Then the Lord Jesus has reduced the whole of the first table to one proposition—Thou shalt love the Lord thy God ; and the whole of the second table to one proposition—Thou shalt love thy neighbor.[3] And then the Holy Ghost has reduced these two propositions to one—love is the fulfilling of the law.[4] Love, therefore, rightly directed and exercised, is the consummation of man's moral obligations, and secures the fruition of the highest spiritual estate which his nature is capable of attaining. And even amidst the ruins of that nature as the fall has left it, and as sin has made it—this is its first, its deepest, its most absorbing, and its most imperishable force. While it has the mastery, we are not utterly lost : for a loving nature, though a depraved, is still a gentle, noble and true nature. But when it is subverted—and the fierce, cruel, bitter and vindictive passions usurp the complete dominion of the soul, the last trace of the moral image of God in the human affections has been effaced.

IV.—1. Grace, Mercy and Peace, say the Scriptures, from God our Father and Jesus Christ our Lord.[5] So that peace flows from mercy, and mercy from grace. And in another place,

---

[1] Rom., iii. 26.   [2] Exod., xx.   [3] Mat., xxii. 36–39.
[4] Rom., xiii. 10.   [5] 1 Tim., i. 2.

they carry us further still : thus, after that the kindness and love of God our Saviour to men appeared, not by works of righteousness which we have done, but according to his mercy he saved us, by the washing of regeneration, and the renewing of the Holy Ghost.[1]   So that God's Goodness is the cause of his Love—his love the cause of his mercy ; his mercy the cause of our salvation : and thus salvation is the effect of them all.

2. As the Goodness of God when manifested toward objects considered in their unworthiness, is called grace ; and when manifested toward objects considered in their desirableness to God is called Love : so when that Goodness is manifested toward objects considered in their misery, it is called mercy : and finally, when manifested toward objects considered in their guiltiness, it is called long-suffering. Mercy, therefore, is that divine propension which leads God to succor the miserable ; and is attributed to him throughout the Scriptures[2] as an eternal, unalterable, necessary, active, and free attribute of his being.

3. Amongst these Perfections of God which bear upon us in the most obvious manner—and of which the evidences are most constant and conclusive, his mercy stands conspicuous. For human misery is an inheritance of the whole race, and of every individual of it—as broad as the sin which produced it at first, and which is continually increasing its bitterness. By disobedience came sin, and by sin death ; and the sin and the death have passed together—through all generations and with unfaltering steps, around the circuit of the whole race. For the sin, the grace of God provides the remedy : for the misery his mercy offers the consolation and the deliverance. And in some shape or other, that mercy is exhibited to every creature that suffers—so long as the creature has not passed out of the state in which mercy is possible. But the mercy of God flows, not only from the same Goodness from which his grace flows ; but, also, from the Grace itself; and Grace and Mercy, both alike have reference to sin—one regarding the unworthiness of the creature, and the other regarding the misery which that unworthiness produces. When, therefore the Grace of God is clean taken away, his mercy also is clean taken away : for it is only in proportion as sin is removed through grace, that the misery produced by sin, can be solaced by mercy. Even the infinite mercy

---

[1] Titus, iii. 4, 5.   [2] 2 Cor., i. 3 ; Eph., ii. 4 ; James, i. 13.

of God, could avail nothing in removing misery without removing the cause of it: and when the cause of it, is not only given over as irremediable forever—but falls under the Justice of God, under the other aspect of sin, which we call guilt—and that even beyond the Long-suffering of God : then it is not only, so to speak, essentially impossible for the mercy of God to avail any thing for the sinning sufferer ; but any attempt to do so, would involve a direct conflict of the divine Attributes.

4. For us to object that the mercy of God is not manifested in an equal degree to all his creatures, is wholly absurd. That would be of itself impossible unless the miseries of all were precisely equal, and the destinies of all not only uniform, but exactly similar ; both of which suppositions are not only inconsistent with the frame of the present universe—but with that of any universe, that could fully exhibit the perfections of God. Moreover, when we consider that whatever mercy any of us receives is, in its very nature, just so much goodness which we did not deserve : and, further, that the mercy of God, of whatever kind and to whomsoever extended, must be exercised with relation to the chief end of his work of creation, of providence and of grace, and must be put forth in accordance with all the perfections of his infinite being : the folly of such repinings is shown to be surpassed only by their presumption.

5. To urge that the mercy of God ought to have led him to prevent the introduction of any suffering into the universe, or to its total extirpation after it had found an entrance, is only saying, on the first point, that God's mercy ought to deprive itself of all possibility of making itself manifest in the universe, and that this ought to be done in subordination to the sins of men : and, on the second point, it is only saying, that God having failed in his grand design of such a universe as he proposed, but could not accomplish, ought now by an irregular and miraculous interposition to subvert the order, and the event of all things, and cure such defects of his plan and operation, as he had not, at first, foreseen and provided for : and that all things ought to be done, by God, to prevent sin from being followed by misery : the whole of which is impious.

6. If it be still further alleged—that God ought to have prevented the introduction of sin itself into the universe—and thereby excluded the possibility of suffering : in addition to

what has been said before, it is obvious to reply, that this cavil of infidelity is levelled more directly at natural Religion than at Christianity ; since sin and misery are actually in God's world, and Christianity only proposes to redress them. As a blasphemous cavil against God for having acted as he has done in the matter of creation, providence and grace—perhaps before we are fully satisfied of our right to make it—and thus to assail him in his being, and all his attributes, we ought to reflect that God is at least as wise, as Powerful, and as Good, as an infidel : that he is at least as much bent on the preservation of his essential glory, and the manifestation of his declarative glory, as any infidel is ; that being such a God, and working to such an end, he is as likely to be right, in the means as any infidel. Especially we ought to reflect, that what things are possible—what things are best amongst those that are possible—and amongst the best possible, which are they that on the whole God ought to prefer, are matters he may as well be trusted with as any infidel : and that —as for us—the undeniable facts of the universe,—as for example—God, creation, and salvation on one side—and sin, misery, and perdition on the other, had as well be accepted as they assuredly exist ; as that we should revolt against God because they do exist ; and accomplish by that revolt, nothing, except one more proof of the things we impiously reject, and one more ground of the certainty and justice of our perdition—along with every infidel.

V.—1. The last of the Perfections of God, which fall under the special aspect which I am now considering, is his Long-suffering. It is, as was before observed, that exercise of his Goodness, which leads him to delay the execution of his just judgments upon the guilty. Amongst the fruits of it are the Patience of God with sinners : the Forbearance of God towards the impenitent : and his slowness to anger.

2. The Scriptures abound with statements of the existence of this perfection in God : and with representations as to the manner and extent of its exercise, towards every fallen creature. He who cannot look upon sin with the least allowance—is so far from wishing sinners to perish in their sins—that he has done all that was consistent with his divine perfections, in order to save them ; and then delayed the destruction upon which the impenitent rush, to the very uttermost. There is no human being of

whom, as we survey their life and contemplate their nature, it is not certain, that if God had sought occasion against them, or been strict to mark iniquity—they must, already, have been consigned to remediless destruction: and every soul of man is obliged to render this verdict of itself. The extent to which the Forbearance of God is manifested personally to every human creature—could be justly estimated, only after we knew the number and turpitude of their transgressions; and could rightly estimate the holiness, the majesty, and the goodness of him, against whom they offended; and could fully appreciate the extent of that necessity produced alike by the exigencies of the universe itself, and by the immediate claims of divine justice, that every disobedience of the creature should receive a just recompense of reward.

3. This immeasurable Forbearance, which is exercised toward each individual in this boundless way—extends also to every class of persons, and to the entire race of men. The children of God were its objects, while they lived in open sin ; and they are still its objects as they strive, with an imperfect obedience, to obey God. The openly profane are its objects, while their day of grace may be supposed to continue ; if possible, still more so— that they are not cast into hell at once, when that day of grace is done. The very damned await till the day of endless doom, for the second death to fall upon them, with all its horrors. And the redeemed throughout every successive generation, find the Long-suffering of God to be Salvation[1]—not only because his goodness leads them to repentance ; but also because but for the riches of his Long-suffering and Forbearance, he would have made a short work, in righteousness, long ago, of a race that having rejected him, crucified his Son ; and the very existence, much less the salvation of all succeeding generations would have been impossible.

4. And now if, notwithstanding such Long-suffering, the guilty will still rush upon destruction; and notwithstanding such mercy, the miserable will continue to choose suffering instead of repentance ; and notwithstanding such grace sin must still abound: what idea of the depravity and perdition of ungodly men can equal the reality? When the Grace, Mercy, and Long-suffering of God, will have been finally exhausted—and the

---

[1] Rom., ii. 4; 2 Pet., iii. 15.

Lord Jesus shall be revealed from heaven with his mighty angels—in flaming fire, taking vengeance on them that know not God, and that obey not the gospel of our Lord Jesus Christ; who can exaggerate either the terror or the justice of that divine wrath, in which they shall be punished with everlasting destruction, from the presence of the Lord, and from the glory of his power.[1]

VI.—1. We proceed next to consider the Justice of God. Amongst all his Attributes not one is more comprehensible by us, or more intimately and universally operative upon us. Mercy and Truth go before his face: but Justice and Judgment are the very habitation of his throne.[2] By it the very bonds of the universe are kept together: and the unalterable distinction between Right and Wrong—True and False—Good and Evil, is preserved and made everlastingly triumphant. And as for man—the sum of all the goodness which has been shown to him by the Lord—and of all the duty that God requires of him, is declared to be;—that while he must love mercy, and walk humbly before God—it goes before both that he must do Justice.[3]

2. Justice may be predicated of God in several distinct senses. It is essential to him as God: that is, it is an absolute Perfection of his nature. It belongs to him as the Sovereign Ruler of the universe: that is—independently of any express commital of himself in any way—his administration of all created things will be spontaneously, perfectly, and universally just. It also appertains to him as the Judge of men and angels, under the actual system of the universe: that is, he will determine, and apply, with unalterable Justice, the system which exists, so that every one shall receive his exact due—and no more and no less—according to its requirements. He is just, as God—just as the Sovereign Ruler—just as the Eternal Judge: his justice is Essential—Administrative—Judicial: and is supreme and invariable—in all three of these aspects. Again: Justice itself may be contemplated under two aspects: one, namely, special, in which is considered only that particular Attribute of God, or that single virtue of man; the other, universal, in which it is embraced as. an element, or a qualification of other perfections of God, or other virtues of man. For religion itself is only the just rendering to God that which is his; and love to our parents is only justice in that form; and justice itself is

______

[1] 2 Thes., i. 7–9.   [2] Ps. lxxxix. 14.   [3] Micah, vi. 8.

but truth in our actions, as truth is but justice in our words. And again, special, or particular justice, may be viewed as being commutative ; that is, the perfect rendering to every one of all that duty requires to be done ; and as being distributive, that is the righteous distribution of deserved punishments and rewards ; which two methods of justice, in a public aspect, we call civil and criminal justice. And again, if the Essential, the Administrative, and the Judicial Justice of God is considered as brought under the distinction of Justice into Special and Universal ; the two former kinds of his Justice would fall under the head of Universal, and the last kind, namely, his Judicial Justice, under the head of particular Justice ; that is, of Justice considered by itself, and as regulated by the conditions of the Special System under which it is administered, and as exercised merely in rewarding and punishing, according to that system, every one who is subject to it.

3. Justice is the giving to every one that which is his. Divine Justice is that natural Sanctity of God by which he is kept perfectly from all imperfection, and most perfectly loves himself and the determinations of his own most holy Will. Nor is it, in any way, a different presentation to say, that the divine Justice is divine Goodness, tempered and administered by divine Wisdom ; for, from these two attributes combined and directed upon every particular matter, with a full view of the whole universe, and its great end, every result would flow, that flows from the direct application of the Justice of God. In the Administrative Justice of God, as before defined, that is, his Justice as the Ruler of the universe, this natural sanctity is specially exhibited in all his works and all his words. For when the prophet saw his train of angels filling the whole temple, and Seraphim cried to Seraphim, " the whole earth is full of the glory of the Lord," they began by a threefold ascription to him—as the holy, holy, holy Lord of Hosts.[1] And among all the grounds of that boundless glory, and all the proofs of that immaculate holiness, the Justice of his nature, and the Justice of his reign, shines forth continually in every act he performs and every word he utters. His work is perfect : all his ways are judgment ; a God of truth and without iniquity, just and right is he.[2] In all his work of creation ; in all his arrangement and administration of

---

[1] Isaiah, vi. 3.   [2] Deut., xxxii. 4.

his divine Providence over all things ; in all the manifestation of his nature and designs, in the salvation of lost sinners, through the sacrifice of his only begotten Son ; he declares himself to have proceeded with a perfect regard to the claims of infinite Justice, whether considered in itself as a perfection of his being, or considered in relation to his acts, as the creator, disposer, and director of all things. And the highest judgment of the human understanding, and the deepest impulses of human nature, alike conduct us to the perfect approbation of every act of God which we are capable of understanding, and to the most absolute trust in his equity, in whatever things the weaknesses of our faculties or the insufficiency of our knowledge may place beyond our capacity to decide. Our sense of dependence, which is universal in our race, is an instinctive testimony of our nature to the being, and the power of God ; and, in the same manner, our sense of accountability is a testimony to his dominion and his justice ; and our sense of blameworthiness is a testimony to the perfection with which the works of God accord with and respond to his acts, and his attributes. For the nature of man, because it is rational and accountable, does not thereby, the less, but does the more, live and move and have its being in God ; and because it has become depraved it does not thereby evade, but only changes the aspect of God toward it, and its response to him. It must be dreadful to human nature to be condemned by God ; but, it would be scarcely less dreadful to it, for God to declare it to be innocent, when it knows itself to be guilty. It would be dreadful that the innocent should be condemned, even through mistake, or by an act of mere power irrespective of their innocence ; but how much more dreadful, that they should be condemned *because* they were innocent !

4. In like manner the Essential and Administrative Justice of God involves the perfection of Truth in him, in all he says as well as in all he does ; for, as has been already observed, justice, considered as universal, is, when applied to our utterances, Truth. This Truth of God, when considered in one aspect, is the Truth of his Divine Essence and Perfection ; that is, the perfect conformity of the essence of God with the divine conception of itself ; and of every perfection with every other, and with the divine essence, and with the divine conception of it. And again, considered in another respect, the Truth of God's Intel-

lect is such that there is a perfect conformity between his conception of all things and objects about which it is exercised and the things and objects themselves ; so that all things must necessarily and infallibly be known to God precisely as they are. And again, considered in another point of view, the Truth of God prohibits the possibility of all error, falsehood, mistake, deception, and trifling with his rational creatures, in every manifestation of himself, by word or act. For while the truth of his creatures is, like their being, contingent, so that they may be untrue in word and act, and their essence remain ; the Truth of God is essential, and therefore immutable and eternal, and can no more not be than he cannot be. In the first aspect of the Truth of God we may call it Metaphysical, in the second Logical, and in the third Ethical. It is impossible, therefore, in every view we can take of the subject, that any manifestation which God makes of himself, and of all things, could be otherwise than infallibly true and certain, that is infallibly conformed with the divine mind, and with the things themselves ; and this is most especially the case with the Revelation he has made of himself, and which is to so great an extent the foundation on which his judicial justice is administered ; which, also, the Scriptures continually assert in the most explicit terms. The Lord is the true God, he is the living God, and an everlasting King :[1] this is the life eternal, that they might know thee, the only true God ;[2] to serve the living and true God.[3] And we know that the Son of God is come, and hath given us an understanding, that we may know him that is true : and we are in him that is true, even in his Son Jesus Christ. This is the true God, and eternal life.[4]

5. Particular Justice, that is, justice considered of itself, when viewed in its Commutative sense, namely, under the notion of rendering to every one according to the obligations binding on us, can be applied to God only in a metaphorical sense ; for the idea of duty or obligation is strictly inapplicable to God. But particular Justice, in its Distributive sense—the rendering of rewards and punishments as they are merited—applies to him in the most eminent sense ; for he is not only the infinite Judge, but he is the infinite Lawgiver, who has established every code, by means of which justice can be judicially administered in things pertaining to himself ; and he is, moreover, the infinitely

<hr>

[1] Jer., x. 10.   [2] John, xvii. 3.   [3] 1 Thes., i. 9.   [4] 1 John, v. 20.

just Ruler, whose laws thus made, and thus judicially applied, find in him the executor of their eternal sanctions. Nor is there any possibility of avoiding this result upon the supposition of the existence of God, and of creatures like ourselves ; for in the very act of our creation, in the nature of our very being, and in the conditions upon which our existence is continued, there occur of necessity relations between God and us which involve what we call the Laws of Nature, of which God is the only Author, and which he must administer or cease to be God. The first point immediately before us is, that from the very nature of the case these laws cannot but be just, and justly administered ; and the next point is, that, under any circumstances, the just admin- istration of any law is wholly impossible, except by means of what is tantamount to their judicial application ; that is, to the complete consideration of them, as applied to the particular cases that arise under them, and the just application of the rule to the case. It follows, therefore, that from the very nature of God, of the case, and of justice itself, it cannot but be that every transgression and disobedience must receive a just recompense of reward ; and every right action must be approved by God. In- dependently of any special Covenant, or Law, or Revelation from God, the conditions upon which the universe exists, reveal to us the necessary and eternal dominion of unalterable justice; not instant in its application it may be, but sure and immaculate.

6. Taking the Scriptures as true, it has pleased God to bind himself to man, and man to him—by two covenants—widely different from each other—and both of them independent, in their origin and obligation, of the law of nature, of which I have been speaking. The first of these, called the Covenant of Works, was made with man in his state of innocency ; the second, called the Covenant of Grace, was revealed to man, and applied for his deliverance after his fall ; but was, as to its absolute nature and origin, a covenant from eternity, between the persons of the Holy Trinity, for the salvation of man, in his foreseen condition of ruin by the fall. The particular discussion of either of these covenants would be out of place here. What is to be considered at present is, that it was impossible for either of them to change in the least particular, any Perfection of God, or to make him known to us, or bind him to us, in any way that was inconsistent with his Being and his Attributes. In particular, as applicable

to the matter immediately before us, the conditions of both these covenants, are of necessity obliged to be unalterably just. To be so, neither of them could possibly permit sin to go unpunished, or possibly deprive righteousness of its reward; and the administration, as well as the nature of both of them, must be perfectly just. Many points of great intricacy must be expected to arise in the details of questions so vast in their compass, and so boundless in their application; but the fundamental principles are clear and may be comprehended by every one. These, as we shall the more plainly see as we the more carefully examine, are not only clearly recognized in both of God's covenants with respect to man, and in every part of his blessed word; but are made the basis of all his methods of dealing with men and angels—throughout every dispensation.

7. So deep and unalterable are these foundations of eternal justice, that even after the covenant of works had ceased, by its breach, to be a covenant of life; this did not hinder it from being a covenant of death—to the whole family of man; for every one had incurred its fearful curse and penalty. And even when the Covenant of Redemption would restore man to the lost image and favor of God; not a jot nor a tittle of that eternal justice of God could be abated. If Christ will reap the glory—even he must take the humiliation and endure the agony. God must be just while he justifies the ungodly. Considered in whatever light, there is no proper necessity that God should save sinners. But if he graciously wills to do it, there is a strict necessity that he should do it justly. And that is the problem, of which there was no solution, but the incarnation and sacrifice of the Son of God. If this universe, and every creature in it, had perished— another universe—nay, many more—under the same or under other auspices, might have replaced it. But what could efface a stain upon the tarnished justice of God?

CHAPTER XXII.

CONSUMMATE ATTRIBUTES OF GOD: SUCH AS APPERTAIN TO HIM
CONSIDERED AS THE SUM OF ALL INFINITE PERFECTIONS.

I. Nature of the Attributes of the Fifth Class.—II. The Life of God: and its Infinite activity and unwasting Fulness.—III. The Majesty of God.—IV. Omnipresence of God.—V. All-sufficiency of God.—VI. Oneness of God.—VII. The Blessedness of God. The participation of this is attainable by man: but only through the Knowledge of God.—VIII. Method, and Spiritual insight: God, and Salvation.

I. THERE remains to be considered another great class of the Attributes of God, which in our mode of conceiving things must be distinguished from each of the classes heretofore treated of. I call them *Consummate Attributes.* Their peculiar characteristic, upon which I base their place and name in the classification I have adopted is, that they must be contemplated, in order to be properly understood, as connected immediately with all the other perfections of God. This may occur either by considering them as results of all the rest united, or as the common matrix of them all: according as one or other method of treating the subject is proposed. Thus occupying a peculiar relation to all the other Perfections of God, and by consequence to the universe, they afford the ground of a distinction, and so of a classification, and thus of knowledge of God's adorable nature: which knowledge is the proper end of all such enquiries.

II. The first of these in logical order, is the *Life* of God, and the infinite *activity* which appertains to that Life. The Scriptures express nothing concerning God, more earnestly, than that he is the *living* God: and I have several times directed attention to those remarkable testimonies—and to the method of their general truth, in the being of God. But there is an aspect in which this Consummate perfection of God ought to be contemplated, more exalted than has hitherto been suggested. Of all the perfections of the divine nature, the whole universe is made partaker of the fruits of this in a manner the most universal—the most copious, and the most enduring. The vital action in God is the infinite power of the infinite essence of God. In it is the living force of every other Attribute of his nature ; and its activity is the source of every manifestation of himself, and therefore of all creation—all providence, and all grace. In every created thing, life according to its kind, is the first blessing that God can bestow and the foundation of every subsequent blessing. Whatever exists has its being in him : whatever rising higher so exists as to move—as the Scriptures express it—also has its being in him : and rising higher still—whatever so exists that we may say specifically it lives—that too has its being in God. The whole universe lives, moves, and has its being in him. From the clod of the valley with all its properties, up through those wondrous forces which pervade the universe in a form non-vital ; and that living power which sustains the inanimate creation ; and that vital principle which fills the earth with living creatures—to its highest known form, in the endless life of man : all, without exception, as without stint, and without exhaustion, either in its source or in its manifestation, is an emanation from the living God—and an unbroken and immeasurable outpouring of goodness and power and wisdom, reaching from the unfathomable depths of the past, fructifying the whole universe, and sweeping onward to eternity ! What an idea does it give us of God, to know that all this required only that he should speak and it was done : and that, in all its utmost glory and beauty, and strength, if he were but to utter the word, it would all pass away?

III. In the midst of this boundless manifestation of the Life of God and of its fruits, we are to consider what idea we can form of him, as of the being to whom all that exists appertains, by absolute and illimitable Right and Dominion. The being who made all things, who owns all things, who rules all things, who in his sovereign, illimitable and irresistible sway, is unto himself, the rule, as well as the cause, and the end. That which we know of all that we behold, is but the smallest part of what may be known. And all that we behold, may be the smallest part of all that exists. And all that can exist, is but as nothing compared with him, in whom it all lives, and to whom it all appertains, by ways, the completeness and imperial absoluteness of which nothing in the universe can do more than faintly illustrate. Conceive of the nature of a dominion like this, whether in its extent or its essential nature; and then conceive of him, who has title to it, and whose perfections fit him to exert it, in a way supremely glorious to himself. After that we may have some faint idea of the perfection of Dominion which belongs to Jehovah of Hosts, and which, because we cannot better express it, we may call the Majesty of God.

IV. We are also to consider that this Living God, with this Infinite Dominion, is of that nature which we express by saying, he is at every instant present with every object and at every point throughout the whole universe. Each particular thing is as completely subject to his personal supervision, as if it alone existed in the universe; and the whole universe is as completely taken in by his all-pervading presence, as if he regarded nothing but its general frame and order. He is an Omnipresent God. It is thus that the infallible exercise of his omnipotence can be rightly directed, on the one hand to all the subordinate ends of his eternal counsel, and on the other to the great end, unto which all things are required, by his infinite will, to tend continually. It is thus that the infinite Intelligence, Will, Power, Knowledge, Wisdom, Goodness and Justice of God, pervade with the distinctness of a personal presence, the entire universe. It is thus that his Simplicity, Eternity and Immensity, forbid the idea of place or time to him at all, in any sense, except that of an eternal and inscrutable omnipresence.

V. In immediate connection with this consummate Attribute of God, by means of which all his perfections are in a manner concentrated; there is another divine perfection, in which we conceive of God, in one view, as competent to all that is brought into immediate contact with him by his omnipresence. He is the All-sufficient God. Infinitude is the characteristic of his nature, of each separate perfection, and of the combination of every perfection in him, considered as a personal God. Without effort, without distraction of mind, without confusion or hesitation in working, without limitation of Power, or defect of Wisdom, or doubt of Justice, or failure of Goodness, or wavering of Counsel; a supereminent perfection is in him. As he lives, as he exerts his illimitable Dominion, as he is omnipresent, thus living and thus ruling: so he is All-sufficient, supereminently Perfect. Whatever perfection there is in the universe, is but an emanation—a shadow—of the perfection, that is consummate in God. All-sufficient to himself, all-sufficient to every creature, all-sufficient to every end in all things: so immeasurably does he transcend all occasions, and all existences exterior to himself, that the very distinctions by which we determine all things, are lost in him. To him nothing is either great or small: and to number the hairs of our head, to feed the young ravens when they cry unto him, and to adorn the lilies of the valley ; or to create, and order, and rule, and sustain, and bless, and punish, principalities and thrones and hierarchies, visible and invisible —with all the exalted interests and complications they exhibit ; are—to him—considered in themselves—works that are alike easy, alike difficult ; and considered with reference to him, are alike great, alike small. Every measure by which such things can be determined, passes out of us—and is lost in the Infinitude, and All-sufficiency, and supereminent perfection of God.

VI. And as the sum and end of all, these two results follow by inevitable necessity, namely : The Oneness—Uniqueness of God, and his Infinite Blessedness. For God, as has been shown, possesses all possible perfections, in the most absolute manner and in the highest possible degree. But if more than one such Being is proposed, the two must differ in some way from each other ; in which case one of them cannot be infinite in all his perfections : or they must be exactly alike ; in which case, it is not in fact two, but only one whose image has been twice repeated, that we conceive of ; for an infinitely perfect being cannot lack unity any more than any other perfection. And nothing but God can be absolutely perfect. There may be an infinite variety of all other existences, and an infinite number of each. But God is infinitely perfect ; so that there can be but one God.

VII. The infinite Felicity of God is continually declared to us throughout the Scriptures. Nor is it possible to conceive how it could be otherwise. For in him there is a continual duration of his blessedness ; an uninterrupted and absolute fruition of the very highest perfections ; the constant and perfect intuition of himself—and of all his perfections ; the absolute fruition of all—always and altogether ; the infinite All-sufficiency of himself, his absolute Independency of all things exterior to himself ! It is impossible to conceive that his Blessedness should not be perfect, or that it should ever be interrupted, or that it could be otherwise than infinite and eternal. It was a participation of this Blessedness which God proposed for man, and for which he fitted him in his original creation. It is a still more exalted participation of it, which he proposes to fit him for, and restore him to the fruition of, by that Great Salvation which is in Jesus Christ. As the Knowledge of himself is the fundamental condition of the perfect and eternal Blessedness of God ; so the Knowledge of God lies at the very root of all blessedness in the creature ; how much more in the ruined creature, whom it is purposed to restore ! And we know that the Son of God is come, and hath given us an understanding that we may know him that is true ; and we are in him that is true, even in his Son Jesus Christ. This is the True God, and eternal life.[1]

VIII. In concluding a subject so immense and so difficult, I may be allowed to refer distinctly to the Classification of the Attributes of God, proposed and discussed in the Seventeenth chapter. If what has been advanced in the five chapters which succeed that one, can be considered a just and true outline of the most intricate part of all knowledge ; then the analysis upon which that classification rests, must be allowed to be so far comprehensive and exhaustive of the vast subject, as to furnish the diligent student of the Scriptures with important suggestions in his endeavors to reduce to a clear and simple method, its sublime revelations touching the nature of the true God. What is supposed to be gained is, a more exact knowledge of God, which is the highest of all knowledge, by means of a more exact method, founded upon distinctions which as to the divine nature are perfectly obvious, and as to our nature are in accordance with its fundamental laws. There can be no doubt that upon such a subject as this, a just method is next in importance to a strict adherence to revealed truth ; if indeed either is possible without the other. As to the knowledge itself, it is decisive concerning all systematic acquaintance with the plan of Salvation. The declarative glory of God is the very end of Salvation ; as it is of every thing in the created universe ; and the display of the nature and perfections of God, is the method of that glory. Whoever has the very least idea of the way in which God saves sinners, has a corresponding idea of the Nature and Perfections of God. Whoever has the most perfect conception of all that is

[1] 1 John, v. 20.

involved in the salvation of sinners, has the most complete knowledge of the Nature and Perfections of God. It is on that very account that it is so much easier to attain a certain knowledge of God through the practical operations of his grace, than through the abstract contemplation of himself. And it is on the very same account that the absolute comprehension of his Word, is no more possible than the absolute comprehension of himself. Without a spiritual insight, no true Knowledge either of God, or of Salvation, is possible. With a spiritual insight, no other limit can be put to the knowledge we may attain of both—except that it cannot be absolutely complete.

THE KNOWLEDGE OF GOD,

OBJECTIVELY CONSIDERED.

ARGUMENT OF THE FOURTH BOOK.

THE three preceding Books have had for their particular subject respectively, Man—The God-Man—and God. In a certain sense the objective knowledge of God unto salvation is fully attained. when we clearly understand what is involved in those three conceptions. But that very knowledge of God is an object of scrutiny of transcendent interest: and that, whether we consider its absolute nature, its precise extent, its source, or our manner of obtaining it. This Fourth Book is devoted to the discussion of that sublime topic. The Twenty-Third Chapter, which is the First of this Book, contains a general survey of the whole matter of our knowledge of God, and establishes the reality of it, the nature of it, and the method by which it is attainable: and as the result demonstrates that God may, and does, manifest himself to our Intelligence as an object of certain knowledge; that he does this after a Natural Method, in Creation and Providence: after a Supernatural Method in the Incarnation and the Work of the Holy Ghost: and after a Method combining both the preceding, in the Sacred Scriptures and in the human soul as created and renewed in his own image; and then proves that except by these Three Methods, and except by the Six applications of them, two under each Method, God does not manifest himself to human Intelligence, and is not an object of knowledge to man. The Six following Chapters are devoted to a thorough discussion of those Six Manifestations of God, considered with special reference to the knowledge they afford us concerning him. The Twenty-Fourth Chapter, which is the Second of this Book, is devoted to the Knowledge of God, as the Creator of all things, derived from the knowledge of his Works, considered as manifestations of himself: wherein the fundamental truth of the creation of the universe is demonstrated, and the perpetual presence of the Creator shown: the method and sum of our knowledge of God through his works, is developed: the relation of this knowledge of God to all other knowledge of him, and the paramount authority of this primeval manifestation of God, are pointed out; and the abnormal condition of the created universe, arising from the introduction of Sin, and its Remedy, is pointed out, and the solution of this great problem given. In the Twenty-Fifth Chapter, which is the Third of this Book, the whole subject of the Infinite Dominion of God, as exhibited in the method, and course, and end of Divine Providence, is developed as a source of our knowledge of God, manifested in his sublime control of all things : wherein, amongst other things, the relations of Providence to every other manifestation of God, are discussed : the relation of the will of God executed in Providence, to the will of God revealed in his Word, is specially illustrated : the point of view from which all Providence is unfolded by God is pointed out : the sublime illustration of Providence in the career of the Messianic kingdom, is detailed : the God and the system revealed in Providence are shown to be identical with the God and the system revealed in creation, in the Sacred Scriptures, and in human reason : and in conclusion, the relation of Providence to the invisible world is disclosed : and therein, the whole question of Angels and departed Spirits, as objects and agents of divine Providence, is briefly discussed. The two preceding Chapters are thus devoted to the only two examples that exist whereby God manifests himself to our Intelligence, by a method purely natural : that is, purely within the sphere of our Intelligence, according to the purely natural use of the faculties with which we are endowed. While the two Chapters which immediately follow, are devoted to the only two examples which exist whereby God manifests himself to our Intelligence by a method purely supernatural : that is, purely without the natural sphere of our faculties, and absolutely demanding a supernatural influence upon us, in order to their just and full appreciation. The Twenty-Sixth Chapter, which is the Fourth of this Book, discusses the whole matter of the Word made Flesh—God manifest in human nature : and therein, the spiritual system, both of God and of the universe, of which that conception is the ruling idea, is disclosed : the origin of the conception, its progress through all time, and its influence upon all other knowledge of God, and upon all possible systems of belief, are exhibited : the utter impossibility of saving sinners; explicating the Scriptures, or comprehending the mode of the Divine Existence revealed therein, without this conception, is set forth : the sum of the Knowledge of God attainable through his Incarnation is attempted to be appreciated, and this shown to be the culminating point : and the unavoidable certainty and irresistible force of this method of the knowledge of God, through Jesus Christ, are demonstrated. The Twenty-Seventh Chapter, which is the Fifth of this Book, is devoted to the Knowledge of God attainable through the manifestation of himself in the New Creation— that is, in the whole work of the Divine Spirit, this being an example of the supernatural method in which the Divine Person especially contemplated, to wit, the Spirit, is as thoroughly distinct from human nature, as the Divine Person of the Son in the preceding example, is thoroughly united with it : and herein the mode of the Divine Existence, and the influence thereof upon the way of Salvation, and upon the method of Divine Manifestation, are explained : the nature of the New Creation—of the work of the Spirit therein—of the posture of the universe when it begins—of its progress, epoch by epoch, from Adam to the Millennial Glory, with the sum of the results in the way of knowledge at each epoch—is stated in detail : and in a special manner the wonderful working of the Spirit as the Author of the New Creation, is developed with reference to Christ the head of that creation—in the constitution of the person of Immanuel—in his perpetual presence with the Mediator in his whole estate of Humiliation—in his creation of the mystical Body of Christ, the Church of the Living God, and every member thereof; the whole being an outline of the way of salvation, from that point of view, as objective knowledge. Both the purely natural and the purely supernatural methods, and the entire examples under each, of the Manifestations of God, being thus passed through; the two succeeding Chapters discuss the third method, which is a combination of the two methods already explained; under which third method, as under each of the others, but two examples have ever been applied by God —both of which are subjected to a careful scrutiny. In the Twenty-Eighth Chapter, which is the Sixth of this Book, the special object of consideration is God manifested in Revelation—the God of the Sacred Scriptures: wherein an attempt is made to appreciate the Sacred Scriptures under the conception of their sublime unity, as the Institutes of the kingdom of God, composed by the Holy Ghost—explicating the kingdom in its origin, progress, and triumph under a threefold aspect; to wit, as the Messianic kingdom, with Christ as its King and Lord, and the world in hostility to it; as the New Creation of which the Holy Spirit is the Author and Christ the Head; and as the Church of God held forth in the members thereof, who are the brethren of Christ, and the children of God: that they are expressly a Divine Treatise concerning God—developed around the Person of Immanuel—with the power of perfect truth, and the efficacy of an infallible method—and that their divine origin and authority are inevitably certain. The Twenty-Ninth Chapter, which is the Seventh and last of this Book, is occupied with the consideration of the human soul, as created and recreated in the image of God, and as being a manifestation to itself in its own conscious existence, of him in whose likeness it was both made and renewed: and herein is a careful scrutiny into human nature, in its original and in its fallen state—in its fundamental unity and boundless diversity—in its rational, moral, and spiritual aspects—analytically and historically—the sum of all being, that the soul knows itself, and in so doing knows God manifested in the created and self-conscious image of himself; and still further, there is a careful scrutiny of the question of Life, considered with special reference to the new Birth—of the question of the image of God in unfallen, depraved, and restored man—of the question of Regeneration, with its nature and effects: and the result upon the soul is shown to be a higher and surer knowledge both of itself and of God: as inevitable upon the data proved —and augmented at every step by the agencies employed by God, the methods used by God, and the effects produced through both in the Renewal and Sanctification of the Soul: doubly therefore, the renewed soul, in its own conscious existence, knowing itself, knows him whose image it is, and who manifests himself both in its creation and in its regeneration. A great multitude of questions, covering in the aggregate a boundless field of enquiry, speculation, and knowledge, are involved more or less directly in the matter discussed in this Book. Such as did not lie directly in my way are passed in silence; such as I was obliged to consider have been encountered, and the results are stated. The fundamental truths supposed to be established are far too numerous to be stated of each divine Manifestation, in a general summary, here. But considering the conception of this entire Book as one great question, bearing with decisive force on the whole idea of the Knowledge of God : then the fundamental truths supposed to be demonstrated in it, may be stated thus : The Knowledge of God, objectively considered, is, in the strictest sense, a science of positive Truth: the great end of that science is Knowledge unto Salvation : the grand divisions of it are, Man—the God-Man—God: the sources of it are the Manifestations which God makes of himself to our Intelligence : the elements of it are, the particular parts of the Knowledge of God obtained by man, through the manifestations which God makes of himself to our Intelligence : God has manifested himself in this manner to man—and has thus become an object, not of complete and perfect knowledge, which is impossible : but of precise and certain Knowledge unto Salvation : He has done this in a limited number of ways, and by a still more limited number of methods—the whole of which are susceptible of exhaustive enumeration, and distinct classification by us : He has done it after a Natural method, with two ways—namely, Creation and Providence : He has done it after a Supernatural method, with two ways—namely, Incarnation and the New Creation : He has done it after a method combining both the preceding methods, with two ways —namely, Divine Revelation and the human Soul as a created and recreated conscious and living image of himself: and finally, the whole relation of that human soul to the whole case is such, that its ignorance of God in its present fallen estate is abnormal, founded in sin, and fruitful only of misery.

CHAPTER XXIII.

OUR KNOWLEDGE OF GOD: GENERAL STATEMENT CONCERNING THE
MANIFESTATIONS OF GOD.

1. Methods of knowing God. Nature of the Inquiry.—2. As an object of knowledge. God is neither perfectly comprehensible, nor wholly incomprehensible.—3. Distinction between material and immaterial essences. This distinction applied.—4. Human nature considered with reference to its capacity of knowing.—5. The most inscrutable of all problems—how God could conceal himself.—6. Our double relation to God, as creatures and as sinners.—7. Our knowledge of God, the product of his manifestations. These considered as natural, as supernatural, and as combining both methods.—8. Creation, Providence: Incarnation of the Son of God, the Work of the Holy Ghost: Divine Revelation, the Human Soul.—9. The domain traversed. The result of the Analysis stated in detail.—10. The posture of Revelation fortified.

1. WE proceed from the direct inquiry concerning the nature and mode of the divine existence, to a detailed examination of the whole question touching the means by which we may certainly know God. Hitherto, all these means have been resorted to and used—some more, some less: what is now to be attempted, is to vindicate in a distinct manner, that use, and to point out clearly what those means are, and that they alone are the true and the sufficient means of our certainly knowing God. The question does not primarily concern the fact of God's existence—which has been proved : nor yet the manner of his existence, which has been largely illustrated : though both of these questions are continually involved. But taking our stand upon all that has been proved and illustrated, what we are to examine and determine next, is the methods by which we can come, and have come, to the certain knowledge of such a God as has been displayed : all the methods, in their nature, and in their order.

2. In some respects, God is wholly incomprehensible by us. In other respects, he is completely comprehensible by us. If he were in every respect wholly incomprehensible—he would be in.

no respect the subject of our knowledge : if he were in every sense the subject of complete knowledge by us, we should know him far better than we know ourselves, or any thing else that exists. On both sides it would be in its result, the abnegation of God : on the one side by banishing him from the intelligent universe, on the other side by degrading him below the creatures of his own hands. Both of these forms of appreciating God have been found at every period of human History—plunging the race into one abyss after another. God is not a purely abstract—and therefore a purely inert being—removed infinitely from us and conceivable only as a metaphysical exaltation, a stranger to his own universe, and alike incapable of manifesting himself, and of extricating himself out of his eternal incomprehensibility. Nor on the other hand, is God a being who so passes into the created universe as to be, in a manner, absorbed in it, exhausted by it, and even more obvious to the creatures he has made than the wonders of their own being are. As the cause of the universe itself, he passes into the universe and is manifested by it, as every cause is manifested in its effects. The heavens declare his glory : all things visible announce some one or other of his invisible perfections : his intelligence, his will, his power, shine forth in all his works ; every thing that is most august in him, is manifest in his transcendent dominion over all things—still more distinctly in the powers and movements of the soul of man—and with perfect fulness in the Word made flesh. Still however, we who are but finite effects of that infinite and perfect cause, can neither manifest perfectly, nor comprehend perfectly that which being infinite must be infinitely comprehended—and to be so must be infinitely manifested : neither of which is possible to finite creatures. God escapes us in that infinitude, which is inaccessible to us, and incomprehensible by us. Yet we have conceptions, simple and primitive, concerning that very infinitude of God, and even concerning that incomprehensible essence of God to which his infinitude appertains: inexplicable, it may be, because they rest upon the furthest term of our intelligence, and because it does not appertain to reason to explain, but to accept those simple and primitive conceptions which are the elements of knowledge and the very highest criteria of Truth. Does any one suppose there can be any effect without a cause; any phenomenon without a substance—any existence without an essence—any thing felt, or thought, or done, without a thinking, sentient, living personality ? Or does any one suppose there can be any cause which is not contained, in some way, in its effects—or any substance which has not distinct relation to its own phenomena—or any essence which makes existence manifest and yet does not exist itself—or any personality whose thoughts, emotions, and acts, do not afford any comprehensible idea of its nature? If we apply these primitive conceptions, to the infinite and incomprehensible being of God—we find them as clear in their relation to him, as in their relation to any other object to which they can be directed. Effects, phenomena, existence, ideas, emotions, personality—springing from an infinite cause, revealing an infinite substance, inhering in an infinite essence, manifesting an infinite nature: or to reverse the statement—an infinite cause, an infinite substance, an infinite essence, an infinite nature—manifesting itself in effects, phenomena, existence, ideas, emotions, acts: how is it possible for rational beings to say—either that these things are not the subjects of knowledge—or to say that they are the subjects of perfect knowledge? How is it possible to say, that God is perfectly comprehensible, or to say that he is wholly incomprehensible ?

3. All things which come within the sphere of our faculties are capable of being reduced into two grand classes—and the whole are separated by a single line of division—fundamental and impassable. On the one side is all that we call *material*, on the other side is all that we call *spiritual:* and compound or decompose them as we may, the ineffaceable and all-pervading distinction abides in its invincible force. Each of these immense classes has one fundamental mark peculiar to itself, and one fundamental negation of the mark peculiar to the other: and neither of them has relatively to the other more than the one fundamental mark and negation; and when both of them are stripped of every thing else, this fundamental mark and negation remains to indicate the nature of that inscrutable portion of each which we call its *essence*. This fundamental mark of the essence of matter is that it has *extension;* this fundamental negation is, that it does not think. This fundamental mark of the essence of Spirit is, that *it thinks;* this fundamental negation is that it has no extension. It is in vain to say that we know nothing of the essence of any thing : for we do know with

absolute certainty, that spirit does think, and is incapable of any extension at all: and with the like certainty, that matter does not think, and is capable of boundless extension.   It is still more vain to say—that it is a mere assumption to claim that any *essence*, either of matter or spirit, exists.   For the word is nothing; it is the thing which is insuperable.   Call it what we may, something exists, which thinks and is indivisible: and something else, which cannot think and is infinitely divisible.   And so certain is this, that we are utterly incapable even of conceiving that a thought could exist without any thing to think it, or that extension could exist without any thing to be extended.   Now it has been demonstrated before, that the infinite God about whose manifestations we are inquiring, is a self-existent Spirit—possessed of all the perfections developed in several chapters of the preceding Book.   It is to the human Spirit, the head of the creation of that Infinite Spirit, that the manifestations of God for which we seek are made: it is these which are of supreme importance to us, and to them is this inquiry especially directed.

4. The truthfulness of our senses, and the truthfulness of our consciousness, is for us the ultimate certainty upon which every other certainty rests.   For us, absolute Truth can go no further ; absolute certainty can repose on no surer basis.   Thus endowed by God, we possess infallible means of knowing what exists and what passes within us, and what exists and what passes without us, to the whole extent that both are the proper subjects of knowledge, and are brought within the circle of our powers.   In our complex nature, the wonderful essences both of matter and of spirit are mysteriously united, to form of both, in each human being, a free personality, which is a distinct, active, and voluntary, but, at the same time, a dependent, force in the universe. On the one hand, all physical things are made tributary to our growth in knowledge and in power; on the other hand, we are made partakers of that universal, absolute, and infallible reason, which, in its relation to us, fallen as we are, is, indeed, no longer a perfect guide ; and are made capable of receiving that eternal truth, which is supreme even to human reason itself, and independent of it, as it appears in man—that intelligence and that truth which are consummate in God, and are of the very essence of the Infinite Spirit.   By whatever means it can be shown that we exist at all, it is shown at the same time that we exist in

such a manner, and with such capabilities, that we cannot avoid knowing, in some form, that which is the proper object of our senses and our faculties, and within their reach ; nor avoid perceiving, that in the things thus known there is that eternal distinction of True and False, responsive to the infinite intelligence of God, and that eternal distinction of Good and Evil, responsive to the infinite Rectitude of God. We cannot err in supposing that our consciousness reports to us these inward acts and states, dependent on the perception of these existences and these distinctions. We are incapable of distrusting the absolute truth of that which our consciousness reports to us ; for to doubt it implies that we might doubt the doubt, which is wholly absurd. All that is left to us is to rely on the reality of the distinctions themselves, or to believe that all things are equally true and false, equally good and bad ; that is, we must subvert the deepest foundations of our nature, and destroy both intelligence and conscience, in order to avoid the necessity of knowing God ! Nor does it avail any thing to urge that our nature is both feeble and limited, by way of disproving its essential character ; any more than it tends to prove we are not what we are, because other natures are far above or far below ours. Our imperfections may prove that our nature is dependent, which is true, or that it is depraved, which is true also ; but it is, nevertheless, dependent human nature—depraved human nature. It is a self-conscious, voluntary, free, rational, moral, and therefore of necessity a knowing nature, with means of infallible, though not complete, knowledge concerning itself, concerning things exterior to itself, and concerning the relations of those outward and inward worlds to each other, and to the author of both of them.

5. How such a state of things as I have now briefly stated could exist independently of such a God as I have heretofore demonstrated is what no human intelligence is able to conceive, however vain and multiplied may have been the attempts of Philosophy, falsely so called, to persuade itself that it had done what human nature repudiates as impossible. Nay, it has been shown again and again, by those who have had the deepest insight into philosophy, and have spoken only in her venerable name—that the fundamental cognitions by which we know our finite selves, and know a finite outer world distinct from ourselves, absolutely involve the insuperable belief of a

substance for every phenomenon, an essence for every existence, a cause for every effect ; in one word the conception of an infinite Creator, without involving the conception of whom, the very simplest acts of our rational nature are incomprehensible and impossible. In the nature of the case the real difficulty would be, for God to conceal himself from us, and for us to conceive how he could accomplish this, even supposing him to desire it. And the only rational presumption would be, that he strongly desired to make himself known to us, and would take care that this result should be effectually secured. With such a nature as ours has been shown to be, how is it conceivable that we should be shut up with such a God as the Living God, in a universe full of him, and still have no conception of him, nor even any assurance of his existence ? We, separate activities restrained at every instant by an infinite activity : we, living intelligences face to face perpetually with the infinite giver both of life and intelligence : we, each one a real though a finite cause, in ceaseless contact with the cause of all causes : we, in whom the useful, the free, the beautiful, the true, the good—are the very elements of all progress—and their triumphs over nature, in society, in all art, in all knowledge, in all religion, are the consummation of all human civilization—living, moving, and having our being in the very bosom of the omnipresent author of them all ; and yet this perfectly glorious being shall be considered as nowhere manifested to us ! Let us not dishonor our nature and insult our Creator by pretending to credit such conceits.

6. We sustain two very distinct relations to God, as has been heretofore clearly explained and repeatedly illustrated. We sustain toward him the relation of creatures, and the relation of sinners, with all that is involved in both. He is our Creator, and he is our Saviour—with all that is involved in his being both. The knowledge which we need of him, is the Knowledge of him in both of these respects, the Knowledge relevant to us considered as occupying both of these relations to him. And the means concerning which we inquire, and whereby that Knowledge must be obtained, are such as are appropriate and real with respect to us, considered both as creatures and as sinners ; and the manifestations of God, whereby we may know him—of whatever kinds they may be—must to be effectual, be suitable to our condition and faculties, just as they are. We are not seeking for methods

by which beings higher or lower than ourselves, on the boundless scale of possible existence, might know God ; but exclusively for such means of knowing him as come within the circle of our nature—within the compass of our powers—within the reach of our faculties, sense, intellect, conscience ; the physical, the rational, the moral ; this, for us, is all. Through either of these, or through any two, or through all three, or by means of any relations which they bear to each other, or to us, or to God ; we possess the means of certain Knowledge. Nor must we forget, that these means if they terminate on the one side upon us, terminate on the other upon God ; and, therefore, if we may not exalt their perfection to the perfection of God, neither can we degrade their weakness to the level of human infirmity. They are the middle term through which all knowledge passes from the infinite to the finite ; and who can tell what boundless riches of Knowledge are lost in the perilous transit, from the unwasting fountain to the frail recipient ! Who can limit the improvement of which these sources of the Knowledge of God are susceptible in us, even in our present state of existence—much less, when they are perfected in eternity ! Who can imagine the boundless store we may gather up, of what is lost to us now !— How clear, and how ennobling is the conviction to which the most rigid analysis conducts us, that whatever knowledge we have or can obtain of God, is not to be distrusted as if it might be unreal ; but contrariwise, is worthy of the most intrepid confidence, because by the very means through which we obtain it, we are made certain that the mine from which some precious particles have reached us, literally overflows with inexhaustible treasures !

7. I have already stated, in various forms, that we cannot launch ourselves beyond the limits of our peculiar nature in search of the knowledge of God : but must content ourselves with such means of the knowledge of him, as he brings within our sphere. I have also pointed out our insuperable ignorance in some respects, of the essences of all things, and our precise knowledge in other respects ; and our primitive and instinctive belief concerning the only essences of which we have any conception, namely the essence of matter and the essence of spirit. There is no form in which the idea of a material existence of God can be stated—which does not result immediately in some

form of Atheism. Moreover, the precise conception we have of the very essence of matter, namely *extension* and by consequence, form, divisibility, and the like, is contradictory of the very conception we have of God—and of every attribute of his nature : while the precise conception we have of the very essence of spirit, namely *thought*, and by consequenc, self-consciousness, intelligence, and the like, is exactly in harmony with the very conception we have of God, and of every perfection of his being. It is impossible therefore, that God should be the immediate object of our senses, or that we should have immediate cognition of him through them. On the other hand it is equally impossible for such finite existences as we are, through the natural exercise of such faculties as ours, upon such conditions as limit their ordinary use, to have any intuition or immediate vision, or direct cognition of a spiritual existence exterior to ourselves. Moreover, we are unable to construe to ourselves the unconditioned, the infinite, in whatever form it may be presented to our intelligence. The direct and immediate cognition of God, in any natural manner and by natural means, is therefore impossible to us. We cannot know him thus by means of our senses, for he is immaterial, and they take cognizance only of matter, and its phenomena. Our Spirits, shut up in their tenements of clay, cannot have a natural intuition and immediate vision of any spirit or of Spiritual existences exterior to themselves. Finite, limited, and acting under conditions which determine the limits of knowledge —and the possibility even of thought—we cannot construe the infinite to our intelligence. The direct Knowledge of God is therefore impossible to us by any natural means. Supernatural means must be resorted to, and supernatural effects must follow their use, if we know God in any manner different from the manner natural to us. It is clear that all our knowledge of God must be derived from Manifestations of himself coming within the sphere of our intelligence. These manifestations may be such as to come within that sphere naturally considered ; or they may be such as to come within it only by means that are supernatural : or they may be such as combine both methods. The manifestations of God in Nature and in Providence, may be considered examples of the first kind. His manifestations through the Word made Flesh, and in the work of his Divine Spirit may be considered examples of the second kind. His manifestations in the written Revelation of his Will, and in the Human Soul may be considered examples of both methods united—that is, examples of the third kind.   As far as our knowledge extends, these examples exhaust in principle, the susceptibility of the case—and in effect embrace all the permanent manifestations of God to man.

  8. What I allege is, that God has created the universe, and that he is the Ruler of it : and that herein are two manifestations of himself, boundless in their extent, permanent in their contact with us, and as means of knowing him within the natural sphere of our intelligence.   What I allege in the second place is, that God through his Son Jesus Christ our Lord, is the Saviour of men, and that God, through his divine Spirit, is the sanctifier of men : and that herein are two additional manifestations of himself, altogether supernatural both in their methods and their effects, but completely within the sphere of our intelligence when supernaturally made known to us.   And what I allege in the third place is, that God has delivered to us, by means of men inspired by him, a permanent revelation of himself, and that in the soul of man as created and as re-created, he has erected a perpetual monument to himself as Creator and as Saviour : and that herein are two additional manifestations of himself, which partake of the method of the first two, in that they are in many particulars within the natural sphere of our intelligence—and which also partake of the method of the second two in that they are in many respects transcendently separated from nature, and capable of being adequately construed to our intelligence, only under a supernatural illumination.   There is no other permanent manifestation of God to man, which does not fall within the compass of one or the other of these.   Nor can we conceive how there could be, or why there should be, any other in our present state of existence.   By means of these the perfect knowledge of God unto salvation, and the complete fruition of God unto eternal life, are attainable by man.   Nay so attainable, as to glorify God and exalt man in the highest conceivable degree, both in the method and in the result—of the knowledge of God made known to man.   Therein our fallen nature recovering its primeval glory, obtains that restoration which in a manner vague, but most powerful, has occupied so large a space in all its hopes and struggles.   Therein man enters upon that better form of life brought to light by the Gospel and

becomes the inheritor of that true immortality which crowns all.

9. They who the most carefully examine, will the most clearly see that the analysis which has brought us, by a process so rigorous, to results so great—has been obliged to touch in its transit, immense questions of all sorts, and vast problems which the human mind has avoided as insoluble, or staggered under even to our day. There is scarcely a sentence that is not necessary to the final result; yet there is scarcely one which announces a truth that might not be enlarged to a chapter, more suitably than compressed into a few syllables. Over this vast domain Christianity has fought innumerable battles with her open enemies and her pretended friends : and there is no portion of it, over which Philosophy has not always wandered and always struggled. Following the order of my method and my thoughts, the objective view of the Knowledge of God led directly across this vast domain, through which a thorough Evangelism and a true Philosophy combined, can alone insure to us a safe footing and a sure way. What I bring from the survey has been stated in the preceding paragraph, in a particular way, and with reference to a special illustration needed there. The six permanent forms of the divine manifestation, which the whole analysis has produced, and which are completely exhaustive of the subject as it is related to our present inquiry—will form the topics of the six succeeding chapters. The object of the present chapter is accomplished, if it is clearly perceived upon what general grounds I maintain, that the true knowledge of the living God is attainable by man : that it is attainable only by means of the manifestations which God makes of himself : and that both the principles and the examples of his permanent manifestations, are distinctly appreciable by man. Summarily stated they appear in the following manner :

(*a*) God may be known by man, as manifested in his works : God the Creator :

(*b*) He may be known, as manifested in his Dominion and Reign : The God of Providence :

(*c*) He may be known, as manifested in Human Nature : The Word made flesh :

(*d*) He may be known, as manifested in the New Creation : God the Spirit :

(*e*) He may be known, as manifested in Revelation: The God of the Sacred Scriptures:

(*f*) He may be known, as manifested in the conscious existence of man : God the maker and renewer of the Human Soul.

10. I have forborne to cite particular passages of the Scriptures, in confirmation of the successive steps of the foregoing development, and in support of the various statements involved in it. All true knowledge of God, no matter how attained, must accord with all further knowledge attainable of him ; and the matter immediately before us, was the settlement of Principles, which in some degree involve the Scriptures themselves as one— or if the statement is better—as the infallible means of our knowing God. Still, however, in order that the Scriptures may be an infallible means—or indeed any means—of our knowing God, it is necessary that God should manifest himself in that manner, and that we should be able to comprehend him when so manifested. That the word of God should be unto us, not only a perfect rule, but the only perfect rule, whereby we may glorify and enjoy him, depends upon principles which involve both the nature of God and that of man, and the relations between the two : principles which determine that there are other most important means of knowing God, and determine what those other means are, at the same time that they determine with certainty on what grounds the Scriptures may be the transcendent means they claim to be. The method pursued embraces all, avoids the cavil of arguing in a circle, and strengthens the foundations of the Scriptures themselves.

CHAPTER XXIV.

I. 1. The Creation of the Universe—according to the Word of God.—2. Appreciation of its Sublime Statements.—3. State of the question—supposing them to be rejected.—4. Additional proofs of the Creation of all things by God.—II. 1. The Relation of created things to their Creator, as manifestations of him, and so means of knowledge of him.—2. Outline of the method and fundamental part thereof.—3. Ourselves and our Creator.—4. Elements of the Problem of the knowledge of God, from the Work of Creation.—5. The Perpetual Presence in the universe, of the Power which created all things. The Living God as fully manifested in, as the Creator is by, all things.—III. 1. Appreciation of the results of this knowledge of God. 2. All the divine manifestations, though distinct, are correlated. Relation of this mode to the rest.—3. Fundamental authority and compass of this Natural Revelation of God.—4. The abnormal condition of this question, by the entrance of Sin and its Remedy, into the Universe. Solution.

I.—1. As a mere question of fact in Revealed Theology, nothing is more clear, nothing can be more direct, than the teachings of the Sacred Scriptures concerning the creation of the Universe. In the beginning God created the heavens and the earth.[1] These are the words with which the Oracles of God commence. They are immediately followed by a comprehensive but circumstantial account of the creation of our world and every thing in it ; of our Solar and Sidereal systems, apparently beyond a doubt; and most probably of the whole physical universe. The statements of this original account of the creation of all things constituting our universe, are repeated innumerable times throughout the Scriptures ; and in their absolute truth lies the fundamental basis of every other truth the Scripture contains which it imports us to know ; since nothing else they state concerning it is comprehensible or can possibly be true, except upon the supposition of the truth of their statements concerning our origin. Nor is it possible for a candid mind to mistake what the Scriptures mean continually to assert. It is creation in the most absolute sense upon which

[1] Genesis, i. 1.

they everywhere insist ; the making of all things out of nothing by God in the space of six days, and all very good. This creation may be called inexplicable—incomprehensible—incredible—impossible : it has been so called. What I insist on here is, that in defiance of all that, the Scriptures do not only assert it, with the most sublime conviction and directness, but that their doing this is one of their most pregnant and fruitful facts, and involves one of their highest titles to be called the word of God. The manner of the creation, the circumstances which attended it, the motives which lead to it, the results which were to flow from it, as all these overwhelming events are explained throughout the Scriptures, give to the subject a grandeur which never loses its influence over the sacred writers, and which it is impossible for a rational creature to contemplate without astonishment and awe.

2. In whatever light we contemplate the Scriptural account of the creation of the universe, it is equally marvellous. Considered as a myth, a creation of the imagination—its grandeur surpasses all conception. Considered as a historical attempt to recover and restore to man the story of his origin, the wonder is that the obscure story outran the sublime record, and that all peoples, who never saw the record, preserved the great outlines, demonstrating the signal point of their own primeval unity in the unity of traditions so remarkable. Considered as a scientific theory meant to account for the actual condition of the universe, how futile are all other theories, such as the fortuitous combination of atoms—the eternal existence of the universe—the gradual development of all things, an endless series of creations, and the like : when compared with the simple, grand and complete solution of the problem offered by Moses, and reasserted throughout the Scriptures ! Considered as absolute truth, recorded through a divine inspiration for human instruction, how amazing is the insight connected with its continual statements, into every other inspired truth ! For example, into the highest mystery of all—the mystery of the divine existence. It is the one God in three persons who created the universe. For when God created the heaven and the earth, the Spirit of God brooded on the face of the waters :[1] yet, it was the Word of Jehovah who made the heavens and His Spirit the Host of them :[2] and yet, once more, it is God the Father of whom are all things, and the Lord Jesus

[1] Gen., i. 2.   [2] Ps. xxxiii., 6.

Christ by whom are all things :[1] and still, it was the Word, who was in the beginning with God, and who was God, who made all things, and without whom was not any thing made, that was made.[2]

3. Now if we reject this wondrous account, we cannot stop there and leave a question of that sort, and so urgent for some solution, in total silence. For that a stupendous universe really exists, and has a voice which we must hear and construe, is palpable to us continually. If it is the work of a creator, it is a most glorious manifestation not only of his being, but of many of his infinite perfections : a manifestation open before us, and soliciting our attention, and profusely rewarding our inquiries. If it be not a created universe, and a manifestation of divine power, and wisdom, and goodness—what is it? A crushing enigma? Phenomena incalculably vast and intricate, without any substance? Existences apparently innumerable, and no essence for any of them? Effects the most wonderful, complex, reiterated—and all without any cause? Overwhelming proofs of design, of a beginning, of adaptation, of final causes, of boundless intelligence, and yet no being to whom we may refer these undeniable proofs of a personal existence pervading the universe and controlling it? These things, according to the primitive laws of our intelligence, are simply impossible. Or if they were possible, we are naturally incapable of believing them to be so : that is we are naturally incapable of accepting such a solution as that, of the problem of the universe. We cannot avoid believing in a creator, unless they will supply his place with that which is at once adequate and credible.

4. Independently of the word of God, and of those psychological considerations which I have suggested, and from both of which sources of proof, the fact of the absolute creation of the universe seems to be positively certain: there are other proofs to the same effect from various quarters, independent of both the foregoing, which appear to be conclusive. For example, there is in all existing things a manifest contingency, dependency, mutation and tendency to decay, wholly inconsistent with the idea of their having an independent and necessary existence. But whatever has not a necessary and independent existence, must have a creator, or must be fortuitous. But if there is any God, then nothing can be fortuitous in regard of him; and he must be the

<hr>

[1] 1 Cor., viii. 6.   [2] John, i. 1–3.

sole Creator. Unavoidably, therefore, if there is a God, there can be nothing else except what he creates. Again: the existence of laws and principles of reproduction, throughout the universe, which are distinct from the creature, which are superior to it, and which are, for the most part, unknown to it; clearly shows the impotence and insignificance of the creature compared with that great and controlling cause—which has subjected their existence to those laws and principles—which of themselves prove that cause to be free, intelligent, and irresistible—that is to be a creator. Again: It is perfectly certain that what begins, must have a creator; for if it be wholly inexplicable how even an infinite creator can give existence to something out of nothing—it is utterly absurd to say this can be done without any creator at all. But it is certain, both historically and scientifically, that the existences in this universe are recent; nay, as compared with eternity are very recent. They have had a beginning—that is they have been created. Moreover: there is no force nor any being in the universe, except God, competent to create any thing : nor is there any work of creation, in any absolute sense, now going on. But while it is perfectly intelligible that a free and personal and infinite Creator might freely create at one time, and cease to create afterward: it is on the other hand, impossible to conceive of the existence of a competent, creative cause which is blind and fortuitous, competent and active in creating at one time, and incompetent and inactive at another time: and yet at the same time self-existent, and therefore eternal and by consequence immutable. And still further: every cause is so manifested in its effects, that no cause can possibly transcend itself, nor any effects transcend their cause. No fortuitous cause can act with design: no blind cause can produce for a foreseen end; no dead cause can produce vital results: no cause destitute of intelligence and will, can produce effects endowed with intelligence and will. Nay it is a mere absurdity to pretend that a finite cause can create any thing. One single act of creation is an incontestable proof of the supreme Godhead of him who performs it. And so every dependent and contingent existence, is of necessity, an incontestable proof that an act of creation has been performed. Just so much as exists beside God—just so much proof of creation and so many manifestations of God, are set before us.

II.—1. It is not for the purpose of proving the existence of God, except as that is incident to the main topic, that the work of creation is specially considered here: but contemplating the created universe as a most glorious manifestation which God has made of himself—it is to seek therein, beyond the palpable proofs that he is, those deeper and more comprehensive ones, that he is the rewarder of them that diligently seek him. Nevertheless we are to remember that the certainty of God's existence, and of our knowledge thereof, are respectively the foundations of all knowledge of God and of all comfort therein; while scepticism is invested with this twofold temptation, that it is a refuge from superstition, and that it ministers a kind of subtle nourishment to pretentious ignorance. As soon as it is admitted that such a universe as this exists, it is capable of being shown that there must be an original and eternal form of self-existence : and that this must be an infinite spiritual form. As soon as it is perceived, that we are obliged to recognize any such thing in the universe as cause, no matter of what kind, and that by a primitive law of our being, we cannot avoid believing that every effect is obliged to have a cause ; then it follows, readily, that all causes and all effects are traceable to one self-existent and eternal cause, infinite in force and intelligence. As soon as it is perceived that all existences except that of the one Infinite and self-existent, not only are, but are obliged to be dependent, finite and contingent ; then it follows inevitably, that they were all created. And as soon as we observe and admit, that all finite existences, manifest in themselves and in their relations, an adaptedness for certain uses and objects and ends, and a want of adaptedness to other uses and objects and ends ; it is impossible to avoid believing that he who created them, did it with design and with intelligence and with power, Now it is in these manifestations of himself, throughout all creation, that we discover proofs of the nature and character of God—and that we obtain true knowledge of him. It is a kind of knowledge perfectly within the sphere of our Intelligence—both as to the nature of it, and as to the means of our obtaining it ; a boundless creation—every part of which is a conclusive proof of God's Existence, and a manifestation of some one or other of his perfections. On the one hand, the infinite God manifests himself in and by means of a created universe : on the other hand, the finite creature man, rises to the knowledge of the infinite God, as he is thus manifested.

2. If we will consider attentively what is involved in proving that God is the Creator of the universe, and will then reflect upon his perfections as they have been classified in a previous chapter: we shall observe, how immense is the knowledge of God which we have actually attained in coming to that point, and how clear the way before us from that point is, to still further discoveries concerning the divine nature. We cannot conceive of any motive being sufficient, or even possible to God as the chief motive in creating the universe—except the manifestation of himself in the way of glory to himself, and in the way of blessedness to the creature. The source of life to all things, he possesses the fulness of life in his own self-existence; and the living cause of all things and of all causes, the infinite actuosity of that self-existence, is clothed with boundless power, directed by infinite intelligence, prompted by infinite goodness, guided by infinite justice, impelled by an infinite will. The result is the universe we behold. Not a development of God; but a work of God by which he makes himself manifest. Not a work as of necessity in the progress of God—a kind of outbirth of himself: but a free purpose of an infinite will, shining forth in every part of that creation, which had been determined in preference to all others. Every part was good as it passed the unfathomable gulf, and emerged from non-existence: the whole was very good, as it sprang forth in glory and beauty, with its new life gushing wildly through every fibre of it, and its new light flashing from breast to breast and from world to world, and the anthem of all created things like a hymn of joy and praise and triumph to the Eternal, swelling throughout the universe! Very good unto the glorious end for which it, amidst and above all boundless possibilities of things, had been chosen and created; very good in its own pure estate—unpolluted as yet—and full of the divine presence, veiled only by the weakness of the creature.

3. It may be well admitted that there are few who possess that knowledge of God considered as our Creator, which all thoughtful persons might easily obtain: few who possess even that knowledge of the works of God, digested into scientific forms, which is within the reach of all educated persons. This,

however, is no more than occurs with regard to every other source of divine knowledge : and shows how the contented ignorance of God in which men abide, is not the fault of the means of knowledge, which God has provided, but is voluntary and sinful, and is justly denounced by the Scriptures as akin to the scoffing of the last perilous times.[1] Yet of all knowledge, the knowledge of nature—which is but another name for God manifested in creation, is the nearest to us, the most immediate and striking in its results, and in its ordinary forms the most certain to be obtained by him who seeks it : for many of those most obvious natural links between us and our creator are so simple and so close, as to make matter almost appear rational, and to make organism appear as if it might almost produce thought. Yet as we advance, God, instead of humbling, exalts himself more and more ; carrying us with him indeed, in his boundless progress—but never allowing us to cross the gulf between the finite and the infinite ; exalting us more and more as we know more and more of him, but exalting himself above us continually ; knowing him better forever, but getting no nearer to him forever. We must not forget, however, that we who thus seek for God in his works—are ourselves the most marvellous part of his creation : and though still competent to know and honor him, that we are fallen very far below the estate in which he created us, and have brought upon the universe that curse of sin, which everywhere obscures the image of the creator, and have brought upon ourselves that depravity which unfits us for perceiving as we might that divine image.

4. Occupying our own stand-point in the created universe, and from it looking out upon all the works of God, the most impressive aspect in which it strikes us, perhaps, is its immeasurable vastness connected with the thought of its absolute production from nonentity by the creative power of the ever-living God. We have no means of making ourselves understood, when we would utter our conceptions of illimitable space and of the innumerable forms of existence, which are scattered through this immensity : indeed we are unable to construe to ourselves the ideas which we would fain make articulate to others. Beneath us there are divisions which seem to be infinite—gradations which appear to be immeasurable—the very existence of many

---

[1] 2 Peter, iii. 3–7.

of which we never could have ascertained by our unaided senses; and again around us, and beyond us, illimitable extension and boundless creation—the very existence of the greater part of which also, art and science have slowly and painfully made known to us. Here, then, in a manner, are four distinct worlds presented to us: the outer one naturally on a level with our faculties: the one beneath us, which minute researches aided by the microscope reveal: then the one which the highest efforts of science aided by the telescope brings within our reach: and finally the one within us, to the bar of which the others are all brought, and which is the most wonderful of them all. We can occupy no position in which presumptuous confidence of knowledge which we do not possess, and imbecile self-abnegation of faculties and means of knowledge which distinguish and adorn our nature, can be more out of place, than when standing thus face to face with our Creator—as seen through his infinitely glorious works. We do not know what a creation of something out of nothing is; but we do know that every finite thing, is a created thing, and that there can be but one creative cause—but one infinite, personal Creator. We cannot conceive of time's having either a beginning or an end, without conceiving of time before the beginning and of time after the end, just as easily as of any other time. We cannot conceive of any space being so small that it might not be smaller, nor so large that it might not be larger. We cannot conceive of matter being so extended, so divided, or so compressed, that it is not equally conceivable as being differently extended, still further divided, or still more compressed. We cannot conceive of existence of any sort without motion, and yet motion as incident even to matter, is perfectly inscrutable, except as the product of an intelligence distinct from the matter. And finally, matter and motion, and time and space—an infinite self-existent Spirit creating all things—a finite created intelligence searching into all created things for the Knowledge of the Creator; behold the elements of the problem of the Knowledge of God from the work of creation. Those elements cannot be combined, so far as we can conceive, in such a manner as to avoid demonstrating a Creator; nor in such a manner as to conceal that Creator, in the fundamental exhibition of his nature and character.

5. Considering the created universe as one whole, one work,

and from thence seeking to deduce its specific characteristics, and the nature of him who executed such a monument of life, of power, of intelligence, and of goodness ; we cannot avoid being struck with the distinct and pervading manifestations of such a power still abiding in the universe, as it has been shown must have created it. To create such a universe—is an inconceivable exertion of all infinite perfections by an infinite being ; but it is hardly less to sustain the action of such a universe in its career and to its end, unto both of which indeed, it was created. What we observe, therefore, is the inextinguishable force of the life that fills the universe and replenishes all things in it. In its origin utterly inscrutable to us ; in its ordinary individual manifestation often the frailest of all things, and of all things the least valued by nature and the most squandered by her ; but as an elemental principle of the universe, recuperative, invincible and all pervading. Life—assimilation—reproduction—death. What is it ? We may not dare to say that the vital force in man as distinguished from his intelligence is the same with that manifested in the lower animal kingdom ; nor that this latter is near akin to that exhibited in the whole vegetable kingdom ; nor that this again is of the same nature as the whole or any part of that irresistible power which pervades the universe in the form of mere affinities and forces. But what must be said, is that the sum of all this boundless and overwhelming power of life, of one sort and another, which replenishes every created thing, in one or other of its forms, emerges from the creation as inexplicably as the creation does from nonentity ; and that it manifests the Living God in the universe, as really as the universe manifests a Creator. Then it behooves us to contemplate the principles upon which this boundless and irresistible life of the universe rests, and through which it acts ; the steadfastness, and yet the versatility, the inconceivable activity, tenacity, and power, with which the principles of that varied life of the universe manifest themselves. A step further reveals to us that these principles manifest themselves through laws which are invariable, irresistible, and immutable ; laws, which with an exactitude perfectly rigorous, and with an intelligence which omits nothing and which usurps nothing, control and direct, throughout every portion of the universe, every manifestation of its varied and immeasurable life. Another step obliges us to suspect that all this life in all its forms, all these principles which express so much of its nature as we have examined and classified—and all these laws through which those great principles operate—are pervaded by a universal tendency of mutual adaptation. And then a little scrutiny reveals to us, that this adaptation of every part of the universe to every other part, and to the whole—is not only the very ground upon which these immeasurable forces can co-exist at all; but therein is found that very *nexus* of the universe itself, which makes it a decreed universe, and not a fortuitous universe. And still one additional step, and we are forced to observe, that all that has been now pointed out, is absolutely beyond the power, independent of the capacity and will, irrespective of the choice, and without regard to the knowledge or the ignorance of the creature. Nor is the slightest attempt made in any part of the manifested life of the universe, to lower this supreme position of the sovereign Creator of all things ; or to make the creation itself appear to the creature to be any thing less or more than it really is, namely, a stupendous manifestation of the wisdom, power, and glory of the true and Living God, in the execution of the free and immutable counsel of his own will.[1]

III.—1. Now it is for us to consider all the perfections of this Infinite being,—and all our relations to him—that we may attain unto that degree of knowledge of him, which may be reached through the works of his hands. His manifestation of himself by means of the universe he has created, is the primeval manifestation : the first of all—the foundation also of all. We cannot recognize God in this relation for a moment, without perceiving that his right to us, in us, and over us and the whole universe, is absolute and unlimited. He has created us from nothing : he has done the like concerning the whole universe, of which each one of us is an almost imperceptible part : he has done all this from considerations originating in himself, and terminating upon himself. That he has a perfect right to use and dispose of us and of all things, merely and absolutely as seems good to himself, is also beyond cavil : and what is more, we may rest assured that there is an unavoidable certainty that this will be done. If in the doing of this, the glory of the Creator is found to be not only consistent with the great blessedness of the creature, but to be

---

[1] Gen., i. 2, 3 ; John, i. 1–5 ; Rom., i. 19–21 ; Rev., iv. 11.

infinitely promoted thereby, and that in a manner supremely satisfying to the Creator: a further insight is thus gained into the moral aspect of his infinite being. Nor is it possible for us to resist the overwhelming conviction, forced upon us by every attempt we make to know God by means of his works, that such a Creator will use such a creation—in a manner corresponding with all his infinite perfections, and for the accomplishment of ends suitable to the wondrous displays made of himself in it.

2. While it is necessary to keep the different sources of the knowledge of God distinct, in so far as neither to confound them with each other, nor to omit any because others may seem to be more perfect : we are not to restrict ourselves in the use of every means as a help—even in the right use of all the rest. Thus those sublime ends proposed by God in the creation of the universe, to which allusion has just been made, become more distinct to us and more comprehensible by us, under every successive manifestation which God makes to us of his nature, his works, and his counsels : and thus our knowledge is increased, while the certitude of it is strengthened from every quarter. The providential use which is made of every peculiarity of nature, makes it continually obvious that the Ruler of the Universe is identical with its Creator : and not to multiply illustrations—the writers of the Inspired Books make it perfectly obvious that they had an insight into the profoundest secrets of nature, and into their providential use, and that they had an insight into the great designs of God, whether considered as Creator, Ruler, or Saviour of the world, which was altogether superhuman upon every one of these vast topics.—Thus the Creator, the Ruler, and the Saviour become identified at the first step of this process of our inquiry into the nature of God ; and even the very latest manifestations of God, through his work in the soul of man, brings its tribute to reward the earnest seeker after God, even from his very first step. For the sense of dependence and accountability in man, is a response of human nature itself to the claims of its divine Creator, Lord, and Master ; and the human conscience is explicable at all, only when it is seen that it is the moral sense of a created and dependent, and yet free and personal existence. Amidst the facts and analogies of the physical universe, the most sublime doctrines of Revealed Religion find themselves illustrated, recognized, assumed ; so that our nature and destiny as deduced from the works of God and as explained

in his word—as ordered in his providence, as controlled by his Divine Son and Spirit—and as exhibited in our own conscious existence, are established with perpetual accumulation of evidence, and invincible assurance, side by side with the knowledge of the Living and true God.

3. Existence is the first gift of God : the gift upon which the possibility of every other gift depends. The work of creation is the foundation of every thing in the universe which is exterior to God : and whatever else God doth, rests upon this, his primeval work. The relations which subsist between God and all created things, are the fundamental relations in the universe ; the laws which express these relations, which we call the laws of Nature, constitute a distinct revelation of God, and from God : and with this primitive revelation, every subsequent one must accord. The rational and moral nature of man are a part of this creation—a part of this original Revelation : natural reason and natural morality—intelligence and conscience—are antecedent to all religions, as being the elemental parts of the religion which results from the primary relations between God and man, considered as creator and creature. Natural Religion is therefore the foundation of all true Religion : and a very large part of Revealed Religion consists in the clear and authoritative re-statement of the fundamental truths of this primary Religion, grounded in this primeval revelation of God in creation. Nor is it concerning Religion alone that statements of this description are so important and so true. It is upon the study of the works of God, and the comparison of the results thus obtained with each other and with all things else, that our knowledge of all things is mainly founded : knowledge which Revelation itself respects, accords with, and assumes to be real. The relations of numbers and quantities ; the laws of the human faculties ; the method of the intellect in stating its own processes ; what are these, and many similar things, but common and permanent operations of nature ? And yet in another point of view they become sciences of the highest order —Mathematics, Metaphysics, Logic. God is not the maker only of the universe ; he is also its sustainer. The universe is from him, and He is in it ; and his infinite perfections are palpable, both ways, and that continually.

4. We rely implicitly upon the stability of the universe, and of the order which we observe in all things. Independently of experience we would not expect any serious change, of the cause

of which we knew nothing; and when such things established themselves before our eyes, as, for example, death, we should not expect any reparation. Death is an inscrutable phenomenon to nature : the resurrection of the body is as unexpected after death as death after life. All these are abnormal occurrences, of which Nature must seek knowledge from Revelation. They are results of the introduction of sin into the universe, and of the introduction of the remedy for sin. And death and the resurrection, stupendous as they are, are but effects ; it is sin and its remedy, which are the cause. And stupendous effects as they are, they are but two out of innumerable effects, produced upon the universe by the entrance of sin into it, and the final purging it of sin. At present, it is a universe lying under the curse of God, but with a promise of deliverance ;[1] a condition in both aspects abnormal. Yet it is under these conditions that we must now contemplate the source, the career, and the catastrophe of the created universe. Conditions which may obscure many aspects of the question of God, considered merely as Creator, but which increase in a still higher degree our means of knowing God in the new relation which the new conditions of the problem impose. God as the Ruler of a Universe depraved but to be purged ; God as the Saviour and sanctifier of sinners ; God as Revealed in his blessed word, and in the conscious existence of the fallen and recovered soul. All these are manifestations of the same God, who created us and all things, and whose glory, simply as Creator, the fall of our own race has temporarily obscured. The shock to the universe by the entrance and diffusion of sin ; the recovery of the universe from the curse and pollution of sin ; the development of the relations of the Creator, so as to involve those of Saviour also ; the final results of all these conditions, normal and abnormal, in the fate of the created universe : all these vast topics, and others like them, dilate naturally from the subject before us, and dilate also our conceptions of it, until the whole dominion of God may become visible from any one position in it, and the whole being of God be made the subject of a scrutiny commencing with any aspect of it. It is the unity of the Living God ; the unity of his infinite being, and work, and perfection, which makes such things not only possible without confusion or distortion, but which solicits them as constituting an exalted method of developing the divine proportion of Faith.

[1] Gen., iii. *passim;* Acts, iii. 19–21.

CHAPTER XXV.

GOD MANIFEST IN HIS INFINITE DOMINION—THE GOD OF PROVIDENCE.

I. 1. General idea of Providence.—2. Its Relations to Nature, Creation, and Grace.—3. Its Relation to God as a manifestation of his infinite Nature, and Eternal Counsel.—4. The irresistible execution of the Will of God, ordinarily through the use of means and second causes, and to the exclusion of Chance, Necessity, and Fate.—II. 1. The Sublime Vision of the Prophet Ezekiel.—2. The aspect of that Universal Providence in the light of Revelation, Reason, Experience, and our Primitive Convictions.—3. The Will of God, executed in his Providence, is not limited to his Will revealed in his Word.—4. The force of that truth, in its relation to the Knowledge of God, and to Duty.—III. 1. The point of view from which all Providence is unfolded by God.—2. The System of Providence exhibits the same God exhibited in Creation, Revelation, and Reason—Special Providence.—3. The sublime illustration of the Nature and Ends of Providence, furnished in the Nature and Career of the Messianic Kingdom.—IV. 1. The universal belief of Mankind that invisible Intelligences were Objects and Agents of Divine Providence.—2. Pure Spirits: Spirits of just men made perfect: Resemblance and Difference.—3. Summary of Christian Doctrine, touching the Angelic Hosts.—4. Their Relation to Divine Providence.

I.—1. THE outward works of God, as it is commonly expressed, are the works of Grace and of Nature. The works of nature are again divided into Creation and Providence ; the latter being, when considered relatively to nature only, a kind of continual creation, but when considered in reference to the whole bearing of God's dominion, being rather contrasted with the work of creation than treated as a kind of prolongation of it. And let it not be disguised, that the moment we admit a Providence we admit a Creator ; because it is only when we admit that the universe is dependent and contingent that any providence over it is possible. For, if it is not dependent and contingent, it is self-existent, eternal, and immutable ; and whatever is either one of these is uncreated, and as much out of the reach of Providence as God himself. In like manner, the moment we prove a Creator it becomes very easy to demonstrate a Provi-

dence. Indeed a created universe, capable of continued existence, without the continued presence of the Creator, is wholly
inconsistent with any idea we can form of any kind of cause or
of any kind of dependent existence. And even if that were not
so, it is obvious that Creation itself is a Providence, if in the
very act of creation the whole future existence of the universe is
foreseen and effectually provided for.

2. What is called nature, is that active force of bodies upon
which their actions depend; and so the nature of the Universe,
is the sum of all those forces which inhere in all the bodies in
the Universe. God, it has been shown, is the Author of Nature. The rational creatures of God taken together and considered separately from the merely physical universe, are called
unitedly the Spiritual World, the City of God, and so on. So
far as we have any positive knowledge these are men and angels:
no other rational creatures are known to exist; and all we know
certainly of angels is by divine revelation. With reference very
especially to rational creatures, but with reference also to the
whole universe, the Providence of God is his most holy, wise
and powerful preserving and governing all his creatures and all
their actions.[1] This Providence of God, so comprehensive over
all his works, taken in its complete sense embraces every act of
God except his work of Creation: and along with that work of
Creation, is the complete execution, according to the infallible
foreknowledge of God, and the free and immutable counsel of
his will, of the eternal decree of God. But the eternal decree of
God, by which his work of Creation was directed, and his work
of Providence is executed, having special reference to his rational
creatures, namely to men and angels, but embracing also whatever comes to pass; is nothing more, nothing less, than the irresistible consummation of the free, wise and holy purpose of
God according to the counsel of his own will, wherein for his
own glory, and from all eternity, he has foreordained whatever
comes to pass.[2] As an attempt to survey the providence of God,
under so wide an aspect as this, would carry us through the
whole field of revealed Religion; we must of necessity restrict
the view to be taken of it here. Nor is there any difficulty in
doing so. For while the work of Providence is very closely con-

<hr>

[1] Ps. ciii. 19; Rom., xi. 36; Heb., i. 3; Math., x. 29, 30.
[2] Eph., i. 4–11; Rom., ix. 15–23.

nected with the work of Creation on one side and the work of Grace on the other, it is not identified with either: and while it may be said to embrace both, yet it has a special province distinct from both, and remarkably connecting them with each other. In the logical order of the manifestation of God to man, Providence immediately arises, as soon as any creation exists: and the course of that Providence conducts immediately through the broken covenant of Works, to God manifest in the flesh, as the result, at once infinitely gracious, and if there be any grace at all then irresistibly logical ! In a certain sense every thing is involved in the Providence of God: but at the same time, there are such realities as Nature, and Creation, and Grace.

3. We are not speaking of God in any vague sense; but of that true and living God, to the knowledge of whom all our past inquiries have been devoted, and concerning whom we have obtained many clear ideas. Nor are we speaking of his Providence in any loose manner; but in a precise method, as he manifests himself in his infinite dominion over the universe and over all things therein, and as thereby made known in what he is to his rational creatures. Supposing there is such a Providence of God, it results necessarily that it must accord with his nature, his essence, his perfections, his designs. For it is absurd and contradictory to suppose and is practically as well as theoretically impossible, that he could create a universe for one object and govern it for a different object; that he should purpose to effect one set of results, and labor to bring about a different set; that his Nature should impel him in one direction and his Intelligence point out another as preferable, and his Will reject both. The whole Providence of God must necessarily accord with the whole purpose of God: and just so far as the former is comprehensible by us, we have, by that means, an insight into the latter, and into the nature and character of God. But the purpose of God is simply the determination of his will, consummated in his decree. Nor does it change the matter in the least, to speak of the decree any more than of the purpose or the will of God as one or as manifold: except that the former is simpler and more accurate. And since the decree of God is no more than the determination of his will, whatever can be asserted of the nature of the latter, is equally and necessarily true of the former. If the determination of the will of God is from Eternity, his de-

cree also is from Eternity. If the will of God is perfectly free and perfectly immutable, so is his decree. If the will of God is not a simple and pure cause, destitute of intelligence and a sufficient reason, neither is his decree. If God can and does will things inscrutable to us, so can he and will he decree them. If God wills all things with reference to all his own perfections, and with reference to the whole universe and its chief end, he decrees all things in like manner: and so of every other aspect of the matter. As has been abundantly shown, the possibility of all things depends on the divine intelligence : their existence depends on the Divine Will : therefore the decree of God neither determines the possibility of things, for that is determined by the Divine intelligence, nor the Existence of things for that is determined by the Divine will : but it determines only the certitude of that existence, which was before not only possible but willed. Of itself it changes nothing in the things themselves. All things remain free, or contingent, or necessary, under the decree of God; precisely as they were free, contingent or necessary when contemplated by the intelligence of God as possible, or by the will of God as existing. In like manner they remain great or small, clear or inscrutable, good or bad, precisely as they were before.

4. Now the irresistible execution of the will of God in all created things is his Providence—He sustains, preserves, and governs all things : all his creatures and all their actions. Under his illimitable dominion, the omnipresent God is so in his universe, that all things *work* and *all* work together. Specially indeed for good to them that love him—but universally to all results, and to the grand result of all things.[1] All his Attributes concur in all his Providence : but his power, his wisdom, his goodness and his justice are most especially manifest. So far from excluding means, and rejecting second causes, the ordinary Providence of God manifests itself through them rather than without them ; and it is with reference to them that the distinctions of free, necessary and contingent have special application to human events : just as it is of the essence of things that God's Providence is said to be preserving, and with reference to the actions of his creatures that it is called concurring, and relatively to the object and end of things and actions that it is said

[1] Rom., viii. 28.

to be governing and controlling.   Those acts of God's Providence which occur without respect to ordinary means and second causes, are sovereign and miraculous interpositions : and the more clearly it can be shown that they do not flow from the antecedent condition of things, nor from the power of second causes, the more certain it is that they are direct acts of God.   In both cases a first cause and the dependence of all things on it, are equally necessary, equally certain : since otherwise, there can be no act or work of God, whether Providential or Miraculous.   As to Chance there can be no such thing under the dominion of God ; and all that can be meant by necessity is, that from given causes appropriate effects must ensue, or on the other hand that there must be an appropriate cause for given effects.   No cause can be fully known except in its effects, nor can any effect be adequately construed except in its cause.   Fate, whether that of the Ancient Stoics, or of the Mohammedans, or of the Pantheists, though differing from each other in that the first denies all freedom to human actions and all contingency to events, while the second, though admitting them both, denies all their force, and the third though subordinating means to the end rejects all contingency from the universe : fate under every conception of it, except that there is an absolute certitude of events and effects founded in a certain order of causes and of things, is inconsistent with the fundamental conception of the Adorable Providence of God.

II.—1. The Prophet Ezekiel had a sublime vision twice vouchsafed unto him, which affords the grandest illustration of the nature, scope and relations of Divine Providence.   Out of the whirlwind and the cloud, and the self-enfolding fire, and the insupportable brightness, there emerged the likeness of four living creatures, which he afterwards knew to be Cherubim.   Strange and diverse, but having some likeness of a man, each with four diverse faces, and each with four wings : united to each other, actuated by one spirit, moving straight forward without turning, and with a common impulse, burning like coals of fire, and flashing as they went, their movement was as the appearance of a flash of lightning. Connected with the four living creatures, were four wheels, which were one even as the living creatures were one ; a wheel within a wheel, resting upon the earth their rings were so high that they were dreadful, and the rings of all four were full of eyes—the appearance of the wheels like a beryl and like a terrible crystal, moving all together, straight forward, by an impulse common to them all, and shared equally by the wheels and the living creatures. And besides the life common to them all, there was a spirit which controlled them all, so that when the living creatures went, the wheels went by them, and when the wheels stood, the living creatures stood, and all were lifted up from the earth together. And as they went the Prophet heard the noise of their wings like the noise of great waters, as the voice of the Almighty, the voice of speech, as the voice of a host ; and when they stood there was a voice from the firmament over their heads, and above that firmament was the likeness of a throne, and upon the throne the likeness as the Appearance of a Man, from the loins up like amber and flame, and from the loins down like fire, and girt about with brightness like the bow of heaven. This, says the Prophet, was the Appearance of the likeness of the Glory of the Lord. And when I saw it I fell upon my face, and I heard the voice of one that spake.[1] Upon a vision so amazing, let us rather be content to say that it illustrates what is otherwise taught, than that we are absolutely sure of its complete interpretation. It is a vision of the glory of Jehovah ; and upon the throne above all this glory is the Divine Redeemer in the likeness of our nature. Out of the chaos and fury of all human things, and the fervor and the vehemence of all human passions, emerges this sublime representation of the All-seeing, All-ruling Providence of God, whose awful wheel resting upon the earth, reaches to heaven, and moving side by side with all living things, and with the immediate symbol of his presence, the wondrous Cherubim, moves by an impulse which directs them all. The prophetic empires of which there were but four—gathered into one in the vision, though the living creatures were yet distinctly four. The empire of Providence, suited to each living empire, gathered into one wheel, though yet distinctly four. The Spirit of all living things the same, no matter how divided ; the Spirit of Providence the same, no matter how dissevered ; the common spirit of both so far united that both relate to the same events and the same movements, and that both march together across the track of ages ; while both alike are subject to the transcendent dominion of a Divine Spirit, directing all living things and all provi-

<hr>

[1] Ezek., i. 15–28, x. 8–22.

dential acts to one most glorious consummation. The movement of the nations, and the peoples, and the empires, however terrible and confused it may seem, and however wild may be the noise of their wings like the noise of great waters, which are their constant prophetic image ; yet all is subject to that voice from the firmament and the throne above it, and the Man who sat on it ; whom the prophet had no sooner seen than he knew the vision to be the appearance of the likeness of the glory of the Lord. He knew it was a representation of the divine glory, as it is manifested in an intimate, irresistible and all-pervading dominion over the created universe. And so I use it.

2. Whoever will consider attentively any one of the immense and apparently boundless elements which make up the sum of the universe, or any one of the innumerable and glorious ends which unite in the transcendent chief end of its existence, will perceive that the idea of the working of such means to such ends, throughout all time, all space, and all existence, independently of an Infinite Providence, is the most transcendent of all absurdities. What then can be said of the folly that denies to all these means and causes, and existences combined ; and to all these ends, and effects, and operations wrought out in one illimitable system ; the necessity of any direction or control—the presence of any concurrence, support, or dominion ! The declarations of the Word of God concerning the reality and the nature of his Providence over all things, are not only well-nigh innumerable, but the very end of any Revelation at all, involves the existence of such a Providence ; and the whole compass of the Revelation actually made implies and rests upon it. Human intelligence in every form in which it can address itself to such a subject, finds itself incapable of escaping the conviction that there is such a Providence over all things ; finds no grounds on which to reject it, except grounds which subvert the primitive laws of intelligence itself, and overthrow the foundations of human knowledge. The experience and observation of every human being is full of proofs to himself that all the events of life have a power and significance, less or greater, but essentially different from that power, which, strictly speaking belongs to them : and that it is this power external to their own essence which, whether by its excess or its deficiency, really gives to all actions, all events, all causes, all occasions, their decisive force. And the entire history

of the human race is one perpetual illustration of the manner in which nature and man are subjected to a controlling and directing power working through both, but predominant in the disposal of both. A power which leaves to human actions whether great or small, whether good or bad, whether free, contingent or necessary, whether absolutely spontaneous or thoroughly considered, all their force and all their character each according to its kind : and which yet, at its pleasure, mocks all that force even when it seems to be irresistible, and at its pleasure, gives to that force even when it is most feeble an uncontrollable efficacy, and at its pleasure leaves that force to its own undisturbed results. So profound is the reality thus asserted by Revelation, by reason, and by all experience, and so thorough is the connection thus established between God and man, that the conviction of a Providence is not only the deepest of those convictions which are primitive in human nature, but the strength of that conviction is the most distinctive mark of every race that has made itself illustrious, of every individual that has lifted himself high above the level of his kind. Nor is there any mystery in this. For not to discern God is the greatest of all imbecility, as knowingly to work against God is supreme folly : while to discern, to trust, and to co-operate with him, is at once the way of wisdom, and the way of triumph.

3. It has been repeatedly said that we occupy two distinct relations to God, in one of which we are considered as creatures, in the other as sinners ; and that God considered as the Creator, and considered as the Saviour is responsive to these relations of man. Natural Religion is the result of the former relation, Revealed Religion is the result of the latter : the covenant of works is the exponent of one, the covenant of grace is the exponent of the other. The Providence of God has reference to both of these relations, to both of these religions, to both of these covenants. The religion of nature—the covenant of works, and man's posture as a creature, are widely modified by Revealed Religion, the covenant of grace, and man's posture as a sinner : yet nothing is absolutely abolished, however different the aspect of God may appear when considered as the author of nature and of the covenant of works, from what it is when he is considered as the Saviour and as the author of Revealed Religion and the Covenant of Grace. These statements are designed to make obvious one

of the most striking, and I may add one of the most unobserved
things concerning the whole course and nature of Divine Providence—namely that the will of God as executed by his Providence, is not limited to the will of God as revealed in his word.
The whole compass of the will of God is not revealed in his word,
but only the whole will of God unto the salvation of penitent
sinners. The whole purpose of God concerning all things is not
revealed in the Scriptures ; but only so much of his purpose as
will suffice to make those Scriptures a perfect rule of faith and
obedience to man in the way of glorifying God and enjoying him
forever. The Providence of God, therefore, as a perpetual illustration of his will and a perpetual execution of his purpose, is at
once a commentary upon his written word, and a supplement
thereto. He acts concerning innumerable things which have not
been the subject of any special revelation : and concerning innumerable things which though revealed in part, are not revealed
as to all the relations in which God's Providence controls them
nor all the ends to which it directs them. Amongst those omitted things, or things only incidentally revealed are to be classed,
in general, all things that do not relate in some manner more or
less distinct, to the Messianic Kingdom, or to the life of God in
the soul of man. And how immense is the mass, and how overwhelming is the complexity of these omitted things, controlled
and directed by Providence, but unnoticed, or very slightly
noticed in the word of God !

4. Let me illustrate what I mean. When the Lord struck the
child which Uriah's wife bare to David, he besought God for the
child, and fasted, and went in and lay all night upon the earth.
In his anguish he refused to be comforted by the elders of his
house, or to eat bread with them. On the seventh day the child
died ; but his servants overcome by his grief feared to tell him.
When David perceived that the child was dead, he arose from
the earth, and washed, and anointed himself, and changed his
apparel, and came into the house of the Lord, and worshipped ;
and then came to his own house and required bread and eat.
His servants greatly astonished, said, thou didst fast and weep
for the child while it was alive, but when the child was dead
thou didst rise and eat bread. And he said, while the child was
yet alive I fasted and wept : for I said who can tell whether God
will be gracious to me, that the child may live ? But now he is

dead wherefore should I fast ?   Can I bring him back again ?
I shall go to him, but he shall not return to me.¹   Now here is
the secret purpose of the Lord, wholly unknown to his beloved
servant, and here is that servant beseeching God to avoid the
execution of that purpose, so long as he did not know what God
would do : but the moment he knew, by a severe stroke of Providence what the will of God was, promptly accepting it and
drawing comfort from its bearings on his own immortal destiny.
It is a great rule of duty for us : a clear illustration of a subject
of the highest importance. The Providence of God falls out
according to his whole will, a very large part of which is wholly
secret as to us, and can be known only by the event. As soon
as it is thus made known, it becomes not only a rule of duty to
us, but is never without elements of consolation to us. But until it is thus put in execution, it is wholly beyond our power to
make it a means of knowledge, of faith or of obedience. And
such is the general order of Providence—and such are the relations of God's secret and God's revealed will to it, to each other,
and to us. We are not to suppose however that the case now
stated is a just illustration of the distinctness with which the
secret purpose of God is ordinarily disclosed to us by his Providence. There are many considerations which ought to satisfy us
of the contrary, and make us perceive that at the most, the
knowledge of the will of God disclosed in his Providence can
only illustrate and supplement, but can never properly control,
much less contradict his will as made known to us by his blessed
word.—It is a means of knowing God : to the wise and pure in
heart a most fruitful and precious means : nay a means very peculiar in itself, and opening up a knowledge of the will of God
not otherwise attainable by man. On these very accounts to be
cherished assiduously, but with that self watchfulness dictated
by a sense of the feebleness of our faculties, the shortness of our
lives as contrasted with the endless sweep of the plans of God,
and the narrow portion of his infinite acts which is submitted to
our personal consideration.

    III.—1. The highest evidence which the Scriptures could
give us of the estimate which they put on the moral nature and
the moral destiny of man, as compared with every thing else
united ; is to be found in the fact that they are in a strict sense,

<hr>

¹ 2 Sam., xii. 15–23.

no revelation at all, and make no claim of being one, except incidentally—touching any thing that does not bear upon that moral nature and that moral destiny: and so they are addressed absolutely to our faith and are a rule of unqualified obedience. Nor is it possible to imagine how they could give a more exalted proof that they mean to teach the Supreme Godhead of the Lord Jesus Christ, than they furnish in not only placing him in the very centre of the moral system of the universe, but in placing him, considered as the Saviour of sinners, absolutely over the moral universe as its ruler, and in ascribing to him as such an uncontrollable dominion over all things.[1] It is from this point of view that providence unfolds itself: and it is to rational creatures considered in this point of view that it is unfolded. The whole progress of the human race is one grand development of Providence: every event in history is an incident in the course of Providence: every result of every act of every human being, is an item in the overwhelming sum of Providence: every co-operation of nature is an element in the stupendous dominion thus exerted. If any thing good and coherent can be deduced from the confused, irregular, and sinful career of individual men, it is far less attributable to human reason and virtue than to the controlling, guiding, and overruling Providence of God. If there has been any real and uniform progress toward whatever is great and permanent, exhibited in the career of the human race, it is far less attributable to any steadfast apprehension and purpose in it, much less to any wise and heroic pursuit of its fixed convictions, along a track stained with blood and wet with tears, than to the supporting care, and the watchful love of the Infinite God who has guided its fierce and erring steps. To say that rational beings can be conducted through endless generations, in such a manner as this, and still fail to obtain any adequate knowledge of him, in whom they live and move and have their being, is to omit the material portion of a problem so strange. All is not expressed when their rationality and their ignorance are thus grouped together, in a manner apparently self-contradictory, as if to excuse them and inculpate God. It is not that they cannot, but it is that they will not know God. They are ignorant because they are depraved, and in defiance of their rationality. The knowledge of God which is attainable they do not

<hr>

[1] Eph., i. 20–23.

like to retain ; so much as they know of him, they use not either for his glory or for their own advancement. And so God gives them up to their own vile affections, to a reprobate mind and to strong delusions. And then no lie is too gross for belief, and no ignorance too deep to be reached, and alas ! no pollution too revolting to be rejoiced in, and no suffering too fearful to be deserved !¹

2. The general resemblance of what may be called the System of Providence, to the general system deducible from the work of creation, and to the general system distinctly taught in the Scriptures, and to the highest and clearest conceptions of human reason ; undoubtedly affords a distinct and impregnable ground of proof of the unity of that Infinite Intelligence, and Will, and Power, which pervade the universe ; as well as a manifold demonstration of the nature of that Infinite Spirit of whom these are distinguishing perfections. If we will carefully consider any one of those great and immutable principles which appear to underlie the whole course of Providence, we will find that it is a principle clearly manifested also in the order of Nature, distinctly stated in the Sacred Scriptures, and fundamental to human nature. Take, as an illustration, the extreme Specialness of the Providence of God : that grand and fruitful peculiarity which gives such distinctness to all God's dealings with men, and which on that very account is so hateful to every form of Infidelity. That this is an invariable principle upon which all Providence proceeds, is self-evident to every attentive observer of it. There is not a human being who cannot recall many instances on which the whole tenor of his subsequent life has been controlled by events or decisions which seemed to him, when they occurred, too insignificant to require consideration. Not one who cannot recall many other events which were unspeakably painful when they occurred, out of which have come by an irresistible chain of other events, the greatest blessings of his life. Not one who cannot recall many other events which were denied to his strongest efforts and desires, and which would have inevitably ruined him, if he had been gratified. Not one who can recall a single event of the very least consequence in his life, which did not require innumerable preceding and concurring events, many of them contingent, many apparently fortuitous, nearly all

¹ Rom., i. 18–32; 2 Thess., ii. 1–12.

minute and apparently inconsequent, to bring about the great, particular and decisive event. Now all this, I repeat, is in a manner self-evidently true of the whole course of Providence : and it involves and reveals one of the clearest and most universal principles upon which all Providence proceeds. If we will now appeal to human reason, nothing can be more obvious than that such a manner of Providence is the only manner in which any Providence at all is possible. Whatever enters into an end, must constitute a part of the means ; for the end is not otherwise attainable ; and in an illimitable series of dependent causes and effects, where every cause is also an effect, and every effect becomes itself a cause, the breaking of a single link in the adamantine chain, annihilates the whole as completely as if every link were destroyed. Upon different principles there may be an infinite succession of miracles, which men may see fit to call a course of Providence : but there can be no ordinary Providence —the very meaning of which as distinguished from chance, and necessity, and fate, is the execution of a foregone purpose, unto a determined end, through the intervention of causes and means. If we will apply next to Created Nature, her response is prompt and direct, that God knows no such distinction as the cavil implies ; for with God nothing is great, nothing is small, nothing difficult, nothing easy. Between him and all created things there is a gulf so immeasurable that distinctions of that sort lose all significance. For any thing more, his whole work of creation is intensely special ; and the order of nature does not more distinctly reveal that there ever was any creation at all, than that every created thing was formed in a manner the most special, and in no other manner, and was formed unto ends most special, and unto no other ends. And now if we will inquire at the oracles of God, their answer is the most precise of all: Are not two sparrows sold for a farthing ? and one of them shall not fall to the ground without your Father : nay, the very hairs of your head are all numbered.[1] And so in all that concerns us, both for time and eternity. The fundamental principle of God's dealings with each one of us is that these dealings are most special. Out of two in one bed, out of two grinding at one mill, out of two found in one field, one shall be taken and the other left.[2] And every one of us shall give account of himself to God.[3] It is not meant, in any of these

____

[1] Mat., x 29, 30.   [2] Luke, xvii. 34–36.   [3] Rom., xiv. 12.

great departments of the knowledge of God, that his special act exhausts itself, or that the special end first attained accomplishes all his purposes. Far otherwise. But it is meant that the Providence of God, like every work, and act, and word of God, the very opposite of being vague, indeterminate, or inefficient, is special, precise, and effective.

3. The grandest illustration which the universe affords of the nature and ends of Divine Providence is that afforded in the career of the Messianic Kingdom, as studied on the one side in the divine record, and on the other side in its actual progress through all time. It is, moreover, that aspect of Providence which is of all others the most important to us; and in the study of it we have this immense advantage, that the vast period through which the perpetual illustration runs is illuminated at every epoch by an inspired narrative of facts, itself confirmed at every step by prophecies already fulfilled, and tested by other prophecies still impending. If we add still further, that whether by means of the Divine Record or by means of the actual life of the glorious Kingdom, every great interest of man in all ages, every empire, every people, every aspect of society, every stage of civilization, is more or less involved in the grand sweep of the inquiry : we have nothing left to be desired toward the completeness and the certainty of the conclusions we may reach. Thus, connecting the history of the world with that of the Kingdom of God in the world, the whole may be divided, upon the very obvious grounds of that connection, into four great periods. The *First* extended from the fall of man to the Exodus of the Ancient People of God out of Egypt, and embraced the whole period during which neither the Kingdom of God nor the world powers had reached a development much beyond that of the household estate, and during which the first Sacrament was given, and circumcision alone, as an outward mark, separated between the world and the Church under its Patriarchal form. The *Second* Period extended from the Exodus to the Babylonian Captivity, and embraced on the one hand the rise, complete development, and fall of the Theocracy, and the giving of the greater part of the Old Testament Scriptures ; and on the other hand embraced the rise and triumph of the Assyrio-Babylonian Kingdom, the first of the universal world powers, and with it the dawn of profane history. The *Third* Period would extend from the Baby-

lonian Captivity to the commencement of the Millennium, toward the close of which period our lots are supposed to be cast ; embracing on the one hand the restoration and subsequent extinguishment of the Jewish Church and State, the advent and ministry of Messiah, the outpouring of the Holy Ghost, the ministry of the Apostles, the giving of the latest portions of the Old Testament Scriptures, and the whole of the New Testament Scriptures, and the establishment and subsequent career of the Messianic Kingdom under the Christian dispensation ; and on the other hand the rise, progress, and overthrow of the Medo-Persian, Macedono-Greek, and Roman Empires, the three remaining universal world powers, the rise and progress of modern civilization and society in its present form, and the rise, culmination, and decay in the bosom, respectively, of the East and the West, of those terrible apostacies of Mahomet and of Rome, which sought to perpetuate in a new form the universal dominion of force, and which have filled the earth with pollution and blood. The *Fourth* Period would embrace the complete and triumphant establishment and glory of the Messianic Kingdom, with its Millennial Reign, the utter destruction of the World Powers, and of all that opposes and exalts itself against God, tho perdition of the enemies of God, the glory of his saints, the resurrection of the dead, the consummation of all things. Now, it is impossible for these questions, so awful in their grandeur, to pass across the mind even in the most rapid and general manner, without our seeing in every statement which embraces any outline that is intelligible; that there is, from the beginning to the end, an invincible connection through and through. There is an unavoidable dependence and result, shining through the whole; an overwhelming though it be an inarticulate force predominating through all generations, over all developments, amidst all manifestations; while its silent and sublime intelligence bends and rules and masters all things, whether free, necessary, or contingent, according to an immutable purpose, by an unalterable will, to a decreed end ! We look back through thousands of years, upon tens of thousands of events. The whole career of man, of nature, of Providence is open before our eyes. Now extricate the idea of Providence from those ages, those events, that career; and what is left ? The attempt is mere folly. The idea of Providence is the very vital principle of the whole. It is by it alone that any unity, any order, any progress, any result is possible. Without it there is first chaos and then annihilation. Practically, the sum of true religion as deduced from the word of God, may be expressed by saying that our will is swallowed up in the will of God. Theoretically the sum of reason and experience as deduced from the course of Providence, is the very same truth, and may be stated in the very same words. A result not less striking and pregnant, than it is certain and conclusive.

IV.—1. This result naturally opens to our consideration another topic directly involved in this inquiry; a topic extremely curious and difficult in itself, having its root in the connection of other intelligences than man—with the course of Divine Providence as it relates to man. Strictly speaking it is only through Divine Revelation that we have certain knowledge of the existence of any rational creatures in our universe except those of our own race. Nevertheless it is to be remarked that the whole human family in all ages, even those nations and races the most profoundly ignorant of the word of God, and those most thoroughly hating and rejecting it, have cherished as a fundamental article of all forms of religion, a belief in the existence of other intelligent beings, not of our race, and a conviction of their intimate connection with our destiny. Every superstition has availed itself of this fixed belief of mankind, and peopled the earth, and the air, and the waters, and the heavens and hell too, with innumerable intelligences. Some ascending to the nature of Gods, and some degraded far below man, but all of them distinct and immortal existences, and all of them concerned more or less, with the interests of our race. A belief so remarkable and so nearly universal, however it may have arisen, must necessarily be grounded in the very nature of man; since its invincible permanence can be accounted for in no other way. The same may be said of an analogous belief of man concerning his own spirit. The nearly universal belief of the human race has been that man thought, and willed, and loved, and hated, and desired and the like, not because he had an organized body, but because he had a spiritual soul; and that after the body had perished the soul would still exist—exist forever—either in connection with other bodies in endless succession, or in a separate state without any body; and that so existing it would concern itself with the course of Providence over human affairs. And this belief, equally universal and equally remarkable as the foregoing one, must like it, necessarily be grounded in the very nature which took it up, without considering whether or not it was able to give a precise account to itself of it, and which cleaves to it with a tenacity wholly disdainful of any account of the matter at all. What the Scriptures teach us concerning this latter subject, namely, the immortality of man, has been separately discussed in a previous chapter. What they teach us concerning the former subject, namely, the separate existence of other intelligences and their relations to the course of Providence, both as its objects and agents, will be briefly explained here.

2. The Sadducees, those philosophical infidels of the ancient dispensation, professed to believe that neither angels nor spirits existed, and that no resurrection awaited man.[1] Touching these great questions, said Christ to them, Ye greatly err : and the cause of your error is your ignorance both of the Scriptures and of the power of God. And then, as to the matter of the resurrection, he asserted its reality and pointed out that it was revealed in the Jewish Scriptures : and as to the condition both of angels and of the Spirits of the Just in the resurrection, he explained what that condition was, and wherein it was alike in both.[2] Neither angels nor the spirits of the just can die ; the latter are equal to the former, and are the children of God and the children of the resurrection ; neither the former nor the latter marry or are given in marriage : in fine, the latter are as the former. Such is the substance of the special refutation offered by Christ to the cavils of the presumptuous unbelievers of that day. The Great Teacher explains the truth as of his own knowledge, and points out how it was contained in their own Scriptures. It will be observed that the distinction between angels of God strictly speaking, and the children of God and of the resurrection, as the spirits of the redeemed are called, is preserved carefully by the Saviour : and that this general distinction covers the entire spiritual hosts. All of them are either complete created spirits ; or are the spirits of human beings, human beings that is in their glorified estate. The latter are not only all one in Christ Jesus, by whom they have been redeemed and sanctified and glorified ;

---

[1] Acts, xxiii. 8.   [2] Mat., xxii. 23, 33 ; Mark, xii. 18-27 ; Luke, xx. 27-38.

but they are all of one original race : no longer indeed marrying and giving in marriage, and therefore multiplying no more, but all originally begotten and descended from the first, and in a strict sense, the only created human being ; for Eve was formed out of the person of Adam, and the human body of Christ was formed out of the substance of the Virgin Mary. The former class, on the contrary, the angels strictly speaking, are all spirits and nothing more ; all separately created, each one an order by himself as really as the whole human race is but one order : and whatever relations may exist amongst them, are wholly different from those that exist amongst human beings ; and whatever special relations may exist between them and the Godhead, are essentially different in many respects, from those which exist between the Godhead and the human race. As for example, neither person of the Godhead has ever taken the nature of any of them into union with the divine nature ; nor have any of them been made partakers of the divine nature, through such regenerating, sanctifying, and glorifying work of the Holy Spirit in them, as has occurred with regard to every saved sinner. We do not know of the existence of any intelligent creatures in the universe, except the two classes herein described ; embracing amongst the angels those that have fallen, and amongst men those that will be finally lost. There are many considerations leading to the presumption, perhaps even to the belief, that there are such creatures, and that their number is incalculable, their diversities boundless, their destinies unspeakably diversified : and that the bright and glorious worlds, if indeed they are worlds, which stud our heavens and seem to crowd illimitable space, are all the habitations of innumerable beings capable of knowing, of enjoying, and of glorifying God. Beings created indeed for the express purpose of illustrating, each race in a different estate and a different world, some peculiar glory of the Lord ; as we, in our world will illustrate the glory of his boundless grace. We do not know, and therefore must not teach as a part of that truth which is profitable unto all things, any thing at all touching these sublime and seductive mysteries.

3. It is most expressly taught in the sacred Scriptures that these angels of God, speaking now of all complete spirits created by him, are as really objects of his adorable Providence as human beings are, and that even more than human beings they are the

agents of his Providence. Their very name is one of Office, rather than of nature.—They are *legates, messengers* of God, especially designed to minister unto him in his universal dominion : the special objects of that ministry being, to proclaim the glory of God ;[1] to declare the purposes of God ;[2] and to execute the decrees of God.[3] They are incorporeal, and therefore invisible :[4] being spirits they are endowed with intelligence, and will and desires : an intelligence transcendently above ours, both in the mode and in the objects of it : a will, in the freedom of which multitudes of them fell,[5] and the rest were joyfully obedient to God :[6] desires, directed always to those things which concern the glory of God.[7] Their power transcends our conception by its vastness, as well as by the methods through which it is exerted : an example of which and of their providential use also is seen in the destruction of a hundred and four score and five thousand Assyrian soldiers in one night, by a single angel, and so entirely without effort on his part, or the power of resistance on theirs, that nothing was apprehended till the dawning day revealed the slaughter of the enemies of God.[8] Their number is altogether inconceivable in its vastness. The Prophet Daniel saw thousand thousands ministering unto the *Ancient of Days*, and ten thousand times ten thousand standing before him.[9] All created at first capable of falling, an immense portion of them, possibly the third part, actually fell.[10] They who fell not are confirmed forever in their estate of glory and blessedness.[11] They who fell are irrecoverably lost.[12] This fall of the angels had, in its results, the most intimate and enduring relations to the career and destiny of the human race : for it was under the temptation of the chief of them, that man fell : and the whole subsequent career of the human race, has been one ceaseless struggle against the tempter ; and its final deliverance at the very end and catastrophe of the life of the world, is to be signalized by his being cast into the Lake of torment.[13] This is that Dragon, that old Serpent, which is the Devil and Satan.[14] Called Satan, with special reference to his prime share in the revolt in heaven, and

---

[1] Isa., vi. 3.   [2] Luke, ii. 10.   [3] Psalm ciii. 20.   [4] Luke, xxiv. 39 ; Psalm civ. 4.
[5] Jude, 6.   [6] Psalm ciii. 20.   [7] 1 Pet., i. 12 ; Eph., iii. 10 ; Exod., xxv. 18–20.
[8] 2 Kings, xix. 35.   [9] Dan., vii. 10.   [10] Mat., xii. 26 ; Luke, viii. 30 ; Rev., xii. 4.
[11] Luke, xx. 36 ; Mat., xxv. 31 ; 1 Tim., v. 21 ; Heb., xii. 22 ; Mark, viii. 31.
[12] John, viii. 44 ; 2 Pet., ii. 4 ; Jude, 6.   [13] Rev., xx. *passim*.   [14] Rev., xx. 2.

the fall of the angels ; called that old Serpent, as the deceiver of our first parents and the destroyer of the human race ; called the Dragon, as the merciless persecutor and oppressor of our race through all its sinful pilgrimage ; and called the Devil, as summing up in one fearful term his appalling character and his appalling fate, the Liar-murderer of the universe, the smoke of whose torment ascendeth, day and night, forever and ever ![1]

4. These innumerable spirits good and evil, fall under the Providence of God in a twofold manner. They are objects of it and they are agents of it. Considered of themselves as the mere objects of Divine Providence, if neither man nor any other part of the universe had been created, these mighty spiritual intelligences—in all their countless hosts, separated by endless gradations into some glorious ordering peculiar to their nature, and divided in twain by the irreparable ruin of those who fell ; present to us the dominion of God in his infinite providence, in an aspect of overpowering extent and grandeur. Considered as the agents of him, whose Providence is executed by messengers who are exalted Spirits, and enforced by ministers who are a flame of fire ; even him, whose infinite reign extends over this boundless created universe, and embraces in a peculiar manner the innumerable beings who constitute the human race : how do they exalt the awful majesty of God, the boundless efficacy of whose reign covers immensity and eternity, and is conducted expressly for the illustration of his glory ! Here, as everywhere in our contemplation of God, the thoughtful spirit receives a twofold impression. On the one side, an impression of the incomprehensible nature of the Infinite, Self-existent Creator and Ruler and Saviour : on the other side, an impression of the distinctness of the proofs of his existence and of his infinite perfections and acts. There is so much that we understand clearly, and there is so much that we cannot understand at all, that our own position in such a scene of things, becomes one of the strangest parts of the great problem of existence. In this, and the preceding chapter, I have passed in review those manifestations of God, which according to the classification previously established, bring that problem within the sphere of our intelligence naturally considered, and by means of the works of God as the Creator and Ruler of the universe, subjected to the scrutiny of that intelligence.

____
[1] John, viii., 44; Rev., xx. 10; Rev., xiv. 9–12.

As we advance, other manifestations of God coming nearer and nearer to us, will be found to confirm every thing we can know in the two ways already pointed out ; and to add continually, both to the extent and the certainty of that knowledge, concerning the means of obtaining which the present inquiry is directed.

CHAPTER XXVI.

GOD MANIFEST IN HUMAN NATURE: THE WORD MADE FLESH.

I. 1. Difference between the manifestation of God Naturally and Supernaturally.—2. The Incarnation of the Son of God. Spiritual system of the Universe from that point of view.—3. Controlling position of the Christ of God.—II. 1. Origin of the idea of God manifest in the flesh. Progress of it across all ages, and all dispensations.—2. Utter impossibility of salvation for sinners without it.—3. The Relation of the knowledge of God through Redemption, to the knowledge of him through Creation and Providence.—4. Sum of the knowledge of God attainable through his Incarnation.—5. Appreciation of Christ, considered in himself.—III. 1. The effect of the idea of the Word made Flesh, when applied to all possible Religious Systems.—2. The effect of its gradual development upon the Scriptures themselves, and upon the Messianic Kingdom.—3. Analysis of the Resemblance and Difference, in principle and proof, of the manifestations of God hitherto considered.—4. Relation of the Analysis to all possible manifestations. The Word made Flesh, the culminating point. Distinctness of the method. Elevation attained. Clearness of further Progress.

I.—1. THERE is a great difference between the manner in which the knowledge of God is brought within the compass of our faculties, as exhibited in the two preceding chapters, and as exhibited in the present chapter, and in the next succeeding one. The work of creation lies open to our scrutiny, and the dominion of God is palpably around us and over us ; and our means of knowing him, both as our Creator and as our Ruler, are such as in their nature are level to the natural capacity of man, and in their reality are as absolutely certain, and as personally cognizant to one generation as to another—to all generations alike. Whatever difference there may be is a difference of degree, and in that respect the latest generations ought to possess the highest degrees ; since the progress of knowledge ought to reveal the Creator more and more clearly, and the progress of time ought to unfold continually the course of Providence. On the other hand, the Incarnation of the Godhead is in itself, and in all its effects, wholly supernatural, and being so must be so considered, if we are to derive therefrom the true knowledge of God: and the presence and operation in the universe of the Divine Spirit with direct and universal relevancy to that Divine Incarnation, is assuredly no less supernatural than it. It is another way of the manifestation of God altogether, from the way hitherto contemplated under the twofold aspect of Creation and Providence. A way which approaches us and influences us after a manner wholy distinct from us, and wholly supernatural in itself. For we are a part of creation and we are immediately involved in the course of Providence ; and in both respects we come directly within the sphere of these sublime manifestations of God. But the Incarnation of God transcendently supernatural as it is, is also exclusive of every individual man except Jesus of Nazareth ; and in that sense absolutely includes human nature, but precludes every other personality of human kind. And the work of the Spirit of God in whatever human being is a work from without, absolutely supernatural in itself. And therefore both the one and the other, though they be transcendent manifestations of God not only to us but in us—become so in a manner not spontaneous to nature, and yet not inconsistent with nature—far less contrary to it : but in a manner beyond nature, and so in strict accordance with the facts, and in strict propriety of speech, in a supernatural manner, whether reference be had to the manifestations themselves, or to their effects upon us. By the former methods, so to speak, the knowledge of God is brought to us ; by the latter methods we are brought to it.

2. The great object of the written Word of God, is God manifest in the Flesh. That written Word may be considered as a divine record, and so an infallible rule of our faith and obedience ; or it may be considered only as the annals of the Jewish race, containing their history, their polity and their literature— embracing in a special manner the lives and institutions of Moses and of Jesus. Considered even in this latter point of view, it is itself the repository of the main facts upon which we are to base our estimate of the reality of the perpetual claim set up therein, to be a divine record, and of the value of the perpetual assurance of the coming of Messiah as God Manifest in the Flesh. Considered in the former light, there is no need that I should recapitulate here, what I have employed no less than seven chapters to illustrate and enforce—namely, the whole doctrine of the Per-

son and Work of Christ, the Son of God and the Saviour of the world. In whatever light we see fit to consider these writings, they present to us in the most distinct manner, the Prophetic Messiah, and the Historic Christ. And it is for us to ascertain that these two are one—to gather up the idea they present of him, to estimate the origin and development of that idea, and to determine for ourselves how justly they ground their invincible conviction that he was Immanuel, and as such, the Mediator between God and man, and so the Great Teacher, the Divine Redeemer, the Infinite Ruler. Whatever else may be obscure, this at least is clear beyond mistake, that herein is a distinct view of the Spiritual System of the universe, totally unknown to human reason and to natural religion. God has passed over from being the mere Creator and Ruler of his creatures and has become Incarnate, that he might be the Saviour of sinners. This stupendous mystery is the one ruling conception of the Scriptures. Its motive, the time and circumstances and mode of its occurrence, its nature as a manifestation of God, its influence upon the fate of the universe and especially upon the destiny of man, the method by which its effects are to be realized upon earth and in heaven, through time and eternity; these are the sublime themes of all Scripture given by Inspiration of God. It is no longer Creation only, nor Providence only, but embracing both—the great topic becomes Grace. All the propositions which involve all knowledge of God, become more intense and more strict. What was an earnest hope, becomes a positive conviction ; for it is a faithful saying and worthy of all acceptation, that Christ Jesus came into the world to save sinners.[1] What was common before becomes personal, what was special becomes specific. Before, God's mercies came upon the good and the evil—his blessings upon the just and the unjust—his goodness upon every living thing. But here are transcendent glory and blessedness ; and insuperable limitations follow. All access to the absolute God is closed forever ; no man henceforward to all eternity, knoweth the Father save the Son, and he to whomsoever the Son will reveal him.[2] This is the first limitation upon the Grace of God, that it must flow through a Mediator ; and the second is like unto it. For as there is but one God, so there is but one Mediator between God and men ; there never was, there

<hr>

[1] 1 Tim., i. 15.   [2] Mat., xi. 27.

never will be another.[1] And the third limitation fixes with infinite precision the person, the motive, and the way. It is the Man Christ Jesus, who is that only Mediator ;[2] for there is none other name under heaven, given amongst men, whereby we must be saved ;[3] for God so loved the world, that he gave his only begotten Son, that whosoever believeth in him might not perish, but have everlasting life ![4]

3. Concerning the existence of God; the stupendous facts which in a manner control all other facts, may be considered such as these, namely, that he is wholly distinct from the universe—that he is an Infinite personal God—that there is perfect unity of his Infinite Spiritual Essence—that there is a Trinity of persons subsisting in that essence. The stupendous facts concerning Human Nature are such as these, namely, that it was created in the image of God, and lost that image by sin—that God has taken it into indissoluble union with the divine nature —that it will be transcendently manifested to the universe at the second coming of the glorified God-Man—that death will deliver it up in a glorious resurrection to an immortal existence. It is this God who is manifested in this human nature. On the one side, the Second person of the Godhead; on the other side, Jesus of Nazareth of the seed of Abraham; of the two natures, one person—the Christ of God. The Word was made flesh and dwelt among us, says the Apostle John, and we beheld his Glory, the Glory as of the only begotten of the Father, full of grace and truth.[5] The form of God and the form of a Servant were united in him; the mind which thought it no robbery to be equal with God, and the mind which became obedient unto death, even the death of the cross; the end of which was, his infinite exaltation over the whole universe, the homage of every creature therein to the name of Jesus, and the confession of every tongue that Jesus Christ is Lord, to the glory of God the Father.[6] And the effect upon us was designed to be, that the same mind should be in us, that was in Christ Jesus. On the one hand a boundless self-abnegation; on the other a true appreciation of our being the children of God and the brethren of Christ; and as the end that we should, as joint heirs with him, obtain an inheritance incorruptible, and undefiled, that fadeth not away, reserved in

[1] 1 Tim., ii. 5.   [2] 1 Tim., ii. 5.   [3] Acts, iv. 12.
[4] John, iii. 16.   [5] John, i. 14.   [6] Phil., ii. 5–11.

heaven for us, who are kept by the mighty power of God, through faith, unto salvation.[1]

II.—1. This conception of God manifested in human nature did not originate with the Scriptures, nor is it equally distinct in every part of them—nor did all the sacred writers possess it to the same extent, nor with the same clearness. During twenty-five of the forty centuries which preceded the birth of Christ, no part of the written word appears to have existed : and the ministry of angels, the immense duration of human life, and the bestowment by God of the spirit of Inspiration upon his servants, supplied the lack of a precise and permanent divine record, such as we now possess. What is to be observed is, that it was from the very beginning that this conception of Messiah makes itself manifest ; not at all as a speculation, and not merely as a belief, but as the very fountain of spiritual life to every child of God, and as the very foundation on which the Spiritual System actually administered by God, was explicable to man. In this manner the sublime conception passed from breast to breast, and from age to age, the very channel of its descent through the generations marked out to us in the very earliest monuments of our race, till it made its lodgement, purely and simply, in the written word at the very origin of this new form of preserving and transmitting divine truth. Thus Moses takes it up, and claiming to speak with God as one speaks with a familiar friend, he attributes to God himself the origin of the conception of God manifest in the flesh ; points out with perfect distinctness its first utterance by God in the very act of passing sentence upon our first parents and their destroyer ; traces its progress, as the living principle of the Messianic kingdom down to his own day ; and then lays it at the foundation of all his own wonderful institutions : institutions whose very object was to organize that very Messianic kingdom in the form of a Theocracy, till the God-man should himself appear. We are not to suppose that the ancient method of transmitting this sublime conception was abolished when the conception itself was reduced to a clear statement and made a part of the written word ; nor that the conception itself, thus lodged in a distinct form in the written word, needed no further development. The truth is far otherwise in both respects. The conception of God manifest in human nature, has dwelt in the

---

[1] 1 Peter, i. 3–9

heart of every child of God, only the more distinctly by the help
of the written word ; and has passed in that way, from heart to
heart, and from age to age, across the generations, since as before. And during about sixteen centuries, beginning with Moses
and terminating with the Apostle John, and embracing every intermediate writer of every portion of the Sacred Scriptures, we
have this overruling idea wrought out continually, and in every
form. Nor is it possible for us to imagine that even yet we have
reached the whole length, and breadth, and depth, and height
of the boundless riches of this mystery of grace. The consummate triumph of the Messianic kingdom is yet future ; the second coming and reign of the Messiah are still before us ; the
glories of eternity are yet to come ; and notwithstanding all the
Spirit of God has revealed unto us, the full amount of what God
has prepared for them who love him, has never entered into the
heart of man.[1]

2. It has been demonstrated, as I think, that the ruin of
the human race is not only absolute but irremediable, when considered from any natural point of view : and that a divine interposition was wholly indispensable in order to prevent its universal perdition. It has also been demonstrated, as it appears
to me, that the Incarnation of the Godhead was the single
method by which an effectual interposition for the rescue of
mankind was possible. But the matter goes even further than
this : for it may be confidently asserted that in the actual condition of man, there is a total impossibility of God's making
himself completely known to man in order to his Salvation—
except by means of the Incarnation of himself ; nay further, that
the divine Scriptures themselves which purport to reveal the
way of our deliverance, become utterly nugatory and incomprehensible as an adequate means of salvation for sinful men—except they are allowed to be grounded on the fundamental conception of the Word made flesh. Our relations to God, and
God's relations to the universe, and the relations of the sacred
Scriptures both to God and to us, and the intimate nature both
of God and of man as both natures are involved in these several relations ; all is inexplicable as tending toward the recovery
of our lost race—all is clear and explicable as tending directly to
our perdition as sinners—until the idea of a Saviour, God-man,

<hr>

[1] 1 Cor., ii. 9, 10.

and so Mediator between God and men, is clearly brought to
light. It is then that a new knowledge, and with it a new and
glorious hope, become our heritage. It is then that we obtain
a distinct knowledge of the mode of God's existence, as being
that of three persons in one essence ; and a clear conception of
the influence of that fact upon our own destiny. It is then that
we arrive at clear views of all the perfections of the Divine Nature, and perceive how they all harmonize through such a Messiah as this, in the restoration of fallen man. It is then that
we are able, through the realization of this superhuman conception, manifested before us in the person of Christ, and developed
in the whole work of Christ ; really to come unto God by him,
and assuredly to experience that whosoever thus comes, will in
no wise be cast out.[1]

3. Now let us observe how every end which is proposed in
creation and in providence, is proposed also in redemption—only
that other glorious ends are superadded : and that the ends
which are common to them all are manifested most clearly by
this last method. It has been shown abundantly, that the subjective reason for the creation of the universe and all things
in it, can be found only in God himself, and that the objective
reason, which alone is to be found in the universe itself, is the
supreme conformity of this particular universe to the subjective
reason existing in God. That subjective reason is the purpose
of God to manifest his own glory to the intelligent universe—
in a way of the greatest blessedness to his creatures. As the
infinite Ruler of the universe, the whole course of his Providence
is directed to the execution of the very same purpose of God :
namely, the highest illustration of all his perfections to his
whole universe ; doing this in such a way as bestowed on his
creatures the greatest felicity consistent with that chief end.
And now the work of Redemption, bearing still more directly
upon the same supreme object, and springing from precisely the
same infinite motive—brings to light a new aspect of the glory
of God, unknown to Providence considered of itself ; just as
Providence had brought to light a new aspect of his glory unknown to creation, considered of itself. And the blessedness of
the creature, as far as the chief end of every work of God allowed
to be possible, which shines so conspicuously as the purpose of

____
[1] John, vi. 37.

God in creation, and becomes so much more illustrious in Providence—rises so high in Redemption as to seem almost inseparable from that very glory of God, which is his chief motive. As if we should say, this blessedness of the creature which seemed to be a great but incidental end in the glory of creation, and to mount almost to equality in the glory of Providence, becomes in Redemption the very manner of the glory itself! To which this is to be added, that whereas in creation we, who are so deeply implicated in every work of God, can be considered merely as creatures, and in Providence can be considered only as the subjects of an infinite moral Ruler, become in Redemption the very children of God! And, to add one more element to the glory of God, and to our own blessedness, we who at the best are but unprofitable creatures, and unthankful subjects, and disobedient children, are made partakers of an infinite weight of glory, only through the eternal love of God, manifested not only, but made efficacious through the sacrifice of his only begotten Son.[1] It would indeed be idle to set about proving that these things teach us somewhat concerning God. They carry us in truth into the heart of God—the very focus of all knowledge of him. And in the very midst we are confronted with that sublime unity of purpose and working which shines forth in every manifestation of God : wherein every thing that precedes, though it seemed complete in itself, becomes still more perfect as a part of all that follows. So that creation becomes more glorious as we view it under the light thrown on it by the course of Providence ; and Providence assumes a more wondrous aspect as soon as its relation to Redemption is disclosed ; and Redemption, too, exhibits new riches, both of Grace and Glory, as it is contemplated from every point of our increasing knowledge, as we advance towards that eternal life which consists in knowing the only true God, and Jesus Christ whom he has sent.[2]

4. If we will carefully consider what it is we actually learn concerning God by means of his manifestation in human nature, we cannot fail to be struck with the infinite scope of the ideas we receive in that manner. Let me suppose that we have a clear conception of the chief of these ideas : the union of the divine and human natures in the being called Jesus Christ, and proclaimed to be the Son of God and the Saviour of men : the office exe-

[1] John, iii. 17.   [2] John, xvii. 3, 4.

cuted by this God-man, namely, that of Mediator of God's eternal Covenant of Grace : the execution of that office of Mediator between God and men, comprehended in his being the infallible Teacher of all truth and all duty ; in his being the atoning Priest and the all prevalent Intercessor for his people ; and in his being the only King and Ruler of the Messianic kingdom, and as such, head over all things : the mediatorial office of this God-man, executed in that threefold manner, first in an estate of infinite humiliation, ending in his crucifixion as an atoning sacrifice, and then in an estate of infinite exaltation upon the throne of God and at the right hand of the Father. And then let me suppose that we have also a clear conception of the chief of the corresponding ideas, concerning the inexpressible change in our own state and destiny, which is designed to be produced through this Incarnation of God : the pardon of sin—the total restoration of our nature—redemption from hell—a glorious resurrection—an immortality of blessedness in a future state of existence. I do not see that there is any thing either in Creation or Providence, more remote from the natural apprehension of man, than these sublime ideas ; nothing assuredly to exceed their infinite scope.—Yet as means adapted to ends, nothing can be more amazingly effective, more perfectly complete. And the new light they throw upon all we knew before concerning the nature, the character, the attributes and the counsels of God, immense as it is, and supernatural as the manner of its production is admitted to be ; is as distinct to the understanding, as that which accompanies our reception of any new truth whatever. It may be confidently asserted that every complicated chain of Providence, and every statement of any act of creation, is incapable of being brought to the intelligence of man with a clearness of apprehension, equal to that we experience in perceiving every capital truth connected with the manifestation of God in the flesh. As a universal test and rule of truth, the very greatest philosophers have held this to be decisive. That there is in truth itself, a light which makes its own nature both manifest and certain, can never be called in question as long as any truth at all can be said to be self evident ; any more than it can be doubted that light, which reveals all things else, also manifests itself. And thus in the very nature of these immense conceptions, it is more certain they did not originate with us, than it is that the ideas of God as the Creator, and of God as the Infinite Ruler, did not originate with us: while in the very distinctness with which we perceive them, and the very clearness with which we construe them to our intelligence, we have an extraordinary proof that they are true.

5. The weakness of our faculties, and the poverty of language as compared with a subject like this, embarrass all our attempts to express precisely our highest conceptions. It is very common to say the Bible is our Religion, which is true in the sense that the Bible is an infallible account of our Religion. But it is strictly true to say, that God manifest in the flesh is the chief part of all true religion, and that no part of it is of any avail irrespective of him. After we have explained in detail every particular thing that relates to the person, and work, and glory of Christ, and explained also the proportion of the whole, we are not satisfied with what we have done, or can do, in that manner, but feel that the grand impression of the whole is not adequately made, not fully brought out. Christ is more in the totality than all the parts we are able to gather up, set forth to our own apprehension. The glory which his fulness of grace and truth makes manifest is the glory of the only begotten of the Father ;[1] and in him dwelleth all the fulness of the Godhead bodily.[2] The declaration that he is the author and the finisher of our faith receives a peculiar light from being connected immediately with the command that we should *look unto him ;*[3] for it is from his fulness we receive grace responsive to grace ; and it is while with unveiled face we contemplate the glory of the Lord that we are transformed into the same image—glory responsive to glory.[4]* All good in the creature, whether of grace or glory, proceeds from Christ—is the product of Christ in us, and is responsive to somewhat in Christ : and the whole image into which we are transformed is the image of Christ. The image we have lost by the fall is the image of God ; and unto that we must be restored, or we must perish. We are restored to it in a new creation of which God is the model, and wherein we are renewed not only in knowledge and in rectitude, but in that especial form of holiness which is the product of divine truth.[5] In all this new creation unto good works, while we are the workmanship of God,

---

[1] John, i. 14.   [2] Col., ii. 9.   [3] Heb., xii. 2.   [4] John, i. 16 ; 2 Cor., iii. 18.
* Χαριν αντι χαριτος—απο δοξης εις δοξαν.   [5] Col., iii. 10 ; Eph., iv. 24.

it is in Christ Jesus that the whole is accomplished.[1] But what has been stated really embraces every thing—the new creation, all grace, all glory, complete restoration generally in knowledge, and righteouness, and specially in that peculiar holiness which divine truth teaches, and is the grand instrument in producing ; that is, the righteousness of the God-man, by which we are justified, and through which we are sanctified. Christ is therefore unto us life itself, in every true and spiritual sense. He is the embodiment of true religion itself—that religion which is the outbirth of the covenant of grace, and which expresses the sum of the relations between a gracious God and sinful men. In him all is presented to us in a personal form, in a concrete, living manner. The written word is, at the most, a form of truth, but Christ is the truth itself. All separate parts of knowledge and of righteousness, precious as they may all be justly accounted, derive a part of their value from some further end to which they lead ; but Christ is the very satisfying end of all ! In the full possession of him, we lack nothing, we need nothing, we desire nothing beyond. If we could extricate the Word made flesh from every thing else in the universe, we should have a complete conception of every perfection of the Godhead, and every thing glorious and lovely in human nature united in one Being. This Being is the Messiah of the Old Testament, the Christ of the New Testament—God manifest in Human Nature.

III.—1. The manner in which the idea of the divine incarnation has been shown to have originated, and to have been propagated among men, is the only one which renders it intelligible. I may add that it is not otherwise possible it should have received the development it did in the Sacred Scriptures, or that it should occupy the position it does toward all possible religious systems. In the latter respect the power of this conception may be illustrated in some degree, by observing that it produces upon the chaos of religious ideas to which man has given birth, an effect similar to that produced by the conception of Providence upon the chaos of events which human passions produce. We cannot, without wholly subverting human intelligence, admit that utter delusion and folly, unmixed with any truth at all, is a possible result in any system which reason and conscience accept : nor could we allow such results to be common with-

---

[1] Eph., ii. 10.

out impeaching our Creator for contriving, and our divine Ruler for steadily conspiring our destruction, under the forms of intelligence and moral sense. Taking every system of morals and religion that exists, or can be imagined, when it is subjected to the test of introducing into its bosom the idea of the Christ of God, precisely as that idea is found, at any stage of its development in the written word : what occurs is, that the system is instantly rectified and reduced to order. What is true and good is discovered and located : what is wholly false is disclosed in its deformity : what is distorted, is reduced to its true proportion. It is as if in every science of positive truth, nothing certain and final could be obtained, by reason of the omission of the one grand truth which regulated the innumerable subordinate truths, and in the absence of which confusion and mistake characterized even the use of truth itself : but as soon as that central truth is restored, every thing falls of necessity into its place, or if it finds no place is rejected as untrue. That so large a part of all human systems of morals and religion, should perish under such a test ; that many of them should save so little from such a wreck ; is only one more proof of the necessity of a divine intervention to prevent the perdition of our race: an immense illustration of the sublime efficacy of the method in which that divine interposition has taken place.

2. And upon the former of the two points suggested at the beginning of the preceding paragraph, the development, namely, which this central idea of true Religion has received in the Scripture ; it may be observed that the Christian dispensation, as compared with the Jewish dispensation, affords the most sublime illustration of the manner in which the mere increased development of this vast conception affects a system in which no error at all existed. It cannot be denied that the Jewish dispensation was not only a dispensation of divine truth, but that this especial truth, in a certain stage of it, was its vital principle : and yet it is not conceivable that the Jewish dispensation could have remained as it was, after the advent of the Saviour of the World. It does not appertain to this portion of the subject to point out the nature of the proof, that the Scriptures are of divine origin, afforded by the manner in which they treat the whole conception of the God-man : but it is pertinent to remark that their manner of treating the subject, incontestably proves that both the idea itself and its whole development are di-

vine. Whoever will connect the primeval intimation that the seed of the woman should bruise the serpent's head, uttered by God at the fall of man; with the apocalyptic visions of the glorified Redeemer, uttered four thousand years afterward by the Apostle John; and will then fill up the chasm between the two, by carefully tracing through all time, all the unfolding of that first utterance, up to the inconceivable Glory and Majesty in which the King of kings and Lord of lords is presented when all revelation concerning him terminates; will find himself as easily persuaded to believe that human force created the universe, and that human wisdom is the vital influence in Providence, as to believe that human intelligence has conceived and developed this most amazing part of all the manifestations of God. It is in this conception that the turn is given to the whole Spiritual System of the universe; speaking after the manner of men. In it lies the nexus between Natural and Revealed religion; between universal morality and evangelical holiness; between a universe of creatures, under the curse of God, and a universe of sinners saved by Grace; between the Glory of God as partially exhibited and the Glory of God as completely made known to his intelligent universe. If it could be rigorously demonstrated that the existence of any God at all is simply impossible; human intelligence, upon a complete survey of all that is involved in this conception of God manifested in the flesh—would firmly insist that he who did all these things ought to have been God.

3. There is a difference, and there is a resemblance, between the nature of the evidence upon which the facts of creation, and the facts of Providence, and the facts of Redemption, are respectively established to the satisfaction of the human mind. This difference and this resemblance, are in many particulars very marked ; but it may be observed in general, that it is a difference and a resemblance founded on the nature of the several cases. In each of them a manifestation of God is propounded ; but in each a manifestation which is widely different from every other ; and, therefore, each one must necessarily be sustained in part by evidence common to all, and in part by that sort of evidence which is peculiar to itself. It may be added that the fact of there ever having been a creation—and the fact of there being any intimate and universal Providence; are facts as subject to be denied, have been as resolutely denied, and are just as necessary

to be proved, and perhaps as difficult to be proved, as the fact of a divine Incarnation. In each case there are three very distinct stages of the inquiry. The first is, the motive which led God to determine, and then to act as he has done in all three cases; and about this, every rational creature feels it to be a matter beyond all cognizance lower than that of God himself; and so this point is taken to be sufficiently explained in each case, when the motive is lodged in the breast of God, and he is allowed to make himself the motive of his conduct. The second stage is the manner in which God executes these great designs, in which he becomes successively manifest as Creator, Ruler, and Redeemer. How does he create a universe out of nothing? How is he omnipresent, being a personal God and distinct from the universe ; and how are those infinite perfections and infinite acts to be explained, which, in the concrete, we call Providence ? How is the Hypostatical union between the divine and human natures, effected, maintained, and directed in the whole matter of the Incarnation and its results ? Here again, the posture of the human mind is the same with reference to each of the three ways of the manifestation of God. The *manner* of. Creation, of Providence, and of Incarnation, is wholly and alike inscrutable to us ; and beginning at the beginning—the first fact, namely, the self-existence of an infinite and eternal first cause, is the most overwhelming fact the mind ever encounters ; and the second fact, namely, the creation of the universe out of nothing, is inferior in its utter inscrutability, only to the self-existence of the Infinite Creator. The third stage of the inquiry brings us in each case to the same point, namely, the actual occurrence of the grand fact; and here again, to a certain extent, our position is precisely similar as to all three methods of the divine manifestation, and as to the evidence required in each case. We desire to be certified of the fact itself ; we desire to comprehend that in reality, it is a manifestation of God; we desire to have developed before us, the significance of them all as means of the true knowledge of the living God. It is at this third stage that these three great manifestations of God develop themselves differently and demand a different kind of evidence, corresponding in each case to their own several natures.

4. The rational faculties of man preside equally over every form of inquiry, and his intelligence must decide equally upon

every species of evidence. So taken, we may consider the evidence of creation and in creation, as being in its nature experimental, inductive, and in effect, proof; the evidence of Providence and in Povidence, as embracing the preceding and adding thereto strictly moral evidence; and the evidence of Incarnation and in Incarnation, beside embracing the two preceding—as to certain aspects of the case—as adding a still higher form of strictly spiritual evidence. Perhaps that is not different from saying that the prevailing aspect of creation is physical; that the prevailing aspect of Providence is moral; that the prevailing aspect of Redemption is spiritual; that throughout the whole of them there is the force of a Divine Will, and over the whole the light of a Divine Intelligence. The particular forms under which the whole, or any part of this evidence, shall be brought forward and arrayed, so as to satisfy our intelligence, belongs to a different department of the great subject of the Knowledge of God. The analysis just made, was necessary to point out how it is that every manifestation of God hitherto considered, whether we call it, with reference to our own nature, natural or supernatural; is equally capable of being construed and established to human intelligence: and if so, then this is also true of every possible manifestation of God. For it was before proved that there are no other manifestations of God, but the three now considered, and the three remaining to be considered : and moreover that the whole six embraced but two methods and the union of the two. That is to say, a natural method in creation and Providence; a Supernatural method in Incarnation and the New Creation; and a union of both methods in Revelation and in the Human Soul. But having fully considered both the fundamental methods, in developing the first three manifestations of God, we have been obliged to consider all the difficulties as to evidence, which the nature of the case, whether natural or supernatural, would allow : and the general subject has reached the point where such an analysis was proper. The particular effect of it here is, to connect the Incarnation of God, in the most precise manner, with the previous works of creation and Providence: and having reached in Christ Jesus the culminating point of the Knowledge of God, to connect that exalted height of knowledge, and that God-man, immediately with every succeeding manifestation of God. In effect, every succeeding manifestation of God, has, as will be seen, an especial relevancy to God manifest in Human Nature ; as both the preceding manifestations tend unto and can be fully explicated only in connection with that of the Word made flesh.

5. Let us suppose that we have a clear idea of God—in so far as that he is an Infinite Being, in whom are all perfections. Let us add, one by one these following ideas : that he is the creator of the universe ; that he is the Ruler of every thing he has created : that he is the redeemer of fallen men : that he is the sanctifier of the sinners he saves : that he is the author of a permanent Revelation, which is a perfect rule of faith and duty unto Salvation : that the soul of man as made and as renewed by God, in which that first idea of God dwells, both apprehends all these subsequent ideas of God and is a living monument of the truth of the whole of them. Is it not clear that every one of these additional ideas, vast as they are, may be considered as lodged implicitly in the first idea of God as possessing all perfections ; and that continually increasing knowledge of God flows from their development, one after another, so far as we have yet subjected them to scrutiny ? Is it not clear that all the knowledge of God thus attainable is coherent, every part with every part ; and the whole of it the result of the successive manifestations which God has made of himself ? It seems to me that nothing can be more certain than the method by which we have reached—in the Word made flesh—the summit from which the whole field of such inquiries may be surveyed. That nothing can be more assured than the position thus obtained, from which to pass onward to the three remaining manifestations of God ; all of which have a direct relevancy to all of those hitherto considered, and especially, as has been pointed out, to God the Saviour of the World.

CHAPTER XXVII.

GOD MANIFEST IN THE NEW CREATION: GOD THE HOLY GHOST.

I. 1. The Mode of the Divine Existence, in its relation to the Universe, and especially to the New Creation.—2. Relation of the Holy Ghost to the Old Creation. —II. 1. The nature of the New Creation. The work of the Spirit therein. The State of Man and the Universe.—2. Special consideration of the Spirit and his work as a means of divine knowledge.—3. Grand epochs in the progress of the New Creation.—4. The Sum of divine knowledge under the Patriarchal Form of the Church during its first three periods, from Adam to Noah—from Noah to Abraham—and from Abraham to Moses.—5. The fourth or Theocratic period— from Moses to Christ. Additional knowledge of God therein.—6. Advent of Messiah. The effect thereof upon his kingdom.—7. In this fifth period it is the whole work of Christ, through the Spirit, in his estate of Humiliation. Appreciation of consummate knowledge.—8. The sixth period of the New Creation. Dispensation of the Holy Spirit since Pentecost.—9. The explicit relation of the work of the Spirit to Christ, to the written word, to the work of Creation, and therein to the nature of man, and to the course of Providence.—III. 1. The wonderful working of the Holy Ghost, as the Author of the New Creation.—2. With reference to Christ, as the Head thereof, in the constitution of his person, as Immanuel.—3. With reference to the whole Mediatorial work of Christ.—4. With reference to the mystical Body of Christ, and the members thereof.

I.—1. GOD is a Spirit, infinitely perfect, of a threefold personality. His Essence is one and simple. That Essence sustains three modes of existence, which are not names, but Persons. These Persons are one in Essence, of a mutual inbeing, and equal in power and glory. They are distinct in their Names, in their Order, in their manner of working and in their personal properties. It is proper to the Father that he neither proceeds, nor is begotten of any, but that the Son is begotten of him, and that the Spirit proceeds from him and the Son : it is proper to the Son that he is begotten of the Father, and that the Spirit proceeds from him and the Father : and it is proper to the Spirit that he is not begotten, but that he proceeds from the Father and the Son. From which properties indeed is the special name of each Person.—These are inscrutable mysteries. They are the ultimate facts of the Divine Existence. They cannot, perhaps, be stated in a simpler form ; and this form of statement is acquiesced in by the whole Orthodox Church of God as containing the result of the innumerable representations of his Divine Word on the subject. Undeniably this is the manner of the Divine Existence, upon the reality of which it depends, that the Scriptures should be either coherent or intelligible ; that the Spiritual System of the universe revealed in them should be possible ; or that the Plan of Salvation they contain should be either true or efficacious. The relation of God, considered absolutely, and the relation of the Father, of the Son, and of the Holy Spirit, considered separately, to the whole work of Creation, of Providence, and of Grace—taken all together, make up the sum of the known relations of God to the universe : unless we should see fit to consider the eternal state of glory as a work of God distinct from Creation, Providence and Grace : in which case, nothing is changed, but our mode of considering the subject, by making four departments of it, instead of three. What is now to be specially considered is, so much of the Relations of God to the universe, as is involved in the manifestation of God to us in the New Creation—as a means to us of the true knowledge of himself. The Manifestation, that is, of the whole work of God considered as the Restorer of his universe from the curse, the penalty, and the pollution of sin, so far as that work may be viewed in the results of it, objectively considered. There is a special work of the Holy Spirit—the third Person in the Trinity, with reference to the New Creation, just as there is a special work of the First and the Second Persons in the Trinity, with reference thereto : and this special work of the Holy Spirit with reference to the New Creation, is not only the means of our transcendent knowledge of himself—but also of the whole Godhead. It is the second of the two purely supernatural methods of the Divine Manifestation, which God has vouchsafed unto man. The first of the two has been considered in the previous chapter—and has its foundation in the union of the divine and human natures. The second, to which this chapter is devoted, is a totally different Manifestation of God—which has its foundation in the perfectly distinct, personal, spiritual existence of God, separate from humanity—separate from the universe.

2. It may be needful to observe that the restriction of this

inquiry to the New Creation, is not to be considered as an intimation that the Holy Spirit took no part in the original, or old
Creation : but is occasioned, after what has been already advanced on the general subject of creation, by that necessity of
compressing these discussions, which limits them continually, and
by the incomparable fulness of the work of the Spirit in the
New Creation. All divine operations, are commonly ascribed
in the Scriptures to God absolutely ; because all the persons of
the Trinity concur in all of them—and because the divine essence is one. In the same manner, when a particular account is
given of any divine operation, it is commonly ascribed pre-eminently to one or other person of the Godhead, or the part taken
in it by each person is clearly expressed. And prevailingly the
order of subsistence of the three persons in the divine Essence
is the order of the operation of the three in all the great works
of God. The beginning of divine operations is usually ascribed
to the Father—of whom, and to whom and through whom are
all things : the sustaining, establishing and upholding all things,
is ascribed to the Son : and the perfecting and concluding all
things, to the Holy Spirit : with a perpetual concurrence, however, of all, in all.[1] The original creation was divided into two
very marked classes—the rational, namely, and the irrational
portions of it ; and in both of these great departments of the old
creation, the part ascribed to the Holy Ghost—beside his co-
operation in the whole, was the completing work of each. The
heavens were garnished by the Spirit, and the host of them rendered glorious and beautiful, wrought and adorned to show forth
God's power and wisdom.[2] And the earth and its host received
their quickening and prolific power, from the brooding of the
Spirit of God upon the face of that formless and void deep which
God had created—and by the same Spirit the face of the earth
is continually renewed.[3] With reference to the creation of man,
the head of the visible creation, the statements of the Scriptures are distinct and remarkable. The Lord God formed man
of the dust of the ground, and breathed into his nostrils the
breath of life : and man became a living soul.[4] Here is the
matter of which he was formed—dust of the ground : the addition thereto, namely, the breath of life : the result of the whole

<hr>

[1] Rom., xi. 32 ; Col., i. 17 ; Heb., i. 3.   [2] Job, xxvi. 13 ; Ps. xix. 1.
[3] Gen., i. 2 ; Ps. civ. 30.   [4] Gen., ii. 7.

manifested in the union of the two—man became a living soul.
How clearly is this wonderful origin of our race—otherwise utterly inscrutable—set before us in one divine sentence ! But
there is more. God said, Let us make man in our own image,
after our likeness: so God created man in his own image, in
the image of God created He him.[1] The creation therefore
of the human soul, the *Spiration* of a vital principle, an immortal existence, breathed from God into man, is the immediate
work, as its very manner shows, of the Holy Spirit.[2] And so
that original intelligence in man by which he might discern the
will of God, that ability and inclination unto his service, that
love of him and conformity unto him : in other words, that
knowledge, righteousness, and holiness wherein so large a part
of man's conformity to the image of God consisted, were pro-
ducts of the operation of the Holy Spirit. There is no marvel,
therefore, that in the renovation of our fallen nature, the restoration of that lost image of God, which was bestowed on us at
first by the Spirit, should be his immediate operation, wherein
by a New Creation he restores his own work to more than its
original glory.[3]

II.—1. The fall of man by transgression against God, produced upon the whole visible universe of which he was the head,
those terrible effects which appertained to transgression by the
primitive constitution of man, and by the penalty of the Covenant of Works ; effects which were to a certain degree intimated
in the sentence pronounced by the Almighty at the time ;[4] which
all succeeding ages have developed ; and which will not cease to
be felt throughout eternity. To retrieve these results in such a
manner as became the glory of God, and to make the whole issue
of them all, in time and in eternity, supremely illustrate that
glory ; was the immediate object of the Covenant of Grace, and
therefore of the Incarnation of Christ, and of the whole work of
the divine Spirit in the New Creation. That New Creation is,
indeed, the sum of the operations of the Spirit, in the practical
application of the Covenant of Grace with all its blessings and
benefits to the universe, as it and all things lay under the penalty of Sin, the curse of the moral law, and the Special Sentence
of God pronounced upon the breach of the Covenant of Works.
The curse of God is upon the Tempter, and upon the man, and

<hr>

[1] Gen., i. 26, 27.   [2] Job, xxxiii. 4.   [3] John, iii. 1–21.   [4] Gen., iii. 14–19.

upon the woman, and upon the earth, and upon all things pertaining to them all : all underlies that curse, and all that is implied in it, and awaits its terrible execution.   As for man he has fallen from his original righteousness : he has lost communion with God : he has become dead in Sin : he is wholly defiled in all the faculties and parts of his Soul and of his body.[1] And from this depraved nature proceed all actual transgressions : and the pollution and the transgressions springing from it, altogether subject us to the wrath of God, and to every misery, spiritual, temporal, and eternal.   And so fatal is the condition, and so deadly is that malady of Sin which alone of all maladies has no result, of itself, but in death, that not a single creature of the race did, of himself, ever escape, or ever could.   For always and without exception, lust, when it hath conceived, bringeth forth sin, and always and without exception, sin, when it is finished, bringeth forth death.[2]

2. It has been largely shown that this fearful condition of man and of the universe, was retrieved by the interposition of God : that the special form of that interposition was through the Incarnatian of the Son of God, the second Person of the Trinity : and that the efficacy of that interposition was secured by the work of the Holy Spirit, the third Person of the Trinity. At present, it is the aspect of that whole dispensation of the Spirit, as the manifestation of God in the New Creation, and so the means unto us of the true knowledge of him in all spiritual things, and not the general discussion of the great doctrine of the Holy Ghost, which is directly before us.   Considered in whatever light, this Dispensation of the Spirit covers every part of the New Creation, every outworking of the eternal Covenant of Grace. It commences, therefore, for its manifestation, with the very uttering of the earliest promise to our race, which was embraced in the threat which closed the divine sentence against their Tempter —I will put enmity between thee and the woman, and between thy seed and her seed : it shall bruise thy head and thou shalt bruise his heel.[3]   From that moment God appears to sinful man not merely as his offended Creator, but also as his merciful Saviour.   Thenceforward Messiah has a revealed relation to man, the New Creation has a positive sense to the human race, and

[1] Gen., iii. 7–9; Rom., v. *passim;* Gen., vi. 5–7; Rom., iii. 10–19.
[2] James, i. 15.   [3] Gen., iii. 15.

the Holy Spirit has a sublime mission of grace in this ruined world. We need not be ignorant of what those innumerable statements intend, wherein we are divinely informed that God gives his Spirit unto us—that he sends the Holy Ghost upon men—that he ministers of the Spirit unto them—that he pours him out upon them ; nor of the meaning of the corresponding statements concerning the Spirit, that he proceeds from the Father and the Son—that he comes to men—that he falls and that he rests upon them—and that he departs from them. Nor need we marvel at those manifold operations through which God attested by signs, and wonders, and mighty works, and still more mighty gifts of the Holy Ghost, the constant progress through all ages, of his glorious work. We need not err : we need not marvel. The key to all these things has been put into our hands by God himself. The motive, the end, the effect, the significance, the cause, the power of all is clearly set before us ; as soon as we will accept in its simple verity, and its divine fulness, that first recorded promise and sentence of God all in one ; at the moment that he opened under one covenant, that way of Life, which had just been closed forever under the other. And this transcendent knowledge, in the first glorious inception of it, is made ours through the manifestation of God in the New Creation. And all the steadfast development of this new light and this new life, whether in its progress through the centuries, or in its growth in our own souls, depends upon the same sublime manifestation of God.

3. I have pointed out in a previous chapter, the manner in which it seemed to me most convenient to contemplate the great epochs and subdivisions of the progress of the Messianic kingdom, when the particular object was to obtain a distinct and comprehensive view of the relations of Providence to that kingdom in its connection with all the world Powers. A different aspect of the Messianic kingdom is presented to us, when we seek to comprehend the perpetual development of the saving knowledge of God in it, and by means of it : since in this light it is the connection of the Saviour and the Sanctifier of that kingdom with each other, as manifested in its own great progress ; and not the connection of the kingdom itself with the course of Providence, which we are especially to consider. The New Creation considered as a perpetual and continually increasing manifestation of God, involves in its widest conception, every element

of our knowledge of God—and in its specific conception rests upon the whole work of the Divine Spirit considered with particular reference to the Covenant of Grace. Though a new and spiritual, there is yet a real creation : though there may be a special aspect of Providence, yet it is not only real but peculiarly glorious : and the work of Christ—the Dispensation of the Spirit —and the Revealed Will of God, have primary reference to the New Creation—while the soul of man is as really the subject of this as of its original creation. The manifestation of God in Christ has been considered ; and his manifestation in Revelation and in the Human Soul will be hereafter considered separately in their order. At present it is the manifestation of God, the Spirit, in the specific relation of that Divine Agent to the whole work of the Restitution of the universe which lies before us. In this vast field of knowledge, there are operations of the Spirit common to all the periods into which his Dispensation can be divided : while there are also grand epochs which mark his Dispensation—as from period to period, his manifestations become more full in themselves, or more subject to human scrutiny. Following these, we may call the period from Adam to Noah the first state of the New Creation : that from Noah to Abraham the second state : that from Abraham to Moses the third state : that from Moses to Christ the fourth state : the personal ministry of Christ the fifth state : and the period from the Ascension of Christ to his Second Advent the sixth state. So far as this inquiry is concerned, all that will follow the Second Advent of Christ may be considered one single State of the New Creation : or we may make the Millennial Reign one state, and the eternal Glory another state : or we may recoil in our weakness and ignorance, from any attempt to connect the Divine Spirit in any particular manner with the glorified state of the New Creation under the immediate dominion of the glorified Saviour, whether on earth or in heaven. Here, as everywhere, the inscrutability of these awful themes presses us the most as we get very near to their consummate result : and divine Revelation refuses to open to us the culminating result of any mystery of God, with the same distinctness that it opens to us, all that is elemental in them all. We cannot too clearly understand, that nothing is revealed merely to our curiosity.

4. We will not pause here to inquire further into the actual

condition of man as created, and his actual condition as fallen, and the precise difference between the two conditions : all of which has been now exhibited in a general manner, and the special discussion of which belongs to other parts of Theology. It is clear that the very first declaration of the Way of Life for fallen man, involved the revelation by God, of truths wholly new and unspeakably grand and vital to man. The first Parents of our race learned that there was salvation for lost men ; that this salvation had its origin merely in Divine Grace ; that it would be exhibited through the future Incarnation of a Redeemer ; that the Redeemer would be at once a Suffering and a Triumphant Saviour ; that his finished righteousness was to be embraced only through faith. If we add to these immense acquisitions in knowledge the Moral Law as the rule of obedience, which abides to this day, and the Institution of Sacrifice, as the mode of worship, which was consummated in the sacrifice of Christ ; we have, perhaps, the sum of Adamic Theology—the sum of the attainment of the Church of God in the knowledge of himself, during its first period extending from Adam to Noah. The first explicit mention of a direct covenant between God and man occurs in relation to the covenant entered into with Noah by the Almighty, after the drowning of the world in the flood.[1] And therein is the rich blessing of God, and immense additions made, through the divine Spirit, to the knowledge of the will of God already possessed by man. The distinct Revelation of the universal steadfastness of nature ; of the purpose of God concerning the future fate of the world and the human race ; of the dominion of man, and of his liberty in the use of all created things ; and of the providential care of God over the human race : to these are added commands now first given to man, upon which rest the foundations of organized governments and all civil authority amongst men : and then God set his bow in the cloud, and made it a token of the covenant between him and the earth.[2] Thus augmented, the sum of Revealed Theology may be considered as occupying this posture during the second period of the church, extending to the call of Abraham. The Jews, who distinguished themselves amongst the nations by calling all mankind the Children of Noah, and adding for themselves the further appellation of the Seed of Abraham, received from the earliest

[1] Gen., ix. 9.   [2] Gen., viii. 15–22, ix. 1–17.

ages, and from sources now unknown, seven precepts called Noacic, binding, as they held, on all mankind, and of which traces are undoubtedly to be found amongst all peoples. They may be summarily stated thus : the first precept was against Idolatry, the second against Profaneness, the third against Homicide, the fourth against Uncleanness, the fifth against Rapine, the sixth against Sedition, the seventh against Cruelty. Passing to the third period, which extended from Abraham to Moses, it is to be noted, that as the Antediluvian period was preceded by the fall of the whole race, so the first two postdiluvian periods were preceded each by a great and general apostasy of the race. Noah and his household alone of all mankind had not forsaken God ; and Abraham himself was not wholly free from that universal idolatry, out of the midst of which God chose him from a race which had thus for the third time rejected him. The supernatural call of the Friend of God was perfectly distinct, and the great object of it precisely stated by God. Get thee out of thy country, and from thy kindred, and from thy father's house : in thee shall all families of the earth be blessed.[1] The augmentation of the knowledge of God in this period of the New Creation was various and immense. The chief things may be summarily stated, thus : God gave to Abraham a clearer and fuller explanation of his first promise of a Saviour : the promise of the Seed in whom all the families of the earth should be blessed was reduced into a distinct covenant with Abraham, and was reiterated to him at least seven times ; a more complete explanation of the Covenant of Grace was made to him ;[2] the Sacrament of Circumcision was established, both as a testimony of God's personal covenant with Abraham, and as a sign and seal of the Covenant of Grace, and therein the first outward and permanent mark of the visible church, and of its complete and Sacramental separation from the world.[3] The precise restriction of the personal promises to the descendants of Abraham, and of the Spiritual promises to mankind through the Seed of Abraham, that is Christ ;[4] the bestowment of all these promises, and all the corresponding privileges, upon the infant seed of those to whom the respective promises appertained ;[5] and, as crowning all, the personal grace bestowed on Abraham individually, whereby he

[1] Gen., xii. 1–3; Heb., xi. 8–10.   [2] Gen., xvii. 1–8.   [3] Gen., xvii. 9–27.
[4] Acts, iii. 25; Gal., iii. 8–16.   [5] Gen., xvii. 7; Rom., ix. 8.

became the Father of the Faithful, the Friend of God, and the perpetual representative both of those naturally and of those graciously inheriting the amazing inheritance covenanted in his seed. The sum of divine knowledge indicated in the foregoing sketches of the first three states of God's Church in the world, is in that respect the measure of God's manifestation in the New Creation, at the Exodus from Egypt, and the foundation of the Theocracy by Moses.

5. It required twenty-five centuries to develop the Messianic Kingdom to the point now reached. The Book of Genesis contains its inspired record through that long course of ages. A few of its earlier chapters are devoted to the Period from Adam to Noah ; a few succeeding chapters to the period from Noah to Abraham ; and the whole remainder of it to the period from Abraham to Moses. With Moses commences that great change in the condition of the New Creation, involved in the bestowment on it by God of a permanent, written Revelation. In the nature of the case, every thing in the Kingdom of Messiah grounds itself upon a Revelation from God ; even such things that enter into it, as are the subjects of natural knowledge, entering into it only in that manner, and to that extent which a divine Revelation shall disclose. It is the Spirit of God which presides over all; it is only the manner of perpetuating the Revelations he makes which is changed, when these Revelations are reduced to a permanent written form. The Revelations made by God during twenty-five centuries before the writing of the Book of Genesis, and which are recorded therein ; stand precisely on the same footing as the Revelations made during sixteen succeeding centuries from Moses to the Apostle John. Their being recorded immediately, or after some years, or after many centuries, is perfectly immaterial as to their intimate nature ; since a watch in the night, yesterday when it is past, and a thousand ages, are alike to God. It was to the same church of God, therefore, and by the same method of a divine Revelation given by the same Spirit of God, that Moses and all the prophets ministered during the fourth period of the New Creation, extending even to Christ, and embracing the whole of the Old Testament Scriptures. By the universal consent of antiquity, sacred and profane, Moses was the first public Lawgiver of the human race, and his writings are, by many centuries, the earliest that are

known to have existed amongst men. It is at the end of nearly thirty-five centuries from his day, that in estimating the career, the Laws and Institutions of this wonderful man, we are obliged to declare that in the whole compass of history, no mere man is comparable to him. The Ten Commandments, which condense into a few propositions the whole sum of the Moral Law, and which he laid as the basis of his Theocratical commonwealth, he plainly tells us were written by the finger of God on tables of stone.[1] And they who are the most competent to judge, and who the most carefully compare this earliest written monument of our race, with all that our race has produced ; are the readiest to admit that any account of their origin, substantially different from the one given, would have been incredible. Pregnant with this immutable and infallible rule of duty, the Books of Moses, and all the divine writings contained in the Old Testament, reiterating all the Knowledge of God imparted to men by the Holy Ghost during the three preceding states of the church—advance that Knowledge very greatly and very variously, but in a way capable of systematic appreciation from the stand point occupied in this survey. It is here we are first taught with such perfect clearness, the fundamental principle of the whole Jewish Dispensation—that divine Revelation is the only adequate foundation, the sole unerring rule of all true Faith, and of all acceptable Worship. The second great and comprehensive principle which pervades that dispensation is, that the righteousness which is acceptable to God, through which pardon for sin, and eternal Salvation are attainable by fallen men ; is only through the promised Seed, who is the Messiah—and that merely of divine Grace. The third grand principle is, that all the Institutions of that Theocratic Commonwealth, however glorious they might be and sufficient for the time, were not permanent, and of themselves an end ; but that every thing was limited, peculiar, transient, ceremonial, and typical ; pointing to more glorious institutions, signifying better things than themselves, and destined to terminate in a more glorious form of the Kingdom of Messiah, and a more exalted knowledge of the true God. Such was the state of divine Knowledge, to which the Manifestation of God in the New Creation, during its Fourth, or Mosaic state, had conducted men ; the glory of divine Reve-

---

[1] Ex., xxxi. 18.

lation, the glory of Sovereign Grace, the glory of the promised Saviour.

6. At length the Son of God appeared. The Seed promised four thousand years before, was manifested in the flesh. That great primeval promise, in which was involved implicitly the whole plan of salvation, the whole economy of all the manifestations of God in the New Creation—developed through so many centuries and such various and cumulative Dispensations ; now came to be simply and completely fulfilled, in its most obvious sense, and in its most fundamental conception, of God manifest in Human Nature. The period of this appearing of the Son of God is marked by two notable designations. It is called *The fulness of the Time*—and it is called *These Last Days*. When the *fulness of the time* was come, says the Apostle Paul, God sent forth his Son, made of a woman, made under the law, to redeem them that were under the law.[1] And in another place, he says, God who at sundry times and in divers manners spake in times past unto the fathers by the prophets, hath in these *last days* spoken unto us by his Son, whom he hath appointed heir of all things.[2] The fulness of the time, according to the eternal purpose of God ; and according also to innumerable utterances by him of that purpose, through the long past ages. The fulness of the time also, according to the working of all things, and the in-working of each upon all, whereby all created things had reached that express juncture and result, when the New Creation could the most signally manifest itself, through the appearing of its own Lord. This fulness of the time on the one side, was coincident on the other with these Last Times of the Theocratic form of the Messianic kingdom, in which he was to be manifested : he who had been fore-ordained before the foundation of the world, as at once the glory of his people Israel, the light of the Gentiles, and the Desire of all Nations.[3] Every promise of God concerning the New Creation, in every stage of its progress, contemplated Him that was to come ; and it lay in the very heart of the Mosaic Institutions—as I have pointed out in the preceding paragraph—that these last times were reached when everlasting righteousness should be fully brought in. The offering up of Christ upon the cross, consummated the very idea of Sacrifice, which was the great outward form of worship from

[1] Gal., iv. 4, 5. [2] Heb., i. 1, 2. [3] 1 Pet., i. 20; Luke, ii. 32; Hag., ii. 7.

Adam to Christ; and the whole Sacrificial System of Moses, and with it, every thing peculiar to that great dispensation, fell of itself. The blood of all atoning sacrifices was sprinkled against the veil of the Temple, as the door leading to the dwelling-place of Jehovah; and on the great day of yearly Atonement the blood was carried through it into the Holy of Holies, by the High Priest. No marvel then, that when the crucified Saviour—crying with a loud voice, It is finished, bowed his head and gave up the Ghost; the veil of the Temple was miraculously rent in twain, from the top to the bottom.[1] It could not have been recognized as standing another hour—without confounding the whole proportion of Faith, and casting doubt upon the certitude with which we are able to follow its great course, as it is perpetually led onward by the Holy Ghost, widening and deepening at every step.

7. In this fifth state of the New Creation, therefore, it is the whole work of the Saviour of the world, during his estate of Humiliation, which becomes, through the Spirit of God, a means unto us of the knowledge of God. What has been advanced in the chapter immediately preceding this, when treating expressly of the Word made Flesh, need not be reiterated here; nor need we anticipate here, what must be taught in the next succeeding chapter when the Manifestation of God by means of a Written Revelation, will be separately considered. The testimony of John the Baptist concerning Christ, as that testimony is compressed, confirmed and recorded by the Apostle John was, that being the only begotten of the Father, and dwelling in his bosom, he hath declared God unto us.[2] And the Apostle Paul intent upon the same course of thought, calls Christ Jesus, the Apostle and High Priest of our profession—exhorts us to contemplate him as such—and pronounces our calling heavenly, and those who partake of it holy.[3] Nothing can be imagined more thorough and comprehensive, than these statements. Being the Son of God, and so of his essence, he had the same infinite cognition and comprehension of all truth, as the Father. As he alone has seen God and had a perfect intuition of him, he alone is perfectly qualified to explicate all things concerning him. As he dwells in the bosom of the Father, he is cognizant of the whole counsel of God; and is possessed of the Holy Spirit with-

[1] John, xix. 30; Mat., xxvii. 30–52.   [2] John, i. 18.   [3] Heb., iii. 1.

out measure ;[1] and of all the treasures both of wisdom and knowledge.[2] As both the Apostle and High Priest of our profession, he has perfectly explained all that can concern God's glory and worship on one side, and our faith and obedience on the other, as all are connected with our heavenly calling; which all who preceded him could but partially comprehend and disclose, each in his order and degree. The counsel, and will, and revelation of God, are therefore complete unto Salvation, in Christ Jesus : and after we have received his teachings, whether directly from himself or whether by means of those chosen thereunto by him, and inspired by his Spirit sent from heaven upon them, there remains no more truth unto salvation for men to know, beyond that thus embraced and consummated. Considered in this light, these great principles and truths peculiarly related to the state of the New Creation in which God is thus manifested, may be summarily stated in the following manner. First : the absolute fulness, completeness, and certainty of the salvation of penitent and believing sinners, by Jesus Christ : and the total impossibility of salvation for sinners in any other way, or upon any other terms. Secondly : the total inability of man in his present fallen state, by any sufficiency of his own or by any means which any creature can offer, to perceive, or to comprehend, or to embrace unto salvation—the truth, the way, and the life made known to man by God. Thirdly : the indispensable necessity of the New Creation of the soul of man, unto salvation : the being born again of the Spirit, that we may become the sons of God, be partakers of the kingdom of heaven and inherit eternal life. Fourthly : the absolute necessity of a life of holiness following after our new birth, and persisted in to the end : whereunto the Revealed Truth of God is the only efficacious instrument, the divine Spirit the only sufficient agent, and the divinely instituted means of Grace, the only sure method. Fifthly : the total separation of the Messianic kingdom in its new state, from this world, and the kingdoms thereof : the supreme headship of the glorified Redeemer in it and over it : the exclusive authority of his Revealed Will as the rule of its life, faith, worship, and form : and the perpetual presence, power, and authority of the Holy Ghost, therein, in the name and place of Christ. Sixthly : the assured certainty of the second coming

[1] John, iii. 34.   [2] Col., ii. 2.

of the glorified Redeemer, and of the absolute consummation of all his gracious promises, and glorious counsels, in the complete triumph of the Messianic kingdom : the restitution of all things, and the recapitulation of all things in Jesus Christ : the resurrection of the dead, the general Judgment, and the eternal retributions to the just and to the unjust.   Such from the point of view here occupied, is an imperfect outline of the divine knowledge predominant in the teachings of the New Testament Scriptures, and immediately dependent upon the relation of the Holy Ghost to the Word made Flesh, and through him to every part of the New Creation.   Simple as the outline is, who can avoid a sense of the transcendent nature of the knowledge thus brought within our reach by the Holy Ghost ?

8. The Sixth state of the New Creation, is that which is now passing over us, and which being fully initiated by the outpouring of the Holy Ghost on the day of Pentecost, will continue until the Second appearing of the Son of God, in his glory.   The great promise of the Old Testament Scriptures was the coming of Christ in the flesh : and the second was the pre-eminent effusion of the Spirit under the Gospel church state.[1]   This is the distinguishing glory of the Messianic Kingdom under the existing form of it ; and is the crowning blessing to that kingdom in its whole militant state.   The doctrine of the divine unity, has been shared with the church of God, by the more enlightened part of the human race : the doctrine of the divine Trinity was known to the church itself from its foundation on earth ; and the doctrine of the Incarnation was its original corner-stone.   But the Dispensation of the Holy Ghost, in the manner witnessed in the Gospel church, never occurred amongst men until Christ was glorified :[2]   and the very existence of it was not suspected even by those who believed the testimony of John the Baptist, and were partakers of his Baptism.[3]   The promise of Christ also, throughout the Old Testament Scriptures, differed in one most striking particular from the innumerable promises of the Holy Ghost : and yet all the promises of both agree in another particular not less striking.   Christ was to come in such a manner as to put an end to the church state, to which his coming appertained ; but the Holy Ghost was to found and perpetuate a new church state : while in Christ's work of demolition the Holy Ghost was to be

[1] Isa., xxxv, 7 ; Joel, ii. 28 ; Ezek., xi. 19.   [2] John, vi. 39.   [3] Acts, xix. 1–3.

all and in all to him, and in the Spirit's work of reconstruction
Christ was to be so truly the author of it all, that the Spirit was
really to be his Vicar therein. The great work whereby God
would glorify himself, was that of the New Creation, which is
through Jesus Christ, the Head thereof, for the recovery and
restoration of all things unto himself.[1] In the whole execution
of this work, God has made the most illustrious displays of himself, and the most glorious discoveries of himself to his universe.[2]
And in no part more illustriously than in the mission of the Holy
Ghost from the Father and the Son, to found the Gospel state
of the church ; to preserve and to perfect the church in that
state ; to accomplish by it all. the designs of God in the New
Creation ; to reap through it, all the glory which is his due ;
and to confer by it, all the blessedness compatible with that
glory.

9. The knowledge of God which is attainable by man
through that particular Manifestation of God in the New Creation, which occurs through the outpouring of the Holy Spirit
under the Gospel Dispensation, is the common inheritance of
all Christians. This is the exact position in which our race now
stands ; the exact point to which the evangelical efforts of every
child of God are chiefly directed in their endeavors to advance
their own souls and to save lost men. The explication of it in
its saving application to the human soul, belongs to that other,
or *Subjective* view of the Knowledge of God, which is the com-
plement of the view herein presented, and which the method I
pursue postpones to a subsequent place, and a separate treatment. I therefore, limit myself here to the statement, in a
systematic manner, of the great principles and truths which appertain to that aspect of the subject under immediate consideration. First : The whole Dispensation of the Spirit unto the
saving knowledge of God by man, has perpetual reference, in
every state of the Messianic Kingdom, to the Head and Lord of
that kingdom : and if we could conceive of any fundamental variation in the universal application of this fundamental truth, it
would occur in the more earnest and thorough application of it in
the gospel state than in any other. But there is no such variation.
There never was any promise of eternal life made to fallen man,
except through the Seed of the woman ; and there never was

[1] Heb., i. 1–3 ; Eph., i. 10–12.   [2] Eph., iii. 8–10 ; 1 Pet., i. 10–12.

any operation of the Spirit conducing unto the eternal life of fallen man except with reference to that Seed. The work of the Spirit can no more be conceived of as transcending or as coming short of the stipulations of the Covenant of Grace—or as dislocated from the work of Christ, than the work of Christ can be conceived of in the same way relatively to the same covenant and to the boundless love and the eternal purpose of the Father, of which the covenant itself is an outbirth, and the work both of Christ and of the Spirit, infinite Manifestations. Secondly : Every operation of the Spirit in its utmost effusion, has relevancy to the Written Word ; the whole of which has been Revealed or Inspired by himself ; the true discernment of which he alone can bestow ; and the saving power of which is the result of his co-operation. Thirdly : The entire work of the Spirit upon the mind, and conscience, and heart of man, in the New Creation, has continual reference to the work of God, considered as the Creator ; and therefore continual reference to the nature of man himself ; the light, the knowledge, the inclination, the ability, the holiness, the life which he imparts, being without violence to the free, intelligent, and moral nature of the creature. Fourthly : In the same manner, the dominion of God as the Providential Ruler of the universe, is scrupulously respected in the whole Dispensation of the Spirit ; insomuch that every act of Providence, innumerable as they are, and inexplicable as they may appear to be, is turned to the good of them that love God, and directed to the certain and complete salvation of the heirs of eternal life. And so the Spirit of God, whose whole work is one of the most glorious manifestations of God, uses all the other manifestations of God, as means of augmenting beyond conception that knowledge of God, which it is inseparable from his own immediate work to bestow. The end of his whole work as directed upon man, is to quicken him into the knowledge of God ; to transform him into the image of God ; and to fill him with the fruition of God. The absolute universality of this condition of man—and that not imperfectly as in us now—but unto absolute perfection in every human being ; appears to be the lowest condition which the Scriptures permit us to ascribe to the Millennial State. Taking human nature as it is, if the causes now at work are competent to produce, and are designed to produce that condition, in its universality and its perfection ; then is it pos-

sible that the Millennium may occur as the consummate restitution of human nature as it is, under the gospel state, and as a
part of it. If otherwise, it must necessarily occur after the gospel state is done ; or to man in some other condition ; or as a
new and separate state of the Messianic Kingdom.

III.—1. The relation between the Spirit and the Saviour is
such, that the work of each of them unto salvation depends in
a very peculiar manner upon the work of the other. The order
of the subsistence of the Spirit in the Trinity as the *Third* person thereof, is founded in his eternal procession from both the
others :—and so being the Spirit both of the Father and the
Son, and being also of one essence with both, a double aspect is
given to all divine operations. All the works of the Spirit are
performed by the same divine power which is common to the one
divine nature, and so they are referred to the one Divine Essence;
and yet the authority of the Father, and the love and wisdom of
the Son are to be considered in all the acts of him who is the
Spirit of them both, while his own peculiar efficacy is also to be
considered. The promise of the Spirit to his disciples by the
Saviour, and the gift of him to the church, was the great legacy
of the Redeemer.[1] And this is equally true whether considered
formally under an apprehension of the infinite preciousness of
the gift itself ; or materially, under the idea of the glorious purposes and ends of such an inestimable gift[2] On the one hand,
the gifts bestowed on the church through him are boundless in
their value and efficacy ; and on the other hand, the profession
required of all believers, has nothing more indispensable than
the avowing of the work of the Spirit of Christ, which if they
have not they are none of his.[3] All that has been advanced in
this chapter, has had a direct bearing upon the nature and the
reality of the Knowledge of God attainable by man through the
New Creation—as one of the perpetual fruits of the manifestation of God the Spirit. What I shall further advance very
briefly, is designed to disclose in some degree the wonderful manner of working, by means of which the Spirit becomes the author
of the New Creation, and therein the giver, of all saving Knowledge of God, through Jesus Christ the Head of that creation.

2. Jesus Christ the head of the New Creation—became In-

[1] Heb., ix. 15–17.   [2] 2 Cor., i. 22; John, xiv. 26–28, xvi. 1–15.
[3] Eph., iv. 10–13; Rom., viii. 9.

carnate by taking human nature into hypostatical union with his divine nature as the Son of God; which has been largely explained. But this assumption of human nature was the only immediate act of the Son; and he alone of the persons of the Trinity performed that act, and became Incarnate.[1] The only necessary consequence of this act, was the personal union of the two natures, in the person of the Son of God, the person of the Man Jesus being swallowed up: a union not capable of dissolution, even by the separation of the soul and body of the Man Jesus, by death; because it was not the union of that soul and body with each other, but the union of both of them with the divine nature, which constituted the person of Christ. Every other result of the union of the divine nature in the person of the Son, upon the human nature united with it, was absolutely voluntary on the part of Christ; the human nature though inconceivably advanced, not being changed in its essence, nor the acts of the divine nature toward it ceasing to be voluntary acts. The Holy Spirit is the immediate efficient cause in all external divine acts; and he is as really the Spirit of the Son, as he is of the Father:[2] he is, therefore, the immediate operator of all divine acts of the Son, even those on his own human nature. Every thing, therefore, involved in the Incarnation of the Son, except the single act of *assuming* human nature, was wrought thereunto by the Spirit. The miraculous conception and formation of the body of Christ, in the womb of the Virgin Mary, and out of the substance of her body, was the peculiar and creating work of Spirit.[3] The Holy Ghost shall come upon thee, and the power of the Highest shall overshadow thee; is the manner of this New Creation.[4] The Spirit of God moved upon the face of the waters; is the manner of the old creation.[5] The primeval promise is fulfilled: for the Son of God is made of a woman, and is made flesh.[6] The innumerable intermediate promises, no matter how special—are all fulfilled. The work of the Spirit, and this act of Christ, this miraculous conception through the Spirit, and this assumption of human nature by the Son, unitedly solve the mystery of Salvation. Here is the New Creation in its head, in its author, and in its ultimate, positive, controlling facts.

3. The human nature of Christ the Second Adam, was in

---

[1] John, i. 14; Rom., i. 4; Gal., iv. 4.   [2] Gal., iv. 6.   [3] Luke, i. 26–38
[4] Luke, i. 35.   [5] Gen., i. 2.   [6] Gal., iv. 4; John, i. 14.

no way implicated in the fate of that of the first Adam. The promise of the Incarnation was not given to Adam until he fell ; and so Messiah was not implicated at all in the Covenant of Works, and the primeval state of man. The fall of Adam brought the curse and penalty of that broken covenant, upon all of whom he was the Federal head : and they were only such as descended from him by ordinary generation : neither of which relations did Messiah sustain towards him. For his connection with human nature, whether the manner of the miraculous assumption of it by him, or the manner of the miraculous formation of it by the Spirit, of the body of the Virgin Mary, or the manner of the original promise of God, be considered ; is a connection with human nature real and complete, but also with human nature pure and perfect. From the moment of its conception, this pure and perfect human nature of Christ, was positively endowed by the Spirit with all grace.[1] The Spirit was given to him without measure.[2] All powers and gifts which human nature could contain were bestowed upon him.[3] Visible and audible pledges were given him from heaven :[4] and his habitual condition was, that he was full of the Holy Ghost :[5] and boundless miraculous power dwelt in him.[6] He was guided, sustained, and comforted by the Spirit, throughout his whole work of humiliation : and in its last fearful act, he offered himself up to God, through the eternal Spirit, a sacrifice, as the great High Priest of his church, to make atonement and reconciliation for his people.[7] In the state of the dead, the angels had outward charge of the body of Christ :[8] and the Holy Ghost, by his peculiar care, accomplished that great promise of God that the Holy One, as David called him—the Holy Thing announced by Gabriel and created by the Spirit, should not see corruption.[9] His human soul, Christ, in the very article of death, had committed to the special care of the Father ; for the Father had engaged himself in an eternal covenant to preserve him even in death ; stipulating expressly that he would not leave his soul in hell, nor suffer his body to see corruption ; but that he would show him again the path of life, and that while his body was under the power of death, his soul should possess the fulness of joy in the presence of God, and

[1] John, xi. 1–3.   [2] John, iii. 34.   [3] Isa., lxi. 1.   [4] Mat., iii. 16, 17.
[5] Luke, iv. 1.   [6] Acts, ii. 22.   [7] Heb., ix. 14.   [8] John, xx. 12.
[9] Ps., xvi. 10 ; Luke, i. 35 ; Acts, ii. 29–31.

partake at his right hand of those pleasures which are eternal.[1] The resurrection of Christ is assigned distinctly to each person of the Trinity, in a special respect, and to the whole Godhead as an undivided act.   As to the Father in respect of his loosing the pains of death.[2]   And to the Son himself, in respect of his infinite power and right, in laying down his life and taking it again.[3] But the peculiar efficiency whereby the body of Jesus was raised from the dead, was that of the Holy Ghost :[4] making manifest thereby, the infinite satisfaction of God in the whole work of Redemption as wrought by Christ.   And again : the Spirit which made the human nature of Christ holy at first—and afterwards quickened it again and restored it from the dead—also made it glorious : meet for its inconceivable and eternal exaltation. When he appears we shall be like him : for he will change our vile bodies that they may be fashioned like unto his glorious body : and this will be done by the same working whereby our souls are renewed in his image, and whereby he is enabled to subdue all things unto himself ; the working, namely, of the Eternal Spirit.[5]   And finally, we must add to this complete and immeasurable working of the Spirit in the person of Christ, and on it, another divine operation immediately concerning Christ, in which also is involved the foundation of the whole office of the Spirit towards the church.   When the Comforter is come, said the Saviour, whom I will send unto you from the Father, the Spirit of Truth which proceedeth from the Father, he shall testify of me.[6]   This divine testimony was constantly appealed to by the Apostles : we are his witnesses of these things, said they, and so is the Holy Ghost, whom God hath given to them that obey him.[7]   And it is a testimony, both as to the form of it and the substance of it, both as it is outward and as it is inward, perfectly complete and conclusive ; God bearing witness, both with signs and wonders, and with divers miracles and gifts of the Holy Spirit, according to his own will.[8]   And now it must be evident, that if what has been advanced in this and the next preceding paragraph can be accepted as a true account of these sublime realities : then the whole matter of the New Creation lies as palpably before us as an object of distinct, though it be supernatural

---

[1] Ps. xvi. 10, 11.   [2] Acts, ii. 24.   [3] John, x. 17, 18.
[4] 1 Pet., iii. 8 ; Rom., viii. 2 ; Eph., i. 17–20.   [5] 1 John, iii. 2 ; Phil., iii. 21.
[6] John, xv. 26.   [7] Acts, v. 32.   [8] Heb., ii. 4.

knowledge, as the matter of the old creation does as an object of knowledge of any kind : nay that nothing can be conceived of as being made known to the intelligence of man more precisely, than that there is a New Creation ; that God is manifested in it as the Word made Flesh who is the Head of it ; and that he is manifested in it again as the Holy Ghost who is the author of it.

4. The great operations which follow that portion of the work of the Spirit which relates to the head of the New Creation, concern first the body, and then the members thereof. The foundation of the Gospel church state lies in the promise of the Holy Ghost ; and the erection and preservation of it lie in the execution of his work.[1] The Saviour being exalted by the right hand of the Father, received of the Father the Holy Ghost in the manner so long before and so often promised : and on the day of Pentecost, shed forth by the bestowment of him, the wonders of grace which were seen and heard that day in Jerusalem. That one body of Christ—the Church which he redeemed with his blood—is made partaker of every gift of God dependent upon and following after the ascension of Christ, through that Spirit : every gift, and for every work, unto that one body from that one Spirit. And in this manner the perfecting of the saints, the work of the ministry, and the edifying of the body of Christ will be carried on—tending always to the unity of the faith, to the knowledge of the Son of God, and to the perfection of man unto the measure of the stature of the fulness of Christ. This is the vocation wherewith we are called.[2] The mystical body of Christ is no less really the work of the Spirit than the natural body of Christ was : and his work of a New Creation appertains as really to every member of this mystical body, as his creating efficiency appertained to the whole of that old creation over which he brooded. The elect of God—the redeemed of Christ—are the matter of this life-giving work—the members of this mystical body unto whom a new principle of spiritual life is imparted by the Holy Ghost. The Scriptures continually assert the necessity and the reality of this New Birth, and continually ascribe it to the Holy Ghost.[3] And thus the second part of the New Creation is completed, and a mystical body is prepared for Christ, as before a natural body had been, by the Holy Ghost.[4] Nor does

[1] Acts, ii. 33
[3] John, iii. 3–6 ; Rom., viii. 1–12.
[2] Eph., iv. 1–16.
[4] Col, iii. 10 ; 1 Cor., xii. 1–12.

the analogy stop here. For it is by the Holy Ghost that the new life implanted in every regenerated soul is preserved, developed, and advanced, step by step, and from one degree of grace and strength unto another, until every one of them in Zion appears before God.[1] The author of this progressive Sanctification of believers is the Holy Ghost: and indeed it is the immediate work of God by his Spirit.[2] The end of which is, that the members of the mystic body of Christ will be brought, even as the natural body of Christ was brought, by the perfect and complete work of the Holy Spirit, to an infinite glory and blessedness corresponding to the infinite exaltation of Christ.[3] And thus the wonderful working of the Spirit, of which the first example has been given with some exactness touching the person of Christ—and the second touching his mystical body and the members thereof only very generally ; might be carried through every state and every aspect, and every relation of the New Creation. As the sum of the whole, I will add but one word. If it can be proved, or if it is admitted, that a solitary case of Spiritual Regeneration ever occurred among men ; then it is infallibly certain that the wonderful facts developed in this chapter are substantially true. Because no other force in the universe is competent to that result except the force here developed : and because no other intelligence in the universe ever conceived of such a result. On the other hand, if it can be proved, or if it is admitted, that no case of Spiritual Regeneration ever occurred ; then it is infallibly certain, that human nature is incompetent to say that any thing whatever is either true or real. Because there is nothing in the whole range of possibilities more overwhelmingly proved by outward testimony and inward consciousness, than that Spiritual Regeneration does occur ; and if this mass ot proof and conviction is utterly deceptive, our nature is utterly imbecile. In attempting to discredit God, we only degrade ourselves.

---

[1] Psalm lxxxiv. 7.   [2] 1 Thes., v. 23.   [3] 2 Tim., iv. 6–8.

CHAPTER XXVIII.

GOD MANIFEST IN REVELATION—THE GOD OF THE SACRED SCRIPTURES.

I. 1. Statement of the question.—2. Historic Relation of the Divine Revelation to the Human Race.—3. If the Scriptures are not divine, it requires a divine Intelligence to state what they are.—II. 1. Both methods of Divine Manifestation combined in the Scriptures.—2. The Kingdom of God and the Word of God, in themselves and in their relation to each other.—3. Scriptural Conception of the nature of the Kingdom of God, and of its Origin.—4. Progress of the Kingdom (a) under the conception of the Messianic Kingom: (b) Of the New Creation: (c) Of the Church of God.—5. Consummation and Triumph of the Kingdom under these three aspects.—6. The Scriptures are a Treatise of God: Developed around the conception of Immanuel: Whose Author is the Divine Spirit.—III. 1. The Scriptures considered in their power, as perfect Truth.—2. In the efficacy of their infallible method.—3. State of the question as to their being Inspired and Revealed. 4. Both inevitable upon the *data* proved.—5. True source of unbelief.

I.—1. THE knowledge of God, as he manifests himself in Creation and in Providence, is addressed to our intelligence after a manner altogether natural; in Redemption and in the New Creation after a manner altogether supernatural. In the Sacred Scriptures, and in the soul of man, the manifestation of God to our intelligence is by both methods combined. These, as has been shown, are the only methods of the divine manifestation to us, and these are the only divine applications of these methods respectively. It is not possible for us to know God by any other methods. By each of these methods, and by all the ways in which they are divinely used, we may obtain perfect assurance of the existence of God, and all the knowledge of him which is appropriate to each particular method and way; and by all of them combined, the perfect knowledge of him, to the whole extent that our nature is competent to its attainment, is made accessible to us. Having completed the investigation of the first two of these methods, and of the divine applications of each of them, we advance to the third method, which is the combination of both the others. Of the two divine applications of this third method, the Sacred Scriptures furnish one, and the soul of man the other. They will be subjected to inquiry in that order, because the soul bears to the Scriptures, as it does to every other manifestation of God, only the relation of a means, while the Scriptures, like all the four preceding manifestations, bear to the soul the relation not merely of a means, but also of an incalculable force.

2. Whatever knowledge we have historically of the human race more ancient than about twenty-five centuries, we derive exclusively from the Old Testament Scriptures. We must accept them as true, or be content to remain in profound ignorance of the origin of mankind, and of the progress of our race during the greater portion of its existence, as recounted by them. Taking our race as a whole, we have no knowledge of its having existed in ignorance of a portion of the Revelations which these Scriptures contain ; and we know positively that portions of the race possessed portions of these Scriptures in their present form, and declared them to be ancient records, at the very earliest period of profane history ; and that the knowledge and the veneration of them have continually widened and deepened amongst men throughout the whole historic period. They contain in a most remarkable manner the connected and exact history of man, in a precise and unbroken channel, from the moment of his creation. Adam, Noah, Abraham, Moses, Jesus. These names, and the eras which they recall, and the record which expounds and connects them all, cover more than forty centuries. These centuries and this record terminate in the very bosom of authentic history, at the culmination of the Roman Empire, the last of the universal World Powers, at the very prime of the Gospel Church State, while the last of the Apostles of the Lord was consummating all the record of the past, and projecting the light of prophecy to the end of time.

3. It is in vain that we would shut our eyes and turn our backs on such a monument as this. So grand, so unique, so decisive of the fate of man ! We must decide upon its claims : we must form some estimate of it : we must render to ourselves, some intelligible account of it : we must confront it. In general, I will limit myself here to two remarks, both of which appear to me to be decisive. The first, which I may say is *positive*

is, that if these Scriptures are allowed to be what they claim to be, namely, the Word of God, then they solve in a manner absolutely complete, every problem, whether moral, cosmical, or historical, which the origin and total progress of the human race taken as a whole—suggests to the mind of man : while, if their claims are rejected there are multitudes of problems both moral, cosmical, and historical, and they of the most vital import, which become at once wholly insoluble : and what is more, that very insolubility arises from causes wholly inexplicable, except as those causes are explained by the very Scriptures we reject. The second remark, which I may say is *negative* is, that while these Scriptures have declared to us from age to age, immense truths perpetually new and perpetually increasing in fulness—as relates both to God and to our own souls : the whole human race during nearly eighteen centuries which have elapsed since the canon of Scripture was closed, has not added to our stock of knowledge one solitary truth respecting God, or respecting our souls : and what is more, the whole human race, during more than forty centuries covered by the period during which the revelation contained in these Scriptures were given to man, never stated even the smallest of the truths touching God and our souls, as distinctly as they are all stated by them : nor is the whole human race competent to do so now, after possessing for nearly sixty centuries, a divine model for such statements. Upon these two grounds it may be confidently asserted, that if these Scriptures are not the product of a superhuman intelligence, it requires a superhuman intelligence to determine what they are the product of.

II.—1. It is in this light, namely, that the Scriptures are the product of a divine Intelligence, that they are to be considered a manifestation of God. It is as though God spoke personally to us : and therefore it is a supernatural method of bringing the Knowledge of God within the sphere of our intelligence. But this is qualified in a peculiar manner ; in the first place, by making human beings like ourselves the channel of these divine communications, so that they are mediate and not immediate ; and in the second place, by giving to the communications themselves, a permanent and connected form, in writing, whereby our intelligence may address itself to their study, as to any other permanent truth. In these two respects, this method of the divine manifestation, adds to what is supernatural in it, much also that is natural to us. The question of the divine influence upon man in order to the production of the Scriptures, and the question of the capacity of man to comprehend them, whether without or with further supernatural aid, are certainly of the deepest import. Both of these will be briefly considered, after we have first endeavored to obtain a clear conception of the Scriptures themselves, taken as a whole, and contemplated in the manner just indicated.

2. These Scriptures present to us every where, the idea of a Divine kingdom which though in this world, is not of it. When we speak of this as the Messianic kingdom, we have special relation to the dominion of the Lord Jesus as Mediator between God and men; and at the same time to the powers of this world as they stand in antagonism thereto. When we speak of it as the New Creation, we have special relation to the same kingdom as founded, wrought out, and perfected by the Holy Ghost. And when we speak of the church of God, we have special relation to the same kingdom, considered as manifested in its own members, gathered out of the world, and become subject by a new creation to their divine Lord. The conception of such a kingdom with which, under the several prevailing aspects just indicated, the Scriptures are pregnant, is founded upon the two ideas of the apostacy of man, and of the purpose of God to reclaim and to punish that apostacy. And that purpose of God to reclaim and to punish, is founded in the design of making himself known to his universe, *first* for the illustration of his own glory, and *secondly* for the blessedness of the creature. Now the Scriptures appertain to this kingdom of God, under the threefold aspect of it, as the Dominion of Messiah, as the New Creation, and as the Church of God, in a manner at once absolute and universal. They contain a complete account of its origin, of its development and progress through all time, and of its infinitely glorious consummation and final triumph. They are the Divine record of this heavenly kingdom, in a manner incomparably more complete, and with an infinitely more exact unity of design, than we can conceive it possible for the history, the laws, the manners, the institutions and the whole literature of any earthly kingdom, to be considered, in their totality, the record of it. For herein, nothing is omitted which is needful to make our knowledge com-

plete : and nothing is introduced concerning any thing exterior to the kingdom, which is not necessary to elucidate something involved in the kingdom itself, in some aspect of it. Here is the kingdom of God as conceived of by himself : and here in his written word is the whole divine record of that kingdom.

3. As connected with the origin of this kingdom of God, these Scriptures give to us a precise account of the creation of man and of the universe. No less exactly, the original and glorious state of man : the covenant of works which God entered into with him : the temptation and fall of the first parents of the race—incidentally the invisible world : and then again precisely, the sentence of God upon the tempter, upon our first parents, and upon the universe now polluted by sin and defaced by misery. In the midst of this scene of ruin, is laid the foundation of that glorious kingdom, of which Messiah is the head, of which the Holy Ghost is the Creator, and of which redeemed souls are the members. And here, at the very moment when all was lost, is the first articulate utterance concerning that eternal Covenant of Grace, by which life and immortality, in a new and more glorious form, are brought to light by the gospel of God. I restrain all comment upon these transcendent themes. But may it not be said in all sobriety, that a few pages of the Word of God from which this imperfect summary is condensed into this brief paragraph, give us a clearer and a more satisfactory account of all of them, than is to be gathered from the whole mass of uninspired writings of the human race, touching any one of them ?

4. Starting from this point, the Kingdom of God, in the threefold aspect of it already pointed out, makes its progress onward and still onward—across the endless generations. It alone survived the catastrophe of the human race at the flood: it alone will survive the catastrophe of the second coming of the Lord : it alone will survive the catastrophe of the final conflagration. Always side by side with this sublime progress, which is also a perpetual and sublime development—always, too, in advance of this progress, by throwing forward a prophetic light upon all future time ; the Revelation of God accompanies the Kingdom of God. It is its rule of duty; it is its rule of faith ; it is the nourishment of the very life which it records ; it is unto it that very manifestation of God which, as I am seeking to show, it is

also to us. And to make this somewhat more distinct, let us consider separately but with great brevity, the progress of the Kingdom of God under each of its three grand aspects.

(*a.*) In developing the nature and recounting the progress of the Messianic Kingdom, from its origin till its consummation, the Scriptures develop prophetically by the side of it the nature, and recount the progress and ruin of all the universal World-Powers. And then develop the nature, rise, progress and ruin of the two great apostacies of Mohammed and of Rome ; which respectively sought to perpetuate in the East and in the West under a new and peculiar form, the dominion of those universal empires ; and which defile some of the fairest portions of the earth, even to our day. Under this combined view, the whole career of the human race, the whole progress of human civilization, are wrought prophetically and historically into the august narrative : and the perpetual contrast of a career and a civilization with the true Knowledge of God, and without that Knowledge—and that commensurate with all time—is laid open before us. In the midst of these vast ideas, two others still more sublime than they preside continually. The idea of a divine Providence in its silent, irresistible, and omnipresent force conducting all things, through all ages, to their predestinated end : and the idea of Messiah himself—the God-man—long promised—finally incarnate ; the teacher of all teachers—the crucified—the risen —the glorified—the giver of the Holy Ghost—the inconceivably glorious King—and Lord—and Restorer of the universe !

(*b.*) Under the conception of the New Creation, another aspect of the progress of the Kingdom of God, with new ideas and wondrous knowledge—is developed throughout the Sacred Scriptures. Fallen man is no longer fit for the service, no longer competent to the enjoyment of God : and the way of life under the Covenant of Works is closed forever. It behooved that the universe must lie under a perpetual curse, and the whole human race must perish ; or that a better covenant must be revealed to man, and a New Creation fit him for its blessings and fit the earth itself for a habitation of God. This New Creation is what the Scriptures reveal to us, in its nature, its form, its design, its progress and its whole effects. With the first steps of its progress emerges the glory of the third person of the adorable Trinity—the author of the New Creation : and therewith as his work advances, the full knowledge of the mode of the divine existence. The struggle of good and evil, throughout all generations is everywhere developed: the malice of hell—the blessedness of Gospel holiness: the successive revelation of divine truth, consummated at last in the Great Teacher. Inspiration reducing the Word to a written form, and dwelling thus during sixteen centuries in holy men of God: Prophecy, attested in its perpetual fulfilment, to every generation of men: miracles avouching every word that proceeded out of the mouth of God: the new birth and the sanctification of believers, demonstrating every day of the whole life of the world, that the Word of God is indeed a Gospel unto man, and that it is a divine power unto Salvation !

(c) The progress of the kingdom of God, considered as his Church, purchased by the blood of his Son, and created anew by his Spirit ; is developed throughout the Scriptures—from the first promise in the garden of Eden, till it is finally delivered up in spotless glory upon the Lamb's Book of Life. It is the grand peculiarity of this manifestation of the kingdom of God, that it is considered chiefly in its members: as in the first of the two preceding it is considered chiefly in its Head, and in the second in its Author. And thus every stage of the progress of the Church, and every step in its development, is presented to us throughout the Scriptures in a manner the most distinct : so that the successive patriarchal conditions of it—Adamic, Noacic, Abrahamic ; and its Theocratic condition under the Mosaic institutions ; and its thoroughly miraculous condition during the ministry of Christ and his Apostles ; and its purely spiritual condition thenceforward to the Millennium under the special dispensation of the Holy Ghost, are the burden of the word of God, whether historically, prophetically, doctrinally, or spiritually considered. To this Church of God, militant throughout all ages, is committed alike the conversion of the world, and the illustration of God's great glory to the universe : and the Scriptures are at once the means, the warrant, the record and the guarantee of her work : and her progress is the progress of the accomplishment of God's Covenant of Redemption, and of the recapitulation of all things in his only begotten Son, the Saviour of the world. She is the Bride of the Lamb, and on her has been bestowed through the long ages, gift after gift, and grace upon grace—all worthy of her eternal Lord, and all marking the fixedness and the boundlessness of his love ; insomuch that if it can be said that God has ever made assured provision for any thing whatever—he has provided that his Church shall know him, and that men may know him through her !

5. I have said that it is not only the origin and the progress of this kingdom of God in this threefold aspect ; but that it is also its infinitely glorious consummation and final triumph in all of those aspects—concerning which the Scriptures are an infallible means of the knowledge of God. It is this point which we now reach. As yet, we have not seen all things put under the feet of Jesus, and the kingdoms of this world swallowed up in the Messianic kingdom. As yet, we have not seen whole nations born at once ; new heavens and a new earth springing into life from the decaying bosom of the old ; and all things restituted in a New Creation. As yet, we have not seen the Church of the living God dwelling in the New Jerusalem come down from God out of heaven, adorned as a bride for her husband ; the tabernacle of God with men ; and all that is worthy of glory and honor in all nations, brought and laid at his feet. We have heard his voice from the cross saying, *It is finished !* We have yet to hear his voice from heaven saying, *It is done !* But we look for all these things, and for the time when we shall know even as we are known ; with confidence exactly proportioned to the power of the new life that has been begotten in us by the Spirit, to the trust we repose in Messiah, and to our fitness to inherit the glory which is to be revealed. The ruin of every enemy of God—the death of death—the millennial reign—the general judgment—the eternal life in the realms of light ! We have behind us nearly sixty centuries of proof. We have around us in our brethren, living monuments of God's redeeming love, God's stainless truth. We have in our hands, the promise of his coming ten thousand times repeated. We have in our souls, the imperishable marks of what he can do and will do. We are not mad ; we only believe. Believe and are sure, upon the ground of ultimate, divine necessities—which are ten thousand times stronger than any ultimate, human necessities upon which we feel ourselves incapable of doubting the realities of our present condition.

6. It is impossible to contemplate the Scriptures in the man-

ner I have pointed out, without perceiving that we are obliged to accept them, on the one side, as a supernatural manifestation of God, and on the other side as manifesting God in a manner more permanently within the sphere of our intelligence than any other method external to us, can be. But there are other things to be taken into our estimate of the Scriptures, which distinguish them still more remarkably, and which intensify to the most exalted degree, both the unity of their scope and the combined fulness and distinctness of the divine knowledge they impart. In the *first* place, it is to be noted, that the Scriptures expressly make God the particular and ultimate subject of all their teachings. From beginning to end, they are a treatise concerning the Divine Being. It is his Creation, his Providence, his Grace, they develop. It is his Covenant of Works whose breach destroyed man, his Covenant of Grace by which man is rescued. It is his love which prompts all, his Son who executes all, his Spirit who perfects all, his Word which reveals all. Messiah is the Christ of God ; the New Creation is the work of God's Spirit ; the Church is the Church of God ; and it is God's Kingdom which embraces all. We can no more understand the Scriptures and still continue ignorant of God, than we can behold the universe without partaking of its light. In the *second* place, the actual development of the grand unity of the Scriptures, considered as a treatise of the Divine Being, is around the person of the Son of God. It is not God infinitely separated from us ; *it is God with us ;* it is Immanuel who is held before us with a perpetual distinctness. It is about his person, and work, and glory, that all things cluster, that all things tend—that the Scriptural conception of God opens itself clearly. If the Scriptures were conceived of as being re-cast, and digested into a connected biography of the second person of the Trinity, no one can point out what portion of them could be omitted without obscuring the idea we have of the divine Teacher, Ruler, Redeemer. In this manner a unity in the highest degree *personal*, is given to elements so immense, so divine and so complicated ; and the knowledge of God thus educed, is delivered to man in such a manner, that he is obliged, as it were, to hide his face from it, in order to avoid it. In the *third* place, the whole of these Scriptures are the product of one single mind, and that a divine mind ; thereby stamping upon them, in another form, that transcendent unity of their great design, that assured truth and coherence of their whole matter, and that infinite perfection of their manifold form, which place them at an immeasurable distance from all other writings. Even in the Book of Nature, as we painfully turn over its gigantic pages, we find nothing so clearly written, as the oneness of the author of it all. And the Book of Providence, with so many countless millions of records which our short pilgrimage does not suffice for us to inspect, and so many countless millions more of which we cannot decipher even so much as the alphabet; yet all we can construe to ourselves, has nothing so obvious as that the image and superscription are the same, and even what is closely sealed against our inspection, has the mark of the eternal King stamped broadly on it all. But what is all this compared to the impression we derive of the uniqueness of the Word of God, as we stand face to face with the Holy Ghost therein? Unspeakably various and difficult as the contents of the Scriptures are, and supreme as is the aspect which they continually present, no volume worthy to be studied was ever placed in the hands of man, of whose general conception a more distinct idea could be formed, and whose grand aim and method were so difficult to be misunderstood.

III.—1. It may be confidently asserted that the result to which the foregoing analysis conducts us, is wholly unavoidable. If God is manifest in these Scriptures in any such manner as has been pointed out, then these Scriptures are an infallible repository of the knowledge of God unto Salvation; and God, objectively considered, is brought completely within the sphere of human intelligence, by a permanent Revelation. Whatever power is in all truth, considered of itself, is also in this truth considered of itself. Natural light, by which all things are manifested, makes itself manifest: and truth performs towards the spiritual essence of man an office analogous—but more perfect—to that performed by light through his organism of sight. What the force of this power may be, in either case, depends partly on the power itself, but partly also upon the recipient of the power. To the blind, light manifests nothing: to an exquisite sensibility its manifestations are inestimable. To the coarse, and narrow, and feeble, and depraved spirit—truth in its very simplest form may be hardly distinguishable: while to the pure and highly gifted spirit, even the highest and remotest truth may come with a self-evident clearness. It is a wondrous power—wondrously neglected by the teachers of mankind. But whatever the power may be, it resides in this truth of God with a potency unknown to every other form of truth. Because this form of truth is wholly unmixed, that is, it has no error in it: and because, again, it is absolutely complete, that is, it has omitted nothing. For the Scriptures restate with perfect clearness and with divine authority, every truth of Natural Religion: and then they add, by Revelation, all new truth that involves Salvation. And then they seal the certitude of both. For it is by Inspiration of God that holy men have been infallibly directed what things to record, of those they might know without Revelation; and what things to add of the unknown, Revealed unto them. They who revere truth of itself—they who justly exalt its sublime efficacy—let them know that God has brought all this within their reach, on themes compared with which all other themes are worthless, and in a form compared with which all other forms are vile.

2. But there is far more. For besides containing unmixed and complete truth—and that delivered in a manner incomparably unique, and with a certitude unapproachable in any other form of truth; the Scriptures add this, namely, that they make known to us a divine method of ascertaining with infallible certainty, and to the utmost extent of our own intelligence—the perfect sense of the truth they contain. This divine method embraces all the outward means provided in the Word of God for perpetuating and extending the knowledge of himself: and all the inward movement of the human soul, so far as it is itself active in these great processes, from the first sense of its own blameworthiness with which its new career commences, onward to the highest attainments possible for it in its new form of life. This latter department of the divine method of knowing God by means of revealed truth, appertains in a special manner, to the subjective view of the knowledge of God; and it would be untimely and impossible to treat it aright here, in a few sentences. The former department embraces all that Christians call the outward means of grace. The church of God, as held forth in her divinely appointed form: the discipline of that divine Institution: her appointed worship, in all its parts, of prayer, praise, the preaching of the everlasting Gospel, the administration of her Sacraments, with alms and fasts, and every good work. I need not add, the diligent study of the truth we desire to under-

stand, nor the diligent endeavor to incorprate practically with our being, so much of it as we know: because these are conditions not peculiar to the revealed method of knowing divine truth—much as they are insisted on therein ; but they are conditions common to the true acquisition of truth under every possible form, and in the absence of which no considerate person can imagine that any truth can be acquired aright. But neither is this the whole of the infallible method by which it is revealed to us, that we may come to the perfect knowledge of all truth unto Salvation. At this point the Scriptures themselves pass, in a peculiar manner, into the subjective part of this sublime topic, and the truth they reveal becomes the instrument of the Holy Ghost in his enlightening, quickening, and sanctifying work in the human soul : the whole discussion of which appertains, to that other aspect of the knowledge of God. A divine method perfect in its abundant outward means—and perfect also in its inward efficacy : a method so thorough, that the portions of it which are outward have a perpetual tendency to the portions which are inward, and finally, in their highest application—pass over into the soul in a manner absolutely peculiar to themselves : a method which commences with the simplest parts of truth— and ends by making the soul the abode of the Spirit of God himself—who is the author of all truth ! Can we dare to say of the Scriptures as a manifestation of God, that their power of imparting the knowledge of him is less than transcendent ?

3. The importance of all that has been said depends upon the certainty of the divine Inspiration and Revelation of the Sacred Scriptures. If it is so that a divine influence has infallibly directed the mind of man in the utterance of these writings, such as we now possess them, then they are, what they claim to be, the Word of God, and their contents come to us with a divine certainty as to the manner of them, and a divine authority as to the matter of them. All this is expressed by saying that the entire portion of them which makes known what man could not naturally discover is Revealed ; and that every part of them, both the naturally knowable and unknowable, is just as it is, because the writers of it all were Inspired. It is of no consequence to the present matter to inquire in what particular manner, or in how many various ways, this divine influence was exerted upon the writers of the Sacred Books ; the grand question is as to the

reality of such an influence. That question resolves itself into two others ; *first* as to the evidence for and against the actual occurrence, and, *secondly*, as to the possibility of the occurrence. The latter is a question of mere Philosophy, the former is one of mere fact. Of the two, the question of fact necessarily controls the question of Philosophy ; for that which has never occurred in fact, Philosophy can only conjecture to be possible, while that which has occurred in fact controls Philosophy. As to the fact that such a divine influence as has been defined was exerted on all the writers of the Sacred Books—this is a question of immense breadth, filling the chief place in the great department of Christian Evidence, the discussion of which, according to the method I follow, stands at the head of the third or relative aspect of divine truth, commonly called Polemic Theology. I have in many instances throughout the preceding chapters stated, in an incidental manner, such considerations as seemed to me conclusive, in support of the fact of such a divine influence ; and I have published a monograph demonstrating, as I think, the divine origin and authority of the Sacred Scriptures, upon the basis of their *Internal Evidence*. It is to be remembered that this question of fact has been debated from the very dawn of knowledge, and has never rested, because, in truth, when it is given up on either side, all is given up. It is as a refuge from total discomfiture, therefore, that they who controvert the fact of divine Revelation and divine Inspiration take shelter under the denial of the possibility of the fact proved, and seek for support in the abuse of Philosophy. In this form of the question the discussion can hardly be said to have any value, either practical or scientific ; because, on supposition, for example, that a man has been born again, and that he has in his own soul the satisfying proof of the fact, to what end are any further denials of the possibility of regeneration ? Or if for any reason such discussions are supposed to be of any value, then, in the actual state of the question, and, to say the very least, with the overwhelming presumption that the divine influence in question has actually been exerted, and has been attested throughout all generations ; it lies on those who deny the possibility of that influence to make good their denial by a demonstration which shall crush and overwhelm the contrary belief of every child of God, and of every speculative believer in him, since the world began ; and shall nullify the grounds upon which human nature itself, whether in its state of purity, in its fallen condition, or in its partial recovery, has rendered its devout testimony to the presence of its Creator. Whatever may be possible with God, such an achievement as this is assuredly, impossible with man.

4. I repeat, it is impossible. For such a conclusion does not lie within the known data, upon which any conceivable demonstration having that result must proceed. Given such a God and such a human nature, as are demonstrated : from the data, it *cannot* follow that it is impossible for God to inspire man—impossible for God to reveal unknown truth to man—impossible for God to exert such an influence as shall produce the Bible we have in our hands. On the contrary the directly opposite conclusion is not only inevitable, but is directly involved in the data. If these data be taken apart and considered separately—the result is the same. For upon supposition of such a God as that whose idea is the great conception of the Scriptures, what difficulty can be imagined as obstructing him in making known to his intelligent creatures, any thing they are capable of knowing, by any method competent to influence the nature he has given them ? The thing is inconceivable. On the other hand, taking man as he perceives himself to be, what is there in his nature which puts him out of the reach of any influence, mental, moral or physical, which his omnipotent Creator may see fit to exert upon him, whether direct or indirect, whether mediate or immediate, whether common or miraculous ? He may well be defied to suggest even as a conjecture—much less to demonstrate as a fatal necessity, any such hindrance to God.

5. In reality such cavils when clearly stated, have a deep meaning beyond the emptiness of their pretended object. It is not meant that it is really impossible for God to reveal himself to man : but that it is improper in God to reveal himself as he has done. The human soul turns away from the account which God gives of himself and of us. It is not such an account as our fallen nature either expects, or desires, or willingly accepts. In our robust sinfulness, we perceive no need of the balm that is in Gilead. It is only after the heart is touched, and the conscience awakened, and the true light has penetrated the mind, that we begin to see that the manifestation which God has made of himself in his blessed Word, is not only infinitely true, but infinitely

fit. There is no marvel greater than the continued, identical, conscious existence of our former self, and of our present self— with that great gulf between the two, on the other side of which, we said of God that his law was foolishness—and on this side of which we say that we esteem every word which has proceeded out of his mouth, concerning all things, to be right!

CHAPTER XXIX.

GOD MANIFEST IN THE CONSCIOUS EXISTENCE OF MAN: GOD THE
MAKER AND RENEWER OF THE HUMAN SOUL.

I. 1. Man.   General statement of his Being.—2. The Human Soul.   Its Creation.
Nature.   Likeness to God.—3. Method of its consideration as a manifestation of
God.—4. Unity and Permanence of human nature in its essence: Nature and
causes of its boundless diversity.—5. The Soul's knowledge of itself and of God.
Insight of inspired men.—6. Analysis of man's spiritual nature, in its original
likeness, and present unlikeness to God.—7. Sense of the True, the Good, and
Duty; in a spirit made in God's image—but fallen from it.—8. Religious nature
of fallen man: analytically and historically considered.—9. The Soul revealed
and known in the *data* of consciousness—is the created image of God.—II. 1. Life.
Creation.   Birth.   Resurrection and Regeneration.—2. The Relation of the image
of God to the soul of fallen man considered analytically and historically.—3. Restoration of that lost image.   Nature and effects of this great change.—4. Surer
and Higher Knowledge, both of God and of ourselves: (*a.*) As the Result of the
Effects produced on the soul, by its Renewal in the image of God: (*b.*) As the Result of the Method, whereby the effects produced in our regeneration occur: (*c.*)
As the Result of the Agencies through which these effects occur in the soul.—5.
The general Result stated: and shown to intensify every particular Result.

I.—1. THE more complete our knowledge is of all the works
of God, the deeper is the conviction with which we can say with
David, that our soul knoweth right well that they are marvellous
works.   And among all these marvellous works, we may safely
adopt his emphatic distinction of our own being, "I am fearfully
and wonderfully made," and devoutly confess with him God's
title to our praise therefor.[1] It was a marvellous creation in
which our being commenced; a fearful aspect of it that it bore
the image of God himself: a being, very wonderful in its separate parts ; still more wonderful in the personal existence constituted out of those united parts.   This crowning marvel of the
works of God, fearful and wonderful, is revealed to us in the
sacred Scriptures as existing under four successive and widely

[1] Ps. cxxxix. 19.

different estates, through all of which it preserves the same nature, no matter how deeply modified ; through all of which it bears one identical, continued, self-conscious, separate existence. Its first estate was perfect but fallible : its second estate is one of lapse and depravity, the original perfection gone, the original fallibility passed over into sin and misery : its third estate is one of regeneration, and great, but not complete recovery, its nature renewed, the soul not perfectly sanctified still dwelling in a body corrupt and perishing : its fourth estate will be one of complete restoration, and of endless glory and blessedness, commencing with the soul at the death of the body, augmented as to the soul and commenced as to the body at the resurrection of the body, and consummated as to both united, throughout eternity. Only the first parents of the race ever occupied the first estate ; and by transgression they lost it. It is only the second estate that is absolutely universal to the whole race descending from our first parents by ordinary generation. The third and fourth estates are peculiar to the redeemed of God, who constitute the New Creation. It is seen at once therefore, how the eternal love of the Father ; the whole work of the Son and of the Spirit ; the whole power of divine truth ; in one word, how the whole power of God unto salvation, and our whole knowledge of God thereunto, enter as controlling elements into the nature and end of the restoration of man, and of the immortality of glory and blessedness secured to him therein. It will be seen also, that our present inquiry has only an indirect relation to the fearful destiny of the impenitent ; since they pass out of the range of a manifestation of God in the creation and renewal of the human soul, as soon as the second part of that manifestation, namely, in their renewal, becomes for them an eternal impossibility.

2. The creation of the soul of man was perfectly distinct from the creation of his body. For God formed man from the dust of the ground, but he breathed into his nostrils the breath of life, and man became a living soul.[1] In two instances since the creation of Adam, the human body has been produced after a supernatural manner : the instance of Eve, who was formed by God out of the rib of Adam,[2] and the instance of Jesus, who was formed by the Holy Ghost, in the womb of the Virgin Mary, and out of the substance of her body.[3]

[1] Gen., ii. 7.   [2] Gen., ii. 21–23.   [3] Luke, i. 31–35

Every other human body has, like every thing else having life, whether animal or vegetable, been the result of a reproductive process peculiar to itself; while every human soul has been created by God, and not produced from other souls.[1] Separately, as well as differently created, and in its essence wholly different from the essence of the body, the soul is so far from being the result of any physical organism, that there does not exist a single quality common to it and to matter, with which it is so closely and wonderfully connected. Its new creation does not affect the natural depravity of the body in which it dwells; cannot prevent its decay and death; and is no part of the efficient cause of its resurrection. And to crown all, the death of the body which reduces it to the dust from which it was formed, so far from damaging the soul, releases it, that it may return to God who gave it; with whom it dwells in this separate state until the resurrection of the body fits it for its eternal habitation; the whole of which has been largely explained in another place. It is emphatically of the soul of man, and with no conceivable reference to his body considered of itself, that the Scriptures declare that God created man in his own image and after his likeness.[2] As a spirit, he is the image and after the likeness of the infinite Spirit; and then as it is successively added that he is a living soul; that he is endowed with intelligence, with will and with power; that he is invested with a distinct personality and with dominion over all things around him; that he is by his very essence naturally a knowing and a free spirit, sustaining to truth all the relations involved in these qualities; we acquire at every step a more complete conception, how it is that man with all these qualities is by creation in the image and after the likeness of the adorable God, with his transcendent attributes. I would avoid all that is illusive; yet I cannot escape the suspicion that the unity of the human race, with the distinct personal existence of every member of it—a type of existence so different from that of all other created spirits of which we have any idea, and so much nigher to the type of God's own being; may have much to do with God's declaration, peculiar to our race, that it was created in his image and after his likeness. At any rate, the unquestionable state of the matter as revealed to us in the Scriptures, is hardly so much as paraphrased, when it is said that

____

[1] Job, xxxiii. 4; Acts, xvii. 25; Eccl., xii. 7.   [2] Gen., i. 26–28.

God, considered as the creator of the human soul in his own image, is manifested to man in his own conscious existence.

3. In this final instance of the manifestation of God to our intelligence, I have alrealy said repeatedly, that we find the second example—the sacred Scriptures being the first—of the combination both of the natural and the supernatural method of the divine manifestation. Considering the human soul both as created and as recreated in the image of God, the method is supernatural : considering it as coming to the knowledge of itself, and by that means coming to the knowledge of its Creator and its Redeemer in whose image and likeness it is, the method is natural. It is true that the distinct knowledge that we are created and recreated in the image of God, is supernaturally revealed to us : but I do not see that it would be possible for the human soul to know enough of itself to be settled in the conviction of its own separate existence, without immediately accepting the existence of God. Instances have existed of men who believed in a certain sense that there was a God, and yet denied the separate existence of their own souls : but the reverse seems to be so entirely inconsistent with the fundamental laws of our nature, that it is impossible to believe, and no one ever did or can believe, in the separate and immortal existence of his own soul, and at the same time not believe in the existence of an immortal God, distinct from the universe, and of whom that soul was an image. And beyond a doubt no one ever believed assuredly in the regeneration of his soul, who did not believe assuredly in a divine Redeemer. No higher evidence could be sought, that God is manifest in the conscious existence of man, as the Creator and Renewer of the human soul in his own image.

4. The fundamental identity of nature in all the individuals of the human race, exists under a perpetual diversity of all the persons of the race one from another. That boundless diversity exists in every physical endowment, taken separately, and in the result of all united in one body ; it exists in every endowment of the soul taken separately and in the result of the whole united in one soul ; it exists in the person made up of the union of the soul and body—all their physical and mental endowments—as compared with every other person. Yet all these persons are identical in nature, identical in the quality, the essence of all their forces summed up, no matter how immense may be the

separate or combined diversities already indicated. We habitually contemplate each other as persons merely; and struck with the constant dissimilitudes which we observe, are prone to overlook the resources of nature, in the elements just pointed out, for the preservation of her steadfast unity, under the production of the most boundless variety. The influence of our souls and bodies upon each other mutually, working out from a new quarter those perpetual differences in the original endowments of both; and then again the influence of external causes upon both soul and body; carry still higher the aspect of the manifold forces to which our common nature is subjected in its manifold development. We can easily see, how high, on one side, such a nature was fitted to rise; how low, on the other side, it may be sunk; while the oneness of its essence is still preserved. But to render possible such results as I have sought to explain, and as we behold every moment of our lives, we must accept as true, a human nature real and permanent, with faculties original, distinct and permanent. Therein again, we have a shadow of the infinite nature with its infinite perfections; an image, dim at first—broken and defaced now—but still an image of God, and capable of a divine restoration. There is but one God, and there is no other God with whom he can be compared; moreover, the living God is infinitely perfect; in him, therefore, but one type is conceivable. The same thing would be strictly true in a lower degree of human nature, if there had been but one man, and he had existed in but one estate. It is still true of human nature considered in its essence, and considering that essence as capable of preserving its identity through four estates, as before pointed out. It is the human soul contemplated in its second or lapsed estate, and contemplated in its third or renewed estate, which to us, now, is the subject of conscious existence; as an image more indistinct in the former, and more distinct in the latter estate, but in both an image, and so a manifestation of God to our intelligence. The whole of this human nature, considered, not in its wondrous diversities, but in its fundamental oneness; and considered in its spiritual, and not in its material element; this is the subject of our present scrutiny.

5. The knowledge of ourselves is the only knowledge, except the knowledge of God, that is of eternal importance to us; and these two knowledges are so dependent on each other, that

neither is attainable, in any true sense, without the other. The wise, even among the heathen, have placed the wisdom of self-knowledge at the head of all human wisdom; and the sacred Scriptures press us with the greatest earnestness, to endeavor habitually after this knowledge; and that in direct connection with our endeavors after the knowledge of God, and after conformity to him as known.[1] Nor is any thing more remarkable in the Scriptures, than their unerring insight into the very depths of the human soul. Our conduct, our motives, our principles, our beliefs; given, either of the four, and the Scriptures will produce out of the secret chambers of the Spirit the other three, with infallible exactness. That which we painfully conjecture of others, that which we obscurely see in ourselves, men who lived thousands of years before we were born, will tell us clearly and unerringly, as a matter palpable in itself, and obvious to them, throughout the interminable changes of the four quantities. And the moment the result is stated, our eyes are opened; for a two-edged sword has passed through the joints and marrow of our being—a discerner of the thoughts and intents of the heart.[2] Nor do they urge with greater earnestness the duty of keeping our heart, out of which are the issues of life,[3] than they explain with all distinctness, the real nature of the difficulty of so doing.[4] Desperately wicked, who can fathom its depths; deceitful above all things, who can know it? The fallen soul, easiest of all things to be led astray; sin, the surest of all things to lead astray; and the very state of the soul, first subjected to our scrutiny, a state of sin; and its only remaining state known to us consciously, a state of but partial deliverance! We need not wonder, therefore, that the true knowledge of the soul, is so difficult of attainment by the carnal mind; nor that the progress of Philosophy has been so slow in developing a nature of whose fundamental conditions as being an image of God, and as being depraved, it took no account. Yet we must not suppose that such vital knowledge is unattainable, or that it is not a proper object of true Philosophy.

6. God is a spirit; the soul of man, made in the image of God, is also a spirit. Understanding, Will, and Power, infinite like his being as an infinite spirit, appertain to God as attributes; they appertain also to man as faculties, finite like his being as a

[1] 1 Cor., xi. 28; 2 Cor., xiii. 5.   [2] Heb., iv. 12.   [3] Prov., iv. 23.   [4] Jer., xvii. 9.

finite spirit, and now depraved with his fallen nature. The possession of those Perfections by God, necessarily involves the Attributes of infinite Knowledge and Wisdom ; the possession of those corresponding Faculties in a finite manner by man, just as necessarily involves that he should be a being knowing and wise, in direct proportion to those finite Faculties in a fallen nature. But these infinite Perfections of Knowledge and Wisdom in God, and the corresponding finite endowments in man, have relevancy on the one hand to the eternal and ineffaceable distinction between the True and the False, as really as they have relevancy, on the other hand, to the Infinite Understanding of God and the finite understanding of man. And while the ability to perceive this distinction of True and False, incontestably proves that man has an understanding, and his having an understanding incontestably proves that he is a spirit : on the other hand, his inability to apply that distinction justly and exactly, and his proneness to err in its application, just as incontestably proves that his capacity of Knowledge and Wisdom, and therefore his understanding, and therefore his spirit, are all depraved together. Passing to the moral nature of God, and to such infinite Perfections as Love, attended by Goodness and Mercy, and ordered in Justice and Long-suffering, we readily see the connection of all such affections with the divine Will : and as we contemplate in man's moral nature the image of this moral nature of God, we perceive the same connections of these qualities with each other, and with his Will. We perceive also, that all such Attributes in God and such affections in man, are not merely related to the Understanding ; but have a further quality which we call moral, by which they have relevancy to the eternal and ineffaceable distinction between the Good and the Evil ; a distinction carrying the previous distinction between the True and the False to a higher pitch, but never justly occurring independently of it. And, therefore, it may be said precisely as it was before, that the untruth of all these affections, as really as the untruth of our knowledge, attests the depravity of our understanding, and so of our spirit ; while, still further, the ability to perceive the distinction of Good and Evil incontestably proves that we have a moral nature, and so a Will, and so are spirits ; and then the inability to apply this distinction justly and exactly, and the constant proneness to err in applying it, proves just as incontestably that our affections, and therefore our moral nature, and therefore our will, and therefore our spirit, is depraved. And thus by a double process, on the one side through our rational nature, and on the other side through our moral nature, we arrive at the same results asserted by God, namely, that we are spirits created in his image, but that at present we are depraved spirits, having his image defaced but not destroyed in us.

7. The idea of duty is connected inseparably with the idea both of the True and the Good. Every duty rests on some ultimate truth, and tends to some ultimate good. In their foundations, our rational and moral nature are but different aspects of the same spirit; and in their results, the True and the Good coalesce in Duty. Just as in God, when we speak of his Attributes, it is himself we mean; and when we speak of his acts as being acts of Justice, of Love, of Power, of Vengeance, and so on, it is still God who performs them all. There is, nevertheless, a wide difference in the influence upon us, of truth considered merely of itself, and of truth considered with the further qualification that it is good; a wide difference between the mere assent of the understanding to the True, and the consent of the conscience to the Good; a wide difference between the perception of the understanding of the merely False, and the perception of the conscience of the Evil. The sense of duty performed, or of duty violated, personally by ourselves, is the highest concrete effect of the True and Good united, or of the False and the Evil united. The sense of satisfaction and of approbation which a good conscience diffuses through the soul, is a shadow of the fruition which God derives from the perpetual intuition of himself: and the sense of blameworthiness which attends every serious intuition of ourselves, until the conscience is seared, is the testimony of the soul itself to its own depraved estate. It is God himself who is the source of all the True and all the Good. So absolute is this, that we have no means of laying a positive foundation for either the True or the Good, except we lay it in God; nor of laying any foundation at all besides him, except we lay it in our own souls; and in the latter case we are conscious of innumerable errors, and never perfectly assured of security from mistake. Relatively to us, so completely is God the sum of all the True and all the Good, that even when we err as to both, we make God himself the objective form of the very error, and deify rapine,

lust, deceit, or whatever, most grossly evil or absurdly false, we happen to suppose to be the perfection of the True and the Good. Thou thoughtest, says God, that I was altogether such an one as thyself.[1] The reflex of God's relations to us as the Creator, Ruler, and Judge of men, is found in that sense of dependence and accountability which is universal in man. Considered as the response of a created and responsible spirit, passing through a probationary into a retributive state, this is a most distinct testimony to God : but if there is no God, or if he is different from what he is revealed to be, it is one of those inscrutable mysteries which thicken at every step of our departure from the true light. And I may add, as not less striking, that in the midst of our acutest sense of blame-worthiness, we cannot escape a profound but obscure sense, that this was not our original condition, and that there remains in us a susceptibility of some kind, to be better off again ; while in the midst of our deepest convictions that we are helpless in our dependence, and that we must sink under the responsibility which awaits us, we find it impossible to extinguish a perennial hope that deliverance will come. These states of the soul are precisely what is inevitable, if the soul be a spirit, created in the image of God, fallen from that image and now depraved, but subject to and awaiting a new creation ; and the existence of such states of the soul, is the most distinct confirmation of the revealed facts which account for them ; and the confirmation becomes overwhelming when the revealed facts which make every thing clear, are beyond the reach of natural knowledge, and when no facts within the reach of natural knowledge, afford any solution at all.

8. Our rational nature grounds itself, therefore, upon that ineffaceable distinction of the True and the False ; and wherever that distinction can exist, it can expatiate, and knowledge is certain and attainable. Our moral nature grounds itself upon that further and ineffaceable distinction of the Good and the Evil ; and wherever that distinction can exist it can expatiate, and moral culture is real, and moral advancement attainable. The idea of Power in the spirit of man, as in God, is indissolubly connected with the understanding and the will ; and in its nature is expressly limited by them. Its resources are all furnished by them, or are such as are also resources to them. As

<hr>

[1] Psalm l. 21.

God is the sum of all the True and all the Good; so in us the
spirit whose very nature is fundamentally relevant to the True
and the Good, would have gone forth toward God with its whole
Power, as its habitual action. This is the knowledge, the service
and the enjoyment of God; this is true Religion; this is the
posture of the case as man was created. In his fallen state,
every human element of the problem is changed; but no element is destroyed, and all of them are capable of restoration.
Man is still impelled toward God; is still, by nature, as inevitably religious as he is rational, or moral, or invested with
spiritual power. His spirit is depraved; by consequence his
understanding, his will, his spiritual power are depraved also.
Whatever we can mean by his religious nature and its results,
are therefore depraved. But there is, nevertheless, a religious
nature still; and there is a sum and there are results thereof.
Of all the aspects of man, the most universal and the most profoundly affecting, are his unremitted struggles toward God, and
his frightful and continual failure in his attempts. His endeavors have been not only real, but anxious and incessant; and his
methods, dreadful as in many respects they have all been, were
not without a certain mixture of truth, and even of an approach
toward goodness. At any rate he did not select them as evil and
false, but as true and good. But they were the endeavors and
methods of a fallen nature; of a nature which could not rest
without God, and yet which could not find God; which saw that
there were such things as truth and goodness, but could not distinguish which they were; which mistook the false for the true,
and chose the evil before the good; which made its misery deeper
and its sin more vile, by the cruel and impure means its very
sense of both, led it to adopt; which outraged and dishonored
God, even when it blindly sought his favor. Yet always, it retained the idea of God, and confessed there was a God; always
it acknowledged itself to be sinful; always it desired reconciliation with God; always it sought this through expiatory sacrifice;
always it expected it through a delivererer who should exhibit
some union of God with man, and who should prove victorious
over death! Wonderful, fearful, is this fallen nature of man;
wonderfully pitiable; fearfully guilty! A wreck now, it once
dimly bore God's perfect image. But even while under God's

curse, it has God's promise of deliverance ; and by a new crea-tion, it can be, and is restored to his lost image.

9. In so far as we are capable of knowing any thing at all, we are capable of knowing what passes within us ; and in so far as we can obtain assurance that we do know any thing, we can obtain assurance that we do know this. The spirit of man, is an existence, not a phantom or an idea ; a living, a knowing, a thinking, a loving, a real existence. To deny to such a being the primary elements of its own cognitions ; to call in question those ultimate facts of which our consciousness assures us ; is to deprive us of the fundamental criteria of truth itself, and make a nature whose grand distinction is that it thinks, and feels, and knows, the mere sport of every delusion. It is indeed, far more than this ; for it is to make the infinite author of our being the author of our delusions, by creating us with intelligence only in order that we may be deceived by untruthful reports of our own soul, which we are incapable of disbelieving. To deny that we are conscious of what we are conscious, is equivalent to denying —the facts of consciousness itself. To deny the truth of the facts which consciousness reports to us, is to deny the possibility of Philosophy, whose very office it is to construe those truths ; to subvert the possibility of knowledge, which rests upon the verity of those truths ; and to annihilate the possibility of belief, whose first and chief nourishment is in those truths. Admitting, on the other hand, that the existence of the facts of consciousness, as phenomena, is just as certain as the existence of the soul itself, whose existence their existence certifies ; and admitting that the veracity of consciousness is just as certain in what it reports, as in the fact that it reports at all : then our feet are set upon a rock. Then philosophy may return from her endless wanderings, to her perennial rest : Knowledge may commence afresh her sub-lime career : and belief may repose in tranquil confidence upon truth, which even the desperate deceitfulness of our depraved hearts, and the desperate deceivableness of sin, cannot shake. God in his infinite knowledge of all things, has a perfect cogni-zance and intuition of himself. Man in his finite knowledge of all things, has an imperfect cognition and intuition of himself. But this is the nearest, the surest, and the most satisfying knowledge naturally attainable by man. And when the soul itself is renewed in knowledge and in rectitude, the image of

God, dim and defaced in all things, and utterly lost in true holiness, is itself restored at the same moment : made more capable of being discerned, while we are made more capable of discerning it. Our most certain means of knowledge, are the means of knowing somewhat of our own souls ; for our consciousness is the most intimate assurance we can possess of any thing. The knowledge we thus obtain is the most certain of all knowledge ; for the least doubt thrown over the certainty of that by which every thing else is known, casts every thing else into a still deeper uncertainty. But when we come to the knowledge of ourselves, we come to the knowledge of the image of God. And this whole analysis, conducted under the testimony of consciousness, runs side by side with the previous analysis of the nature of God, conducted under the light of revelation ; as that divine nature is exhibited under such Attributes as can be reflected in the human soul ; especially such as distinctly appertain to what we may call the spiritual, the rational, and the moral nature of God. As the Creator of the human soul, therefore, God is manifest in the self-conscious existence of that soul, which is an image of himself.

II.—1. There are four ways, widely different from each other, by which that inscrutable gift which we call life is bestowed on man. The first of these is creation, in which the race itself commenced : the second is birth, according to a peculiar reproductive process, wherein each individual existence commences : the third is the resurrection of the body, which follows and conquers death : the fourth is the one we are now to speak of, that renewal of the soul by means of which the life of the second Adam, who was a quickening spirit, supplants in it, the life of the first Adam, who was but a living soul.[1] Concerning this last way of communicating a real life to man, the most obvious thing is, that it is continually explained to us in the word of God, by calling our attention to all three of the other ways in which life is given to us, and by constantly applying to it the names of all of them. It is expressly and repeatedly declared that the new man is created ; and the analogy to the original creation is made more complete, by declaring that this is done in Christ Jesus, after the image of God, by the Holy Spirit.[2] The divine Saviour, in making the whole matter of this great change in man plain to Nicodemus, in private and express instruction concerning it ; holds

[1] 1 Cor., xv. 45.

[2] Eph., ii. 10, iv. 23, 24; Col., iii. 10.

his discourse steadily to the point, that it is a second birth, spiritual indeed, and from above, but yet real not only, but the first, the simplest and the most indispensable part of the new life.[1] That it may be most distinctly explained as a resurrection, we are repeatedly told not only that we were children of wrath, but that we were dead in sins, and that God, who is rich in mercy, and for his great love wherewith he loved us, quickened us together with Christ, and hath raised us up together, and made us sit together in heavenly places in Christ Jesus.[2] And when the method of this new creation, second-birth, quickening from spiritual death, is set before us in the distinct efficiency that produces it ; we are plainly and repeatedly told that it is according to the working of the mighty power of God : and as if to render mistake impossible, it is added that it is the same which wrought in Christ, when God raised him from the dead, and set him at his own right hand in heaven.[3] The great risk we run is that of understating, and not that of overstating the work of God in the renewal of the soul of man ; and the consequent danger is of obscuring too much, and not of exhibiting too broadly, the manifestation of God in that renewed soul, and so in the conscious existence of man.

2. We are to comprehend distinctly this great matter, both as it is revealed to us by God and as it is manifested in our own consciousness. So far as the essence of our being is concerned, we are still spirits, and are still endowed with the same nature, and with all the faculties we had at first, and will have forever ; and in all these, and in innumerable particulars appertaining to them, many of which have been pointed out, what is meant by saying, we have lost the image of God, is not that any of them are destroyed, but that all of them are polluted, depraved, and corrupted. This latter is true of the very essence of the soul, and of the very essence of the body also ; and by consequence of all the faculties of the former, and of all the parts of the latter. It is most signally true of all that touches our ability to distinguish truth and to pursue it, and to discover falsehood and to shun it ; and of all that touches our ability to discover the good and to choose it, and to perceive the evil and to hate it. As God is the sum of all perfection, whether considered in the light of the true or the good, what I have just said amounts

<hr>

[1] John, iii. 1–13.   [2] Eph., ii. 3–6.; Col., ii. 12–13.   [3] Eph., i. 19, 20.

to this, namely, that we are no longer capable of seeing God as he really is, nor capable of choosing God as he really is, for the portion of our souls ; but, on the contrary, we are prone, and that both naturally and continually, to see and to choose all things, and especially all spiritual things, in a manner always different, and often exactly opposite, from the manner in which God sees and chooses them. If we could suppose it possible that we had come without fault into such a state as this, we might make some claim that we were merely victims. As the case stands we are really criminals, and that even upon the testimony of our own conscience. The misery of our condition is not only most proper but wholly secondary : it is its sinfulness that accounts for all, nay, that is its essential and controlling feature. So taken, there are two aspects of the matter which immediately concern us here. In the first place, the retention of the image of God, in any proper sense, by the fallen soul ; and, in the second place, the restoration of that image to the soul. The second point I will consider in the next paragraph. Touching the first, this paragraph was designed to state its true sense, the sum of which is this: in so far as human nature is identical with itself throughout all its estates, to that extent it preserves the image of God through them all ; in so far as it varies through successive estates, its likeness to God increases or diminishes ; in so far as it loses entirely in one estate some striking mark of conformity to God which it possessed before, as, for example, true holiness, it has therein wholly lost the image of God ; and in like manner of the defacing and obscuring of God's image, either partially of certain qualities or totally of the whole nature ; and also of the restoration, augmentation, and consummate perfection of God's image in man. What is insisted on is, that a self-conscious intelligence cannot well be conceived of as totally ignorant of the creator and perpetual sustainer of it, more especially if he continually and in various ways manifests himself to it ; but that this ignorance, if possible at all, is purely voluntary, if the self-conscious intelligence bears the image of its creator. Nor is it possible for subsequent changes in the creature, provided they do not destroy its essence, to destroy totally the image of the creator, and the means of knowing him thereby. If it were possible for that to occur, the effect would be that a totally new form of existence would occur, which would not be human nature, whatever it might be. For us the universal consciousness of the race, responsive to the continual testimony of the Scriptures, puts the matter at rest. Man's whole career is one sustained response to this universal consciousness of the race—this continual testimony of God ;—one great, blind, misguided struggle to recover the lost image of God, and achieve the promised deliverance ; one perpetual demonstration that he needs, that he desires, and that he is capable of restoration, but that he does not understand it, is unable to accomplish it, and is repugnant to the method in which alone it is possible !

3. The strange conviction of mankind, that they were authorized to hope for a better state, and that it would be the fruit of divine mercy ; however it may have arisen or been propagated, was not without the surest foundation. God's eternal Covenant of Grace pointed exactly in that direction : and the unanimous testimony of his children, in all ages, has been that the renewal of the human soul is a great reality. It is of God : it is through Jesus Christ ; it is by the Holy Spirit ; it is under the light and power of divine truth ; in it the understanding is enlightened, the will is renewed, the conscience is sanctified, the affections are purified ; the result is a new ability and a new desire to know, to serve, and to enjoy God. This universal testimony of every one concerning himself, is confirmed by every one of all the rest, and by the Word of God concerning the whole ; of which divine word, this new creation of the soul of man, in the necessity, the reality and the nature thereof, is as it relates to us the most peculiar and pregnant part. It is this new life of the soul, in which every thing that practically distinguishes all Christian people, primarily consists. In the varieties of its manifestations, founded more or less upon previous individual diversities, but founded also upon that sovereign will upon which all other diversities ultimately rest ; consist the wonderful diversities of the people of God, both in gifts and graces. There are, however, matters in which no diversity can be ; and they are supreme. There must be a restoration to the lost image of God ; a new creation of the soul by the Holy Ghost of which God himself is the model, and which is wrought by the Holy Ghost in the name and for the sake of the Lord Jesus. Neither the old creation, nor the natural birth, nor the resurrection of man, is a complete image of this new birth. For in neither of those wonderful

works, was a living, thinking, feeling, self-conscious spirit, the subject of the amazing change. A change wrought, not by it, nor even of it, but in it, and that by God himself: a change in which it was indeed a subject and not an agent, and under which its condition was one not of activity but of passivity. Nevertheless it is a passivity of a most peculiar kind. Not that of the dust, or the fœtus, or the dead, as in the three other cases. But that of a living, thinking, feeling, self-conscious spirit, which incurs a divine and spiritual renewal, toward which it has no efficiency of its own. Thus renewed, the new life of this spirit must be, of necessity, a real and vital existence, tending unto and nourished continually by him who gave it ; adorned with some gift of God, crowned with some grace of the Spirit, manifesting in some way or other a light, the very nature of which is, that it cannot be hid. And finally, the two invariable manifestations of the new life of this renewed soul ; the two unalterable tendencies of the restored spirit ; the two grand offices of spiritual religion as a power in the regenerate heart: Faith, namely, and Repentance, must show forth themselves and their fruits. The reality of the new creation of the fallen spirit ; the reality of the new life of the soul thus restored ; the reality of its union with Christ its Saviour, and of its possession of the Holy Spirit its sanctifier : These are realities which no more admit of uncertainty or variety, than the realities of our existence as spiritual, rational, moral, and fallen, admit of them.

4. Whether we consider the effects which are thus produced in us, or the methods by which they occur, or the agencies through which they are effected ; we are equally conducted to a surer and higher knowledge both of God and of ourselves. And are conducted again, through the peculiar knowledge of ourselves thus obtained, and by means of our increased capacity for divine knowledge ; to a still higher and nearer knowledge of God. Let us endeavor to observe this more closely.

(a) The allegation is, that the effects produced on us by the renewal of our nature, are of such a kind as to augment our knowledge of ourselves not only, but our knowledge of God also ; and the latter in various ways. The immediate effect is, that a new life analogous to that of the quickening spirit Christ, supplants in us the old life analogous to that of the living soul Adam. The old man with his deeds is put off, and the new man is put on. But it is expressly declared that the old man was corrupt according to the deceitful lusts, and that the new man is renewed in knowledge after the image of him that created him, and that after God he is created in righteousness and true holiness.[1] We were spirits before, and are spirits still ; the nature, understanding, will, power, affections which we had before, we have still ; but before, their state was, as compared with their present state, corrupt, deceitful, lustful, and every way evil ; while their present state as compared with their former, is one of knowledge, righteousness, and true holiness, all of which are in the image of corresponding Perfections of God, who has renewed, created again the soul thereunto. Resting here upon the first steps of this new life of God in the soul of man, the objective view of which alone appertains to the present stage of our inquiry, the mere statement of the case seems to be conclusive. Every effect upon us, which is indicated, or which upon that line of progress is possible, is an effect whereby the knowledge of ourselves is necessarily and continually increased ; and whereby the knowledge of God in us becomes clearer, higher, and more intimate ; and whereby at every step of our progress we become more and more conformed unto him, and therefore, in a like degree, qualified and inclined to know and to enjoy him. These results are involved in the terms of the proposition, and are inevitable. They would occur with absolute uniformity, if it were so that God in his sovereign good pleasure never withdrew his spirit, nor hid his face for a time from his children ; or if his children never backslid through the power of indwelling sin, the remains of depravity in a nature not perfectly sanctified. These and other causes which interrupt the uniform progress of our new life, appertain to another place, and neither space nor a proper method allows them to be treated here.

(*b*) The methods by which the effects produced on us in our regeneration occur, are subject to a similar statement, as the effects themselves, concerning their influence upon our knowledge of God and of ourselves. However various these methods may be, they all respect the actual nature to which they are applied ; all tend to the purification and exaltation of that nature. They are methods by which new truth is brought before our intelligence, and all truth is made more obvious ; by which new

----

[1] Eph., iv. 22–24; Col., iii. 9, 10.

and higher forms of grace are exhibited to our moral nature, and all goodness is made more distinct to the conscience; by which the true nature of all that is false and all that is evil, is continually set before the soul. They are methods which, considered as applied from without inwardly upon the soul, are the result of a superhuman insight of its nature, and a divine recognition of its condition and capabilities; and considered as working within the soul itself, they involve at every step accomplished, its own free and enlightened consent. Did any one ever hear of a soul regretting that it was born again? Did any one ever imagine that the struggles of an awakened soul under the burden of its sin, tended toward any thing evil, as long as they tended toward Christ? Or that the penitent and believing soul, ever charged any divinely-appointed means of grace with being a burden, a violence, or a snare? Did any one ever complain that violence had been done to the freedom of his nature, because God had not left his boasted self-determining power in such total ignorance, and blindness, and imbecility, as to what was true and good, as rendered all choice impossible, capricious or uncertain; or that it was a further violence that God, whether by natural means or through an intimate and even supernatural influence upon the soul, or through a fundamental renovation of the spirit itself, had controlled the free determination of the will, unto the true and the good, that is unto himself? The manifestation of God is our only means of knowing him, everywhere and in every way. But this manifestation occurs in the very soul itself, which is the seat of knowledge; and occurs by methods expressly devised in infinite wisdom, for the renewal of that soul in knowledge itself; and by the perfect application of those methods, with a divine power even to the extent of a new creation: these are the terms of the problem. The demand is, does an augmentation of our knowledge of ourselves and of God necessarily result from such a manifestation of God in us? Surely but one answer can be given.

(c) Concerning the agencies through which all the methods of divine manifestation are conducted in the soul of man unto his regeneration and sanctification; a statement precisely similar to those made concerning the methods adopted and the effect produced, as means of increasing our knowledge of God and of ourselves, must be made. Using the word agencies in its widest sense, and remembering that the great end of them all is the complete restoration of man's spiritual being, and that chiefly in the sanctification of his conscience ; we shall see at once, as the chief of them are suggested, how directly and how powerfully their action upon the soul and in it, must reveal to the soul its own nature and state; must make God manifest to it; and must constantly augment its fitness and its desire for the knowledge and enjoyment of him. (1.) The great agency is God himself. He created man ; he regenerates man ; he sanctifies man. The Father and the Son and the Holy Ghost, each as a divine person, and the Godhead in which all three unitedly subsist in one essence ; it is this adorable God, considered as one God in three persons, who is the sole efficient agent in the entire work of man's new creation. This has been so largely and variously shown, that nothing more is needed here, than to call attention to the manifest impossibility of such a work, by such an agent in such a soul, without its result being exactly such as is now insisted on.   Indeed, I must go further, and assert that by means of the Plan of Salvation practically exhibited and inwardly applied, such insight and enjoyment of God is possessed by every penitent and believing soul, as is possessed by no other created being, and as is wholly unattainable by any other.   (2.) This agency of God is attended continually by the agency of divine truth; truth, that is, having relation to divine things, and chosen and uttered and applied by God for this very end. Concerning which it is enough to repeat here, that truth considered of itself being the immediate object and aliment of the understanding, and considered as good being the immediate object and aliment of the conscience ; it cannot but be, that such a use of it in its highest form, and attended with a divine power, must produce its highest possible effects ; that is, the highest knowledge and enjoyment of God attainable by man, must be the product of these causes. That divine truth is the only efficient instrument in the sanctification of the soul, is not disputed amongst the children of God. That it is used also in the very work of regeneration itself, is probably their common, though not universal judgment ; a point the less necessary to be discussed out of its place, as it is not disputed, that in whatever the soul itself takes any part, the agency of divine truth is employed by God. (3.) Amongst outward agencies, of which the number is so great, embracing all the stated means of grace, all of which are means of instruction; and embracing also innumerable opportunities and occasions from other quarters; I ought not to omit particular mention of the special providence of God. No proof can be greater that God, in all his grace toward us, respects his own previous work as our Creator, and acts within us regardfully of the nature he has given us; than that, instead of doing the least violence to our free, knowing and self-conscious, though depraved spirit, he resorts to outward and providential means, of bringing us to the effectual knowledge of, and willing subjection unto, all inward means. The mercies which crown our lot, and the sorrows which darken it, are both alike connected with God's inward dealings with our souls in a manner so exact, that the most thoughtless cannot overlook it, nor the most obdurate wholly disregard it. So deeply seated in human nature is the recognition of this connection, that probably no great movement of God upon the soul of man has ever occurred, without being associated in the thoughts of him who was the subject of it, with some outward movement of God's special providence. That is to say—so far as relates to the matter before us, in all God's work of grace, he respects his work of creation in us; and subordinates his work of providence over us; toward the making of his grace effectual, in building us up in the knowledge and fruition of himself. (4.) As to the soul itself, there is one remarkable aspect of it, in which it may be said to be an agency employed in its own growth in the knowledge of God under every manifestation he makes of himself; and amongst the rest, very especially under that manifestation of him which occurs in its own conscious existence. I have already pointed out that the soul incurs, sustains, is the subject of this new creation; and that there is no conceivable sense in which it can be said to exert an efficient activity thereunto; while its passivity, nevertheless, is the peculiar passivity of a self-conscious spirit, upon which a vital process passes, by a divine power. And these distinctions, though they may appear over nice, and not very important, are really wholly decisive in the present state of Philosophy and Casuistical Theology —of many questions which enter vitally into Christian doctrine and experience. But the soul has one remarkable power; the power, namely, of directing, of fixing, of changing, of sustaining the attention; the fruits of whose exercise or neglect, are transcendent, and are in their origin, voluntary. When it is considered that there is no way known to us, by which any faculty of the mind, or any emotion of the soul, can be cultivated, except by its own exercise : and when it is further considered how decisive is the part played by the attention in the exercise, and therefore in the cultivation, of our mental powers; it is easy to see how justly the Apostle Peter charges that our ignorance of divine things is voluntary ; and how justly he denounces it as most sinful and most insulting to God.[1] On the other hand, it is obvious, how surely any method by which God is pleased to control and sustain the attention of the human soul --much more of the regenerate soul, directed upon itself, and upon the divine manifestations in itself ; must augment our knowledge both of him and ourself, and must increase our capability of the further knowledge of both. The result thus reached is the common experience of all Christian people ; for nothing is more certain than this very increase of the power and compass of the new life in the soul of man, under its fixed and habitual attention to God's dealings with it.

5. The sum of the matter, stated in a form at once exact and general, is to this effect, namely : God is the Creator and the Renewer of the human soul : both that creation and that renewal are in the image of God himself : the soul, therefore, in knowing itself, has a double means of knowing God, one as it knows his image, and that in a twofold manner, and the other as it knows his presence and operation, sustaining, renewing and advancing the soul, and his own image therein. The fall and recovery of the soul, taken altogether, so far from weakening, strengthens the case, by reason of such a manifestation of God in the renewal of the soul as would not otherwise have occurred ; and by reason of such proofs of his being and nature, and such insight and fruition of him by the soul, as were impossible upon any other conditions. The existence of man being the existence of a self-conscious spirit, to whose nature it appertains that it thinks, feels, knows and desires ; it follows inevitably from the nature of the case, that God as the Creator and the Renewer of the human soul, is manifest in the conscious existence of man. This great and decisive result assumes a new importance, when we reflect, that what is thus shown to be absolutely certain from

---

[1] 2 Peter, ii. 2–10.

the nature of the case, is conclusively established, beside, by the independent testimony of God himself, on one side ; and of the soul of man on the other ; the Word of God and human experience uniting in the most precise assurances, that God is thus known by man.   Starting from this point, and remembering that every other manifestation of God to man is a manifestation to this living and knowing soul, to which God is already manifested in itself, as its Creator simply, or doubly as its Creator and its Renewer ; that much additional force is to be given to every other source of the knowledge of God, that the search into it is not in reality made by a rational soul still in a state of darkness, but by a rational soul already illuminated by the candle of the Lord.   It is not easy to say in how many ways the depraved soul of man can resist, evade, and pervert the truth ; nor to estimate the depth of that marvellous hatred it can reach, of all that God propounds to it as good.   But this does not impeach the contrary powers, and capabilities, and tendencies of the soul ; much less does it impeach the means by which God manifests himself as the sum of all that man ought to know and desire.   It only sets before us one edge of those great problems which lie at our next step, directly in our path, and the discussion of which completes the objective side of the Knowledge of God : namely, the application of all our Knowledge, both of God and of ourselves, to the solution of the questions of our first and our last estates : the beginning and the end of our career : the sum and result of all divine knowledge as relates to all human existence.

THE KNOWLEDGE OF GOD,

OBJECTIVELY CONSIDERED.

ARGUMENT OF THE FIFTH BOOK.

THIS Fifth Book is in one respect, a re-survey of the fundamental basis of the argument which the preceding four Books may be said to rest upon; being a careful deduction from the creation of Man downwards to the point, at which the whole Treatise took its start, in the Study of Man as he actually exists. In another respect, it is a supplement to the preceding four Books; being the application of their sum and results, to the whole questions of God, of Man, of the Mediator and of the Knowledge of all—as they unitedly bear on the grand problems of religion and upon their sum and result. In still another respect a course of enquiry, very simple at first—becoming more and more difficult with every successive step—may be said to be completed at the end of the fourth Book; and now, in this fifth Book, it is applied in its immense results, to those vast and intricate questions which commence with the origin of the human race, control its whole career, and preside at its final catastrophe. Taken by itself, it is a treatise of Mortal existence and divine Truth, face to face: taken as the conclusion of the four preceding Books, it is an exposition of their theoretical and practical results. The Thirtieth Chapter, which is the First of this Fifth Book, discusses the Primeval State of Man—his creation in the image of God—his glory and blessedness—his perfection and fallibility—his special consecration to God: therewith, the nature of duty and responsibility—the measure of both—the certainty of redress: the conception of a covenant added to such a system—the fundamental difference between the two—and the indestructible nature of the results of that primeval condition of man, throughout every subsequent condition in which he can exist. The Thirty-First Chapter, which is the second of this Book, treats of the Covenant of Works—commencing with a settlement of the moral relations of the Creature to the Creator merely as such, and the modification thereof by express Covenant—with an appreciation of this particular Covenant. Then follows a detailed analysis of the scriptural statements concerning this Covenant—the principles upon which it rested—the end it was designed to produce—the scope of it—and the sanctions of it: then a demonstration of the perpetuity of the Moral Law—an enquiry into the conception of Man on which the Covenant of Works was based—and into the nature of perfection in created and dependent beings: the sovereignty of God and the dependence of man, are shown to be fundamental elements of Religion, in itself—the modification of the Primeval State of Man by the Covenant of Works to have been greatly to the advantage of man—and all the objections thereto to be mere cavils against God's sovereignty in Creation, in Providence or in Grace: in conclusion, the immutability of the fundamental principles of Religion, irrespective of the form Religion may put on, is demonstrated—and the chief of those principles are stated, illustrated and applied. The Thirty-Second Chapter, which is the Third of this Book, discusses the whole question of the breach of the Covenant of Works, the Fall of Man, and thereby the entrance of Evil into our universe: the discussion begins with the question of Evil—and shows that its Philosophical solution is clear, but conditional: the solution of the whole matter given by the Apostle Paul, in connection with the Fall and Recovery of Man, is carefully examined: and then the account of the matter by Moses, is thoroughly considered: the relation of the whole transaction to the state of mind of all the parties involved in it—to the Moral Law and the question of duty—and to the eternal purpose and counsel of God, is explicated: then follows an examination of the personal and immediate effects of the Fall—the sentence of God upon the Offenders—the appreciation of that sentence and of the state of man and the universe under it—the passing of a perfect nature through its fallibility, over to pollution: and in conclusion, a thorough consideration of Original Sin, and briefly the distinction between penal and incidental consequences of the Fall of Adam.—The Thirty-Third Chapter, which is the Fourth of this Book, is an attempt to apply the sum of the great truths established, to the explication of the whole career and destiny of the human race; beginning with an exhibition of the efficiency of the Method pursued, and the certainty of the Truths reached—it is shown how close the connection is between the Knowledge of ourselves and the Knowledge of God, and between the Objective and Subjective Knowledge of God: then the human race considered as a whole—throughout its whole career—is estimated—together with the bearing of both Covenants upon it, and the influence of divine knowledge on it: its condition is shown to be perilous and transitory—its impending catastrophe to be the extinction of its mortal existence, at the second coming of the Lord—and its estate, together with that of the visible church, and that of individual professors at that period is pointed out, and the solution of every problem, now unsolved, shown to be perfect then: the individual destiny of men is then discussed, and it is shown that both Covenants contemplated those embraced under them, individually: it is pointed out how and when individual pollution occurs, how and when individual restoration— and the doctrines of Reprobation and Election, and the resemblance and the difference between the career of the Reprobate and the Elect are explained: then the grand solution of the problem of mortal existence is shown to be double, not single—Salvation and Perdition—with the method of the Glory of God in both—and the infallible certainty of our knowledge thereof.—The Thirty-Fourth Chapter, which is the Fifth and last of this Book, and the last also of this Treatise, is an attempt to account for the apparent conflict between many of the clearest truths concerning God and many of the clearest concerning ourselves, and to point out the influence and effect of this state of case: it is shown that the Finite and the Infinite coalesce in the very nature of Religion—that these double results occur along that line—and are, in the nature of the case unavoidable: that their denial or even mitigation, is absurd—and that overpowering as they may be, the human soul accepts them not only as real and inevitable, but as the very strongholds of spiritual life: that God has solved some of the most august of them—that the combination of a thorough Evangelism, and a sound Philosophy solves many more—that even the most insoluble are perceived, by the renewed soul, not to be contradictions, but to be the sublimest realities, whose solution lies in some generalization higher up than we can reach—but to which a higher form of spiritual life may yet bring us. And now, if I may venture, amongst questions so numerous, so vast, and so enduring, to select such as are most fundamental and to state them in a connected form, it seems to me that those which follow are clearly proved, in this Book, namely: The human race is a created race, and an image of God—and was at its creation consecrated to God in a most special manner: Its primeval condition was one of great glory and blessedness, perfect in itself, but fallible, and therefore probationary:—The Covenant of Works was a most gracious act of God, added in order to lighten and shorten the probation of Man, being a covenant of life with the single condition of obedience: The posterity of Adam was embraced in the reward, the peril, and the penalty of this trial of him their root—and by his Fall incurred with him, every thing involved in his Fall: Evil of whatever kind, entered and fell upon the human race by reason of Adam's Fall—the chief parts thereof being sin and misery under the penalty and curse of which the whole race lies: The Covenant of Grace was declared by God, in its fundamental provision for the salvation of men before he passed sentence on Adam, and thereby the absolute condition of our fallen race was utterly changed: The actual condition of our race since that utterance by God, is that of a fallen race out of which God will save, by grace through the divine Redeemer, his own Elect—and the Remainder will perish in their sins: The relation of Adam to the whole race, and the relation of the Redeemer to the portion saved out of the race, bear the closest resemblance to each other—a resemblance existing also between the fundamental principles of the two Covenants of which they were the head respectively—and between the relations of the two Covenants to the moral law, and to the nature of Man: These grand truths, all of which are revealed truths, solve every problem in the career and destiny of the human race, whether taken as a whole or taken individually, whether considered as originally perfect, as now fallen, or as to be finally saved or lost: The mortal existence of the human race is temporary and most perilous, and will be extinguished at the Second Coming of the Lord—when every problem of human existence, whether mortal or immortal, will be openly solved to the infinite glory of God: The times and seasons of that Second Coming are absolutely unrevealed: The sum and result of our Knowledge of God, and of the whole career and destiny of man, have a precise and determinate relation to each other: So much as is inexplicable by us is so far from being false, that its reversal would subvert the foundations of Knowledge: And finally, the Knowledge of God attainable by man is absolutely certain—and its result is perfectly sure in the salvation of penitent and believing sinners.

CHAPTER XXX.

THE PRIMEVAL STATE OF MAN.

I. 1. Posture of the question stated.—2. Relation of our natural Reason and Instincts, to the Revealed Knowledge of our origin, career and destiny.—II. 1. Multitudinous creations of pretended science: one of the Bible.—2. The creation of Man in the image of God.—3. Statement of the condition of Man as thus created. —4. Appreciation of that condition.—5. God's consecration of Man to himself; and therewith the consecration of the Sabbath. Significance of these Acts.—6. The Dominion, Glory and Blessedness of our race, as created.—III. 1. The nature of duty and responsibility as connected with the primeval State of Man.—2. The measure of both.—3. Measure and certainty of redress.—4. Conception of a covenant, added to such a system.—5. Fundamental distinction between the primeval condition of man, and his condition under the Covenant of Works.— 6. Indestructible results of the former condition.—7. Importance of the analysis herein attempted.

I.—1. The whole of this attempt to develop, in an objective point of view, the nature, the extent and the sources of that Knowledge of God which is attainable by us, took its start with an inquiry into the actual state of man. The result to which that inquiry led in its first stage, and which was developed in the third chapter, was that the actual condition of the human race is a condition of universal sin and misery ; and that, except by means of some divine interposition, unsearchable to human reason, this ruin of the race is irremediable. At that point, the general subject separated into two branches, of which one had relation to the preceding history of the human race, and the other to its immediate career: along one or other of which it behooved to pursue our inquiry into the knowledge of God. The latter, which we took, carried us directly at the first step to the actual interposition of God : at the next step to the Person, Work, and Glory of the Saviour of the world : and then, with him exalted to the throne of the universe, not only as its Ruler and Redeemer, but as its Teacher also, our inquiries into the Nature and Perfections of God, and then into all the manifestations of God—have conducted us in a natural and rigidly consecutive manner, through that branch of the subject, to its end, as a means of divine knowledge. The inquiry recurs now to the portion of the subject, left at the close of the third chapter. It was left with a brief explanation to this effect, namely: That it did not belong to Christianity, any more than to all other systems which propose to redress the ruin of man, to explain how that ruin had been incurred: yet, the perfect ability of Christianity to give a complete explanation, when contrasted with the utter inability of all other systems to give any explanation at all; and the complete accordance of the remedy afforded by Christianity with the nature and mode of occurrence of the ruin itself; raised such a presumption that Christianity was itself the very divine interposition the case required, that we might well accept her initiative explanation of a topic common to all systems, till we had carefully considered the remedy peculiar to herself, which she had to propose. That has now been done. And under the perfect conviction that the balm that is in Gilead is a sovereign remedy for all the sin and all the misery of man; we may take up again the account of the great Physician of souls, concerning our primeval condition, the origin of our ruin, the exact mode of our present condition, and the precise results of all things under it. The inquiry opens to us the sum and result of the knowledge of God objectively considered.

2. What I have several times intimated concerning our total ignorance of our own origin and destiny, as a race, is worthy of very attentive consideration. Except in the Word of God, we have no distinct account worthy of a moment's consideration, even of the primitive condition, much less of the actual origin of mankind: nor is there, except in it, any certain grounds for even a probable conjecture as to our ultimate fate considered as connected with this earth. On both points, indeed, the human mind, even in its most advanced condition, has gone wholly astray from the truth; notwithstanding its access to the primeval knowledge possessed by the first parents of the race, and to the revelations of God so often given, during so many ages, and so widely scattered over the earth. It has gone utterly astray, as to our original condition: supposing it to have been very low at first, and to have advanced greatly, in the progress of ages; whereas its first, was its highest estate—lost, and tending to a deeper degradation—

never yet recovered. It has gone astray also, as to our destiny in its connection with this earth : supposing our connection with it to have been from the most remote antiquity, whereas it is but of yesterday, when compared with all the past : and supposing it will be perpetual in our present condition, whereas compared with all the future, it will be most transitory. And yet there were always instincts of the race, wiser by far than its boasted reason : common convictions dwelling in the universal heart and mind of the race, truer by far than the conjectures of its pretentious knowledge. Man always felt that he was blameworthy : and why should he not experience that relief from unrest, which certain knowledge can impart, when he is clearly taught how it is that he came to be so guilty, and his sense thereof so just ? He always felt that somehow and somewhere, human nature had been or would be a better and higher human nature than his now is : and some how, or somewhere, had been or would be, a worse and lower human nature than his now is. He had conceptions immeasurably purer, higher, better, nobler, than he was himself : he had conceptions immeasurably lower, viler, baser, than he was himself : he had boundless hopes and aspirations : he had fearful misgivings and apprehensions. It was idle to call these things idle: they were always *felt* to be the greatest of all realities. And they were. And when the light of heaven came to him, and the page of his mysterious being and destiny was fairly read by him, then it was all plain enough. His very nature was a testimony, and his whole life was another, to the truth of God's account of his primeval state—of his career and of his end. Much of the inscrutable mystery of his being, in all its aspects, is cleared up as soon as a few sentences of divine truth have laid bare his primeval condition, and the true causes of his present estate.

II.—1. The creation of man was the last creative act of God on the last of the six days of creation. There is no intimation that there had ever been any cosmical act of creation put forth by God, before that creation recorded by Moses ; but there is much in the account which it is extremely difficult, if not impossible to reconcile with any belief or admission on the part of Moses, that any previous cosmical creation had ever occurred : and all the sacred writers follow and confirm Moses. It is certain that no subsequent act of original creation is intimated in the Scriptures as having occurred : and that no proper creative person, or power, or force, has ever existed in the universe, or is conceiveable by us, except God only. The Scriptures abound with declarations concerning the creation recorded by Moses, of all things out of nothing in the space of six days : they abound with declarations concerning the New Creation, by means of which God's spiritual kingdom is brought forth, sustained, and made victorious over all things : and they abound with declarations concerning the catastrophe which awaits the whole visible creation. But they are profoundly silent touching those multitudinous previous creations, and that continuous subsequent creation, concerning which the most modern ignorance, differs from the most ancient ignorance, chiefly in that the ancient, in its modesty, put forward as conjectures, what the modern, in its ostentation, puts forward as science. As yet, no one, I believe, has had the courage to discover a fossil man, with whom to confront Moses : a very curious forbearance of creative nature and her believing expositors, whether Christian or infidel. And as our inquiries relate almost exclusively to man, we may thankfully accept the respite, and for the present continue to suppose that as man really exists, it is quite as capable of belief that God created him, as that he created himself, came by chance, or existed from eternity : and that on supposition of his being created by God, the proof of our credulity is not humiliating when we accept the veracity of God, pledged throughout his Word, as to the time, the manner, the circumstances, the object, and the result of that creation.[1]

2. The first parents of our race, were created in the maturity and perfection of all their faculties, of body and of soul : and they alone of all their race, entered upon existence in such a condition as this. Not mature only—but also sinless, the existence into which they thus bounded, was cast in a scene of things undefiled by sin—unclouded by suffering—and which God himself, as he surveyed every thing he had made, pronounced to be very good. First, man's physical part was separately created by God—dust of the ground : and then God breathed into his nostrils the breath of life : and man became a living soul.[2] Dust of the ground : the breath of life : a living soul : God the author : man, male and female, the product. This creation, thus simply and directly announced, is repeatedly declared to have been, in the

---

[1] Genesis, i. 26–31.   [2] Gen., ii. 7 ; 1 Cor., xv. 45.

image and after the likeness of God: that is, summarily, God created a being, in general resembling the divine being, and possessing a nature and endowments copied after the nature and perfections of God. There is first, a physical organism, the most perfect, the most wonderful, the most comprehensive, the most exalted of all the visible works of God. This organism is so complete, that although it has been the special object of scrutiny from its creation, and although it is probably better understood than any other great work of God, and although every portion of it has yielded to the unremitting study of so many centuries immense stores of knowledge: nevertheless, the end of complete knowledge is so far from having been reached, that scarce a single organ can be said to be perfectly understood, scarce a single function of a single part to be thoroughly comprehended, scarce a single tissue to be thoroughly appreciated. This exquisite organism, worthy, if we can presume to say any thing is worthy, of the workmanship of God, undefiled as yet by sin, was animated by an immediate spiration from God—he breathing into its nostrils the breath of life. Man's vital existence is not the product of his organism, nor necessarily connected with it: but was added by a separate and most peculiar act of God, to the finished organism: and is capable of continued connection with the organism even while it is in a condition of indefinite disorganization and decay: and is capable of being separated from it, while the organism is in its most perfect state—and in fact is separated from it, by death, in every case. What the nature of this vital principle is, is utterly inscrutable. It is the breath of God communicated to the first man, in an immediate and creative act, and propagated in a peculiar manner to his whole race. It becomes, in each individual, indissolubly united with the spiritual part of man—his soul—which seems to be intended in calling man a living soul, and seems to express its proper immortality. This indissoluble union of the vital principle with the soul, explains the instant death of the body as well as the continued existence of the soul, after the separation of the soul and body of man. This living soul—which it is said man became—is the basis of his resemblance to God, and itself the fundamental part of the divine image which he bore, the divine likeness in which he had been created.

3. The primeval state of man is thus clearly made known to

us by God. He was created with a perfect and exquisite organism, to which God added a spiritual soul, uniting indissolubly to the latter the principle of life, which animated the body also : and by these wonderful unions of two created things, the body and the spirit, and the spirated breath of life from God, the new and glorious being stood before his Creator ! It is a new spirit, endowed with a life which shall never end, with activity which cannot rest, with faculties in the likeness of the Attributes of God, with endowments after the image of the Perfections of God ; a new race, indeed, of spirits ; the absolute oneness of the race, a vast image of the oneness of God himself ; the distinct personal existence of each member of the race, as a separate force and yet an insparable portion of the one whole, like a dim shadow of the divine personal plurality ; and the very form of the oneness and the plurality of the divine existence, as made known to us, the idea of eternal paternity, of eternal filiation, and of eternal procession from both to each other, exhibited, as far as nature could, in the relations of this new race upon itself—fathers and sons, in an endless oneness of plurality, endlessly united ! But nearest of all, perhaps, to the present purpose, man's primeval estate was in the image and after the likeness of that infinite Rectitude of God which is the very essence of his moral nature.[1] Therefore we were worthy to be called the offspring of God,[2] to be declared to be the image and glory of God ;[3] and therefore when we put on the new man we are expressly said to be created after God in righteousness.[4] It was also in the image and after the likeness of the infinite knowledge of God, and of the infinite understanding and will to which that knowledge is related, and of the infinite Spiritual Essence, to which they all appertain. And therefore our renewal in the image of him that created us is declared to be a renewal in knowledge ;[5] a restoration produced by our being renewed in the spirit of our mind ;[6] a new product of God's workmanship, created in Christ Jesus unto the good works which were our original ordination ;[7] a new bestowment of that eternal life which consisted originally in the knowledge of the only true God, and which consists now in that same knowledge divinely restored, with the knowledge of Jesus Christ, whom God hath sent, divinely superadded.[8] It was also

---

[1] Eccl., vii. 29.   [2] Acts, xvii. 29.   [3] 1 Cor., xi. 7.   [4] Eph., iv. 24.
[5] Col., iii. 10.   [6] Eph., iii. 23.   [7] Eph., ii. 10.   [8] John, xvii. 1–3.

in the image and after the likeness of that infinite Perfection of God which is called true Holiness ; by which I understand that infinite sanctity of God out of which truth flows, and in the perfection of which it is not only said that *God is Truth*, as spoken continually of the Godhead, but the same statement is made, with great emphasis, of the Son and of the Holy Ghost, through whom all divine truth is brought nigh to us.[1]   There was something more than Rectitude, something more than the Knowledge of God, the image and likeness of which man possessed ; and this is expressed by a periphrasis showing the relation of these two perfections to each other, and the result thereof.   Rectitude and Knowledge, that is Righteousness and Truth ; the result, True Holiness, that is the sanctity which God's Truth found responsive to it in man, and which God's Truth now nourishes in man : literally, the original man was created, and the new man is restored, not only in the image and likeness of God's Knowledge and Righteousness, but of that divine perfection also which rests in a peculiar manner upon both the others, and which we call true Holiness.[2]

4. Such a condition as this—the chief features of which only have been gathered from the statements of the sacred Scriptures, and set forth in their most elemental form, is not difficult of a general appreciation by us, even in our fallen estate, much less in our recovered likeness to God, and above all when we are directed at every step by the perpetual light of the Divine Word. It is very evident that in our primeval condition, we were capable of knowing and seeing, of loving and enjoying God.   We were the objects of divine approbation, both in our nature and our acts ; and were permitted to enjoy and did enjoy, a constant and very near intercourse with God.   We were full of light and of blessedness, and were capable of immeasurable advancement and felicity.   We were exempt from error, from sorrow, and from shame ; and had no knowledge of disquietude, or pain, or sin.   We were not subject to sickness, or decay, or death ; and no evil of any sort—physical, mental, moral, or spiritual had any place in our being.   We were put in possession of an endless life of glory and blessedness ; and were made capable both of enjoying and preserving it for ourselves, and of perpetuating it to an innumerable race of our own descendants through endless gene-

<hr>

[1] John, xiv. 6; 1 John, v. 6.   [2] Eph., iv. 24.

rations. In all this career of boundless exaltation to ourselves, the universe itself would have rejoiced forever in the estate of perfection in which it came forth from the hand of God, fashioned expressly as the habitation of a race so glorious: and every inferior creature, each after its own kind, would have rejoiced always in its satisfying share of that infinite goodness of God, which was over all his works. And then to crown all, the great chief end of the creation, and the great subordinate end of it, would have been perfectly accomplished, both together: for the declarative glory of God would have been permanent and eternal by means of such sublime manifestations of himself; and the blessedness of the whole creation would have gone hand in hand forevermore, with the boundless glory of God! If we could conceal from ourselves, for a moment, the manner in which the wreck of all this glory and blessedness, was repaired by the grace of God; we could appreciate in a manner far more just and adequate, both that which we and the whole universe lost by the fall of our race, and that which we and the universe have incurred of boundless misery, through fearful guilt.

5. Beyond what was involved in the very nature of man, and in the very nature of his original estate, and its relations to God and the universe; much was superadded by God, in a way of sovereign and merciful dealing with him, in immediate connection with his creation. Besides the divine attestation to the whole creation, and to man as the chief part of it, that it was all very good, God added his special blessing both to the man and the woman: an immeasurable act of favor and protection—a crowning proof of his love, wherein he appropriated the race to himself, after the peculiar manner of God. All that he had made, and all connected with it—were delivered over to a common glory and unto a common fruition: except that two things were drawn unto God himself with a special nearness. Man his chief work, he consecrated to himself by his special blessing; and the Sabbath day, the everlasting memorial of what he had done, and the peculiar means of making effectual that consecration of man—God blessed and sanctified, as most singularly his own.[1] Nothing can be more striking and decisive than both of these divine acts, so carefully recorded for everlasting instruction. And in the whole subsequent dealings of God with the human

---

[1] Gen., i. 28, ii. 3.

race, nothing is more distinctly and perpetually kept before the human mind—nothing is more carefully placed in the very front of every aspect of every dispensation of Grace, than these two primeval claims of God, lodged in the very bosom of creation itself. The race that was made in the image, and after the likeness of God himself, was from the beginning a blessed race, consecrated to God. When he retrieves it, he reclaims but his own; when even in its desperate madness of sin, his unchangeable love answers by the sacrifice of his Son, it is no new fervor, but the inextinguishable purpose from eternity to have a seed to serve him! And this sacred time of God—memorial alike of creation and of redemption—type alike of primeval, and of renewed, and of eternal fruition of God—lodged in the very heart of natural Religion, before the existence even of the Covenant of Works—embedded in the moral law as the speciality of all duty toward God, inseparable from Gospel holiness; it is unto man, a proof that he was once free and holy—a help and joy to his endeavors after perfect restoration—and a token that an endless triumph awaits him! Man cannot be wholly lost as long as these two primeval claims of God, find a response within him: as long as the idea of his own primeval consecration—and the idea of consecrated time, as a token thereof—between him and God —both still asserted by God—are not wholly obliterated from his soul.

6. Thus created in God's image, and thus consecrated to God's service, man was divinely invested with an absolute and unlimited dominion over the earth, and over all things in it.[1] Let us make man in our image, after our likeness, and *let them have dominion ;* these are the words in which the divine purpose is announced : and to the man and the woman, after their creation—*have dominion,* are the words of the boundless investiture. Even the fall of man, and the total apostacy and almost total destruction of the race, did not extinguish this grant : for more than sixteen centuries after it was made and forfeited, God delivered to Noah after he came forth from the ark, all earthly things, and added as applicable even to the fallen condition of the race, that the fear of man and the dread of man should be upon them all.[2] At first, it was a grant of all things, not in trust, but with absolute fulness. Subdue the earth, use it, oc-

---

[1] Gen., i. 26–28. [2] Gen., ix. 2.

cupy it, possess it, enjoy it—it is thine.   And then he bade them replenish it also.   Increase and multiply ; be fruitful—subdue—replenish.   Fill the earth with beings having this dominion over it : exalted beings—all holy and wise—all of one blood and race —all united in boundless glory, perfection and felicity.   The whole race, forever, to be one immeasurable expanse of all goodness and all greatness : and every individual of it to be united to every other individual of it, by ties which should never be broken, and by love which should know no interruption.   And so deep and so fixed were these additional ordinances of God, both in the divine purpose and in the nature of man ; that the fall which produced a catastrophe so fatal to man and to the universe, did not extinguish them.   The blessing of Adam, was reiterated to Noah : the dominion of the race was re-affirmed to him : the command to be fruitful, to multiply and to replenish the earth, was repeated to him : and the sacredness of his life which had borne the image of God, was assured by new guaranties.[1]   God will find a way to retrieve and to punish, the apostacy and ruin of man.   After a respite of sixteen centuries, during which man had shown himself to be only evil and that continually, the wrath of God in its just fierceness swept away the whole race, except Noah and his household, in the flood of waters.   So much was due to God.   And this besides, that in re-peopling the earth, under a second head, and with a fallen race, the principles which had sustained the original fabric of the moral universe when all was pure, should be shown by the power of their working when all was corrupt, to have been infinitely complete and efficacious unto the end for which they were designed at first.   Nothing can be more complete, than such a proof as this of the glory and blessedness of the primeval state of man.   Let any one consider the nature and the force of that single idea of the universal brotherhood of man—lost by the fall and restored in Jesus Christ : and he may find opened to him clearly, the method of a general estimate of the divine conception of the glory and blessedness of our first estate, not one sublime principle of which but was pregnant with unalterable truth and boundless goodness.

III.—1. It is manifest that out of such a state of things as I have described, there would arise obligations on the part of man,

[1] Gen., ix. 1–6.

corresponding to the relations which he found himself sustaining, to the capacities with which he was endowed, and to the blessings which were bestowed on him. The moment we acknowledge that we are creatures, there arise, immediately, the ideas of dependence and obligation : for we are his, who made us. As soon as we allow that we are rational and moral, we are obliged to allow the distinctions of True and False, Good and Evil : for otherwise there would be no possibility of exercising, much less of showing the existence of, either reason or conscience. The existence of a creator, and at the same time of rational and moral creatures, involves the existence of duty on the part of such creatures. The measure of the duty on the one hand, and on the other of the responsibility if it is not performed—is to be sought, in the absence of positive rules, in the respective conditions of all the parties, and the particular relations of each.

2. In the very nature of the case, therefore, it is not possible for such creatures to exist, otherwise than in a condition of obligation and accountability, of some sort or other. Their very nature is at once a law and a proof unto them : and the very nature of God is alike a measure and a revelation of his claims upon them. But the claims of God under such circumstances, and upon such creatures as we have been considering—whether we contemplate God in what he is or in what he has done for them, are perfectly immeasurable claims upon the gratitude, the love and the obedience of the creature. And on their side, the corresponding obligations of the creatures, are only to be limited by their utmost capacity to please and honor God, in whatever way he may indicate his pleasure to them.

3. In the event of failure there must be adequate redress, of some sort or other, supposing that there is steadfastness in the system under which the failure occurs, or power or wisdom in him who established it, or justice or truth in him who administers it. Supposing all these things to combine in any one system, as they all do in the system of God's universe—the redress for every failure of duty is not only inevitable, but is inevitably certain to work itself out as a part of the system itself, inherent in its original constitution, and unchangeably certain as the result of its progress. And the measure of that redress is unavoidably determined, in like manner, by the claims of God who has been offended, and by the obligations of the creature which have been

violated : that is, by the truth and rectitude upon which the whole system is founded, and to which the reason and conscience of the creature respond.

4. Under such a system as that at the head of which man was placed, there were no sins, as yet, to punish : of course, therefore, there were none to pardon : and of course, once more, there was no such notion as pardon, possible, under it. A perfect creature under a perfect system, administered by a perfect Ruler, whose laws were written on the hearts of his subjects, could have but one rule and one reward. Do and live : this embraced at once all duty and all felicity.—But, at the same time, every failure and every shortcoming, sufficiently grave to involve redress, immediately and irrecoverably defeated the whole scheme, as to every one thus failing. And if instead of the personal risk thus run by each creature as it might exist under such a system, the risk were run all at once, by the common head of all before any of the members existed, and as a common representative of all : this, in the first place, could only be in consequence of a positive divine constitution ; and in the second place, if it were so, by virtue of such a constitution, it is obvious that the result whatever it might be, would be as comprehensive as the constitution under which it had occurred.

5. That a covenant, such as that just intimated, was made by God with Adam, we know, and the result of it : both of which will be considered in their order. At present we are to observe that before and independently of any such covenant, the ordinances of God which have been recapitulated as immediately connected with the creation of man, and the relations which subsisted between God and man which have been generally exhibited, and the very natures of God and of man which have been summarily explained, unitedly coerce a system of the most precise kind, and of the most prodigious extent. It is not difficult to separate the three elements of such a system above stated, and to conceive of each one of the three as forming a separate system, or the separate parts of one system. What is most important is, that they are all necessary, permanent, indestructible elements of every system by which the human race is to be affected so long as it exists. Whatever else man may become, he will never cease to be a creature, nor will God ever cease to be his Creator : he can never cease to possess a nature which was originally pure and

upright, and to underlie all the consequences, good and evil, of that primitive and imperishable truth : and so of all the rest. It is on this account that it is of such vital importance to us, both as a decisive question of speculative truth, and as a transcendent practical force in our eternal experience, to understand clearly, and to appreciate fully, what our primeval estate really was anterior to the institution of the Covenant of Works by God.

6. From these indestructible elements of our primeval estate, there results of necessity a system of natural knowledge, a system of natural reason, and a system of natural morality : or to speak more exactly, a system of man, having these three aspects, which system in every original aspect of it, is simply and purely of divine authority. For God is the sum of all the True and all the Good : and man created pure and upright, spiritual and immortal, in God's image, would habitually and naturally cleave to the True and the Good, that is to God, with all the power of his free, knowing, and loving nature. The forms of knowledge must accord with the forms of his understanding ; the Laws of Nature must accord with the distinctions which he perceives to exist between the True and the False : Natural Religion is the exposition of his sense of the Good and the Evil. All this seems to be perfectly evident, perfectly unavoidable. And though there may be by subsequent catastrophes immense degradation in the estate of man, yet so long as the essence of his nature is not destroyed—so long as his identical existence is continued—these primeval verities abide in that degree. Thus the Moral Law, written at last by God on tables of stone and given to Moses, had been written by God on the heart of Adam twenty-five centuries before. And fallen as all men were, all the time from Adam to Moses, all men yet had in their natures the traces of that law. And though when God reproduced that law for Moses, the whole human family united could not have done this, yet not a human being then or since, who was not judicially blinded, could behold that divine reproduction, without recognizing it as good even when it condemned him.

7. In some respects this, like every other subject that nearly concerns the infinite being and eternal counsel of God, lies out of the range of our poor faculties. Here, as everywhere else, it behooves us to advance steadily to the utmost limit that our ability will reach—to recognize the impassable barrier when we

come distinctly to it—and there to bow our spirits in thankful
docility to him who has led us that far, and in adoring confidence that all that is beyond is well, since it is all with him.   It
is good for us, no doubt, to know as nearly as we can, what
things they are we cannot know ; for then we can the more safely
strive for what we may obtain ; and then, too, our unrest ought
to cease.   Those aspects of this vast subject, therefore, which lie
merely in conjecture, I have not presumed to touch : and this all
the more because I desired to separate two immense events which
appeared to me to be wholly distinct, but which are usually confounded in the treatment of them ; the Primeval state of man,
namely, and the Covenant of Works.   When that distinction is
firmly established, a new light is thrown on the primitive condition of our race, and so on all its subsequent career : and we have
reached therein the furthest term of our inquiries in that direction.

CHAPTER XXXI.

THE COVENANT OF WORKS.

I. **1.** The moral force of the Relation of Creator and Creature, considered of itself.—2. How this condition is modified by express Covenant.—3. The Covenant of Works.—4. An Additional and most merciful Dispensation.—II. 1. The Scriptural Testimony to the facts of the case (*a.*) The Garden of Eden: (*b.*) The Tree of Life: (*c.*) The Tree of Knowledge: (*d.*) Sanctions of the Covenant: (*e.*) General Aspect of that Covenant.—2. Its idea as a Covenant of Works.—3. The Posterity of Adam expressly and unavoidably involved in this Covenant.—4. Obedience, the single condition of the Covenant.—5. Scriptural Statements concerning the Tree of Life: (*a.*) Man, as a sinner, is deprived of its Use: (*b.*) Its relation to man considered as penitent and righteous: (*c.*) Its relation to the Cherubim: (*d.*) To victorious Saints: (*e.*) To the New Jerusalem: (*f.*) To the endless Blessedness of the righteous: (*g.*) To the general Development of Salvation.—6. Scriptural Statements concerning the Tree of Knowledge.—7. Sacraments of the Covenant of Works.—8. The inherent nature of every Dispensation merely Legal.—9. The Covenant of Works was a Covenant of Life, with transcendent promises.—10. Nature and bearing of the penalty annexed to it.—III. 1. Eve. Duty. The Moral Law.—2. The conception of Man, on which the Covenant of Works rests. 3. The fallibility of dependent creatures. The peril, and yet the divine mercy of Adam's trial.—4. The Sovereignty of God and the Dependence of the creature, fundamental in the nature of Religion.—5. In so far as the Covenant of Works modified the Primeval condition of Man, it was in divine Mercy, and to our advantage: (*a.*) The violation of the moral Unity of the race was averted: (*b.*) The probation of the race became specific, temporary, exact, instead of being perpetual, universal, indefinite: (*c.*) The immense personal advantages of Adam, inured to the benefit of his race : (*d.*) The trial itself, was the lightest that can be conceived of: (*e.*) The probability of Adam's success, greater than that of any other human being: (*f.*) Every objection to this trial, is reducible to one directly against creation, providence, or grace.—6. Immutability of the ultimate elements of Religion. Those most important stated, generally: (*a.*) Special example, The principle of Positive Covenant—Headship—Substitution—Imputation: (*b.*) Fitness for the Favor of God must exist, to justify the continuance of that favor.

I.—1. IF God had placed man upon no particular trial, man would have been upon a universal and perpetual trial. If God had affixed no particular penalty to any particular transgression, there would nevertheless, have been an adequate penalty connected with every transgression. Because there was, as has been abundantly shown, in the very nature of man, of God, and of the relations between them considered as creator and creature, that which had all the force of the most positive laws, and consequences as inevitable as the most distinct covenant could provide.

2. It pleased God to modify this condition. He did it in infinite wisdom and goodness, and with the design of consummating man's estate of innocence and perfection. He reduced this general state of things to a speciality : concentrated the trial of man's universal obedience, upon one special proof of it. Still further, it pleased God in his great grace, to put the whole race upon trial, in its great, original, representative head ; to particularize the exact redress which would be exacted, in case of transgression ; to add and to express a great reward in case of obedience ; to reduce the whole case to a distinct statement, and to communicate it clearly to Adam, in the form of a positive covenant with him.[1]

3. This is what is commonly known in all Christian Theology as the *Covenant of Works.* It is often called the *old covenant,* as being the first explicit covenant made by God with man. It is also called the *Legal Covenant,* to distinguish it from every manifestation of the Covenant of Grace ; though it was itself a most gracious covenant, after its peculiar manner. And it is called the *Sinaitic Covenant* because it was from Mount Sinai that the eternal and immutable law of God, written first by him upon the soul of man, was written a second time by his finger on tables of stone, and proclaimed openly from heaven as the universal rule of rectitude, and the sum of the moral law.[2] This multiplicity of names however indicates some danger of indistinct conception of a subject which it is of the last importance to understand clearly.

4. The whole of the preceding chapter is based on the idea that the *covenant of works* was a separate and distinct dispensation of God toward man, in the estate in which he was created, and blessed, and invested with dominion, and commanded to subdue and replenish the earth, and made acquainted with the hallowed rest of the Sabbath day.[3] It was a further and additional exhibition of God's infinite goodness to man. It followed, it accepted, and, in that manner, it embraced whatever had gone before ; but

---

[1] Gen., ii. 8–17 ; Hosea, vi. 7 ; Rom., iii. 27, x. 5.
[2] Ex., xx. 3–18 ; Mat., xxii. 37–40.   [3] Gen., i. 27, ii. 3.

it stipulated nothing that had gone before ; it stipulated nothing but what was new. Its conditions were revealed, not natural conditions ; its promises were positive, not inherent ; its penalty was expressly regulated, not left to the infinite, unuttered discretion of God. As to what had already taken place, it was all immutable, all eternal, all to be taken for granted in every conceivable Dispensation of God toward man afterwards to occur, so long as man continued to possess a conscious, identical existence, and to occupy any state of probation. So taken, it is all a part of the *Covenant of Works ;* so it is also of the *Covenant of Grace;* differently, no doubt, in the two covenants, in some respects very differently. But both covenants, and their results, are as distinguishable from creation, and its immediate consequence, as they are from each other. A new and most gracious form of probation was proclaimed by God.

II.—1. The statement of the case, in the Sacred Scriptures, concerning the origin, nature, and provisions of the Covenant of Works, is very precise ; and every part of the Divine Word takes for granted the reality of that covenant, and the perpetuity of its consequences, using the word consequences in its largest sense, while many passages of that word treat the subject expressly. The passages already cited, and those which will follow, confirm these statements. Summarily, the main facts are these, namely :

(*a*) After the creation of man, and in addition to all that was involved therein, and also in those great commands, mercies, and gifts bestowed on him in direct connection with creation in God's image, God prepared a garden in Eden, and put therein the man whom he had formed to dress it and to keep it.[1]

(*b*) The garden of Eden contained every fair, pleasant, and fruitful tree, and amongst them, in the midst of the garden, the *Tree of Life.* Divine permission, in the form of a command, was expressly given to Adam, to eat freely of every tree of the garden, *except one,* which was distinctly named, and which excepted tree was not the Tree of Life ; so that the access of man was complete, and permission unlimited, to eat the fruit of the Tree of Life. Indeed the form of the grant being, by way of command, and its substance, " *eating thou shalt eat,*" involved the idea of a perpetual, universal, successive right, duty, and use in man to

---

[1] Gen., ii. 8–15.

Eden, and all its fruits, omitting the one prohibited, and including the Tree of Life.[1]

(c) The prohibition was explicit and single. In the midst of the garden was the *Tree of the Knowledge of Good and Evil.* "Thou shalt not eat of it," was the express command of God. "Ye shall not eat of it, neither shall ye touch it"—is the form in which Eve understood and repeated the prohibition.[2]

(d) The sanction affixed by God both to the command which carried the right and duty of man to use the fruit of the *Tree of Life;* and to the command which prohibited to him the use of the fruit of the *Tree of Knowledge of Good and Evil;* were the very highest that can be conceived of. The penalty was expressed in these words, "For in the day that thou eatest thereof, thou shalt surely die."[3] The reward, if we may so express it—the promise annexed to the keeping of the two forestated commands of God, was man's confirmation in his state of perfection, and an assured inheritance of everlasting life.[4]

(e) Whatever we may endeavor to persuade ourselves was the design, the nature, the implied compass, conditions or results of the *covenant of works;* if we may confide in the statements of the divine word, and if we are able to gather up the exact outline of these statements, here is the covenant itself set before us. It was a dispensation of God to man ; following man's creation in the image of God ; synchronous with man's abode in the garden prepared for him by God ; anterior to the existence of any of the human race but Adam and Eve ; the terms of which were few and simple ; the sanctions of which were infinite and eternal both ways ; the immediate effect of which was to test man's obedience to God ; and the method of that test twofold—namely to partake of the fruit of the *Tree of Life,* and to reject the fruit of the *Tree of the Knowledge of Good and Evil.* It will be our surest way of comprehending all this more precisely —to consider in succession all the capital elemental ideas, which enter into the case ; separating, as we proceed, such as, strictly speaking, cannot be so taken.

2. We need not hesitate with the church of God in all ages, and with God himself by the mouth of inspired men to call this

---

[1] Gen., ii. 9–16.   [2] Gen., ii. 17,* iii. 3.
[3] Gen., ii. 17.   [4] Lev., xviii. 5 ;   Mat., xix. 16, 17.

* מוֹת תָּמוּת : *Dying thou shalt die.*

Divine Dispensation, a covenant between God and Adam ; nor to add, that it was a *covenant of works.* We are told in so many words that Adam broke covenant with God ; a passage somewhat obscured to the English reader, by an erroneous rendering.[1] And indeed there is no way in which we can understand the innumerable assertions, that the covenant of Redemption is either *new* or *better*, as compared with all that had been manifested before it was manifested ; or that the Gospel state is *new* or *better* as an exhibition of the Covenant of Grace, than all preceding manifestations of that, and all other covenants : if indeed no other covenant had existed.[2] As to this being a *covenant of works;* that is manifest on the face of the whole matter. For the required obedience manifested by outward acts—and in its own nature performed by Adam himself—and performed perfectly, or not at all, could have no other nature, in his case. Whatever might be Adam's relations to his posterity—which will be considered presently, it is very obvious that to derive any benefit either to them or himself under such a covenant, he cannot plead either an imperfect obedience of his own, or a vicarious obedience of any one else ; both of which, it is conceivable that his posterity might have plead before the infinitely good God, under this very covenant if Adam had received its reward ; and both of which it is certain, we all must plead under Christ and the covenant of Grace, or all perish. But Adam's individual work could no more be any thing else—but a personal and perfect work, than Christ's individual work could be ; and the covenant of Works, as a covenant of life, was staked on the personal and perfect obedience of Adam—exactly as the covenant of Grace as a covenant of Life, was staked on the obedience— even unto death—of the Son of God. In reality, as I have before pointed out, we can form no conception of a created and dependent being standing related to our infinite Creator and Ruler—which does not involve the ideas of law and covenant. And when these ideas become positive and specific, they carry with them, always, something added in the way of mercy on the part of God, and of benefit to the creature. This reaches its height in the sacrifice of Christ, in our room and stead.

3. It is perfectly certain that the whole posterity of Adam, descending from him by ordinary generation, were intended to be

---

[1] Hosea, vi. 7, viii. 1.   [2] Jer., xxxi. 31–40; Heb., viii. 6–13.

involved, were actually involved, and could not but be involved, in the result of this great trial of the first progenitor and federal head of his race. Yet it is equally clear that these results all depend upon the one fact of there being a positive, and not a virtual covenant between God and Adam, as I have before explained. It is therefore, clear, that the more strictly we distinguish between the Law of Nature, properly so called, and the *covenant of works;* the more certain it is that the Moral Law must survive both the keeping and the breach of the *covenant of works*, and that the whole human race must underlie the curse and the penalty of that Covenant, if it be broken—and must reap its promises if it be kept. The question here is, nakedly, as to the range of the covenant. To suppose that it embraced Adam only, is to suppose that it was a divine contrivance whose only certain effect would be to separate Adam from all his posterity; which, in that case it was obliged to do, let it end as it might. And the total object of that most preposterous result, would seem to be to reverse by a divine constitution, the order of nature just before established in the work of creation. For by it, the unity of the human race and the steadfastness of the whole universe were made to depend upon the uniformity of causation : now expressly and doubly violated—upon the hypothesis —in the very nature of man, who is the chief work of God. Is it possible for us to suppose the whole work of Christ to have been absolutely fruitless, with regard to every human soul but that of the Man Jesus ? Then how are we to suppose a similar absurdity of him who was his type ? Moreover, what is gained by denying Adam's Federal Headship, and then polluting us all, by merely natural means, to which we were no party, in any sense ? As both the common progenitor and the common representative of all, Adam's position, as the root of the human race, explains all. And to this intent, and by means of this covenant, is the whole current of divine testimony.[1]

4. The condition—the solitary condition—of the *covenant of works*, was obedience ; covenanted obedience—for himself and for all his posterity, by Adam. Observe, Adam was yet innocent—perfect—but fallible ; and God had before this covenant, and independently of it—exercised toward him all those great acts of providence, up to the placing him in Eden—of which

---

[1] Acts, xvii. 26; Rom., v. 12, 19; 1 Cor., xv. 21, 22, 45–49.

repeated mention has been made. Naturally, as has been repeatedly said, the understanding of this exalted image of God went forth to all that was True—his will to all that was Good—and both with all the power of his pure Nature. That is only to say, in other words, it was the pure, incessant and powerful impulse of his nature to love, to obey, and to enjoy God—as the sum of all the True and the Good. It is not very easy for us to see how such a being as this could be put on any trial at all—except as touching some act of outward obedience—founded upon some positive command. At any rate the condition of the Covenant of Works adopted by God was exactly of this kind. Still however it touched Life on one side, and Good and Evil on the other: those eternal, and inscrutable realities! And these sublime relations of the command on the one side, and the prohibition on the other, made the obedience of Adam all the more natural, as the test leaned over from a mere positive character, toward some accordance with the high instincts of his own spirit. It cannot be disputed amongst Christians, that the prohibition to eat the fruit of the Tree of Knowledge of Good and Evil, was most precise; because in this part of the trial of Adam's obedience, the words of God are express.[1] It is without sufficient warrant that the command of God touching the use of the fruit of the Tree of Life, is construed into a mere permission.[2] We shall see that its use was a high and sacred duty; it was the positive side of man's obedience. And if it were permitted to us to assert that he could have won the eternal life set before him, perhaps it would be proper to add that the sacramental use of the Tree of Life was the appointed means of his triumph.

5. Concerning the *Tree of Life*, what has been already said amounts to this, namely: that it was in the midst of the garden of Eden—that Adam not only had free access to its fruit, and the clearest intimation of the importance of its use, but all this was introduced with a divine command: that both the form and substance of God's covenant with Adam, involved the habitual, hereditary, perpetual, and covenanted use of the fruit of the Tree of Life, by man.[3] The Scriptures speak with great frequency and distinctness of the Tree of Life. The most remarkable statements concerning it, which throw light upon the subject now under consideration, may be digested under the following heads:

[1] Gen., ii. 17   [2] Gen., ii. 9, 16.   [3] Gen., ii. 8–17.

(*a*) That man considered as a sinner, is absolutely deprived of its use : his moral condition after the fall, and considered with reference to his knowledge of good and evil, being wholly incompatible with its use ; an immortality of sin and misery being the only effect of its use by such creatures.[1]

(*b*) That to the penitent and the righteous divine Wisdom and true Holiness, are as the Tree of Life.[2]

(*c*) That God hath placed Cherubim, and a flaming sword to keep the way of the Tree of Life.[3]　A wonderful proof, that eternal life, no longer attainable by man's obedience, was attainable through God's mercy.[4]

(*d*) That Christ Jesus will give to every victorious saint—to eat of the Tree of Life which is in the midst of the Paradise of God.[5]　Nay this immortal gift, is the first and the foundation of all the immeasurable fruits of endless triumph, which he who hath the keys of death and hell, proclaimed through the beloved Apostle to be the inheritance of " him that overcometh."

(*e*) That in the midst of the street of the New Jerusalem, which is paved with pure gold, transparent as glass ; and on both sides of the river of the water of life, clear as crystal, proceeding out of the Throne of God and of the Lamb ; stands the Tree of Life, bearing twelve manner of fruits, yielding fruit every month, and the leaves of the Tree are for the healing of the Nations.[6]

(*f*) That a large part of the blessedness of those who keep the commandments of God, consists in their right to the Tree of Life and their free and abundant access to it, through those gates each one of which was a separate pearl, into that city built of gold which came down from God out of heaven ; and from which are eternally excluded all the enemies of God.[7]

(*g*) In a word, however our ignorance, stupidity, and depravity, may incline us to treat as unmeaning, insignificant and unworthy of the majesty of God, the symbols of his original dealings with our race, in the way of an express covenant ; it is perfectly manifest from the whole tenor of Scripture, that God himself held the matter in a widely different estimation.　Eternal Life—and good and evil—and God's covenants concerning the whole scope of both ; in one sense—these are mysteries—

---

[1] Gen., iii. 22.　　[2] Prov., iii. 18, xi. 30.　　[3] Gen., iii. 24.
[4] Exod., xxv. 17–22.　　[5] Rev., ii. 7.　　[6] Rev., xxii. 1, 2.　　[7] Rev., xxii. 13–15.

but they are sublime mysteries. And the great current of divine truth, so far from obliterating any vestige by which they can be made more distinct ; heaves up more and more conspicuously as it widens and deepens, even to the end, whatever, from the very beginning, had any permanent connection with the eternal purpose of his will.

6. Concerning the *Tree of Knowledge of Good and Evil,* the direct declarations of the Scriptures have already been, in great part, stated, and may be summarily recapitulated thus : that it like the Tree of Life, stood in the midst of the Garden of Eden : that Adam had continual and free access to it : that the eating of the fruit of it was the only prohibition laid on him : that he was expressly forbidden to eat that fruit : that he was distinctly informed that the result of his disobedience would be utterly fatal : that both the form and substance of the covenant with him would involve all his posterity in the ruin his disobedience would bring on himself : that intimations he could not misunderstand were made to him, that the command to eat of the Tree of Life and the prohibition to eat of the Tree of Knowledge of Good and Evil, though positive precepts, had an infinite relevancy to the very essence of his nature and his destiny : and that the knowledge prohibited to him was incompatible with the exalted form of life he then possessed, and with the still more exalted form of life offered to him by this covenant.[1] The statement of the Scriptures bearing indirectly upon the subject, are nearly innumerable ; some of which will be examined. In the mean time we must observe that the fall of man brought the whole matter into a concrete form, in which the subject was to be dealt with practically, and in which all merely didactic expositions were superseded by the fearful reality, as it stood palpably before the universe. It is this which causes the difference of treatment observable in the Scriptures, after the fall of man, of the question of the Tree of Life and that of the Tree of Knowledge. The one has accomplished the ruin to which it was competent : and that ruin is before our eyes. The other remains as a type of the blessedness we have forfeited, and will recover through a better covenant and a more glorious head.

7. We are in the habit of connecting the idea of a Sacrament with the Covenant of Grace, chiefly if not exclusively. There is

[1] Gen., ii. 8–17.

no reason in the nature of the case, and none is intimated in the Scriptures, why every Covenant of God with man, should not be equally fit to be held forth in sacred ordinances, which should be signs and seals of it. I do not see that the Sabbath day, or the garden of Eden which some have considered Sacraments of the Covenant of Works, can be so accepted. The former as I have shown in another place, did not appertain to the Covenant of Works—but to the primeval consecration of man himself to God, and to that universal and immutable law of his being which is the basis of all religion ; God by a singular providential act anterior to the Covenant of Works, having instituted this sacred and perpetual ordinance as expressive at once of man's nature and obligations, and of God's nature, works, and dominion. In like manner the Garden of Eden, whether considered as the habitation of man, the scene of his trial and fall, or a type of the New Jerusalem, or of heaven itself ; cannot be considered a Sacrament. The case is different with the *Tree of Life* and the *Tree of Knowledge.* Both of them—the former perhaps somewhat more obviously than the latter—may be considered both signs and seals of the Covenant of Works, and therefore Sacraments. They were both perpetual admonitions and remembrancers of the probation our first parents were passing through, and of the Life and Death that waited on the issue. One of them was a means of strength, by the participation of it : similar to the use of the Sacrament of the Passover or the Lord's Supper. The other by the prohibition of it, the sight of it, and the refusal of it, a means of strength also : unlike any other known Sacrament, but yet most appropriate to the peculiar covenant—to which it appertains. Taken together, they taught and enforced precisely the essence of the truth of which they were signs and seals ; and this is the very essence of a proper sacrament. They taught that there were two conditions to which man was liable : one, namely, of present blessedness and glory, capable of being unspeakably augmented : the other of mixed good and evil, in which the evil would gain against the good forever, and which could end, if left to itself, only in the eternal ruin of the whole race. They taught and enforced, moreover, that man was precisely then passing through the ordeal which was to decide between these two estates : and their united force was, a ceaseless urgency that he should know and possess the one, and that he should not seek to know and make trial of the other, but should shun and reject it. The inward desire for the one state, and the inward repugnance to the other state—were as near as could be, answerable to these outward signs.

8. It remains to examine more carefully the sanctions annexed to this covenant : the penalty if it should be broken—the reward if it should be kept. In general it is true, that while no legal dispensation can exist, or be conceived of without adequate penalties for transgression, on the other hand it does not appertain to such dispensations to bestow upon obedience any other reward than such as appertains to the obedience itself. All law in its own nature, simply approves, acquits, applauds the righteous ; for it is a rule of rectitude prescribing and defining that which is of itself right—duty, and which all men were already morally obliged to do ; or where it goes further than this, it is a rule of positive obligation, prescribing such things, indifferent in their moral nature, as those who have the right to prescribe, judge to be of themselves, advantageous. Whatever advantage can exist or result in such cases, is in the obedience itself, and neither is nor can be more than its own natural fruit ; that is, it is not properly of the nature of a reward. On the other hand, transgression is, in its own nature, not only the violation of duty, but the perpetration of wrong ; and therefore every transgressor not only deserves punishment, but the possibility of the continuance of any dispensation of law, depends on its preventing or redressing transgression. If Adam had never lost his primeval condition, but had kept exactly every law of his nature, his nature and his condition would nevertheless have remained forever as they were at first : but if he had violated any law of his nature, there was no possibility of his escaping the consequences of that violation : and these consequences would have been strictly penal, just so far as they were unalterably connected with the transgression, whether naturally or by some positive law of God. It seems, therefore, altogether impossible that the Covenant of Works should have been made with Adam, if it did not contemplate some favorable change in his previous condition : some result to which no merely legal dispensation was adequate. No greater penalty could exist than the one affixed by God to this Covenant, so that in that respect, nothing was gained by Adam. On the other hand, if no positive reward in case of continued

obedience had been added to the natural fruit of the obedience itself, in this respect also, Adam could gain nothing. But in fact, this covenant was an act of infinite goodness and mercy, and not a nugatory, much less a harsh dealing of God with the creature whom he had already so greatly honored and blessed. We are therefore to seek in both sanctions of the covenant, both in its reward promised and its penalty threatened, and especially in the former, for evidences of God's gracious intentions, similar to those we have seen pervade every other part of this wonderful transaction.

9. I have already pointed out, in the commencement of this chapter, the general nature of the change produced upon the primeval state of man, by the Covenant of Works. The promises annexed to that covenant, by way of reward for the obedience that should fulfil it on the part of Adam—are less insisted on in the Scriptures than the nature of the penalty annexed to its breach. And the reason is most obvious. Whatever those promises could have produced, became impossible by the fall of man ; and besides more than they could have secured for us, is now secured in Christ : while the penalty has actually been incurred by man, and it imports us all, as we value our souls, to understand it and the way of escaping it. Still those promises were transcendently great. The very essence of the Covenant was, that it was a Covenant of Life—the very sign and seal of which was the Tree of Life, of which the earliest and the latest pages of God's Word are alike full, now in the beginning of time as a Sacrament in Eden—and again in the end of time as an infinite truth in Paradise.[1] But we know expressly and in many ways of divine statement—amongst the rest by the very penalty of this Covenant, that *death* had no place in the world before the fall of man.[2] A divine Covenant of *Life,* therefore with a glorious being, as yet not subject to death ; a Covenant whose very object was to remove all risk of lapse—and to advance still higher the glory and blessedness of the creature ; is, in a most exalted sense, a Covenant of promise. This therefore was the sanction of the Covenant, on that side, namely : the perpetual confirmation of Adam and his whole race, in their primeval state of innocence and perfection, the augmentation and eternal dura-

---

[1] Lev., xviii. 5; Gal., iii. 12.   [2] Gen., ii. 17; Rom., v. 12.

tion of this glory and blessedness.[1]   Nothing can give us a clearer idea of the infinite glory of the Covenant of Grace, and of the infinite love which prompted it—than that it secures to fallen man a higher estate, than was thus put in the reach of man before he fell.

10. What the penalty annexed to the breach of the Covenant of Works was intended to mean, and who were designed to be embraced by it, might be said not to admit of any doubt, if it were not for the fierce and reiterated assaults which have been made upon this portion of the dealings of God with his creatures. In the day that thou eatest thereof, thou shalt surely die.[2] Nothing could be more explicit than this.   Nor is it less so, when we are told, that death entered into the world by sin, and has passed upon all because all are sinners : and that the sin thus entering into the world was an act of disobedience of one man, and that man Adam.[3]   Nay, the form of the penalty in its first utterance, has been confirmed not only by all Scripture, but by the whole sum of human experience, and by the intimate consciousness of every human being—*Dying thou shalt die.* As soon as you eat the forbidden fruit you will cease to be the head of a living, and become the head of a dying race.   As if he had said, your soul and body shall separate, which is *temporal* death :[4] your soul and body shall both be separated from the favor of God during this life, which is *spiritual* death :[5] your whole man, soul and body, shall be eternally banished from God's heavenly presence and glory, and have their part in the lake which burneth with fire and brimstone, which is the *second* death.[6]   And is it not so ?   Is not our race a dying race ?   Does not every human heart know that it is a sinful race ?   And are not our just and terrible apprehensions of the retributions of eternity, the testimony of nature herself to the perdition of ungodly men ?   Nor is it possible for any thing to give us a higher conception than such a penal sanction as this annexed to the covenant does, of the desire of God to deter, as before to persuade man from its violation, and of the terrible guilt of that violation, and of the fearful nature of the catastrophe it would produce. I have said before, that no penalty could be greater than this ; and I have added, that we must, nevertheless, find in this very

---

[1] Mat., xix. 16, 17 xxii. 32; Luke, x. 25 ; Rom., viii. 3.   [2] Gen., ii. 7.
[3] Rom., v. 12–19.   [4] Gen., xxv. 11   [5] Luke, i. 79.   [6] Rev., xxi. 8.

penalty some proof of God's beneficent intentions toward man in this very covenant. The same apparent paradox confronts us in a still higher degree in the aggravation of the ruin of the impenitent by reason of their rejection of Jesus Christ. These are the two highest manifestations of the solicitude of God for the advancement of man; and they are attended by the two highest proofs of his abhorrence of sin. In both instances, while we tremble at the severity of God, we perceive that any other line of conduct on his part would not be an evidence of love to us, but of indifference to his own glory. We have yet learned but little of God, or of the only foundation of our own blessedness, until we comprehend that his refusal to look upon sin with the least allowance, is precisely the point in which the penitent and believing heart the most earnestly desires conformity unto him. It is not immunity in sin, it is deliverance from sin, that either covenant proposed, or any child of God ever desired. The covenant of works would have prevented our ruin; the covenant of grace would retrieve it. In both instances sin is the dangerous, the hateful, the fatal thing. The solution was against us in Eden, for us at Calvary. In both instances the proof of God's hatred toward sin augmented the proof of his love for us.

III.—1. It is noteworthy, that notwithstanding the important part played by Eve in the sequel, the covenant of works was not made with her; but she, like all the rest of the human race, was embraced in it representatively—a very pregnant fact, resting, perhaps, in part upon her relation of permanent dependence upon Adam, and chiefly upon her being really, though in a peculiar way, as completely a part of himself as his descendants were. In like manner it is to be observed, that both before the covenant and under it, there was the distinct recognition and the outward application to Adam, of all three of those great classes of duty which appertain to man in every possible condition of mortal existence, and which unitedly embrace every duty obligatory upon him in this life. What we owe to God, what we owe to our neighbor, and what we owe to ourselves, embraces every thing. The sanctification of the Sabbath day, the institution of marriage, and the command to dress and keep the garden of Eden, were stated, outward, and revealed instances in all these great classes, each of supreme importance in its class. These duties, like the moral law, which is the eternal rule of rectitude, are liable, no doubt, to various modifications under the perpetual course of divine providence, and the interminable vicissitudes of all things. But the moral law itself, and the principle of duty to God, to our neighbor, and to ourself are both immutable. They preceded the Covenant of Works; they would have survived if that covenant had been executed, as they have survived its breach; and so far from being discharged by the Covenant of Grace, they not only receive their fullest realization by means of it, but the great Apostle of the Gentiles protests that faith establishes the Law, and that it would be a fatal objection to faith if the Law was made void through it.[1]

2. The whole idea of the Covenant of Works proceeds on the assumption that man in his original condition, though perfect, was fallible: just as the whole conception of the Covenant of Grace proceeds on the assumption that man, though fallen and depraved, is capable of being restored. The fallibility of the most perfect dependent creature, is an absolute condition of its existence. If it were infallible it would be immutable; and being immutable, it must necessarily be eternal; and if eternal, it can neither be created nor dependent. Moreover, if it is infallible it must be without any limitation of any attribute, whether in the number or the perfection of its attributes; but a being with an infinite number of infinite attributes, is an infinite being. And again, to be infallible, it must be absolutely perfect; but absolute perfection is the negation of dependence and creation, as well as of fallibility. And so on through all the phases of existence. As far as we can understand, the alternative offered to God—was the creation of dependent and fallible creatures, or no creation at all: and after their creation, a covenant answerable to their created nature, or no covenant at all: and after their fall, a recovery answerable to their fallen nature, or no recovery at all.

3. An infinite God might, in any contingency, give to any fallible creature sufficient aid, of whatever kind, to keep it in its actual estate. But this is a keeping founded on the aid of God, and not on the infallibility of the creature. It is an aid, moreover, founded on the idea of *Grace*—not on the idea of law, of trial, of reward, or even of conditional promise. And thus even the final perseverance and consequent salvation of the saints,

<hr>

[1] Rom., iii. 31.

does not depend at all upon their infallibility, much less upon their free will : but it depends upon the efficacy of the work of Christ—the abiding of the Spirit of God within them—the nature of the Covenant of Grace—and the immutability of God's eternal decree. There is, however, something more as to the intimate cause of this eternal steadfastness of the redeemed, which can only be glanced at here, as illustrative of the general question of the fallibility of dependent creatures—and the guarding against it only through grace. We are told that as Christ's brethren were partakers of flesh and blood, and so liable to death, and to the temptation of him who had the power of death— Christ himself became incarnate, that through death he might destroy the Devil and deliver the children of God.[1] When the destruction of Satan is fully consummated, all fallible creatures will, therefore, be delivered from such temptation as destroyed Adam, and has kept his race in bondage. To this it is added, that they who hold the beginning of their confidence steadfast to the end, are made partakers of Christ :[2] and still further, that amongst the exceeding great and precious promises which are given to us through our Lord and Saviour Jesus Christ, one of the chief is, that having escaped the corruption that is in the world through lust, we should be partakers of the divine nature:[3] and finally, that being changed from glory to glory, we shall attain to the image of the Lord the Spirit, and to the liberty in which he abides.[4] So that besides eternal freedom from temptation, there will be an exaltation passing beyond the possession of God's image into the possession of God's nature ; and, therefore, no more possibility of lapse. To the present purpose it is of no consequence, whether we take this in its simple and sublime verity, as I incline to do, or take it merely as expressive of our infinite security through grace. Either way, it suffices to illustrate the wide difference between a fallible creature under the Covenant of Works, and a fallible creature under the Covenant of Grace ; and to explain how Adam, tempted by Satan, and tried under a Covenant of Works, was necessarily in fearful peril ; and yet how that specific trial diminished the peril and increased the reward of a universal and perpetual trial, without any positive covenant at all.

4. The absolute dominion of God over man, and the complete

<hr>

[1] Heb., ii. 14, 15.   [2] Heb., iii. 14.   [3] 2 Peter, i. 1–4.   [4] 2 Cor., iii. 17, 18.

dependence of man on God, are fundamental truths of all religion, whether natural or revealed, whether practical or speculative. The inherent poison of every form of religious error, whether it be manifested in life or in doctrine—when stated in its most general form, is the rejection, in one way or other, of this dominion of God over man ; or this dependence of man on God. The Covenant of Works, considered in its widest sense, is the complete recognition and direct application of both of these fundamental truths. Even in the narrowest view that can be taken of it, it still proceeds upon both of them, and applies them both to a particular divine constitution, designed to determine practically and in the first instance, the condition of the human race ; and to exhibit clearly the result of these two great truths, when applied to a perfect but fallible creature placed under certain specified conditions. The Covenant of Grace applies the same test to the same creature—placed under conditions fatally modified by the breach of the previous covenant, and under a divine constitution answerable to that changed condition. It is still the absolute dominion of God—the complete dependence of man. Why was the second result of the combined application of divine sovereignty and human dependence to a condition so much worse than the first—as full of blessedness as the other was of misery ? Whatever answer to that question will solve the difficulty, will at the same time exalt to the highest pitch, both of the truths I am asserting. The whole difference lies absolutely in divine grace.

5. From the very constitution of our minds we are prone to scrutinize the conduct, even of our Creator, and to determine for ourselves, and according to such light as we have, all things whatsoever. If this is done with sincerity and sobriety, the issue should always be to the honor of God and the comfort of our souls. Of all that God has done, nothing perhaps is more worthy to be thoroughly scrutinized by us than his creation of man, and his dealings with him in his primeval estate, and through the Covenant of Works : for without these things, what are all things to us ? In these attempts we encounter, of course, questions far out of the reach of our intelligence ; other questions abstruse to the last degree, but yet not utterly closed against patient thought ; other questions boundless in their pregnancy, but still rich in their wonderful disclosures. Sitting

down at the feet of Jesus Christ, with the divine word in our hands, and the divine Spirit in our hearts, we can never rise up without feeling our spirit tranquillized by whatever search into these wonderful transactions. Confining this suggestion for the present, to the special subject of this chapter, this much seems certain, that in whatever respect the primeval condition of man, exalted as that was, can be considered as having been modified by means of the Covenant of Works; it was to the advantage of the human race and to the praise of the goodness of God. In illustration of which, let it be considered :

(*a*) That by means of this covenant this much would necessarily be gained, that a mixed condition of the human race would be assuredly avoided ; a possible condition analogous to that of Angels and Devils living together, rendered impossible. Let the trial of Adam issue as it might, the unity of the race would be preserved ; to its infinite blessedness if he stood ; and even if he fell, to its unspeakable advantage in this, that it would still be in a position to receive as a whole, what none could otherwise receive at all, namely, whatever ulterior overtures of mercy, the infinite resources of divine beneficence might suggest.

(*b*) This further and immense advantage was obtained—that as the covenant was made with Adam, and had reference to specific proofs of his obedience—the probation of the race became personal to one man, instead of universal to all men— specific of certain acts of his, instead of perpetual of all acts of all men ; temporary and definite, instead of endless and indefinite. Add to which, whatever additional strength could be imparted to a pure and great soul, thus situated, by every just and exalted motive drawn from a sense of duty to his own innumerable posterity through endless ages, thus added to the duty already binding on him both to God and to himself.

(*c*) Other and conclusive facts made this probation of the race in Adam more favorable to it, than any other imaginable probation of it could be. He had been personally created by God—created in a state of perfection—and in the complete maturity of all his faculties. He personally knew God. He had every advantage and help which it was possible any creature similar to himself ever could have, and some which none ever could possess ; he escaped innumerable occasions of temptation and causes of weakness to which every future man would be exposed.

(*d*) One trial, by one precisely similar series of acts ; directed to a single object ; under one single command, and that toward a duty we cannot conceive to have been difficult ; one single prohibition, and that directed against a sensuous act most of all under the control of the will : all surrounding circumstances as favorable as they ever could be to any similar attempt ! If the Scriptures had omitted to state the particular seduction under which Adam fell, how could we imagine his failure to be possible ?

(*e*) With the perfect knowledge beforehand of the trial and the risk—the danger and the reward : with the image of God full upon him, and the law of God written in his heart ; there can be no doubt that if he failed, it was not in the nature of the case possible for any one to succeed who was inferior to him, nor probable that any one not superior to him could do so. But of his race none could be superior to him ; while, as has been shown, none could be, in all respects, equal to him, for this great service. Yet if he had succeeded, all his race would have reaped all the blessings and benefits of his obedience.

(*f*) It seems to me that we are left without any ground on which to doubt or hesitate, unless we deem it right to repine that God created our race at all, or that having created them, he had purposes of infinite beneficence toward them. If our objection is, that he created our race fallible ; the answer is that an infallible creature is as really a contradiction in terms as an uncreated creature. If it be that we object to the probation of a fallible creature ; the answer is again this is a contradiction in terms, because to be fallible is to be on probation. If it be that we object to the particular probation ordained by God in the covenant of works ; the answer is again, this is a contradiction in terms, because while it admits the general necessity of *a* probation, by excepting to the particular probation, it retracts the admission in which the exception itself rests ; since the particular probation excepted to, is of all that can be imagined the very best for him that is to be tried. Alas ! what hurts us is, not that we were tried—but that we failed.

6. The immutability of God, and by consequence the immutability of the sum of the True and Good, and therefore the immutability of the ultimate elements of Religion, necessarily reproduces under every form which true Religion can put on, those great principles which are involved in its very nature. This

necessity is no less obvious on the side of our own nature, which being in all its estates and under all its mutations, essentially the same nature, can never escape in one condition any immutable principle or truth, which stood related to its essence in any other condition. Our condition as fallible creatures, our condition as sinful creatures, our condition as regenerate creatures, our condition as glorified creatures, and I might add our condition as finally lost creatures, is each time peculiar ; but we are essentially the same creatures through all conditions. Illustrating at present the immense truth involved herein, by contemplating only so much of our destiny as is involved in our primeval estate, in the covenant of works, and in the development, until now, of the covenant of grace ; we have seen continually and especially in this and in the preceding chapter, how numerous and how controlling are the ways in which it makes itself manifest. The perpetuity of the principle of duty—the immutability of the moral law, the unalterable necessity of obedience —the eternal force of man's primeval consecration to God, and of the obligation to render a corresponding outward worship— the illimitable sovereignty of God over man—the unavoidable dependence of man on God—the possession of the image of God by man as the one condition of his being rational, moral, and immortal, the one condition of his primeval innocence, his present susceptibility of restoration, and his capacity to be forever glorified—the utter impossibility of created perfection that shall be absolute and infallible, short of a union with God so close as to justify the Scriptures in calling it a partaking of the divine nature : these are among the eternal and immutable realities which are wholly irrespective of the form which true religion may put on—but which exist equally and unavoidably under all its forms as primitive laws or elements of its very essence. It is, of course, very evident that the successive forms which Religion may put on, may educe additional principles, not manifest before ; or even new principles peculiar to these forms ; and these whether of one or the other sort, may be of the most transcendent importance, and may become thenceforward not only immutable but paramount. As, for example, the revelation and establishment of the principle of a *positive covenant* between God and man, as the basis of all special mercy. I will add two specifications to those already stated generally ; one of them connected with the example just cited, the other with both classes of truths ; both of them having the highest importance.

(*a*) The principle of a positive Covenant carried with it the principle of Representation—Headship : and that involved the principle of substitution—Imputation. Adam, as the covenanted head of his race, represented the race, was substituted in the probation, for the race. Inevitably, therefore, his acts involved the race ; that is, the race would be treated precisely as if every member of it had done, personally, exactly what they did representatively. The merit of Adam's obedience—the demerit of his transgression, would be imputed to them as much as to him : and this imputation would be grounded, not on any vague generality, nor on any arbitrary constitution ; but upon the very nature of the covenant itself, and upon the very wisdom, and goodness, and reason, wnich dictated the covenant. This does not express the whole case ; because Adam was, in addition, the progenitor of the whole race. As such, his acts were not imputed, but his nature was inherited : which completes the case. He was the root of the race. Now this is precisely analogous to what occurs under the covenant of grace. Christ is the Head, the Representative of the Redeemed : the merit of his obedience and sacrifice—which was obedience unto death—is imputed to them, precisely because it was rendered in their stead, that is, it was vicarious. And, moreover, every one of them inherits through Christ, and by a new birth, a new life—a renewed nature : which, as before, completes the case : and as before, in the very nature of the covenant. Adam, under the Covenant of Works, is the Federal and Natural Head of all who are embraced in that Covenant. Christ, under the Covenant of Grace, is the Federal and Supernatural Head of all who are embraced in that Covenant. So exact is the analogy, and so immutable is the principle, that the two applications of it in the two covenants, mutually restrain each other, if I may so speak. For the unrestricted finality of Adam's work would have been the utter perdition of the whole race : that of Christ's work its total restoration. In so far as Christ's work actually saves any body—the work of Adam is actually repaired : and in so far as Adam's work causes or ends in the destruction of any body—Christ's Salvation lacks that much of being actually universal.[1]

<hr>

[1] Rom., v. *passim.*

(*b*) The great principle on which human nature still insists on saving itself, is precisely the one on which human nature stood in its primitive estate : *Do and Live.* It is the same principle which in a new form was tested by Adam, under the Covenant of Works : *Do that others may Live.* It is the same principle which in its last form Christ fully wrought out : *Do for sinners, that they may Live.* The application of the principle in its most difficult form, by Christ, was complete and triumphant. Its application in its second form, by Adam, was a total failure. Its application, in its first form, by man in his primeval estate, was superseded by the publication of the Covenant of Works : which was a great and merciful modification of it. Its application in that first form, now by sinful men, is a mere expression on the one side, of their natural conviction that man cannot be saved, and should not be saved, in sin ; and on the other side, of their stupid and deadly unbelief. Taken altogether, we have the testimony of human nature itself, under all its manifestations, and we have the testimony of God under every form in which he has dealt with man, that the principle upon which the Covenant of Works was based, was a merciful form of the very principle upon which the universe itself is sustained, and which neither God nor man can forego, while the universe endures. A fitness for God's favor must exist to justify the continuance of that favor. The fall of man brought an utterly ruined world, and that immutable principle, face to face. The solution of the tremendous problem was—Christ Crucified !

CHAPTER XXXII.

ORIGIN OF EVIL: BREACH OF THE COVENANT OF WORKS: FALL OF
MAN: RUIN OF THE HUMAN RACE.

I. 1. The relations of the questions of the origin of Evil and the manner of its occurrence, to Philosophy and to Theology.—2. Method of their solution.—3. The Logical solution clear but conditional.—II. 1. These questions, as stated and solved by the Apostle Paul.—2. The remedy as stated by him, side by side with their solution.—3. As questions of Reason, of Fact, and of Revelation, they are solved by the Fall of Adam.—4. The connection of the human race with Adam, in that Catastrophe. He was its natural Progenitor.—5. He was its Covenanted, Federal Head.—6. This principle of Representation illustrated in Redemption.—III. 1. Detailed Analysis of the Facts attending the Fall of Man, as they are stated by Moses, and accepted throughout the Scriptures.—2. State of mind of Satan, and of our first Parents, proximate to the Fall.—3. The outward act—and its immediate Effects.—4. The relation of this Event and its consequences, to the eternal Counsel and Purpose of God.—5. Intimate cause of Adam's first sin.—6. The effects of the Fall upon the question of duty, and the nature and measure of accountability.—IV. 1. Detailed Analysis of the personal Facts, and personal Effects upon our First Parents, immediately consequent on their Fall.—2. The sentence pronounced by God, upon Satan, upon the Earth, and upon Adam and Eve.—3. Appreciation of that sentence, and of the new condition of man under it.—4. The passing over of a fallible nature from Perfection to Depravity. Original Sin: (*a.*) The Guilt of Adam's First sin: (*b.*) Want of Original Righteousness: (*c.*) Corruption of our whole Nature.—5. Distinction between the strictly Penal, and the merely Incidental Results of the Fall.—6. Under the curse of God, but with his promise of Deliverance.

I.—1. THE questions which we encounter at this point give rise to some of the most disputed problems of Theology, as well as some of the most difficult points in Philosophy; and yet the facts connected with them are as distinctly stated in the Scriptures as any other connected with the nature or the history of man; and are as intelligible as any others that are fundamental in the scheme of his existence or destiny. The existence of evil, either moral or physical, as a question of Philosophy, may be altogether inscrutable, but as a question of fact there can be no rational difference of opinion. In like manner the mode of its occurrence, and even the mode of its propagation, may be wholly incapable of determination by us when left to ourselves ; or various conceivable modes may be suggested, alike possible in point of reason, and alike defective in proof. But as soon as that divine interposition is allowed which is the fundamental principle of Revealed Religion, and the whole scope of which is recorded in the Scriptures, then both questions, namely, the existence of evil and the manner of its occurrence, though they must still occupy their place in the domain of Philosophy, become fundamental in Revealed Theology.

2. Why evil should be allowed—and how—are questions precisely similar to the questions, why should there be any creation—and how ? They are all to be solved only, and precisely in the same manner—namely by God himself—upon the supposition that God has interposed and made a Revelation. No doubt, if in solving them, the reason or the conscience of man should be outraged, or the established facts of the universe should be disallowed : a powerful and just presumption would arise that the solution was not of God, and that the record which contained it was not divine. But this goes to the question of a divine interposition and a divine record of it : not to the question whether such a record ought to solve, or does in fact solve such mysteries. In like manner—though men see fit to dispute concerning the true significance of the actual solutions given by God : this is no more than they see fit to do concerning every question great and small, whether of Natural or Revealed Religion—or indeed of every thing else, in very near proportion to their ignorance and presumption.

3. We can readily understand, that God in determining whether he would create a universe or not, would decide according as one course or the other would be most pleasing to himself ; and that this would depend upon which course would result most to his own glory. If he should create—we can easily see that he would select such a universe as would most perfectly answer the ends he had in view : and that these ends, if they were many, could not contradict and defeat each other : and that the rest must necessarily bend before the sufficient and chief end. Touching the matters now before us we may add, that it is plain enough his infinite purity would lead him to exclude all sin--and his infinite goodness to exclude all misery from the

universe, to the whole extent this could be done consistently
with his main and sufficient end.　And seeing we know so little
of God compared with infinite knowledge—so few of his perfections compared with their infinite number—and so little of each
one of them compared with its infinite scope ; we may make our
very ignorance a just basis of confidence.　Because if what we
do know makes it certain that he would act in a particular way
—the threefold infinite beyond our reach immeasurably exalts
the certainty, that if all were known, our ground of confidence
would be immeasurably increased.　But now we reach the end.
For imagine it to be possible that the very existence of sin and
misery, may tend in the very highest degree, to promote the very
main and sufficient end of any creation at all—namely the declarative glory of God in making himself known to the universe :
then we are obliged to cross our track abruptly, for in that case
we cannot avoid seeing, that sin and misery are logically certain
in a created universe.　And when we see in fact, that sin and
misery are in the Universe—and see further that the chief part
of the certain knowledge we have of God comes to us through
the plan of salvation—which never had existed if sin and misery had not existed ; we are not exactly in a position to assert,
that it is impossible for the case to arise, upon which the logical
certainty of their existence occurs.　Our best way is, having
reached our own poor limit—to stand reverently before God, and
hear what he is pleased to say.

II.—1. He who was not a whit behind the chiefest of the
Apostles has expounded to us, after his manner, these great
mysteries.　He has done it expressly, and in the very connection
which of all others would make them most clear and most impressive.　He has placed the origin of evil, and its cure—side by
side—and explained both together.　The fall and the recovery
of man are held up together to our view, and are made to illustrate each other.　The headship of Adam and the headship of
Christ, are set face to face, and a parallel is run between them.[1]
The whole of both cases may be intelligibly stated in a few sentences.

(a) Sin entered into the world by Adam ; and death came
by sin.[2]

(b) This was the result of one single offence ; and the par-

---

[1] Rom., v. 12–19.　　　　　　　　　[2] Rom., v. 12.

ticular nature of that offence was, that it was an act of disobedience.[1]

(*c*) The death which came by sin passed upon all men, and this in a twofold sense ; they not only actually die in him,[2] but they do so because they sinned in him.[3]

(*d*) If there could be any doubt of these facts or of the principles upon which they rest, the sum of the facts of man's being and God's government over him, would put them beyond question.[4]

2. Now the cure of sin, the recovery of man, the final triumph of grace, all proceed on these same principles. Only in this case there is an abounding power and glory—an abounding application of the remedy for sin ; by means of which, not only is the restoration of man to be made complete, but he will be exalted far beyond what he could have attained, if he had never fallen: and God's declarative glory will far exceed what it would have been, if sin had never entered into the world. Here as before, a few sentences may make the matter intelligible :

(*a*) The first man, who was only a living soul, was the figure of him that was to come :[5] even the last Adam, who was a quickening Spirit, and the Lord from heaven.[6]

(*b*) So complete a figure was the former of the latter, that as soon as we comprehend what part the one had in our ruin, we can comprehend the part the other has in our recovery. And if we comprehend the latter best, we may by it comprehend the former.[7]

(*c*) The abounding fulness and power of the latter over the former, still scrupulously respected the exact analogy between the two cases. The ruin was by means of a single act of disobedience : the recovery by means of a universal obedience and an infinite sacrifice. The ruin was propagated by means of natural generation ; the recovery is consummated by means of a supernatural regeneration. Where sin abounded, grace shall much more abound : where death reigned through sin, eternal life shall reign, through righteousness, by grace.[8]

3. Such is the explanation given by the Apostle Paul of the entrance of Evil into our world, of the ruin of our race thereby

---

[1] Rom., v. 17–19.   [2] 1 Cor., xv. 21, 22.   [3] Rom., v. 12.
[4] Rom., v. 12–19; 1 Cor., **xv.** 21, 22, 44–49.   [5] Rom., v. 14.
[6] 1 Cor., xv. 45–17.   [7] 1 Cor., xv. 48, 49.   [8] Rom., v. 15–19.

and of the result of the whole. Side by side with this, is his account of the recovery of man. The covenant made by God with man, which has been carefully explained, was broken by a direct act of disobedience, knowingly transgressing the only positive prohibition which the Creator imposed on the creature. That act was a formal renunciation of the authority of God; a deliberate incurring of the threatened penalty ; a wilful surrender of the promised reward. So far as Adam was personally concerned, nothing can be more obvious than the grounds of his condemnation. Supposing him to be bound in any way to God, whether as his Creator, his Ruler, or his Saviour, it is not possible for us to imagine a state of case, in which it could be more simply and precisely shown, that transgression had fundamentally violated and changed the relations between God and man. For the nature of that violation and change, considered as a question of mere reason, we must look into the nature of the case itself ; considered as a question of fact, we must look into its results as exhibited in the actual state of man without the Gospel ; considered as a question of Revelation we must look to the penalty affixed to the prohibition violated, as that penalty is expounded in the Scriptures.

4. I have shown in the previous chapter, when expressly considering the Covenant of Works, that the whole family of man was necessarily and was expressly embraced in its stipulations— and must, as the case might be, receive its reward, or incur its penalty. Treating now of the penalty alone, it may be proper, before proceeding to the statement of the exact manner in which it was incurred by Adam, to point out precisely the grounds upon which, under the case as it stood, that penalty must embrace all his ordinary posterity in the same ruin which overtook him. There are two great facts, both of them clear and transcendent, which unitedly control the case. The *first* is, that Adam was the natural head and common progenitor of his race. The human family is not only of one blood, as has been proved in another place, but the blood of Adam is that one blood. The whole Scriptures are subverted, and human life is the grossest of all enigmas, if this be not true. If it be true, nothing is more inevitable than that whatever change may have been produced on the whole nature of Adam by his Fall—of which I shall speak presently—before the existence of any of his issue, must

have been propagated through all succeeding generations. If there is any thing perfectly assured to us, it is the steadfastness of the order of nature, in the perpetual reproduction of all things after their own kind. If the fall produced no change on the nature of Adam, it could produce none on the nature of his descendants. If it did produce any change upon his nature, it was his nature thus changed, and not the form of his nature before his fall, which his posterity must inherit. If it be demanded, why then does it not occur that believers should propagate a believing offspring? the answer is clear and various. (1) They are neither the original, the common, the exclusive, nor the representative head of their issue; they are but a part of a common race. (2) Regeneration is wholly a moral change—and in that sense a partial change of human nature: it is in no degree whatever, a physical change: the physical change analogous to regeneration, takes place at the resurrection of the just: in this life regeneration leaves out entirely that part of man's nature by which the race is propagated. (3) The moral change produced on man's nature is not, in this life, absolute; the remains of indwelling sin continue in it, and that in a form so virulent, that every believer would relapse, if God's Spirit were taken from him. (4) In effect, to demand that a believer—should by natural generation propagate believers, is to demand that the influences of the Holy Ghost should be propagated by natural generation through a being whose moral nature is imperfectly sanctified, and whose physical nature is utterly depraved; which is both absurd and impious.

5. The *Second* of the two great facts alluded to is, that Adam was the Federal, the Representative, the Covenanted head of his race, as well as its natural head. That this was his position in his trial and his fall, is the explicit testimony of the word of God, and the unavoidable effect and direct purpose of the Covenant of Works—as has been abundantly shown. It is his first transgression only, with which his race has this connection. For that sin terminated his trial, involved his fall, changed his nature, introduced death into the world, and rendered Adam incapable of any further representation of his race in a Covenant of Life, and incapable of any Covenant with God, upon the condition of obedience. The covenanted headship of Adam, has been already shown, in another place, to have been every way advan-

tageous to his race, in its great trial; advantageous if he succeeded, advantageous even if he fell: securing all things—or if
all were lost, securing the best possible result compatible with
such a loss, and demonstrating at the same time that no other
form of trial of the race, or any member of it, would have been
more fortunate. This, it may be alleged, is simply admitting
that a fallible race must fall, if strictly tried. What then? I
know of no ground on which the contrary can be asserted. An
infinite series of events all terminating in the same way, out of
two equally possible ways, is absurd: and the first fall, is ruin.
But a fallible being may as readily fall as not fall each time he
is tried: that he fell the *first* time, only showed the strength of
the certainty that he must fall sometime, if his trial goes on. If
it is answered, that God ought not to create fallible beings, this
is only to say that he ought not to create any beings at all: for
as has been shown, an infallible created being is a contradiction
in terms. If it is said, God should not put a fallible being on
trial, this is merely to say that God should not create him; for
he cannot exist and act, without being on trial—until his trial is
passed. If it is said, God should not make a positive covenant
with a fallible being, this is merely to refuse such aid as God
may give him by reducing the difficulties of probation, diminishing the evils of failure, and increasing the motives to success.
If it is said, that God ought to help him at his need, this is
merely to confess that, virtually, he is already fallen, and only
stands by grace, which is passing out of the principles of a fallible, into the principles of a fallen state. If it is said, God had
better create him a sinner at once, this is absurd: for God
neither is, nor can be, the immediate author of that which is the
opposite of himself, the immediate creator of that which is hateful to himself, the immediate former of sin. In fine, we are unable to conceive of the direct creation of either an infallible, or a
sinful being: a perfect but fallible being, is the only kind of rational and moral being whose creation appears to be possible:
certainly the only kind that ever was created. The creation
and fall of a perfect, but fallible being, is the only conceivable
way in which a sinful being can be originally produced; and the
two principles of natural and covenanted headship united, furnish the only imaginable solution of the actual posture of the
human race. I may add that, logically, the Covenant of Grace

is not only a nullity, but an impossibility, except as the sequence, in thought, of the broken Covenant of Works.

6. The principle of Representation, therefore, completes the explication of the whole case, which, without it, is insoluble in many of its aspects. It is clearly stated in the Scriptures, and in one form or other pervades the universe. Without it, not merely the progress, but the efficient existence of human society, is impossible. So that we are hardly in a position to find fault with its application in a case where that application was altogether inevitable, and might be unspeakably advantageous, while it could not possibly increase our danger, or augment the evils of failure. Still, however, if we demand further satisfaction, we have only to turn our eyes to Calvary, and behold the Sacrifice of Christ in the room and stead of his people. This was the repetition in a form transcendently gracious of that same principle of Representation. The issue of its first application in its ordinary form was our ruin, through the first Adam, under the Covenant of Works: the issue of the second great and gracious application is, endless glory, through the second Adam under the Covenant of Grace. He who has said—as by one man's disobedience many were made sinners, has added in the same breath —so by the obedience of one shall many be made righteous.[1] To reject the principle, or to deny the record of our death in Adam, is at the same time to reject the principle, and to deny the record of our life in Christ.[2]

III.—1. Going back now to the original record of the case whose explication in the New Testament has been carefully considered—we find the statement of the Fall of Man made in the earliest pages of the Old Testament, to embrace the following leading facts:

(*a*) The original suggestion of disobedience to God, and the first temptation to it, came from one of God's creatures of a different race from man, called in connection with this transaction, the Serpent:[3] and called in other portions of the Scriptures— the Great Dragon—That Old Serpent—the Devil—and Satan.[4] This remarkable fact is full of significance in a great variety of aspects; and appears to have had its influence in a great variety of ways, upon the whole economy of redemption.

(*b*) This temptation was addressed not to Adam but to Eve;

<hr>

[1] Rom, v. 19   [2] 1 Cor., xv. 21, 22.   [3] Gen., iii. *passim.*   [4] Rev., xii. 9, xxii. 2.

and her fall appears to have preceded any direct attempt upon Adam.[1] This important fact is also made account of in various ways, in all the subsequent conditions of the human race, and in all the relations of the sexes to each other—relations which so deeply affect its destiny.

(c) The temptation and fall of Adam appear to have occurred through the immediate agency of Eve, after her own transgression under the temptation of Satan.[2]

(d) As to the particular method of the temptation : both Adam and Eve were seduced and deceived : Eve by Satan—then Adam by Eve. They were not only tempted, but tempted by great allurements, which were false : and in the case of Adam the personal influence of Eve was superadded.[3]

(e) They were assured that the penalty denounced against transgression would not be inflicted : that the act of disobedience suggested would be attended with great increase of knowledge, and followed by the exaltation of their condition in the knowledge of good and evil to the condition of God : to prevent which, it was insinuated, was the reason of the prohibition of the Tree of Knowledge to them.[4]

(f) Thus tempted, the woman, seeing the fruit of the tree to be good for food, and pleasant to the eyes, and to be desired to make one wise, took thereof and ate ; and then gave to her husband, and he ate.[5]

2. The particular state of mind of all the parties to this fearful transaction, seems to be capable of distinct appreciation. Satan, who had himself fallen, revolted against God and been cast out of heaven, was actuated by hatred against God, and malice against man.[6] The Saviour describes him as a murderer from the beginning—a liar also, and the father of lies ; applying to him those very epithets, and declaring him to be the father of the wicked, and to be consumed by the same lusts that are manifested in them.[7] The state of mind of our first parents, precipitating their ruin, seems to have been one of unbelief toward God, especially with regard to the threatened punishment of transgression ; and of inordinate desire to obtain forbidden knowledge by forbidden means, and thereby as they vainly

[1] Gen., iii. 1–6, 13 ; 2 Cor., xi. 3,   [2] Gen., iii. 6–12, 17 ; 1 Tim., ii. 14.

[3] Gen., iii. 4–13 · 2 Cor., xi. 3 ; 1 Tim., ii. 14.   [4] Gen., iii. 4, 5.

[5] Gen., iii. 6.   [6] Rev., xii. 7–9.   [7] John, viii. 44.

hoped a certain equality with God.   Nor does the narrative permit us to overlook the suggestion of so low an impulse as intemperate appetite ; or to omit their mutual weakness springing from inordinate mutual affection, which led Eve to become the instrument of Adam's seduction, and Adam to yield to that influence.   These things are infinitely remarkable, as opening to us an insight upon divine authority, into the workings of perfect but fallible souls, and into the actual state of them proximate to their fall.   So far from being worthy of the supercilious contempt of shallow unbelief—they are the sole fragments of a psychological state utterly and forever departed, out of which we are to construe, as we may, the widest and the most intricate of all problems.   Unbelief—inordinate desire of forbidden knowledge —presumptuous aspirations after equality with God—the pride of the eye—the lust of the appetite—the inordinate mutual devotion of loving hearts : now add to these, credulity under skilful temptation—and we have all the known immediate elements of the inward state, which resulted in the first transgression.

3. The outward transgression followed as a result of this inward state.   The soul, thus working, yielded under the temptation with which it was assailed.   The outward act was the unmistakable proof of the previous inward consent.   Its perpetration put the whole case out of the reach of any remedy belonging to the Covenant under which man stood, or the immediate scheme of things under which he was created.   The trial was over : the reward was forfeited : the penalty was incurred. The Covenant of Works was no longer a Covenant of Life.   The Religion of Nature was no longer adequate : for man had passed over from the condition of a creature only, to the condition of a sinner.   And God must execute with unalterable justice the Laws of Nature, and the penalty of his violated Covenant, or he must supplement his relations of infinite Creator and Ruler, with the new relation of infinite Redeemer !   What has been done may, as we now know, be repaired by some mystery of Grace : but it can never be undone.

4. The issue of the trial of the human race in Adam—and by consequence the issue of the Covenant of Works, must have been as well known to God before as after the event.   It must also have been as well known to him before as after, what course he would take with the human race, upon the fall of man.   But

this is only another mode of stating, that the Fall of Man, and the course to be taken afterwards, were as much considered and provided for—that is, were as really parts of the great scheme of Creation and Providence, as any other parts thereof.   Nay the manifestation of the Covenant of Grace, incident to the Fall of man, and the development of it through time and eternity, was the great means foreordained for the glory of God in connection with the whole scheme of Creation and Providence.   There is, no doubt, a very wide difference between knowing and determining : and therefore between foreknowledge and foreordination.   But when the knowing and the determining, the foreknowledge and the foreordination, are united in the same infinite mind and become acts of the infinite intelligence and infinite will, of the very same omniscient and omnipotent being, who is himself the ground, and cause, and end, as well of all things known, as of all things actual : such distinctions cease to afford any refuge against the naked and sublime light which blinds us.   Moreover, to us who are the dependent objects both of the foreknowledge and the foreordination of the one, and the only, infinite and personal God, who is not only the infinite First Cause of all things, but the Omnipresent Ruler of all things ; these distinctions are of no particular moment, and have no practical force.   Nothing can be known as actually existing that does not actually exist ; and nothing can exist actually, but by the will of God : while all that is known by God as merely possible—is nothing to us. In this great case we have the whole Word of God and the whole Providence of God, added to the unavoidable conclusions of our own reason, attesting the reality of God's foreordaining as well as foreknowing action, touching the overthrow of the Covenant of Works as a Covenant of Life—the entrance of sin into the universe—and the ruin of the human race.   This great catastrophe did not take God by surprise.

5. Whatever method we may see fit to adopt in order to discover or explain the intimate cause of Adam's first sin, we must see, and we must acknowledge when we deal fairly with ourselves and the great theme, that the result was the consequence, not of any want of ability on the part of God, but of his exact adherence to the principles of the scheme he had adopted.   It is impious to say that God cannot do any thing that does not involve a contradiction ; it is equally impious to say he can do anything

wrong. In effect, nothing is more universal, even to the unregenerate, than that they are restrained by God : nothing is more universal to believers than that they are delivered from temptation. It will not do for us to say absolutely that God could not have bestowed upon Adam strength adequate to his trial ; all we can say is, that this could not be done upon the principles of the precise trial then made. For the Fall of Man to have been prevented by the interposition of God, would have required the whole economy of the Covenant of Works to have been arranged upon different principles and to widely different ends ; and therefore we must say, of necessity, that such an interposition could not have occurred according to the special method and objects of that covenant and that trial under it. Upon this general basis we may proceed with our explanations : saying that Adam fell because he was left to the freedom of his own will ; or saying that the Fall was the result of the abuse of his moral liberty ; or saying, as I have done, that, first or last, it was the inevitable result of a strict and permanent trial of a perfect but fallible creature, and was hastened and assured in this case by great external temptation ; or we may give any other account that pleases us of that most difficult and obscure matter, provided we will scrupulously respect on one side the absolute sovereignty of God, and, on the other side, the absolute dependence of man.

6. Let all that, however, be as it may, we are not to suppose for a moment that the claims of God upon us are reduced in the least, much less that they are set aside, by the breach of the Covenant of Works and the Fall of Man. Adam was as much obliged by the law of his being to obey God in all things, as he was obliged by the Covenant of Works to obey God in the additional matters specified in that Covenant. Those additional matters touched his deliverance, on one side, from the risk of ruin which attached to his fallibility, and, on the other side, the confirmation, security, and eternal augmentation of the blessedness which attached to his perfection. But they were the farthest possible from contemplating the least diminution, in any event, of God's infinite dominion or man's absolute dependence and accountability. We might as well say the law of the land is abolished as soon as it is transgressed. Whatever force the Law of Man's being, the Law of Nature, the Moral Law, or the Covenant of Works ever had, as a rule of duty, a rule of judgment, or

a rule of punishment, remained after the fall of man precisely
as before ; and if God had added nothing more after that catastrophe, nothing as to any of those Laws had been changed, except that neither by all of them, nor by any of them, could man
any longer obtain the favor of God. None of them had any
thing to do with transgression but to reveal it, to forbid it, to
condemn it, and to punish it. Thus they still abide in all their
force, and however modified or supplemented by the Covenant
of Grace, they are not only respected but executed under that
Covenant ; all of which is clearly set before us in the condition
of man immediately consequent upon his fall, and in the sentence passed by God upon all the parties to that fall, to which
we now proceed.

IV.—1. The immediate effects of transgression upon Adam and
Eve are recorded in the Scriptures, briefly indeed but with great
emphasis. The evidences that their perfection was gone, that
their fitness for communion with God was lost, that sin, and
shame, and terror had become the heritage of our fallen race, are
set before us. The mode in which this intimate change was produced in the nature of man by transgression is, like all the great
problems of our being, full of intricacy in its last analysis.
Something will be said about it presently in explicating the nature of original sin. The facts are these, namely :

(*a*) The eyes of Adam and Eve were opened, as soon as they
had eaten of the fruit of the Tree of Knowledge of Good and
Evil. The fatal knowledge they had sought at so great a cost,
was obtained. They now knew Evil as well as Good. They
already knew whether this would make them as Gods, according
to the promise of Satan—or cast them down from their high
estate, according to the threat of God.[1]

(*b*) They were immediately filled with shame : the particular object of it being their own nakedness, of which it is expressly said they had not previously been ashamed : and the
general cause of it being their sense of exposure, depravity, and
self-aversion. The first use of their fatal knowledge is to discern
that shame is the first fruit of a transition from life to death—
from the service of God to the service of Satan.[2]

(*c*) They were immediately filled with terror of God : they
fled from the voice of God : they avoided his presence : they

<hr>

[1] Gen., iii. 7.   [2] Gen., iii. 8, 10, 11.

sought to hide themselves from him. Then came the fearful challenge of God—the direct personal representation of their guilt—their own confession and account of their transgression—both of them and Satan confronting one another, and confounded before God.[1]

2. Then followed the formal sentence of God upon these fallen creatures—and upon their tempter—and upon the earth itself for man's sake. In the day that thou eatest thereof thou shalt surely die.[2] They had eaten, and their plea had been heard. The woman thou gavest me, said Adam—to be with me, she gave me of the tree, and I did eat.[3] Exactly true—but wholly insufficient : mercies bestowed are the last excuse for the sinful use of them. The Serpent beguiled me—said Eve—and I did eat.[4] True again—but insufficient: dallying with temptation, she was easily seduced herself, and became at once the willing seducer of her husband—for which last wickedness she offered no excuse. Satan offered no plea.

(*a*) And the Lord God said unto the Serpent, Because thou hast done this, thou art cursed above all cattle, and above every beast of the field : upon thy belly shalt thou go, and dust shalt thou eat all the days of thy life : and I will put enmity between thee and the woman, and between thy seed and her seed : it shall bruise thy head, and thou shalt bruise his heel.[5]

(*b*) And unto the woman he said, I will greatly multiply thy sorrow and thy conception : in sorrow shalt thou bring forth children ; and thy desire shall be to thy husband, and he shall rule over thee.[6]

(*c*) And unto Adam he said, Because thou hast hearkened unto the voice of thy wife, and hast eaten of the tree, of which I commanded thee, saying, thou shalt not eat of it, cursed is the ground for thy sake ; in sorrow shalt thou eat of it all the days of thy life : thorns also and thistles shall it bring forth to thee ; and thou shalt eat the herb of the field. In the sweat of thy face shalt thou eat bread, till thou return unto the ground ; for out of it wast thou taken : for dust thou art, and unto dust shalt thou return.[7]

(*d*) Then came the commencement of the execution of this sentence of God. It is, so to speak, an interlocutory sentence,

---

[1] Gen., iii. 8–13.   [2] Gen., ii. 17.   [3] Gen., iii. 12.
[4] Gen., iii. 13.   [5] Gen., iii. 14, 15.   [6] Gen., iii. 16.   [7] Gen., iii. 17–19.

extending from the fall till the final judgment ; when the complete result of the whole penalty of transgression will be made finally manifest, and full and eternal sentence pass, in the presence of all worlds. God drave forth the man from the Garden of Eden, from the Tree of Life, and from his own presence. Man's toils and sorrows on earth began. And Cherubim, and a flaming sword turning in all directions, kept the way of the tree of life. Who shall find a way of return for a race thrust out by God himself ?[1]

3. Terrible as this sentence is—let us comprehend clearly that it is not the full—the final sentence of the great day : that the complete penalty denounced by God upon transgression, is stayed, both as to its reutterance and execution. The great thing to be noted is, how completely every part of the case, and every word uttered by God, proceeds upon the idea that our race is undone, that sin has made its lodgment in the earth—that all things underlie the curse of God and the penalty of death. The curse of God is denounced on Satan, for his part in the ruin of man. For man's sake, who pollutes the earth—it also is cursed. Upon woman, sorrow, and subjection : sorrow mixed up forever with her tenderest cares and joys—subjection clouding forever the course of her truest love : sorrow and subjection recalling even as she gives life and as she confers bliss, that the ruin of the universe came through her weakness and by means of her seduction. Upon the man—toil—endless, unrequited toil : bread painfully earned—eaten in bitterness—coined out of his very life : life itself—boundlessly degraded from its glorious primeval form— lost in fruitless struggles having no higher aim than its own weary continuance—and no loftier hope than the dust from which he came, and to which he tends. All this too, but the beginning of wo : but the first line of an existence to be written always in tears, and polluted with blood—always : but the outer form of a being of which the inner life is steeped in sin and misery. Alas ! is not Evil in the world ? Have we not found its source—its origin ? Can any mortal transport himself into the Garden of Eden the day before the fall of man—and do it again the day after that fall—and doubt any longer ?

4. The mode in which human nature passed over, by transgression, through the channel of its fallibility, from a state of

<hr>

[1] Gen., iii. 22–24.

perfection to a state of depravity—may be understood as fully by saying, it has lost the image of God, as we are capable of understanding it.   The natural condition of the human race, after the point now reached in its career, is one of sin and misery—as I have shown at large, in another place.   Misery being only the product of sin and inseparable from it, need not be specially considered here : and all actual sins, in all their forms, being the product of original sin, which is their source and root, may also be passed over at present.   That state of our nature which we express by the words *Original Sin*, consists in the guilt of Adam's first sin, the want of that original righteousness in which he was created, and the corruption of our whole nature itself.   By calling this *Original Sin*, we intend to say, it is a state and not an act, and that it is congenital.   By *Nature* we mean the sum of all the forces, spiritual, moral, intellectual and physical, which make up our being, and give it its peculiar character.   This therefore is the sense of the general statement; having by the fall lost the image of God in which we were created, we are fallen into an estate of sin, and the present condition of our nature is a condition averse to God, opposite to him, and hateful to him.   The elements of this condition, that is the nature of this congenital or original sin, summarily stated above, may be more fully set forth, as follows :

(*a*) Its first element is the guilt of Adam's first sin.   By which is meant that on account of our natural and covenanted relations with Adam, we are considered and treated precisely as we would have been, if each one of us had personally done what Adam did.   The guilt of Adam's first sin is imputed to his posterity.   There is doubtless a wide difference between imputed sin, and inherent sin.   We however have both—and that naturally ; and it tends only to error to attempt to explicate either of them in disregard of the other, or to separate what God has indissolubly united, namely, our double relation to Adam.   It is infinitely certain, that God would never make a legal fiction a pretext to punish as sinners, dependent and helpless creatures who were actually innocent.   The imputation of our sins to Christ, affords no pretext for such a statement ; because that was done by the express consent of Christ, and was, in every respect, the most stupendous proof of divine grace.   Nor is the righteousness of Christ ever imputed for justification, except to the elect : nor ever received except by faith, which is a grace of the Spirit peculiar to the renewed soul.   In like manner the sin of Adam is imputed to us, but never irrespective of our nature and its inherent sin.   That is, we must not attempt to separate Adam's federal from his natural headship—by the union of which he is the *Root* of the human race : since we have not a particle of reason to believe that the former would ever have existed without the latter.   Nay Christ to become our federal head, had to take our nature.[1]

(*b*) The second element in Original Sin, is our natural destitution of that original righteousness, in which Adam was created. We have not only lost the image of God in knowledge, righteousness, and true holiness, and had that image defaced in all things : but we are naturally destitute of those communications of God's grace, whereby the image of God was kept alive in the soul of Adam.   Perfection and fallibility can consist together ; that is, perfection can so exist in a dependent creature as to be capable of being lost by disobedience to God.   But it would be absurd to say it can exist after it is lost : that is after the fallibility has ended in transgression.   And this is what occurred to Adam : and what by reason of our connection with him as our natural and federal head re-appears in us.   The guilt of his sin is not only imputed to us, but the effects of that sin upon his nature, are also manifested in us : the most immediate of which effects is the terrible loss and destitution herein set forth, and by reason of which our nature has ceased to be competent to the enjoyment of God, or fit for his service.[2]

(*d*) We must add as the third element the corruption of our whole nature.   It is not enough to say, sin is justly imputed to us : it is not enough to add, that our nature has incurred the most fearful privations, even to the extent of being dead in sin :

it is meant, that in point of absolute truth and in the estimation of an infinitely right mind—our nature is thus utterly depraved. And our depraved moral sense which calls good evil and evil good, so far from lowering the tone of the just judgment of God concerning our polluted nature; only makes it the more manifest how thorough and how universal that depravity must be, which pollutes our only natural guide in what is good—the conscience itself.[1]

5. Having, partly for the sake of brevity and partly under the force of a strict method, omitted the consideration of all actual sin, as well as of the misery which flows from sin : it may be the more proper to reiterate the universal sweep of this original sin, which is the root in us of all sin and all misery. The soul itself and all its powers, the mind and all its faculties, the body and all its parts, the essence of the soul and the essence of the body and all the issues of both : all these are but parts of that one nature of man—which is but the sum of all the forces that make up his being. All are under the curse of the broken Covenant—under the penalty of the violated law of God. Each in its degree and according to its kind, and all unitedly underlie the divine malediction. In our attempts to analyze a subject so immense, as is presented by the practical operation of a power like this upon the life of the human race ; it is of the greatest account to discover, if we can, some exact principle upon which we may distribute, in a satisfactory manner, such results of the fall of man as are strictly penal, and such as are to be considered merely incidental, in the case of each particular person. I content myself with offering, without comment, the following solution. In the *first* place, all sin of every kind, is a penal result to every human being—exactly to the extent that it is incurred ; and every one is liable to incur it all. In the *second* place, every form of misery which is indissolubly connected with every form of sin is penal to him on whom thus falls : but those forms of misery —of which the number is so great and the suffering so sharp— which come upon us by other means than our own sins, are not to us penal : but are only incidents to our general sinful condition and to our abode in a world that is accursed, and do always work together with all things else, for good to them that love God.[2]

<hr>

[1] Gen., vi. 5; Mat., xv. 19, 20.   [2] Rom., viii. 28.

6. It is worth while to remember what we lost by sin, and what it may still further cost us : and thus keep before our minds and hearts the solemn account of our fall. Even the most partial summary is full of awful import. For we have lost the image of God, his favor and all communion with him. We have lost our exalted dominion over the creatures. Our lives have been curtailed to a span. We have become slaves to our commonest physical necessities, our very existence being a mere struggle for food and raiment, and against disease and pain. We have lost that vast intelligence, and that boundless capacity for knowledge which made us like God ; and have forfeited that perfection and felicity which made us blessed in ourselves, lovely to each other, and objects of satisfaction to God himself. We have surrendered all claim upon every promise of God for a future life of blessedness, have become naturally destitute even of the assurance that there is such a life, and darkness, and wo, and ruin, have settled upon our race. Moreover, we underlie an eternal sentence, which is only respited till we awaken from this dream of life. We have incurred the penalty of the violated law of God, and the curse of his broken Covenant. A penalty and a curse, which press upon us every moment of our lives, and weigh us down and bind us for time and for eternity. And to crown all, there is no conceivable way of escape for us, nor one ray of light or mercy, except in the infinite love we have outraged, the infinite goodness we have despised !

7. As we look out from a condition so appalling, what hope have we ? Our first parents, as they passed out of the gate of Eden, departing to return no more, saw that strange and bewildering, but universal token of the divine presence, God's Cherubim, standing there beside the flaming sword. And then they might recall, what in their terror they had overlooked. God had not executed outright, the full penalty of transgression. He had not even reuttered it in all its extent : and his divine forbearance must have a meaning. Then they would remember, that when he cursed Satan, he dropped some wondrous words about a Promised Seed, and a great Warfare, and a strange Victory ! I will put enmity between thee and the woman, and between thy seed and her seed : it shall bruise thy head and thou shalt bruise his heel.[1] Let God be forever blessed and magni-

---

[1] Genesis, iii. 15.

fied, for these infinitely pregnant words! They changed, instantly and forever, the destiny of the human race and of the whole universe. It was no longer a race and a universe under the mere curse of God: but it became a race and a universe, under God's curse, *but with God's promise of deliverance!* That is the exact posture still: under God's curse, but with God's promise. Every succeeding age has witnessed the progress of this promise to completion. The whole career of man is one endless struggle under that curse, toward that promise. The whole Scriptures are one perpetual development of this primeval utterance of the Covenant of Grace. The entire course of Providence is one vast amplification of it. A single utterance of sovereign goodness, filling up the gulf between the first Way of Life, closed forever—and the new and better Way of Life, which no one is able to close. The ruin of the Fall, and the glories of Redemption, face to face for the first time. How can we fill our minds with the import of this promise, and contemplate what has resulted from it, without feeling the profoundest conviction that these are indeed the words of God? Behold, after so many thousands of years, how they are still replenished with divine fidelity and power, bearing all things forward to their sublime and eternal consummation!

CHAPTER XXXIII.

THE SUM AND RESULT OF HUMAN EXISTENCE: WITH THE SUM AND
RESULT OF THE KNOWLEDGE OF GOD OBJECTIVELY CONSIDERED.

I. 1. Efficacy of the method pursued, and certainty of the results reached.—2. The
closeness of the union between the Knowledge of ourselves and of God.—3. And
between the Objective and Subjective Knowledge of God.—II. 1. General appreciation of the human race, considered in its unity.—2. General statement of the
divine acts and means, directed toward its recovery.—3. Effects of divine Knowledge upon it.—4. Its perilous and transitory Estate.—5. Its impending catastrophe. Its period known only to God. Condition of the human Race, of the Church
of God, and of individual Professors, when it shall occur.—6. Solution of all
things, at the second coming of the Lord.—7. Sum and Result of Mortal Existence, responsive to the sum and result of the Knowledge of God.—III. 1. Our
destiny personally considered, under the sum of the Truths reached.—2. Both
Covenants contemplated, individually, every being embraced in them.—3. How
pollution occurs to every soul. How restoration occurs to every Elect soul.—4.
Reprobation and Election.—5. Career of the Reprobate and the Elect: how far
common, how far different: exposition of both.—IV. 1. Solution of the grand
Problems of Mortal Existence.—2. Perdition of Man.—3. Salvation of Man.—4.
Method of God's Glory, in both.—5. Infallible certainty of the Knowledge of
God.

I.—1. WITH regard to the condition of the human race in its
present estate, we have now arrived at the same result by two
different methods, and from two opposite quarters; and these
the only methods by which we could ascertain that condition
with certainty, the only quarters from which we could obtain
certain knowledge. In the commencement of our inquiry in
the earlier Chapters of the First Book, by a method intended
to be inductive and exhaustive, man was subjected, as he lives
before us, to a careful scrutiny: and again, at the end of our inquiry, in the preceding Chapters of this Fifth Book, mounting to
the original creation of man, and pursuing a method intended
to be deductive and exhaustive, God's work of creation and his
original dealings with man, and man's conduct and destiny
therein, have been subjected to a similar scrutiny. In this way,
and by the use of all the light allowed to us in the settlement of

questions of this sort, we arrive at certain knowledge concerning the present condition of man, and concerning the manner in which that condition became what it is : and the exact accordance of the result which our first scrutiny proved to be actual, with the result which our second scrutiny showed to be inevitable, is a conclusive proof of the efficacy of the method, and of the certainty of the result thus doubly reached.

2. In the whole of both of these processes a certain amount of the knowledge of God was involved at every step ; and that knowledge necessarily increased from step to step. It would be perfectly natural and obvious now to proceed with the development of the whole remaining Knowledge of God attainable by man, from the point reached in the close of the last chapter, and recapitulate, from that point of view, the substance of all remaining divine truth exhibited throughout this Treatise. Starting from the position each one of us actually occupies to-day, and going steadily onward in the natural development of the whole attainable knowledge of God, we soon discover that our knowledge of what God now is and does, involves the knowledge of what God has always been and done, and will hereafter be and do ; and that the complete present knowledge, even of ourselves, involves not only the knowledge of all our past and all our future, but also the Knowledge of God. The knowledge of our present condition and the knowledge of the manner in which it occurred, is completely attainable only through the Knowledge of God : and so much of it as is attainable without the Knowledge of God, is utterly inexplicable without that knowledge. But the whole of our future destiny lies in the grossest darkness, except as the light of God himself chases that darkness away. And most especially, all that can be of the least advantage to us in delivering us from our present estate of sin and misery, and from the eternal perdition which we see no means of escaping ; must come to us along with the true Knowledge of God, and must come from God himself: so intimately is all our true knowledge of our own nature, origin, condition, and destiny connected with our true Knowledge of God.

3. It is in this manner that the question of the Divine Existence, and the question of the Immortality of man, lie so close to each other at the foundation of every profitable method of inquiry into this great subject. It is in this manner that the

whole Scriptures connect the whole revealed Knowledge of God, immediately with the whole question of salvation for man. It is in this manner that the whole of this attempt to present the outward and positive Knowledge of God as a system distinct from the inward and experimental effects produced by means of that knowledge, never loses sight of the controlling fact that it is the Knowledge of God unto salvation, and that the object of its separate presentation is its more distinct perception, and thereby a clearer appreciation both of itself, and its effects. Between the inductive inquiry into the state of man, which occupies the opening chapters of this Treatise, and the deductive inquiry into the state of man, which occupies its closing chapters, it is the Knowledge of God unto Salvation, made known by God to man, which is the sum and substance of the whole. And at the close of a survey of this Knowledge of God unto Salvation, thus, objectively considered, we unavoidably turn to the corresponding posture of man ; and incidentally, of the universe, as exhibited under the whole knowledge thus collected and systematized. How are these vast causes, and agencies, and forces, to affect us ? and what is to be our destiny, individual and general ? In what manner is the universe involved in the result of our destiny ? In what way, and to what extent does our destiny or that of the universe affect the glory of God ? It is such inquiries as these which arise of themselves in every thoughtful mind, when it attempts to embrace as a whole, the system of the Knowledge of God : and they reveal the grandeur of that knowledge. The detailed answer to such questions is nothing less than another vast system : it is the subjective view of the Knowledge of God. It is the reality of *that* which gives its true value to *this*. And as every particular portion of this, has its answering result in *that;* so also there is a general sum of the whole peculiar to each of these general aspects of Divine truth. Let us briefly attempt to sketch, for the one we have been considering, some of the great outlines, as we contemplate all things from the point now attained.

II.—1. At the end of nearly six thousand years from the creation of man, one generation of the human race, numbering a thousand millions of souls, finds itself here in possession of this earth. At every instant multitudes are passing beyond the river of death—other multitudes of new beings are bursting into life,

This enormous multitude of immortal creatures, equally divided as to sex, differs, each individual from the rest, to the utmost limits of nature—providence—chance—fate, in all things else. The change of the generation is incessant and irresistible, and after a little will be absolute and universal: but it is so gradual and so silent, as to produce no shock—so imperceptible that no one knows or can know when one generation is gone, and another generation is come—or to what particular generation he, or any thing else exactly appertains. We are the children of Adam ; unitedly in our day, we present for an instant, and at each successive instant, that one living, undivided race ; and the next instant, and every successive instant it is changed, and yet not changed : and presently it is all changed, and yet it changes never ! The part at any time on earth, compared with the part in eternity, is like one grain of sand to the mass of the whole earth : and compared with the part yet to come—who knows, or can even conjecture, any thing ? Of all these millions whose appalling number even our imagination cannot distinctly apprehend, not one was ever asked whether he would exist or not ; nor what condition he would prefer to be born to ; nor in what land or age. Not one was ever permitted, let him desire it ever so ardently, to pass into annihilation—or ever will be. Not one ever had power to change, in the least particular, the essence of his nature ; to avoid the infinite dominion of God ; to escape the stroke of death ; to shun the single and infinite alternative of being the friend, or the enemy of God ; or to evade the judgment-seat of Jesus Christ in the great day, and the eternal retributions which are to follow. Whatever there is of evil in this wonderful condition, is abnormal, and is the fruit of the Fall of the first man.

2. It is a race once perfect, then fallen and polluted, and, as such, lying under the wrath and curse of God, and the penalty of every Divine law and covenant which was ever a rule of obedience unto them. But it is also a race capable, through Divine grace, of restoration to the lost image of God. And Divine grace, promised even before sentence after their Fall, and before their expulsion from the Garden of Eden, has been brought to light by successive and continually increasing manifestations ; until, through the incarnate, crucified and glorified Son of God,

the complete knowledge of God, through Grace unto salvation, has been manifested among them for nearly two thousand years. And now for almost two thousand years, the Spirit of God has been poured out upon men ; the Word of God in a complete and permanent form has been in possession of men ; the kingdom of God in the glorious form of the Gospel Church has been set up among men. And the proclamation of free pardon to all men, and the restoration of all men to the image and enjoyment of God in this life, and to inconceivable glory and blessedness in the life to come, upon condition of Faith in the Divine Saviour, and Repentance for sin, has been the grand and peculiar mission of this gospel church to this ruined race. It has always been the immediate duty of every pardoned sinner, and the aggregate duty of the whole gospel church, to make this proclamation, in season and out of season, to every human being ; and the single and unalterable conditions of discipleship have always been— deny thyself, take up thy cross, and follow Jesus Christ in the Regeneration. So great is the urgency of God in the matter of his grace, that to enjoy and to make known that grace, is the peculiar manner in which he requires his people to manifest their love for him and to advance his glory : and so exact is his fidelity to his promise of pardon and restoration, that no penitent and believing soul ever called upon the name of the Lord that was not saved.

3. The knowledge of God is the means of the recovery of man : and the sacred Scriptures are the infallible rule of the whole of that knowledge, as well as the repository of the chief part of it. There is a high sense in which other means of the knowledge of God are not only important, but are Divinely appointed. Some of which, indeed, are transcendent means, such as the incarnation of Christ and the work of the Spirit. Every manifestation of God is an object of positive knowledge, considered of itself ; nay of the widest and most exalted knowledge. But over and above this, and besides their independent position as vast sciences, they are the only means of knowledge of God himself—and that is the indispensable means of our salvation. No work of the Spirit fails to augment the knowledge of God ; all Providence tends directly to that end ; the whole work of Christ is unto us a light and a power ; and to be our Teacher is that part of his Mediatorial Work whereby he makes all the rest intelligible

to us. It is not, of course, meant to question the enlightening, quickening, and regenerating work of the Holy Ghost as the means of our very fitness to know God aright: nor that this very work of the Spirit depends upon the sacrifice of Christ; but to say, that all is unto the true knowledge of God in us ; all are parts of that very knowledge ; all in its application to us uses that knowledge. And such is the efficacy of all divine knowledge, that even when it does not work in us its whole effects, it still accomplishes that whereunto it was sent ; and the soul in which it finds any lodgment, if it refuses to have peace with God, can no more have peace without him.

4. When we consider that from the moment of the first promise of God after the Fall of man, this great united race of rational creatures descended from that one man, were never so situated that they ought to have lost the knowledge of that promise, superadded to all that remained of their primeval knowledge ; we might have expected our condition to be far better than it is, even if God had left the race to itself from that moment to this. But when we recall the wonderful dealings of God with our race from that primeval promise to the present hour, all directed to the perpetuity, the increase, and the efficacy of Divine Knowledge among men ; and then attempt to estimate the course and the vicissitudes of this interminable struggle between light and darkness, and to sum up the result in a full and just appreciation of the present condition of our race ; astonishment, humiliation and despair on one side, and a sense of the infinite grace, mercy, and long-suffering of God on the other side, are the natural emotions which the whole survey excites. We cannot imagine that God will permit such a struggle to be eternal ; and the Scriptures assure us that he will not. The present condition of our race on earth, is perfectly anomalous. It will be, compared with any measure we can apply to God, or to eternal things, extremely transitory. In that sense speedily, and moreover suddenly and when the enemies of God the least expect it, the mortal career of the race will be closed—its mortal existence will be blotted out—and all the immense problems connected with its mortal state will be eternally solved.[1]

5. At what period of time, at what point of the mortal existence of the human race, this great catastrophe will occur, is de-

____
[1] Mat., xxv. 31–46 ; Rev., xx. *passim.*

clared in the Scriptures to be wholly unrevealed—utterly unknown except to God himself. The disciples asked the Lord as they sat together on the Mount of Olives, to tell them when the great events he had warned them of should be, and what should be the sign of his coming, and of the end of the world.[1] His answer, which is full, is one of the most remarkable passages of the Divine Word, and has been most variously interpreted. I have suggested in a former chapter that the Doxology he affixed to the Prayer he gave his disciples as a model of all prayer, enables us to understand such passages clearly. As to the sign of his coming of which such frequent mention is made in the Scriptures,[2] and concerning which he tells us it will be like lightning shining from one part of heaven to the other ;[3] he answered his Apostles by saying it should appear after the sun had been darkened, and the moon had ceased to give her light, and the stars had fallen from heaven, and all the powers of the earth had been shaken : that it should be accompanied by the mourning and wailing of all the tribes and kindreds of the earth because of him, as they shall see the Son of man coming in the clouds of heaven, with *power* and great *glory;*[*] and that it would be immediately followed as an inseparable incident of it, by his sending his angels with a great sound of a trumpet to gather together his elect from the four winds, from one end of heaven to the other.[4] He added two remarkable statements : *first,* that heaven and earth should pass away, but his word should not : *secondly,* that the personal dispensation set up by himself and embracing his kingdom, power, and glory (so I understand the words rendered—*this generation*)[†] should not pass away, till all he had been uttering should be fulfilled.[5] Having thus fully answered, except as to the time when these stupendous events should occur, his reply as to that part of the inquiry was most specific. But of that day and hour knoweth no man ; no, not the angels of heaven, but my Father only.[6] Not only, no man and no angel, but not even the Son, as Mediator, knows that day.[7] Even the ancient prophets knew that Jehovah alone knew

---

[1] Mat., xxiv. 3.   [2] Dan., xii. 13 ; Mat., xxvi. 64; Rev., i. 7–13, xiv. 14.

[3] Mat., xxiv. 27 ; Luke, xvii. 24.   [*] Μετα δυναμεως και δοξης πολλης.

[4] Mat., xxiv. 29–31; Rev., i. 7; Acts, i. 11.   [†] Η γενεα αυτη.

[5] Mat., xxiv. 34, 35, xvi. 28; Mark, xiii. 30; Luke, xxi. 27, 32.

[6] Mat., xxiv. 36.   [7] Mark, xiii. 32.

that awful day.[1]   And the Apostolic Churches knew this so fully, that Paul told the Thessalonian Christians there was no need of his saying any thing to them about times and seasons, connected with an event which they perfectly knew would be as secret and as sudden, as it would be overwhelming in its ruin to all the wicked.[2]   For in the very last interview of the Apostles with the risen Lord, they had desired to be informed of the glory of Israel, and of the immediate relation of Christ's present work, and their own mission, to a matter which lay so near their hearts.   And he had put their minds at rest by telling them that the times and the seasons which the Father had put in his own power did not belong to them even as his Apostles, either in a way of knowledge, or as appertaining to their great work : but that they behooved to be witnesses for him, and would soon be anointed by the Holy Ghost for their own, and widely different mission.[3]   Still, however, this great catastrophe of all mortal things, is not left as a matter distant from us, as well as indeterminate as to the time of its occurrence. In the same interview on the Mount of Olives to which I alluded at first, the Lord Jesus, after answering the inquiries of his Apostles about the events he had been predicting, and about his second coming and the end of the world ; proceeded to explain in succession the condition of the human race, the condition of the visible church, and the condition of believers taken one by one, as he would find them when he should come.   The condition of the world in the days of Noah is made the type of the condition of the impenitent at the coming of the Son of man :[4] the condition of the church at large when the bridegroom shall come, is set forth in the parable of the Ten Virgins ;[5] and the condition of individual members of it in general, when their Lord shall come and reckon with them, is set forth in the parable of the Talents.[6]   And then immediately follows the account of the judgment of all nations by the Son of man in his glory.[7]   What is to be most heedfully noted is, the manner in which all this sublime revelation is interspersed with urgent commands to all men in all ages, to watch for this overwhelming consummation, as an event personally and infinitely momentous to themselves. Watch, therefore, said the Saviour, for ye know not what hour your Lord doth come : watch, for ye know neither the day nor

---

[1] Zech., xiv. 7.   [2] 1 Thes. v. 1–3.   [3] Acts, i. 4–8.   [4] Mat., xxiv. 36–41.
[5] Mat., xxv. 1–13.   [6] Mat., xxv. 14–30.   [7] Mat., xxv. 31–46.

the hour wherein the Son of man cometh : be ye also ready, for in such an hour as ye think not, the Son of man cometh.[1]   And to the same purport is the whole testimony of Scripture.   Nor can it lie in the mouth of any being except God himself to say *when* an event he has concealed in his own bosom, and reserved under his own sovereign and unrevealed will, must or must not, should or should not occur : nor is any mortal in possession of any knowledge which justifies him in saying one single word, more or less, than God has said concerning it.   What we do know is, that this scene of things will pass utterly away ; that this will occur in connection with the second coming of the Son of God ; that this is, in some sort, the sum of the mortal result of the grand problem of humanity ; and that it imports every human being to act with reference thereto, as he would with reference to its actually impending over him.

6. The obscurity which envelops the time in which God will perform these stupendous acts, and the occasions he will use to accomplish them ; does not envelop the subject in such a way as to prevent the diligent student of the Divine Word from perceiving, to a great extent, what things will precede, what will accompany, and what will follow the extinction of the mortal existence of the human race at the second coming of the Lord.   In the preceding paragraph, I have already repeated, after the words of the Saviour, various events of the most amazing grandeur, under each of those categories : and probably not a single impending event connected with the whole career of the human race, and with all God's dealings with it, but might be located in like manner, with reference to this great glory of Christ, and this great catastrophe of humanity.   Indeed how could it be otherwise ?   Is not Christ the Creator of all things ?   Is he not the only Redeemer of men ?   Is he not the Head of the New Creation—the Prince Messiah, and the only Ruler in Zion—the Husband and Lord of the Church—and so the Head over all things ?   Is it not against him that the heathen rage, that the kings of the earth conspire, that the people madly imagine all vanity ?   Is it not from him that all Apostacies depart ?   Is it not his saints with whose blood every Antichrist is drunk ?   Was it not his brow on which the greatest of the world-powers put the crown of thorns in mockery ?   Is it not his saints who are to

[1] Mat., xxiv. 42–44, xxv. 13.

take the kingdom? Is not he the promised Seed who is to crush the head of the old Dragon—to put every enemy under his feet—and at last to triumph over death and hell? Where else but in him are we to look for the end, any more than for the cause of all things? And how can there be any final solution of any thing except in his presence, under his power, and to his glory? The wonder is not that the Scriptures cluster every thing around him, more and more as all things converge to their sublime conclusion; but the wonder is that any saint should wonder at it; and the greatest of all wonders would be if any thing different could have happened.

7. There are two very different ways in which it is possible to contemplate this countless multitude which is made up of all the individuals of the human race during its entire mortal existence. We may consider them in the *first* place as a race restored by the work of Christ, in such sort that the portion which will perish at last are exceptional cases of very peculiar heinousness, the stated and common fate of the race being salvation. Or we may, in the *second* place, consider them as a fallen and depraved race, the whole of whom would perish notwithstanding the work of Christ, but for the infinite love and grace of God which make that work effectual, in saving out of the race such as are brought to the obedience of faith. It is indeed alleged that they are all saved; which, as it is utterly inconsistent with our whole knowledge both of God and man, need not be taken into consideration in this incidental way. And it is even alleged that they are not a sinful race in any serious sense, and are not therefore in any danger of perdition; which being contrary to the common conscience of the race, requires no attention in this connection. The two methods of considering the race, first stated above, differing very widely, agree at least in this, that the final destiny of the race is not single, but is double; and that the work of death, and the work of life; the Fall of man and the recovery of man; the headship of Adam and the headship of Christ; the glories of heaven and the damnation of hell; are all eternal verities. They agree, therefore, that there is an infinite reality in the Divine truth to which all our inquiries have been directed; an infinite fitness in it all to the nature of man under all the vicissitudes of that nature; and an infinite response to the sum of it, in the sum

and result of the destiny of the human race. But alas ! how erroneously do we judge of human nature, and how sadly do we mistake the word of God, and how thoroughly do we confuse the proportion of Faith, when we reverse exactly the parts of this fundamental posture of the human race, responsive to the sum of all our knowledge of God objectively considered. The human race is not a restored race, out of which a certain number are lost ; but it is a fallen and depraved race out of which a certain number are saved. It is, logically, immaterial what the proportion of the lost and saved to the whole race, and to each other may be ; but the question as to the mode is vital as regards the possibility of any salvation at all. For it is absolutely certain from the Word of God, and clear to reason and experience, that the absolute condition of human nature as we know it to be, after all that God has done for the human race taken as a whole, and as the absolute sum of the whole case for all, is not an estate of salvation ; nor one that, of itself, tends to, or terminates in salvation. To make perdition exceptional to such a state as this, is in effect to put an end to the possibility of salvation by denying both its nature and its necessity. By accepting salvation as exceptional to the actual condition and logical destiny of the race, as every thing now stands, we make account of every thing exactly as it is. It is still a fallen race, lying under the penalty of death, but susceptible of Divine recovery : with the primeval promise of a Saviour completely fulfilled by God, and the means of restoration fully brought to light : but these means are rejected and defeated except just so far as they are made effectual by the further and special grace of God ; and the race is lost, with a portion of it— far the greater portion it may be—saved through the free, sovereign, efficacious, special grace of God.[1]

III.—1. It will simplify the matter in some respects to consider it in a strictly individual light. And this is the aspect of the subject which above all is important to each particular being. For however each of us may be involved with others in common mercies, calamities, sympathies, and responsibilities, and that so greatly that no one liveth to himself, and no one ever dieth to himself ; and however we may be all stamped with a universal nature, and enveloped in a universal progress, and

<hr>

[1] John, xvii. *passim;* Rom., xviii. 28–39.

united in a universal brotherhood ; still we enter one by one each a separate personality, upon our strange and endless existence ; we struggle thus, we depart thus ; and thus will we stand before God and give account to him in the great day.[1]

2. God has created the human race, as a whole, in no other sense than that he has created all the individual beings who unitedly make up that race. In the Divine mind the exact number of these individuals, and the precise condition of each during its whole existence, was as clear and as certain before the creation of the first man as they will be after the fate of the last man is sealed. In his eternal Covenant of Grace, the fact that God knoweth them that are his, is declared to be the very seal of the steadfastness of the foundation of God.[2] Nor is it conceivable how that covenant, or the Covenant of Works, could be made by an omniscient Creator, concerning beings created by himself, in such a way as to shut his eyes to facts, which, whether as Creator or as Omniscient, he was obliged to know ;— facts which, as he is the Infinite First Cause, were obliged to have the root of their possibility in his Divine Intelligence, and the root of their future actual existence in his Divine Will. Whoever and whatever will exist in time, is obliged to be known and willed from eternity by God : each separate and responsible existence, represented in the Covenant of Works by Adam, was obliged to be individually known and willed by God from eternity ; each separate and responsible existence embraced in the Covenant of Grace through Christ was obliged to be separately and individually known and willed from eternity by God. In effect this is only saying that things cannot be known to be what they are not ; and that nothing can exist without the knowledge or against the Will of God ; and that nothing can exist with both his Knowledge and Will, otherwise than as his Knowledge and Will saw and determined from eternity. It is wholly immaterial to the present matter what the result may be in all cases, or in any case ; the thing is, that let every case, or any case, be as it may, it is absurd to say it transcends the Knowledge of God, or is independent of the Will of God.[3]

3. Contemplated from eternity, as creatures to commence an existence in time, and thenceforward to exist forever ; contemplated, as they actually would be, in connection with Adam, as

---

[1] Eccl., xii. 14; 2 Cor., v. 10.   [2] 2 Tim., ii. 19.   [3] Eph., i. 11; Rom., xi. 33.

his descendants, and as united with him in the Covenant of Works ; contemplated, therefore, as fallen and depraved, each soul created in time by God, and neither pre-existent nor pro-created, becomes actually polluted from the instant of its connection with the flesh it is to inhabit ; that is, from the instant of the actual occurrence of its connection with Adam, through whom, as the original progenitor and covenanted head of this individual being, its pollution came ; that is, from the instant of its actual contact with the pollution with which its contact had always been thus contemplated by God. This is the fate of every human soul that ever existed, except three, namely, the souls of Adam and Eve, which fell, and the soul of Jesus, which did not fall ; and it will be the fate of every future human soul. Now, by means of the Covenant of Grace a remedy is provided adequate, in its own nature, for the perfect restoration and sal-vation of these fallen human souls—indubitably adequate in the case of all that will be saved, and, though it concerns not the present matter, adequate also, as far as we can see, to have saved whatever infinite number besides, God might have been pleased to create and save. All that will be saved, who are properly called the Elect of God, and who will infallibly be saved, be-cause, being the Elect of God, they will be so dealt with, through infinite grace, as to insure their salvation—are contem-plated from eternity as fallen in Adam and born in sin, as before shown, and as united with Christ, their covenanted head, in the Covenant of Grace : they are contemplated as being redeemed by Christ and regenerated by the Holy Ghost ; and from the mo-ment that the righteousness of Christ is actually imputed to them, and actually received by Faith, and they are actually regenerated by the Holy Ghost, that which had been always contemplated by God concerning them actually occurs, and they are pardoned and restored to the lost image of God. Just as in the other case, so in this ; from eternity they were contemplated, in connection with their covenanted and natural head in one case, and with their convenanted and supernatural head in the other case ; and from the moment of their vital contact with their head, that becomes actual which God had always contem-plated as certain.[1]

4. That portion of the human race that will be finally lost

<hr>

[1] Rom., v. 12–19 ; 1 Cor., xv. 21–49 ; Eph., i. *passim*.

we know perfectly, from the Scriptures, will be condemned for
their sins, and will, in their own judgment, and the judgment of
men and angels, as well as in the judgment of God himself,
richly deserve their condemnation ; nor is it possible to imagine
that they would be condemned under any other circumstances.
As I have already shown, even the elect are chosen of God
from eternity, not in contemplation of them as pure and deserving God's love, but in contemplation of them as polluted
and so as needing the infinite Sacrifice of Christ and the infinite work of the Holy Ghost, the motive for all being the infinite glory of God in the manifestation of his infinite beneficence.
It is, therefore, impious and absurd to say that God passes by
and reprobates those who will perish, in the contemplation of
their being pure and worthy of his love. They never were contemplated as pure ; they never were pure ; they were always
polluted from the first moment of their existence ; were contemplated as such from eternity; were passed by and reprobated
being such ; will be condemned as such to all eternity. God's
infinite grace, we may make bold to say, would lead him to for-
give all the sin in the universe, to the utmost extent that was
consistent with the chief end of all his works, namely, the manifestation of himself for his own glory. And God's infinite mercy in like manner, would lead him to assuage all the misery in
the universe, upon precisely the same condition. That there is
either sin or misery in the universe, therefore, is for reasons that
even the infinite grace and the infinite mercy of God respect,
and will respect forever. On the other hand, it will not do to
say that God passes by and reprobates lost sinners, merely on
account of their sins either original or actual; because as to original sin, the elect were as deeply polluted as the reprobate, and
as to actual transgressions, the great glory of the Saviour is, that
he is able to save unto the uttermost, them that come to God by
him. The case, as it actually occurs, is this, namely : It is the
unalterable law of God's being to punish sin, whose wages is
death ; while it is the unalterable purpose of God's love to bestow eternal life upon sinners through Jesus Christ, our Lord.
Upon this human race of fallen sinners, both of these aspects of
the nature of God are exhibited to his eternal glory : on the
one hand, through his electing love taking sinners out of their
lost race, giving his Son to be a sacrifice for their sins, and sav-

ing them to the glory of his sovereign grace: on the other hand, in his immaculate rectitude, leaving sinners in their sins to perish to the glory of his infinite justice: but doing both in such a manner that, on one side, he is infinitely just while he justifies the ungodly; and on the other side, infinitely long-suffering to them that perish, insomuch that neither they, nor any one else can see how they came to be damned, except that they preferred to have sin with death, rather than holiness with eternal life, even through the blood of Christ.[1]

5. The career of each particular human being will be, on the whole, and in the sum of it, answerable to the single and universal fact of the fallen and depraved nature of all; modified by the equally universal fact that this fallen and depraved nature is still a spiritual, religious, knowing, rational, and moral nature, capable of restoration to God; and modified by the still further fact that portions of the knowledge of which we have treated throughout, have always been within reach of an immense multitude of them, and that the whole of it is required by God to be made known to every one. The sum of the career of each particular human being of whom the grand and single additional fact is true, that they are pardoned by God, regenerated by the Holy Ghost, and become, through sovereign grace, penitent and believing disciples of the Lord Jesus Christ; will be answerable to the influence of that fact added to, and modifying the facts before stated concerning their fallen and depraved condition. And the issue of the career of each individual in another life, will be answerable to the sum and result of its career in this life; so that the eternal and unchangeable state of each particular person, is the obvious and certain effect of all the foregone facts of its whole existence, and all the influences which, under those facts, have produced the final result. A primeval estate, perfect, but fallible; the Covenant of Works; the breach of it; the fall, and universal depravity of man; the manifestation of the Covenant of Grace; and at last, the coming and work of the Saviour of sinners; the dispensation of the Holy Ghost, and the proclamation of the Gospel to the whole family of man; the struggle of good and evil in every human soul, and the manifestation thereof in every human life; the victory of evil in every case; all this is common to man. Then comes the difference. Evil is allowed to have its course, and ruin is per-

---

[1] Rom., vi. 23; John, iii. 16–21; Rom., ix. 22, 23; 1 Peter, i. 2–5.

mitted to come, and hell is opened from beneath. But God will not be left destitute of a seed to serve him; the blood of Christ cannot be allowed to be fruitless: the eternal purposes of God's love and mercy cannot be defeated. And so, through sovereign grace specially and effectually applied by God himself, a new kingdom, peculiarly his own, of which his Son is the Head, his Spirit the Creator, his Word the light, and his Elect the members, is taken out of this lost race, at its extremity and while endless ruin was impending. The solitary question which lies out of the reach of all human conjecture, and upon which God has never deigned to offer a syllable of explanation, is precisely why he saw fit to choose the particular persons he did choose in their extremity, and why he saw fit not to choose the particular persons he did not choose. Why Adam instead of any other out of the countless millions of possible human beings, was made the head of the first creation; or why the man Jesus was taken instead of any other of the countless millions of possible individualizations of humanity, as the head of the New Creation; or why any other act of absolute sovereignty should be performed as it is, and not otherwise by God: it is extremely doubtful whether we should be able to judge, even if it had pleased God to reveal to us as much of his infinite thought, and motive, and purpose, as our poor nature could contain. So far is certain—that but for this choosing of some by God to eternal life, no one would have obtained that life; that they who obtain eternal life, do so through no desert of theirs, but merely through the sovereign grace of God; and that the rest who perish do so under circumstances which, so far from impeaching the infinite rectitude of God, even his infinite grace cannot impeach.[1]

IV.—1. We have now reached such solutions of the immense problems of existence, as the sum of all our knowledge of God, objectively considered, seems to me to conduct us to with an irresistible force; which I have calmly and reverently followed, without the slightest purpose or desire to evade any result, or to force any. The total extinction of the mortal existence of our race; the eternal continuance of its existence in a future state of being; the double issue of eternal misery to a portion, and eternal blessedness to the other portion of the race; the connection of both of these issues with the whole previous career, both personally and representatively, back to the fountain of the race in Ad-

---

[1] Mat., xxii. 1–14; Rom., viii. *passim;* Rev., xx. *passim.*

am, of each individual upon whom each issue falls.   These, I must allow, are propositions which nothing but divine knowledge can make certain ; but unitedly, I must insist that they afford a sublime and perfectly exhaustive solution, so far, of the whole subject.

2. But the solution goes far deeper.   The primeval condition of man was a perfect, but fallible condition : in this condition God entered into a covenant with Adam, the object of which was to assure to him and his posterity the endless possession and perpetual increase of his primeval glory and blessedness : Adam, by his fall, lost the estate he had, and forfeited the better estate promised : all his posterity, corrupt and accursed, are born in sin and misery : and thus coming into existence, the depravity of their nature insures their sinfulness and misery in this life, their temporal death and their endless perdition.   Here, again, each one of these statements, I admit, must rest for its support on divine knowledge : but here also, I insist that unitedly they completely explain the sinful career of man in this world, and his endless perdition in the next.   What they do not explain is, how any human being escapes perdition.

3. That problem is also solved in two stages, thus : Man, after his Fall, retained his original nature, and continued his identical self-conscious existence : this original nature, depraved but not destroyed, was capable of being divinely restored to the image of God which it had lost ; the method of that restoration lay in the miraculous Incarnation of the Son of God in human nature ; and then in this divine Saviour's making, by the obedience of his perfect life, and the vicarious sacrifice of his death, such a satisfaction to divine justice that man might be pardoned ; this Redeemer, being God-man, and Mediator between God and men, became the infallible Teacher of men, as well as their infinite Ruler and their atoning Priest, and crowned all by the purchase through his blood, and the sending from heaven of the Holy Ghost to apply, inwardly to men, his whole work of salvation— and to set up and perpetuate on earth the Gospel Church expressly for the conversion and sanctification of every penitent and believing sinner, who would accept salvation through Jesus Christ.   Once more, I admit, that each of these statements requires a divine confirmation : but I likewise insist that they contain an exhaustive solution of the reason why the whole human race was not lost.   Perhaps what would require explanation, would rather be, why all were not saved.

4. If we should stop here, it would prove that we did not rightly apprehend either God or ourselves. In effect, so terrible is the depravity of man, that instead of accepting the Son of God, they slew him. And from that day to this, the human race with one accord and when left to themselves, have rejected him, despised his Word, grieved his Spirit, and persecuted his followers. If it had not been for the special and unsearchable grace of God, and his eternal and unalterable purpose to have a people, a church, and an eternal inheritance taken out of this fallen and depraved race of sinners, as monuments of his own glory to his whole universe throughout eternity, not one human being would have been saved at all. So that, not loving us because he had given Christ to us, but giving Christ for us because he loved us with an eternal and unalterable love ; God saves us, so to speak, by reason of the fidelity of that love, of his jealousy for his own glory, his own purpose, his own covenant, his own decree ; after we had not only deserved destruction, and rendered ourselves incapable of life except through grace, but had also rejected that grace, denied the Lord that bought us, and slain the Prince of life. Finally, I admit that these statements also can be accepted only on the testimony of God himself ; but I insist, that they contain a perfectly exhaustive solution of the fate of the human race, as that fate has been proved to be. If they be true, there is no marvel that God's reprobate enemies should perish ; no marvel even that his elect should not be allowed to perish.

5. But the statements upon which those conclusions rest, which develop the sum and result of human existence, have been shown, one by one, throughout this Treatise to be inseparable portions of that truth which is divinely made known to man for his salvation ; and to enter as to the sum and result of them, fundamentally into our knowledge of the being, nature, attributes, and works of God. We have, therefore, the highest assurance we are capable of obtaining, whether from the nature of knowledge itself, or from its forms, that we have obtained the knowledge of God objectively considered, as a science of Positive Truth. The inward effects of this knowledge constitute a second and separate view of Divine Truth. It is the remaining portion of what is commonly called Didactic Theology ; according to the method I adopt, it is the *Knowledge of God considered Subjectively ;* and will be treated by itself.

CHAPTER XXXIV.

THE FINITE AND THE INFINITE COALESCE IN RELIGION: GOSPEL
PARADOXES: THEIR INFLUENCE AND SOLUTION.

1. Union of the Finite and the Infinite in Religion.—2. Double Results. Their Position. Mode of Solution.—3. Their influence upon our religious Belief and Experience.—4. Struggles of earnest souls: Shallowness of unbelief.—5. Exaltation of the Gospel: confirmation of the soul.—6. Spiritual appreciation of these sublime Paradoxes.

1. THERE are two elements in religion, one of them Infinite and the other Finite, both of which must be constantly estimated, if we would have clear views of its nature, or habitual satisfaction of mind in resting on the whole compass of its truth. On the one side is God himself; that perfect, divine, and all-pervading element, infinite, both in truth and force, and infinite also in incomprehensible mystery. On the other side is man—ourself—that frail and erring element, which it is our first necessity to comprehend, not only of itself and positively, but also relatively to God, and so to the very object of religion itself—as God is its very source. These two elements are to be appreciated in every theoretical and every practical view of religion: and every system must bring its results into some form that will bear to confront the settled truths of each of these elements, considered both jointly and separately.

2. It is the extreme difficulty of doing this—indeed in some most important respects the apparent impossibility of doing it, which begets what we call, for the want of a better name, the Paradoxes of the Gospel. Those double results, which are so numerous and so capable of perplexing us; some of which, God has solved and united with such sublime light; some of which men dispute over interminably; multitudes of which superficial minds never trouble themselves to consider. Two things appear to be clear concerning all of them. The first is, that they are all to be found located along that line, in which the infinite and the finite—the divine and the human elements in religion, at once

unite and are separated ; and therefore all belong, not so much to a separate consideration of any particular part of religion, as to a general estimate of religion as a system. The second is, that the only method of their solution, is the application to them of a simple evangelism, and a thorough philosophy, combined : for the lack of which, on the one side or the other, there is sometimes found so much extravagance, and at other times so much shallowness, in the mode in which the most important truth is stated.

3. It is extremely obvious that the success of our attempts to solve these Gospel Paradoxes to our own satisfaction, must have a controlling influence upon the tenor both of our systematic belief, and of our spiritual life. For, on the one side, it is an inexorable demand of the human intellect, that there must appear to it to be a pervading order and coherence in all that it recognizes as truth and knowledge ; to effect which, it will steadfastly labor upon all the parts and proportions of all truth, and till it has accomplished what satisfies it, is only the more eager and anxious, in proportion as its love and pursuit of truth are the more thorough and absorbing. And on the other side, the inner life of man cannot be nourished with inconsistent and contradictory, with empty and inconclusive things ; any more than his poor tabernacle of clay can be fed by husks, any more than it can be fed by jewels : but the soul lives by a nurture, various and deep in its exquisite assimilation—and it pines when its heavenly food is heterogeneous, either in itself, or with regard to it.

4. We often speak of the difficulties of religion as presented in the works of infidels and heretics. But they are not worthy to be so much as once thought of, when placed by the side of the difficulties which the soul of the true believer has mastered. Satan does not reveal his strength to his willing followers. The spirit which rests in the shallow doubts which outlie the wide frontiers of divine truth, never approaches the real problems over which the heart agonizes, and before which the intellect recoils. If the inward struggles of any earnest Christian spirit in the progressive development of its divine life, were distinctly recorded, so that they could be carefully considered by others ; they would show nothing more clearly than the utter insignificance and hollowness, the pitiable ignorance and baseness, of the common pretexts of unbelievers. These great spiritual battles are fought around and within these citadels — these

strongholds of God, in each of which is intrenched one of these great Gospel Paradoxes. And if our eyes were opened so that we could see at one glance the whole vanguard of the church militant, we should behold encamped around, or lodged within these very battlements, the chief captains of the army of the Lord; some safely and serenely reposing on the bosom of Christ, having won the great victory; some discomfited, yet still renewedly girding themselves for the life battle; some calmly watching and pondering, till the signal falls for a new onset; some in the very heat and desperate grapple of the imminent deadly breach! Who can pass his eye, even in thought, around their glorious ranks, without wonder, and love, and joy: without perceiving under a new aspect, the high communion of the redeemed of God—in this form of their union with and in Christ!

5. It is a fatal error to imagine that we gain any thing, either in the power or the distinctness of our spiritual experience, by avoiding these sublime meditations. And it is another error not less fatal, to suppose that the Gospel is commended to the soul of man, by our poor attempts to lower the terms of these grand paradoxes, on one side or the other, or on both. The difficulty is not created by the Gospel: it lies in the infinite nature of the case—and in the eternal nexus wherein God stands related to his own universe. As I have intimated before, so much of the difficulty as can be solved at all, can be solved only through the most intense application of the plan of Salvation, to the most profound realities of the case; a result to which all superficial philosophy and all shallow evangelism, unitedly or separately, are utterly incompetent. Open them, as bottomless chasms across the pathway to eternity: pile them up, as impassable mountains in the way toward the New Jerusalem: and then you will not only tell the whole truth—but you will so tell it that the soul of man can both understand and believe it. It is after that, only, we can know—or that we care to know, how these mountains can be brought low, these valleys be filled, these rough places be made smooth, these crooked ones become straight, and a highway be made for the Lord and for his redeemed!

6. And after all it is not by means of the logical faculty, that man escapes perdition. Our faith does not stand in the wisdom of man, but in the power of God. It is with the heart that man believeth unto righteousness. It is not merely—nay, it is

not even chiefly—upon what we call our reason that the power
of God's grace manifests itself in the new creation ; and so it is
not mainly, much less merely, by means of philosophy—no matter how pure and deep, that God can be fully comprehended,
much less embraced.   How do men blush, when they know God,
at the bare thought of the unspeakable folly and littleness of
their former cavils against the grand truths of the Gospel—
nay, against the Gospel itself—when they were spiritually dead ?
On the other hand, how many are there, who never questioned
a single one of those glorious truths, nay, who saw and received
them all separately in their power and their simplicity, as a mere
light, but who, at the same time, did not, and knew all the while
that they did not, receive a single one of them, in the divine
love, and the divine power thereof—much less in the unction
and fulness of the divine proportion of them all ?   The things
of the Spirit must be spiritually discerned, if they are to produce any Spiritual effect.   And we must content ourselves to
accept only the sense of the letter that killeth, and perish therein;
or we must be born again.   And then we must content ourselves, again, with such growth as is possible from the nourishment of each simple truth accepted by itself ; or if we would go
on to perfection, we must be strengthened with might in the
inner man.   The power in the understanding and the power in
the soul—the philosophy and the evangelism, by which the proportion of faith itself becomes the grandest of all powers, next
after the immediate power of God's Spirit ; these are all Spiritual powers—in the absence of which all the Paradoxes of the Gospel must remain utterly incomprehensible to man.   In their
presence, most of them are capable of a solution felt to be complete, and generally capable of being clearly expressed.   And
such as are not yet mastered by us, are felt to be, not contradictions, but the sublimest truths ; whose reversal would disorder
the universe, and derange the very foundations of universal
Knowledge ; but whose solution lies in some exalted generalization, higher up in the bosom of God, than our poor measure can
yet attain.

INDEX.

ABBREVIATIONS.—B., book; ch., chapter; p., page; par., paragraph pass., *passim;* sec., section; let., letter; id., idem.

A

ANTHROPOLOGY. See argument of the First Book, *passim.*

APOSTLES OF CHRIST. B. II., ch. vii., sec. ii., par. 8.

ATTRIBUTES OF GOD, general classification of the Divine perfections. B. III., ch. xvii., *passim.* Primary Attributes, ch. xviii. Essential Attributes, ch. xix. Natural Attributes, ch. xx. Moral Attributes, ch. xxi. Consummate Attributes, ch. xxii.

ANALYSIS of our knowledge of God, and of our capacity and means thereof, B. IV., ch. xxiii., *passim : idem,* ch. xxvi., sec. iii., par. 3, 4.

ANGELS, the doctrine with regard to, B. IV., ch. xxv., sec. vi., par. 1, 2, 3, 4.

ADVENT of Messiah, B. I., ch. iv., *passim :* B. II., ch. vii., sec. ii., par. 1, 2, 3, 4: B. IV. ch. xxvi., sec. ii., iii: *idem,* ch. xxviii., sec. ii., par. 6, 7.

B

BEING OF GOD, the mode thereof determines the plan of salvation, B. III., ch. xv., sec. v., par. 1, 2, 3, 4: *idem,* sec. i., par. 1, 2, 3: *idem,* sec. ii., par. 1, 2, 3: the perfections thereof, B. III., ch. xvii., general classification: ch. xviii., first class: ch. xix., second class: ch. xx., third class: ch. xxi., fourth class: ch. xxii., fifth class: secondary demonstrations of the being of God, by methods both *à priori* and *à posteriori,* B. III., ch. xviii., sec. i., par. 4.

BAPTISM OF CHRIST, B. II., ch. vii., sec. ii., par. 1, 2.

BEING OF MAN, considered in its immortality, B. I., ch. vi., *pass.:* considered in its absolute nature and totality, as a manifestation of God, B. IV., ch. xxix., *passim :* considered in its creation and primeval state, B. V., ch. xxx., *passim.*

C

CHRISTOLOGY. See Argument of Second Book, *passim,* pp. 71, 72.

CHRIST, relation of his sacrifice to the perpetual Ministry, B. II., ch. vii., sec. ii., par. 7: His Humiliation, B. II., ch. x., sec. i., ii.: His Exaltation, *idem,* sec. iii.: necessity of both, *idem,* sec. iv.: the great Teacher, B. II., ch. xi., *passim :* His parables, *idem,* sec. iii., par. 6: His miracles, *idem,* sec. iv., par. 4, let. *a, b, c, d :* His priesthood, B. II., ch. xii., *passim :* His kingly office, B. II., ch. xiii., *passim :* His incarnation, as a manifestation of God, B. IV., ch. xxvi., *passim.*

CREATION considered as the first and constant manifestation of God, B. IV., ch. xxiv. *passim*: relation of the Holy Ghost both to the Old and the New Creation, B. IV., ch. xxvii., sec. i., par. 1, 2: sec. ii., par. 1: creation of man, B. V., ch. xxx., sec. ii., par. 1, 2, 3, 4, 5, 6.

COVENANT OF WORKS, B. V., ch. xxxi., *passim*: its effect upon the primeval state of man, *idem*, sec. i., par. 1, 2, 3, 4: scriptural account of it, *idem*, sec. ii., par. 1, 2, 3, 4, 5, 6, 7, 8, 9, 10: effect of it on the principle of Duty, the Moral Law, etc., *idem*, sec. iii., par. 1, 2, 3, 4; its advantages, *idem*, par. 5, letters *a, b, c, d, e. f:* breach of the covenants of Works, with the cause, manner, and consequences thereof, B. V., ch. xxxii., *passim*.

CATASTROPHE impending over the human race, B. V., ch. xxxiii., sec. ii., par. 4, 5, 6, 7.

CERTAINTY, infallible, of the knowledge of God, B. V., ch. xxxiii., sec. iv., par. 5.

D

DOXOLOGY OF THE LORD'S PRAYER, peculiar significance of, B. II., ch. x., sec. i., par. 5, 6.

DIVINE PERFECTIONS, B. III., ch. xvii., general classification: ch. xviii., perfections of God as an infinite being: ch. xix., as an infinite personal spirit: ch. xx., those of his infinite *rational* nature: ch. xxi., those of his infinite *moral* nature: ch. xxii., consummate perfections.

DIVINE GRACE, nature and fruits thereof, B. III., ch. xxi., sec. ii., par. 5.

DUTY, the true idea and nature thereof, B. IV., ch. xxix., sec. i., par. 7: duty and responsibility, B. V., ch. xxx., sec. iii., par. 1, 2, 3, 4, 5, 6, 7: effect of the fall of man upon it, B. V., ch. xxxii., sec. iii., par. 6.

DETAILED ACCOUNT of the Fall of Man, B. V., ch. xxxii., sec. iii., iv.

DOUBLE RESULTS, in religious truth, their cause, difficulty, nature, and solution, B. V., ch. xxxiv., *passim*.

E

EXALTATION OF CHRIST, B. II., ch. x., sec. iii., iv.

ESTATES OF CHRIST, B. II., ch. x., sec. i., ii., iii., iv.

EXPIATION, B. II., ch. xii., sec. i., par. 1, 2, 3, 4, 5.

ESSENCES, material and immaterial, B. IV., ch. xxiii., sec. iv.

EXISTENCE, mode of the Divine, B. I., ch. v., sec. i., par. 4, 5, 6, 7: B. III., ch. xv., *passim*: B. IV., ch. xxvii., sec. i., par. 1.

EPOCHS of the New Creation, B. IV., ch. xxviii., sec. ii., par. 3, 4, 5, 6, 7, 8, 9.

ELEMENTS OF RELIGION, their immutability, B. V., ch. xxx., sec. iii., par. 6.

EVIL, origin of, B. V., ch. xxxii., *passim*: penal and incidental, distinction between, *idem*, sec. iv., par. 5.

EXISTENCE, sum and result of mortal, under the whole dealings of God, B. V., ch. xxxiii., *passim*.

ELECTION AND REPROBATION, analysis of both, B. V., ch. xxxiii., sec. iii., iv.

F

FUNDAMENTAL TRUTHS. See end of Argument of B. I., p. 2: end of Argument of B. II., p. 72: end of Argument of B. III., p. 198: end of Argument of B. IV., p 320: end of Argument of B. V., p. 445: fundamental elements of religion, B. V., ch. xxx , sec. iii., par. 6, let. *a, b:* fundamental truths of it, B. V., ch. xxiii., sec. iv., par. 1, 2, 3, 4, 5.

FALL OF MAN, and origin of evil, B. V., ch. xxxii., *passim*.

FINITE AND INFINITE, their coalescence in Religion, B. V., ch. xxxiv., *passim*.

G

GOD, a demonstration of His being and of the manner thereof, B. I., ch. v., *passim*: His Revealed Names, B. III., ch. xiv., *passim*: Mode of Existence, B. III., ch. xv., *passim*: Divine Perfections, general classification, B. III., ch. xvii., *passim*: Primary Attributes, *idem*, ch. xviii.: Essential Attributes, *idem*, ch. xix.: Natural Attributes, ch. xx.: Moral Attributes, ch. xxi.; Manifestations of God, see Argument of B. V., *passim*, and ch. xxiii., *passim*: the Creator of all things, B. IV., ch. xxiv., *passim*: the Ruler of all things, B. IV., ch. xxv., *passim*: Incarnate, B. IV., ch. xxvi., *passim*: Manifested through the New Creation, *idem*, ch. xxvii., *passim*: in the sacred Scriptures, *idem*, ch. xxviii.: in the human soul, ch. xxix.

H

HUMAN RACE, its Ruin, universal and irremediable, B. I., ch. iii., *passim*: Unity of the Race, *idem*, sec. i., par. 2, letters *a, b, c, d, e, f, g*: Misery of its condition, *idem*, sec. ii., *passim*: Christianity accepts and solves this problem, *idem*, sec. iii., *passim*.

HUMILIATION OF CHRIST, B. II., ch. x., sec. i., ii., iv.

HOLY GHOST, Doctrine of, B. III., ch. xvi., *passim*: Author of the New Creation, B. IV., ch. xxxviii., *passim*.

HUMAN NATURE, God manifest in, B. IV., ch. xxvi., *passim*: considered as a means of knowing God, by itself, in its fallen state, B. IV., ch. xxix., sec. i., par. 1, 2, 3, 4, 5, 6, 7, 8, 9: in its restored state, *idem*, sec. ii., par. 1, 2, 3, 4, 5: Ruin of it, by the Fall, B. V., ch. xxxii., *passim*.

HEADSHIP of Adam, and of Christ, B. V., ch. xxxii., sec. ii., par. 1, 2, 3, 4, 5, 6.

I and J

INTERPOSITION OF GOD, to save man, B. I., ch. iv., *passim*: sovereign, gracious, and effectual, *idem*, sec. i., par. 1, 2, 3, 4: method and principle of that Interposition, *idem*, sec. ii., par. 1, 2, 3: motive, manner, fact, and mode thereof, *idem*, sec. iii., par. 1, 2, 3, 4.

JESUS OF NAZARETH, the Historic Christ, B. II., ch. vii., *passim*.

IMMANUEL, the mystery of the Incarnation, B. II., ch. viii., *passim*: His person, *idem*, sec. i., par. 1, 2, 3, 4, 5, 6: God and man, *idem*, sec. ii., par. 1, 2, 3. 4, 5, 6, 7, 8, 9: true idea of, B. IV., ch. xxvi., sec. ii., par. 1, 2; sec. iii., par. 1, 2.

INCARNATION, the highest manifestation of God, B. II., ch. viii., sec. ii., par. 9: B. IV., ch. xxvi., *passim*.

INTERCESSION OF CHRIST, B. II., ch. xii., sec. iv., par. 1, 2, 3, 4.

INSPIRATION AND REVELATION, B. IV., ch. xxviii., sec. iii., par. 1, 2, 3, 4, 5.

INDIVIDUAL aspects of both Covenants, B. V., ch. xxxiii., sec. iii., par. 1, 2, 3, 4, 5.

K

KINGLY OFFICE OF CHRIST, B. II., ch. xiii., *passim*: Christ Royal and Divine, *idem*, sec. i., par. 1, 2, 3, 4: distinctive facts, *idem*, sec. i., par. 5, let. *a, b, c, d, e, f, g*: titles, *idem*, par. 6, 7, 8, 9, 10, 11: Kingly aspect of the mediatorial kingdom, *idem*, sec. ii., par. 1, 2, 3, 4, 5, 6.

KNOWLEDGE, sources of unto salvation, and certainty of, B. IV., ch. xxiii., *passim:* of God through Creation, B. IV., ch. xxiv.: through Providence, *idem*, ch. xxv.: through the Word made Flesh, *idem*, ch. xxvi.: through the New Creation, *idem*, ch. xxvii.: through Divine Revelation, ch. xxviii.: through the human soul, ch. xxix.

KINGDOM OF GOD, true conception of, B. IV., ch. xxviii., sec. ii., par. 2, 3, 4, 5.

L

LIFE of all created things a perpetual proof of a Creator, B. IV., ch. xxiv., sec. ii., par. 5: life, creation, etc., B. IV., ch. xxix., sec. ii., par. 1, 2, 3, 4, 5.

M

MAN, his actual condition, individually considered, B. I., ch. i., *passim:* socially considered, Household, B. I., ch. ii., sec. i., par. 1, 2, 3, 4, 5, 6: Civil Society, *idem*, sec. ii., par. 1, 2, 3, 4, 5: His Religious Nature, *idem*, sec. iii., par. 1, 2, 3, 4, 5, 6, 7: Divine Interposition to save man, B. I., ch. iv., *passim:* His Immortality, and the true nature thereof demonstrated, B. I., ch. vi., *passim.*

MEDIATOR between God and men, B. II., ch. ix., *passim:* Necessity and nature of, *idem*, sec. i., par. 1, 2, 3, 4, 5; his Dispensation, *idem*, sec. ii., par. 4, let. *a, b, c, d, e, f, g, h, i, j:* Redemption by him as a way of life, *idem*, par. 5: his two Estates, B. II., ch. x., *passim:* his Offices, B. II., ch. xi., sec. i., par. 1, 2, 3, 4, 5.

MIRACLES of Christ, B. II., ch. xi., sec. iv., par. 4, let. *a, b, c, d:* the nature of miracles, with a short demonstration of them, B. III., ch. xviii., sec. ii., par. 4.

MORAL DISTINCTIONS, the true ground thereof, B. III., ch. xxi., sec. i., par. 2, 3: *idem*, sec. vi., par. 4, 5.

MANIFESTATIONS OF GOD, the whole of them stated and classified, B. IV., ch. xxiii., par. 7, 8, 9: in Creation, *idem*, ch. xxiv.: in Providence, ch. xxv.: in the Flesh, ch. xxvi.: in the New Creation, ch. xxvii.: in Revelation, ch. xxviii.: in the Human Soul, ch. xxix.

MORTAL EXISTENCE OF MAN, its sum and result, but general and particular, B. V., ch. xxxiii., *passim.*

N

NAMES OF GOD, their importance and import, B. III., ch. xiv., sec. i., ii.: Jehovah, *idem*, sec. ii., par. 1, 2, 3, 4, 5, 6, 7: I Am and Jah, *idem*, sec. iii., par. 1, 2, 3: El, *idem*, sec. iv., p. 2: Lord of Hosts, *idem*, par. 3, 4: Most High, *idem*, sec. v., par. 1: Adonai, *idem*, par. 2: Shaddai, *idem*, par. 3: Elohim, *idem*, par. 4.

NEW CREATION, whole doctrine of, as a work of the Spirit, and a manifestation of God, B. IV., ch. xxviii., *passim.*

NATURE OF MAN, exposition of it, considered as an image, and so a manifestation of God, B. IV., ch. xxix., *passim.*

O

OFFICES OF CHRIST, Prophetic Office, B. II., ch. xi.: Priestly Office, B. II., ch. xiii.: Kingly Office, B. II., ch. xiii.

ORACLES OF GOD, true conception of, B. IV., ch. xxviii., sec. ii., par. 6: their power, *idem*, sec. iii., par. 1, 2: their origin, *idem*, par. 3, 4, 5.

ORIGINAL SIN, B. V., ch. xxxii., sec. iii., par. 1, 2, 3, 4, 5, 6.

P

PROPHETIC OFFICE OF CHRIST, B. II., ch. xi., *passim:* true idea of it, *idem,* sec. ii., par. 1, 2, 3, 4, 5; its actual exercise, *idem,* sec. iii., par. 1, 2, 3, 4, 5, 6, 7 Divine confirmation of it, *idem,* sec. iv.

PARABLES, as distinctive of Christ's teaching, B. II., ch. xi., sec. iii., par. 6.

PERSON, meaning thereof, as applied to the Godhead, B. III., ch. xv., sec. iv., par. 1, 2, 3.

PROVIDENCE, the whole doctrine considered as a manifestation of God, B. IV., ch. xxv., *passim.*

PRIMEVAL STATE OF MAN, B. V., ch. xxx., *passim.*

PERDITION AND SALVATION, B. V., ch. xxxiii., sec. iv., par. 1, 2, 3, 4.

POLLUTION AND REGENERATION, analysis of both, B. V., ch. xxxiii., sec. iii., par. 1, 2, 3, 4, 5.

PARADOXES OF THE GOSPEL, their nature, source, and effects, B. V., ch. xxxiv., *passim.*

R

REVELATION, the primeval form of it by means of the names of God, B. III., ch. xiv., *passim:* the created universe considered as a Revelation of God, B. IV., ch. xxiv., sec. ii., par. 1, and sec. iii., par. 1, 2, 3.

RETRIBUTION, unavoidable certainty thereof, B. III., ch. xxi., sec. vi., par. 1, 2, 3, 4, 5, 6.

RESTORATION of man to the lost image of God, B. IV., ch. xxix., sec. ii., par. 1, 2, 3: increase of divine knowledge thereby, *idem,* par. 4, 5.

RESULTS, certainty of those reached, B. V., ch. xxxiii., sec. i., par. 1, 2, 3.

S

SOUL AND BODY, distinction between them—union—and endless existence of both, B. I., ch. vi., sec. iii., par. 1, 2, 3, 4, 5, 6.

SACRIFICE, B. II., ch. xii., sec. i., ii., iii.

SPIRIT, doctrine of the Holy Ghost, B. III., ch. xvi., *passim:* Nature, person, and work, *idem,* sec. i., par. 1, 2, 3: his relations to Immanuel, and to Revelation, *idem,* sec. ii., par. 1, 2, 3, 4, 5: to our knowledge of God, *idem,* sec. iii., par. 1, 2, 3, 4, 5: sin against the Holy Ghost, *idem,* sec. iv., par. 1, 2, 3, 4, 5, 6: Work of, B. II., ch. xxvii., *passim.*

SALVATION, in its immediate relation to the Moral Attributes of God, B. III., ch. xxi., sec. ii., iii., iv., v., vi.

SPECIAL PROVIDENCE, the doctrine explained, B. IV., ch. xxv., sec. iii., par. 1, 2.

SACRED SCRIPTURES, God manifested therein, B. IV., ch. xxviii., *passim:* their conception of the kingdom of God, *idem,* sec. ii., par. 3, 4, 5, 6.

SOUL OF MAN, concerning its nature and immortality, B. I., ch. vi., *passim:* considered as an image of God, B. IV., ch. xxix., *passim.*

SABBATH, its origin and nature, B. V., ch. xxx., sec. i., par. 5, 6.

SACRAMENTS OF THE COVENANT OF WORKS, B. V., ch. xxx., sec. ii., par. 7.

SOURCES OF DIVINE KNOWLEDGE. See Argument of B. IV., pp. 317–320.

SATAN, his connection with the Fall of Man, B. V., ch. xxxii., sec. iii., par. 1, 2 · *idem,* sec. iv., par. 1, 2, 3.

SUM AND RESULT of Divine Knowledge. See Argument of B. V., *passim.*

T

THEOLOGY. See Argument to B. III., *passim*, pp. 197, 198. See Preliminary State-ment, *passim*.

TRINITY, Doctrine of, fully discussed, B. III., ch. xv., *passim*.

THE TRUE AND THE FALSE, relation of that ineffaceable distinction to God and to man, B. III., ch. xx., par. 7: the true, the good, and duty, B. IV., ch. xxix., sec. i., par. 6, 7, 8, 9.

TREE of Life, and of the Knowledge of Good and Evil, B. V., ch. xxx., sec. ii., par. 5, 6.

U and V

UNITY OF ESSENCE AND TRINITY OF PERSONS, Nature and effects of this manner of the divine existence, B. III., ch. xv., sec. iii., iv., v., vi.

UNPARDONABLE SIN, B. III., ch. xvi., sec. iv., par. 1, 2, 3, 4, 5, 6.

UNIVERSE, the created, God manifested therein, B. IV., ch. xxiv., *passim*.

UNITY of the human race, B. I., ch. iii., sec. i., par. 2, letter *a, b, c, d, e, f, g*: unity of human nature in its essence, B. IV., ch. xxix., sec. i., par. 4.

W and X

WILL, distinction between the Secret and the Revealed Will of God, B. IV., ch. xxv.. sec. ii., par. 3, 4.

WORD, THE, made Flesh, B. II., ch. viii., *passim*: B. IV., ch. xxvi., *passim*.

WONDERFUL WORKING of the Holy Ghost, B. IV., ch. xxviii., sec. iii., par. 1, 2, 3, 4.

329301

Made in the USA